THE ROUTLEDGE HANDBOOK
OF SMUGGLING

The Routledge Handbook of Smuggling offers a comprehensive survey of interdisciplinary research related to smuggling, reflecting on key themes, and charting current and future trends.

Divided into six parts and spanning over 30 chapters, the volume covers themes such as mobility, borders, violent conflict, and state politics, as well as looks at the smuggling of specific goods – from rice and gasoline to wildlife, weapons, and cocaine. Chapters engage with some of the most contentious academic and policy debates of the twenty-first century, including the historical creation of borders, re-bordering, the criminalisation of migration, and the politics of selective toleration of smuggling. As it maps a field that contains unique methodological, ethical, and risk-related challenges, the book takes stock not only of the state of our shared knowledge, but also reflects on how this has been produced, pointing to blind spots and providing an informed vision of the future of the field.

Bringing together established and emerging scholars from around the world, *The Routledge Handbook of Smuggling* is an indispensable resource for students and researchers of conflict studies, borderland studies, criminology, political science, global development, anthropology, sociology, and geography.

Max Gallien is a Research Fellow at the Institute of Development Studies (IDS) located at the University of Sussex, a Fellow at the International Centre for Tax and Development (ICTD), and a Senior Fellow at the Global Initiative against Transnational Organised Crime (GITOC). He is a political scientist specialising in the politics of informal and illegal economies, the political economy of development, and the modern politics of the Middle East and North Africa.

Florian Weigand is the Co-Director of the Centre for the Study of Armed Groups at the Overseas Development Institute and a Research Associate at the London School of Economics and Political Science. He works on armed conflict, illicit economies, and international interventions, and explores the politics and societal dynamics of conflict zones, borderlands, and other complex environments. He is the author of *Conflict and Transnational Crime: Borders, Bullets & Business in Southeast Asia* and *Waiting for Dignity: Legitimacy and Authority in Afghanistan*.

THE ROUTLEDGE HANDBOOK OF SMUGGLING

Edited by Max Gallien and Florian Weigand

LONDON AND NEW YORK

Cover image: © Fernanda Morales Tovar

First published 2022
by Routledge
2 Park Square, Milton Park, Abingdon, Oxon OX14 4RN

and by Routledge
605 Third Avenue, New York, NY 10158

Routledge is an imprint of the Taylor & Francis Group, an informa business

© 2022 selection and editorial matter, Max Gallien and Florian Weigand; individual chapters, the contributors

The right of Max Gallien and Florian Weigand to be identified as the authors of the editorial material, and of the authors for their individual chapters, has been asserted in accordance with sections 77 and 78 of the Copyright, Designs and Patents Act 1988.

The Open Access version of this book, available at www.taylorfrancis.com, has been made available under a Creative Commons Attribution-Non Commercial-No Derivatives 4.0 license.

Trademark notice: Product or corporate names may be trademarks or registered trademarks, and are used only for identification and explanation without intent to infringe.

British Library Cataloguing-in-Publication Data
A catalogue record for this book is available from the British Library

Library of Congress Cataloging-in-Publication Data
Names: Gallien, Max, editor. | Weigand, Florian, editor.
Title: The Routledge handbook of smuggling/edited by Max Gallien and Florian Weigand.
Description: New York, NY : Routledge, 2022. | Series: Routledge international handbooks | Includes bibliographical references and index.
Identifiers: LCCN 2021031294 (print) | LCCN 2021031295 (ebook)
Subjects: LCSH: Smuggling--Case studies. | Borderlands--Case studies. | Emigration and immigration--Case studies. | Violence--Case studies.
Classification: LCC HJ6619 .R68 2022 (print) | LCC HJ6619 (ebook) | DDC 364.1/336--dc23
LC record available at https://lccn.loc.gov/2021031294
LC ebook record available at https://lccn.loc.gov/2021031295

ISBN: 978-0-367-48953-3 (hbk)
ISBN: 978-1-032-15927-0 (pbk)
ISBN: 978-1-003-04364-5 (ebk)

DOI: 10.4324/9781003043645

Typeset in Bembo
by MPS Limited, Dehradun

CONTENTS

Lists of illustrations	*ix*
List of contributors	*x*

1 Studying smuggling   1
Max Gallien and Florian Weigand

PART I
Methods and approaches   **17**

2 Localising smuggling   19
Gregor Dobler

3 Smuggling ideologies: Theory and reality in African clandestine
   economies   30
Kate Meagher

4 Lorries and ledgers: Describing and mapping smuggling in the field   45
Nikki Philline C. de la Rosa and Francisco J. Lara Jr.

5 Quantifying missing and hidden trade: An economic perspective   61
Sami Bensassi and Jade Siu

6 Research in dangerous fields: Ethics, morals, and practices in the
   study of smuggling   77
Thomas Hüsken

Contents

PART II
Borderlands and their people

93

7 Making borders, closing frontiers and identifying smuggling:
Comparative histories
Paul Nugent

95

8 Borderlands, frontiers, and borders: Changing meanings and the
intersection with smuggling practices
Sergio Peña

107

9 Trading spaces: Afghan borderland brokers and the transformation
of the margins
Jonathan Goodhand, Jan Koehler, and Jasmine Bhatia

118

10 Scales of grey: The complex geography of transnational cross-border
trade in the African Great Lakes region
Timothy Raeymaekers

134

11 Smuggling as a legitimate activity? The OPEC Boys as social bandits in
Northern Uganda
Kristof Titeca

144

12 Tall tales and borderline cases: Narratives as meaningful contraband
Mareike Schomerus and Lotje de Vries

156

13 Gender and smuggling
Caroline E. Schuster

168

PART III
Smuggling goods

181

14 Cocaine smuggling: Between geopolitics and domestic power struggles
Angélica Durán-Martínez

183

15 Sharing the load: The distributive nature of the opium trade in,
and from, Afghanistan
David Mansfield

196

16 Arms trafficking
Nicholas Marsh and Lauren Pinson

213

Contents

17 Reconciling competing policies for combatting wildlife trafficking and preventing zoonotic pandemics 228
Vanda Felbab-Brown

18 Cigarette smuggling: Trends, taxes and big tobacco 247
Max Gallien

19 Theft and smuggling of petroleum products 260
Tim Eaton

20 Old routes, new rules: Smuggling rice in the porous borders of the Sulu, Celebes, and South China Sea 272
Eddie L. Quitoriano

21 The intersections of smuggling flows 286
Annette Idler

PART IV
Smuggling and mobility 301

22 Humanitarian smuggling in a time of restricting and criminalizing mobility 303
Ilse van Liempt

23 Migrant smuggling and the social organisation of cross–border mobility 313
Luca Raineri

24 Human smuggling, gender and labour circulation in the Global South 326
Priya Deshingkar

25 Human smuggling in the time of COVID-19: Lessons from a pandemic 341
Lucia Bird Ruiz-Benitez de Lugo

PART V
Smuggling and conflict 353

26 The illicit trade and conflict connection: Insights from US history 355
Peter Andreas

27 Smuggling, survival, and civil war economies 369
Aisha Ahmad

vii

Contents

28 Checkpost chess: Exploring the relationship between insurgents
and illicit trade 384
Shalaka Thakur

29 Rebels, smugglers and (the pitfalls of) economic pacification 397
David Brenner

PART VI
Addressing smuggling **409**

30 Blue frontiers: In pursuit of smugglers at sea 411
Carina Bruwer

31 Communities and crime wars: Adaptation and resilience 431
Matt Herbert, Tuesday Reitano, and Siria Gastelum Felix

32 The "war on smugglers" and the expansion of the border apparatus 444
Lorena Gazzotti

Index *455*

ILLUSTRATIONS

Figures

4.1	Economic value chain of cross-border trade in Sulu and Tawi-Tawi	54
5.1	Difference between "missing trade" and "hidden trade"	62
5.2	ICBT survey points monitored by governments of Nigeria and Benin	67
9.1	Map of Afghanistan, highlighting locations referred to in the case illustrations	125
11.1	Poster of a (fictional) film on the Arua Boys smugglers	150
12.1	The border stone that is the only official demarcation of the border between South Sudan and CAR	157
12.2	The South Sudan/CAR borderstone in the vast bushland	162
15.1	Map showing southwest Afghanistan and the province of Nimroz bordering Iran and Pakistan	199
15.2	Imagery of the Iranian border wall south of the provincial capital Ziranj, Nimroz	200
15.3	Imagery of the abandoned border village of Kruki in Kang district, Nimroz	201
15.4	Map of Nangarhar, showing the main smuggling routes into Pakistan	204
15.5	Mapping of the border fence built by the GoP with an initial focus on the Mohmand tribal areas north of Torkham	207
16.1	An illustration of the national pool of illicit arms	220
21.1	Illicit supply chain networks	290
29.1	A palm oil smuggler on the Moei River that marks the border between Myanmar and Thailand	403
30.1	Maritime zones	414

Tables

9.1	Typology of trading corridors	123
15.1	Costs incurred by an opium trader of transporting 1 kg of opium from Bakwa to Iran	202
15.2	Costs incurred by an opium trader from transporting 1 kg of from Sherzad to Pakistan	206
15.3	Estimate of the number of traders and smugglers in Nangarhar	209

CONTRIBUTORS

Aisha Ahmad is an Associate Professor of Political Science at the University of Toronto, the Director of the Islam and Global Affairs Initiative and a Senior Researcher of the Global Justice Lab at the Munk School of Global Affairs, and the Chair of the Board of Directors of Women in International Security-Canada. She is the author of the award-winning book *Jihad & Co.: Black Markets and Islamist Power* (Oxford University Press, 2017). She has conducted fieldwork in Afghanistan, Pakistan, Somalia, Mali, Kenya, Iraq, and Lebanon, and has advised both government and international organizations on global security.

Peter Andreas is the John Hay Professor of Political Science and International Studies at Brown University. He holds a joint appointment between the department of Political Science and the Watson Institute for International and Public Affairs. Andreas is the author, co-author, or co-editor of eleven books, including *Smuggler Nation: How Illicit Trade Made America* (Oxford University Press, 2013), *Policing the Globe: Criminalization and Crime Control in International Relations* (Oxford University Press, 2006), *Border Games: Policing the U.S.-Mexico Divide* (Cornell University Press, 2000, 2nd ed. 2009, 3rd ed. 2022), and, *Killer High: A History of War in Six Drugs* (Oxford University Press, 2020). He is currently working on a new book, *The Illicit Global Economy: What Everyone Needs to Know* (under contract with Oxford University Press).

Sami Bensassi is a Reader in Development Economics at the Birmingham Business School. After completing a PhD in Economics (University of Paris Nanterre, France), he joined the University Jaume I (Spain) in 2009. In Spain, he led a research project on the impact of maritime trade on Mediterranean countries for the Centre for Research on the Mediterranean Economies (CREMED). He joined the Birmingham Business School in January 2013. Since 2013, he has worked extensively on smuggling in North Africa and West Africa across two projects in cooperation with the World Bank and the AGRODEP network.

Jasmine Bhatia is an Expert Advisor with the European Institute of Peace working on the Afghanistan Peace Process. Prior to this role, she was a Postdoctoral Research Fellow in the Department of Development Studies at SOAS. Her research interests include civil wars, insurgent movements, and sub-national political settlements in violent contexts. In 2018, she received her doctorate in Politics from Oxford University, which involved several rounds of mixed-methods fieldwork in Afghanistan. In addition to her academic projects, Jasmine has worked as a consultant for the United Nations and on several UK government-sponsored international development projects, primarily in Afghanistan and the Middle East.

Lucia Bird Ruiz-Benitez de Lugo is Director of the Observatory of Illicit Economies in West Africa at the Global Initiative Against Transnational Organized Crime, with longstanding experience researching and analysing human smuggling and trafficking markets internationally, alongside other forms of organized crime. Lucia was previously a practising lawyer, and worked as legal and policy adviser to the Punjab Government, Pakistan, and the Ministry of Finance, Ghana. During this time, Lucia was affiliated with Oxford Policy Management, a development consultancy headquartered in the UK.

David Brenner is Lecturer in Global Insecurities in the Department of International Relations at the University of Sussex's School of Global Studies. His research explores the intersections among conflict, security, and development. It is informed by long-term field work in the restive border areas between Myanmar, China, Thailand and India. David is author of *Rebel Politics: A Political Sociology of Armed Struggle in Myanmar's Borderlands* (Ithaca, N.Y.: Cornell University Press).

Carina Bruwer holds a PhD in Public International Law from the Centre of Criminology at the University of Cape Town, South Africa. Her doctoral research focused on combating transnational organized crime at sea. She holds LLB and LLM degrees from Stellenbosch University, is an admitted attorney and has worked for the United Nations Global Maritime Crime Programme. She is currently working in conservation and wildlife crime in southern Africa.

Nikki Philline C. de la Rosa is Country Director of International Alert Philippines. She has over two decades of professional experience in politico-economic research and program management, working with international and local NGOs and academia. She holds an undergraduate degree from the University of the Philippines and an MSc in Development Studies (with distinction) from the London School of Economics. Nikki co-authored the section "Robustness in Data and Methods: Scoping the Real Economy of Mindanao" in Alert's publication *Out of the Shadows: Violent Conflict and the Real Economy of Mindanao*, which won the 2017 National Book Award for social science.

Lotje de Vries is an Assistant Professor at the Sociology of Development and Change Group of Wageningen University. She is an editor of *Secessionism in African Politics: Aspiration, Grievance, Performance, Disenchantment* (Palgrave Macmillan 2019) and *The Borderlands of South Sudan: Authority and Identity in Contemporary and Historical Perspectives* (Palgrave Macmillan, 2013) and has published widely on security, authority, and state-building in borderlands, drawing on extensive field research in the Central African Republic and South Sudan.

Priya Deshingkar is Professor of Migration and Development at the University of Sussex. She specialises South-South migration, poverty and development with a focus on forced migration, precarious work, human smuggling and trafficking and gender. She led the ten-year DFID-funded Migrating out of Poverty Consortium with projects in five global regions and 11 countries across Asia and Africa. Prior to joining Sussex, Priya was a Research Fellow at the Overseas Development Institute in London. Priya has a PhD in Development Studies and has published extensively on migration related topics.

Contributors

Gregor Dobler is Professor of Social Anthropology at the University of Freiburg, Germany. An economic and political anthropologist focusing on Southern Africa and Western Europe, he is one of the founders of the African Borderlands Research Network and has published widely on borderland issues.

Angélica Durán-Martínez is an Associate Professor of Political Science at the University of Massachusetts-Lowell and Director of the Global Studies PhD Program. She holds a Ph.D. in Political Science from Brown University, an M.A. in Latin American and Caribbean Studies from New York University, and a B.A. in Political Science from Universidad Nacional de Colombia. She is the author of *The Politics of Drug Violence: Criminals, Cops, and Politicians in Colombia and Mexico* (Oxford University Press, 2018), winner of two awards. She has published several book chapters and journal articles on issues of crime, violence, and insecurity in Latin America.

Tim Eaton is a Senior Research Fellow with the Middle East and North Africa Programme at Chatham House, where he focuses on the political economy of conflict in the Middle East and North Africa and in Libya, in particular. He was lead author on a 2019 report on the development of conflict economies in the Middle East and North Africa that was listed among the University of Pennsylvania's top research papers of 2019.

Vanda Felbab-Brown, a Senior Fellow at the Brookings Institution, is the director of the Initiative on Nonstate Armed Actors and several other projects and initiatives at Brookings. She is the author of several books and numerous articles and policy reports, including *The Extinction Market: Wildlife Trafficking and How to Counter It* (Hurst and Oxford University Press, 2017).

Max Gallien is a Research Fellow at the Institute of Development Studies (IDS) located at the University of Sussex, a Fellow at the International Centre for Tax and Development (ICTD) and a Senior Fellow at the Global Initiative against Transnational Organised Crime (GITOC). He is a political scientist specialising in the politics of informal and illegal economies, the political economy of development and the modern politics of the Middle East and North Africa.

Siria Gastelum Felix is the Director of Resilience at the Global Initiative. A former Emmy award winning journalist, she also worked at the International Narcotics Control Board's Secretariat in Vienna and the United Nations Global Initiative Against Human Trafficking. She currently leads GI-TOC's programming in Latin America and works on technology applications to empower civil society leaders to collaborate.

Lorena Gazzotti is the Alice Tong Sze Research Fellow at Lucy Cavendish College and CRASSH, University of Cambridge. Her research explores elusive border control and ephemeral carcerality at the Spanish–Moroccan border. She has published in the Journal of Ethnic and Migration Studies, the Journal of North African Studies, and the Sociological Review, amongst others. Her first book, *Immigration Nation. Aid, Control, and Border Politics in Morocco*, is forthcoming with Cambridge University Press in November 2021.

Jonathan Goodhand is Professor of Conflict and Development Studies, in the Department of Development Studies at SOAS, University of London, and an Honorary Professorial Fellow at the University of Melbourne, School of Social and Political Sciences. He is the Principal

Contributors

Investigator of a four-year Global Challenges Research Fund project 'Drugs & (dis)order: Building sustainable peacetime economies in the aftermath of war.' His research interests include the political economy of conflict, war economies, war-to-peace transitions and the role of borderlands, with a particular focus on Central and South Asia

Matt Herbert is the Research Manager for the North Africa and Sahel Observatory at the Global Initiative Against Transnational Organized Crime. He is a political scientist who has worked throughout North and West Africa, specializing in security sector reform, border security, and transnational organized crime. Max Herbert holds a PhD in International Relations from The Fletcher School of Law & Diplomacy, Tufts University.

Thomas Hüsken is a German ethnologist who teaches at the University of Bayreuth. His main fields of research are political anthropology, borderlands studies, and the anthropology of development. He has conducted extensive fieldwork in Egypt, Yemen, Jordan, and since 2007, in the borderland of Egypt and Libya in particular. Thomas Hüsken is the author of *Tribal Politics in the Borderland of Egypt and Libya* (2019). He is co-founder and member of the executive committee of the African Borderlands Research Network (ABORNE).

Annette Idler is the Director of Studies at the Changing Character of War Centre, Senior Research Fellow at Pembroke College, and at the Department of Politics and International Relations, all at University of Oxford. She is also Visiting Scholar at Harvard University's Weatherhead Center for International Affairs. She works on the interface of conflict, security, and transnational organized crime and has conducted extensive fieldwork in and on Venezuela, Colombia, Ecuador, Myanmar, and Somalia. She is the author of *Borderland Battles: Violence, Crime, and Governance at the Edges of Colombia's War* (Oxford University Press, 2019), published in Spanish as *Fronteras Rojas* (Penguin Random House, 2021), and co-editor of *Transforming the War on Drugs: Warriors, Victims, and Vulnerable Regions* (Oxford University Press/Hurst, 2021). Her work has appeared in journals such as *World Politics, Third World Quarterly*, and the *Journal of Global Security Studies*.

Jan Koehler is Research Associate at SOAS with focus on Afghanistan, Pakistan, Central Asia and the Caucasus region. He received his first degree from the Freie Universität Berlin in Social Anthropology and did his PhD in Political Science on institution-centred conflict research. The emphasis of his academic research is on the impact of interventions on local patterns and dynamics of social order, subnational governance and conflicts. As part of a group of researchers Jan developed systematic mixed method research designs, combining more inductive qualitative case-studies with deductive quantitative hypothesis-driven approaches.

Francisco J. Lara Jr. is currently a Peace and Conflict Adviser to International Alert and teaches at the University of the Philippines – Diliman. He is co-editor of the book, *Out of The Shadows: Violent Conflict and the Real Economy of Mindanao* (2013) which won the 2017 National Book Awards in the Social Sciences, and authored the book *Insurgents, Clans, and States: Political Legitimacy and Resurgent Conflict in Muslim Mindanao, Philippines* (2013). He holds an undergraduate degree from the University of the Philippines and an MSc and PhD from the London School of Economics.

David Mansfield is an independent consultant. He has been conducting research on rural livelihoods and poppy cultivation in Afghanistan since 1997. This research has involved over

Contributors

16,000 in-depth household interviews in rural Afghanistan. David has a PhD in development studies and is the author of *A State Built on Sand: How Opium Undermined Afghanistan*, and produced more than 75 research-based products on the illicit economies and rural livelihoods in Afghanistan.

Nicholas Marsh is a Senior Researcher at the Peace Research Institute Oslo. He has written tens of articles, chapters, and reports on the acquisition and use of weapons by non-state groups, the global licit and illicit trade in small arms and light weapons, and national and international laws and regulations governing arms transfers. He has been the Chair of a European Science Foundation funded research network on small arms, and a consultant to the UN Office on Drugs and Crime and to the Small Arms Survey. His work has involved the NISAT project which for 17 years collected data on the licit and illicit trade in small arms and light weapons.

Kate Meagher is an Associate Professor in Development Studies at the Department of International Development, London School of Economics. She specializes in research on African informal economies, and has done extensive fieldwork-based research on cross-border trade and regional integration at the Nigeria-Niger and Uganda-DRC borders. She has also published widely on informal institutions and hybrid governance, taxing the informal economy, and informality and economic inclusion in Africa. Recent publications include *Globalisation, Economic Inclusion and African Workers: Making the Right Connections* (Routledge 2016, co-edited with L. Mann, L. and M. Bolt).

Fernanda Morales Tovar is a visual artist whose work explores the analogies and dialectics existing in the environment that promote the conjunction of nature and urban devices in everyday life. She constructs a visual archeology based on the interpretation and proposal of signs of the intersection of spaces, the human being, the stories, the ruin, and the landscape, through the use of paint. She earned her MFA and BFA in Visual Arts from the National Autonomous University of Mexico. She did an Academic Research Stay at the Complutense University of Madrid, Spain (2019). Her work has been exhibited in various museums and institutions in Mexico and the Netherlands, as well as being part of the Lumen-Mexico Collection.

Paul Nugent is Professor of Comparative African History, the University of Edinburgh with a specialism in African borderlands. Paul is the holder of an ERC Advanced Grant for the AFRIGOS project, comparing transport corridors, border towns and port cities across four regions of Africa. He has most recently published *Boundaries, Communities and State-Making in West Africa* (CUP, 2019) comparing border and state dynamics in Ghana/Togo and Senegal/Gambia. Paul is the founder and chair of the African Borderlands Research Network (ABORNE) and a member of the Africa-Europe Strategic Taskforce dealing with transport and connectivity.

Sergio Peña currently works at El Colegio de la Frontera Norte. He holds a doctoral degree in urban and regional planning from Florida State University. His research agenda focused on studying urban planning and planning theory, crossborder planning, governance, and cooperation processes between the U.S. and Mexico. He is the co-editor-in-chief of the Journal of Borderlands Studies (JBS). He has published several articles on borders and the most recent publication is: Peña, S., & Durand, F. 2020. Mobility planning in cross-border metropolitan regions: the European and North American experiences. *Territory, Politics, Governance*, 1-18.

xiv

Contributors

Lauren Pinson is Assistant Professor at the University of Texas at Dallas. Her research focuses on small arms trafficking, drug trafficking, and international assistance aimed at preventing those trades. Her fieldwork on small arms has included interviewing officials in government and regional organizations in more than a dozen countries. In collaboration with Nicholas Marsh, she constructed a dataset on illicit small arms seizures while she was a visiting researcher at PRIO. She has also worked as a consultant to the UN Office on Drugs and Crime and briefed OSCE's Forum for Security Co-operation on illicit small arms issues.

Eddie L. Quitoriano has been affiliated with International Alert-Philippines since 2011, in the field of shadow economies and violent conflicts with focus on the Southern Philippines, Nepal, Aceh and Myanmar. He earned a Bachelor of Arts from Xavier University-Ateneo de Cagayan in 1973, after which he got immersed in rebellion and insurgency that brought him to North Africa, the Middle East, South and Central America and North Korea. Largely auto-didactic, much of his knowledge on shadow economies and conflicts are drawn from experience and mentorship. His independent consultancy includes assignments for the World Bank, GIZ and other international development agencies.

Timothy Raeymaekers is Senior Lecturer in political geography at the University of Zurich. His research focuses on resource frontiers, including mineral extraction and agricultural plantations in Central Africa (Democratic Republic of Congo) and Southern Europe (Italy). His broader interests involve questions around territory, borders and sovereign power in the context of supply chain capitalism.

Luca Raineri is Researcher at the Sant'Anna School of Advanced Studies of Pisa, Italy. His areas of expertise include security studies, international relations, African politics and transnational governance. His research investigates transnational flows of security relevance and extra-legal economies, focusing in particular on the Sahara-Sahel region, and has been published in several scholarly journals. Dr Raineri has consulted for several NGOs, IOs and think tanks dealing with security and its nexuses with human rights and development, with a particular focus on Africa.

Tuesday Reitano is the Deputy Director of the Global Initiative Against Transnational Organized Crime. She previously worked in the UN system, on organized crime, fragile states and development. She has authored a number of policy orientated and academic reports with leading institutions such as the UN, World Bank and OECD on topics ranging from organized crime's evolution and impact in Africa, on human smuggling, illicit financial flows, and the nexus among crime, terrorism, security and development.

Mareike Schomerus is Vice President at the Busara Center in Nairobi and Research Director of the Secure Livelihoods Research Consortium at ODI in London. She directs Busara's work on 'the mental landscape', which links ethnographic research with behavioural science to better understand situations of crisis and how to design human-centred solutions. Having published widely on violent conflict, peace processes, borderlands, as well as behavioural mechanisms in post-conflict lives, her most recent book is *The Lord's Resistance Army: Violence and Peacemaking in Africa* (Cambridge University Press, 2021).

Caroline E. Schuster is a Senior Lecturer in the School of Archaeology and Anthropology at the Australian National University, having previously held research fellowships at the Harvard

Academy for International and Area Studies and the Center for the Study of Gender and Sexuality at the University of Chicago. Her research on the production of gendered economic subjects through microcredit appears in her book *Social Collateral: Women and Microfinance in Paraguay's Smuggling Economy*. Her current research is supported by an Australian Research Council Discovery Early Career Researcher Award (DECRA) and focuses on financialization and climate insurance.

Jade Siu is a Researcher at the Oxford Department of International Development. She researches refugee economies and informal cross-border trade in East Africa, focussing on the border costs imposed on traders. Previously she was a consultant in the field of international development and trade. She obtained her PhD in Economics at the University of Birmingham.

Shalaka Thakur is a PhD candidate at the Graduate Institute, Geneva. Her research explores how political order is constructed in conflict zones. She has been conducting fieldwork along the Indo-Myanmar border since 2013, engaging with non-state armed groups, state security forces, civil society and businesses to understand how wartime orders connect to questions of peacebuilding. Shalaka has been a research associate at the London School of Economics and Political Science (LSE) and has an MSc in Conflict Studies from LSE.

Kristof Titeca is an Associate Professor at the Institute of Development Policy, University of Antwerp. His work focuses on governance and conflict in Central and Eastern Africa, with particular attention to the Uganda-DRC borderlands. His latest books are *Rebel Lives: Photographs from inside the Lord's Resistance Army* (Hannibal Books/FOMU) and *Negotiating Public Services in the Congo* (with Tom De Herdt, ZED Books).

Ilse van Liempt is Associate Professor in Urban Geography at Utrecht University. She is the Research Leader of the UU wide Focus Area Migration and Societal Change and has published widely on irregular migration, refugees and processes of inclusion and exclusion. Her PhD research was published with Amsterdam University Press and is called *Navigating Borders: Inside Perspectives on the Process of Human Smuggling into the Netherlands*.

Florian Weigand is the Co-Director of the Centre for the Study of Armed Groups at the Overseas Development Institute and a Research Associate at the London School of Economics and Political Science. He works on armed conflict, illicit economies, and international interventions, and explores the politics and societal dynamics of conflict zones, borderlands, and other complex environments. He is the author of *Conflict and Transnational Crime: Borders, Bullets & Business in Southeast Asia* (Edward Elgar, 2020) and *Waiting for Dignity: Legitimacy and Authority in Afghanistan* (Columbia University Press, 2022).

1

STUDYING SMUGGLING

Max Gallien and Florian Weigand

Smuggling is an economic activity that is politically defined and socially embedded.[1] In its functional essence, smuggling is typically trade, anchored in the demand for certain products and the costs of their movement. At the same time, it is segmented from legal trade through laws, which are, along with their enforcement, deeply political, tied into processes of state-formation and demarcation, economic regulation and prohibition, and geopolitics and conflict. Unlike most trade, smuggling in its perception and study is also intimately tied to the figure of the 'smuggler' and the particular social space of the borderland in which they are imagined to operate – as a risk-taker, a broker, a hustler, a worker, a profiteer, a villain, or a local hero. Consequently, the study of smuggling always has attracted a range of disciplines: anthropology; geography; economics; sociology; history; law; and political science. Even so, it rarely has been genuinely multi-disciplinary. Discussions are frequently siloed along regional, disciplinary, and methodological lines that are connected insufficiently with each other. Frequently, smugglers appear not just on the geographic margins of states but on the margins of arguments that are primarily not about them and are imagined and framed to fit the respective assumptions, theories, and ideologies.[2]

This handbook is intended to work against these tendencies and toward what might be called 'smuggling studies.' Its aim is to bring diverse disciplinary perspectives on smuggling together in one place and in conversation with each other, to highlight themes that emerge across different areas: the complex relationships among smugglers, states, armed groups, and globalised markets; the role of and impact on borderland communities; the sometimes counterintuitive effects of conflict and 'anti-smuggling policies;' and the drivers of heterogeneous dynamics across goods and routes. It also seeks to reflect on the methods and politics that have shaped the study of smuggling and to outline pathways for future research and collaboration. First and foremost, it seeks to present the value of understanding smuggling by placing smuggling at the centre of a field of study, not casting it at the margins, merely as a policy implication or a bogeyman. The remainder of this introduction is split into two broader sections. The first summarises key observations in the study of smuggling, highlighting central themes around conceptions, routes, actors and regulation, while also tracing some of the key developments and fault-lines in this field of study itself. The second section then provides an overview of the purpose, perspective, and content of this volume.

DOI: 10.4324/9781003043645-1

Defining smuggling – in time and space

We define smuggling as the purposeful movement across a border in contravention to the relevant legal frameworks.[3] It should be clear from this that smuggling, as an activity and as a field of study, is fundamentally politically defined. Both the borders that make smuggling cross-border trade and the laws that make it illegal are social and political constructs. This of course means that the boundaries of smuggling are movable and embedded as much in the context of an activity than in the activity itself. Critically, they are conditional not just in space but also in time. As historical studies of cross-border trade have often highlighted, the same exchange of food and livestock between two settlements can over the years and without any variation in its practice change from a neighbourly exchange to legal international trade to smuggling.

As many contributions in this volume have highlighted (for example, Nugent; Andreas, in this volume), the history of smuggling, deeply entwined with the processes of border-making, colonialism, and the territorial expansion of states, is an excellent illustration of this dependency on politics. It highlights again the fundamental contextuality of the topic at hand, as different goods and trade corridors have been criminalised and decriminalised across history, while borders have been drawn, erased and re-drawn. While it is frequently referred to as the 'shadow' or 'dark side' of globalisation, trade or border making, a more historicised approach to smuggling takes away some of the perceived neutrality or inevitability of the dividing line between the legal processes and its 'underbelly.' It notes that what is today often taken self-evidently as 'global drug smuggling' would have been incomprehensible to an observer from 200 years ago, not just because the borders across which these goods move have changed, but because the very conception of 'drugs' as a particular set of criminalised medically harmful recreational substances is distinctly contemporary (see Porter and Hough, 1996).

Naturally, these processes of rule-making and boundary-making have not been shaped merely by geography, changing social norms and their legal codification, but also by political and commercial interests (see for example Durán-Martínez, in this volume). Here, the political drivers behind the historical geographical expansion of the nation-state and of empires have shaped critically the making of borders, the creation of borderlands and the construction of a global legal trade system. Smuggling today often happens across borders that were drawn by colonial powers through communities that remain closely connected (see for example Titeca, in this volume). As historical scholarship has often highlighted, the expansion of state and imperial structures has not demarcated only smuggling, but often not shied away from encouraging it or drawing on it where it was useful, from arms supplies to blockade busting to the opium wars (Andreas, 2014; Harvey, 2016). Opium in particular of course highlights the complex relationship among empire, economic interests, bureaucratic development, and the criminalisation of certain trades (Kim, 2020). It also fits into a wider picture, especially with a view to narcotics, that serves as a reminder that the colonial and imperial history of the making of smuggling both through border-making and the making of global rules of trade and consumption have been embedded deeply in unequal power structures and consequently have been racialised (Koram, 2019) and gendered starkly (Schuster, in this volume). As we note below, the politics of making smuggling – and making smugglers – still disproportionately affects communities not just at geographic but also political margins of the modern state system, from travellers to nomadic pastoral communities. This is especially true given how closely connected modern policy on smuggling is with language around 'poor governance,' 'weak states,' and 'under-development,' considering the power structures that have shaped its context necessarily unsettle common de-politicised conceptions of smuggling and anti-smuggling policy.

Studying smuggling

While the making of laws and of borders has shaped smuggling, smuggling can also do the same trick in reverse. As a range of contributions in this volume have highlighted, smuggling has actively shaped how borders and borderlands have developed. While Scott famously framed borderlands and their mobility as essential resistance against the 'last enclosure' of the state (2009), historians have frequently highlighted the ways in which border communities and smugglers have at times themselves contributed to shaping and legitimising border structures (Nugent, 2002 and in this volume). At the same time, smuggling has been connected to the rise of vast state enforcement apparatuses, both within countries and acrossborders. It has contributed to the justification of state and imperial expansion and contributed to the shape of modern bureaucracies and state structures (Andreas and Nadelmann, 2008), and influenced legislation, from tariffs to prohibition.

Naturally, none of these dynamics are merely historical: legislation around trade and taxation, prohibition and tariffs still are constantly evolving and re-shaping the barriers between legal and illegal trade. In the last few years, a legal global trade in cannabis products, long almost entirely limited to smuggling, has been developing again. Taxes and tariffs on different goods are constantly re-negotiated, and arguments around smuggling are still actively shaping lobbying efforts – for example around taxes on tobacco products (see Gallien, in this volume). While the past decades have seen fewer borders being re-drawn, customs unions and trade agreements are changing the boundaries and barriers of the global trade system, simultaneously accompanied by new trade infrastructure and industries of border fortification, shaped again, by discourses of smuggling and porosity (see Andreas, 2009; Andersson, 2014; Gazzotti in this volume).

As the politics and the violent history underlying the creation and maintenance of modern state and legal systems have created the boundaries that characterise smuggling, they naturally have complicated its definition. Similarly, they have shaped how scholarship has conceptualised, characterised and named smuggling. Somewhat unsurprisingly, the literature on the topic currently has not endorsed one universal set of terms. Researchers, including the authors in this volume, have used a variety of conceptions of the term, or sub-sections of it, and a variety of language around it, from illicit trade to contraband to shadow trade to informal cross-border trade (ICBT) to trafficking. This tapestry typically becomes even more diverse when we leave the language of academia and talk to those engaged in smuggling themselves. Here, some may speak of "livelihood trade," others of "informal trade," and others just of "business." Given the politics of the 'boundaries of smuggling,' it should be unsurprising that the language around it has become varied and contested, as academics, policy practitioners and smugglers all seek to establish and subvert these boundaries and the connected normative claims about the activity, the political context that names it illegal, or the local social context that may frame it as immoral or heroic.

The term 'smuggling' in particular, may be seen by some as endorsing a statist perspective towards the activity. We would like to highlight here that this is not our intention – we trust our audience not to read a normative position in the term, and defer to the importance, in evaluating smuggling, of its aforementioned context, of which this volume provides riches. We feel it critical to maintain both the fact that the defining features of smuggling are socially constructed and the conviction that this does not make them meaningless in practice. Our aforementioned definition groups within its conception of smuggling some practices which are entirely normalised and tolerated, and which would see both those involved in the trade and some of those studying it balk at the term. We note, however, that the illegality of an activity still can have critical consequences for those involved in it, even if activities are normalised. It can shape the routes or profits available, the payments traders must make, or the violence they may be subject to, including at the hand of the state.

We do not seek to and did not impose a uniform terminology, definition, or perspective on the authors of the individual chapters, as will be evident to the reader. Instead, the claim that we seek to make here is that, within this diverse language, and within these contingent and shifting boundaries, there lies a field of study to which a variety of methodological and disciplinary perspectives are making contributions that can speak to each other and be legible across terminological differences.[4] Finally, it is worth noting that while smuggling requires borders, these do not necessarily have to be (or lay claim to being) national borders between states. Goods can be smuggled into a prison, past a barricade into a city under siege, or from an area controlled by an armed group to a territory dominated by a different group. The focus of this volume, however, lies primarily in smuggling across international borders, alongside the particular geographic, social and political structures that they give rise to.

The content of smuggling

The study of smuggling has seen the development of numerous sub-divisions and sub-categorisations of its titular activity, some structured around the scope of the activity (such as bootlegging vs wholesale smuggling), the actors involved (see Dobler, 2016 or Goodhand et al., in this volume), or the routes taken (such as maritime smuggling, see Bruwer in this volume). Other distinctions have categorised territory according to its position in a wider smuggling macro-structure, dividing between spaces of production and transit, and between entrepot and consumption territory (Igue and Soule, 1992; Bennafla, 2014). While we do not expand on these here, we think it worth expanding on some distinctions and observations that are based on the goods that are being traded. Again, some preliminary conceptual points are in order.

First, some chapters in this volume reference a distinction between 'licit' and 'illicit' smuggling. This distinguishes between the smuggling of goods for which a legal trade corridor exists that is not subject to additional restrictions, such as rice (Quitoriano, in this volume) or gasoline (Eaton, in this volume), and the smuggling of goods for which it does not, which typically includes goods such as firearms (Marsh and Pinson, in this volume), narcotics (Mansfield; Duran-Martinez, in this volume), or rare wildlife (Felbab-Brown, in this volume).

Second, this volume also includes chapters on the smuggling of people. We have included them not because we understand the smuggling of people and the smuggling of goods as essentially the same, or because we seek to understand humans merely as 'cargo.' As each of the respective chapters highlight, human smuggling spurs unique dynamics: it complicates the roles of smugglers and of law enforcement and gives rise to further distinctions around consent and relationships between smugglers and smuggled that are not applicable to the smuggling of goods. However, we have decided to include these studies in this volume because we believe that the two areas of scholarship can benefit from closer communication, especially given the rich and critical history of scholarship on human mobility. As the different contributions in this volume powerfully illustrate, the study of smuggling of people has made contributions to our understanding of the role of networks, the politics and effects of anti-smuggling policies, and the entanglement between smuggling and livelihoods that provide critical interventions into our understanding of smuggling more widely (see Bird; Deshingkar; Gazzotti; Raineri; van Liempt, in this volume).

Historically, the study of smuggling has not been characterised only by disciplinary and methodological divisions, but also often by segmentations based on the study of different goods, with particularly active sub-fields developing around the smuggling of different narcotics, hydrocarbons, and agricultural products. The chapters on different smuggled goods in this volume can be read as empirically rich single case studies on commonly smuggled goods. Read

Studying smuggling

alongside each other, they provide an illustration of the power that comparisons between different goods can have in the study of smuggling. Contributions to the study of particular goods again demonstrate how much the dynamics of smuggling are subject to the particular contexts in which they operate. They provide an important reminder that this is not just context-dependent on laws and borders, although both can also be good-specific, but also one shaped by value chains, industries, and markets.

Studying smuggling with a focus on particular goods also situates the role of illegal movement across borders within the larger life of these commodities. It can point to the importance of different production economies – some of which are highly labour intensive and connected to politically tolerated livelihood strategies. This can be observed in the case of some agricultural production of narcotics such as cannabis in Morocco; others also are an important source of revenue for competing authorities such as in the case of opium in Afghanistan (see Mansfield; Ahmad, in this volume). Similarly, consumption markets can shape the politics of smuggling, as has been particularly noticeable in the context of firearms (Pinson and Marsh, in this volume) (where actors are worried about the effect on the capacity for violence of the end-user), or in foodstuffs, (where smuggling routes have often been central to maintaining livelihoods) (see Scheele, 2012; or Quitoriano, in this volume).

Focusing on particular goods can also help illuminate the heterogeneity in power, access and profit along smuggling value chains and the different actors involved (see for example Mansfield, in this volume). It also demonstrates that smuggled goods don't exist always as smuggled goods – while some value chains are entirely illegal, others dip in and out of legality as they cross borders and boundaries, passing from export processing zones to free ports and to consumption markets. Consequently, they closely tie in to the changing politics of trade liberalisation, regulation, and taxation in recent decades (Meagher, 2003). Here, work on the smuggling of licit goods, in particular, has foregrounded the importance of examining the role of legal industries in smuggling as well. While they often frame themselves as victims or competitors of smuggling, work on cigarette smuggling or wildlife trade, for example, has highlighted both the role of formal sector actors in smuggling economies and the continuous re-negotiation of the boundaries between legal and illegal trade (see Felbab-Brown; Gallien, in this volume). Furthermore, focusing on value chains frequently points to the importance of formal and informal finance, of licit and illicit financial flows, and of money laundering and currency exchange as critical features of smuggling today. These issues are particularly prevalent if we consider where smuggling typically is studied.

Localising smuggling

As this volume shows, there has been a strong theoretical and empirical connection between the study of smuggling and the study of borders and borderlands, particularly in African countries and low- and middle-income countries across the globe. In a sense, this is unsurprising – moving goods across borders is a defining part of smuggling, state capacity to limit these types of activities is arguably lower in low-income countries, and the production centres for some of the most studied smuggled goods, such as cocaine or opiates, lie in the so-called 'Global South.'

However, as a range of contributions in recent years has illustrated, it is important to complicate this picture. Scholarship on bordering and the externalisation of borders (see Pena, in this volume) has shown that borders themselves are often more complex and geographically expansive institutions than the proverbial line in the sand. A focus on borders themselves, however, also risks over-emphasising one particular aspect of smuggling activities – the logistics of movement – at the expense of dynamics of production, consumption and in particular financing, which are more frequently located in the political and economic centres (see

5

Meagher, in this volume). Seeking to understand the relationship between the centre and the periphery – geographically, politically, legally, economically – has been one of the central contributions of the study of smuggling to social sciences more widely, but also remains an ongoing challenge.[5]

The frequent focus of the study of smuggling on low- and middle-income countries presents a parallel dynamic. As many of the chapters in this volume highlight, they present particularly important and insightful places of study, where smuggling overlaps with ongoing state transformation processes, and where some of the most visible changes and intense human costs and suffering in connection with smuggling are concentrated. It is critical, however, to locate these as nodes in wider networks which also feature high-income countries – as key consumption markets for narcotics, as key financial centres for the movement and investment of capital, as logistical centres for global transport networks, or as drivers of the rules of global trade and mobility that shape legal and illegal trade structures alike.

Building on these considerations, it is important to recognise that just like legal trade, smuggling today is a truly global phenomenon. Naturally, there are different corridors and geographic weights to the trade of different goods, and some countries more frequently take the role of production, consumption, or transit space. However, not only is there no country on the globe today that is not in some way implicated in smuggling structures, but smuggling is also deeply embedded in the increasingly globalised economy and its structures and infrastructures of finance, shipping, mobility, and technology. Consequently, it is critical to take a wider look at the geography of smuggling and consider it more explicitly in the context of the development of the global trade system more broadly. While many of the most visible dynamics around smuggling may lie in borderlands, it is important both to connect these developments to dynamics that lie in the political and commercial centres, and re-evaluate the role of these spaces in smuggling.

Parallel to discussions on the spaces of smuggling lies increasing scholarship that asks how different smuggling actors and networks intersect, particularly in borderland spaces. One strand of the literature has frequently highlighted the potential for new connections to be formed between different smuggling networks in these spaces (see Idler, in this volume). In these strategic nodes, where the flows of various smuggled goods, licit and illicit, converge, different actors at times share a labour pool, local interlocutors, routes, information, or interests. That argument has often been extended to point to the risk, or perhaps the suggested proclivity of smuggling networks to engage closely with other non-state actors in these spaces, to form 'dirty entanglements' (Shelley, 2014) with organised crime groups or particularly terrorist organisations. Naturally, these arguments have been focused in particular on spaces of conflict and contested governance.

Recent years, however, have also seen scholarship seeking to 'untangle' these suggested entanglements, and highlight the complex and often adversarial micro-dynamics between these different actors on the ground. Authors have shown that alongside entanglements often lie segmentations between different actors and networks, based on different risk trade-offs, different normative evaluations of different activities, or different regulatory structures in which smuggling is embedded (Gallien, 2020). The question then becomes how and when different actors connect in borderlands. Here, a rich history of scholarship on borderlands has once again highlighted the importance of local political and social contexts to understand processes of brokerage, social and economic capital accumulation, moral economies, and practical norms that shape these interactions (see Goodhand, Raeymaekers and Titeca, in this volume; as well as Roitman, 2004; Titeca and Herdt, 2010; Raeymaekers, 2014; Hüsken, 2018; Raineri, 2019, among others). This connects to another central theme in recent scholarship.

Studying smuggling

Regulating smuggling

Unsurprisingly, the way in which things are smuggled varies significantly across goods, routes, and regions. Some smuggling routes pass across rural and barely noticeable borderlines, others through heavily fortified checkpoints or across the high seas (Bruwer, in this volume). While many goods are hidden from the eyes of state officials while they pass across borders, this is not always the case. One of the most notable themes in recent scholarship on smuggling is also perhaps one of the most counter-intuitive with respect to common portrayals of smuggling as a lawless game of cat and mouse. As multiple chapters (e.g., Raeymaekers, in this volume) and recent scholarship have more broadly highlighted, smuggling is typically conducted neither in a 'lawless zone' nor entirely under the radar of the state. Instead, smuggling is itself embedded in various forms of regulation.

Some regulation is inherent in smuggling operating as a trade – it is affected by formal legal frameworks, laws of demand and supply, by price differences and changes in these parameters. While these can introduce fluctuations and uncertainty into the life of smugglers, much other regulation is often intended to increase predictability for actors involved. This includes regulation created among and between smugglers – cartels on the more well-known end of the spectrum, but also arrangements around insurance, debt and divisions of retail territory. Most remarkably perhaps, scholarship has also shown that the relationship between smugglers and state agents is often substantially more regulated than commonly assumed. For example, looking at the Congo-Uganda border, Raeymaekers (in this volume) shows that many 'borderland bandits,' which play an important role in the smuggling economy and the way it is governed, owe their position to connections with the state. Rather than being characterised by mere evasion or perhaps unstructured petty corruption, recent scholarship has described a variety of more structured relationships, regulating how goods can be smuggled, at what price and under which conditions (i.e., Titeca and Herdt, 2010; Ahmad, 2017; Gallien and Weigand, 2021; Raineri and Strazzari, 2021). This can be found throughout the chapters in this volume, a few of which have further demonstrated that these dynamics take on an additional complexity when they are set in a context where also non-state armed groups are active (see Brenner; Thakur, Ahmad, in this volume). These examples highlight not merely that smuggling is often more structured and regulated than common imaginaries suggest, but also point to the complex interplay between such arrangements and ideas of legitimacy and local normative conceptions.

Here, communities themselves can emerge as regulatory actors. Local understandings of what type of smuggling is and is not appropriate, moral, or religiously permitted might not always present a unified evaluation of smuggling practices or by themselves drive out less accepted variants. Being highlighted frequently across these chapters (see for example Titeca; Quintaro; Schomerus and de Vries, in this volume), they present another level of regulation that smugglers engage with as they negotiate their relationships with their communities as customers, employees, neighbours, brokers, or customary governance actors (see also Goodhand et al, in this volume). Critically, acknowledging different community-centred perspectives on smuggling present an alternative account of smuggling to one that is solely focused on compliance with formal legal frameworks. They can help widen the vocabulary and categories relevant in describing and understanding smuggling. As particularly the chapters in the 'borderland' sections in this volume highlight, community perspectives can locate evaluations of smuggling in the political, economic and social environments of borderland communities, in local livelihoods or the history of community interaction across borders.

The smuggler

As we have noted above, the study of smuggling has often stood at the margins of separate academic enquiries, with smugglers being cast in supporting roles to support theories and policy recommendations that were not grounded in an in-depth analysis of smuggling itself, be it in studies on trade liberalisation, globalisation or war economies. Consequently, research that has sought to centre smuggling in its analysis has often struggled not merely with the terminology but also the figure, imaginary, and common perception of 'the smuggler' itself. As scholarship on human smuggling in particular has noted (see for example Sanchez, 2014; Gazzotti, in this volume), the figure of the 'smuggler' has increasingly become a boogeyman in the policy literature. Here, it has functioned not merely as an analytical shorthand, but also has provided a canvas to project blame for the horrific human costs at the intersection between modern systems of mobility, smuggling, and state policies. While this dynamic is somewhat less developed in the context of the smuggling of goods, here, too, a closer look at recent empirical scholarship on smuggling offers at least three important correctives.

First, as recent scholarship on the issue, and a range of contributions in this volume demonstrate, there is enormous and analytically relevant diversity in the people who are involved in smuggling (see for example Dobler, 2016; Sanchez, 2014; Goodhand, in this volume). While common conceptions of 'the smuggler' are typically associated with men, women play a variety of visible and less visible roles in smuggling networks around the globe. Schuster (in this volume) illustrates the "powerful modes of feminine concealment work" in her study of Ciudad del Este, on the Paraguayan side of the Tri-Border Area with Argentina and Brazil. Similarly, actors from varying class and social backgrounds can be involved in smuggling networks, which can at the same time present tools for social mobility and contain highly uneven and oppressive divisions of risk and profit. While the distinction between 'small fish' and 'big fish,' between bosses and their more vulnerable employees in common accounts of smuggling capture some imbalances of power, modern networks are often not just hierarchical structures but complex and dynamic assemblages of capital, labour and relationships.

Second, a simplistic focus on the figure of the 'smuggler,' even if more broadly conceived, also risks misrepresenting the way in which people engage in smuggling networks. Frequently, as ethnographies on smuggling, in particular, have noted, smuggling is not a full-time activity, and does not define comprehensively, economically, socially, or politically those involved in it. On the one hand, framing smuggling as something that is only done by 'smugglers' risks ignoring the degree to which smuggling is also practiced or facilitated by tourists and migrants crossing borders, or neighbouring pastoral communities keeping up long-standing exchanges of goods, or doctors, lawyers, and architects making a bit of money on the side (e.g., Peraldi, 2001; Scheele and McDougall, 2012). On the other hand, framing everyone involved in these activities as a 'smuggler' often risks expanding normatively charged terms to huge groups of people, and deepening prejudices around borderland communities.

Third, the figure of the 'smuggler' also risks limiting the driving role and agency of smuggling to those involved in moving goods across borders, and conceptually segments them from the wider networks of relationships that make up smuggling today. As noted above, smuggling does not exist always in antithesis to or competition with state law enforcement, but is embedded in structured relationships with state- and non-state governance providers. Focusing merely on the figure of the smuggler risks drawing a firm line through complex networks of facilitation, toleration, accountability, and profit that involve state- and non-state actors. It also risks drawing too firm a line between legal and illegal trade. Business communities have frequently relied on the figure of the 'smuggler' in order to lobby policymakers. Adopting their discourse risks overlooking that legal and illegal trade are also shaped by each other – migration systems are perhaps the most striking but by far not the only example of this. See for example the chapter on cigarettes in this volume. It presents businesses in contrast to smugglers, camouflaging that formal enterprises themselves sometimes are involved in activities such as tax and tariff evasion. They may tolerate smuggling if it brings their goods cheaply into a different market, or engage in smuggling themselves.

Clearly, the solution here is not to do away with the term altogether – it is used frequently throughout the volume by authors who still manage not to fall prey to the pitfalls outlined above. We believe the best way forward is instead to continue to contextualise and complicate the term, to highlight the diversity of activities, and to present scholarship that takes a wider view at the wider networks and political economy structures in which smuggling is embedded.

Smuggling and conflict

Smuggling can be a crucial aspect of armed conflicts, ensuring the survival of civilian populations, financing warring parties, and even creating economic incentives to continue fighting (Keen, 2007; Andreas, 2008; Kaldor, 2013). Consequently, smugglers frequently feature in the literatures on war economies, conflict, and security. Recent work on smuggling and conflict, including contributions in this volume, has sought to unpack the complex interplay among these phenomena (see for example Walther and Miles, 2017; Duran-Martinez, 2018; Walton et al., 2018; Brenner, 2019; Idler, 2019).

On the one hand, wars and armed conflict often shape the dynamics of smuggling. Armed conflicts create new demands and, in the context of evolving war economies, new opportunities for smuggling. For example, armed groups often depend on smuggled weapons and goods (Pinson and Marsh, in this volume). Meanwhile, the needs of civilian populations during armed conflict give rise to survivalist smuggling activities as well as the rise of "smuggling tycoons," who accumulate considerable wealth (Ahamad, in this volume). Armed conflicts create new opportunities for "network specialists." Goodhand, Koehler and Bhatia (in this volume) illustrate the crucial role of brokers, who act as intermediaries among the various parties involved in the smuggling economy. Perhaps counterintuitively, state actors in armed settings frequently feature among those that benefit from smuggling economies (see Weigand, 2020; Mansfield, in this volume).

However, scholarship on smuggling and conflict has noted that armed conflict can also inhibit smuggling, and many smugglers try avoiding conflict zones on their transit route as they are notoriously difficult and expensive to navigate (Gallien and Weigand, 2021). Successful smuggling in conflict zones frequently requires negotiations with and payments to numerous authorities, including state actors and non-state armed groups (Ahmad, 2017; Thakur and Brenner, in this volume). Profit margins in the smuggling economy of conflict zones are often low due to the high costs of transportation, even in the smuggling of high value goods. In his detailed analysis of the opium trade in and out of Afghanistan, Mansfield (in this volume) shows that smuggling is only profitable for the numerous involved actors, if conducted in large volumes.

Meanwhile, peaceful or stable environments are more conducive to smuggling. Thakur (in this volume) illustrates how political agreements, such as ceasefires, between armed groups and state actors at the India-Myanmar border have exacerbated the smuggling economy, while enabling the various political authorities to collect more taxes and levies from smugglers. Conversely, states have tried to intervene in the smuggling economy with political objectives. However, such interventions have not always had the desired consequences. Brenner (in this volume) shows how US policies aimed at curbing the revenues generated by armed groups through 'conflict minerals' in the Democratic Republic of the Congo, shifted how those armed groups generated revenue and ultimately resulted in more violence.

Disciplines, methods and motivations

We started this introduction noting that despite the existence of substantial work on smuggling in different disciplines, and despite overlapping themes and concerns, there often has been relatively little interaction and conversation among them. As in adjacent fields, some of this has been shaped by broader disciplinary and methodological divisions, as well as different conceptions of what 'data' on smuggling looks like, and the types of contexts in which this is accessible. From a methodological point of view, this relative 'siloing' likely has done a particular disservice to the generation of knowledge on smuggling. As methodological work on researching smuggling and illegal activities more widely has pointed out (see i.e., Ellis and MacGaffey, 1996; Gallien, 2021; Siu and Bensassi; Dobler; De La Rosa and Lara, in this volume), the particular challenges in researching these activities make work across methodologies and across disciplines particularly important and potentially particularly productive. Furthermore, different methodologies share wider challenges around ethics and risks (see Huesken, in this volume) and the trade-offs of localising smuggling (see Dobler, in this volume) that can provide a starting point for conversations across disciplinary divides.

Beyond methodologies, it appears that another dynamic that has deepened gaps among disciplines are disciplinary assumptions about the motivations of smuggling and smugglers. Consequently, one central feature in strengthening the literature's ability to interact and bridge the gaps among them is to emphasise that as the features of smuggling are diverse, so are its motivations, and the two should not be conflated or assumed to be singular. Smuggling is an economic activity and price differences, tax rates or transaction costs often feature in the calculations of smugglers. A broader view at different literatures on smuggling cautions against suggesting, based on that observation, that smuggling is exclusively motivated by economics, or that by definition it is essentially equivalent to tax evasion (Pitt, 1981). Similarly, as we have noted above, smuggling is defined and shaped by politics, and can be in itself a highly political activity. Political effects and motivations don't always overlap, however, and the micro-politics of smuggling can be complex and counter-intuitive. Hence, a wider look across different literatures and disciplinary traditions also cautions against assuming, a-priori, that smuggling is necessarily also politically motivated, or, more importantly, that its politics are always inherently subversive and antagonistic toward the state.

Similarly, smuggling has deep historical roots, and much of what today is framed as smuggling routes across borders created in colonial contexts are in fact trade routes that pre-date both the borders and the laws that make the trade illegal. While it is worth highlighting this fact as a relevant complication of more criminalising approaches to smuggling, here too it remains important to remain cautious in transitioning from a feature to a motivation, noting that smuggling, even if it is along the same routes, is not always motivated by a historical continuity or path dependency. As much historical work on smuggling has shown, trade across similar routes can transform substantially and swiftly over time as its economic, political, and social environment shifts.

A similar point is true for the observation that smuggling is socially normalised in borderland environments. As scholarship in borderland studies has often found, smuggling frequently is part of the everyday lives of borderland populations, no matter how much external observers may be scandalised by it. Scholarship on these issues also cautions that here, again, it remains important

Studying smuggling

not to draw a line from the everyday normalised practice to conclusions about the beliefs and motivations of people involved in the trade. Recent work in borderland studies, in particular, has highlighted critical diversities – while some smuggling may be normalised in communities, other activities might be tolerated grudgingly. While some smuggling activities may be embedded socially and central parts of borderland livelihood strategies, other activities at the same time may have unleashed dynamics of profit, competition, and violence that communities observe with unease (for example see Meagher; Titeca, in this volume).

Examining the conceptual challenges in studying smuggling and pointing to underlying common themes, previous sections in this introduction have noted the various possible points of connection for work on smuggling among different disciplines that have worked in this space; particularly anthropology, sociology, history, political science, and economics.[6] These considerations of methods and motivations further highlight the way communication between disciplines can strengthen work in this area, and provide new avenues for collaboration and complicating dominant assumptions. Challenges around ethics and localising smuggling for example, as discussed in this volume, exist across disciplines and would benefit from closer conversations. Similarly, work across different perspectives can help embed localised ethnographies in transnational analyses or challenge macro-level discussions through more critical perspectives. Legal scholarship and anthropological accounts of practical norms typically have different starting points, but both contribute to analyses of the different regulatory levels that surround smuggling. This leads us directly to the purpose and structure of this volume.

This book

This book aims to provide the first systematic introduction and comprehensive mapping of research on smuggling in a variety of disciplines, with a view to aiding the formation of a more well-connected field of 'smuggling studies.' We aim both to provide an entrance and reference for new scholars of the field and a point of connection and inspiration for collaboration, and new perspectives for established researchers. As we have argued above, research on smuggling has been produced in various disciplines. Geographic sub-fields have frequently been segmented from each other by disciplinary boundaries, ideological divergences, methodological differences, and linguistic gaps. Hence, our intention is to move the study of smuggling from the edges of different discussions and disciplines to its own centre, creating a cornerstone for a more thorough investigation that draws on the insights of the various disciplines that consider the topic.

The book is structured around larger thematic debates. It covers themes ranging from the methodological challenges in researching smuggling to its central conceptual histories and debates. It provides introductions of how selected goods are smuggled around the world, offering empirical texture and comparative insight. In addition, it seeks to link smuggling scholarship to central discussions in social sciences, such as the nature and development of the state, the construction of borders, mobility, and armed conflict.

The handbook begins with a discussion of the methodologies, terms and perspectives that have shaped how smuggling has been studied in different disciplines. This first section of the handbook has two main functions. On the one hand, it aims to provide an introduction and methodological toolkit to those readers who are new to the field, and are thinking about conducting research on the topic. On the other hand, as the book also seeks to reflect critically on the knowledge generated on smuggling so far, it seems only fitting to begin it by discussing the tools and ideas that have been used to help trace blind spots and ways forward. After addressing the question of where to go to study smuggling and discussing the way localising smuggling shapes its study (Dobler, in this volume), a chapter on 'smuggling ideologies' (Meagher, in this volume) traces the distortions that overly ideological or programmatically driven perspectives on smuggling have introduced into its study. The following chapters discuss different quantitative (Siu and Benassi, in this volume) and qualitative approaches (de la Rosa and Lara, in this volume) that have dominated the study of smuggling, as well as the ethics, risks and security challenges that are linked to and have influenced the study of smuggling (Hüsken, in this volume).

The second section of the handbook looks at borderlands and their people. Building in particular on the rich literature on borderland studies, this section zooms in and takes a closer look at the dynamics of smuggling at the local level to provide an understanding of how borderlands function, how smuggling is understood locally, and the role of communities, brokers and other actors in the local smuggling economy. The section begins by tracing the historical creation of borders (Nugent, in this volume) and reviewing how different scholarship has conceptualised borders, borderlands, and frontiers (Peña, in this volume). After investigating the role of brokers in local smuggling economies (Goodhand, Koehler, and Bhatia, in this volume), the section looks at the politics of smuggling and the role of the state in the smuggling economy at the local level (Raeymaekers, in this volume) and analyses the role of smugglers in their local communities (Titeca, in this volume). The following chapters explore local narratives, memories and histories in the context of smuggling (Schomerus and de Vries, in this volume) and unpack the role of gender in the smuggling economy and how gendered tropes shaped our perception of the topic (Schuster, in this volume).

The third section provides an overview on various goods that are frequently smuggled, identifying common routes, practices, and procedures. In doing so, the handbook considers both licit and illicit goods and a range of case studies from around the world. The section begins with a discussion of goods that are widely considered to be illicit, such as cocaine (Durán-Martínez, in this volume), opiates (Mansfield, in this volume), weapons (Marsh and Pinson, in this volume), and wildlife (Felbab-Brown, in this volume). It then proceeds to a discussion of goods that are commonly viewed as licit, such as cigarettes (Gallien, in this volume), petroleum products (Eaton, in this volume), and rice (Quitoriano, in this volume). The final chapter of the section investigates the intersection between the flows of different goods (Idler, in this volume).

The fourth section focuses on the smuggling of people and the intersection between mobility and smuggling. It both introduces central concepts in this literature and discusses the effect of restrictions on and the criminalisation of mobility (van Liempt, in this volume). It provides an introduction to the networked structure and the social organisation of migrant smuggling (Raineri, in this volume), and examines its relationship with wider structures of labour circulation, considering, in particular, its gendered effects (Deshingkar, in this volume). The final chapter of this section uses the effect of the Covid-19 pandemic on borders around the globe to draw out lessons on human smuggling more widely (Bird, in this volume).

The fifth section then explores the role of smuggling and conflict as the two topics are often portrayed as closely linked. On the one hand, armed conflict and wars are commonly associated with bolstering smuggling economies. On the other hand, illicit trade is often viewed as a driver of armed conflict, providing income opportunities for armed groups and corrupt state actors alike, and incentivising the continuation of war. This section aims at providing a more nuanced understanding of what frequently is called the 'conflict-crime nexus.' After looking at the role of smuggling in historical wars (Andreas, in this volume) the section looks at smuggling and war economies (Ahmad, in this volume) and explores the role of armed groups in smuggling economies (Thakur, in this volume). In the conclusion of the section, the handbook analyses the effects of policies aimed at curbing smuggling to fight insurgencies or to reduce armed conflict (Brenner, in this volume).

Studying smuggling

The final section of the handbook engages with how smuggling currently is addressed and could be addressed differently, also providing a stepping stone for policymakers thinking about how to engage with the topic. Following a discussion of maritime borders (Bruwer, in this volume), the handbook takes a critical look at policing and law enforcement in the context of smuggling (Gazzotti, in this volume). The section and the handbook conclude with a chapter that takes us back to the local level, exploring community adaptation and resilience (Herbert, Reitano, and Gastelum Felix, in this volume).

While we tried to cover a large range of perspectives and approaches in this handbook, it is naturally not without limitations. The set of goods covered here is limited and selective. It is meant to provide an introduction to the diversity of goods and the factors that drive their unique dynamics, not to diminish the relevance of smuggled goods that we do not cover here, such as amphetamines, electronics, alcohol, garments, or works of art and heritage. Crucially, the role of financial flows requires further investigation. There is also a disciplinary bias within this book – while we have aimed to bring together different perspectives here, our focus has been on the social sciences. This has been shaped both by our own perspective on the field and an intention to seek out literatures that may speak to each other particularly well, and is not meant to discard work on smuggling in the arts and humanities.[7] Geographically, the handbook engages primarily with smuggling in low- to middle-income countries, while also arguing in a range of chapters for a wider global view of these activities that include the role of consumption markets and networks in high-income countries. We recognise that representation in this handbook does not reflect these goals fully. While we have managed an equal distribution of genders among the authors, authors from or based in low- to middle-income countries are still under-represented among the contributors to this book. Nevertheless, we hope that the book contributes to a deeper knowledge and further networking within the field that also strengthens connections among fields and will further shift these balances in future volumes.

As this handbook aims at providing an overview of the entire field of what we describe as smuggling studies across disciplines, perspectives, and worldviews, it also illustrates tensions within this field. Different scholars in this handbook engage with different types of questions and relate their work to different strands of literature. They take different positions on the frameworks, meanings, and definitions of smuggling, and especially on the role of state and policy actors in relation to these activities. Some chapters in this volume focus on suggesting ways to advance our thinking within the frameworks and languages provided by states and policymakers, especially in order to develop ways to address pressing issues in a relatable way on the short term. Others focus on a more critical engagement with the assumptions and definitions that are proposed by states and make suggestions for how to change our thinking about smuggling – how we study it, what we think the problem is, and what answers could be – in a more substantial way. As throughout the different issues presented here, we see value in this diversity, and hope that our readers share this view.

Notes

1 We would like to thank Peter Andreas, David Brenner, Gregor Dobler and Shalaka Thakur for their comments on earlier drafts of this chapter. More importantly, as we draw here on chapters throughout this handbook, we would like to thank all the authors in this volume for their thoughtful contributions and for sticking with this project during what was for many a challenging time. We would like to thank Rosie Anderson and Helena Hurd at Routledge, and Camilla Ridgewell at the LSE. We acknowledge and are grateful for the funds provided by the ESRC and the London School of Economics and Political Science in order to make this handbook open access. If you're surprised that we've snuck

a whole acknowledgement section into a footnote – this is a handbook of smuggling. What did you expect?

2   For an illustration of this point in the context of African borderlands, see Meagher (in this volume).

3   This is typically conceptualised as the movement of goods or people, but could similarly refer to capital or information.

4   We note that this field naturally has a close overlap with what is usually referred to as 'borderland studies' – this will be evident throughout this volume, which has a large set of contributions from leading scholars typically associated with this field. As we note in the section below, the two do not precisely map on top of each other: not all borderland studies focuses on smuggling, and not all analysis of smuggling can or should be located in borderlands, as scholars might instead focus on financial actors in economic centres, on policy makers in political centres, on larger transcontinental networks or on maritime smuggling.

5   Dobler in this volume provides a deeper discussion of this issue.

6   This also applies to connections between different fields of study, such as borderland studies, work on war economies, the study of transnational organised crime or of informal economies.

7   One exception to this perhaps represents the cover of this handbook – a painting by Fernanda Morales Tovar, entitled "Displaced nexus." From her series "Archeologies of the environment," the image spoke to us as an illustration of the fact that institutions such as borders are constructed not merely architecturally but socially, and benefit from an analysis that centres people's role in their emergence, maintenance, and perhaps subversion. We were glad to find an illustration that moves away from common visual representations of borders merely as lines or walls, and of smugglers merely as masked men. We hope that the readers will find their own connections between the artwork and the chapters in this volume – our favourite is that the painting's central object shades the landscape behind it in a different colour, mirroring the description of the border as a prism for stories and perceptions in the chapter by Schomerus and de Vries in this volume.

Works cited

Ahmad, A. (2017) *Jihad & Co.: Black Markets and Islamist Power.* Oxford, New York: Oxford University Press.

Andersson, R. (2014) *Illegality, Inc.* Oakland, CA: University of California Press.

Andreas, P. (2008) *Blue Helmets and Black Markets: The Business of Survival in the Siege of Sarajevo.* Ithaca, NY: Cornell University Press.

Andreas, P. (2009) *Border Games: Policing the U.S.-Mexico Divide.* Ithaca, NY: Cornell University Press (Cornell Studies in Political Economy).

Andreas, P. (2014) *Smuggler Nation: How Illicit Trade Made America.* Oxford: Oxford University Press.

Andreas, P. and Nadelmann, E. (2008) *Policing the Globe: Criminalization and Crime Control in International Relations.* Oxford, New York: Oxford University Press.

Bennafla, K. (2014) 'État et illégalisme: quelle géographie? Une approche par les flux marchands depuis l'Afrique et le Moyen-Orient,' *Annales de geographie,* n°, 700(6), pp. 1338–1358.

Brenner, D. (2019) *Rebel Politics: A Political Sociology of Armed Struggle in Myanmar's Borderlands.* Ithaca, NY: Cornell University Press.

Dobler, G. (2016) 'The Green, the Grey and the Blue: A Typology of Cross-border Trade in Africa★,' *The Journal of Modern African Studies,* 54(1), pp. 145–169. doi: 10.1017/S0022278X15000993.

Duran-Martinez, A. (2018) *The Politics of Drug Violence: Criminals, Cops and Politicians in Colombia and Mexico.* Oxford, New York: Oxford University Press.

Ellis, S. and MacGaffey, J. (1996) 'Research on Sub-Saharan Africa's Unrecorded International Trade: Some Methodological and Conceptual Problems,' *African Studies Review,* 39(2), pp. 19–41.

Gallien, M. (2020) 'Informal Institutions and the Regulation of Smuggling in North Africa,' *Perspectives on Politics,* 18(2), pp. 492–508. doi: 10.1017/S1537592719001026.

Gallien, M. (2021) 'Researching the Politics of Illegal Activities,' *PS: Political Science & Politics,* 54(3), pp. 467–471. doi: 10.1017/S1049096521000317.

Gallien, M. and Weigand, F. (2021) 'Channeling Contraband: How States Shape International Smuggling Routes,' *Security Studies,* 30(1), pp. 79–106. doi: 10.1080/09636412.2021.1885728.

Harvey, S. (2016) *Smuggling: Seven Centuries of Contraband.* Chicago: University Of Chicago Press.

Studying smuggling

Hüsken, T. (2018) *Tribal Politics in the Borderland of Egypt and Libya.* 1st edition. 2019. New York, NY: Palgrave Macmillan.

Idler, A. (2019) *Borderland Battles: Violence, Crime, and Governance at the Edges of Colombia's War.* Oxford, New York: Oxford University Press.

Igue, J. O. and Soule, B. G. (1992) *L'etat entrepot au Benin: commerce informel ou solution a la crise.* Paris: Karthala.

Kaldor, M. (2013) *New and Old Wars: Organised Violence in a Global Era.* New York: John Wiley & Sons.

Keen, D. J. (2007) *Complex Emergencies.* 1st edition. Cambridge, UK; Malden, MA: Polity.

Kim, D. S. (2020) *Empires of Vice.* Princeton, NJ: Princeton University Press.

Koram, K. (ed.) (2019) *The War on Drugs and the Global Colour Line.* London: Pluto Press.

Meagher, K. (2003) 'A Back Door to Globalisation?: Structural Adjustment, Globalisation & Transborder Trade in West Africa,' *Review of African Political Economy,* 30(95), pp. 57–75.

Nugent, P. (2002) *Smugglers, Secessionists and Loyal Citizens on the Ghana-Togo Frontier: The Lie of the Borderlands Since 1914.* Athens, Oxford: Legon, Ghana: James Currey.

Peraldi, M. (2001) *Cabas et containers. Activités marchandes informelles et réseaux migrants transfrontaliers.* Paris: Maisonneuve & Larose.

Pitt, M. M. (1981) 'Smuggling and Price Disparity,' *Journal of International Economics,* 11(4), pp. 447–458. doi: 10.1016/0022-1996(81)90026-X.

Porter, R. and Hough, M. (1996) 'The History of the "drugs Problem",' *Criminal Justice Matters,* 24(1), pp. 3–5. doi: 10.1080/09627259608552771.

Raeymaekers, T. (2014) *Violent Capitalism and Hybrid Identity in the Eastern Congo: Power to the Margins.* New York, NY: Cambridge University Press.

Raineri, L. (2019) 'Cross-Border Smuggling in North Niger: The Morality of the Informal and the Construction of a Hybrid Order,' in Polese, A., Russo, A., and Strazzari, F. (eds) *Governance Beyond the Law: The Immoral, The Illegal, The Criminal.* Cham: Springer International Publishing (International Political Economy Series), pp. 227–245. doi: 10.1007/978-3-030-05039-9_12.

Raineri, L. and Strazzari, F. (2021) 'Drug Smuggling and the Stability of Fragile States. The Diverging Trajectories of Mali and Niger,' *Journal of Intervention and Statebuilding,* pp. 1–18. doi: 10.1080/17502 977.2021.1896207.

Roitman, J. (2004) *Fiscal Disobedience: An Anthropology of Economic Regulation in Central Africa.* Princeton, NJ: Princeton University Press.

Sanchez, G. (2014) *Human Smuggling and Border Crossings.* London, New York: Routledge.

Scheele, D. J. (2012) *Smugglers and Saints of the Sahara: Regional Connectivity in the Twentieth Century.* Cambridge: Cambridge University Press.

Scheele, J. and McDougall, J. (eds) (2012) *Saharan Frontiers: Space and Mobility in Northwest Africa.* Bloomington, IN: Indiana University Press.

Scott, J. C. (2009) *The Art of Not Being Governed: An Anarchist History of Upland Southeast Asia.* New Haven, CT: Yale University Press.

Shelley, L. I. (2014) *Dirty Entanglements.* New York, NY: Cambridge University Press.

Titeca, K. and Herdt, T. de (2010) 'Regulation, Cross-border Trade and Practical Norms in West Nile, North-Western Uganda,' *Africa,* 80(04), pp. 573–594. doi: 10.3366/afr.2010.0403.

Walther, O. J. and Miles, W. F. S. (2017) *African Border Disorders: Addressing Transnational Extremist Organizations.* London, New York: Routledge.

Walton, O. et al. (2018) *Borderlands and Peacebuilding: A view from the Margins.* Conciliation Resources. Available at: https://researchportal.bath.ac.uk/en/publications/borderlands-and-peacebuilding-a-view-from-the-margins (Accessed: 7 June 2021).

Weigand, F. (2020) *Conflict and Transnational Crime: Borders, Bullets and Business in Southeast Asia.* Northampton, MA: Edward Elgar Publishing, Incorporated.

PART I

Methods and approaches

2

LOCALISING SMUGGLING

Gregor Dobler

Where would you go if you wanted to study smuggling?

The different answers scholars give to that question structure the emerging academic field of studies on smuggling. On the one side, scholars in security studies or international relations often look upon smuggling networks as global or at least regional phenomena that are not associated with specific sites as much as with a flow of goods and a counter-flow of money. These scholars study smuggling from a bird's eye perspective, using all available data to understand the direction, amounts and consequences, of illegal trade flows. Very often, they do not "go" to any specific research site.

On the other side are those (often academically at home in anthropology, geography, history or the more qualitative brands of sociology or political sciences) who study smuggling as the illegal transport of goods across a national boundary – a site-specific activity mostly happening in borderlands, where smuggling networks turn into local realities and can be understood in their consequences.

This handbook brings together scholars from both perspectives. My own outlook on smuggling to a great extent has been shaped by the second approach. I came to the field with a primary interest not in smuggling, but in borderlands. When I started doing fieldwork in a border region, I found smugglers at work, so I had to become interested in smuggling. Similar things apply to some of my closest colleagues, many of them loosely organised in the African Borderlands Research Network (ABORNE). Our fascination with the borderlands has given rise to a huge and very useful corpus of empirically nuanced, theoretically sophisticated studies on smuggling that have collectively changed our understanding of borders and their consequences for societies. These studies have allowed us to understand better how states and societies forcefully interact in borderlands, how practical norms are renegotiated in border situations, and how money is being made and boom towns are emerging, only to decline again a few years later. Borderlands are places where things happen. Since often enough, these 'things' are shaped by smuggling, borderlands research has also become a catalyst for new perspectives on smuggling.

Such studies in borderlands typically *localise* smuggling in a double sense. On the positive side, they are uniquely placed to understand the consequences smuggling has for the people who engage in it and for the societies and governance processes shaped by it. They make smuggling visible as a real-life practice of human beings, a practice in which different societal

DOI: 10.4324/9781003043645-2

fields intersect to generate unforeseen consequences, and they show both smuggling's wide variety and its embeddedness into local social, political, economic, and cultural contexts.

There is a downside to localising approaches, as well. Borderland studies are rarely able to capture the complex, globe-spanning smuggling networks into which local activities on the border are embedded, and they are not well suited to addressing smuggling that does not happen on the border, but is organised from corporate offices in the world's capitals. Focusing on the consequences smuggling has for a local society may make us overlook a bigger picture – and may lead policy practitioners to understand smuggling as a problem that can be addressed by policing the borderlands.

Both on the positive and on the negative sides, the methodological decision to localise smuggling in the borderlands has consequences for what we see (see also the Introduction to this volume). In this article, I first lay out what I see as major strengths of a localising approach. In a second step, I analyse some shortcomings and potential blind spots of studying smuggling from a borderlands perspective. Finally, I suggest ways of expanding the reach of borderland studies without losing the advantages of localised research, and of combining localised with more systemic approaches. Since my own expertise is in the borderlands, the entire paper rather sums up my experiences with localised research than offering advice on how to use systemic approaches. Analysing where systemic approaches find their sites of research and suggesting ways to improve them would need a second, corresponding article – written by somebody much more grounded in that perspective than I am.

Understanding smuggling: the strengths of a localised perspective

I can best illustrate the strengths of a localising approach to smuggling by using examples from my own research on the borderlands between Namibia and Angola (Dobler 2008a, 2008b, 2009, 2014, 2017). Localised research, I will argue, allows us to gain a real-world perspective on smuggling. It helps us to understand the intricacies of moving goods across a border – intricacies that have hidden consequences for wider networks, as well – and to analyse the ways smuggling is embedded into other activities and into the surrounding society. Without such a real-world understanding of smuggling, we run the danger of isolating smuggling from its social environment and to misunderstand it as a class of activity set apart by its nature, where often enough the only thing that sets it apart from other trade activities is the state's (or the researcher's) gaze.

Oshikango is a Namibian town on the border to Angola that experienced massive trade-led growth after the end of the Angolan civil war. The town is situated at the point where regional transport corridors from the Southern African harbours of Walvis Bay and Durban cross the Angolan border. During the 2000s, the lack of infrastructure in war-torn Angola coupled with currency regulations and differently structured trade networks in both countries turned Oshikango into a necessary nodal point between two segment of international trade networks: the segment in which goods produced in different parts of the world reached Southern Africa, and the second, separate segment in which Angolan-based traders organised the cross-border movement of goods into Angola. A large percentage of all goods consumed in the southern regions of Angola not only had to pass through Oshikango, but were offloaded here and stored into bonded warehouses. From these warehouses, Angolan trades acquired them and imported them into Angola, paying cash in US dollars even for huge truckloads of whisky worth a hundred thousand dollars or more.

As a consequence, Oshikango was more than just a border post through which goods were exported. It was the meeting point between trade networks and the place in which the transfer

Localising smuggling

between two national realms of regulation could be negotiated. If you had enough local knowledge here, you could circumvent taxes and import duties and multiply your profits. Smuggling networks did not only pass through the town; they were organised here.

For me, this turned the town into an ideal place to understand both the technicalities of smuggling and the consequences of smuggling for society in a borderland. For both aims, I needed quite a lot of local embeddedness and a long presence in everyday life. For some time, I compiled the daily account statements in a liquor warehouse; I worked with UNCTAD's Asycuda software used for processing export papers, sat around in offices and spent the evenings hanging out with warehouse owners, clearing agents, or local politicians. In this, my approach was very typical of localising studies. Like many colleagues, I found that I could acquire in-depth local knowledge that would not have been accessible in any other place and by any other method. It allowed me to develop a real-world understanding of smuggling, and to identify structures that were important far beyond the local level. Let me only mention three points as examples.

First, I learned to understand that nothing about cross-border trade in Oshikango was straightforward. I realised how many difficult decisions had to be taken when filling in a customs form in Asycuda. I understood how customs officials could, in all legality, make life difficult for traders by taking slightly longer than necessary to process papers – in particular where warehouses had to have bank guarantees for road bonds, so that a new shipment could only be made after the papers of an earlier one had come back from the border and the road bond had been cleared. This, in turn, made good relations between warehouse owners and local state agents crucial; being there allowed me to witness how such relations were kept up in everyday practice. I began to see how Chinese traders could, through fake invoices in a cross-border business conducted in US dollars, get their hands on unregistered hard currency very useful at home, or how customs officials had to use a fine judgment to evaluate invoices – not necessarily to separate real values from fake ones, but to maximise their own profits without being exposed to sanctions from their superiors. I understood why Angolan importers often chose the long detour to the next border post some 300 km east, where import duties on the Angolan side more easily could be avoided.

Through each of these examples, I began to understand how extensive the grey zone between outright smuggling and completely legal cross-border transactions was. In Oshikango, very few goods crossed the border in completely illegal and unregistered ways. On the side of petty smuggling, local residents carried goods for everyday consumption or for village trade across the border; at the other end of the spectrum, cocaine and stolen diamonds were brought in from Angola clandestinely. Most money, however, was made in the huge zone between these extremes – the zone in which people needed the right stamps on the right paperwork in order to bring goods across the border. Goods were officially registered as exports on the Namibian and as imports on the Angolan side, and cross-border profit was hidden in the interstices of both sets of paperwork.

Was this smuggling? Was it legal trade? What in a bird's eye view might look like two different sets of practice done by two different sets of people ('traders' and 'smugglers') became visible on the ground as positions on a sliding scale which the same actors occupied in different situations. "Clear distinctions between the good and the bad," as Thomas Hüsken put it referring to Paul Nugent's study on the Ghana-Togo frontier (Nugent 2002), "are often misleading or part of self-legitimizing narratives" (Hüsken 2019, p. 166).

Secondly, the difficulty in telling traders apart from smugglers shaped local perceptions and the local embeddedness of cross-border actors. Nobody I spoke to in Oshikango had a clear moral view on 'smuggling.' Oshikango's smuggling networks did not operate in a shady underworld, and they were not set apart from the world of upright citizens by the illegality of their actions. The boundary between right and wrong was just as difficult to draw as the boundary between smuggling and trading. People did make moral judgments about variants of trade, but their criteria differed from the legal judgments by state authorities.

Much has been written on the difference between 'illegality' and 'illicitness' (Roitman 2008), and often, scholars have identified local 'practical norms' that define the borders of licit behavior and govern the interaction between state authorities and traders (Titeca and Herdt 2010; de Sardan 2013; Meagher 2014; Heitz-Tokpa 2019; Gallien 2020a; Tazebew and Kefale 2021). In Oshikango, there were indeed a certain number of practical norms that a researcher could have codified at any given moment. Few of them, however, applied to transactions in any abstract sense. Everybody might know what honest trade should look like, but deviations from that model were judged concretely and in relation to the parties involved, not merely in relation to rules. Defrauding individuals was worse than defrauding institutions, and defrauding people or institutions close to oneself was worse than defrauding distant others. Nobody cared much about tax avoidance in China, and few people cared deeply about tax avoidance in Namibia. Even when traders were known to sell defective goods to an anonymous buyer, this affected their reputation and undermined trust in them, but it did not usually generate a strong moral judgment. If a trader defrauded a close business partner, however, the treachery this involved made the transaction reprehensible in the eyes of most.

As a consequence of this relational character of moral evaluations, a researcher needs deep knowledge about the local context even to begin understanding what constitutes a licit or an illicit transaction. This, in turn, complicates our understanding of smuggling. Each individual cross-border transaction has consequences on the local level; it affirms or changes rules of acceptable behavior, affects social ties among the people involved, re-draws social boundaries and generally contributes to the reproduction of society. The outcome of this process is not predictable without understanding how that particular transaction links to the everyday life of people in the borderland.

Thirdly, research in Oshikango made me understand that smugglers and state institutions are not in any naturally antagonistic relation. Both need each other and cooperate with each other. "In practice," as Hüsken sums up his findings about smuggling between Egypt and Libya, "smugglers, soldiers, customs officers, policemen and the ordinary citizen are very much intertwined actors for whom smuggling is a field of economic cooperation, social arrangements and political strategies" (Hüsken 2019, p. 166). Most ethnographies of cross-border situations come to similar conclusions (Egg and Herrera 1998; Raeymaekers 2009; Titeca 2012; Ng'askie 2019; Gallien 2020b; Weigand 2020; Gallien and Weigand 2021). Smugglers do not by-pass the state; they use it selectively. State agents, in turn, do not fight smuggling as such. They rarely care much about the legality of transactions on the other side of the boundary, and if they insist on legal practices on their own side, this is often a means to increase demand for their own co-operation.

These three examples should illustrate how much a localised perspective on smuggling can add to our understanding of smuggling and its consequences for society. I could multiply the examples, both from my own work and from that of many colleagues. The question I am concerned with here, however, is not whether localised studies allow us to understand the borderland, but in how far they help us to understand global smuggling networks. Why should we care how a concrete load of goods crosses the border, what paperwork is involved, and what different people living in the borderlands think about that transaction – as long as the goods, in the end, pass to the other side, evading state scrutiny and regulation and often enough causing a lot of harm to people in the receiving society? What, in short, can localising perspectives teach us about smuggling networks?

I will address this larger question in two steps. First, I want to take a step back and show what elements of smuggling might remain hidden from a localising perspective. An entirely localised perspective, I will argue, indeed creates the dangers of overlooking important aspects of smuggling and ultimately of romanticising smuggling as a local practice.

In a second step, I then try to show that ignoring the borderlands and their localised dynamics to focus on the big picture instead is no solution either. Smuggling networks are crucially shaped by the local contexts in which they are embedded, and small changes on the ground may lead to their re-organization or even abandonment. Just as a perspective solely grounded in the local cannot fully grasp the entire network, a systemic analysis alone cannot make us understand these links between local and global dynamics of smuggling; by necessity, it remains ignorant of far too many defining features of smuggling networks.

Understanding smuggling: blind spots of a localising perspective

Localising perspectives could distort our image of smuggling in two ways. First, they could tempt us to over-emphasise elements which are crucial on the local level, even if they have few consequences for the entire smuggling network.

To take just one example, borderlands scholars have placed a huge emphasis on local power structures. How does state power interact and intersect with the power of formal or informal non-state actors? What role do smuggling networks, violent gangs, private security firms, or local youth associations play in maintaining public order in borderlands? What kinds of governance emerges at the margins of the state, and how can we conceptualise it? Such questions are crucial for describing and understanding border situations in general; the more volatile and dynamic situations tend to focus the attention of border scholars in particular. They have become the focus of a wide array of fascinating studies and have enriched our empirical knowledge and theoretical understanding of border situations. These qualities might, however, tempt us to overestimate their importance for understanding smuggling: borderland studies have such interesting things to tell us that we might assume that the borderland indeed is where the only relevant action is.

Even for the goods that shape local networks of power, though, the borderland often is only *one* segment in a wider network of trade. If weapons smuggled across a border fuel a local conflict or change power relations between the state and a local militia, this is very pertinent for the local society. Is it also a defining feature of the entire arms smuggling network, or just the random local consequence of larger structures? The power that youth gangs acquire by smuggling petrol across a border may change local governance structures, but does that tell us anything about the entire trade network between refineries and consumers? A localised perspective on smuggling might tempt us to overlook other, more mundane aspects of wider smuggling networks. Smuggling tends to become visible and have observable societal consequences in borderlands, but that should not make us assume that what becomes visible in borderlands is a defining feature of the entire smuggling network, or even that the variants of smuggling important for the borderlands are important for countries at large.

This brings me to the second way in which a localising perspective could distort our image of smuggling. Important variants of smuggling never touch the borderland at all, or simply pass through it unhindered, invisible, and without generating changes on the local level. I see four main variants of smuggling which cannot (or can only with huge difficulties) be observed in the borderlands and might disappear from view in a localised perspective: high-stakes smuggling in illegal goods; goods by-passing border situations by air, sea, or in pipelines; illegal trade in legal goods; and virtual transactions.

The first variant, high-stakes smuggling in illegal goods, is simply very difficult to access with the means of localised social research. Researchers usually find it relatively easy to obtain information about the smuggling of legal goods – goods that can be legally traded within a country and that, as soon as they have crossed a border illegally and successfully entered a different regulatory realm, once again become indistinguishable from non-smuggled goods. Accessing smuggling networks that focus on goods whose possession and trade are illegal in themselves is much harder. Smuggling hard drugs, military weapons, or counterfeit currency are cases in point, as is illegal trade in ivory, rhino horn, or other material protected by international conventions and national laws (Hübschle 2014, 2016; Minnaar 2015; McCurdy and Kaduri 2016; Haysom 2020). Their very existence has to remain hidden, and by definition successful traders manage to keep them secret – from their social environment as well as from researchers. Reliable information on their trade can be obtained much more easily by investigative work covering the entire market, than by localised fieldwork in a cross-border situation.

The second variant of smuggling that can escape a localised perspective concerns goods that are either too small to be visible on the border, or that travel on different routes bypassing border posts. In mid-2000s Oshikango, rumors about diamond smuggling from Angola abounded, and many people suspected local warehouse owners of buying illegal stones. If such trade indeed happened, however, nobody but those directly involved in it had reliable information about it. Diamonds could be concealed much too easily, and the proceeds from diamond smuggling hidden among other large cash transactions. From the neighboring country Zambia, gold (a by-product of industrial copper mines) is flown to South Africa for refinement in company helicopters; if some of that gold escapes registration (as it routinely did until 2010), that variant of smuggling remains completely invisible from the borderlands (personal communication from field data by Rita Kesselring). On a rather different scale, oil or gas pipelines often pass through border regions, but no borderland actors are involved in selling or buying the commodities transported through them. If we want to know whether oil or gas is appropriately taxed and registered, the borderlands are not the best places to start.

A third variant of smuggling bypasses borderland actors, as well: smuggling organised by actors elsewhere in goods that could be legal, and which pass through border regions without changing hands or being offloaded. In the Southern African border regions I am most familiar with, timber trade would be a case in point. Illegal logging frequently leads to the export of timber from protected forests, but borderlanders (or researchers with local knowledge in the borderland) usually are in no position to assess the legality of the truckloads of tree trunks they see passing (Lescuyer and Tal 2016; Lukumbuzya and Sianga 2017, see also Cerutti et al. 2018).

Finally, and most importantly, while borderlands are often helpful places to understand the movements of bulk goods, they are not the best places to learn about the ownership of goods in transit, or movements of capital. Smuggling comes in many guises. An ethnography of a border town in Southern Africa – say, Oshikango, Chirundu, Musina or Kasumbalesa – can teach us a lot about medium-scale traders who doctor invoices or use transit trade regulations for round-tripping of goods. From a local perspective, these variants of smuggling are important; they generate wealth and power, change statehood and governance and, by privileging certain economic activities, channel investment and growth into specific regions and sectors. Seen on the national scale or in a global perspective, their effects are dwarfed by other, less localised phenomena.

In Chirundu, for example, a border post between Zambia and Zimbabwe, most of the trucks passing through carry copper cathodes. Copper in various forms accounts for roughly 80% of

Zambia's exports. This trade certainly leaves traces in border towns; truck stops, motels and bars are just as important elements of the local economy as clearing agents and freight forwarders' offices. The commodity itself, however, just passes through once the load is cleared. Most copper loads that cross the border are owned by international trading firms, more often than not subsidiaries of the companies who own the mines (Dobler and Kesselring 2019). If smuggling happens here, it is not organised by a local strongman whose good relations with a particular customs officer on night shift allows him to bypass regulations. It is organised, with all paperwork in perfect order, in global corporate offices and facilitated by tax advisors and accounting firms. Its techniques are not visible in the borderland. They consist of intra-firm profit shifting, in tax-optimization strategies, in the gentle overpricing of supplies or the declaration of mining supplies as investment goods in order to make use of tax exemptions, to name but a few (Lundstøl et al. 2013; Readhead 2016, 2017; Guj et al. 2017; Brugger and Engebretsen 2020). Researchers (and customs authorities) usually find it even more difficult to obtain reliable information on such practices than on, say, diamond or drug smuggling, and they leave few traces in the borderlands.

In an earlier paper (Dobler 2016), I developed a typology of cross-border trade that also applies to smuggling, differentiating between 'green,' 'grey,' and 'blue' trade. I call 'green' trade the local trade carried out on foot or on bicycle away from official border posts and under the radar of border authorities. 'Grey' trade is in goods transported in lorries on roads; it needs the border post and its paperwork, relies on local knowledge in the border region and thrives in the economically, politically, and socially dynamic sphere of the borderland. For 'blue' trade – trade across the oceans and through the air – borderlands are often a nuisance, and the ideal of crossing a border would be the frictionless transport corridor with paperless one-stop border posts.

Since 'green' and 'grey' trade are the domain of the borderland and of borderlanders, localised research in borderlands privileges them compared with 'blue' trade and smuggling. The dynamism of the borderland can make us forget what is invisible here, and lead us to reproduce a somewhat romantic image of the resilience of local practice in the face of global supply chains. This is not a problem of localised research as such. Ethnographies of commodity traders, tax advisers, or shipping companies could keep the strengths of localised research while providing access to different movements of goods. Gaining access and research authorization for such variants of localised research is usually far more difficult than localising one's perspective in the borderlands.

In Bert Brecht's *Threepenny Opera*, the villain Mack the Knife rhetorically asks: "What is a picklock to a bank share?" Just as qualitative social scientists often find access to criminal subcultures easier than to corporate elites, borderland scholars find it easier to focus on people involved in 'grey' smuggling networks, whose trucks, forged invoices, and bribes are more akin to picklocks than to bank shares, than on those organising blue trade across the globe. The real money, and the real harm, is not in smuggling Chinese sneakers or barrels of petrol across an African border; it may not even be in the illegal supply of small arms to a local militia. It is in the respectable smuggling networks of the corporate world that are all but invisible from the borderland.

How to remain localised without being restricted to the local

This brings me back to my initial question: where would you go to study smuggling?

My own choice has been to study smuggling in the borderland, using the method I am most familiar with and most competent in: long-term participation in other people's everyday life. I find I can best understand what life means in any given place by living in that place and sharing the everyday interests of the people who are constantly busy remaking this place.

Since I remain convinced by the strengths of this approach, I have started this article by outlining some of them. I also have come to realise limitations of this approach for understanding smuggling, and enumerate some of them in this paper. For me, the practical consequence of acknowledging these limitations should not be to give up on localising smuggling. Rather, research on smuggling should move beyond the alternative of *either* localising *or* adopting a systemic, bird's eye approach (for similar arguments, see Malik and Gallien 2020; Walther 2018 and the Introduction to this handbook).

Some important aspects of smuggling can be understood only through localised research. The consequences of smuggling for governance and the workings of state institutions, for example, cannot be deduced from above. The technicalities of smuggling, the everyday organization of smuggling networks, the large grey zone between legal and illegal trading practices and the links between them – all these themes need careful, empirically open research on the ground. If the aim of such research is not only to understand one particular borderland, but to analyze the organizational and social consequences of smuggling, we cannot do without information that remains invisible for a localised perspective anchored in a borderland.

Seen from the other end of the spectrum, systemic perspectives can teach us a lot about smuggling routes, about the overall extent of smuggling, about the integration of states into the global economy and about the links between legal and illegal segments of global commodity chains. Without grounding and testing such knowledge in real-life perspectives gained through localised research, however, our ideas about the consequences of such systemic aspects in a local context will remain mere conjectures.

More importantly still, the local embeddedness of smuggling can have consequences for smuggling networks that reach far beyond the local arena. Global networks of 'blue' trade might be antagonistic to borderlands dynamics and try to replace them by more frictionless structures, but they still pass through the borderlands and interact with state institutions as they are. As long as these institutions and their governance effects are shaped by the localised practices of 'grey' traders and other borderland actors, they also influence practices of global trade flows. One last Southern African example can illustrate this point: copper mined in the DRC is usually transported to the Southern African harbors in two segments. The first segment runs from the mines to offshore warehouses in the Zambian Copperbelt. It uses different trucking companies and different truck drivers than the second segment, which links the warehouses to the harbors in Durban or Walvis Bay – simply because navigating each different local state and each different border situation needs a distinct set of skills, of local knowledge and of local political connections. The difference between both segments is not so much shaped by the 'blue' trade networks as by borderland interactions among more local actors, but all traders and smugglers have to deal with the resulting structures. 'Grey' and 'blue' trade interlink and influence each other. To understand the global trajectories of goods, we also need an understanding of their local pathways, the comparative advantages of different transport routes and their structuring effects on global networks.

It is of course easy to argue for a combination of localised and systemic perspectives, but how can we achieve the combination in practice? No individual research project can do everything at once. Researchers have to decide what methodology to adopt, how to use their limited resources, and how to write in accordance with the preferences of their own field. IR specialists are not going to turn into anthropologists. How can we broaden our perspectives?

For each individual project, the salient point is of course that the method fits the research question. Both localising and systemic approaches have to be self-critical in this regard.

Localising smuggling

Localising studies in borderlands are excellent for some purposes, but they cannot answer all questions. Generally better suited to understanding a local society than to assessing the extent of global networks, they might distort our image of what smuggling is if we do not move beyond them.

To some degree, we can avoid such distortions without leaving a particular borderland. By broadening localised research designs, we can avoid letting the field alone structure what we find. To people living in a borderland, for example, trucks with copper passing through might remain irrelevant, since their presence does not affect local society directly. Their social invisibility must not prevent us from including them in our analysis.

Often, simple hand-made statistics can offer a first corrective to local perspectives and allow us to control for our own biases. What goods are passing through? What do we know about their trade? Who owns the trucks passing through, and who owns the loads? Who is involved in their trade, and what do we know about the larger networks to which that trade is linked? How well can we understand these networks from the local perspective? Such simple questions often have allowed me to perceive blind spots in my own outlook.

A second corrective is offered by a broader view on the economy of a country and a region. What goods *should* pass through a border? Are some invisible, and why? Who would know about their trade, and where would they cross the border? If we know that cocaine is consumed in the capital, we can start asking how it reaches the country; if we know that gold is transported to be refined in a different country, we can ask how it gets there. We still might not be able to get in-depth information about these variants of trade from the borderlands, but integrating them into our overall analysis will give us a better assessment of the border situation.

A third corrective is provided by a question I find much more difficult to answer in practice: Where do profits from cross-border trade end up? How much actually stays in the borderland, how much flows elsewhere? Here, as well, the borderlands will not provide all answers we may seek, but asking these questions will change how we perceive the borderlands and their integration into wider commodity chains.

Taken together, such correctives allow us to link our in-depth knowledge about a specific border post or a specific cross-border situation with other perspectives generated through different methods. Ultimately, however, we can only understand smuggling networks *collectively* – through co-operation among different researchers using a wide variety of methods in many different places. Smuggling networks link specific places and regions; in each place, they engender different forms of social change. Studies that concentrate on the structure of the networks alone will not be able to grasp their local embeddedness and the changes they bring to local societies, and will fail to explain how the network's structures are influenced by localised dynamics. Studies that concentrate on the local alone will struggle to see the full extent of the network and to evaluate how important those interesting developments in the borderland are for the bigger picture. Taken together, however, both perspectives can link up and illuminate each other. Just like smuggling, research on smuggling needs teamwork that links up people with different specializations.

Such teamwork comes with its own challenges. Localising and systemic perspectives on smuggling are usually pursued by different disciplines, each of which naturally sees the others' methodological choices as misplaced and its results as largely irrelevant to the questions that *really* matter. We peddle in different goods and often see each other as competitors rather than as partners. With this, we ignore a lesson smugglers could teach us: that a certain degree of trust in the other, cooperation, and a healthy division of labor according to expertise and positionality increase each party's benefits.

The most stimulating research on smuggling has, to my mind, emerged from networks which have managed to overcome such antagonistic tendencies and have brought the different approaches into a real dialogue. I think here of the collaborative work done by ABORNE, or of *Valueworks*, a collaborative research project on copper's value chain organised by Rita Kesselring and funded by the Swiss Network for International Studies. Although it was not focused primarily on smuggling, *Valueworks* could serve as a model for smuggling studies, as well. It combined localised studies in Zambia, Switzerland and China with cross-cutting perspectives on global production networks, financialization or tax regimes – and brought both into dialogue with civil society groups and activists. The cooperation has been eye-opening for everybody involved, and has brought fascinating results (see Kesselring 2019 for an overview).

Cooperation needs patience, tolerance, and curiosity (and sometimes the right funders), but in my experience, the outcome justifies the additional effort. Cooperation enables us to describe more accurately what smuggling is and what consequences it has, and it helps us to theorise smuggling in more accurate and more helpful ways. This handbook is in itself a vivid testimony to the potential of a collaborative approach to the study of smuggling, and it shows what we could gain by constructively linking localising and systemic research perspectives.

References

Brugger, F. and Engebretsen, R., 2020. Defenders of the status quo: making sense of the international discourse on transfer pricing methodologies. *Review of International Political Economy*, online first.

Cerutti, P.O., Gumbo, D., Moombe, K., Schoneveld, G., Nasi, R., Bourland, N., and Weng, X., 2018. *Informality, global capital, rural development and the environment: Mukula (rosewood) trade between China and Zambia*. Bogor: CIFOR.

Dobler, G., 2008a. Boundary-drawing and the notion of territoriality in pre-colonial and early colonial Ovamboland. *Journal of Namibian Studies*, 3, 7–30.

Dobler, G., 2008b. From Scotch whisky to Chinese sneakers: international commodity flows and trade networks in Oshikango, Namibia. *Africa*, 78(3), 410–432.

Dobler, G., 2009. Oshikango: the dynamics of growth and regulation in a Northern Namibian boom town. *Journal of Southern African Studies*, 35(1), 115–131.

Dobler, G., 2014. *Traders and trade in colonial Ovamboland, 1925-1990: elite formation and the politics of consumption under indirect rule and apartheid*. Basel, Switzerland: Basler Afrika Bibliographien.

Dobler, G., 2016. The green, the grey and the blue: a typology of cross-border trade in Africa. *The Journal of Modern African Studies*, 54(1), 145–169.

Dobler, G., 2017. China and Namibia, 1990 to 2015: how a new actor changes the dynamics of political economy. *Review of African Political Economy*, 44(153), 449–465.

Dobler, G. and Kesselring, R., 2019. Swiss extractivism: Switzerland's role in Zambia's copper sector. *The Journal of Modern African Studies*, 57(2), 223–245.

Egg, J. and Herrera, J., eds., 1998. *Echanges transfrontaliers et intégration régionale en Afrique subsaharienne*. Paris: Ed. de l'Aube [u.a.].

Gallien, M., 2020a. Informal Institutions and the regulation of smuggling in North Africa. *Perspectives on Politics*, 18(2), 492–508.

Gallien, M., 2020b. Smugglers and states: illegal trade in the political settlements of North Africa. PhD Thesis. The London School of Economics and Political Science (LSE).

Gallien, M. and Weigand, F., 2021. Channeling contraband: how states shape international smuggling routes. *Security Studies*, 30(1), 79–106.

Guj, P., Martin, S., Maybee, B., Cawood, F., Bocoum, B., Gosai, N., and Huibregtse, S., 2017. *Transfer pricing in mining with a focus on Africa*. Washington, DC: World Bank.

Haysom, S., 2020. From the maskani to the mayor: the political economy of heroin markets in East and Southern Africa. *ENACT Research Paper*, 13, 60.

Heitz-Tokpa, K., 2019. Mande hunters and the state: cooperation and contestation in post-conflict Côte d'Ivoire. *African Studies Review*, 62(1), 148–172.

Localising smuggling

Hübschle, A., 2014. Of bogus hunters, queenpins and mules: the varied roles of women in transnational organized crime in Southern Africa. *Trends in Organized Crime*, 17(1–2), 31–51.

Hübschle, A., 2016. *A game of horns: transnational flows of rhino horn*. application/pdf. Cologne: IMPRS-SPCE.

Hüsken, T., 2019. *Tribal politics in the borderland of Egypt and Libya*. Cham, Switzerland: Palgrave Macmillan.

Kesselring, R., 2019. *Valueworks: effects of financialization along Copper's value chain*. SNIS Working Paper. Geneva: Swiss Network for International Studies.

Lescuyer, G. and Tal, M., 2016. Intra-African trade of timber: the Cameroon-Chad case in 2015 [online]. Available from: https://agritrop.cirad.fr/580185/ (Accessed 31 Mar 2021).

Lukumbuzya, K. and Sianga, C., 2017. *Overview of the timber trade in East and Southern Africa*. Cambridge, UK: Traffic.

Lundstøl, O., Raballand, G., and Nyirongo, F., 2013. *Low government revenue from the mining sector in Zambia and Tanzania: fiscal design, technical capacity or political will?*, SSRN Scholarly Paper No. ID 2411451. Rochester, NY: Social Science Research Network.

Malik, A. and Gallien, M., 2020. Border economies of the Middle East: why do they matter for political economy? *Review of International Political Economy*, 27(3), 732–762.

McCurdy, S. and Kaduri, P., 2016. The political economy of heroin and crack cocaine in Tanzania. *Review of African Political Economy*, 43(148), 312–319.

Meagher, K., 2014. Smuggling ideologies: From criminalization to hybrid governance in African clandestine economies. *African Affairs*, 113(453), 497–517.

Minnaar, A., 2015. The supply, demand, trafficking and smuggling of drugs in South Africa: a situational review. *Acta Criminologica: African Journal of Criminology & Victimology*, 2015(sed-3), 1–28.

Ng'askie, P.O., 2019. *Fusing formal and informal trading: Emerging practices in the livestock value chains between Kenya and Somalia*. Working Paper No. 2019:12. DIIS Working Paper.

Nugent, P., 2002. *Smugglers, secessionists & loyal citizens on the Ghana-Toga frontier: the life of the borderlands since 1914*. Legon, Ghana: Sub-Saharan Publishers.

Raeymaekers, T., 2009. The silent encroachment of the frontier: A politics of transborder trade in the Semliki Valley (Congo–Uganda). *Political Geography*, 28(1), 55–65.

Readhead, A., 2016. *Transfer pricing in the mining sector in Zambia*. London: National Resource Governance Institute.

Readhead, A., 2017. *Toolkit for transfer pricing risk assessment in the African mining industry*. Bonn: GIZ.

Roitman, J., 2008. The ethics of illegality in the Chad Basin. *In*: J. Comaroff and J. Comaroff, eds. *Law and Disorder in the Postcolony*. Chicago: University of Chicago Press, 247–272.

de Sardan, J.-P.O., 2013. The bureaucratic mode of governance and practical norms in West Africa and beyond. *In*: M. Bouziane, C. Harders, and A. Hoffmann, eds. *Local Politics and Contemporary Transformations in the Arab World: Governance Beyond the Center*. London: Palgrave Macmillan UK, 43–64.

Tazebew, T. and Kefale, A., 2021. Governing the economy: rule and resistance in the Ethiopia-Somaliland borderlands. *Journal of Eastern African Studies*, 15(1), 147–167.

Titeca, K., 2012. Tycoons and contraband: informal cross-border trade in West Nile, north-western Uganda. *Journal of Eastern African Studies*, 6(1), 47–63.

Titeca, K. and Herdt, T. de, 2010. Regulation, cross-border trade and practical norms in West Nile, North-Western Uganda. *Africa*, 80(4), 573–594.

Walther, O., 2018. Regional integration. *In*: T. Binns, K. Lynch, and E. Nel, eds. *Handbook of African Development*. London: Routledge, 286–299.

Weigand, F., 2020. *Conflict and transnational crime*. Cheltenham: Edward Elgar Publishing.

3

SMUGGLING IDEOLOGIES

Theory and reality in African clandestine economies

Kate Meagher

Introduction

In Africa, clandestine economies get an identity change about once every decade. From the mid-1970s to the mid-1980s they were associated with economic distortions (May 1985; World Bank 1981); from the late 1980s to the mid-1990s they were about indigenous entrepreneurship and regional integration from below (Egg & Igue 1993; MacGaffey 1991; World Bank 1989). From the late 1990s through much of the 'noughties' they have been linked with corruption and criminalization of the state (Bayart et al. 1999; Reno 2000); from the late 'noughties' clandestine trade was all about real governance and more authentic forms of state formation (Menkhaus 2006/7; Raeymaekers 2010). Recently, a more selective approach distinguishes 'acceptable' clandestine trade that creates employment for women and youth, from criminal revenue streams for rebels and global terrorists (Van den Boogaard et al. 2021; Kodero 2020; Maguire and Haenlin 2016; Titeca 2019). With so many changes of character, it is pertinent to ask whether these reflect shifts in the nature and effects of clandestine economies themselves, or shifts in the way they are perceived by international researchers and development practitioners.

A close empirical examination of African clandestine economies (or informal cross-border trade, aka 'smuggling') reveals that they have always involved a variety of elements, ranging from responses to economic distortions through indigenous entrepreneurship to criminalization, depending on which countries or regions one is looking at, and when. In some countries, such as Nigeria, clandestine trade has weakened industrialization efforts and undermined the formal economy; in others, such as Benin or the Gambia which derive significant revenue from operating as local import hubs, it is central to the organization of the formal economy (Bach 1999; Golub & Mbaye 2009; Igué 1977; Sall & Sallah 1994). In still other countries, such as Sierra Leone or the Democratic Republic of the Congo (DRC), clandestine economies are bound up with rebels and rogue military forces that ravage the state and society, while in contrasting cases, such as Senegal, clandestine trade has actually contributed to social stability and processes of state formation (Babou 2002; Lindley 2009; Malcolmson 1996; Reno 2003; Renton et al. 2007).

In this chapter, I will consider the role of ideological framing and international policy objectives in shaping and reshaping our understanding of African clandestine economies,

30

DOI: 10.4324/9781003043645-3

focusing on the ongoing tension between criminalizing smuggling activities and portraying them as developmental sources of state building and poverty alleviation. I argue that prevailing development perspectives on African clandestine economies often obscure rather than clarify the changing effects of illicit trade on governance and development in various African contexts. To trace the gap between smuggling ideologies and smuggling realities, I will focus on informal cross-border trading systems in West Africa during the 1990s and their role in underpinning criminalization discourses, and on violent Eastern African cross-border trading complexes in the 2000s centred on the Great Lakes region, which have been central to hybrid governance narratives of the constructive role of smuggling networks in African state formation. In both cases, the liminality of smuggling and a tendency to pathologize or essentialize African realities provide a palette for theorizing illicit trading activities around international notions of the 'right' kind of order, rather than around the national political and economic processes and popular development aspirations.

African clandestine economies and model shopping

African clandestine trading systems have played havoc with conventional theories of states and economies – they expanded rather than contracted in the face of liberal market reforms, and became entwined with rather than replaced by the formal institutions of the state (Egg & Herrera 1998; Hibou 1999; Meagher 2003; Nabuguzi 1994). By the late 1990s, the recognition that smuggling was neither reined in by liberalization, nor transformed into a seedbed of liberal entrepreneurship turned from disillusionment to alarm as African trading networks began to seize the opportunities of liberalization and globalization to expand their clandestine reach into the global economy (Duffield 2000; Meagher 2003). This set the stage for the rise of criminalization perspectives, which defended the Weberian model of the rational-legal state by pathologizing African clandestine trade as mechanisms of violent predation, 'war economies' and 'shadow states' (Bayart et al. 1999; Collier & Hoeffler 2000; Reno 2000).

A decade later, these Afro-pessimist interpretations have given way to more sanguine views of the developmental capacities of non-state forms of order. Weberian models of the bureaucratic state have been overtaken by models based on Olson's stationary bandit and Tillyan notions of state formation as a violent process. In the process, the developmental implication of Africa's smuggling networks are being rehabilitated across the continent. What is going on? Have African clandestine economies changed the way they operate, or have researchers developed better approaches to understanding their impact on development, or is something else afoot?

Two main processes seem to be at work here, one practical and the other theoretical. On the one hand, a recognition of the poor performance and high cost of conventional approaches to state-building are encouraging a search for alternative means of restoring order in hard-to-govern regions of the continent (Menkhaus 2006/7; Reno 2004; see also Meagher 2012). As Thomas Bierschenk (2010:2) points out, decades of detailed anthropological work on informal and non-state forms of organization have revealed that 'political order is possible without the state,' leading to a rethink of imported Weberian models of the rational bureaucratic state, increasingly regarded as an unnecessary luxury for Africa's fragile regions. On the other hand, emerging theoretical perspectives that focus on the notion of 'hybrid governance' suggest that violence and rival forms of order and authority may be part of more authentic processes of state-formation rather than symptoms of criminality and state failure (Boege et al. 2009a; Hagmann & Peclard 2010; MacGinty 2010; Menkhaus 2008; Vlassenroot & Raeymaekers 2008). Non-state forms of order not only offer better value for money, but a new theoretical packaging suggests they may be acceptable and even preferable paths to development (Boege et al. 2009a:14). Similar to Keebit von Benda-Beckman's notion of 'forum shopping,' prevailing development thinking seems to have gone shopping for new models of African clandestine trade to fit changing political and developmental objectives (Benda-Beckmann 1981).

In the process, thinking about clandestine economies has shifted away from Weberian models of economic and political institutions, to a realization that the opposite of rational bureaucratic order is not disorder and corruption, but informal forms of order. The image of a 'shadow economy' regulated by a 'shadow state' is giving way to the recognition of a range of indigenous institutions that create local forms of order in the shadow of the state. This has been facilitated by an improved institutional understanding of informal forms of order, and a realization that they can be enlisted to create a measure of stability at lower cost. As James Ferguson (2006:208) argues in his provocative book *Global Shadows*, engaging with informal systems of order and authority means that 'capital investment can be institutionalized in a way that makes it possible to cut out the "overhead" of a national-level societal project and to provide political order "flexibly" on an as-needed basis, to restricted and delimited non-national spaces.' This 'aha moment' has been followed by an explosion of interest in arguments by Charles Tilly and Mancur Olson that violence and protection rackets are not necessarily signs of criminality and regulatory collapse but harbingers of new, more locally-embedded forms of order (Olson 1993; Tilly 1985). While Tilly (1985:170) stresses the interdependence among war making, state making and organized crime, Olson (1993:569) critiques the denigration of predatory states, arguing that 'the metaphor of predation obscures the great superiority of stationary banditry over anarchy and the advances on civilization that have resulted from it.'

While Tilly expressed reservations about the extension of his theories from early modern Europe to contemporary developing countries (Tilly 1985:185–186), recent research on cross-border trade and informal markets has revealed greater confidence in the applicability of these ideas to twenty-first century Africa. Contemporary studies of clandestine trade in the DRC, Uganda, Somalia and various parts of West Africa have all drawn explicitly on the work of Tilly or Olson to suggest that large-scale smuggling activities and violent forms of regulation are not instances of African regulatory pathologies, but represent the replacement of imported and unworkable ideal types with more embedded systems of order and state formation (Boege et al. 2009b:601; Chalfin 2010; Menkhaus 2006/7; Raeymaekers 2010; Reno 2009; Titeca 2011:61).

In addition to bringing new scholars of African clandestine trade to the fore, some more established proponents of criminalization perspectives have shifted gear. William Reno initially associated 'illicit economies' with corrupt 'Shadow States' using corruption and violent predation to dismantle rational bureaucracies (Reno 1997, 2000, 2006). In subsequent work, Reno has turned to Tillyian and Olsonian notions of violence as an alternative source of order, and uses them to show how violence and war economies in contemporary West Africa can lead to 'indigenous … as opposed to internationally scripted transitions' (Reno 2009:317). He highlights the shift from predation to peaceful economic competition in West African contexts, as networks of violence and plunder built up during conflict are transformed into legitimate political and business relationships, leading to the claim that 'These developments represent the emergence of new forms of governance outside the framework of imported notions of reform and state-building' (Reno 2009:313).

This greater appreciation of local institutional process, warts and all, is certainly to be welcomed. The bizarre twist in this theoretical rehabilitation of African clandestine economies, however, is that they tend to be applied to contexts in which cross-border trading activities are empirically more violent and criminal than those conventionally cited to support the older criminalization narratives. Examples of the criminalization of African states and economies in

Smuggling ideologies

the late 1990s tended to be drawn from relatively peaceful informal business systems in West and West Central Africa (Egg & Herrera 1998; Flynn 1997; Grégoire 1992; Gregoire & Labazee 1993; Igue & Soule 1992; Meagher 2003). By contrast, contemporary 'hybrid governance' views of clandestine trade as transformative tend to be drawn from contemporary cross-border trading complexes in Eastern Africa, where violence and criminality have made cross-border trade increasingly inimical to popular welfare (Amnesty International 2005; Eichstaedt 2011; Global Witness 2009; Human Rights Watch 2005). Examining why largely peaceful informal commercial networks were represented as criminal, and largely violent smuggling systems are being represented as sources of stability and political transformation raises important questions about the ways in which prevailing interpretations of African clandestine trade are shaped by ideological agendas rather than by empirical realities.

The criminalization of smuggling in West Africa

Many of the most iconic cases of the criminalizing influence of cross-border trade have been drawn from West African clandestine trading systems, as exemplified in the work of Bayart et al. (1999), Janet Roitman (2004) and Mark Duffield (2000; 2001). Likewise, Daniel Bach's (1999) research on informal trade and regional dis-integration draws heavily on West African examples which dominate the Francophone literature (Egg & Herrera 1998; Igue & Soule 1992), and William Reno's (1997, 2000, 2006) model of the shadow state rested heavily on research in Sierra Leone and Nigeria.

Similar research on clandestine trading networks in Zaire/DR Congo was occasionally featured in criminalization narratives of the 1990s (Reno 1998; Bayart et al. 1999), but was much less prominent, owing in large part to the limited global presence of Congolese trading networks. As recognized by Janet MacGaffey and Remi-Bazenuissa-Ganga (2000), Congolese trading networks of the 1980s and 1990s lacked the institutionalized corporate organization of their West African counterparts, confining them to relatively low-level international trading activities. By contrast, West Africa's dynamic smuggling networks used liberalization for a dramatic expansion of their engagement with the global economy, raising alarm in the international community by their ability to bypass formal regulatory structures and subvert the intentions of economic reforms (Meagher 2003). Yet a closer look at the evidence shows that, despite the perceived threat in international policy circles, the vast majority of West African smuggling activities were neither criminal nor violent. They were dominated by trade in legal commodities through illegal channels, and were much less involved with war, illegal goods, or the creation of peripheral centres of power in the 'borderlands.'

War economies vs empirical evidence in West Africa

Criminalization perspectives of the late 1990s routinely linked the highly organized clandestine trading systems of West Africa to 'violent modes of accumulation' based on war, criminality, and trade in illegal goods. The core actors of cross-border trading networks were frequently represented as 'warlords,' 'mafia entities,' and 'rebels' or armed youth, whether the indigenous commercial groups at the heart of these networks had anything to do with war or not (Duffield 2000; Reno 1998; Reno 2000; Roitman 2004). Reno (2000:434) states bluntly that 'this commerce accompanies armed conflict, and plays an important role in provoking and prolonging much of the warfare in Africa.'

In other cases, the link between transnational smuggling networks and violence has been made by dismissing any meaningful distinction between violent and peaceful modes of clandestine trade. Roland Marchal and Christine Messiant (2003:100) express exasperation with the tendency of commentators on war economies to create an impression of clandestine trade as a 'belligerent factor by definition.' David Keen's (1996) notion of war as 'the pursuit of economics by other means' has been used widely to merge the notion of clandestine trading networks with war economies, even where there is no evidence of war or violence. Reno (2006:31) contends that smuggling networks 'fuse the exercise of political power to violent predation in informal and clandestine markets ... well before these places come to international attention as conflict zones.' Similarly, Mark Duffield (2000:79–80) claims that

> Given the general characteristics of transborder trade, it is possible to argue that there is a similarity between peace economies and war economies ... Even when violence is not visible, similar processes of exclusion and oppression can be in operations but at a lower key ... War and peace are relative rather than absolute conditions.

Many of the criminalization narratives also focus attention on illegal goods as the core commodities involved in smuggling networks. Reno (2000:433), Bach (1999:12), Bayart et al. (1999) and others represent African clandestine economies as a nexus of drug smuggling, piracy, blood diamonds, arms, and human trafficking. Janet Roitman (2004:155) gives a similarly nefarious list of smuggled goods in the Chad Basin. Mark Duffield (2001:156) concedes that African smuggling networks are not necessarily associated with war and illegal goods, but contends that the same networks used for trading medicine and manufactured goods are used for money laundering and arms trading, without providing any supporting evidence for this claim.

Closer empirical examination reveals that the bulk of cross-border trade in West Africa is made up of legal goods, has little to do with conflict, and is centred on a dynamic of currency conversion rather than money laundering (Chalfin 2010; Egg & Herrera 1998; Egg & Igue 1993; Igue & Soule 1992; Meagher 1997, 2003). Numerous studies have documented that the driving force behind the expansion of cross-border trade in West Africa has not been war or the lure of high value minerals, but fiscal and monetary disparities created by the patchwork of Francophone and Anglophone colonies across the region. In particular, disparities in tariff and subsidy regimes in neighbouring countries, and the existence of the internationally convertible CFA Francs side-by-side with the inconvertible currencies of most Anglophone economies have animated cross-border trade (Herrera 1997; Igué 1977; Meagher 2003). A wealth of detailed empirical research conducted by Francophone as well as Anglophone researchers in Nigeria and neighbouring countries has shown that the commodities involved in West African smuggling networks throughout the 1980s and 1990s were dominated by legal goods such as agricultural goods, textiles, cigarettes, used cars, pharmaceuticals, electronics, and other manufactured consumer goods (Egg & Herrera 1998; Meagher 1997; Meagher 2003; Moussa et al. 2010). While drug and diamond smuggling have increased in the region, they are not carried out by the main cross-border trading groups and remain peripheral in terms of value. West Africa is only a transit point for drugs, and diamonds have played a relatively minor role in the value of the region's clandestine trade (Meagher 2003; Reyskens 2012). Even at the height of West African drug smuggling in the mid-2000s, the total value of West African drug smuggling has been estimated at $2 billion, which is less than 2% of West African clandestine economies (African Economic Development Institute 2013).

The largest cross-border trading complex in West/West Central Africa, centred around Nigeria, is almost entirely made up of states that are not at war, including Nigeria, Benin, Togo, Niger, Cameroun and Chad. Only one of these states, Chad – the most economically peripheral

Smuggling ideologies

– could be defined as a 'conflict state' in the heyday of West African clandestine trade. Nigeria, the hub of this clandestine trading complex, hosts the largest informal economy in West Africa. Nigeria's informal economy is estimated at about 60% of GDP in a country that accounts for 60.5% of West Africa's GDP (Economic Commission for Africa 2007; Meagher 2010). This puts Nigeria's clandestine economy alone at about 40% of West African GDP. Transit and re-export trade in Benin and Togo have been put at about 75% of their GDP, most of it informal and based on legal goods (Golub 2010:24).

Beyond the Nigerian cross-border trading complex, the next major centre of cross-border trading networks is in the Senegambian region, where again, the core activities revolve around consumer goods and peaceful trading activities (Babou 2002; Diouf 2013; Ebin 1993; Lambert 1989; Sall and Sallah 1994). The World Bank puts Senegal's informal economy at 60% of the country's $14 billion GDP, or about 2% of West African GDP (Golub & Mbaye 2009; World Bank n.d.). The Mouride trading networks that dominate Senegal's clandestine economy encourage a strict moral code of piety, frugality and hard work, and their expanding involvement in cross-border trade since the 1970s has underpinned one of the most stable democratic states in Africa. The long-standing conflict in the Senegalese region of Casamance has been so low key that some have dubbed its combatants 'part-time rebels,' and it has little role in Senegal's clandestine trading activities (Evans 2003; Foucher 2003). Indeed, Martin Evans (2003) argues that the term 'war economy' is inappropriate to the Casamance conflict.

The only parts of West Africa where classical war economies have predominated during the latter part of the twentieth century are in Liberia/Sierra Leone and in Chad, areas largely peripheral to West Africa's major cross-border trading systems. None of West Africa's major indigenous globalized trading networks, including the Hausa, Igbo, and Mourides, are based in these areas, though Lebanese networks have been more active. Clandestine economies in Liberia and Sierra Leone involved instrumental arrangements with foreign networks and militias rather than institutionalized commercial networks based on local commercial norms and values. Moreover, the entire combined economies of the Liberia and Sierra Leone is less than half of the clandestine share of Senegal's economy, and less than one percent of the GDP of the West African region (Global Finance Magazine 2011a; Global Finance Magazine 2011b; Smillie et al. 2000). The same is true of Guinea Bissau, dubbed Africa's first 'narco state.' While drug trafficking is estimated at twice the country's gross domestic product, this still amounts to less than 2% of clandestine trade in the West African region (Madeira et al. 2011; Reyskens 2012; United Nations Office on Drugs and Crime 2011).

A pluralization of regulatory authority?

Criminalization narratives of West African informal economies have sought to understand not only how clandestine economies restructure flows of goods and resources, but how they reorganize the sources and sites of power in the process of shifting it outside formal regulatory structures of the state. Notions of a criminalized 'shadow state' saw power largely exercised through networks of 'front men' including corrupt officials, strong men and armed youth, sometimes engaging with global corporate linkages operating outside legal regulations (Bayart et al. 1999; Chabal & Daloz 1999; Hibou 2004; Reno 2000; Reno 2004). Using an ethnography of clandestine trading networks, Janet Roitman (2004) mapped the regulatory transformations taking place, which were said to generate new sites of power operating at the borders rather than in capital cities.

While initiating important debates on the regulatory restructuring effected by large clandestine economies, these representation of clandestine power networks are sorely in need of a reality check. Those familiar with the structure of smuggling activities in the countries of the 'Chad Basin' know that prior to 2010, Hausa-Fulani commercial groups rather than military or rebel groups have been the central players, and the regulatory centre of these networks is not at the borders, but in the inland commercial capitals of informal trade, such as Kano in Nigeria, and Maradi in Niger (Hashim & Meagher 1999; Grégoire 1992). The same is true of the Mouride trading networks, which are not intertwined with the military or with rebels, and have their informal organizational capital in the inland city of Touba, not at the borders (Babou 2002; Malcolmson 1996). Not only are these main West African trading networks not geographically peripheral, they are not socially or politically peripheral either. Both the Nigerian and the Senegalese trading networks hail from major national power-holding groups within their respective societies. The Hausa-Fulani block have been at the centre of state power for much of Nigeria's post-colonial history, and the Mourides have had close relations with systems of power in Senegal since colonial times (Beck 2001; Dahou & Fouchard 2009; Diouf 2013). Far from creating new sites of power, these networks have played a key role in consolidating state power through socio-political linkages with and dependence on supportive relations with the state.

The key point here is that West African smuggling networks have been represented as criminal, violent and disruptive of constituted authority when the evidence suggests that in most of West Africa they were predominantly peaceful commercial systems that reinforced state power. What is intriguing is that now that the pendulum is swinging back toward a more positive view of African smuggling networks, attention is shifting away from largely peaceful West African networks to focus on much more violent, militarized and politically disruptive smuggling networks operating in Eastern Africa. In short, what was peaceful was represented as violent and disruptive, and what is violent and disruptive is now being represented as developmental.

The ideological rehabilitation of smuggling in Eastern Africa

Since the mid-2000s, Eastern Africa has displaced West Africa as the epicentre of empirical research and theoretical debates on clandestine cross-border trade. In the Eastern African context, I will concentrate on the largest clandestine trading complex operating in the Great Lakes region, involving the DR Congo, Uganda, Sudan and Rwanda, along with Kenya and Tanzania as key entry ports.[1] Recent studies of clandestine cross-border trade in Eastern Africa emphasize the cooperative relations among smugglers, military actors, state officials and popular forces, who have created practical regulatory solutions to the problems of governance created by state predation and collapse. Negotiations among these actors in the Uganda-DRC-Sudan border regions are seen as a source of 'practical norms' that fill the gap between the legal and the possible in difficult circumstances, leading to a shift of regulatory authority from the decrepit structures of weak or collapsing states to 'military-commercial networks' that restore order and reconnect the region with the global economy (Raeymaekers 2010; Titeca 2012; Titeca & de Herdt 2010). In other words, violent clandestine trading networks are being reimagined as 'law makers' rather than 'law breakers.' A closer look at smuggling networks in the region raises questions about the optimistic interpretation of the transformations underway, calling for a more detailed consideration of their association with violence, the role of licit versus illicit goods, and their impact on regulatory authority.

Smuggling in Eastern Africa has a long history dating back to pre-colonial times, involving trading networks that link the Eastern DRC to the global economy through ports in Kenya and Tanzania, via Uganda, as well as interaction with networks in neighbouring Sudan, Rwanda

Smuggling ideologies

and Burundi (Meagher 1990; Titeca 2012; Vlassenroot et al. 2012). Since the late 1980s, however, these trading systems have been transformed by constant waves of conflict in the region. Unlike West Africa, violent conflict affecting virtually all of the countries in this cross-border trading complex has raged for much of the last three decades, including the war in southern Sudan, the First and Second Congo War, the Rwandan genocide, the conflict in Burundi, and the Ugandan civil war and enduring low-intensity conflict of the LRA and other rebel groups in northern Uganda.

In the process, clandestine trade has been reshaped by military activity, rebel incursions, and waves of refugees moving back and forth across borders, leading to a significant militarization of previously largely commercial cross-border trading networks. In contrast to West Africa's smuggling networks, military forces and rebel militias are central players in clandestine economies of the Great Lakes. In the DRC, Timothy Raeymaekers and Koen Vlassenroot have documented the collaboration of cross-border traders with local rebel groups (Raeymaekers 2010; Vlassenroot and Raeymaekers 2008). On the Ugandan side, a number of scholars have noted that many of those involved in clandestine trade are rebels, former rebels or soldiers (Titeca 2006; Titeca & de Herdt 2010; Vlassenroot et al. 2012). Titeca (2012:52–53) and others have detailed the increasing involvement of the Ugandan military and state officials in cross-border trading activities in northern Uganda from the late 1980s, leading to a genuine 'military-commercial nexus' that has intervened significantly in the regulation of clandestine trade, collaborating with Congolese rebels across the border to ensure access to the product of Ituri gold fields (Human Rights Watch 2005; Titeca 2011; Vlassenroot et al. 2012). Vlassenroot et al. (2012:5) state that 'during the Congolese wars, these networks' mode of exploitation and commercialization became entirely militarized.' The involvement of Rwandan officials and the military in the cross-border mineral trade in Eastern Congo is well documented, making the conflict in Eastern Congo a 'self-financing war' (Jackson 2002:24). The Sudanese branch of this trading complex is equally militarized, with rebels and soldiers displacing local commercial groups in cross-border trading activities (Shomerus & Titeca 2012; Walraet 2008).

Militarization has been accompanied by the replacement of commercial relations with increasingly violent forms of regulation. While cross-border trading relations in West Africa were regulated by institutionalized commercial practices and reputation-based sanctions, Eastern African clandestine trade is dominated by 'violent modes of accumulation.' In the DRC, militarized trading monopolies have marginalized independent traders, and have developed coercive and often violent relations with society (Human Rights Watch 2005; Jackson 2002; Meagher 2012; Raeymaekers 2010). Accounts from DRC and Uganda speak of forced labour, violent treatment of uncooperative local officials, and the manipulation of ethnic antagonisms for the violent restructuring of production and trading networks (Titeca and de Herdt 2010; Vlassenroot et al. 2012).

The key goods involved in these Eastern African trading networks also show a strong leaning toward illicit rather than legal commodities. While manufactured consumer goods play a role, the driving force behind the trade is conflict minerals and arms. In Uganda, Titeca (2012:2) notes that '[t]he export of manufactured goods to Congo and the import of gold remain the basis of the cross-border contraband trade ...' Plundering Congolese gold and timber are key incentives to cross-border trade in Uganda, where gold now plays a prominent role in the country's official exports, despite the fact the Uganda has virtually no gold mines (Human Rights Watch 2005). In Rwanda, a range of conflict minerals, including tin, tantalum and tungsten ores, are central incentives to continued cross-border trade with the DRC. By the late noughties, tin ore rose to become Rwanda's largest export by value, (Garrett & Mitchell 2009:39; UNCTAD 2010:10). The return trade for these conflict minerals includes arms as well as manufactured goods (Human Rights Watch 2005; Renton et al. 2007; Titeca 2012). In short, conflict minerals and arms play a central role in Eastern African clandestine trade, in contrast to the central role of legal goods and convertible currency in West Africa.

Finally, the notion that these militarized smuggling networks are becoming new sources of legitimate authority in their respective regions is not supported by the evidence. Raeymaekers maintains that militarized trading networks in Eastern DRC are engaging in 'state-like functions,' owing to their increasing involvement in taxation and the provision of a range of infrastructure and social services, including roads, health centres, schools and electricity. Titeca (2012) notes similar activities on the part of cross-border traders in northern Uganda. However, the assertion that this creates local legitimacy clashes with evidence that relations between militarized trading networks and local people are highly coercive, based on forced labour, fear and violence. Stephen Jackson (2002:35) argues that smuggling networks, once accepted as legitimate sources of popular livelihoods and accumulation, are widely regarded by local populations to have been 'criminalized' by the process of militarization. Indigenous regulatory systems have increasingly been replaced by illegitimate authority based on violence and military might, riding roughshod over local political, social and commercial governance norms (Tegera & Johnson 2007; Tull 2003).

In the context of violent reallocation of power and resource control, Eastern African clandestine economies seem to be shifting regulatory authority away from the state. In contrast to the situation in West Africa, the groups involved in Eastern African cross-border trading activities are peripheral rather than central to national constellations of power. In Eastern DRC, the Nande and Banyarwanda communities at the helm of the main militarized trading networks in the region are peripheral groups in the post-independence national power equation, which has been dominated by the more politically central Lunda, Luba and BaKongo (Tegera & Johnson 2007; Turner 2007). Even within Eastern DRC, the Nande historically have been economically rather than politically influential, and the framing of the Banyarwanda as foreign migrants has made their political standing inherently precarious and dependent on patronage from the centre (Renton et al. 2007; Turner 2007). Both groups have forced their way onto the national political agenda by using spoilers' tactics of violent control of resources in the border regions, leveraging international support to punch above their weight in national politics. Similarly, the Lugbara who dominate smuggling networks in northern Uganda are marginal to the national commercial and political equation in Uganda, (Meagher 1990; Titeca 2009; Titeca 2012).

Moreover, these claims to power from the periphery are dependent in all of these cases on influential external players who use peripheral local groups as proxies for strategies of illicit access to local markets and resources. Neighbouring countries and international political and economic interests are heavily implicated in backing East Africa's militarized cross-border traders in the violent reassignment of property rights and access to global markets (Global Witness 2009; Human Rights Watch 2005; United Nations 2012). Far from supporting more authentic processes of state formation, these smuggling networks are contributing to the hollowing out of the state, both politically and materially, as they seize unaccountable regulatory control over local populations and divert resources from the state coffers into private pockets and circuits of international capital, undermining public accountability and national resource control.

In a further ironic twist, as African clandestine economies become associated with positive transformations, even the peaceful clandestine economies of West Africa are taking a violent turn in the face of chaotic governance, rising poverty and expanding unemployment. Since the

Smuggling ideologies

late noughties, illegal oil bunkering linked to militarized networks of former Niger Delta militias represents an expanding share of the Nigerian clandestine economy, and the violent Islamic group known as Boko Haram has relied increasingly on the clandestine fish and pepper trade from the Chad Basin, with increasing involvement of the Nigerian military (Salkida 2020; Wallis 2012). Similarly, the Mourides networks of Senegal became increasingly politicized under the former President Wade, weakening their stabilizing and legitimating influence on governance (Beck 2001; Babou 2013). This makes a shift in the political economy literature toward an increasingly positive interpretation of clandestine economies even more puzzling (Golub & Mbaye 2009; Reno 2009).

Conclusion

The question raised by this chapter is whether prevailing theories about the developmental implications of smuggling networks are driven more by empirical realities or by international policy agendas. The cases of West African smuggling complexes in the 1990s, and Eastern African smuggling networks from the late noughties suggest that ideological agendas from above play a greater role in the way we think about appropriate forms of order and disorder than empirical processes from below, particularly in African contexts. The vast majority of West African smuggling activity prior to 2000 was dominated by legal goods, had little to do with war economies, and in many cases tended to reinforce rather than undermine state power. Yet smuggling was widely represented as criminal networks based on violence and war that were inimical to state building.

By contrast, smuggling networks between East Africa and the DRC have been more widely associated with war economies, conflict minerals, arms trading, and state instability. New development ideologies, however, now deploy economic and political models drawn from Tilly and Olson to represent these violent networks as the beginnings of more authentic processes of African state formation. It is perhaps no accident that these ideologies help to legitimate processes that diffuse power and resource control away from the state, and facilitate efforts by local strongmen to assert contractual control over labour and property rights in the service of direct economic linkages with the global economy.

This raises two key questions about the broader trajectory of research on clandestine economies. The first is about models, and the second is about motives. Regarding models, the use of the Tillyan and stationery bandit models in explaining the developmental implications of contemporary smuggling networks demands closer scrutiny. As Anna Leander (2004) and Charles Tilly (1985) have pointed out, the dominance of external resource flows prominent in many developing country contexts undermine the very dynamics of centralization and civil accountability that turns war making into state making. Likewise, Brenda Chalfin (2010:234) argues that the pluralisation and externalization of regulatory authority retools rather than weakens African states, but acknowledges that the shift 'comes at the expense of accountability and the formulation of clear lines of authority in relation to the public ...' New models of how smuggling affects state formation need to be attentive to the implications of existing international conditions on processes of civil accountability.

Regarding motives, it is worth asking why Weberian ideal types of the modern state have been so unceremoniously dropped in favour of new models of engagement with informal order and authority. The answer seems to lie in a growing sense that the international economy can work with informal institutions, which has liberated worried ideologues from their dependence on states as the key agents for maintaining order in the developing world. Roitman (2004:205) was one of the first to point out that, although clandestine trading systems rested on "nonliberal" forms of order, 'the regimes of exchange and non-state-based forms of economic regulatory authority that prevail in the Chad Basin are not averse to free-market principles ...'

Similarly, research on Somalia by Reno (2003) and Menkhaus (2006/7) found that peripheral orders built on clandestine economic networks could, in the right combination of circumstances, be compatible with order, peace-building and global economic integration. This new political economy of clandestine trade seems to offer a solution to vexing development problems by providing mechanisms of stability and market integration that bypass uncooperative states with a growing range of more pliable local regulatory forces. As Reno (2003:40) explains, informal local actors and regulatory systems:

> offer at least the possibility of ... successful integration into the world economy on the basis of transnational family and clan cultural networks rather than the centralizing administrative projects that scholars of early modern European state-building describe (and which the World Bank and other officials increasingly prescribe).

This leaves us with a few nagging questions about how ideologies of appropriate order influence the way smuggling is theorized. Do new forms of order and authority emerging from clandestine trading networks in border regions really give rise to more authentic forms of state formation à la Tilly and Olson, or does their appeal lie in their capacity to bypass the state and respond to global market incentives? The contemporary role of smuggling networks in terrorist financing suggests that a responsiveness to free market principles may not always ensure constructive or compliant forms of order. This raises the further question of who decides which types of clandestine networks foster more legitimate forms of governance and which types are oppressive or criminal? Answering these questions in the interest of progressive economic transformation requires greater attention to whose priorities of order and authority are being promoted in the way that we theorize clandestine trade.

Note

1 Somalia is also a regionally important player in clandestine trade which fits the East African pattern, but will be excluded for reasons of space.

References

African Economic Development Institute (2013). West Africa and Drug Trafficking, www.africaecon.org/index.php/africa_business_reports/read/70.

Amnesty International (2005). Democratic Republic of Congo - North Kivu: Civilians Pay the Price for Political and Military Rivalry, AI Index: AFR 62/013/2005, 5 July.

Babou, C. A. (2002). Brotherhood Solidarity, Education and Migration: The Role of the Dahiras among the Murid Community of New York. *African Affairs*, 101, 151–170.

Babou, C.A. (2013). The Senegalese "Social Contract" Revisited: The Muridiyya Muslim Order and State Politics on Postcolonial Senegal, in *Tolerance, Democracy and Sufis in Senegal*, ed. M. Diouf, Columbia University Press, 125–146.

Bach, D. (ed.) (1999). *Regionalization in Africa: Integration and Disintegration*, Bloomington; Indianapolis: James Currey; Indiana University Press.

Bayart, J.-F., S. Ellis & B. Hibou (eds.), (1999). *The Criminalization of the State in Africa*, Oxford; Bloomington: James Currey; Indiana University Press.

Beck, L. (2001). Reining in the Marabouts? Democratization and Local Governance in Senegal. *African Affairs*, 100, 601–621.

Smuggling ideologies

Benda-Beckmann, K. v. (1981). Forum Shopping and Shopping Forums – Dispute Settlement in a Minangkabau Village in West Sumatra. *Journal of Legal Pluralism*, 13(19), 117–159.

Bierschenk, T. (2010). States at Work in West Africa: Sedimentation, Fragmentation and Normative Double-Binds, Working Paper No 113, Maintz, Germany: Johannes Gutenberg University.

Boege, V., A. Brown & K. Clements (2009a). Hybrid Political Orders, Not Fragile States. *Peace Review: A Journal of Social Science*, 21(1), 13–21.

Boege, V., A. Brown, K. Clements & A. Nolan (2009b). Building Peace and Political Community in Hybrid Political Orders. *International Peacekeeping*, 16(5), 599–615.

Chabal, P. & J.-P. Daloz (1999). *Africa Works: Disorder as Political Instrument*, Oxford; Bloomington, IN: James Currey; Indiana University Press.

Chalfin, B. (2010). *Neoliberal Frontiers: An Ethnography of Sovereignty in West Africa*, Chicago: University of Chicago Press.

Collier, P. & A. Hoeffler (2000). *Greed and Grievance in Civil Wars*, Washington, DC: World Bank.

Dahou, T. & V. Fouchard (2009). Senegal Since 2000: Rebuilding State Hegemony in a Global Age, in *Turning Points in African Democracy*, eds. A. R. Mustapha & L. Whitfield, Woodbridge: James Currey.

Derks, M. (2012). *Improving Security and Justice through Local/Non-state Actors: The Challenges of Donor Support to Local/Non-state Security and Justice Providers*, The Hague: Clingendael Institute.

Diouf, M. (ed.) (2013). *Tolerance, Democracy, and Sufis in Senegal*, New York: Columbia University Press.

Duffield, M. (2000). Globalization, Transborder Trade, and War Economies, in *Greed and Grievance: Economic Agendas in Civil Wars*, eds. M. Berdal & D. Malone, Boulder, CO: Lynne Rienner, 69–89.

Duffield, M. (2001). *Global Governance and the New Wars: The Merging of Development and Security*, London: Zed Books.

Ebin, V. (1993). Les commerçants mourides a Marseille et a New York: regards sur les strategies d'implantation, in *Grands commerçants d'Afrique de l'Ouest*, eds. E. Gregoire & P. Labazee, Paris: ORSTOM-Karthala.

Economic Commission for Africa (2007). *The Relevance of Traditional Institutions of Governance*, Addis Ababa: Economic Commission for Africa.

Egg, J. & J. Herrera (1998). Echanges transfrontaliers et integration regionale en Afrique subsaharienne: Introduction. *Autrepart*, 6, 5–27.

Egg, J. & J. Igue (1993). *Market-Driven Integration in the Eastern Subregion: Nigeria's Impact on its Immediate Neighbors*, Montpellier, Paris, Cotonou: INRA-IRAM-UNB.

Eichstaedt, P. (2011). *Consuming the Congo: War and Conflict Minerals in the World's Deadliest Place*, Chicago: Chicago Review Press.

Evans, M. (2003). Ni pais ni guerre: The Political Economy of Low-level Conflict in the Casamance, HPG Background Paper, London: Overseas Development Institute.

Ferguson, J. (2006). *Global Shadows: Africa in the Neoliberal World Order*, Durham, NC and London: Duke University Press.

Flynn, D. (1997). We Are the Borders: Identity, Exchange, and the State Along the Benin-Nigeria Border. *American Ethnologist*, 24(2), 311–330.

Garrett, N. & H. Mitchell (2009). *Trading Conflict for Development: Utilizing the Trade in Minerals from Eastern DR Congo for Development*, London: Resources Consulting Services.

Global Finance Magazine (2011a). Country Report on Liberia, http://www.gfmag.com/gdp-data-country-reports/ (accessed 28 May 2012).

Global Finance Magazine (2011b). Country Report on Sierra Leone, http://www.gfmag.com/gdp-data-country-reports/ (accessed 28 May 2012).

Global Witness (2009). *Faced with a Gun, What Can You Do? War and the Militarization of Mining in Eastern Congo*, London: Global Witness.

Golub, S. (2010). The Role of Transit and Re-export Trade in Togo's Economy, Unpublished Paper, prepared for Togo DTIS/CEM. p. 24.

Golub, S. & A. Mbaye (2009). National Trade Policies and Smuggling in Africa: The Case of Gambia and Senegal. *World Development*, 37(3), 595–606.

Grégoire, E. (1992). *The Alhazai of Maradi: Traditional Hausa Merchants in a Changing Sahelian City*, Boulder; London: Lynne Rienner.

Gregoire, E. & P. Labazee (eds.) (1993). *Grands commerçants d'Afrique de l'Ouest. Logiques et pratiques d'un groupe d'hommes d'affaires contemporains*, Paris: Karthala-ORSTOM.

Hagmann, T. & D. Peclard (2010). Negotiating Statehood: Dynamics of Power and Domination in Africa. *Development and Change*, 41(4), 539–562.

Hashim, Y. & K. Meagher (1999). *Cross-Border Trade and the Parallel Currency Market: Trade and Finance in the Context of Structural Adjustment: A Case Study from Kano, Nigeria*, Uppsala: Nordiska Afrikainstitutet.

Herrera, J. (1997). Les Echanges transfrontaliers entre le Cameroun et le Nigeria depuis la devaluation: estimation de flux frauduleux d'essence nigeriane et de leur impact au Cameroun et au Nigeria, *Working paper No. 1997-04/T* DIAL.

Hibou, B. (1999). The 'Social Capital' of the State as an Agent of Deception, in *The Criminalization of the State in Africa*, eds. J.-F. Bayart, S. Ellis & B. Hibou, Oxford; Bloomington and Indianapolis: International African Institute, in association with James Currey; Indiana University Press.

Hibou, B. (2004). From Privatising the Economy to Privatising the State: An Analysis of the Continual Formation of the State, in *Privatising the State*, eds. B. Hibou & J. Derrick, London: C. Hurst and Co. Publishers, 1–46.

Human Rights Watch (2005). *The Curse of Gold: Democratic Republic of Congo*, New York: Human Rights Watch.

Igué, J. (1977). *Le Commerce de contrebande et les problèmes monétaires en Afrique occidentale*, Cotonou: CEFAP, Université Nationale du Benin.

Igue, J. & B.-G. Soule (1992). *L'Etat-entrepot au Benin*, Paris: Karthala.

Jackson, S. (2002). Making a Killing: Criminality and Coping in the Kivu War Economy. *Review of African Political Economy*, 29(93/9), 517–536.

Kodero, C. U. (2020). Development Without Borders? Informal Cross-Border Trade in Africa, in *The Palgrave Handbook of African Political Economy*, eds. S. Oloruntoba and T. Falola, Cham: Palgrave Macmillan, 1051–1067.

Keen, D. (1996). *The Economic Functions of Civil Wars*, Adelphi Papers 303, Oxford: International Institute for Strategic Studies.

Lambert, A. (1989). *Espaces et reseaux marchands au Senegal – les echanges cerealiers avec la Gambie et la Mauritanie*, Montpellier: INRA-UNB-IRAM.

Leander, A. (2004). War and the Un-Making of States: Taking Tilly Seriously in the Contemporary World, in *Copenhagen Peace Research: Conceptual Innovation and Contemporary Security Analysis*, eds. S. Guzzini & D. Jung, London: Routledge, 69–80.

Lindley, A. (2009). Between 'Dirty Money' and 'Development Capital': Somali Money Transfer Infrastructure Under Global Scrutiny. *African Affairs*, 108(433), 519–539.

MacGinty, R. (2010). Hybrid Peace: The Interaction Between Top-Down and Bottom-Up Peace. *Security Dialogue*, 41(4), 391–412.

MacGaffey, J. (ed.) (1991). *The Real Economy of Zaire: The Contribution of Smuggling & Other Unofficial Activities to National Wealth*, London, Philadelphia: James Currey; University of Pennsylvania Press.

MacGaffey, J. & R. Bazenguissa-Ganga (2000). *Congo-Paris: Transnational Traders on the Margins of the Law*, Oxford: James Currey.

Madeira, L. F., S. Laurent & S. Roque (2011). The International Cocaine Trade in Guinea-Bissau: Current Trends and Risks, Noref Working Paper, Norwegian Peacebuilding Centre.

Maguire, T. & C. Haenlin (2016). An Illusion of Complicity: Terrorism and the Illegal Ivory Trade in East Africa, RUSI (Royal United Services Institute) Occasional Paper, London: RUSI.

Malcolmson, S. L. (1996). West of Eden: The Mouride Ethic and the Spirit of Capitalism. *Transition*, 71, 24–43.

Marchal, R. & C. Messiant (2003). Les guerres civiles à l'ère de la globalisation. *Critique internationale*, 18, 91–112.

May, E. (1985). Exchange Controls and Parallel Market Economies in Sub-Saharan Africa: Focus on Ghana, World Bank Staff Working Paper No. 711, Washington, DC: World Bank.

Meagher, K. (1990). The Hidden Economy: Informal and Parallel Trade in Northwestern Uganda. *Review of African Political Economy*, 17(74), 64–83.

Meagher, K. (1997). Informal Integration or Economic Subversion? The Development and Organization of Parallel Trade in West Africa, in *Regional Integration and Cooperation in West Africa*, ed. R. Lavergne, Oxford and Paris: OUP/Karthala.

Meagher, K. (2003). A Back Door to Globalisation? Structural Adjustment, Globalisation and Transborder Trade in West Africa. *Review of African Political Economy*, 39(95).

Meagher, K. (2010). *Identity Economics: Social Networks and the Informal Economy in Africa*, Oxford: James Currey.

Meagher, K. (2012). The Strength of Weak States? Non-State Security Forces and Governance in Africa. *Development and Change*, 43(5), 1073–1101.

Menkhaus, K. (2006/7). Governance without government in Somalia: Spoilers, State Building, and the Politics of Coping. *International Security*, 31(3), 74–106.

Menkhaus, K. (2008). The Rise of a Mediated State in Northern Kenya: The Wajir Story and Its Implications for State Building. *Afrika Focus*, 21(2), 23–38.

Moussa, T. A. M., B.-G. Soule & A. S. Afouda (eds.) (2010). *Échanges et réseaux marchands en Afrique*, Paris: Karthala.

Nabuguzi, E. (1994). *Structural Adjustment and the Informal Economy in Uganda*, Copenhagen, Denmark: CDR Working Paper 94.4, Centre for Development Research.

Olson, M. (1993). Dictatorship, Democracy, and Development. *American Political Science Review*, 87(Sept.), 567–576.

Raeymaekers, T. (2010). Protection for Sale: War and the Transformation of Regulation on the Congo-Ugandan Border. *Development and Change*, 41(4), 563–587.

Reno, W. (1997). African Weak States and Commercial Alliances. *African Affairs*, 96(383), 165–185.

Reno, W. (1998). *Warlord Politics and African States*, Boulder: Lynne Rienner.

Reno, W. (2000). Clandestine Economies, Violence and States in Africa. *Journal of International Affairs*, 53(2), 433–459.

Reno, W. (2003). Somali and Survival in the Shadow of the Global Economy, QEH Working Paper No. 100, Oxford: Queen Elizabeth House, University of Oxford.

Reno, W. (2004). Order and Commerce in Turbulent Areas: 19th Century Lessons, 21st Century Practice. *Third World Quarterly*, 25(4), 607–625.

Reno, W. (2006). Insurgencies in the Shadow of Collapsed States, in *Violence, Political Culture and Development in Africa*, ed. P. Kaarsholm, Oxford/Athens, OH/Pietermaritzburg: James Currey/Ohio University Press/University of KwaZulu-Natal Press, 25–48.

Reno, W. (2009). Illicit Markets, Violence, Warlords, and Governance: West African Cases. *Crime, Law and Social Change*, 52(3), 313–322.

Renton, D., D. Seddon & L. Zeilig (2007). *The Congo. Plunder and Resistance*, London; New York: Zed Books.

Reyskens, M. (2012). Drug economy (?): Africa and the International Illicit Drug Trade. *Consultancy Africa Intelligence*, http://www.consultancyafrica.com/index.php?option=com_content&view=article&id= 964:drug-economy-africa-and-the-international-illicit-drug-trade-&catid=60:conflict-terrorism-dis-cussion-papers&Itemid=265.

Roitman, J. (2004). *Fiscal Disobedience: An Anthropology of Economic Regulation in Central Africa*, Princeton: Princeton University Press.

Salkida, A. (2020) 'How Boko Haram Sustain Operations Through International Trade in Smoked Fish,' *Premium Times*, 26 April.

Sall, E. & H. Sallah (1994). Senegal and the Gambia: The Politics of Integration, in *Le Senegal et ses voisins*, ed. M. C. Diop, Oxford: Oxford University Press.

Shomerus, M. & K. Titeca (2012). Deals and Dealings: Inconclusive Peace and Treacherous Trade along the South Sudan-Uganda Border. *Afrika Spectrum*, 47(3), 5–31.

Smillie, I., L. Gberie & R. Hazleton (2000). The Heart of the Matter: Sierra Leone, *Diamonds and Human Security*, Ontario: Partnership Canada.

Tegera, A. & D. Johnson (2007). *Rules for Sale: Formal and Informal Cross-border Trade in Eastern DRC*, Goma: Pole Institute.

Tilly, C. (1985). War Making and State Making as Organized Crime, in *Bringing the State Back In*, eds. P. B. Evans, D. Reuschemeyer & T. Skocpol, Cambridge: Cambridge University Press, 169–186.

Titeca, K. (2006). Les OPEC boys en Ouganda, trafiquants de pétrole et acteurs politiques. *Politique africaine*, 103, 143–159.

Titeca, K. (2009). The Changing Cross-Border Trade Dynamics Between North-Western Uganda, North-Eastern Congo and Southern Sudan, Working Paper 63, Crisis States Research Centre, London: London School of Economics.

Titeca, K. (2011). Access to Resources and Predictability of Armed Rebellion: The FAPC's Short-lived "Monaco" in Eastern Congo. *Afrika Spectrum*, 46(2), 43–70.

Titeca, K. (2012). Tycoons and Contraband: Informal Cross-Border Trade in West Nile, North-Western Uganda. *Journal of Eastern African Studies*, 6(1), 47–63.

Titeca, K. (2019). Illegal Ivory Trade as Transnational Organized Crime? An Empirical Study into Ivory Traders in Uganda. *The British Journal of Criminology*, 59(1), 24–44.

Titeca, K. & T. de Herdt (2010). Regulation, Cross-Border Trade and Practical Norms in West Nile, North-Western Uganda. *Africa*, 80(4), 573–594.

Tull, D. (2003). A Reconfiguration of Political Order? The State of the State in North Kivu. *African Affairs*, 102, 429–446.

Turner, T. (2007). *The Congo Wars. Conflict, Myth and Reality*, London; New York: Zed Books.

UNCTAD (2010). Rwanda's Development Driven Trade Policy Framework, New York and Geneva: UNCTAD and the Ministry of Trade and Industry of Rwanda.

United Nations (2012). Report of the UN Group of Experts on the Democratic Republic of the Congo. UN SC.

United Nations Office on Drugs and Crime (2011). UNODC Director, Guinea Bissau's Leaders Address Concerns about Drug Trafficking in West Africa, www.unodc.org/lpo-brazil/en/frontpage/201/10/2 8-unodc-executive-director-guinea-bissau's-leaders-address-concerns-about-drug-trafficking-in-west-africa.

Van den Boogaard, V., W. Prichard, & S. Jibao (2021). Norms, Networks, Power and Control: Understanding Informal Payments and Brokerage in Cross-border Trade in Sierra Leone. *Journal of Borderlands Studies*, 36(1), 77–97.

Vlassenroot, K., S. Perrot & J. Cuvelier (2012). Doing Business Out of War. An Analysis of the Updf's Presence in the Democratic Republic of Congo. *Journal of Eastern African Studies*, 6(1), 2–21.

Vlassenroot, K. & T. Raeymaekers (2008). Governance without Government in African Crises. *Afrika Focus*, 21(2).

Wallis, W. (2012). Nigeria Losing $1bn a Month to Oil Theft, *Financial Times* 26 June.

Walraet, A. (2008). Governance, Violence and the Struggle for Economic Regulation in Southern Sudan: The Case of Budi County (Eastern Equatoria). *Afrika Focus*, 21(2), 53–70.

World Bank (1981). *Accelerated Development in Sub-Saharan Africa: An Agenda for Action*, Washington, DC: World Bank.

World Bank (1989). *Sub-Saharan Africa: From Crisis to Sustainable Growth*, Washington, DC: World Bank.

World Bank (n.d.). Senegal: Country Brief. http://web.worldbank.org/WBSITE/EXTERNAL/COUNTRIES/AFRICAEXT/SENEGALEXTN/0,,menuPK:296312~pagePK:141132~piPK:141107~theSitePK:296303,00.html (accessed 28 May 2012).

4

LORRIES AND LEDGERS

Describing and mapping smuggling in the field

Nikki Philline C. de la Rosa and Francisco J. Lara Jr.

Introduction

The inherent complexity in the nature and characteristics of smuggling makes it notoriously difficult to study. Early efforts to shine the light on the underbelly of cross border trade with its hidden activities, shadow networks, and violent entrepreneurs were fraught with many difficulties and challenges. People who knew or were involved in smuggling were unwilling to divulge its operations because they benefitted from the continuance of this illicit trade and they knew the threats that lay behind exposing the shadow authorities and criminal networks behind the enterprise.

Traders are understudied because of their tendency to lie, evade, or not talk at all (Harris 1992, p. 138; Mines 1972, p. 47; Neale et al. 1965, p. 33). Consequently, research on trade, whether legal or illegal, is often descriptive in nature, limited in scope, and offers few explanations beyond notions of illicitness and embeddedness and the role of kinship ties and customs in shaping economic activity in local communities.

Meanwhile, the methods that are used to investigate smuggling are activity shaped by people's perceptions of the "dual" nature of shadow economies such as smuggling that exist and operate on the "margins of the law" (Lara and de la Rosa 2016 p. 50, 253; MacGaffey and Bazenguissa-Ganga 2000, p. 9). On the one hand, smuggling often conjured images of illegality, coercion, and danger when it involved the illegal transport and entry of deadly substances and materials such as drugs, guns, and explosives. A menu of illicit goods could turn the data gathering process into a difficult, covert, and sometimes dangerous experience.

On the other hand, smuggling was foreshadowed by a vibrant cross-border trade in food items, prestige goods, and other benign consumer products long before states were formed in these areas. The reappearance of these goods as smuggled items seemed to many as merely a continuation of the previous trading arrangements that were seen as sustainable livelihoods and a form of coping or survival economy for poor communities. They were thus treated differently and often leniently by state agents.

Indeed, in many places, these enterprises were a boon to disadvantaged groups such as small women traders or indigenous peoples who had marginal capital and often transported food products across borders. The distinctive perception that such unregulated trade was

DOI: 10.4324/9781003043645-4

"not illicit or illegal" continues to have traction especially in places where entitlements and livelihoods have collapsed from civil wars, complex emergencies, and pandemics.[1]

Distinguishing between what is "illegal" and what is "criminal" is a constant dilemma for state agents at the borders.[2] For many border enforcers, this is determined by the type of goods that are traded, the relative size of the transaction, and the power and influence of the smuggler, which in turn influences perceptions about what type of smuggling should be prohibited and what could be allowed.[3]

This chapter sheds light on the qualitative methods that are used to penetrate both the "illegal" and the "criminal" aspects of the smuggling apparatus that thrives side by side with formal cross-border trade and has been the subject of many studies of informal economies around the world. We train the spotlight on at least three of these methods, including (1) the use of participant observation to scope trade routes and uncover smuggling networks, (2) the use of in-depth interviews and trialogues to generate primary data from insiders and other key informants and, (3) the use of new mapping techniques using Global Positioning System (GPS)/ Geographic Information System (GIS) technology.

Finally, there are old and new sources of secondary data including archival material and global trade databases that are examined in this chapter, including analytical approaches such as value-chain analysis and network mapping.

Brief background

Smuggling is an enterprise where criminal activities and survival strategies overlap — a peculiarity that shapes the research method used, leading to a combination of data gathering processes that include those conducted openly and aboveground, as well as those that require secrecy and stealth.

For example, tapping into the rich knowledge and experience of government officials, business groups, law enforcers, port laborers, and transport workers, to name a few, could be undertaken openly through structured or unstructured interviews, group discussions, survey studies, and field visits.

Meanwhile, secrecy and stealth may be necessary in cases where interview subjects are engaged directly in the smuggling of prohibited and deadly contraband such as narcotics and illegal drugs or illicit guns and munitions, or when researchers closely observe, examine, and monitor smuggling activities and behavior, including the accompanying corruption and violence that activity involves. In these instances, key informant interviews, mediated interviews, and participant observation are useful tools.

Qualitative studies have opened the door to the vibrant and robust existence of shadow economies and their economic logic and embeddedness, including the social networks surrounding them. In Africa, studies of illicit cross border trade used research methods such as participant observation and the mapping of entire transport and trade routes in countries such as Zaire (Democratic Republic of Congo or DRC), where people and goods travelled for thousands of miles aboard lorries and trucks (McGaffey 1991), or in Nigeria, where the rise of informal yet dynamic and ethnic-based enterprise clusters produced high-quality garments and shoes that were smuggled to other countries (Meagher 2010).

In Nigeria and Somalia, armed extremist groups such as Boko Haram and the Al Shabaab militias continued to engage in the national and transnational trafficking of weapons (Musa 2013; Petrich 2018; Onuoha 2013). Interviews and observations of how nomadic pastoralists and herders used specially crafted skin or thatched bags attached to camels, donkeys, and cows to conceal guns and move these across borders enabled researchers to shed light on the smuggling of small arms and light weapons (SALW) in the region. Boko Haram members are said to stuff their weapons in goods that are transported via heavy trucks, trailers, and lorries, passing security and border officials with very little or no scrutiny at all. Continued access to smuggled weapons explains why the conflict in Nigeria continues to thrive despite a series of military attacks against Boko Haram. The continued smuggling of weapons in Nigeria reveals why the security of the border is synonymous with the security of the state.

Meanwhile, studies of weapons smuggling undertaken by the El Shabaab extremist group in Somalia was made possible when they functioned as a shadow state handing out receipts for illicit payments and illegal taxers collected from gun traffickers. Access to those "receipts" would be a windfall for any researcher. "Unlike the state, al-Shabaab does not double-tax people. The group also continues to function as a shadow government in areas that it no longer physically controls, replacing the state as the provider services, including Islamic courts, humanitarian aid and healthcare" (Petrich 2018).

In Southeast Asia, the practice of documenting illicit payments made in various coastal trading outposts in the Southern Philippines, Malaysia, and Indonesia across the Sulu and Celebes Seas followed similar processes common to Africa (Quitoriano 2019; Villanueva 2016). Granular studies about the smuggling of drugs, gems, motorcycle vehicles and other transport vehicles, including endangered animals saw the use of cross-border transactions and in-depth interviews with border guards to ascertain the existence of a parallel "globalization from below" (Van Schendel and Abraham, 2005).

Studies about the smuggling of weapons and their licit and illicit links in domestic gun markets are crucial. Cukier and Schropshire (2000, pp. 105-26) state how on the global level, "information about the legal firearm trade is limited," but the "information on illicit trafficking is even more incomplete." They used primary data gathered from field observations including CCTV footage, and secondary data from customs reports, purchase orders, and invoices documenting import and export transactions. They found out from field reports that the cross-over of firearms from the international to the local level matched the same period when the cross-over from the legal-formal to the illegal occurred. Their study exposed how army stocks of weapons and munitions are plundered, straw purchases and resales of weapons are made, export documents are falsified, and the reactivation of decommissioned weapons is undertaken.

Lorry riders and maritime voyagers

Robust observations of smuggling behavior, practices, and networks were generated through a data-gathering and documentation process that gathered granular details from long and painstaking fieldwork on land and seagoing vehicles.

Three investigative methods have been used to capture their dynamics. The first entails researchers joining lorries and truck convoys as *participant observers* to monitor and determine the scale of formal and informal payments in stations and checkpoints along the way (MacGaffey 1991; Scheele 2012). The second entails *locating yourself at a particular boundary crossing* or major port to observe, monitor, and sketch the flow of goods and examine the various actors involved in the smuggling process (Quitoriano 2019). The third entails examining the content and volume of goods transported by informal freight vehicles to be stored in stockpiles, warehouses, ice plants and cold storage facilities before comparing these with customs duties and port authority collections (Villanueva 2016).

Using informal interviews and participant observation techniques saw many researchers boarding lorries and trucks or joining seagoing vessels that traversed maritime borders to observe the commodities, transactions, and actors engaged in illicit trade.[4]

Some researchers went beyond mere observation and directly engaged in the procurement and transport of tradeable food and clothing products through borders without paying duties so they could intimately study the smuggling process.[5] Lower-middle class women, oftentimes teachers or local government employees, were also involved in the smuggling of consumer goods such as rice, cooking oil, and petroleum across the Sulu and West Philippine Sea and shouldered the increased overheads from bribing customs and port authority agents.

The use of ledgers to record minute as well as major transactions is important in documenting both qualitative and quantitative data that can be parsed to determine temporal trends in the prices of goods and the different mark-ups that bloat the price of smuggled items as they move towards their destination. The women traders are eager to record their transactions in such ledgers or notebooks that are rich sources of data. Their notes are also important in drawing up a cost–benefit analysis of transactions to indicate where most of the profit goes after overhead costs, including illegal payoffs are accounted for.

Observations on the road and on the sea also became a familiar method for evaluating the activities of indigenous economic networks operating behind smuggling activities. In fact, trucking and lorry-rider studies were so effective that even The World Bank (2006) engaged in the monitoring of tollgates in Aceh, Indonesia, and in other landlocked areas of Central and Western Africa to determine the amount of illicit taxes or illegal toll fees paid by entrepreneurs and traders across trade routes. Researchers were able to calculate and document the total amount of bribes collected in various checkpoints and the added overhead costs that were shouldered by traders.

A study on the economics of extortion in Aceh (Olken and Barron 2009). used the same methodology of participant observation by local Acehnese research surveyors and enumerators accompanying Indonesian truck drivers on 304 trips to and from Aceh. The research observed over 6,000 illegal payments to police, soldiers, and weigh station attendants. Results revealed that bribe rates were sensitive to critical changes in the external context, such as the political agreement between Indonesia and Aceh and the withdrawal of over 30,000 police and military troops from Aceh province. Bribery rates also fluctuated due to factors such as the distance of toll gates and checkpoints to point of origin, the type of trucks used, and the different geographical borders along their route.

Border observation methods in studying trader activities in informal cross border trade in Africa quantified trade flows at border crossings and the rents needed for smooth entry and exit of goods and people (Morrisey et al. 2015). Granular data from direct observation and inferences from secondary data were crucial sources of information for understanding the intricacies of illicit trade.

Other studies were based upon observations on a seagoing vessel traversing the Sulu Sea carrying smuggled rice and other commodities that enabled researchers to draw detailed flowcharts of illicit transactions (Quitoriano 2019; Villanueva 2016). In the port of Tawi-Tawi, data gatherers stationed themselves near warehouses to count the number of *pokol-pokol* trucks carrying sacks of rice from ships at anchor towards their destination warehouses and later compared the volume of rice traded with the public records of imported rice and their corresponding duties.

The researchers were able to identify the most sought-after goods that were transported across the sea from Malaysia and Indonesia that were allowed entry without duties, the marginal cost of transporting goods at each stage of the journey, and the different set of actors (state and non-state) that facilitated the entry of these goods and their distribution.

Travelling by boat across maritime borders allowed researchers to observe and interview traders to distinguish the different types of vessels, the types of goods being transported, and the

Lorries and ledgers

routes used – between pernicious and deadly and the coping trade of foodstuffs, beauty products, and fighting cocks. Group discussions with the women traders produced graphic value chain maps and detailed cost–benefit analysis.

Key-informant interviews and trialogues

Primary data generation from key actors who know about or are directly involved in smuggling can be generated through in-depth interviews, life histories, and "mediated conversations" or "trialogues." Interviews can be layered according to the nature of the goods and the type of trader-actor and state agent involved. There are at least three layers of respondents that can be interviewed to examine the links between the formal-legal, illegal, and the criminal.

The first layer includes those respondents embedded in the formal trade apparatus and are knowledgeable about all the legal institutions and processes that need to be examined to acquire an understanding of how the system is supposed to operate. Potential respondents include officers of government agencies such as treasury and customs officials and port authority personnel. Another vital source of information are the banks and other financial intermediaries that provide credit and capital. Finally, they include revenue and licensing offices of local government units who know the strengths as well as the loopholes in the system that allows smuggling to thrive.

The second layer refers to the illegal traders who smuggle food commodities, fuel, and other non-lethal but strictly regulated commodities. The big buyers that stockpile supplies for the wholesale and retail markets belong in this category, together with the thousands of small entrepreneurs, mostly women, who are engaged in a trading business that is embedded in kinship ties and various social networks. They are the traders who traffic prohibited goods and evade all duties and taxes on their entry, conspiring with the drivers and captains of vehicles and vessels and their crew. It is that side of cross-border trade that "depends heavily on personal relations because of the importance of trust for activities that are often outside the law and which therefore lack its sanctions" (MacGaffey and Bazenguissa-Ganga 2000, p. 7)

Finally, there is the third layer of respondents who are often covert, armed, and very capable of using deadly force to penetrate regions and countries to trade their illegal contraband. They possess considerable resources and assets, including a fleet of vehicles, ships, and aircraft and strategically located warehouses to transport and stock their contraband. Some of them are regionally connected such as the Triads and the South American cartels and they buy protection from local police and security forces. They trade various weapons, drugs, protected wildlife, and are sometimes engaged in human trafficking as well. Some are involved in trading nuclear material and chemical agents sanctioned under international laws.

Key informants and unstructured in-depth interviews

In-depth interviews are often used throughout these layers because the method offers a "far wider and more open-ended" elaboration of the topic (Nichols 1991, p. 13). In contrast to the structured interview that is often used in survey studies, in-depth interviews are unstructured, and are especially useful for lengthy discussions about the nature of a particular business, their open and hidden aspects, and the participation of numerous actors in transactions.

The interviewer begins by first sketching the outline of a particular trading transaction from the procurement of the commodity, its transport and distribution, the gauntlet of rent seekers from source to buyer, and the prices at the end of the transaction. The sketch is then used to arrive at a list of issues and questions that serves as a guide for the interviewer's examination, instead of a fixed set of questions. Based on the in-depth interviews conducted with various actors in an entire smuggling chain, the researcher will be able to determine the total cost of corrupting the various state and non-state actors or shadow authorities along the way.

Family histories

In-depth unstructured interviews can also be utilized to produce a family history of actors engaged in the business of illicit trade. Individual and family life histories are critical in the study of illegal economies embedded in kinship ties and identity groups. This is particularly important and useful in places such as DRC, where "traders rely on personal ties based on the bonds of kinship, ethnicity, friendship, religion, and nationality" (MacGaffey and Bazenguissa-Ganga 2000, p. 110). In their remarkable study of transnational traders, MacGaffey and Bazenguissa-Ganga (2000, pp. 111–116) demonstrate how illicit trade and smuggling was undertaken using family histories and kinship ties from the DRC to Paris, France. Using case histories of family businesses, they described and explained three histories of people importing African foodstuffs to Paris through the help of family members living in Africa.

The use of life histories has also been used to determine the effects on youth socialization of the illicit trade in weapons. Lara (2014, pp. 88–89) describes the life history of a young Muslim and how the smuggling of AK-47 rifles to support the Moro insurgency revealed the class cleavages in Muslim society and made him aware of the rival identities that rewarded some insurgents with the best rifles, while the others had to contend with old M14 and M16 rifles.

Mediated interviews or trialogues

Finally, mediated interviews or trialogues are "difficult" conversations that can only be conducted with the participation of a third party who is known and trusted by the respondent.[6] Trialogues are utilized when confidential in-depth interviews of key resource persons, including persons formerly or still involved in smuggling, are sought for the insights that they can provide. The method has been used in investigating and studying dangerous smuggling enterprises such as the illicit weapons and drugs trade, human trafficking and smuggling, or kidnap-for-ransom activities Gutierrez 2014; Quitoriano 2016).

The mediated interview fills the trust gap between the researcher, who is new, to the respondent, who is involved in what is considered a criminal activity that could be penalized with a steep fine or imprisonment. For example, in the case of illegal guns, the risk of punishment is high. Even those legally involved in gun trading and smuggling were reluctant to divulge their identities. The conversations were repetitive, requiring two or more meetings with a subject over a fortnight to get in-depth details and enable the researcher to debrief with the third-party interviewer and adjust guide questions as the topic progressed and new insights were uncovered.

Access of the researcher to trusted interlocutors to mediate conversations with actors in the trade was key. Trust between the researcher and the interlocutor and trust between the respondents and the interlocutor determined the level of information and the quality of analysis that was generated.

The mediated conversations were primarily organized around the time, location, topic, and pace determined by the respondents. The choice of respondents was determined by mediators who possessed personal, professional, and functional links to the subjects. The mediators were in turn chosen based on the level of trust they had established with the researcher.

In one study of gun smuggling, the mediator was himself a part-time trader in guns, particularly the low-cost guns preferred by low-income buyers such as taxi drivers. Because of the sensitivity of the theme and the nature of the interviews done, a blind list of all respondents whose names and interview dates were withheld for security purposes, and later submitted by the researcher to the editors and the academic consultant of the research for proper verification (Quitoriano 2016).

In another study, interviews with law enforcers and retired military officers revealed the smuggling of hardware, electronics, dry goods, and pirated merchandise, as well as the trade in black-market petrol, stolen four-wheel-drive vehicles, ivory, horns of rhinoceros, gold, arms, and drugs. A discharged former military man stated that "Over time, I understood that, even if the border zones are poor, one nonetheless makes big money there" (Roitman 2005, p. 155).

Mapping and geo-tagging techniques

Capturing the complex market information essential to exposing smuggling requires an interoperable approach to monitor, track, and document the trafficking of goods across land and sea. The use of mapping and GIS technologies is one such interoperable system that can monitor and geotag smuggling-related sightings and incident reports, enabling the identification of smuggling routes, the tracking of vehicles and vessels carrying illicit goods, and the potential ports of entry and exit of prohibited commodities.

In the much-traversed Sulu and the South China Sea where all seagoing vessels *en route* to China from the Indian Ocean pass, naval and coast guard authorities have used the mapping and geotagging of incidents to produce spatial maps that graphically show where smuggling activities are happening.[7]

The process entails the gathering of secondary data from customs and port authority officials of smuggling incident reports on land and sea and geotagging the location of those incidents on a land and sea map.[8] Once they are placed on a map they can demonstrate where smuggling incidents are happening and provide leads to where these incidents will re-emerge. They can geographically reference data that could then be overlaid to other datasets. They are also a useful fusion of both evidence gathering and presentation processes of data and visualization.

Secondary data in archives and global databases

Studying smuggling entails the gathering of robust secondary data that can provide information about incidents, actors, and costs. Researchers can look back in time and assess historical data about the bustling entrepots where cross-border trade occurred over time and look at archival material that can be a rich source of ethnographic material, narratives, and stories about the porous borders where people traded freely from pre-history to the contemporary period.

Other researchers have used financial reports from customs and port authorities in mainland, air, and coastal ports where smuggling incidents abound. Cases of smuggling, especially those that lead to violent conflict, can also be found in police and military incident reports, and in newspaper and other media reports. These reports include data on the date when the smuggling incident occurred, when and how it was disrupted, the actors involved, the type and volume of commodities seized and their estimated market prices.

Archival documents

Using personal accounts in historical source documents is important in the depiction of the actors themselves of the realities observed temporally and contextually. These source documents include original letters and reports, diaries of colonial residents, appeals for support, reward, and promotion, long-winded recommendations, and decrees inspired by local obstruction of government goals (Scott 1976).

They also include historical records of smuggling activity that were accompanied by violent clashes between smugglers and border guards as the demand for consumption goods grew in the eighteenth and nineteenth century. For example, Kwass (2014, p. 5) pointed to the evolution of the consumer revolution in France and its links to the global context to explain, through the use of after-death inventories and probate records "that list, in exquisite detail all the movable goods an individual possessed at the moment of his or her death," revealing how "probate inventories placed French consumption on the map."

Kwass looked at these historical records as important sources of evidence about the causal impact of consumption on the trade of goods, but he also admonished researchers about the inadequacy of the data because "inventories reveal little about where goods came from, who produced them, and what path they took before reaching consumers." The missing data may hide smuggling behavior, requiring additional research to understand the "boisterous and often violent world of production and exchange that brought goods to market in the first place."

Meanwhile, Andreas's (2013, pp. 9–15) classic study of American smuggling underscored the significance of smuggling activities in America as both a barrier but also an enabler of rapid development. He argued that despite the paltry quantitative data available, historical accounts provided other sources of data that were just as important. Historians trained the spotlight on the "uneven balance in cargo between incoming and outgoing ships, private correspondence, and travel accounts." Their studies showed the "magnitude of the illicit trade in molasses is revealed by the discrepancy between official imports and the amount of molasses actually needed to keep colonial distilleries running." These findings would help usher the wider use of global trade data.

In pre-colonial, colonial, and post-colonial Mindanao in the Southern Philippines, genealogical documents such as the *tarsilas* of Muslim families and clans, including maps, descriptions of scientific findings and colonial governance structures, maritime journals, and historical accounts of incidents and patterns of smuggling and border formation are plentiful and have been used in scholarly work.[9] These historical journals, dating at least a century-old, uncover the authentic early descriptions, terminologies, and references to routes and places, motivations, and personalities involved in cross-border trade (Majul 1977; Scott 1978, p. 174; Tagliacozzo 2005).

New insights can also be culled from these old and original documents – or pieces of "incidental intelligence," – referring to data that was unintentionally gathered, or mentioned in passing, that contain more historical relevance than what the authors wanted to say (Scott 1978: 182). Correspondingly, such accounts from historical source documents, written or visualized in maps, illuminated border formation and the evolution of what is licit and illicit – such definitions are a reproduction of colonial power – and how illicit trade was also a form of resistance by the colonized (Schendel and Abraham 2005; Tagliacozzo 2005).

Global database

Another robust source of secondary data are the descriptive statistics made available by recently established global databases containing data that graphically reveals the hidden income streams and profits from smuggling activities.

Lorries and ledgers

In the past two decades, quantitative data has been used as a powerful component of qualitative research. The establishment of the United Nations Commission on Trade (UN Comtrade) has been a helpful secondary source of data that can give leads on the importance and magnitude of certain commodities that are traded and their effects on revenue generation, or the lack of it, in countries where smuggling is rampant. It widened the possibilities for comparative analysis of country performance in monitoring cross-border trade.

The UN Comtrade institutionalized the harvesting of official and hence formal country trade data that can be used for comparative assessments of trade output and to determine trends in the expansion or contraction of commodity trade in the world.[10] It speeded up the work of other multilateral financial, developmental, and security agencies involved in determining smuggling activity, corruption in customs taxes and other revenues, money laundering activities, including drug trafficking.

In the case of gun smuggling in the Philippines, UN Comtrade data was crucial in exposing how (1) weapons were being smuggled into the Philippines through the ports of Manila rather than from the porous borders of the Sulu Sea and (2) that there was a yawning gap between the numbers and prices of weapons exported to the Philippines versus the official reports of importation at the border (Quitoriano 2016). Meanwhile, the use of UN Comtrade data in Myanmar exposed smuggling in the gems market (precious and semi-precious stones, except diamonds) when contrasted with reports of exports and imports of gems to China, Thailand, and other importing countries.

Analytical approaches

Value chain and network analysis are useful analytical approaches for assessing the data on illicit cross border trade. Value chain analysis involves a process of meticulous investigation and analysis of the entire structure of production, trade, and distribution and assessing the importance or value (monetary or otherwise) of each stage in the process. Illicit trade can be better understood if each stage of the process is subjected to a cost-benefit analysis, including the flow of contraband among a different set of actors.

In gathering the evidence to test how costs and profits are distributed in illicit cross-border trade, many studies of smuggling across the Philippines, Malaysia, and Indonesia featured cost-benefit studies to establish the amount of income/profit generated from illicit trade among value chain actors (i.e., small traders, brokers, *kumpit* boat operators, state regulatory agencies, port operators/owners, laborers and haulers) using mainly primary data from personal accounts and life stories of small traders and key informant interviews with customs and trade officials, local government officials, port personnel and laborers, drivers/haulers, warehouse owners, and wholesalers and retailers[11] (Figure 4.1).

The studies discovered the huge rents that accrued to state agents, and the beneficial income streams that flowed to various stakeholders including vessel owners and laborers, women traders, and youth workers hired to prepare the vessels. Profits range from 100% to 150% of investments made prior to each maritime "shopping trip" and back across the Sulu and Celebes Seas (Villanueva 2016). The value-chain analysis also revealed the various social networks based on true and fictive kinship ties built on trust established over many years of dealing with each other across "free trade areas" such as the Sulu Sea.

Other studies of smuggling presented modes of organization built along clan, ethnic, or tribal linkages that were central to successful involvement in illicit cross-border trade. Studies by Gallien (2019), Chouvy (2013), Olken and Baron (2009), and Schendel and Abraham (2005) examined the distinct and efficient modes of organization that fitted the nature of the activity

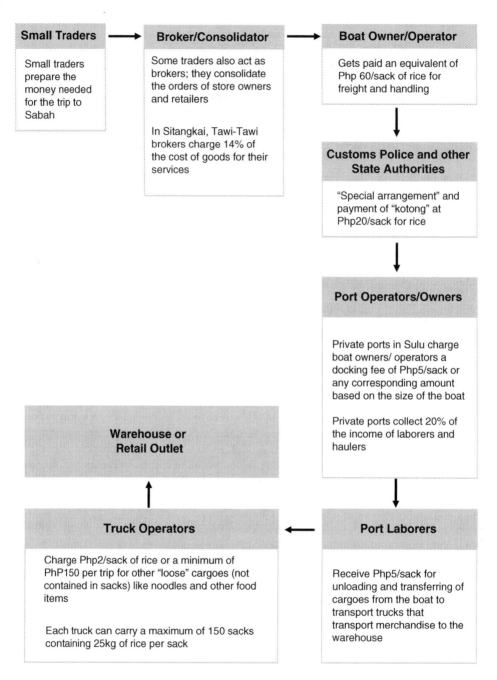

Figure 4.1 Economic value chain of cross-border trade in Sulu and Tawi-Tawi (Villanueva 2016).

being undertaken. For example, traders engaged in the transport of benign products had their own social network and distinguished themselves from the 'truly unlawful' and 'highly illegal' elements of the cross-border trade engaged in kidnap for ransom, drug trafficking, human trafficking, and illicit weapons.

Lorries and ledgers

Other studies of network economies were also the focus of the study of livestock marketing in Northern Kenya. Mahmoud (2008) used case history and participant observations of livestock markets and travelled in livestock trucks on a 48-hour journey along the Moyale-Nairobi road to uncover and understand trust relationships embedded in horizontal social networks as an effective risk-minimizing strategy for traders in highly economic and politically volatile contexts.

Limitations in qualitative studies of smuggling

Despite the strength of the qualitative methods mentioned above, there are several challenges and limitations for each of these methods and processes that need to be understood to enable researchers to avoid mistakes, mitigate weaknesses, avoid pitfalls, and to be honest in declaring the strengths and limitations, the nuances and caveats of each study. Four of the more important limitations are discussed here.

One, *there is always a challenge in making claims about the nature of the general population engaged in cross-border trade based on the limited observations that can be generated in qualitative studies.* The frequent use of unstructured, in-depth interviews and participant observation leads to smaller observations that can be criticized for providing evidence that is seen as wanting, when it comes to the creation of anti-smuggling policies and actions.

In addition, the use of mapping techniques cannot produce real-time information, as access to satellite technology is expensive and often beyond the reach of the researcher, except if the study is funded by the government.

However, these may all be true, but big-N studies are not really a requisite in understanding smuggling and in countering or prevent it. Qualitative data, despite its limitations, has been used to identify loopholes and leakages in tax collection and has enhanced revenue generation. A good case in point is cigarette smuggling in Europe and the networks around the world that feed the illicit enterprise. Joossens and Raw (1998, pp. 66–69) showed how a simple comparison of exports and imports plus the monitoring of smuggling routes and some arrests helped bring about the tighter regulation of cigarette trade, including an international transport convention, and a total ban on transit trade – sale by the manufacturers to dealers, who sell on to smugglers.

Indeed, unstructured interviews, mediated dialogues, and participant observation are methods that can enable an explanation of the logic behind smuggling, the processes and outcomes that occur, the costs and benefits, and most importantly, the actors and networks involved – with more certainty and reliability than quantitative studies can deliver. Besides, looking at the conceptual is as important as assessing the empirical and understanding the logic of the illegal, as opposed to the criminal, represents a new way of conceptualizing smuggling. Moreover, a solid analysis from small observations is infinitely better than an erroneous interpretation of large datasets.

Nevertheless, to mitigate concerns about the validity of the evidence, quantitative studies such as surveys can be undertaken, including attitudinal and perception studies with the use of Likert scales. Mapping that uses Google Earth and ARC-GIS software can reproduce maps more easily and can be made more widely available by governments.

Two, *knowing what information is needed and what indicators are available is burdened by the few secondary quantitative studies that can provide leads for deeper qualitative analysis.* Indeed, studies of smuggling fall into the set of subject matters that "lies beyond the margins of calculation" (Duffield 2001, p. 143) and is seen as impenetrable to social scientific investigation because robust data is difficult to get, and the true picture is not recorded in national accounts.

Some tactics that have been used include "doorstepping," where the researcher goes directly to the target respondent in the hope of getting an extensive interview, which of course is easier said than done.[12] Another method is the conduct of repeated interviews starting with pre-pilot and pilot interviewing. In contrast to doorstepping, the piloting process promotes a no-rush approach, taking time, and doing a baseline interview (Olsen 1992, p. 67).

Another way is to start with media reports or journalistic studies, which may in turn lead to questionnaires and interview guides. However, journalistic methods must be used with caution as they may entice respondents to shut up, instead of warming up to the interviewer. What really helps in these circumstances is to get the respondent to lead you into the discussion and to enumerate the leads themselves. An inductive approach can go a long way in identifying the key issues that could be discussed in-depth.

Three, *mediated dialogues rely on finding traders to talk to, and in learning to manage conversations and meetings with them* (Harris 1992, pp. 139–147). The problem arises from the typically low sample of traders that are willing to talk and are actually chosen in a sample to talk. Another problem is managing conversations and meetings in private and getting the respondents to behave in a way that enables the researcher to get the information needed.

Finding traders who are genuinely knowledgeable about the hidden world of smuggling and can provide valuable knowledge of all three layers of formal, illegal, and criminal trade is difficult. Catching one is often treated as a singular chance to interrogate a key informant and to employ mediated dialogues to keep them engaged and comfortable.

However, oftentimes the respondent refuses to be recorded or will only allow the use of some and not all the information gathered. There are additional challenges in recording the process while conducting the interview as well, especially in the absence of technical support. The bigger challenge also lies in recalling or remembering all the valuable and necessary details that emerge.

Additionally, managing meetings with traders is difficult because they have acquired a style and tendency to test the interviewer's knowledge of trade, so tricking the interviewer is common and unavoidable. It is the result of years of partaking in subterfuge and the consequent "wisdom of the streets."[13]

One way of mitigating this difficulty is to conduct iterative interviews with subjects to enable the researcher to return to the salient topics discussed, not only to check the validity of the recorded conversation, but also to instigate the respondent to add more detail, or to get wider consent for the type of information that can be shared. Mediated dialogues can also be planned in such a way that the third person in the room takes on some of the tasks of recording the discussions.

Four, *there are clear ethical issues about field research, especially the use of participant observation methods or mediated dialogues that may entail breaking the law, which is clearly the case when one participates directly in smuggling activities (even if the contraband is not criminal in nature), or meets with a crime lord on the run from authorities.* Even in cases where the researcher is only indirectly involved as an observer, there is still a thin line here between observing something illegal taking place and tolerating it by not reporting it to the authorities.

Another ethical danger is to be an "advocate" on behalf of those who engage in the illegal yet socially embedded feature of smuggling activity, which redounds to tolerating illegality or illicitness because "they are not of a criminal nature." Among others, James Scott's (1985, 1976) studies have suggested that these activities can be viewed as "weapons of the weak" or part of an alluring "moral economy" where social capital abounds. A related danger here is "brokerage," where a non-partisan and non-controversial researcher provides information about a covert world, for example, and justifies releasing sensitive and confidential information because you believe that your role is to interpret that world (Wilson 1992, pp. 179–184).

All of these are well and good, but they do not lessen the fact that smuggling does exacerbate the nature of fragile and weak states and is certainly a drag on the state-building project. Also, it is important to recognize that engaging in brokerage can be misinterpreted and misused. It is always important to recognize that your knowledge and judgement as a researcher is limited, and it is better simply to let the subjects speak, instead of speaking on their behalf.

Indeed, the most effective response to the ethical dilemma is to ensure that direct participation in illegal activity is avoided and observation and advocacy are only directed towards raising the voice that is unheard and the profiles that are not seen. In short, participant observation can be ethical if it goes beyond proclaiming good and evil, but instead "enables the reader to hear the voices and appreciate the actions of as many of the different people involved as possible." Other practical steps can also be undertaken, such as getting consent from the respondents before each interview, revealing the interests and organizations behind the study being conducted, and guaranteeing confidentiality and anonymity to all respondents.

Conclusion

Smuggling and other forms of illicit trade are difficult to trace and deter, not because they are hidden from view, but because few have undertaken qualitative studies that reveal the logic and inner workings of smuggling activities beyond the analysis that comes from quantitative data that is at best inadequate, and at worse, misleading. There are few studies that link trade to market changes, political opportunities, or the social milieu that surrounds trade, whether illicit or not (Chouvy 2013). This inadequacy leads to two outcomes: *one*, data is concealed; *two*, trade flows become invisible.

Recent years have seen greater strides in exposing smuggling activity through the use of qualitative research. At the same time, states, development workers, academics, and community organizers are generating fresh data that offer the numbers and the stories that deepen our understanding of smuggling activities. These methods have been tested repeatedly by researchers around the world to strengthen their academic and policy research and the creation of countervailing strategies and organizational responses against smuggling.

The use of in-depth interviews and participant observation in the analysis of smuggling, plus wider access to archival or historical accounts remain the mainstay in studies of illicit cross border trade. Some enhancement is happening through new mapping and geo-tagging techniques provide clearer visual evidence of smuggling. New global databases such as the UN Comtrade provide secondary data that can be compared and contrasted to help expose the illicit flow of goods and monies generated from smuggling.

There are new discoveries and counter-intuitive findings of how smuggling operates, how much of it is hidden, and how much of it is part of an effective governance toolbox for managing supply and demand of vital or deadly commodities, preventing crisis and unrest, or strengthening legitimacy and authority.

Indeed, it is important to recognize at the outset that smuggling is not completely outside the gaze of the state, as evidenced by different studies showing how illicit activities are undertaken in both a clandestine or open manner by actors who might also be agents of the state (Schendel and Abraham 2005; Villanueva 2016). Empirical data can also be distinguished as to whether smuggling economies are pernicious and criminal or are mainly coping and survival in nature, hence illuminating the interplay between the illicit and clandestine, and the "embedded and instituted" nature of these economies.

These distinctions are important and sensitivity to the dualistic nature of smuggling is crucial in insulating the scholar or researcher from being turned into an accomplice in the state's business of curtailing all forms of economic informality (Lara and Schoofs 2016; Lara and de la Rosa, 2016).

This chapter has reinforced the importance of qualitative methods for examining smuggling activity around the world. Examining smuggling remains difficult and challenging, and still requires a lot of flexibility and adaptation, combined with a fair measure of luck and the use of investigative skills to generate data. Smuggling will continue to involve different degrees of circumvention, secrecy, and rule breaking, and a stronger effort must be made to open this sector to research and investigative studies.

Notes

1 Villanueva (2016, p. 272) notes how traders and law enforcers categorize contraband goods smuggled into the porous borders of the Sulu Sea as either "allowable" or "highly illegal." Ford and Lyons (2012) note the same perceptions about smuggling in their study of Riau Islanders who engage in trade between Indonesia and Singapore. For the Islanders, smuggling is viewed as a legitimate response to local needs and the perceived failures of the national government and legal system—a fact that points to the need to explore local ecologies of licitness (and illegality) not just in terms of community perceptions but also in terms of different levels of the state.

   Mayer (2018) makes the same argument in the case of West Africa. She points out that media and policy reports often portray human smuggling or irregular migration as a greedy and unscrupulous enterprise, despite the fact that "many migrants from countries such as Senegal treat their handlers as friends rather than criminals and do not see themselves as "smuggled," but rather as people "making calculated choices to migrate based on a host of social factors."

2 Interview with a Philippine Port Authority officer. Zamboanga City. Name and date withheld.

3 Losby et al. (2002) underscored the difference between what is illegal and what is criminal. The informal economy includes both illegal and legal aspects that are often defined by the nature of the enterprise or the goods and services concerned. Many of these enterprises are "not intrinsically unlawful" but violate some rule or law, such as the failure to pay taxes or license fees for microenterprises. They are illegal but not necessarily criminal.

4 Harris (1992, p. 142) argues that "in the field study of trade, the researcher is necessarily always an outsider ... as the 'participant observation' of trade is never undertaken."

5 Interview with a professor from the Mindanao State University in Tawi-Tawi, Mindanao who has made countless trips from Tawi-Tawi to Sabah and Sandakan to engage in the so-called barter trade. Name and date withheld.

6 These are difficult processes because they require strict confidentiality and even stealth especially if the key informant is on the run. It is normally used in cases where the respondent is directly involved in smuggling activity that is criminal in nature, as in the smuggling of narcotics and guns. Journalists are skilled in conducting trialogues.

7 Active Philippine Coast Guard Officer interviewed about the smuggling of weapons and the entry routes used by ISIS militants in the Sulu Sea towards Sulu and Zamboanga. The same official noted how they mapped the location of floating cocaine bags picked up by fishermen from the sea to interdict cartel operations in the surrounding waters of Mindanao. Name and date withheld.

8 International Alert Philippines (2015) Bangsamoro Conflict Monitoring System (BCMS) report included smuggling incidents recorded in police conflict data with latitude and longitude information that enabled the identification of smuggling-related conflict incidents in the high seas.

9 The *tarsila, zarzila* or *tarzila* is a genealogical map that traces the ancestry of Muslim clans and is often annotated by economic and political signifiers.

10 United Nations, Department of Economic and Social Affairs, Statistics Division. (2020). Download trade data. UN Comtrade. Available at https://Comtrade.un.org/data/.

11 *Kumpit* are sea-faring vessels that regularly traverse the maritime borders and can carry as much as 200 tons of cargo. *Pokol-pokol* refers to the flatbed lorries that are usually powered by a Toyota 4K engine and used to transport goods over land.

12 "Doorstepping consists simply of knocking on someone's door, talking your way inside and subsequently emerging triumphantly with the desire information" (Johnson-Thomas 2000, p. 13).

13 They tried to get me to pay for the costs of food and some liquor at the start of an interview, which I refused. However, they got me inspired when they started talking and revealed who among the government authorities had the real "vetting powers" in the illegal import of weapons. I succumbed to their request and gave them a round of beer Filipino researcher-writer on cross-border trade (name and date withheld).

References

Andreas, P. (2013). *Smuggler Nation: How Illicit Trade Made America*. New York: Oxford University Press.

Chouvy, P. (ed) (2013). *An Atlas of Trafficking in Southeast Asia: The Illegal Trade in Arms, Drugs, People, Counterfeit Goods and Natural Resources in Mainland Southeast Asia*. London: I.B. Tauris.

Cukier, W. & Shropshire, S. (2000). 'Domestic gun markets: The licit-illicit links' in Lumpe, L. (ed.). *Running Guns: The Global Black Market in Small Arms*. London: Zed Books.

Duffield, M. (2001). *Global Governance and the New Wars: The Merging of Development and Security*. London: Zed Books.

Ford, M. & Lyons, L. (2012). 'Smuggling cultures in the Indonesia-Singapore borderlands' in Kalir, B. and M. Sur (eds). *Transnational Flows and Permissive Polities: Ethnographies of Human Mobilities in Asia*, pp. 91–108. Amsterdam: Amsterdam University Press.

Gallien, M. (2019). 'Informal institutions and the regulation of smuggling in North Africa'. *Perspectives on Politics*, vol. 8, no. 2, pp. 492–508. Cambridge: Cambridge University Press.

Gutierrez, E. (2016). 'Bandits, Villains and Bosses: Kidnappers of Southern Philippines' in Lara, F. and S. Schoofs (eds). *Out of the Shadows: Violent Conflict and the Real Economy of Mindanao*. Quezon City: Bughaw.

Harris, B. (1992). 'Talking to traders about trade' in Devereux, S. and J. Hoddinott (eds). *Fieldwork in Developing Countries*. London: Harvester Wheatsheaf.

International Alert Philippines, (2016). *Violence in the Bangsamoro and Southern Mindanao, 2011-2015*. Quezon City, Philippines: International Alert Philippines.

Johnson-Thomas, B. (2000). 'Anatomy of a shady deal' in Lumpe, L. (ed.). Running Guns: The Global Black Market in Small ArmsLondon: Zed Books.

Joossens, L. & Raw M. (1998) 'Cigarette smuggling in Europe: Who really benefits?'. *Tobacco Control*, vol. 7, pp. 66–71.

Kwass, M. (2014). *Contraband: Louis Mandrin and the Making of a Global Underground*. Cambridge, MA and London: Harvard University Press.

Lara, F. (2012). 'The new face of Mindanao's strong men: The politico-economic foundations of legitimacy in Muslim Mindanao'. *Asian Studies: Journal of Critical Perspectives on Asia*, vol. 48, nos. 1& 2, pp. 55–68. Quezon City: Asian Center, University of the Philippines Diliman.

Lara, F. (2014). *Insurgents, Clans, and States: Political Legitimacy and Resurgent Conflict in Muslim Mindanao, Philippines*. Quezon City: Ateneo De Manila University Press.

Lara, F. & de la Rosa, N. (2016). 'Robustness in data and methods: Scoping the real economy of Mindanao' in Lara, F. & S. Schoofs (eds). *Out of the Shadows: Violent Conflict and the Real Economy of Mindanao*. Quezon City: Bughaw.

Lara, F. & Schoofs, S. (eds). (2016). *Out of the Shadows: Violent Conflict and the Real Economy of Mindanao*. Quezon City: Bughaw.

Losby, Jan, Else, J. et al. (2002). *Informal Economy Literature Review*. Washington: The Aspen Institute.

MacGaffey, J. (1991). *The Real Economy of Zaire: The Contribution of Smuggling and Other Unofficial Activities to National Wealth*. Philadelphia: University of Pennsylvania Press.

MacGaffey, J. & Bazenguissa-Ganga, R. (2000). *Congo-Paris: Transnational Traders on the Margins of Law*. International African Institute.

Maegher, K. (2010). *Identity Economics: Social Networks and the Informal Economy in Nigeria*. Oxford and Ibadan: James Currey and HEBN Publishers.

Mahmoud, H.A. (2008). 'Risky trade, resilient traders: Trust and livestock marketing in Northern Kenya'. *International African Institute*, vol. 78, no. 4, pp. 561–581. Cambridge: Cambridge University Press.

Majul, C.A. (1977). 'Principales, ilustrados, intellectuals, and the original concept of a Filipino national community'. *Asian Studies: Journal of Critical Perspectives on Asia*, vol. 46, no. 1, pp. 78–97. Quezon City: University of the Philippines Diliman.

Mayer, S. (2018). 'Out of Africa: Human smuggling as a social enterprise'. *The Annals of the American Academy of Political and Social Science*, vol. 676, no. 1, pp. 36–56.

Mines, M. (1972). *Muslim Merchants: The Economic Behaviour of an Indian Muslim Community*. New Delhi: Shri Ram Centre. Cited in Harris, Barbara. (1992). 'Talking to traders about trade' in Devereux, S. and J. Hoddinott (eds). *Fieldwork in Developing Countries*. London: Harvester Wheatsheaf.

Morrisey, O., Lopez, R. & Sharma, K. (eds.). (2015). *Handbook on Trade and Development*. United Kingdom: Edward Elgar Publishing.

Musa, S. (2013, April 20). 'Border Security, Arms Proliferation and Terrorism in Nigeria'. *Sahara Reporters*. Available at http://saharareporters.com/2013/04/20/border-security-arms-proliferation-and-terrorism-nigeria-lt-col-sagir-musa.

Neale, W., Singh, H. & Singh, J.P. (1965). 'Kurali market—a report on the economic geography of marketing in north India.' *Economic Development and Cultural Change*, vol. 13, pp. 129–168. Cited in Harris, Barbara. (1992). 'Talking to traders about trade' in Devereux, S. and J. Hoddinott (eds). *Fieldwork in Developing Countries*. London: Harvester Wheatsheaf.

Nichols, P. (1991). *Social Survey Methods a Field Guide for Development Workers. Development Guidelines*, no. 6. Oxford, UK: Oxfam GB.

Olken, B. & Barron, P. (2009). 'The simple economics of extortion: Evidence from trucking in Aceh'. *Journal of Political Economy*, vol. 117, no. 3. Chicago: The University of Chicago.

Olsen, W. (1992). 'Random sampling and repeat surveys in south India' in Devereux, S. and J. Hoddinott (eds). *Fieldwork in Developing Countries*. London: Harvester Wheatsheaf.

Onuoha, F. (2013). *Porous Borders and Boko Haram's Arms Smuggling Operations in Nigeria*. Doha, Qatar: Al Jazeera Centre for Studies.

Petrich, K. (2018, December 18). 'Guns, pirates, and charcoal'. *Global Initiative Against Transnational Organized Crime*. Available at https://globalinitiative.net/somalia_untocwatch/.

Quitoriano, E. (2016). 'Shadow economy or shadow state? The illicit gun trade in conflict-affected Mindanao' in Lara, F & S. Schoofs (eds). *Out of the Shadows: Violent Conflict and the Real Economy of Mindanao*. Quezon City: Bughaw.

Quitoriano, E. (2019). 'From "Canton Goods" and Rebellion to Piracy and Violent Extremism'. Unpublished manuscript.

Roitman, J. (2005). 'The pluralization of regulatory authority' in *Fiscal Disobedience: An Anthropology of Economic Regulation in Central Africa*, pp. 151–199. Princeton; Oxford: Princeton University Press.

Scott, J. (1976). *The Moral Economy of the Peasant: Rebellion and Subsistence in Southeast Asia*. Connecticut: Yale University Press.

Scott, J. (1985). *'Weapons of the Weak: Everyday Forms of Peasant Resistance.'* Connecticut: Yale University Press.

Scott, W.H. (1978). 'Crack in the parchment curtain'. *Philippine Studies*, vol. 26, no. 1, pp. 174–191. Quezon City: Ateneo de Manila University.

Scheele, J. (2012). *Smugglers and Saints of the Sahara: Regional Connectivity in the Twentieth Century*. New York: Cambridge University Press.

Schendel, W.V. & Abraham, I. (2005). *Illicit Flows and Criminal Things: States, Borders, and the Other Side of Globalization*. Bloomington: Indiana University Press.

Tagliacozzo, E. (2005). 'Secret trade, porous borders: smuggling and states along the Southeast Asian frontier'. *Journal of Southeast Asian Studies*, vol. 39, no. 1, pp. 180–182. New Haven: Yale University Press.

The World Bank. (2006). *Trucking and Illegal Payments in Aceh*. Available at http://documents1.worldbank.org/curated/en/486401468048915010/pdf/376070IND0Truc1yments1Aceh01PUBLIC1.pdf.

Villanueva, S. (2016). 'Cross-border illicit trade in Sulu and Tawi-Tawi: the co-existence of economic agendas and violent conflict' in F. Lara & S. Schoofs (eds). *Out of the shadows: violent conflict and the real economy of Mindanao*. Quezon City: Bughaw.

Wilson, K. (1992). Thinking about the ethics of fieldwork. in Devereux, S. and J. Hoddinott (eds). *Fieldwork in Developing Countries*. London: Harvester Wheatsheaf.

5

QUANTIFYING MISSING AND HIDDEN TRADE

An economic perspective

Sami Bensassi and Jade Siu

1. Introduction

Quantifying smuggling is necessary for researchers and policy makers to understand its connection with the political, economic, and social system. It is also a necessary step to answer policy questions, such as those related to public finances, trade and industrial development. Despite its necessity, measuring smuggling activities is inherently difficult. Researchers are continuously confronted with the challenge of assessing the extent to which the data they have on the characteristics, activities, and behaviours of smugglers are accurate and complete. To what extent can we trust what respondents report? What type of smuggling activities are we able to capture and what type of activities are we not able to capture? How are the data which we collect affected by those who collect them?

Another challenge in quantifying smuggling arises from the fact that the (il)legality of trading activities is not a binary concept. The degree to which traders are compliant with the law varies, and could be visualised as a spectrum. On one end of the spectrum, there exist traders who are complying fully, paying all necessary taxes, abiding by regulations, and registering officially. Trading activities away from that end of the spectrum could be labelled as smuggling. Due to the heterogeneous nature of smuggling, quantifying smuggling becomes complex and perhaps seemingly impossible. In this chapter, we provide a starting point to break down this complexity. We categorise two types of smuggling activities: "missing" trade and "hidden" trade. We define "missing" trade as the trade of goods which are declared correctly in the custom office of one country but not in the office of another country. For example, some goods might be misclassified as another product or under-invoiced so as to reduce the amount of tax which needs to be paid. Scholars have been taking advantage of this characteristic to detect smuggling activities by uncovering discrepancies, or "missing" trade, existing between flows recorded by the custom offices of the exporting and importing countries for the same bilateral exchange. These methodologies have evolved from using aggregated country-level trade flow datasets, which are usually publicly available, to using highly disaggregated custom-level data.

There are trade flows which do not pass through customs at all. Accordingly, unlike "missing trade," these trade flows are "hidden" and cannot be detected by examining statistical discrepancies in customs records (see Figure 5.1). Nevertheless, they are prevalent in land borders, and there has been an increasing recognition amongst governments and scholars that

DOI: 10.4324/9781003043645-5

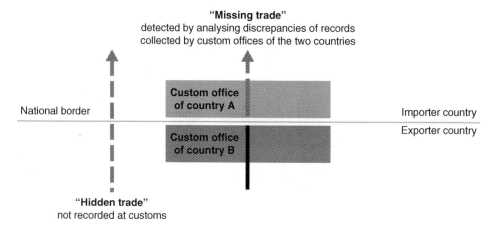

Figure 5.1 Difference between "missing trade" and "hidden trade".

ignoring "hidden trade" would lead to an underestimation of the size of smuggling. In this chapter, we review the relevant methodologies used to quantify "missing" and "hidden" trade.

While estimating the size of smuggling is a useful starting point to gauge its importance in an economy and to explore factors associated with smuggling at a macro level, more information is needed to delve into the nuance behind the motivations and behaviours of various actors involved in smuggling. Why do smugglers smuggle, and how? What are the incentives of other actors, such as customs officers? What would change their behaviours? Even if incentives could be designed to adjust their behaviour, would this be socially and economically desirable? In the past few years, economists have begun to explore these questions quantitatively using micro-data on individuals and firms who engage in smuggling in some way.

While these studies have provided new insights by quantifying the extent of associations, causes and consequences of smuggling at a micro-level, the literature remains thin, and richer analysis using mixed methods is needed.

We begin the Chapter by reviewing the earlier attempts to test economic theories on smuggling. We then examine the developments of various tools to detect "missing trade" after the seminal work by Bhagwati (1964) in Section 3. In Section 4, we review the progress made to capture the size of "hidden trade." In Section 5, we discuss recent quantitative studies using micro-data. We conclude in Section 6 by discussing the future research agenda to better quantify the size of smuggling, and its impact on different aspects of our lives. This Chapter focuses on the smuggling of goods which are legal themselves, as opposite to goods, such as narcotics, wildlife products and arms, which are illicit. The trade activities which we describe are also known as informal cross-border trade (ICBT), and can occur in both land borders and at ports. Our examples are mainly drawn from East and West Africa, the area of our expertise, but these methods are applicable to other regions with porous borders. Due to our background, we put greater focus on discussing the economics literature but we also draw on quantitative studies beyond the field of economics when appropriate.

2. From theory to data

During the 1960s and 1970s, trade economists were keen to understand whether smuggling enhances or reduces welfare. The pioneering work by Bhagwati and Hansen (1973) provides a

Quantifying missing and hidden trade

model to understand the welfare effect of smuggling by incorporating smuggling into trade theory involving two goods which can be traded with transportation costs. This framework examines whether the presence of smuggling enhances welfare through increasing overall levels of trade, or reduces welfare, through diverging trade.[1] They found that if tariffs are not prohibitive, smuggling is generally welfare-reducing.

Theoretical models of smuggling have evolved since Bhagwati and Hansen (1973) to incorporate more realistic smuggling behaviour and market structures which provide a better understanding of the mechanisms through which smuggling can affect welfare. For example, theories have sought to refine the modelling of costs and risks faced by smugglers, such as cost of goods being confiscated and fined (Sheikh 1974), costs of packaging to hide smuggled goods (Thursby et al. 1991), as well as the stringency of enforcement (Martin & Panagariya 1984). Even so, models fail to take into account that smuggling is most perverse in economies where weak institutions and poor infrastructure have pushed up trade costs. With that in mind, by extending Bhagwati and Hansen's (1973) model, Deardorff and Stolper (1990) found that smuggling is in general, welfare-enhancing. They argue that in African economies where there are large market inefficiencies, traders conduct informal trade for survival, rather than purely to evade tax. The inefficiencies which they refer to are trade regulations imposed by governments, such as quotas and price controls. Instead of modelling smuggling requiring an extra resource cost, they model smuggling as a cheaper option than formal trade when regulations are too cumbersome and costly. More recently, using a modern bilateral trade model, Dutt and Traca (2010) theoretically modelled tariff evasion and corruption, and found that the welfare effect of corruption associated with tariff evasion is ambiguous, and is dependent on the level of tariffs.

Despite working with limited reliable data at the time, scholars made innovative use of key macroeconomic data, such as prices and exchange rates, to test these theories. For example, Pitt (1981) directly tests Bhagwati and Hansen (1973)'s theory by defining the incentive to smuggle as the black market exchange rate divided by official effective exchange rate for rubber export in Indonesia. He argues that Bhagwati and Hansen (1973)'s model is inconsistent with his data. Against the backdrop of the implementation of structural adjustment programs, which includes devaluation, Dercon and Ayalew (1995) compares incentives for smuggling coffee, which is affected by the parallel market exchange rate, before and after the revolution in Ethiopia (from 1974).

Estimating the extent of smuggling has also become more sophisticated as more up-to-date and disaggregated data on prices and production of goods become available. Golub and Mbaye (2009) demonstrate the usage of several key economic indicators to estimate the size of smuggling between The Gambia, a country with a relatively free trade regime, and Senegal which takes a more protectionist approach to its trade policies. While it is widely known that there are large volumes of re-exports from The Gambia to Senegal, the official trade statistics collected by the Senegalese customs show that there is almost none. Golub & Mbaye (2009) firstly quantify the amount smuggled from The Gambia to Senegal by making use of the fact that, in absence of smuggling and measurement errors, domestic consumption is equal to domestic production plus net imports (imports minus exports). They construct a simple ratio of net imports minus production over domestic consumption for Gambia. If all trade is recorded, this ratio should be 100%. A ratio larger than 100% suggests that there exists some trade activities not recorded by the customs. They found that in 2004, this ratio for sugar was 400%, indicating a large volume of sugar imported into Senegal is unrecorded. They also used a second method to understand the incentives behind smuggling. They compared the wholesale prices of relatively homogenous goods, such as sugar, rice and wheat, in Banjul, The Gambia and Dakar, Senegal. They found that there were substantial price differences between the two places, and this was especially pronounced in the case of sugar, in line with the first evidence. Similarly, sugar was found to have especially large differences in trade taxes between the two countries. This study provides a good example of how to make effective use of different data sources and methods to triangulate the size of smuggling.

3. Quantifying "missing" trade

One of the most widely adopted methods of detecting smuggling today is the one originally proposed by Bhagwati (1964). This method focuses on estimating a specific type of smuggling. This type of smuggling, or "quasi-smuggling" as labelled by Bhagwati and Hansen (1973), involves goods that are transported through customs offices, but under-invoiced to reduce the amount of tax which needs to be paid. For example, a trader evades taxes by misreporting the price of the product or the quantity of the product. The method of quantifying this "missing" trade involves comparing the data provided by national customs agencies of the exporting and importing countries for the same trade flow in a given time. In particular, trade statistics provided by the exporting country tend to be more accurate than trade statistics provided by the importing country, since traders have the incentive to evade import duties. The method, known as mirror statistics or trade gaps, has the advantage of simplicity. It involves a computation of straightforward subtractions, and makes use of publicly available data, such the UN COMTRADE database, which is the principal source of trade data.

Bhagwati (1964) was also clear about the limitations inherent to this method. It is not possible to rule out other reasons such as time differences in reporting, errors in reporting, or the use of third country in international trade (entrepots economies) to explain the observed discrepancies. He states "'proof' [of smuggling] is thus impossible; only 'plausibility' can be procured by the method proposed" (Bhagwati, 1967, p. 70).

For three decades, Bhagwati's (1964) mirror statistics method attracted very few interests. It was not until the seminal paper of Fisman and Wei (2004) when Bhagwati's (1964) method was applied into econometric analysis. Using disaggregated trade data between Hong Kong and mainland China, Fisman and Wei (2004) found that there is a strong positive relationship between the extent of trade gap and tariff rates: one percent point increase in tariff rates is associated with 3% increase in trade gap. (5.1) shows the formulation of the trade gap which they adopted, and have since been extensively used in other studies. The subscripts i; j; k and t indicate that the gap value is calculated for the trade flowing from country i to country j, for a category of product k at a specific time t.[2]

$$\mathrm{gapvalue}_{ijkt} = \log\left(\mathrm{exportvalue}_{ijkt}\right) - \log\left(\mathrm{importvalue}_{ijkt}\right) \tag{5.1}$$

Fisman and Wei (2004) also extended Bhagwati (1964)'s method to not only detect tax evasion by firms underreporting the value of imported goods but also to detect tax evasion achieved by firms purposefully misclassifying products. By intentionally mis-reporting the classification of the product, traders are then subject to lower taxes compared the taxes if they were to declare the importation of the actual good. Fisman and Wei (2004) investigates the extent of tax evasion through misclassification by calculating the average tax rate of a group of products which are "similar," defined as being in the same four-digit category of the Harmonized System code. They found that, keeping tax rates as constant, trading a good in a group of "similar" products with a lower average tariff increases the trade gap.

Javorcik and Narciso (2008) extend this method by examining the extent to which tariff evasion is more prevalent for products which are more "differentiated" (e.g., shoes) than products which are homogenous (e.g., Irish potatoes), as it is harder for the customs officer to assess the true price of a "differentiated" product. In addition, they distinguish the channels through which tariff evasion is implemented: is it by misreporting quantity or is it by mis-reporting price? They do this by first examining the differences in quantity recorded by exporting and importing countries (which should be close to zero if there exists no quantity misreporting), and then separately examine the differences in unit values recorded by the exporting and importing countries (importing country should have higher unit value than exporting value as it includes cost of freight and insurance). They found evidence that tariff evasion between Germany and Eastern European countries are through the channel of misreporting price rather than through misreporting quantities.

Several studies followed, quantifying the associations between trade gaps and tariffs measures for various countries and products. Mishra et al. (2008) found that higher trade gaps between India and its top 40 trading partners are associated with higher tariffs, with an association stronger for differentiated products. Similar results are found for Kenya, Mauritius and Nigeria (Bouet & Roy 2012), trade between Kenya and Tanzania (Levin & Widell 2014) and for Ethiopia (Mengistu et al. 2018).

The method of trade gap is then applied to understanding beyond the association of tariff evasion and tariff measures. These include studies which examine the relationship between trade gap and corruption (Berger & Nitsch 2008, Jean & Mitaritonna 2010, Worku et al. 2016, Kellenberg & Levinson 2019), political connections (Rijkers et al. 2017), trade agreements (Stoyanov 2012, Sequeira 2016, Javorcik & Narciso 2017), export restrictions (Vézina 2015) and VAT (Ferrantino et al. 2012). These studies show that the trade gaps can be large and are observed in various settings (between developing nations, between developed countries, and between developing and developed countries). They have provided consistent evidence that these gaps are connected to the level of tariffs in the importing country and corruption in the importing and exporting countries.

Another method which makes use of customs data is the price filter method. First proposed by Paul et al. (1994), this method has been used in a number of studies (de Boyrie et al. 2005a, de Boyrie et al. 2005b, 2007). One of the benefits of the price filter method is that it is practical. It makes use of data that customs agencies gather on a day-to-day basis. The method detects fraud by comparing the reported price of a particular shipment with what could be considered the arm's length price, or an objective price, of the goods traded. If the reported price is abnormal – above or below the arm's length price range – the record of the shipment is considered suspicious. This arm's length price can be calculated in different ways. For example, if a market price is available, the market price plus or minus a certain percentage can be used as the arm's length price. In occasions when market prices are not available, one can use the average price of shipments of similar goods (WCO 2018). This corpus of research also has been valuable in showcasing and perfecting this method to help customs agencies flag potential unlawful behaviours.

Nonetheless, the arm's length price thresholds used to compare prices could be ad-hoc. Customs officers may not be well-informed about the actual value of the goods and thus unable to determine whether the value declared by the importer is accurate or not. By using a randomized control trial (RCT), Chalendard et al. (2020) found that providing more detailed and precise valuation information to customs officers at the ports of Mozambique can increase fraud detection. There are also other countries which seek to provide additional information to customs officers through pre-shipment inspection of imports (PSI), where a private firm provides a report to the importing customs, verifying the classification and valuation of the goods before shipment. While this could reduce tax avoidance of the goods which require such a report to be issued, total tax avoidance may not have decreased if there are alternative methods to smuggle, as found in Yang (2008) in the ports of the Philippines.

Recently, Demir and Javorcik (2020) proposed a new method which makes use of a statistical test to detect import tax evasion. More specifically, they make use of the Benford's law, which provides the probability a number will appear as a leading digit[3] in a dataset. They found that while export statistics and import statistics of goods which are not subject to tariffs conform with the law, import statistics of goods which are subject to taxes do not. This provides an indication that deviation from the law is related to import tax evasion.

They then measured the extent of import tax evasion by calculating the deviation from the law. They also found that their results, when using this new method of detecting import tax avoidance, are consistent with using the trade gap method proposed in Fisman and Wei (2004).

Despite the extensive usage of these indirect methods, the "original sin" of these methods comes back to haunt economists interested in smuggling and tax avoidance as soon as it is used in institutional and political debates connected to these questions. A telling example has been the controversy followed by the publication of the 2016 UNCTAD report on illicit financial flows. Denouncing the behaviour of specific countries based on the trade gap method opened a stream of justified criticisms vis-a-vis the origin of the gaps and risked a rebuke of any analysis based on this methodology. As cautioned by Bhagwati (1964), there could be various reasons other than smuggling activities, which explain the presence of discrepancies in trade statistics. Forstater (2018) highlights some of these factors, which include discrepancies between trade statistics provided by UN COMTRADE and those provided by national statistical offices. The use of mirror statistics also relies on one reporting country having an accurate set of trade statistics, which could be the case for trade flows involving a high-income country. This could be problematic when attempting to detect smuggling between two low-income countries which may have low statistical capacity. In addition, while trade statistics aggregated at a high level are easily accessible to all researchers, mirror statistics are most revealing when using highly disaggregated trade data.

If these indirect methods are able to provide only a partial picture of smuggling occurring at customs, it does not provide any information about trade flows which are not recorded either side of the border. Such trade flows are prevalent among low-income countries. This issue of "hidden trade" has been known through qualitative and case studies for a long time (Igue & Soule 1992, Titeca & Celestin 2012, Walther 2015, Bensassi et al. 2017). The next section of this chapter is dedicated to discussing methods used to reveal this trade.

4. Quantifying the "hidden" trade

Much of the "hidden" trade, although not recorded in national statistics, is highly visible in real-life. While some traders intentionally avoid customs offices to evade taxes, other traders are crossing borders which were part of historic trading routes before the borders were drawn (Golub 2015). In recent years, there has been a shift in perspectives, by some governments and international organisations, from criminalising these activities to acknowledging that some of this informal trade could play a role in reducing poverty and food insecurity (Afrika & Ajumbo 2012, Koroma et al. 2017).

As part of this shift, there has been increasing effort by governments to collect data on these informal trade activities. In the perspective of a government, understanding the level of informal trade is not only for the purposes of law enforcement and tax revenue collection, but also for basic accounting purposes. For countries with porous borders, relying on official trade statistics will skew the actual trade balance. For example, Uganda has found that their trade balance figures from Bank of Uganda (BoU) were USD 500 million higher than those recorded by the Ugandan Bureau of Statistics (UBOS) on the expenditure side of the National Accounts. They later were able to reconcile the gap, explained partly by informal cross-border trade (UBOS 2006).

Data collection efforts by governments are varied. In the case of sub-Saharan Africa, to our knowledge, Uganda has implemented the longest-standing systematic survey on informal cross-border trade. The pilot took place in 2004, and the full survey has been implemented every month since then. Its neighbouring country, Kenya, has also implemented a similar data collection exercise, but only for one month in 2011 and 2012 (KNBS 2012). We show the border crossings which have been monitored through these efforts in Uganda and in Kenya in Panel A of Figure 5.2. Rwanda also has been monitoring informal trade at all its border crossings since 2012 (NISR 2014). In West Africa, Nigeria has conducted a similar survey in 2013 and 2014 (CBN 2016), and Benin in 2010 and 2011 (INSAE 2011). Although the data collection in Benin was only implemented for one month in 2010 and 2011, the survey covered

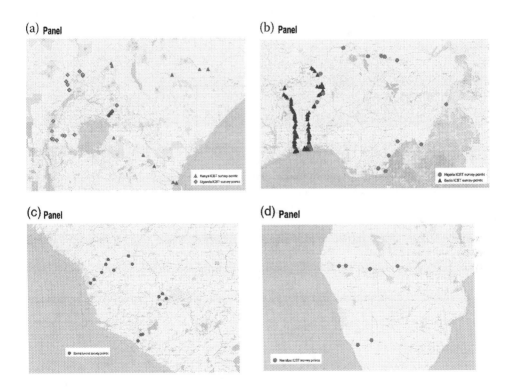

Figure 5.2 ICBT survey points monitored by governments of Nigeria and Benin.

Notes: Panel A are the border crossing points monitored by the governments of Kenya and Uganda. Panel B are the border crossing points monitored by the governments of Benin and Nigeria. Panel C are the border crossing points monitored by Jibao et al. (2017), requested by the government of Sierra Leone. Panel B are the border crossing points monitored by the government of Namibia. Authors approximated the GPS coordinates by gathering information about the locations of the border crossings reported in UBOS (2006), KNBS (2012), CBN (2016), Jibao et al. (2017) and EAN (2016). Coordinates for the border crossings in Benin are obtained in Bensassi et al. (2018).

more than 150 border crossings, with many being in remote border crossings. Panel B of Figure 5.2 shows the density of crossings which were monitored along Benin's borders. Responding to the request from the Head of the Trade Promotion Authority, Jibao et al. (2017) monitored 12 informal border crossings and seven official border crossings in Sierra Leone (Panel C of Figure 5.2). In Southern Africa, Namibia monitored informal trade at six of its border crossings from 2014 to 2016 (Panel D of Figure 5.2) (EAN 2016). Mozambique and Malawi have also implemented similar surveys (IMF 2020). In addition, there have been systematic data collection efforts by non-governmental organisations. Famine Early Warning Systems Network (FEWS NET) collect monthly data on informal cross-border trade of main staples at various border crossings across the African continent to monitor food security. Regional Agricultural Trade Intelligence Network (RATIN) also records informal cross-border trade of key agricultural goods along the borders between East African countries. While the availability of these datasets are a stepping stone to understanding ICBT, data collection efforts of governments and agencies could be shaped by various political and economic agendas, many of which are not known to researchers. As a result, researchers should be aware that depending solely on them may provide a skewed picture of the composition of goods and the extent of cross-border trade globally.

The governmental surveys have mainly been guided by the methodology documented by Ackello-Ogutu (1996). It details the methodology which the researchers followed when estimating informal trade at the borders between Kenya and Uganda, and those between Tanzania, Malawi, and Mozambique and their neighbours. This methodology consists of a two-stage process. The first stage is to obtain a list of commonly-used border crossing points, which are usually close to border towns and customs points (Ackello-Ogutu 1996). By consulting with different actors and visiting border posts, the research team eliminates border posts which do not fit a set of predefined criteria, such as prevalence of trade activities and security. In the second stage, the research team decides how frequently they will monitor the border crossing points. For example, due to resource constraints, the research team from the Ugandan government enumerates only two weeks each month. An up-rating computation can then be conducted to obtain a monthly statistic. This method of up-rating accounts for seasonality across months and days of the week. During enumeration weeks, enumerators are stationed at various points of established informal border crossings to enumerate products as traders pass by.

While this method of direct observation is cost effective, there are several factors which could lead to an underestimation of informal cross-border trade. First, direct observation places importance on the experience and attentiveness of enumerators. Enumerators could miss products travelling across borders. This is particularly the case in border crossings where the flow of goods is high and goods are varied. It is also difficult to enumerate goods which are transported in trucks and cars. Second, traders could change their behaviour when the enumerators are present. Traders might be wary of the enumerators, especially if they are known to be from the government. This could, however, be less of a concern with repeated data collection efforts as traders start to recognise that enumerators are not there to arrest them. Third, due to security concerns, enumeration only takes place during daylight. This means the quantity of goods moved at night is unknown and may be significant. Lastly, while it may be true that most informal cross-border trade activities occur in established border crossings, there still exists smuggling outside these established crossings.

One way to verify the degree of mismeasurement in these estimations is to compare data collected in the same border crossing monitored by separate governments. For example, there are overlaps in the Kenyan and Uganda data collection in the southern part of the border (Panel A in Figure 5.2). Regardless of the degree of underestimation, these surveys have shown that this type of informal crossborder trade is large in magnitude, in comparison with official trade recorded at the customs. For example, Bensassi et al. (2018), using the data collected by the Benin's National Institute of Statistics (INSAE), estimated that the size of informal exports from Benin to Nigeria is five times the size of formal exports. In a smaller magnitude but still substantial, BoU and UBOS estimated that informal exports from Uganda to its neighbours valued USD 538 million in 2018, which was 38% of formal exports to its neighbours (UBOS 2019).

Having gauged the size of informal trade through these surveys, research questions on causes and consequences of informal "hidden" trade at a macro-level can be investigated. There has been a particular focus on the relationships between trade policies and smuggling. For example, Bensassi et al. (2017) observed that there are few overlaps between formal and informal trade of goods between Benin and its neighbours, and found that import bans and tariffs have a positive and significant impact on the volume of goods traded informally. Eberhard-Ruiz and Moradi (2019) and Siu (n.d.) make use of the ICBT survey dataset collected by UBOS and BoU to estimate the impact of trade policies on informal trade flows between Uganda and its neighbours. Using data collected by FEWS NET, Burke and Myers (2014) used informal trade volumes among Southern African countries in their price model and found that, in general, for trade routes with high levels of informal trade and limited government oversight, there is rapid price transmission – a way of measuring how the prices in one market affect another market. They found this result to be different when governments are heavily involved in the import of grain (Myers & Jayne 2012), suggesting that government regulations are not impacting informal trade the same way it is impacting formal trade. Also analysing prices of staples, Porteous (2017) attributes the lack of effect of maize export bans on price differences between markets in East and Southern Africa to imperfect enforcement and the prevalence of informal trade.

5. Quantifying behaviours

In recent years, scholars have started to move from relying on macro-level data to collecting micro-level data on different actors involved with informal trade to understand motivations and incentives better. There have been a number of quantitative studies which make use of original surveys to document the profiles of traders. As expected, these surveys are usually conducted at border points where informal trade is known to be prevalent, for example along the border crossing points between DRC, Rwanda, Burundi and Uganda (Brenton et al. 2011, Titeca & Celestin 2012, Croke et al. 2020), important land borders in Sierra Leone (Jibao et al. 2017, Van den Boogaard et al. 2018), main border crossing points into Botswana (Ama et al. 2013), as well as border towns between Uganda and Kenya (Tyson 2015, Siu n.d., Wiseman 2020). There are other considerations as well. Tyson (2015) made her selection based on its prevalence of smuggling, whether a relevant policy intervention has been implemented, its population density and safety concerns. While these criteria allow research to take place ethically, safely and cost effectively, these criteria can also lead to research bias where too many scholars focus on a specific location. Apart from conflict borders, there could be other border points where informal traders operate but in a less clustered manner. These traders will not be captured by surveys which focus on areas where informal trade activities are most well known.

Designing the sampling strategy is challenging in the context of smuggling. In order to ensure their sample is representative of the population, scholars pay great attention to the sampling strategy. Generally, the most practical way for a scholar to define the sampling frame is to access a list of firms/people of interest. For instance, Sequeira and Djankov (2014) and Sequeira (2016) obtained a list of all official clearing agents in Mozambique and South Africa, and randomly drew clearing agents to track. This, however, often is not available when surveying informal traders. Some scholars draw a random sample participants without a predefined list. For example, Titeca and Celestin (2012) conducted interviews with "every fifth trader to arrive" in all the four sites they had selected around the Great Lakes Region, and Jibao et al. (2017) chose every twentieth trader who crossed the border. This method is difficult to implement systematically on the ground, and the choice of respondents could be influenced by the enumerator's ways of working.

In the absence of a readily available list of the population to draw from randomly, some scholars seek to create their own list. Siu (n.d.) and Wiseman (2020) defined the sampling frame geographically, which involved listing traders within a predefined distance away from the official border post. Brenton et al. (2011) implemented a two-step process in their sampling strategy. They firstly listed small-scale crossborder traders who were passing through selected border crossings within a one-week period. They were informed of which markets these traders operate in. The enumeration team then went to these markets and selected the traders to survey.

Scholars collecting representative samples of informal traders have so far focused on those who trade in small volumes (e.g., Brenton et al. 2011, Titeca & Celestin 2012 and Wiseman 2020). This particular focus could lead to research bias. For example, using their survey data, Titeca and Celestin (2012) found that small-scale informal cross-border trade in the Great Lakes region is dominated by women. While this provided an important insight, this gender ratio may not be the same when examining larger-scale informal traders.

Designing a sampling strategy such that the sample of respondents represents the population of interest is not always applicable, such as when studying networks among individuals or firms. Walther (2015) provides an approach to analyse social networks between cross-border traders. Using existing trade data, he first identifies the products important for his analysis of cross-border trade operating in the border markets located between Niger, Nigeria and Benin. He then identifies the key actors involved in trading these products. As he explains, the next steps in deciding whom to interview is fundamentally different from the sampling strategy described above.

In contrast to traditional surveys that consider social actors as independent units that can be added until they constitute a representative sample of the population, our data refer to non-independent observations. Sampling a population would not work in our case because we don't know how the social actors are intertwined with each other before we start our analysis and, by randomly selecting some of them, we would miss a large number of relevant connections. In order to address this issue, we used snow-balling techniques. Snowball sampling is particularly adapted to the study of cross-border traders, who don't belong to a formal professional institution in which insiders could easily be distinguished from outsiders, and whose number and activities are extremely difficult to evaluate from the investigator's perspective.

This approach has been applied to different settings and questions, such as understanding the role of gender in rice trade networks (Walther et al. 2019) and livestock trade networks in West Africa (Valerio et al. 2020) Beyond deciding whom to interview, collecting quantitative data on illegal activities are challenging. It is hard to distinguish "true" information from "cheap" talk (Fisman 2009), in particular regarding bribes payment associated with informal trade. While it is impossible to know for certain, there are ways to improve the quality of the responses and to check the extent of over/under-reporting.

A starting point is to use local terms in the questionnaire, making use of the fact that "legitimacy" is not objective and fixed (Titeca & Flynn 2014, Van den Boogaard et al. 2018). In Siu (n.d.), the questionnaire asked which border crossing s/he crossed by naming the border crossings, instead of imposing labels such as "informal" and "official" routes. Researchers should also be conscious about who is asking the questions and how that would affect the responses. For example, an interviewer who is also a trader working in the area might be able to gain consent from more traders to participate in the interview, but the respondents could also be dishonest when speaking to someone they know. The responses could then suffer from social desirability bias. Alternatively, traders could be suspicious of an interviewer who is not from the area, and may not agree to be interviewed.

There are also innovative methods to verify how the data collection process has altered the responses. Some traders might choose not to answer questions related to bribe payments. Bensassi and Jarreau (2019) check whether these traders have characteristics that differentiate them from other surveyed traders using econometric analysis. In Sequeira (2016), they are concerned about the reliability of the bribe data self-reported by clearing agents. To address this, they randomly selected clearing agents to be monitored by observers with experience in the shipping industry. This reduces suspicion from the clients. They found that reports of bribes are lower for clearing agents who have been monitored. However, this under-reporting is less so for cases when both the clearing agent and the client gain from the corruption activity; i.e., when tariff rates are higher.

Mixed methods also allow triangulation of information gathered using quantitative and qualitative methods. In Van den Boogaard et al. (2018), the researchers gathered information by using a quantitative survey and using qualitative methods. They highlighted that the coherence in their qualitative and quantitative data has provided them confidence that the responses which they obtained are credible.

There are other methods used in quantitative studies of other topics which could be applied in the context of smuggling. Blattman et al. (2016) proposes to verify responses to sensitive questions, such as those on crime, in quantitative surveys by randomly selecting a subset of those who were interviewed to be followed up by a qualitative researcher. The qualitative researcher then work to build a relationship with these selected respondents and elicit responses of the same questions. There are also other methods which might be more feasible if scholars are time-constrained in their data collection period. This includes the use of list experiments where respondents are randomly provided with a list of statements: one set has a sensitive statement and the other does not (McKenzie & Siegel 2013). They then verify survey responses using administrative data (Deming 2011).

Quantitative surveys are not only a tool to collect information about the characteristics of traders and other actors, but also are used to answer questions, such as, "What changes the behaviour of actors?" and "How do the behaviours of actors change over time?". One method to answer these questions is for scholars to design and evaluate a programme which may affect traders' behaviour over time. Croke et al. (2020) test whether a training programme targeted at small-scale informal cross-border traders reduces bribery payments by using a randomised control trial (RCT). Within their sample of 628 cross-border traders, they randomly selected half to participate in a training workshop. With this method, they were able to compare the outcomes of those who participated in the workshop and those who did not. While this methodology is common in quantitative studies, applying it to smuggling-related research can be particularly challenging. One challenge is to trace the participants, as the authors admit that some traders provided false names at baseline. Two years after their baseline, out of their original sample of 628 cross-border traders, they were only able to track 84% of the sample.

Other studies examine changes in the behaviour of actors by combining both macro and micro-level data. Sequeira (2016) examines what happens to tariff evasion (measured by the trade gap) and the amount of bribes paid (measured using firm-level data) as a result of a policy aiming at reducing tariffs for certain imports into Mozambique. Some products have changed tariffs, while others have not. This variation allows the author to compare outcomes of these two groups. Similarly, Siu (n.d.) first uses macro-level formal and informal trade flow data to understand whether a border facility has reduced informality, and then she gathers trade-level data to understand who chooses to cross the border informally. Chalendard et al. (2020) uses both administrative and survey data to examine how customs officers' behaviour changed as a result of being provided third-party information on import values. After using administrative data to understand changes in inspection actions change, as described in Section 3, they investigate whether better information provided by the in-house team improved customs performance using a RCT. By using both methods, they are able to understand how information affects customs performance in a more nuanced manner.

6. Future research agenda

This chapter provides a dissection of the general term "smuggling" for quantitative analysis. Equation 5.2 describes the value of total bilateral trade for a specific product.

$$Total\ Trade = Reported\ Trade + Missing\ Trade + Hidden\ Trade \tag{5.2}$$

For too long, Missing Trade has been ignored and Hidden Trade has been considered negligible. The assumptions on which this relies are wrong. By using creative methods, scholars have revealed that missing trade can be important even for trade between developed countries (Stoyanov 2012). Recently, with governments and international organisations shifting their perspectives away from thinking about informal trade as a purely criminal activity, scholars have made inroads into quantifying "hidden" trade. As captured by previous qualitative studies, this type of smuggling is found to be a fundamental component of trade among developing nations (Bensassi et al. 2018). These studies show that the size and characteristics of hidden trade vary across country pairs on the basis of trade barriers, currency movements and the state capacity of the countries concerned.

True, missing trade and hidden trade are inherently difficult to measure. As we have seen in the past, however, this endeavour is worth pursuing. Working with a largely theoretical economics literature on smuggling, Bhagwati (1964) took up the huge empirical challenge of quantifying smuggling with basic trade statistics readily available. His method of mirror statistics has paved the way for the next generation of scholars. By applying Bhagwati's (1964) method into econometric analysis, scholars have made great strides in quantifying the extent to which trade and tax policies, as well as institutional factors such as corruption, affect smuggling. Efforts in collecting data on hidden trade have provided governments with a more accurate view of their country's trade balance. Scholars collecting micro-data on different actors have provided important insights into the mechanisms behind smuggling and the incentives of different actors. Scholars have also begun to quantify the extent to which behaviours adapt when faced with operational and environmental changes.

Despite recent headway, quantitative studies on smuggling remain relatively thin, with many questions still unanswered and challenges left untackled. First, precision in detecting missing trade can be improved by designing new quantitative methods beyond the use of mirror statistics. There are fresh opportunities to use transactional data at the customs level, as more customs offices work towards digitalising and automating their operations. Some governments have even been working towards linking previously siloed administrative datasets, such as transactions data at customs and income taxpayer data, for research purposes. To improve

Quantifying missing and hidden trade

knowledge about hidden trade, we call on governments of nations where there is a high prevalence of informal trade (revealed through qualitative evidence) to follow the example of Uganda and systematically estimate informal trade at land borders. By publishing these estimates, scholars can then make use of these resources to generate better knowledge of the interdependence between informal and formal trade, and to quantify the extent to which these activities can contribute to or hinder economic development goals.

At a micro-level, more attention is needed to understand how survey respondents answer questions related to smuggling. Scholars can adopt methods designed for other research areas, as we have highlighted in this Chapter. More pertinently, scholars should complement qualitative approaches with quantitative methods. Triangulation of different data sources, across disciplines, will not only reduce the likelihood of inaccurate conclusions based on biased data, but will also provide a more holistic picture of the research question at hand. This direction could overcome some of the existing challenges in understanding actors involved in smuggling activities over time, the true incentives behind their decision-making, and their real responses when faced with new barriers and opportunities.

Future studies should venture beyond the current focus of existing quantitative studies. We should acknowledge that scholars have only begun the journey of estimating "hidden" trade. We still know little about the prominence and size of trade activities in remote areas, far away from key border towns where most studies have been situated. Night trade activities, due to safety concerns, are also less quantified. With the focus on smuggling of legal goods, methods to quantify smuggling of illicit goods remain elusive. Yet with the help of technology and new ways of data collection, such as collection of user data by the mobile phone app Sauti (which is targeted towards supporting cross-border traders), some of these barriers could be overcome in the future. There should be a shift away from focusing on small-scale traders to understand how and why traders of different sizes enter, thrive, survive, and exit the profession. There should also be a better spread of studies in different countries and continents, from countries in Africa, where most research on informal cross-border trade takes place, to Asia and South America. A more diverse body of studies will enable researchers to verify the extent to which these methods are applicable in different contexts. By further refining and expanding the toolbox of methods to quantifying smuggling, we then can understand better the extent to which informal trade is operated and incentivised differently across cultures, climates and institutions. A collective effort to reduce research bias will be a promising way forward to produce richer and more relevant research which would not provide benefits only to a selected convenient few.

Notes

1　Azam (2007) and Golub (2015) provide a good summary.
2　Notice that this formulation has to be modified to take into account of the case where only one of country has reported a trade flow and is similar to calculation of the trade gap as a share of the import value of the good: gapvalue = (Export − Import)/Import.
3　For example, the leading digit of 187 is 1.

References

Ackello-Ogutu, C. (1996), Methodologies for estimating informal crossborder trade in Eastern and Southern Africa: Kenya/Uganda border, Tanzania and its neighbors, Malawi and its neighbors Mozambique and its neighbors, Technical Paper No. 29. http://hdl.handle.net/11295/49521.

Afrika, J.-G. K. & Ajumbo, G. (2012), *Informal cross border trade in Africa: Implications and policy recommendations*, Africa Economic Brief, AfDB, Abidjan: African Development Bank. https://www.afdb.org/fileadmin/uploads/afdb/Documents/Publications/Economic%20Brief%20-%20Informal%20Cross%20Border%20Trade%20in%20Africa%20Implications%20and%20Policy%20Recommendations%20-%20Volume%203.pdf.

Ama, N. O., Mangadi, K. T., Okurut, F. N. & Ama, H. A. (2013), 'Profitability of the informal cross-border trade: A case study of four selected borders of Botswana', *African Journal of Business Management* 7(40), 4221–4232.

Azam, J.-P. (2007), The welfare implications of unrecorded cross-border trade, in J.-P. Azam, ed., *Trade, Exchange Rate, and Growth in Sub-Saharan Africa*, Cambridge University Press, Cambridge, chapter 2.

Bensassi, S., Brockmeyer, A., Pellerin, M. & Raballand, G. (2017), 'Algeria-Mali trade: The normality of informality', *Middle East Development Journal* 9(2), 161–183.

Bensassi, S. & Jarreau, J. (2019), 'Price discrimination in bribe payments: Evidence from informal crossborder trade in West Africa', *World Development* 122, 462 – 480. URL: http://www.sciencedirect.com/science/article/pii/S0305750X19301433.

Bensassi, S., Jarreau, J. & Mitaritonna, C. (2018), 'Regional Integration and Informal Trade in Africa: Evidence from Benin's Borders', *Journal of African Economies* 28(1), 89–118. https://doi.org/10.1093/jae/ejy016.

Berger, H. & Nitsch, V. (2008), *Gotcha! A Profile of Smuggling in International Trade*, Working Paper Series, Munich, Germany: CESifo.

Bhagwati, J. (1964), 'On the underinvoicing of imports', *Oxford Bulletin of Economics and Statistics* 27(4), 389–397.

Bhagwati, J. (1967), Fiscal Policies, the Faking of Foreign Trade Declarations, and the Balance of Payments, *Bulletin of the Oxford University Institute of Economics & Statistics* 29(1), 61–77. https://doi.org/10.1111/j.1468-0084.1967.mp29001004.x.

Bhagwati, J. & Hansen, B. (1973), 'A theoretical analysis of smuggling', *The Quarterly Journal of Economics* 87(2), 172–187.

Blattman, C., Jamison, J., Koroknay-Palicz, T., Rodrigues, K. & Sheridan, M. (2016), 'Measuring the measurement error: A method to qualitatively validate survey data', *Journal of Development Economics* 120, 99–112.

Bouet, A. & Roy, D. (2012), 'Trade protection and tax evasion: Evidence from Kenya, Mauritius, and Nigeria', *The Journal of International Trade and Economic Development* 21(2), 287–320.

Brenton, P., Bucekuderhwa, B., Hossein, C., Nagaki, S. & Ntagoma, J. (2011), 'Risky business: Poor women cross-border traders in the great lakes region of Africa', *Technical Report 11*, Washington, DC: World Bank.

Burke, W. J. & Myers, R. J. (2014), 'Spatial equilibrium and price transmission between southern African maize markets connected by informal trade', *Food Policy* 49, 59–70.

CBN (2016), Measuring informal cross-border trade in Nigeria, Report, Abuja: Central Bank of Nigeria.

Chalendard, C. R., Duhaut, A., Fernandes, A. M., Mattoo, A., Raballand, G. J. & Rijkers, B. (2020), 'Does better information curb customs fraud?', World Bank Policy Research Working Paper No. 8371. https://ssrn.com/abstract=3633656.

Croke, K., Garcia Mora, M. E. Goldstein, M., Mensah, E. & O'Sullivan, M. (2020), 'Up before dawn: Experimental evidence from a cross-border trader training at the Democratic Republic of Congo–Rwanda Border', World Bank Policy Research Working Paper No. 9123. https://ssrn.com/abstract=3526525.

de Boyrie, M. E., Pak, S. J. & Zdanowicz, J. S. (2005a), 'Estimating the magnitude of capital flight due to abnormal pricing in international trade: The Russia–USA case', *Accounting Forum* 29(3), 249 – 270. Tax avoidance and global development. http://www.sciencedirect.com/science/article/pii/S0155998205000268.

de Boyrie, M., Nelson, J. & Pak, S. (2007), 'Capital movement through trade misinvoicing: The case of Africa', *Journal of Financial Crime* 14, 474–489.

de Boyrie, M., Pak, S. & Zdanowicz, J. (2005b), 'The impact of Switzerland's money laundering lawon capital flows through abnormal pricing in international trade', *Applied Financial Economics* 15(4), 217–230. https://EconPapers.repec.org/RePEc:taf:apfiec:v:15:y:2005:i:4:p:217-230.

Deardorff, A. V. & Stolper, W. E. (1990), 'Effects of smuggling under African conditions: A factual, institutional and analytic discussion', *Weltwirtschaftliches Archiv* 126(1), 116–141.

Deming, D. J. (2011), 'Better schools, less crime?', *The Quarterly Journal of Economics* 126(4), 2063–2115.

Demir, B. & Javorcik, B. (2020), 'Trade policy changes, tax evasion and Benford's law', *Journal of Development Economics* 144, 102456. http://www.sciencedirect.com/science/article/pii/S030438782030031619.

Dercon, S. & Ayalew, L. (1995), 'Smuggling and supply response: Coffee in Ethiopia', *World Development* 23(10), 1795–1813.

Dutt, P. & Traca, D. (2010), 'Corruption and bilateral trade flows: Extortion or evasion?', *The Review of Economics and Statistics* 92(4), 843–860.

EAN (2016), Informal cross-border trade report, Report, Namibia: Economic Association of Namibia.

Eberhard-Ruiz, A. & Moradi, A. (2019), 'Regional market integration in East Africa: Local but no regional effects?', *Journal of Development Economics* 140, 255–268.

Ferrantino, M. J., Liu, X. & Wang, Z. (2012), 'Evasion behaviors of exporters and importers: Evidence from the U.S.–China trade data discrepancy', *Journal of International Economics* 86(1), 141–157. http://www.sciencedirect.com/science/article/pii/S0022199611000924

Fisman, R. (2009), 'Measuring tariff evasion and smuggling', *NBER Reporter Online* (3), 8–10.

Fisman, R. & Wei, S.-J. (2004), 'Tax rates and tax evasion: Evidence from "missing imports" in China', *Journal of Political Economy* 112(2), 471–496.

Forstater, M. (2018), 'Illicit financial flows, trade misinvoicing, and multinational tax avoidance: the same or different?', *CGD policy paper* 123, 29.

Golub, S. (2015), Informal cross-border trade and smuggling in Africa, in O. Morrissey, K. Sharma & R. A. López, eds, *Handbook on Trade and Development*, Edward Elgar Publishing, chapter 10.

Golub, S. S. & Mbaye, A. A. (2009), 'National trade policies and smuggling in Africa: The case of the Gambia and Senegal', *World Development* 37(3), 595 – 606. http://www.sciencedirect.com/science/article/pii/S0305750X08002234.

Igue, J. O. & Soule, B. (1992), *L'Etat Entrepôt au Bénin: Commerce Informel ou Réponse a la Crise?*, Khartala: Paris.

IMF (2020), Nigeria: Informal trade with neighboring countries, Technical report, IMF. https://www.imf.org/en/Data/Statistics/informal-economy-data/Reports/nigeria-informal-trade-with-neighboring-countries.

INSAE (2011), Enquête sur le commerce non enregistré au cordon douanier, Rapport, Institut National de la Statistique et de l'Analyse Economique, Cotonou.

Javorcik, B. & Narciso, G. (2008), 'Differentiated products and evasion of import tariffs', *Journal of International Economics* 76(2), 208–222. https://EconPapers.repec.org/RePEc:eee:inecon:v:76:y:2008:i:2:p:208-22220.

Javorcik, B. S. & Narciso, G. (2017), 'WTO accession and tariff evasion', *Journal of Development Economics* 125, 59–71. http://www.sciencedirect.com/science/article/pii/S0304387816300840.

Jean, S. & Mitaritonna, C. (2010), 'Determinants and pervasiveness of the evasion of custom duties', *CEPII, WP N 2010–26*. https://doi.org/10.22004/ag.econ.115432.

Jibao, S., Mahoi, I. & Sandy, J. F. (2017), The realities of cross-border trade from Sierra Leone to other Mano River countries, Report, International Growth Center. https://www.theigc.org/publication/realities-cross-border-trade-sierra-leone-neighbours/.

Kellenberg, D. & Levinson, A. (2019), 'Misreporting trade: Tariff evasion, corruption, and auditing standards', *Review of International Economics* 27(1), 106–129. URL: https://onlinelibrary.wiley.com/doi/abs/10.1111/roie.12363.

KNBS (2012), Informal cross border trade 2012, Documentation, Kenya: Kenya National Bureau of Statistics.

Koroma, S., Nimarkoh, J., You, N., Ogalo, V. & Owino, B. (2017), Formalization of informal trade in Africa: Trends, experiences and socio-economic impacts, Report, Food Agric. Organ. Accra. http://www.fao.org/3/a-i7101e.pdf.

Levin, J. & Widell, L. M. (2014), 'Tax evasion in Kenya and Tanzania: Evidence from missing imports', *Economic Modelling* 39, 151–162.

Martin, L. & Panagariya, A. (1984), 'Smuggling, trade, and price disparity: A crime-theoretic approach', *Journal of International Economics* 17(3-4), 201–217.

McKenzie, D. & Siegel, M. (2013), 'Eliciting illegal migration rates through list randomization', *Migration Studies* 1(3), 276–291.

Mengistu, A. T., Molla, K. G. & Mascagni, G. (2018), 'Tax evasion and missing imports: Evidence using transaction level data in Ethiopia', *ICTD Working Paper* 101.

Mishra, P., Subramanian, A. & Topalova, P. (2008), 'Tariffs, enforcement, and customs evasion: Evidence from India', *Journal of Public Economics* 92(10), 1907–1925.

Myers, R. J. & Jayne, T. (2012), 'Multiple-regime spatial price transmission with an application to maize markets in Southern Africa', *American Journal of Agricultural Economics* 94(1), 174–188.

NISR (2014), Informal cross border trade statistics in Rwanda, Presentation made in Addis Ababa.

Paul, K., Pak, S., Zdanowicz, J. & Curwen, P. (1994), 'The ethics of international trade: Use of deviation from average world price to indicate possible wrongdoing', *Business Ethics Quarterly* 4(1), 29–41. http://www.jstor.org/stable/385755721.

Pitt, M. M. (1981), 'Smuggling and price disparity', *Journal of International Economics* 11(4), 447–458. https://ideas.repec.org/a/eee/inecon/v11y1981i4p447-458.html.

Porteous, O. (2017), 'Empirical effects of short-term export bans: The case of African maize', *Food Policy* 71, 17–26.

Rijkers, B., Baghdadi, L. & Raballand, G. (2017), 'Political connections and tariff evasion evidence from Tunisia', *The World Bank Economic Review* 31(2), 459–482.

Sequeira, S. (2016), 'Corruption, trade costs, and gains from tariff liberalization: Evidence from Southern Africa', *American Economic Review* 106(10).

Sequeira, S. & Djankov, S. (2014), 'Corruption and firm behavior: Evidence from African ports', *Journal of International Economics* 94(2), 277–294.

Sheikh, M. A. (1974), 'Underinvoicing of imports in Pakistan', *Oxford Bulletin of Economics and Statistics* 36(4), 287–296.

Siu, J. (n.d.), Formalising informal cross-border trade: Evidence from One-Stop-Border-Posts in Uganda, Technical Report. Retrieved from https://papers.ssrn.com/sol3/papers.cfm?abstract_id=3854156.

Stoyanov, A. (2012), 'Tariff evasion and rules of origin violations under the Canada-U.S. Free Trade Agreement', *Canadian Journal of Economics/Revue canadienne d'économique* 45(3), 879–902. URL: https://onlinelibrary.wiley.com/doi/abs/10.1111/j.1540-5982.2012.01719.x.

Thursby, M., Jensen, R. & Thursby, J. (1991), 'Smuggling, camouflaging, and market structure', *The Quarterly Journal of Economics* 106(3), 789–814.

Titeca, K. & Celestin, K. (2012), Walking in the Dark: Informal Cross-Border Trade in the Great Lakes Region, Technical report, International Alert. http://hdl.handle.net/1854/LU-4161492.

Titeca, K. & Flynn, R. (2014), '"Hybrid governance" legitimacy, and (il) legality in the informal cross-border trade in Panyimur, northwest Uganda', *African Studies Review* 57(1), 71–91.

Tyson, J. (2015), 'Effect of sub-Saharan African trade corridors on vulnerable groups', *ODI Report*. London: ODI.

UBOS (2006), The informal cross border trade survey report, Technical report, Kampala: Ugandan Bureau of Statistics.

UBOS (2019), The informal cross border trade survey report, Technical report, Kampala: Ugandan Bureau of Statistics. 22.

Valerio, V. C., Walther, O. J., Eilittä, M., Cissé, B., Muneepeerakul, R. & Kiker, G.A. (2020), 'Network analysis of regional livestock trade in West Africa', *PloS one* 15(5), e0232681.

Van den Boogaard, V., Prichard, W. & Jibao, S. (2018), 'Norms, networks, power and control: Understanding informal payments and brokerage in cross-border trade in Sierra Leone', *Journal of Borderlands Studies* 33 pp. 1–21.

Vézina, P.-L. (2015), 'Illegal trade in natural resources: Evidence from missing exports', *International Economics* 142, 152–160. Economics of Global Interactions. http://www.sciencedirect.com/science/article/pii/S2110701714000481.

Walther, O. J. (2015), 'Business, brokers and borders: The structure of West African trade networks', *The Journal of Development Studies* 51(5), 603–620.

Walther, O. J., Tenikue, M. & Trémolières, M. (2019), 'Economic performance, gender and social networks in West African food systems', *World Development* 124, 104650.

WCO (2018), Illicit financial flows via trade mis-invoicing, Technical report, Brussels: World Custom Organisation.

Wiseman, E. (2020), Trade, informality and corruption: Evidence from small-scale traders in Kenya during Covid-19, Working paper.

Worku, T., Mendoza, J. P. & Wielhouwer, J. L. (2016), 'Tariff evasion in sub-Saharan Africa: The influence of corruption in importing and exporting countries', *International Tax and Public Finance* 23(4), 741–761.

Yang, D. (2008), 'Can enforcement backfire? Crime displacement in the context of customs reform in the Philippines', *The Review of Economics and Statistics* 90(1), 1–14.

6
RESEARCH IN DANGEROUS FIELDS

Ethics, morals, and practices in the study of smuggling

Thomas Hüsken

Introduction

Writing about cultural habits and practices that are labelled as illicit is difficult, particularly when those who practice them are your hosts, conversational partners, and friends. The *Oxford Learner's Dictionary* tells us that smuggling is "the crime of taking or bringing goods secretly and illegally into or out of a country."[1] Etymologically, the roots of the word come from the Low German *schmuggeln*, which means "to lurk."[2] Thus a smuggler is not only a person involved in the clandestine transportation of goods and people, but is also someone who lurks (behind bushes) and is potentially dangerous as well as morally ambivalent. On the other hand, smuggling has often been a topic of romantic discourses that portray smugglers as social rebels, or situate smuggling in the context of political resistance (Girtler 2006) against state authorities and their territorial regimes. States label forms of trade and exchange as smuggling when these activities collide with border regimes, taxation laws or other legal regulations. History reveals how these regulations change in time and thus turn practices that were once legal into something illegal.[3] Smugglers themselves also have varying perceptions of their conduct. They may see (or present) themselves as part of a moral economy of the underprivileged (Wagner 2010, 80ff), or just follow a rational logic of profit maximization. Even ordinary people judge and deal with smuggling in quite different ways. At times, they are the customers of smugglers and purchase goods on black markets without a sense of guilt; at others, they consider smugglers criminals who endanger law and order. Seminal studies like Nugent's *Smugglers, Secessionists & Loyal Citizens on the Ghana–Togo Frontier: The Lie of the Borderlands since 1914* (2003) have shown that clear distinctions between the good and the bad are often misleading or part of self-legitimizing narratives. This applies, for example, to the distinction between the smuggler as a criminal and the morally superior ordinary citizen or to state authorities as representatives of law, order and justice. In practice, smugglers, soldiers, customs officers, policemen and the ordinary citizen are very much intertwined actors for whom smuggling is a field of economic cooperation, social arrangements and political strategies. Thus, the distinctions between legal and illegal or formal and informal economies have little relevance in the empirical study of smuggling and the real practice of borderland economies and beyond (Hüsken 2019, Gallien

DOI: 10.4324/9781003043645-6

2020). What smuggling is and what it is not seems to depend on the position or situation of the person, group, institution or regime defining it.

There is certainly no room for such ambivalence in the perspective of governments, international intervention regimes or the politics of migration control (van Schendel and Itty 2005, Raeymaekers 2014, Gaibazzi, Bellagamba, and Dünnwald 2017). Here, smuggling is discussed as a threat to state-centred definitions of sovereignty, territoriality and citizenship, and as the adversary of the formal economy. It is seen in the context of human trafficking across borders, as part of the transnational drug trade or the illicit trading of arms, or in relation to global jihadist terrorism. Smuggling has thus become a major object of the securitization policies (Scheele 2012, Amar 2013, Hüsken 2019) conducted by states, intelligence services, and military interventions. In the context of civil wars and the disintegration of nation states, non-state actors such as militias and organized crime networks also seek to control or appropriate transregional and cross-border trade routes and resource flows. In this context, borderland populations and their transgressive practices are exposed to state and non-state policies led by the imperative to control or suppress what is labelled as illegal or as unwanted connectivity. Likewise, researchers and their counterparts can become the objects of state and non-state repression, threat and violence simply by the fact of their interactions in the field.

When risk, safety, security and securitization become important issues in fieldwork, fundamental questions are raised about methodology, ethics and the integrity of academic knowledge production. This article tries to find answers to this complex issue. However, my contribution is neither intended as a research ethics guide, nor as a methodological toolbox. Instead, I try to review discourses and practices related to the notion of morality and research ethics in the study of smuggling and the social sciences. The article begins with a discussion of institutionalized ethics review boards as a means to ensure ethical compliance in research and academic knowledge production. It then proceeds with an exploration of the concept of an implicitly reciprocal and negotiated morality that develops through the interactions between researchers and their counterparts[4] in the field. This is followed by an examination of covert research practices that have emerged in the context of the securitization of fieldwork. The last section of the article then considers how risk can be anticipated by embedding research in local safety practices and the joint anticipation of risk as well as by methodical pluralism and every day diplomacy.[5]

Ethics review boards

Ethics review boards are a mandatory, albeit not undisputed practice in the social and cultural sciences of the anglophone world (Dingwall 2012).[6] Ethics review boards can be found in university departments, national academic associations, and national funding institutions or can exist as national committees. In the case of the United States, they are, for the time being at least, part of national legislation (Sleeboom-Faulkner et al. 2017). In addition, an increasing number of journals request evidence of ethics review as part of the submission process leading to publication. Here, ethical approval has come to act as a kitemark or official endorsement not only of the safety of the research method used in a particular piece of work, but also regarding the integrity and probity of the researcher. Boards and commissions made up of fellow scientists or academics from fields other than that of the researcher, and representatives responsible for gender, diversity, and ethics who likewise may be unfamiliar with the researcher's field or region of study, now play an important role in the process of approving or rejecting research projects.[7] The recent debate in Germany, Austria, and Switzerland reveals some of the controversial points related to this development. In an article published in 2017, the German medical anthropologist Hansjörg Dilger (2017, 192) argues that research ethics in German Social and Cultural Anthropology should no longer be characterized by an "voluntaristic and self-imposed muddling through." Instead, he argues for a professional and institutionalized ethics review process based on the internationally established norms documented in most of the ethics declarations of professional science associations such as the Association of Social Anthropologists of the UK (ASA),[8] the American Anthropological Association (AAA),[9] or the American Political Science Association (APSA).[10] The envisaged professionalization and standardization is understood as a proactive initiative to catch up with the natural sciences and clinical studies where institutionalized ethics review boards have been established since the beginning of the new millennium (Marshall 2003). At the same time however, the necessity to sensitize research-promoting institutions and ethics review committees to the special conditions of qualitative field research has been underlined. Furthermore, it has been noted that "qualitative researchers find it far more relevant to promote ethical reflexivity in teaching and research practice than to introduce ethics review boards" (von Unger, Dilger, and Schönhuth 2016, 1). It appears that the motivation of the authors is to find a balance between "doing anthropology ethically" and "doing ethics anthropologically." For now, the German Anthropological Association provides questionnaires such as a "reflection sheet"[11] (to be completed and peer reviewed in dialogue before fieldwork) and a so-called "risk analysis"[12] (to be completed before travel) for voluntary use and for self-assessment only. In addition, anthropologists have presented tutorials on research ethics for self-study or for use in workshops (Schönhuth 2021). Again, these tutorials are voluntary and do not deny researchers the right to make independent decisions.

It seems that the anglophone world has already passed through this process, albeit with different trajectories. While the administration of research ethics in the United States appears to be in the process of returning the responsibility for ethics review to the research professions and departments, Europe is increasingly institutionalizing and centralizing the issue of research ethics, thereby risking or accepting estrangement from the research professions. Not only leading funding programmes for research such as Horizon 2020 of the European Research Council (ERC), but also important national funding institutions like the German Research Association (DFG), require extensive and detailed information on research methodology, sex, gender and/or diversity, and ethics in project applications.[13] In addition, some countries of the global south have established national ethics review boards in order to safeguard the ethical conduct of (foreign) research.[14] In the case of Horizon 2020, the research ethics screening process includes an ethics self-assessment (in the proposal), an ethics review (two stages), and ethics checks and audits (during the project and up to two years afterwards if necessary).[15] Committees and science officers can reject research in regions that are not considered safe for empirical field research or withdraw approval if the security situation changes. They can also sanction unethical conduct (any conduct supposedly violating the ethical principles of the ERC) of the researcher in the course of the project.[16] While ethics review boards seem to be accepted in the natural sciences, they have received criticism in the social sciences and especially in social and cultural anthropology (Dingwall 2012, Sleeboom-Faulkner et al. 2017). The critique points out that ethics review processes are legalistic procedures that fail to address the processual, unforeseeable and often ambiguous character of fieldwork based on qualitative methodology. It is argued that the concept of ethics review boards assumes that "social science researchers control the research process and are in charge of the research situation, which is not the case in most qualitative, ethnographic research" (von Unger, Dilger, and Schönhuth 2016, 8).

A nonreflexive application of ethics screening along selective cultural, moral and legal standards can cause far-reaching ethical dilemmas for researchers. For instance, the guideline for "Ethics in Social Science and Humanities" by the ERC prescribes that criminal activity witnessed or uncovered in the course of research must be reported to the responsible and appropriate authorities, even if this means overriding commitments to participants to maintain confidentiality and anonymity.[17] Confidentiality and anonymity, however, are an indispensable part of the research ethics declarations of all professional associations in the social sciences. Thus, the policy of the ERC not only creates a moral dilemma for researchers but virtually generates unethical behaviour. In the case of my research in the borderland of Egypt and Libya this would have meant exposing my counterparts to the prosecution of the Egyptian and Libyan authorities, who consider most transgressive practices in the borderland as criminal. A similar critique has been directed at the principle of informed consent[18] in the social sciences. While informed consent is indispensable in medical science, it simply cannot be so easily applied in the social sciences and in research on smuggling. Not only is the researcher unable to anticipate with whom, for how long, to what end, and where they will work, but also people like smugglers (who are acting under the suspicious eye of states, services and organizations) will certainly not sign papers that reveal who they are and what they are doing.[19]

However, there is an even more fundamental problem. Ethics review boards are obliged to follow the security regulations (including travel restrictions) of state departments. The professional assessment of the researcher is not considered sufficient. If there is a travel warning from the respective foreign ministry, research trips will not be approved or only permitted under safety precautions that are difficult or impossible to meet for researchers. With a few exceptions, such as in the case of the DFG, which leaves the decision with the university and the respective scientists, this is true throughout Europe. As a result, an increasing number of researchers have stopped conducting research trips. Instead of ethical compliance, the uniform and formalized structure of such ethics reviewing provokes counter strategies by researchers. This can include the customization of rigid ethical principles and standard research models by stretching the meaning of planned activities to tick the right boxes (Sleeboom-Faulkner et al. 2017, 73). It can also mean, though, that the real practice of research is concealed in order to avoid a negative evaluation by the committee. Here, the strictness of the guidelines leads to actual unethical behaviour, namely the pretense of conforming, or concealment, as strategy and tactic. In practice, conflicts between researchers and ethics committees are frequent, and have led to a new form of mediation conducted by experts (often fellow researchers) who are commissioned to moderate between the two parties. In particular, the ethics screening and reporting in the course of a research project forces researchers to hide the ambiguities of the research practice and to translate them into a code that conforms with legalistic terms. The rendering of the ambiguities of research into bureaucratic and legal codes calls to mind what has been described as the "anti-politics machine" (Ferguson 1994) of development, where politics are rendered technical in order to process them within the framework of development cooperation. Instead of ethical compliance, a culture of "hidden transcripts and practices" (Scott 1990) is established that is not only an indication of the over-bureaucratization of science but also represents a culture of distrust.

Morality and ethics in the practice of fieldwork

The different ways of perceiving and defining smuggling – as a transgressive practice and culture of borderland populations or as an illegal or illicit action (see above) – highlight the fact that smuggling is a controversial and conflicted field of practices and worldviews (Hüsken 2019).

Research in dangerous fields

Thus, research on smuggling too contains epistemological, social, political and moral ambivalences and ambiguities for researchers and interlocutors alike. Because of this, a non-normative empirical approach based on the merits of cultural relativism as advocated by Franz Boas and many generations of anthropologists (King 2019) is the essential premise in the study of smuggling. In the sense of Meyer Fortes and E. E. Evans-Pritchard's introduction to their seminal volume *African Political Systems* (1940, 4), we should not ask ourselves how things ought to be done but direct our attention to the ways they are done by people. In other words, our interest must be the emic perspective and the lived practice of people. Thus, the adoption of normative epistemologies centred around statehood, formal economy, legalism and securitization do not make sense in our approach to smuggling and smugglers. As independent researchers, we need openness without prejudice paired with curiosity and empathy. However, even a non-normative approach does not free us from the ambivalences and ambiguities of smuggling as a practice and a field of study. Counterparts may be dangerous or endangered, malevolent or vulnerable. Practices and contexts can be shaped by risk, danger and securitization, or be surprisingly uncomplicated, ordinary and even officially tolerated. Within this fuzziness, called practice, researchers and counterparts alike are constantly making decisions that constitute the morality, the sociality and the politics of fieldwork. Because morality and ethical judgments can vary widely within and among cultures, societies, milieus, groups and individuals, this process is certainly complex. I agree with the German ethnologist Annette Hornbacher, who sees moral decisions in fieldwork as "responsible judgments in view of complex challenges and sometimes aporetic dilemmas, especially in transcultural practice" (Hornbacher 2017, 214). In my view, research ethics must be based on an implicitly reciprocal and negotiated morality that develops through the social interactions between researchers and counterparts, and cannot be delegated to a set of positive laws or normative rules imposed, monitored and safeguarded by specialists, for example, ethics review boards. This process can be complex, contradictory and conflictive, but is also an essential and indispensable part of research practice. In this context, ethics declarations and tutorials can certainly play an important role as a benchmark for compliant scientific work. Even here, however, we always must reflect carefully on their boundedness in certain cultural traditions and revisit their adequacy in the context of every piece of research.

Since the days of Bronislaw Malinowski (1884–1942),[20] the critical reflection of fieldwork as a complex social process with eminent moral issues has been part of the identity of cultural and social anthropology. The alleged scandal in connection with the posthumous publication of his diaries in 1967 does not contradict this but rather confirms this thesis (Malinowski 1967). The debate about the crisis of ethnographic representation (also known as the writing culture debate) initiated by Clifford and Marcus (1986) was certainly another important step in the critical self-reflection of the discipline and its methodology. More recently, colonial and postcolonial studies and queer and critical race theory have produced a growing body of literature that engages with the critical revision of existing hegemonies in academic knowledge production (Ashcroft, Griffiths, and Tiffin 2013). In this context, fieldwork and participant observation are examined and critically reviewed, and authors and activists call for a fundamental moral, ethical, methodological and political revision of all aspects of fieldwork which goes beyond the established ethics declarations of professional science associations.[21] All this has certainly broadened our perspective; however, as Lewis (2014) has argued, the debate has left little room for contributions that do not deal with criticism and deconstruction. The focus on alleged hegemonic power structures (mostly defined as white, male, heteronormative, or Western) and their impact on academic knowledge production obscures the actual polycentricity of power relations in research practice. In this practice, the relationships between the strong and the weak, the powerful and the powerless, the vulnerable and the malevolent, the good or the bad, or the right or the wrong, are complex, multilayered and dynamic. Within this complexity, the vulnerability of researchers and counterparts is certainly an important aspect, but is one which is always accompanied (if not counteracted) by agency and resilience.

If we instead leave the negotiation of morality and research ethics where it belongs, namely in the hands of the principal actors involved (researchers and their counterparts), we therefore need to discuss the elements involved in this negotiation process. Almost every introduction to anthropological fieldwork emphasizes the necessity of trust and empathy as significant resources, and in fact these are the basis of all social interaction in ethnographic research, particularly participant observation and in-depth interviewing. In classical ethnographic fieldwork carried out over a one-year period, or through repeated research over longer periods (Spittler 2014), researchers and their counterparts can begin an interpersonal dialogue or negotiation about the good in (their) human practice, which is what ethics as a theoretical consideration about morality is actually about. Ideally, this dialogical negotiation opens the way for the social and moral contextualization of the research among reliable local partners and the gradual development of stable relationships with key informants based on shared and mutually practised (moral) principles such as confidentiality, accountability and trust (Hüsken 2019, 22ff). Together, they form what has been called the "ethics of reciprocity" (Schönhuth 2021, 50). As anthropologists, we know that this process is fundamental to how and what kind of knowledge is gained.

However, this is only an ideal model, and I do not wish to advocate a false romanticization of ethnographic fieldwork here. Fieldwork and participant observation are only in retrospect a coherent endeavour. In fact, fieldwork can be an experience of unpredictability and insecurity. The negotiation of a shared morality can therefore be controversial, and there is no guarantee of its success. However, ethical judgements and decisions are an expression and a consequence of human freedom, reason and responsibility. This includes decisions that involve risk and safety. Commissions, screenings and ever new rules can neither anticipate nor replace this process. Again, we must leave these decisions in the hands of the researchers and their interaction partners in the field, accepting the possibility of success or also failure. If questions of morality and ethics have to be lived through anew in every research project, then we must expect an honest and transparent disclosure of this process. Although most colleagues involved in the study of smuggling underline that ethnographic fieldwork has been the foundation of their empirical work, we hear relatively little about what this actually meant in detail and almost nothing about moral and ethical challenges. With the promotion of ethical reflexivity in teaching and research practice we can respond to critique without falling into forms of postmodern hyper-reflexivity. Instead of a critical philosophy of science (much needed in other contexts), we should stick to the pragmatism of empirical studies. If there is a paradigm to follow, then I would suggest Robert Chambers' words about the merits and pitfalls of empirical research: "Start, stumble, fall, stand up and use your own best judgement at all times" (quoted by Schönhuth (2021, 106).

Hidden practices and the securitization of fieldwork

The issues of risk, safety and security in fieldwork are now the subject of broad discussion across the social and cultural sciences. With regard to the Middle East and North Africa, some authors argue that recent political developments have turned the region into "no countries for anthropologists"[22] where (ethnographic) fieldwork on the ground is hindered, prohibited and threatened. The detention of researchers by security apparatuses – albeit not a new

Research in dangerous fields

phenomenon – is becoming more common and can be lethal, as the tragic case of Giulio Regeni, a doctoral student at the University of Cambridge shows.[23] The empirical study of smuggling has so far been spared such tragedy. In some border regions of Tunisia, even border officials talk unreservedly about their involvement in formalized smuggling systems with fixed tariffs and conflict resolution mechanisms. In the Libyan region of Fezzan however, any open conversation on illegal transborder trade (such as human trafficking and slave markets close to the border) can cause severe safety issues (including persecution by organized crime networks and militias) for researchers and their counterparts alike (reported by an Algerian historian and ethnologist working in Fezzan who wishes to remain anonymous). Other examples of such issues include the experience of German ethnologist Georg Klute, who during his field studies in Guinea-Bissau in 2010, recognized Italian mafia gangsters (engaged in drug trafficking) in the streets and restaurants of Bissau. His local counterparts strongly advised him to avoid any contact (including eye contact) with these actors due to safety issues. An American colleague, who wishes to remain anonymous here, has also been under United States police surveillance since his research on the United States–Mexico border, while colleagues working in the border area of China and Central Asian states report systematic surveillance by Chinese authorities.

In a conference contribution in Zürich in 2018,[24] David Shankland, Director of the Royal Anthropological Institute, reported about his own experience of vulnerability when he was abducted by drug smugglers in Morocco. According to Shankland, the current situation and developments require researchers to develop strategies and tactics of protection. As a consequence of increased security risks in recent years, social science departments may either prevent researchers from going to unstable areas or introduce security protocols similar to the ones deployed by humanitarian organizations to protect their staff. This would restrain the researcher's movements and require regular contact with local security services, and might impede the ability of researchers to participate in everyday life (Akcinar et al. 2018, 38). These developments are, albeit to different degrees, not exclusive to the African continent or the Middle East. The securitization of fieldwork on smuggling also takes place regarding the borderlands of Russia, central Asia and China (Ibañez-Tirado and Marsden 2020). Meanwhile, the issues of the possible risk involved for and the potential vulnerability of counterparts have been addressed by David Spener (2009) in his book *Clandestine Crossings: Migrants and Coyotes on the Texas-Mexico Border.*

Despite the debate and the obvious relevance of the topic, only some authors reveal the related methodological and ethical problems of their research. This has to do in no small part with the difficult role of the ethical review processes discussed above. Another reason for this may also be the fact that disclosing problems or even failure in the research process is not very conducive to a successful academic career at a time when the publish or perish paradigm applies more than ever. Instead, a hidden securitization of research practices has emerged, that is again seldomly openly discussed. In a recent publication, Peter and Strazzari (2017) have taken the important and commendable step of ensuring more transparency in this field. Based on research experience in Mali and Darfur, they uncover the ongoing securitization of fieldwork in so-called "zones of danger." Securitization is understood in two ways: "research is increasingly framed as a security concern; and it is framed by security concerns. In both cases, extraordinary means and procedures are invoked in the name of security" (Peter and Strazzari 2017, 2).[25] Thus, researchers who deal with sensitive issues or contested fields receive special attention from state, military, intelligence, development, and non-state actors (Hüsken 2019, 20ff). By defining and securitizing zones of danger, these actors can approve or deny access as well as influence researchers and research (Peter and Strazzari 2017, 3). In this respect, zones of danger are a direct result of securitization and differ from the notion of dangerous fields put forward by

Kovats-Bernat (2002). Peter and Strazzari identify three emerging practices that have significant consequences for research and academic knowledge production: remotely managed research; the outsourcing of logistics and fixers; and embedded research (Peter and Strazzari 2017, 7–8). The following considerations take their contribution as a reference point for further discussion.

The practice of remotely managed research is based on the contracting of local researchers to gain access to dangerous areas and to circumvent travel restrictions. These local researchers are used for data acquisition and processing, and often only receive a limited amount of research training from the principal researchers. In such a practice, the principal researcher never personally experiences the context he is studying. The local researchers are often graduate students, local activists, local non-governmental organizations (NGOs), or development employees. Their participation in research can be an attractively paid service, but their work usually does not allow them to further pursue an academic career (as in the case of a doctoral student who carries out fieldwork for a collaborative research project), nor is it recognized as an independent academic contribution. When empirical research and contact and interaction with counterparts rests on the shoulders of often only superficially trained research assistants, questions are raised not only about the quality and reliability of information gathered but also, and even more so, concerning the academic knowledge production based on it. In addition, the local team and its interlocutors are the people ultimately potentially placed at risk. In the study of smuggling in warzones such as Fezzan in Libya, this practice is well established within think tanks, among journalists and in development agencies. However, the local researchers involved are seldom mentioned in publications; instead, the principal researcher appears as the genuine author and expert. Equally ambivalent is the fact that field research of longer durations in zones of danger[26] relies to a great extent on professional researchers of local or regional origin. These researchers are not research assistants but fellow academics. Their local belonging and regional ties, language and cultural skills often allow them to circumvent travel restrictions and access the field. However, their research is dangerous and often only possible as undercover research or on the basis of pure observation. Nevertheless, their contributions flow (often anonymized for security reasons) into the publications of Western scholars who can afford to publish openly. This practice delegates risk to a group of academics who are already politically and financially precarious. Furthermore, it enhances the asymmetries and unequal relations between Western and non-Western academic production on the global south, in which the latter has been and continues to be underrated and overlooked or serves as the provider of local collaborators for Western researchers.

Remotely managed research has also increased through the digitalization of communication via social media and the internet. Digital ethnography relies (among other things) on content analysis of social media or blogs, mobile phone communication, and online focus and discussion groups, and is undoubtedly an important field of study (Pink et al. 2015). However, digital discursive and performative practices are not necessarily congruent with the non-digital lived practice of people. Emerging research techniques such as the real-time interviewing of local interlocutors or experts via social media and video tools (Peterson 2015) that are integrated into workshops or conferences evoke a questionable representation of reality. In the video stream, local interlocutors (similar to the old-school live reporting of war reporters in television) seem to report directly from research sites where professional researchers cannot go. Reality, it seems, is streamed in real time into the office, meeting or conference room. Although the professional researcher or the academic participants of workshops and conferences are not able to contextualize who these speakers actually are and with what kind of authority they speak, these informants are nevertheless treated as authentic representatives of the real issues on the ground.[27] In addition, encounters in digital spaces are far from safe. The digital surveillance

Research in dangerous fields

techniques (tracking) of intelligence services can expose local experts and interlocutors to persecution when they speak about sensitive issues.[28] Thus this variant of remotely managed research may protect the professional researcher but not necessarily their counterparts.

In the second practice identified by Peter and Strazzari[29] – outsourcing of logistics and fixers – fixer agencies provide services to the researcher such as transport and accommodation, guides, translation and interpretation, and research assistance (see above). In 2005, Robert Fisk used the term hotel journalism[30] to criticize international journalists in Iraq who instead of doing independent research, wrote reports based solely on the services of fixers and research assistants. The role of fixers and research assistants in academic research and knowledge production is still a blind spot and unclear to the academic and broader audience. It marks, however, the shift from independent research based on fieldwork among real people and in concrete localities, towards a commodification of information in a market of knowledge brokers. In countries that are experiencing intense conflict or civil wars (such as Libya), individual brokers or broker networks (often in the institutional form of think tanks or NGOs) have developed into a major source for academic knowledge production. Information and knowledge brokers can be committed to science, they may have purely monetary interests, or deliver knowledge according to particular political goals. All three motives are unfortunately seldom openly reflected by researchers, who nevertheless claim to have authentic information.

In the third practice Peter and Strazzari identify – embedded research – the researcher participates (or is employed) in military operations and international intervention regimes, cooperates with intelligence services, or gains access to zones of danger by benefiting from the security architecture of an international organization. This practice is undoubtedly the one most disputed in the social sciences. This is particularly true for the Human Terrain System (HTS), a United States Army support programme employing personnel from the social sciences, for example, anthropology, sociology, political science, regional studies and linguistics, to provide military commanders with an understanding of the local population in Iraq and Afghanistan. In 2007, the Executive Board of the American Anthropological Association (AAA) published a statement opposing HTS as an unacceptable application of anthropological expertise that conflicted with the AAA's Code of Ethics.[31] Most anthropological associations around the world follow the AAA's Code of Ethics.[32] In addition, social scientists who officially work for the military have been challenged by critical academic and public debates (Lucas 2008). Some have nevertheless become official parts of the military apparatus and its related institutions (Haugegaard 2020). A more hidden reality of embedded research occurs with regard to the role of intelligence services. All over the world, intelligence services pursue an active recruitment policy which focusses on researchers who work in danger and conflict zones or deal with illicit practices such as smuggling. Intelligence services offer concrete advantages such as payment, visas and travel permits, and technical equipment to their academic collaborators, but they may also appeal to the civic duties of researchers as loyal citizens to convince scientists to collaborate.[33] Due to the secrecy policies of intelligence services and the lack of transparency among academics, it is difficult to say how many researchers are involved in these practices and how their academic work is affected by this form of embeddedness. In any case, involvement with intelligence services draws science into the logics of spying and secrecy, which makes an open and trusting collaboration between researchers and counterparts impossible. A much more common form of embedded (or assisted) research in zones of danger takes place in the context of international organizations, peace missions, and development cooperation. International organizations can provide security, and can also facilitate access to the field or even offer the opportunity to conduct fieldwork in the context of the security architecture of an international organization. However, embeddedness and involvement come with consequences that can compromise research. Interlocutors and local populations may identify the researcher with the respective international organization. Thus, the interaction between researcher and counterparts can take the form of a donor–beneficiary relationship that clearly differs from a relationship based on reciprocal learning and exchange. Just as local populations may identify the researcher with an international organization, the researcher too may adopt the normative perspective and the organizational interests of the security provider.[34] A particular case is the ensuring of security for researchers by regional or local security forces. These forces may belong to the state, but they can also be local militias or vigilante groups. Here, the researcher can become entangled in conflict formation and dynamics (Kovats-Bernat 2002) that are difficult to anticipate and may affect his position as an independent researcher.

Based on my own research experiences in Libya and the research for this article, the practices described are currently increasing.[35] They are thus the effects of the global trend of securitization inscribed in independent research. This is certainly a worrying prospect. However, there may still be valid ways out of securitization. In the concluding section, I would like to explore these.

Hic sunt leones! Sed autem socii!

The seminal volume *Fieldwork under Fire*, edited by Nordstrom and Robben (1996), discusses the effects that violence, threat and confrontation with suffering can have on researchers and research. At the same time, it exemplifies how local populations organize normality in war or in risk-filled and violent circumstances. The empirical cases show how agency, resilience and inventiveness confront and overcome vulnerability. This does not mean that vulnerability disappears or no longer needs to be addressed, but the cases nevertheless help us not to overvalue it. All over the world, the populations of borderlands are showing remarkable resilience to state-orchestrated policies of control or to the threat of non-state actors such as organized crime networks or militias. These populations assert historical cross-border connectivities and use them in productive ways, even in difficult times (Scheele 2009; Feyissa and Hoehne 2010; Korf and Raeymaekers 2013, Hüsken 2019). Researchers can benefit from these experiences and skills if they achieve local acceptance and, ideally, are able to embed their research in local safety practices. In a recent article, Henig, Marsden, and Ibañez-Tirado (2016) have highlighted skilled forms of "everyday diplomacy" which distinguish local populations in their capacity to handle challenges (such as securitization). This is in my experience particularly true for the provision of safety in insecure fields of action such as borderlands. From mid-2012 on, my own research in the borderland of Libya and Egypt was confronted with criticism, avoidance and then also with threats by radical Islamist groups. I was stopped, held and interrogated at militia checkpoints several times. In 2018, I spend two weeks doing research in Tobruk with my passport held at Tobruk airport by local tribal security personnel. However, I could always rely on the safety networks of my counterparts – not only those of local politicians, entrepreneurs, and tribal leaders, but also those offered to me by ordinary people. Based on their local knowledge and learned competency, these counterparts either prepared me for problems, showed me limits, or solved precarious situations pragmatically and competently. Even more valuable than this was the fact that the awareness and joint anticipation of risk and potential vulnerability proved a key element in relationships of trust and reciprocal solidarity (Hüsken 2019, 15ff). Thus, the researcher can find allies even when there are lions around. Embedding research in local assessments of risk and local safety practices can be a way out of the "security archipelago" (Amar 2013) created by the regimes of securitization described above. Of course, this form of embedding and the safety that comes with it only succeeds via repeated research over longer periods. It also requires courage (including the courage to accept and admit failure) and the willingness to engage in thick participation.[36]

However, I do not wish to downplay risk, nor do I intend to glorify or romanticize research in dangerous fields. Risk requires safety precautions, methodological pluralism and a particular form of everyday diplomacy. Useful and pragmatic guidelines for safety precautions in dangerous fields have been provided by a number of authors (Kovats-Bernat 2002, Goldstein 2014) and these need not be repeated here. It goes without saying that methodological pluralism is a potent remedy in difficult research fields. The methodological developments and advances of the last few decades offer an almost inexhaustible reservoir of possibilities, which is exemplified in many textbooks (Iphofen and Tolic 2018). Multi-sited ethnography (Marcus 1995), tandem and team research (Lecocq et al. 2013; Schlehe and Hidayah 2014), indirect questioning, pure observation, choosing neutral places for conversation, etc., have great potential for the study of smuggling. In addition, online tutorials (Schönhuth 2021) include checklists and self-tests on assessing risks, methods, and research ethics.

In dangerous fields, and even more so in securitized zones of danger, the researcher enters a complex field of relationships, negotiations, compromises, and research adaptation that can be anticipated only partly by the above-mentioned prescriptions. Here, researchers need to develop a particular form of everyday diplomacy in order to cope with these challenges. Caution, a realistic assessment of the possibilities and limits of research (involving local expertise), and a critical reflection of the possible consequences of one's own actions for others must be the basis for responsible diplomatic judgements and practices. This refers to ways of coping, avoiding, or cooperating with international organizations and the military, and includes negotiations and forms of coexistence with border authorities (Spener 2009, 1ff). It also requires careful tactical distance (including exit options) from violent groups such as militias or organized crime networks and other potentially harmful counterparts in the field; last but not least, it concerns our responsibility for our counterparts in the field.

The everyday diplomacy of fieldwork, however, must allow for tactical behaviour on the part of researchers too, as long as they do not compromise the ethical principles laid out in the declarations of our associations. In an earlier publication, I have suggested the notion of discretion (Hüsken 2019, 18ff) as a way to cope with the challenges of research in times of turmoil in Libya. In the novel *The King David Report* by the German writer Stefan Heym (1973), a historian assigned by King Solomon to write the official history of King David is confronted with the complex process of writing a political history. In order to protect himself and his work, he develops the concept of "discretion" and defines it as "truth domesticated by wisdom" (94). I believe that for any researcher confronted with risk or actors who try to compromise the freedom of academic research, a practice of discretion is necessary and legitimate.

I agree with Peter and Strazzari that whenever access to people and areas is determined by policies and practices of securitization, we as researchers must pay particular attention to methodological transparency and ethical reflexivity. Only by revealing the limitations and dilemmas of our research can we improve the quality of our scholarship and enhance the actual security of researchers travelling to zones of danger. When we disclose and share the conditions, processes, and practices of research and knowledge production without omitting the difficulties, ambiguities and dilemmas, we are doing what we ought to do: good science.

Notes

1 See Oxford Learner's Dictionaries, Oxford University Press, last modified 2018, http://www.oxfordlearnersdictionaries.com/definition/english/smuggling.

2 See Duden, Verlags Bibliographisches Institut GmbH, last modified 2018, http://www.duden.de/rechtschreibung/schmuggeln.

3 For example, this is true for the prohibition of the production, sale and transportation of alcoholic beverages in the United States between 1920 and 1933.

4 With the term "counterparts" I refer not only to informants, interlocutors, associates, collaborators, consultants, hosts and friends, but also to wider networks of relationships.

5 Empirically, this article is based on my own research in the borderland of Egypt and Libya (Hüsken 2019: 13ff). In addition, in 2020 and 2021, I conducted 18 conversations (open talks on the issue of research ethics) with fellow researchers, experts (i.e., members of think tanks and development organizations), journalists, and other interlocutors (such as local politicians), from Egypt, Germany, Libya, Mali, Tunisia, the United Kingdom, and the United States. I have integrated some sections from Hüsken 2019. All of these sections have been partly rewritten and adjusted for this article. I would like to thank Daniel Rolph for copy-editing this article.

6 See https://www.theasa.org/ethics/ethnav/nine.

7 See https://www.theasa.org/ethics/ethnav/seven.phtml.

8 See https://www.theasa.org/ethics/guidelines.html.

9 See http://ethics.americananthro.org/category/statement/.

10 See https://www.apsanet.org/TEACHING/Ethics.

11 See https://en.dgska.de/wp-content/uploads/2020/04/GAA_Research-Ethics-Reflection-Sheet.pdf.

12 See https://en.dgska.de/wp-content/uploads/2020/04/GAA_Risk-Assessment-Sheet.pdf.

13 The importance of research ethics for the DFG can be measured by the fact that it exceeds the scientific part of the application. See https://www.dfg.de/formulare/54_01/54_01_en.pdf.

14 In practice, these boards (for instance, in the case of Rwanda) are also used to prevent politically unwelcome research.

15 See https://ec.europa.eu/research/participants/docs/h2020-funding-guide/grants/from-evaluation-to-grant-signature/grant-preparation/ethics_review_en.htm.

16 In the recent case of an approved project on Mauritania, fieldwork was limited to such an extent that qualitative empirical research in the country became impossible. (Information given by a fellow researcher who wishes to remain anonymous).

17 See https://ec.europa.eu/info/sites/info/files/6._h2020_ethics-soc-science-humanities_en.pdf.

18 In medical science, informed consent is a process for obtaining permission (in the form of a written statement) before conducting a healthcare intervention on a person, for conducting some form of research on a person, or for disclosing a person's medical information.

19 For a more detailed discussion on informant consent, see the following blog by Carmen Delgado: https://interpreting-ideas.com/2017/09/.

20 Bronislaw Malinowski was an anthropologist whose writings on ethnography, social theory, and field research have had a lasting influence on the discipline of anthropology.

21 See Schramm 2005, Rooke 2009, Faria and Mollett 2016, and Hanson and Richards 2019.

22 Adapted from the title of the international conference: No country for anthropologists? Contemporary ethnographic research in the Middle East, University of Zürich, November 2018.

23 On 25 January 2016, the anniversary of the Egyptian revolution, Giulio Regeni, a 28-year-old Italian PhD student at the University of Cambridge and visiting scholar at the American University in Cairo (AUC) was kidnapped in the Egyptian capital. Regeni was conducting participant observation on informal trade unions opposing the post-2013 regime. On 3 February 2016, Regeni's corpse was found beside the Cairo–Alexandria desert highway, displaying clear signs of torture.

24 At the international conference: No country for anthropologists? Contemporary ethnographic research in the Middle East, University of Zürich, November 2018 (Akcinar et al. 2018).

25 See also Buzan, Wæver, and De Wilde 1998.

26 Based on my research, this is particularly the case in Northern Mali, Northern Niger, Chad, Sudan, and the Libyan region of Fezzan.

27 I personally witnessed this practice in several international workshops dealing with Libya. In addition, a large proportion of recent publications about Libya are based almost exclusively on survey techniques via the internet or mobile telephone.

28 For some time now, my Egyptian and Libyan counterparts have preferred not to talk about sensitive issues via social media at all.

29 In the original text, this is practice number three. For the sake of clarity, I have treated it as the second one here.

Research in dangerous fields

30 See https://www.independent.co.uk/news/long_reads/robert-fisk-iraq-hotel-journalism-baghdad-b1
639391.html.
31 See https://www.americananthro.org/ConnectWithAAA/Content.aspx?ItemNumber=1952.
32 See paragraph 6 in the Code of Ethics of the AAA: "Responsibilities to one's own government and to host
governments" states that "no secret research, no secret reports or debriefings of any kind should be agreed to
or given." http://www.americananthro.org/ParticipateAndAdvocate/Content.aspx?ItemNumber=1656.
33 See Hüsken 2019, 20.
34 See Hüsken and Klute 2015, 321.
35 Peter and Strazzari (2017, 16) do not seem too optimistic about transparency in this field when they
state "that the trend within the social sciences seems to be in the opposite direction."
36 Thick participation involves training and practice, the complementarity of observation and questioning, and the involvement and productive use of all the senses: listening and watching, touching,
smelling and tasting, and physical and mental feeling (Spittler 2014, 213).

References

Akcinar, Mustafa, Daniele Cantini, Aymon Kreil, Shirin Naef, and Emanuel Schaeublin. 2018.
"Conference Report: No Country for Anthropologists? Ethnographic Research in the Contemporary
Middle East." *Bulletin de la Société Suisse Moyen Orient et Civilisation Islamique* 47: 33–36.
Amar, Paul. 2013. *The Security Archipelago: Human-Security States, Sexuality Politics, and the End of
Neoliberalism.* Durham, NC: Duke University Press.
Ashcroft, B., G. Griffiths, and H. Tiffin. 2013. *Post-Colonial Studies: The Key Concepts.* 3rd ed. London:
Routledge. doi: 10.4324/978023777855.
Brenneis, D. 2005. "Documenting Ethics." In *Embedding Ethics*, edited by L. Meskell and P. Pels,
239–252. Oxford: Berg, Wenner-Gren Foundation.
Buzan, Barry, Ole Wæver, and Jaap De Wilde. 1998. *Security: A New Framework for Analysis.* Boulder, CO:
Lynne Rienner.
Christensen, Maya M., and Rikke Haugegaard. 2017. *Connecting Culture: A Handbook on Cultural Analysis
in Military Planning.* Copenhagen: Royal Danish Defence College.
Clifford, James, and George E. Marcus. 1986. *Writing Culture. The Poetics and Politics of Ethnography.*
Berkeley: University of California.
Dilger, Hansjörg. 2017. "Ethics, Epistemology, and Ethnography: the Need for an Anthropological
Debate on Ethical Review Processes in Germany." *Sociologus* 67(2): 191–208.
Dingwall, Robert. 2012. "How Did We Ever Get into this Mess? The Rise of Ethical Regulation in the
Social Sciences." In *Ethics in Social Research. Vol. 12 of Studies in Qualitative Methodology*, edited by
Kevin Love, 3–26. Bingley: Emerald Group Publishing Limited.
Faria Caroline, and Sharlene Mollett. 2016. "Critical Feminist Reflexivity and the Politics of Whiteness in
the 'Field'." *Gender, Place & Culture* 23(1): 79–93. doi:10.1080/0966369X.2014.958065.
Fassin, Didier. 2006. "The End of Ethnography as Collateral Damage of Ethical Regulation?" *American
Ethnologist* 33: 522–524.
Ferguson, James. 1994. "The Anti-Politics Machine. Development and Bureaucratic Power in Lesotho."
The Ecologist 24(5): 176–181.
Feyissa, Dereje, and Markus Hoehne, eds. 2010. *Borders and Borderlands as Resources in the Horn of Africa.*
Woodbridge: James Currey.
Fortes, Meyer, and Edward E. Evans-Pritchard. 1940. *African Political Systems.* New York/Oxford: Oxford
University Press.
Gaibazzi, Paolo, Alice Bellagamba, and Stephan Dünnwald, eds. 2017. *EurAfrican Borders and Migration
Management. Political Cultures, Contested Spaces, and Ordinary Lives.* New York: Palgrave Macmillan.
Gallien, M. 2020. "Informal Institutions and the Regulation of Smuggling in North Africa." *Perspectives on
Politics* 18(2): 492–508.
Girtler, Roland. 2006. *Abenteuer Grenze. Von Schmugglern und Schmugglerinnen, Ritualen und heiligen
Räumen.* Vienna: Lit-Verlag.
Goldstein, Daniel M. 2014. Qualitative Research in Dangerous Places: Becoming an "Ethnographer" of
Violence and Personal Safety. DSD Working Papers on Research Security: No. 1. Drugs, Security and
Democracy Program, Social Science Research Council, Brooklyn.

Hanson, Rebecca, and Patricia Richards. 2019. *Harassed. Gender, Bodies, and Ethnographic Research.* Berkeley: University of California Press.

Haugegaard, R. 2020. "Culture as Operational Enabler: Training Danish Officers to Understand the Interaction Between Cultural Dynamics and Military Operations." In *Warriors or Peacekeepers?*, edited by Kjetil Enstad, and Paula Holmes-Eber, 97–116. Cham: Springer. doi:10.1007/978-3-030-3 6766-4_7.

Hedgecoe, Adam. 2009. "A Form of Practical Machinery": The Origins of Research Ethics Committees in the UK, 1967–1972." *Medical History* 53(3): 331–350.

Henig, David, Magnus Marsden, and Diana Ibañez-Tirado. 2016. "Everyday Diplomacy: Insights from Ethnography." *The Cambridge Journal of Anthropology* 34(2): 2–22.

Heym, Stefan. 1973. *The King David Report.* New York: G. P. Putnam's Sons.

Hornbacher, Annette. 2017. Comment to the Contribution by Hansjörg Dilger. *Sociologus* 67(2): 213–218.

Hüsken, Thomas. 2019. *Tribal Politics in the Borderland of Egypt and Libya.* Palgrave Series in African Borderland Studies. New York: Palgrave Macmillan. doi:10.1007/978-3-319-92342-0

Hüsken, Thomas, and Georg Klute. 2015. "Political Orders in the Making: Emerging Forms of Political Organization from Libya to Northern Mali." *African Security* 8(4): 320–337.

Ibañez-Tirado, Diana, and Magnus Marsden. 2020. "Trade 'Outside the Law': Uzbek and Afghan Transnational Merchants between Yiwu and South-Central Asia." *Central Asian Survey* 39(1): 135–154. doi:10.1080/02634937.2020.1716687.

Iphofen, Ron, and Martin Tolic. 2018. *The SAGE Handbook of Qualitative Research Ethics.* New York: Sage Publishing.

King, Charles. 2019. *Gods of the Upper Air. How a Circle of Renegade Anthropologists Remade Race, Sex, and Gender in the Twentieth Century.* New York: Doubleday.

Korf, Benedikt, and Timothy Raeymaekers. 2013. "Introduction: Border, Frontier and the Geography of Rule at the Margins of the State." In *Violence on the Margins. States, Conflict, and Borderlands*, edited by Benedikt Korf, and Timothy Raeymaekers, 3–28. New York: Palgrave Macmillan.

Kovats-Bernat, Christopher J. 2002. "Negotiating Dangerous Fields. Pragmatic Strategies for Fieldwork amid Violence and Terror." *American Anthropologist* 104(1): 208–222.

Lecocq, Baz, Gregory Mann, Bruce Whitehouse, Dida Badi, Lotte Pelckmans, Nadia Belalimat, Bruce Hall, and Wolfram Lacher. 2013. "One Hippopotamus and Eight Blind Analysts: A Multivocal Analysis of the 2012 Political Crisis in the Divided Republic of Mali." *Review of African Political Economy* 40(137): 343–357.

Lederman, Rena. 2006. Introduction: "Anxious Borders between Work and Life in a Time of Bureaucratic Ethics Regulation." *American Ethnologist* 33(4): 477–481.

Lewis, Herbert S. 2014. *In Defense of Anthropology: An Investigation of the Critique of Anthropology.* New Brunswick: Transaction Publishers.

Lucas, George R. 2008. "The Morality of 'Military Anthropology'." *Journal of Military Ethics* 7(3): 165–185. doi:10.1080/15027570802376144.

Malik, Adeel, and Max Gallien. 2020. "Border Economies of the Middle East: Why Do They Matter for Political Economy?" *Review of International Political Economy* 27(3): 732–762.

Malinowski, Bronislaw. 1967. *A Diary in the Strict Sense of the Term.* Stanford: Stanford University Press.

Marcus, George E. 1995. "Ethnography in/of the World System: The Emergence of Multi-Sited Ethnography." *Annual Review of Anthropology* 24: 95–117.

Marshall, Patricia A. 2003. "Human Subjects Protections, Institutional Review Boards, and Cultural Anthropological Research." *Anthropological Quarterly* 6(2): 269–285. www.jstor.org/stable/3318401.

Nordstrom, Carolyn, and Antonius C. G. M. Robben, eds. 1996. *Fieldwork Under Fire: Contemporary Studies of Violence and Survival.* Berkeley: University of California Press.

Nugent, Paul. 2003. *Smugglers, Secessionists and Loyal Citizens on the Ghana–Togo Frontier: The Lie of the Borderlands since 1914.* Athens: Ohio University Press.

Peter, Mateja, and Francesco Strazzari. 2017. "Securitisation of Research: Fieldwork under New Restrictions in Darfur and Mali." *Third World Quarterly* 38(7): 1531–1550. doi:10.1080/01436597.201 6.1256766.

Peterson, Mark Allen. 2015. "New Media and Electronic Networks." In *A Companion to the Anthropology of the Middle East*, edited by Soraya Altorki, 509–525. Chichester: John Wiley & Sons.

Pink, Sarah, John Postill, Larissa Hjorth, Heather A. Horst, Jo Tacci, and Tania Lewis. 2015. *Digital Ethnography, Principal and Practice.* Los Angeles: Sage.

Raeymaekers, Timothy 2014. "Introduction Europe's Bleeding Border and the Mediterranean as a Relational Space." *ACME: An International Journal for Critical Geographies* 13(2): 163–172.

Rooke, Alison. 2009. "Queer in the Field: On Emotions, Temporality, and Performativity in Ethnography." *Journal of Lesbian Studies* 13(2): 149–160. doi:10.1080/10894160802695338.

Scheele, Judith. 2009. Tribus, États et fraude: la région frontalière Algéro-Malienne. In *La tribu à l'heure de la globalisation*. *Études rurales* 184: 79–93.

Scheele, Judith. 2012. "Saharan Connectivity in Al-Khalīl, Northern Mali." In *Saharan Frontiers: Space and Mobility in Northwest Africa*, edited by James MacDougall, and Judith Scheele, 222–237. Bloomington/Indianapolis: Indiana University Press.

van Schendel, Willem, and Abraham Itty. 2005. *Illicit Flows and Criminal Things: States, Borders, and the Other Side of Globalization*. Bloomington: Indiana University Press.

Schlehe, Judith, and Sita Hidayah. 2014. "Transcultural Ethnography: Reciprocity in Indonesian-German Tandem Research." In *Methodology and Research Practice in Southeast Asian Studies*, edited by Mikko Huotari, Jürgen Rüland, and Judith Schlehe, 253–272. Houndmills: Palgrave Macmillan.

Schönhuth, Michael. 2021. *Ethics in Ethnographic Fieldwork: A tutorial for self-study and workshops*. Trier: University of Trier.

Schramm, Katharina. 2005. "You Have Your Own History: Keep Your Hands off Ours! On Being Rejected in the Field." *Social Anthropology* 13(2): 171–183.

Scott, James C. 1990. *Domination and the Arts of Resistance. Hidden Transcripts*. New Haven/London: Yale University Press.

Shweder, Richard A. 2006. "Protecting Human Subjects and Preserving Academic Freedom: Prospects at the University of Chicago." *American Ethnologist* 33(4): 507–518.

Sleeboom-Faulkner, Margaret, Bob Simpson, Elena Burgos-Martinez, and James McMurray. 2017. "The Formalization of Social-Science Research Ethics: How Did We Get There?" *Hau: Journal of Ethnographic Theory* 7(1): 71–79.

Spener, David. 2009. *Clandestine Crossings: Migrants and Coyotes on the Texas-Mexico Border*. Ithaca, NY: Cornell University Press.

Spittler, Gerd. 2001. Teilnehmende Beobachtung als Dichte Teilnahme. *Zeitschrift für Ethnologie* 126: 1–25.

Spittler, Gerd. 2014. Dichte Teilnahme und darüber hinaus. *Sociologus* 64(2): 207–230.

von Unger, Hella, Hansjörg Dilger, and Michael Schönhuth. 2016. "Ethics Reviews in the Social and Cultural Sciences? A Sociological and Anthropological Contribution to the Debate." *Forum Qualitative Sozialforschung/Forum: Qualitative Social Research* 17(3), Art. 20. http://nbn-resolving.de/urn:nbn:de:0114-fqs1603203

Wagner, Mathias. 2010. Die moralische Ökonomie des Schmuggels. In *Alltag im Grenzland. Schmuggel als ökonomische Strategie im Osten Europas*, edited by Mathias Wagner, and Wojciech Lukowski, 73–89. Wiesbaden: VS Verlag.

PART II

Borderlands and their people

7
MAKING BORDERS, CLOSING FRONTIERS AND IDENTIFYING SMUGGLING

Comparative histories

Paul Nugent

Although there as many histories of border-making as there are lines on a map, most either involve some progression from a frontier to a border, or are the result of the splintering of an existing state/empire in which case internal borders are typically externalized. The frontier exists in the imagination of state actors, representing an area outside their conception of effective control. Their spatial reading, though, is not always shared by populations whose conception of the landscape of power may differ significantly. The border is more of an empirical reality and represents the point at which the writ of one authority definitively ends and another conceivably begins. The delimitation of a border by map and/or treaty may not result in immediate demarcation of a physical boundary, thereby contributing to a measure of uncertainty. When it comes to maritime borders, it stands to reason that proper demarcation is well-nigh possible. A popular misconception is that there is a sequence according to which states are formed and set out to define their borders, whereas these are generally simultaneous processes. As Peter Sahlins (1988, 1989) has demonstrated in relation to the protracted process of border-making between France and Spain in the Pyrenees, the border was initially actualized through the territorialisation of local identities. The territorialisation of the state itself, which involved the transplanting of institutions such as Customs officials to the margins, came much later – and the demarcation of the boundary line later still. This pattern holds for colonial states as well, as I have recently argued in the case of the Senegambia and the trans-Volta in the nineteenth century (Nugent 2019).

Ultimately, it is those who represent the sovereign authority who stipulate what may legally cross the border and under what conditions – and hence who also define what constitutes smuggling. Clearly, none of this resides inherently in the nature of the goods that are transacted: at certain times and places, the trade in narcotic substances (notably opium) has been considered legitimate, while seemingly innocuous goods like textiles and groundnuts have been identified as contraband. The act of labelling with a view to sanctioning is closely bound up with the aspirations of those who purport to rule, but what this means in practice depends on an underlying capacity to make a preferred version of order stick. If policing is intended to stamp out smuggling, the very act of cementing a border ironically renders contrabanding more attractive.

DOI: 10.4324/9781003043645-7

Borders have historically magnified differences, both because of the differential pace of infra-structural development and because of different regulatory regimes pertaining to taxation and consumption. Moreover, the riskier it becomes to move people and goods across the line, the greater the associated rents and the rewards that come with success. It is only at highly mili-tarized land borders that flows are reduced to a trickle.

Inevitably, this is all bound up with contests over the moral as much as the physical terrain. Whether smuggling is driven by need or motivated by greed is fundamental to establishing the limits of acceptable behaviour amongst border populations – which has an important bearing on the ease with which enforcement is carried out. A prior question is whether the laws themselves are underpinned by any conception of the greater good. In this regard, it is worth recalling Adam Smith's sympathetic depiction of the smuggler as

> a person who, though no doubt highly blamable for violating the laws of his country … and would have been in every respect an excellent citizen had not the laws of his country made that a crime which nature never meant to be so. (quoted in Evensky 2011, p. 260)

In border regions, it is not uncommon for populations to distinguish between smuggling that is considered harmless and that which is considered anti-social (Scheele 2012, pp. 95–124). This relates not just to the scale of the operation, but to the nature of the goods. Where the border is not considered legitimate in the first place, local actors may present smuggling almost as an act of social conscience. In cases where related populations straddle the line, as is true of the Awlad 'Ali of the Liberian/Egyptian borderlands, smuggling may even be integral to the reproduction of larger kinship networks (Hüsken 2019). Conversely, where the border is a consequence of a successful secessionist pitch, populations may be more inclined to co-operate in efforts to protect local agriculture and industry from goods entering from the other side. These shifts and nuances are what makes smuggling such a fascinating topic for historical en-quiry and comparative reflection. In this chapter, I will seek to amplify these broad observations with reference to a range of different contexts in West Africa, South-East Asia, Western Europe and North America. These cases demonstrate that the logics of border-making have shaped patterns of smuggling, while the latter has been constitutive of social relations and political order.

Border logics

Frontiers are inherently ambiguous spaces: while underlying 'lawlessness' is associated with unpredictability and risk, frontiers also represent arenas of possibility for a multiplicity of actors. Indeed, states themselves may derive some benefit from loose arrangements – as with the slaving frontier exploited by the Dahomean kingdom in West Africa. The starting point is, therefore, to understand why states have found fixed borders desirable in the first place. In the European instance, prior to the emergence of properly defined borders, there were often overlapping and/or competing claims made by religious authorities, local nobles and of course rival states-in-the making (Sahlins 1989). Delimiting the border was about laying exclusive claims to populations and territory, while demarcation was an exercise in removing lingering ambiguities. In nineteenth-century Europe, this was associated with more effective technologies of mapping and better communications between the capital and the peripheries. Much of this technological know-how was transferred in short order to empire-building projects in Asia and Africa (Tagliacozzo 2005, pp. 28–47, 76–99).

Making borders, closing frontiers

More specifically, there are a number of underlying patterns in boundary-making that are worth briefly mentioning here:

a. Firstly, states have often acted according to a defensive logic. In mountainous regions, claiming the heights of the land was typically justified on the grounds of establishing better surveillance and/or defensible positions. Creating a string of fortifications, or walled towns, as well as settling loyal populations in border regions, afforded a means for states to restrict the mobility of populations. Across Eurasia, the major threat historically came from men on horseback – as Chinese and Russian empire-builders learned to their cost along the expanse of the great Steppe (Barfield 1989; Khodorkovsky 2002). Colonial regimes that were struggling to assert their authority tended to place great store by securing their borders in the belief that dissidents were likely to take advantage of open frontiers. Although they were often in active competition with one another, colonial authorities had an incentive to co-operate in controlling the movements of potential rebels, as well as restricting the flow of firearms and ammunition. During the Cold War, highly militarized borders were intended to prevent almost any form of interaction across the line. This was reflected in the heavily mined border between Finland and the Soviet Union following the cession of Keralia and the excision of Finnish populations at the end of the Second World War (Paasi 1999). The land border between North and South Korea is an ongoing case where very little gets through (Kim 2014).

b. Secondly, borders have been drawn with the control of resources very much in mind. In densely settled regions, such as in western Europe and much of Asia, there was an incentive to lay claim to populations who were the ultimate source of revenue – whether directly in the shape of taxes or through labour service and levies on the products of the land. Cadastral mapping was an essential aid to improved systems of tax collection in Europe (Scott 1998, pp. 44–52), and the same technologies became fundamental to the demarcation of international borders. More counter-intuitive is the proliferation of mapping 'from below' which underlines the ways in which border populations became active participants in the creation of borders – a theme that emerges strongly in the cases of Alsace and Lorraine and Ghana/Togo (Dunlop 2015, Nugent 2002). Equally, states have had an interest in laying exclusive claims to natural resources – that is, wildlife, forests, fishing grounds, coal and deposits like copper and gold. The conversion of the resource frontier into something enclosed by state borders is exemplified by the manner in which the large swathes of open frontier that were exploited by fur trading companies were folded into imperial Canada.

c. Thirdly, asserting control over trade routes has been fundamental to the logic of border-making. Controlling coastlines with accessible ports, as well as the flanks of navigable waterways, has been a key strategic consideration. In Europe, the main river systems – notably the Rhine and the Danube - have been fundamental to commercial flows, but also were the point at which state borders came together. Across much of Africa, ecologically-based trade – for example between the coast, the Sahel and the Sahara in West Africa – was of considerable importance in the history of state formation. The taxation of goods in transit – such as copper, gold, salt and slaves – provided the material foundations upon which state builders consolidated their position. Although this did not necessarily require well-defined borders, rulers were careful to control chokepoints such as river crossings. Colonial regimes had a particular penchant for deploying rivers as borders for many of the same reasons – often choosing to locate the capital on the river. The twin capitals of Brazzaville and Leopoldville (Kinshasa) that face each other across the Congo river arose out of commercial and logistical considerations on the part of the French and the Belgians respectively (Gondola 2016, pp. 32–35). Inevitably, there was substantial traffic across the river during the colonial period, and this remains one of the most active theatres of smuggling to this day.

The most telling difference is not between colonial and non-colonial cases, but between the variable capacities of polities in general – ranging from states to more decentralized entities – to shape a clear agenda. Historically, weak states have tended to rely on intermediaries such as tax farmers and regional lords to manage their domains – building on bonds of allegiance rather than on territorial exactitude. In colonial contexts, the exploitation of resources was often left to private concessionary companies that exercised some of the vestiges of sovereignty on behalf of the metropolitan government. This was true of much of Central and Southern Africa and of South-East Asia (notably, Borneo). Where states had a greater capacity to intervene, they were more likely to post their own officials to designated border regions. But much depended on the willingness of local intermediaries to supply information and to co-operate in day-to-day enforcement of the regulations. Un-demarcated borders were perceived as a gift to local populations who were the masters of their own terrain and adept at exploiting lingering uncertainties. But they also increased the potential points of friction between neighbouring polities. In the case of the Cerdanya, Sahlins (1989, pp. 233–234) observes that it was the frequency of disagreements about where the border ran – typically when Customs officials were in hot pursuit of smugglers – that informed the decision to delineate this section of the Spanish-French border. In colonial Africa, where aspiring colonial powers rubbed up against each other, bouts of feverish competition were generally followed by efforts to settle rival claims by treaty. Around Lake Kivu, Gillian Mathys 2014, pp. 127–128) reveals how the decision by the Belgians and the Germans to set up border posts mirroring each other at Goma/Gisenyi and Bukavu/Cyangugu between 1900 and 1906 was an exercise in setting down markers in what remained a disputed zone. The actual demarcation of the boundary between the Congo and Rwanda followed some years later. Although physical demarcation by boundary commissions was often delayed by decades, colonial regimes used maps and local agreements to navigate a way around potential misunderstandings. However, even agreeing on where the border ran did not necessarily translate into active co-operation when it came to regulating border flows – except when security was a serious issue. Colonial regimes feared the loss of people (and cattle) and often discouraged crossings into neighbouring territory whilst seeking to poach population from the other side. Those regimes that felt less affected by smuggling went through the motions of practising surveillance, but devoted minimal resources to it. At times, as we will see, they even provided their tacit consent.

In what follows, I will turn to three different patterns in the relationship between border-making and smuggling with reference to specific case-studies: those where smuggling was a response to colonial revenue imperatives; others where the intention was to restrict the flow of commodities, substances and people deemed dangerous; and still other cases where the border suddenly emerged in a moment of political rupture.

Colonial revenue logics in West Africa: the Trans-Volta and the Senegambia

In West Africa, most states reproduced themselves through taxes on trade, whether in the interior or at the coastal ports. It was much less attractive to tax populations directly – although in some places like the Sokoto Caliphate this was practised. A particularly well-documented

Making borders, closing frontiers

polity is Asante which regulated the Hausa caravan trade from the Sahel. Hausa traders were directed to the trading town of Salaga and were not permitted to continue their journey to the capital. The trade to Kumasi and the metropolitan provinces was reserved for state traders and favoured merchants. Asante customs officials also taxed the goods which passed along the Volta river towards the coast. Ivor Wilks (1975, pp. 58–49) has identified a branch of the central bureaucracy whose specific role was to police the 'great roads' from designated control posts and to deal with the incidence of smuggling.

In the later nineteenth century, as the Europeans sought to exert influence well beyond the coastal trading posts, they came into direct conflict with inland states like Asante. The escalating costs of conflict became a source of concern for metropolitan governments. The response of local officials to the revenue imperative fell into an established groove. That is, they initially sought to establish their own control over chokepoints along the interior trade routes, to rebuff the efforts of internal polities to impose their own taxes, and finally to channel the trade to their own ports. However, the attempt to operate within the logics of the frontier became increasingly difficult, and as European rivalries intensified there was more of an interest in establishing spheres of influence and eventually colonies with defined borders. The emergence of the Gold Coast conforms to this pattern. After the British invasion of Asante in 1874, the kingdom lost control of the Hausa routes which increasingly passed down the eastern side of the Volta River. While the British authorities were under pressure from merchants to ensure that the trade from the interior came to them rather than their European competitors, the fledgling administrations at the coast desperately needed to raise income – especially once the Gold Coast colony (minus Asante) was formally consecrated in 1874. The failed attempt to introduce a poll tax culminated in a colonial state that balanced precariously on Customs duties. No sooner had the British defined their eastern border than a vigorous smuggling trade grew up at its eastern margins. In an effort to deal with the problem, the British shifted the border eastwards to include the town of Aflao in 1879 (Marguerat 1993, pp. 23–27). The pattern was repeated as traders from across the sub-region (including Hausas, Minas and Sierra Leoneans), and even some European firms, established themselves just beyond Aflao where there had previously been only a cluster of small fishing villages sandwiched between the sea and the lagoon. Hence Lomé, the present-day capital of Togo, owes its existence to its sudden emergence as a highly cosmopolitan haven for smugglers seeking to evade Gold Coast Customs controls (Marguerat 1998, Spire 2007). The favourable conditions for the contraband trade endured for some years before the Germans arrived on this stretch of coastline in 1884 and staked their own claim to what became the colony of Togo. The emergence of a rival colonial power required the British to agree on a formal border separating the two colonies, which closed the frontier once and for all. The result was the straight line border that remains in place today, running due north from the coast at Aflao and then taking a sharp deviation to the west. This was in no sense a natural border and in many ways provided the perfect conditions for the pursuit of smuggling.

After some years, the Germans decided to relocate their capital to Lomé and set about constructing a modern city with a wharf to handle ships and three railways to carry cash crops from the interior. The Germans and the British had initially agreed to harmonize their Customs duties, but this was abandoned by the Togo authorities when they needed to augment their revenues to finance the infrastructural push. Higher import duties in Togo resulted in considerable smuggling of manufactured goods from the Gold Coast. The Volta River constituted the border for much of its length and provided an easy route for contraband goods travelling in both directions. After the First World War, when France and Britain divided the German colony in two, the southern border remained intact, but further north it was shifted eastwards. For much of its length, the boundary was delimited and later demarcated along the line of the

Togoland hills, in the hope that it might constitute a more natural border. However, the routes through the forested mountains proved extremely difficult for the Gold Coast Customs Preventive Service (CPS) to patrol. Meanwhile, at the coast it was business as usual. British trading firms operated stores in Lomé that notionally catered to the local market. Many of the imported goods that they sold, however, were transported across the border into the Gold Coast, either by pirogues along the lagoons or the sea-route, or overland along countless trails. The most important single item in the contraband trade was Dutch gin. The British relied overwhelmingly on import duties, and the greatest single contributor to these was the duty on gin, followed by textiles and tobacco (Nugent 2019, p. 262). The French maintained head taxes and minimized the level of import duty. Although much of the contrabanding was carried out by small traders, some of the seizures effected by the CPS pointed to something altogether more organized (Nugent 2019, 262–268). Whereas the CPS devoted considerable energy to the campaign against smuggling in the 1920s, the French authorities devoted minimal resources to this aspect of border control.

In the Senegambia, the picture was somewhat different because the control of labour was closely intertwined with the flow of commodities. The British and the French initially established trading posts at Bathurst and Saint Louis with a view to tapping trade along the Gambia and Senegal rivers respectively. However, by the mid-nineteenth century, the production of groundnuts in proximity to the coastal ports had shifted the centre of economic gravity. In the 1880s, the French resolved to claim the entirety of the Senegambia, pegging the Portuguese backwards towards Bissau and encircling the British in the process. Given vocal opposition to relinquishing Bathurst, the question of defining a border between the Gambia and Senegal became a practical necessity. In the western sector, a major consideration for the British was slave raiding. By settling on a border in 1889, and securing French co-operation, the British hoped to establish the conditions that would enable the Jola to cultivate groundnuts in peace. The boundary was drawn according to a simple expedient – comprising a straight line from the coast, followed by one that tracked the contours of the Gambia river at 10 kilometres from either bank (Nugent 2019, pp. 120–122). Again, this was anything but a natural boundary, even if it shadowed a natural feature.

Just as British firms controlled much of the trade in Lomé, it was French firms that dominated the trade of the Gambia, which they conducted from wharf towns dotted along the river. Once slave raiding had been eliminated, the Gambian groundnut economy depended heavily on seasonal labour, or 'strange farmers,' drawn from French territory. Part of the attraction for these workers was to acquire access to British manufactured goods. In addition, Senegalese producers smuggled their own groundnuts into the Gambia in order to be able to purchase these same commodities from the wharf towns that were substantially closer. Moreover, the Gambia suffered from a chronic food deficit, especially at times when the migrant labourers were present in large numbers. Although the Gambia imported rice to cover the shortfall, much of it was smuggled in from French territory. All of this was convenient for the Gambian authorities because they were able to maximize their groundnut exports and also to increase the sale of British manufactures, both of which were taxed.

In significant ways, British and French priorities were aligned very differently. While the French endeavoured to maintain a tight Customs cordon, the British displayed little interest in regulating what crossed the border – other than firearms, the occasional marabout (or religious leader) and stolen cattle. However, the two sets of authorities did have a shared interest in formalizing the strange farmer system. The latter was fundamental to the economic viability and public finances of the Gambia, but migrants also earned money that enabled them to pay their head taxes in Senegal and Mali. The authorities co-operated to ensure that they were registered and did not criss-cross the border at will. However, this depended on the co-operation of the *alkalos* (village chiefs) in the Gambia who managed the system. While the *alkalos* received their cut, there was inevitably some temptation to let migrants enter beneath the radar of the two administrations. While the British favoured permanent settlement, they sought to stamp out the practice of short-term migrants bypassing the controls. Although they co-operated in managing migration, the Senegalese authorities suspected their Gambian counterparts of actively poaching population with a view to promoting permanent settlement. This became a hot issue during the First World War when many people crossed the border to escape conscription.

The trans-Volta and Senegambia cases throw up some interesting parallels and differences. In the Senegambia, the flows that were regulated were people as well as commodities, and the latter included a cash crop (groundnuts), food crops and imported consumer goods. In the trans-Volta, some cocoa was produced, but its production did not depend on labour from across the border, while the trade in foodstuffs was less important. The importance of everyday consumer goods, however, was as evident, even if alcohol featured less in the list of Gambian smuggled goods. In both cases, the leading commercial enterprises were complicit in the contraband trade. British firms in Lomé were well-aware that the imported commodities that they sold were likely to end up in the Gold Coast, although their standard defence was that they had no control once the goods entered the hands of their customers. In the Gambia, French firms sold the British manufactured goods that made their way across the Senegalese border, while they purchased contraband groundnuts that travelled in the opposite direction. In each case, the huff and puff surrounding the campaign against smuggling on one side of the border contrasted with the almost complete lack of interest on the other. Finally, populations who found themselves located on either side of the line adapted creatively to these realities. Borderlanders knew the inland waterways intimately and they were able to make use of the many paths and tracks that criss-crossed the landscape. The difference was that whereas Senegambian smugglers made extensive use of horse and donkey carts, their trans-Volta counterparts were more dependent upon the headloading of smuggled goods. In no sense can smuggling be considered something that existed in ignorance of the border – although such a defence was frequently invoked by those who were caught red-handed. Much like in Cerdanya, populations were well-aware of where the borders ran, even if these were not always clearly demarcated on the ground. A.I. Asiwaju (1976, p. 201) has referred to the emergence of linked markets all along the colonial border between Benin and Nigeria, underlining the ways in which populations appropriated the border. Much the same was true of the trans-Volta and the Senegambia where rotating markets became a defining feature of the borderlands.

Dangerous goods, noxious substances

Aside from taxing goods, the other main source of smuggling resulted from efforts to control the movement of commodities deemed dangerous to some conception of morality and/or social order. This was a particular consideration in an imperial context where hegemony often dangled by a very flimsy thread. The passage of Muslim religious tracts was monitored very closely across West Africa, especially texts that were thought to harbour seditious intent and possibly a coded call to jihad. Firearms loomed large for the obvious reason that they afforded the means to mount resistance. In the Arabian Sea (Mathew 2016, pp. 82–112) and in the watery expanse of South East Asia (Tagliacozzo 2005, pp. 260–282), there was a very substantial traffic in firearms that European consuls and colonial regimes struggled to contain. The lack of clear maritime borders – despite the agreement of the British and the Dutch to draw a line through the Straits of Melaka in 1871 (Tagliacozzo 2005, p. 29) – together with the sheer scale of the trading zone, made this an almost impossible task. The Dutch faced a particular problem subduing the rulers of Aceh in the early 1870s and endeavoured to impose a blockade. In the West African colonies, the French opposed permitting African access to firearms whereas the British were more inclined to accept a case for their use in hunting and to tax their purchase accordingly (Sané 2008). In the Senegambia, there was a vigorous illicit trade in arms and ammunition between the Gambia, the Casamance region of Senegal and the Portuguese colony of Guinea Bissau which was closely bound up with moments of armed resistance. The same pattern was evident on the border between Benin and south-western Nigeria, where arms and ammunition smuggled into the former was deployed in opposition to French rule (Asiwaju 1976, p. 200).

In the case of narcotics, the disastrous social consequences of opium addiction were well known from the Chinese experience. In the East Indies, the British and Dutch authorities were keen to prevent a spillover into their own domains. However, they did not seek to ban the drug, but rather to regulate its supply and consumption. Hence, the rights to sell opium were generally farmed to Chinese merchants in return for a commission. Tagliacozzo (2005, p. 201) points out that populations were subject to distinct rules relating to consumption of narcotics, while the cost of the opium 'farms' differed between the British and Dutch territories. Not surprisingly, therefore, smugglers moved opium from where it was relatively cheap to where it was more expensive. In addition, smugglers imported their own supplies of opium to the region, with Singapore serving as a conduit into the Dutch possessions. The numerous islands and broken coastlines of the sub-region provided the perfect environment in which opium smugglers could transport and conceal consignments of a relatively low bulk, high value commodity.

A strikingly similar story unfolded in the far western borderlands between the United States (US) and Canada. Here, a straight-line border had been drawn along the forty-ninth parallel in 1846, but it was a line on a map and was not really enforced to start with. The Customs presence was minimal, especially along the coast where some areas remained in dispute (Moore 2014, pp. 15–16). Stephen T. Moore indicates that British Columbia had always been more closely connected to neighbouring American states than the rest of Canada, while populations and consumer items like cotton goods and tobacco had moved relatively freely across the line. The borderlanders themselves regarded such smuggling as morally acceptable and, as is so often the case, took a certain pride in running rings around the revenue men. However, it was the passage of items deemed subversive to the social order in the US that led to a more sustained attempt to police the border. Opium was banned in the US in 1914, but not in Canada, which meant that there was a lively trade from one to the other. Moreover, following the American decision to forbid Chinese immigration in 1882, an active trafficking route through British Columbia opened up (Moore 2014, p. 17). As in South-East Asia, much of the smuggling was conducted by water along a broken coastline that was very difficult for an under-resourced coastguard to patrol (Moore 2014, p. 19). The extensive land border made detection equally difficult, not least because of the terrain.

The other item that was of increasing interest to the US authorities was alcohol. Temperance ideas took root on either side of the border in the later nineteenth century, re-flecting the manner in which missionaries and activists criss-crossed the line. Although British Columbia itself went dry during the First World War, this changed just as the Americans passed the Eighteenth Amendment that enshrined Prohibition in the US Constitution. Under the Canadian Constitution, the regulation of alcohol production and alcohol was a federal matter, and the government had no desire to co-operate in the banning of alcohol exports to the US which were a source of much-needed taxes. Much of the alcohol that was notionally destined for Central and South America was instead channelled to US ports. Running alcohol across the border became a major business which the Canadian Customs authorities did conspicuously little to address. Indeed, they even tolerated it as long as the perpetrators refrained from the drugs trade (Moore 2014, p. 61). The contraband business ultimately benefited brewers and distillers, the bootleggers and the public exchequer in Canada. It also enjoyed the sympathy of border populations, especially those living closest to the line. A comparable story can be told for the Mexican border (Martinez 1975, pp. 57–77). Canadian manufacturers were the most vocal critics for the reason that as alcohol went south, items such as tobacco and textiles were smuggled northwards. In the end, it was the repeal of the Eighteenth Amendment that brought the bootleggers' boom to an end.

The irruption of the border

When a border was newly established, governments generally felt impelled to make a statement by establishing control posts. The practical consequences, however, depended on how amicable the divorce settlement had actually been. One instructive example of the ways in which borders can create an environment conducive to smuggling follows the carving of the Free State out of Ireland in 1922. While 26 Catholic-majority counties joined the new state, a rump of six counties remained within the United Kingdom as Northern Ireland. The two governments immediately established Customs posts where none had existed before, despite the fact that there were many unresolved issues about where the border ought to run. Peter Leary (2016, pp. 41–45) observes that Catholics tended to be concentrated on marginal lands in the hills, while Protestants predominated in the more fertile low-lying areas. Catholics and Protestants had tended to frequent different market towns, but the net result of the border was that many discovered that these were located on the other side of the border. Although farm produce was initially exempt, it was necessary to pay duty on everyday items like soap, tea and cigarettes. Moreover, border shoppers were required to use approved crossings even if the goods were not dutiable, and this frequently involved an inconvenient detour. While the Customs regulations were not wildly divergent to start with, this changed as inter-governmental relations deteriorated. In Dublin, the mood was in favour of protectionism after 1932, while the British authorities introduced hefty duties on Irish goods as a form of retaliation. Following tit-for-tat exchanges, even agricultural products were covered by duty. The imposition of a 40% duty on Irish cattle entering Northern Ireland was particularly stiff (Leary 2016, pp. 130–131). While nationalist sentiment justified imposing higher duties, these potentially had a detrimental impact on border populations who depended on supplies from the other side. The inevitable consequence was that smuggling flourished, and while governments on the two sides might appeal to patriotic duty, this enjoyed little traction – for reasons that Adam Smith would certainly have understood. Poor Catholics found a way to fashion an income from smuggling, while Protestants grandees in the north were secretly implicated. Apart from cattle, whisky and cigarettes and clothing were widely smuggled. In 1938, the two governments attempted to call a halt and signed a treaty covering trade co-operation. However, the shortages of the war years, during which Ireland remained neutral, led to the systematic smuggling of everyday items like bread, sugar, flour and tea. By this point, there was no real doubt about where the border ran. On the contrary, it was fundamental to the dynamics of the contraband trade.

The redrawing of European borders after the Second World War and the rapid onset of the Cold War, followed by the eventual collapse of the Soviet Union, involved massive population displacements and acute consumer shortages that were reflected in smuggling. In post-colonial Africa, by contrast, the borders remained remarkably stable despite their supposed artificiality.

Paul Nugent

There has been, though, a proliferation of armed insurgencies in which rebel movements move back and forth across borders to escape detection. Crucially, they also finance their operations, re-arm themselves and nourish their fighters, from the profits of smuggling – typically based on the trafficking in natural resources like timber, precious metals and cattle. However, where movements have been able to secure de facto control over territory, they have tended to mimic the revenue-collection practices of state entities. In a handful of instances, rebel movements have aspired towards creating their own breakaway states, in which cases smuggling has actually been the hand-maiden of border-making. This is true, for example, of the Sudan Peoples' Liberation Movement/Army (SPLM/A) which was always deeply implicated in cross-border trade across the sub-region (Walraet 2013, 179–180). Once formal separation has taken place, it is difficult for post-liberation governments to turn off the tap. In the case of South Sudan, the transition was particularly messy because the border with Sudan, which contains valuable oilfields, remained in dispute, while fighting between factions of former SPLM/A stood in the way of the creation of an effective central government. Hence the performance of border rituals and bureaucratic formalities along particular borders crossings (De Vries 2013, p. 154) has co-existed with systematic involvement of the protagonists in the contraband trade.

Conclusion

Drawing on a wide range of case-studies, this chapter has distilled some underlying patterns in the relationship between border-making and smuggling which can now be summarized. Firstly, the manner in which the border took shape has had a significant bearing on the trajectories of smuggling. In cases where frontiers solidified into borders, the desire to regulate the flow of people and goods was fundamental to the decisions to delimit and eventually to demarcate. This is apparent from the works of Sahlins on the Spanish-French border (1988, 1989) and Tagliacozzo (2005) on colonial South-East Asia. Holding the line generally went together with an official discourse on the evils of smuggling, although states and their minions often benefited from it. Across these cases, what is clear is that while the authorities fretted about unclear boundaries, border populations were well-aware of where the lines ran and profited accordingly.

Secondly, where the border was located wielded an important influence on the capacity of governments to exercise meaningful control. Maritime borders were largely un-demarcated, even if they were minutely detailed on maps, and this always created some leeway for inter-pretation. Mountainous borders were demarcated, but only up to a point. In unforgiving terrain, the dice were generally loaded in favour of the smugglers. Thirdly, the dynamic of any given border was closely bound up with the ways in which states pieced together their revenue streams. In colonial West Africa, the balance between import duties and direct taxes created a context in which goods were smuggled routinely while people crossed borders to evade direct taxation and conscription. Fourthly, the intent behind tightening borders was often related to the traffic in commodities that were deemed injurious to the public good – including firearms, alcohol and narcotics, even if each of these was also taxed in particular instances. Finally, where borders came into existence abruptly, the same dynamics manifested themselves, but often in a telescoped manner. Borders on paper needed to be translated to the landscape. Nationalists have also been tempted by the benefits of protectionism. Border populations have generally been sensitive to everyday inconvenience, but also to the opportunities that the existence of the border presents. As the Irish and US/Canadian cases illustrate, however, engagement in smuggling is not in and of itself an indicator of the illegitimacy of a given border. In Africa, engagement in contrabanding was paradoxically what enabled borders to be internalized

(Nugent 2002). Borderlanders generally came to accept the downsides of partition because of the livelihoods that smuggling sustained. At the same time, contraband has underpinned kinship relations and regional religious networks, as indicated by Hüsken (2019), whilst forging new kinds of connections between commercial centres embedded within larger systems of connectivity as demonstrated by Nugent (2019) and Scheele (2012) for West Africa. In that sense, smuggling has had productive effects that are not fully captured by the association with deviance and evasion.

References

Asiwaju, A.I., 1976. *Western Yorubaland under European rule 1889–1945*. London: Longman.

Barfield, T.J., 1989. *The perilous frontier: nomadic empires and China 221 BC to AD 1757*. Oxford: Blackwell.

De Vries, L., 2013. Pulling the ropes: convenient indeterminacies and the negotiation of power at Kaya's border checkpoint. In C. Vaughan, M. Schomerus and L. de Vries eds. *The borderlands of South Sudan*. New York: Palgrave Macmillan, 143–172.

Dunlop, C.T., 2015. *Cartophilia: maps and the search for identity in the French-German borderland*. Berkeley, Los Angeles & Oxford: University of California Press.

Evensky, J., 2011. Adam Smith's essentials: on trust, faith, and free markets. *Journal of the History of Economic Thought* 33(2), 249–267.

Gondola, C.D., 2016. *Tropical cowboys: westerns, violence, and masculinity in Kinshasa*. Bloomington: Indiana Press.

Hüsken, T., 2019. *Tribal politics in the borderland of Egypt and Libya*. New York: Palgrave Macmillan.

Khodarkovsky, M., 2002. *Russia's steppe frontier: the making of a colonial empire, 1500–1800*. Bloomington & Indianapolis: Indiana University Press.

Kim, S.-Y., 2014. *DMZ crossing: performing emotional citizenship along the Korean border*. New York & Chichester: University of Columbia Press.

Leary, P., 2016. *Unapproved routes: histories of the Irish border, 1922–1972*. Oxford: Oxford University Press.

Marguerat, Y., 1993. *Dynamique urbaine, jeunesse et histoire au Togo: articles et documents (1984–1993)*. Lomé: Presses de l'UB.

Marguerat, Y., 1998. Les deux naissances de Lomé: une analyse critiques des sources. In N. Gayibor, Y. Marguerat and K. Nyassogbo eds. *Le centenaire de Lomé, capital du Togo (1897–1997)*. Lomé: Presses de l'UB, 59–77.

Martinez, O.J., 1975. *Border boom town: Ciudad Juarez since 1958*. Austin & London: University of Texas Press.

Mathew, J., 2016. *Margins of the market: trafficking and capitalism across the Arabian Sea*. Oakland: University of California Press.

Mathys, G., 2014. *People on the move: frontiers, borders, mobility and history in the Lake Kivu region, 19th–20th Century*. Thesis (PhD). University of Ghent, 2014.

Moore, Stephen T., 2014. *Bootleggers and borders: the paradox of prohibition on a Canada–U.S. borderland*. Lincoln: University of Nebraska Press.

Nugent, P., 2002. *Smugglers, secessionists and loyal citizens on the Ghana-Togo frontier: the lie of the borderlands since 1914*. Athens & Oxford: Ohio University Press & James Currey.

Nugent, P., 2019. *Boundaries, communities and state-making in West Africa: the centrality of the margins*. Cambridge: Cambridge University Press.

Paasi, A., 1999. Boundaries as social practice as discourse: the Finnish-Russian border. *Regional Studies* 33(7), 669–680.

Sahlins, P., 1988. The nation in the village: state-building and communal struggles in the Catalan borderland during the eighteenth and nineteenth centuries. *Journal of Modern History* 60(2), 234–263.

Sahlins, P., 1989. *Boundaries: the making of France and Spain in the Pyrenees*. Berkeley, Los Angeles & Oxford: University of California Press.

Sané, S., 2008. *Le côntrole des armes à feu en Afrique occidentale française 1834–1958*. Paris & Dakar: Karthala & CREPOS.

Scheele, J., 2012. *Smugglers and saints of the Sahara: regional connectivity in the twentieth century*. Cambridge: Cambridge University Press.

Paul Nugent

Scott, J.C., 1998. *Seeing like a state: how certain schemes to improve the human condition have failed.* New Haven & London: Yale University Press.

Spire, A., 2007. Kodjoviakopé à Lomé: le temps et la constitution d'un terroir urbain. In P. Gervais-Lambony and G.K. Nyassogbo eds., *Lomé: dynamiques d'une ville Africaine.* Paris: Karthala, 189–210.

Tagliacozzo, E., 2005. *Secret trades, porous borders: smuggling and states along a Southeast Asian frontier, 1865–1915.* New Haven & London: Yale University Press.

Walraet, A., 2013. State-making and emerging complexes of power and accumulation in the Southern Sudan-Kenyan border area: the rise of a thriving cross-border business network. In C. Vaughan, M. Schomerus and L. de Vries eds., *The borderlands of South Sudan.* New York: Palgrave Macmillan, 173–192.

Wilks, I., 1975. *Asante in the nineteenth century: the structure and evolution of a political order.* Cambridge: Cambridge University Press.

8

BORDERLANDS, FRONTIERS, AND BORDERS

Changing meanings and the intersection with smuggling practices

Sergio Peña

1. Introduction

The objective of this chapter is to contribute to the understanding of smuggling practices through the conceptual lenses of borderlands, frontiers, and borders. The analysis is based on the premise that smuggling is a multidimensional phenomenon that cannot be understood without considering its spatial and temporal dimensions, in which borders play a key role. Smuggling is an activity that thrives by taking advantage of structural differences of spaces, adjacent or not, for economic gains. The chapter analyzes specifically the intersection between smuggling and bordering practice.

It is important to clarify the meaning of three concepts that are used interchangeably in the literature: borders, borderlands, and frontiers. The three conceptual categories are not only economic, social, political, and cultural, but also spatial constructs that have meaning and content. Thus, the chapter dissects each category to search for its meaning and how it is linked to smuggling practice. The main question the chapter poses is: *How does bordering affect smuggling practice?*

The second section focuses on discussing how borders have been studied to have a grasp of theories and concepts that could help us explain how smuggling has been approached and defined through the different lenses of bordering practice. The main dimensions discussed are ontological and epistemological aspects related to the production of knowledge of borders, spatial and temporal conceptions of borders, borders and scalar notions, and borders and actors.

The third section discusses in more detail the intersection between bordering and smuggling. The main emphasis is on explaining how smuggling has adapted to the emerging practices of bordering in different epochs; for example, how smuggling changed with globalization and the notion of a borderless world, and how it has adapted to the post-9/11 world of security and re-bordering.

There are two key arguments made throughout the chapter. First, borders are no longer understood as material, static, homogenous, and binary categories where a line separates and differentiates the "in" and "out," and the State determines what is allowed and what is proscribed. Second, borders instead are now understood as a social product that is heterogenous,

DOI: 10.4324/9781003043645-8

107

polysemic, and dynamic where multiple actors are engaged in the process of creating meaning and symbolism. This chapter shows that perceptions and practices of smuggling have been affected by this emerging ontological and epistemological frame. New actors besides the State have emerged, the scope and scale have also changed, as well as the perception of smuggling and the smugglers from local folk heroes to transnational dangers.

2. Borders, borderlands, and frontiers

This section explores the meaning and definition of three concepts that often are used interchangeably in border literature. The main goal is to see if there are meaningful differences and to what extent those help us understand smuggling practice. I argue that even though there are some important differences in their meanings, the concept of *borders* has become the dominant one. *Frontiers* was used more to denote the expansion and control of newly acquired territories and it has lost importance as borders are settled and less likely to change. *Borderlands* is restrictive to a region, often defined by local or national governments, at the border and does not consider that bordering practices can take place away from the border line. The concepts of *borderlands* and *frontiers* have become less prominent because they are still grounded in what scholars (Agnew, 1994, 2008; Newman, 2006a, 2016; Paasi, 2012, 2014) call the classical notion of territorialism that assumes border as "fixed" and a material "thing." Additionally, it is argued that bordering practices can also be found in places not necessarily located at the international border line; the argument is that borders can be found "everywhere" (ÓTuathail, 1999; Balibar and Williams, 2002; van Houtum and van Naerssen, 2002; Lyon, 2005; Rumford, 2006) in places such as airports, highways, etc.

Frontiers and borderlands

The study of Frederick J. Turner originally published in 1893 was very influential in early works of frontiers (Stoddard, 1991; Newman and Paasi, 1998; Newman, 2001; Kraudzun, 2012). Turner's views on frontiers are closely related to the context of the American expansion and settlement of the West's "empty areas" (Baud and van Schendel, 1997, p. 213); Turner's view of the frontier is a cultural deterministic approach that separates the civilized and un-civilized cultures, particularly the white settlers from the native populations, a perspective that reinforces the view of natives as "out of step with modern society" (Stoddard, 1991, p. 2). Furthermore, House (1980, p. 459) states that frontier was a concept used in the diplomatic world and defines the frontier as a "buffer zone," often 10 kilometers in width on either side of the boundary. Peripherality is another dimension that is employed in the study of frontiers (House, 1980; Stoddard, 1991). House (1980) argues that frontiers face a double peripherality because looking at the frontier from both sides, two peripheral zones face each other.

According to Newman (2001), the study of the frontier moved away from the Turnerian cultural deterministic perspective towards a political problematization of the concept. The shift towards understanding the frontier as a political problem opened other views as well, including economics, administration, inter-state conflict, etc.

Finding a substantial difference in the conceptual definition of frontiers and borderlands in the literature is difficult; often they are used interchangeably. Stoddard (1991, p. 8) attempts to differentiate between the two, arguing that "border zone" and "frontier zone" have been used as synonyms, but the border zone normally is used to denote an administrative area whereas the concept of frontiers is fuzzy and not clearly defined. Because of the fuzziness (Newman, 2016) of defining frontiers scholars opted for the use of borderlands because it can offer a better conceptualization of the phenomenon. One advantage of using borderlands, according to Baud and Van Schendel (1997) is that the phenomenon can be approached through its "spatial dimension." Newman and Paasi (1998, p. 190) point out that the concept of borderlands allowed scholars to approach the topic from the perspective of "conflict, separation, partition and barriers" rather than "peace, contact, unification and bridges" which could open a new line of inquiry.

The above analysis shows that it is a futile exercise to try to define clearly the meaning and difference between frontier and borderlands. Scholars in recent years have instead opted for employing the concepts of borders and bordering for the following reasons. First and foremost, frontiers and borderlands are associated with the traditional positivist notion of geography as a physical object or "thing," thus overlooking the hermeneutic and subjective aspects of borders and meaning. Second, from the perspective of politics and international relations, borderlands were narrowly studied from a perspective of territorialism and conflict, facing the same limitations of what Agnew (1994) called the "territorial trap" (discussed in more detail in the next section). Third, the process of integration (e.g., European Union, North American Free Trade Agreement or NAFTA) and globalization during the 1980s that relaxed and softened borders forced us to conceptualize borders in a non-territorial way and problematize borders in hermeneutic and relational terms. Finally, the terrorist attacks of 09/11 revived the analysis of re-bordering and security, reinforcing the notion of borders as fortress.

3. Borders and bordering practice

The noun "border" and the verb "bordering," that denotes practice and action, have become dominant. Also, in the last few decades border studies have gained ground because of globalization processes that created interest in a "borderless world" (Newman, 2006b, 2016; Paasi, 2012). In the next paragraphs the concepts of border and bordering are scrutinized based on five categories: ontology and epistemology; spatial; temporal; scales; and actors. The aim is to explain how these categories help with our understanding of smuggling practice, which is the central purpose of the chapter. For instance, the section describes how smuggling is explained from a positivist versus a constructivist ontology of borders and what it means in terms of methodology.

The production of knowledge about borders has oscillated between two schools of thought – positivist and constructivist – also referred to as scientific and hermeneutic approaches. Earlier studies of borders adopted an ontological view of "naturalized" borders or assumed that reality was independent of the social agents (Kolossov, 2005); physical geography became among the first fields to study borders from an objective perspective. The decision to engage or not in smuggling practice is modeled as a game theory where actors behave rationally and evaluate the probabilities of success and failure. Methodologically, the positivists focus on modeling and predicting flows across borders by applying models derived from the hard sciences such as physics; borders are usually incorporated as a distance or friction variable in the gravitational models. This approach had considerable influence in the globalization, international trade, and borderless world studies (ÓTuathail, 1999; Balibar and Williams, 2002).

Critical theory of border studies has relied on hermeneutical or interpretivist approaches; these studies consider the role of subjectivity in the formation of identity and narratives of differentiation, symbolism, and memory of border places (Newman and Paasi, 1998; Lapid 2001; van Houtum and van Naerssen, 2002; Newman, 2006a; Paasi, 2014). In short, the border is considered something that is socially constructed instead of being independent of the social agent's subjectivity (Kolossov, 2005).

Borders are also analyzed from the perspective of space. The study of borders, from a spatial perspective, revolves around two approaches. On the one hand, there is the classical view of borders and space defined as the "territorialism perspective." The territorialism perspective is defined by the intersection of three categories: territory/sovereignty/borders. Agnew (1994, p. 59) identifies three key assumptions of territorialism: (1) territory and state are one and the same and have been "reified as a set of fixed units of sovereign space;" (2) studies focus on dichotomies such as national/international, domestic/foreign, overlooking some processes that operate at a more local and regional scale; and (3) "the territorial state has been viewed as existing prior to and as a container of society," ignoring local society's history. The idea of the state having all the tools and capability to keep the "container" self-enclosed and under control is one of the most criticized assumptions because borders are dynamic and fluid, not in stasis (Massey, 2005), and often the national and local interests do not work perfectly in tandem (Brunet-Jailly, 2005). Paasi (see Johnson et al., 2011) argues that instead of looking at borders as the domain of territorial sovereignty, the focus should turn to problematizing the relationship between state power and space, which is more visible at borders.

On the other hand, the relational view of space and borders incorporates issues of power and space as suggested above by Passi (2012). The relational view pays attention to social relationships and how these produced and reproduced space. Social networks are one specific tangible form of relational space (Paasi, 2012); borders are the site where a great multiplicity of social juxtapositions exist, characterized by movement and diversity rather than stasis and homogeneity (Massey, 2005; Johnson et al., 2011). Space is co-produced, renegotiated, and contested daily; culture, identity formation, and local social practice become subjects of the relational view.

A new emerging approach is "borderscapes" (Brambilla, 2015) and "borderities" (Amilhat-Szary and Giraut, 2015) which, unlike territorialism, place the emphasis on the intersection of State/security/mobility. These studies rely on Foucault's concepts of biopolitics, and governmentality as spatial practice aimed at controlling, punishing, and disciplining bodies.[1] The body or mobility of bodies (e.g., international migrants) is the subject of study, particularly how biometric technology has merged the border and the body to create data and algorithms for risk analysis (Lyon, 2005). Some studies (Balibar and Williams, 2002; Lyon, 2005; Rumford, 2006) have put forward the notion that borders are "everywhere," arguing that borders have become a-territorial/a-spatial; this is, functions traditionally thought to take place at the border (e.g., passport control, customs, surveillance, etc.) now happen in any location, such as airports, and city streets and become part of everyday life (Amilhat-Szary and Giraut, 2015), and how these bordering practices are resisted and subverted (Anderson and O'Dowd, 1999; Kraudzun, 2012).

The spatial dimension needs to be complemented with the time dimension that pays attention to history. One entry point to the time dimension is the evolutionist approach that sees progress as sequential and the new replacing the old; for instance, Marx's view of history as evolution of modes of production from slavery to capitalism. Another entry point is the time-space-social simultaneity where the new does not necessarily replace the old but rather they relate dialectically, and space and time are fluid rather than in a state of stasis (Soja, 1996; Massey, 2005). Earlier literature of borders focused on developing evolutionary typologies of borders; for instance, Martinez (1994), a historian himself, argues that borders move from alienated to coexisting then interdependent and finally integrated. Baud and van Schendel (1997) identify five evolutionary cycles – embryonic, adolescent, adult, declining, defunct.

Another temporal framework is to break time into modernism and post-modernism. The modern is the world that emerged from the renaissance where science and reason are the main sources of knowledge. The nation-State, according to Max Weber (2009), is an institution that

Borderlands, frontiers, and borders

modernity created to organize society by rational principles where efficiency is highly valued. According to ÓTuathail (1998) the modern view of borders is associated with the Westphalian nation-State system, and border studies reproduce the "territorial trap" assumptions (discussed earlier); the most important aspect to highlight is the notion that states have the monopoly or exclusive right over their territory, and they emphasize the role of the state as a source of administrating and imposing a spatial ordering to meet national interest goals. The post-modern view of the world challenges the "state-centric" approach and focuses on how non-state actors (e.g., corporations, mafias, gangs, terrorist organizations, etc.) make the container "leak" (Agnew, 1994) and move towards "deterritorialization" processes; in other words, from the post-modern perspective, national borders as material "things" or lines that separate are obsolete and thus borders need to be approached as social and economic processes that are "boundless."

Between the modern view of a "compartmentalized" world of sovereign states and the "borderless" narrative of post-modernism, there is the view of selective "de-territorialization" (Newman and Paasi, 1998; Lapid, 2001; van Houtum and van Naerssen, 2002; Newman, 2006b) arguing that the state still maintains the monopoly of territorial ordering by making the border easier to cross for some and harder for others, especially migrants with lower skills or human capital. van Houtum and van Naerssen (2002) referred to this as a process of bordering, ordering and othering. Finally, an alternative view is the one that argues that the discussion should move away from the temporal frame of modern/post-modern, and instead adopt Ulrich Beck's (1992) view of the risk society[2] and focus on "de-territorialized threats" and "global dangers" (ÓTuathail, 1998) (e.g., terrorism, drugs, and human trafficking, etc.) across borders.

Border analysis from a scalar perspective moves among the notions of scale as a "container," fuzzy boundaries, and polycentric networks. The Russian dolls known as matryoshka are used as an analogy to illustrate the scalar notion of a container where one scale fits into another; the largest scale is the national, then the state, and the local is the lowest scale. Processes (economic, social, and political) are contained within those scales, and functions are divided in a hierarchical and functional way (Jessop, 2002). This scalar notion of a container is a normative "straw-man" model of how things ought to be within a political/administrative order. However, the container model crumbles with reality. Scales are often reconfigured by state and non-state actors who employ their power to re-order or re-scale processes to ensure the profitability of capital (Swyngedouw, 1997); scales become fuzzy, and power is polycentric across borders. In summary, the border moves from being a hard and well-marked edge or line around the container to an amorphous object for which it is hard to know where something starts or ends.

Finally, it is important to discuss border and actors. To uncover who the key border actors are, the important question is: Who borders and for what purpose? (Kolossov, 2005; Johnson et al., 2011; Newman, 2016). Border studies have demonstrated that the State is still an important actor that borders. However, new studies have shown that state and local governments as well as non-State actors (e.g., corporations, white supremacist organizations, immigrant advocates, etc.) are important; Cooper, Perkins and Rumford (2016) referred to this phenomenon as the "vernacularization" of borders. The discussion thus far has shown that one of the main actors in the bordering process is the State, since the Westphalian arrangement gave the State sovereignty powers and the monopoly to control its territory and borders (Agnew, 1994). However, the State is an abstract concept that is too limited to explore this issue more in depth. It is more important to explore who is in charge of administering the border and whether those agents are in tune with the State's goals (Brunet-Jailly, 2005). Border bureaucracies (Heyman, 1995) (e.g., border patrol, customs, immigration, army, navy, etc.) are important to study, including to what extent they have their own agenda and interests (e.g., likelihood of being corrupted, enforcing the law in a strict sense).

Multi-national corporations and local business are also important actors that lobby for de-bordering. Asymmetries between neighboring countries often play an important role in the de-bordering process so that the border becomes a fixed locational asset (Boehmer and Peña, 2012). How border bureaucracies interact with economic forces is important to explore. Bureaucracies could be gatekeepers that enforce the law by the book. They could also facilitate exchanges by doing selective enforcement to their own benefit (rent-seeking predatory behavior) or simply be *laissez-faire* (Heyman, 1995). Border society in general is another important actor and the issues of identity and culture play a key role; society could ask for stricter enforcement of the border (narratives of differentiation and "othering") or make the border invisible due to shared values and identities ("usness") (van Houtum and van Naerssen, 2002). Social attitudes towards "deviant," "contesting" or "subversive" behaviors that often take place at the border are important to consider (Brambilla, 2015). For example, borders normally are associated with illegal activities so the question to explore is whether deviancy is rejected or embedded and part of the border social ethos (Baud and van Schendel, 1997). Lastly, while borders have become more and more difficult to cross for some populations, new actors are emerging in defense of human and civil rights that have been violated in the process of migrating (Brambilla and Jones, 2020).

4. Borders, bordering and smuggling practice

The focus in this section is on answering this research question: How does bordering affect smuggling practice? Smuggling is presented as a transgressive social practice that challenges borders and formal institutions. The intersection between border spatiality and smuggling also brings important insights. What follows is a discussion of three border approaches--the "territorialism" view, the relational view of borders, and the notion of borders "everywhere," or mobile borders. By using the conceptual categories (ontology and epistemology, spatial, temporal, scales, and actors) of the previous section, I unpack how smuggling and bordering have evolved.

The territorialism view of borders and smuggling points towards defining smuggling as a transgressive practice to the State's sovereign power and border control. The question that is often raised is: To what extent does the State have the capacity and resources to perform its panoptical function and prevent smuggling? An important track of analysis in this regard looks at bureaucracies as the front line or the most visible face of the State at the border. For example, Heyman (1994, p. 55) argues that "the networked and flexible organization of smugglers possesses significant advantages over bureaucratic action, especially in a boundary situation where smugglers have a safe zone." In short, from a territorialism perspective, the problem is framed as the contradiction of spatial "fixity" and the "fluidity" (Massey, 2005) of illicitness.

From a relational perspective of space, the focus is placed on the social relationships and networks created among smugglers, bureaucrats, and society. Territorialism assumes that the State and bureaucracies are in tandem and both work in perfect harmony, and the latter is professionally trained in the mirror image of Max Weber's rational organization; however, bureaucracies and State goals are not always on the same page. There are examples, particularly in the context of a weak or failed State, when bureaucracies act on their own interest as rent-seeking, thus colluding with smugglers (Basu, 2014). van Schendel (2005. p. 51) defines this arrangement between bureaucracies and smugglers as the *"pax mafiosa"* and highlights two models of organization that show how smuggling and social networks operate at the border – "the double-funnel" (abundance of people involved at the point of origin but few at the points of importation) and the "capillary pattern" (many people at the points of origin and destiny).

Borderlands, frontiers, and borders

In recent years, particularly after 09/11, the idea of borders "everywhere" or "mobile" borders has gained ground in the literature (discussed earlier). This approach emphasized that the focus of the State shifted from controlling territory to assessing risk associated with mobility (people and goods). Border scholars (ÓTuathail, 1998; Balibar and Williams, 2002; Lyon, 2005; Rumford, 2006; Amilhat-Szary and Giraut, 2015; Brambilla and Jones, 2020) argued that as States adopt stronger security measures and surveillance functions (e.g., passport control, citizenship IDs, etc.) these are deployed in many locations away from international borders (e.g., airports, highways, neighborhood, etc.). The spillover effect of border securitization is the increasing costs of smuggling; therefore, the potential profits have attracted new players such as cartels and mafias that have either incorporated "local" smugglers or displaced them. The tactics of smugglers have become more violent, becoming "deterritorialized threats" and "global dangers" (ÓTuathail, 1998; Andreas, 2003), thus the social embeddedness between smugglers and society has been somewhat broken. Finally, as States re-territorialize their borders, enhance surveillance, criminalize smuggling (i.e., from misdemeanors to heinous crimes), and make the land border physically impossible to cross, smugglers "jump scales" and turn to other routes such as sea, air, and underground tunnels.

The attention now is turned to the temporal category and how the symbiosis between borders and smuggling has changed, particularly in the transition between modernity and post-modernity. The thread that links together the border and smuggling is the practice of bordering, particularly the dialectic between open and closed borders.

Within the modern epoch, the State used borders (regulating the flows in and out) to pursue a "national interest" of inward development and only traded to acquire inputs not found inside the nation. Empirical evidence shows that nations have developed at different rates and not in synchronicity. Thus, there can be borders where relative asymmetries are minimal (e.g., USA and Canada, Western Europe, Brazil and Argentina) or large (e.g., USA and Mexico, Brazil and Paraguay, Dominican Republic and Haiti); smuggling is present in both situations, but it is more intense where asymmetries are the largest. Smugglers take advantage of these asymmetries created by bordering practice or economic development policies (e.g., import substitution vs. export oriented). In brief, the modern approach is a State-centric in the sense that the State is the only actor with bordering capacity.

In contrast, the post-modern view is that multiple actors, in addition to the State, have the capability of re-bordering and de-bordering. For instance, transnational corporations' (TNC) revenue and stock value are higher than the entire gross domestic product (GDP) of some sovereign nations. While economies in the post-modern world became integrated and globalized, so did smuggling; as a matter of fact, drug smugglers re-organized into different organizational forms (e.g., cartels) and expanded the scale and scope of their activities (ÓTuathail, 1998; Andreas, 2002) and control substantial amount of financial resources. According to the World Economic Forum, drug smuggling accounts for half the assets of illicit economies and the financial assets are estimated at $320 billion (equivalent to Colombia's GDP of $331 billion) (World Economic Forum WEF, 2016). Anti-immigrant and xenophobic groups have emerged in receiving countries and they have played a key role in re-bordering, therefore, smuggling, particularly human trafficking, has become the center of this re-bordering and criminalization.

Scales are also reconfigured by actors, including smugglers, who seek advantages in the de-bordering process. The important question to be addressed is: How do smuggling, borders, and scales interact and how have they changed? Several authors argue that borders are experiencing a phenomenon of "scale jumping" (Newman and Paasi, 1998; Abraham and van Schendel, 2005van Schendel van Schendel 2005; Rumford, 2006). This is, the traditional dichotomies of domestic/foreign, and national/international, according to Agnew (1994, p. 59), "obscure the interaction between processes operating at different scales." From a scalar perspective, smuggling practices have transformed their scope of action from local-local or cross-border regional to transnational. When smuggling becomes a transnational phenomenon, territorial borders (i.e., borderlands) lose their fixed locational advantages. Instead of being a central node in the flows of smuggled consumer goods such as cigarettes, electronics, etc., they become just another player in the wider and more complex network of transactions; smugglers could "jump scales" and bypass borders. Some border cities as commercial nodes of smuggled consumer goods have lost not only their fixed locational advantage but also the benefits of arbitrage economies were diminished with globalization and the opening of the economy; consumer goods can be shipped or transported without needing to cross a territorial border. The border as location is affected as well as the enterprise of smuggling goods that now are widely available through the formal economy at more competitive prices (Gereffi et al., 2009). Thus, smugglers must turn to other enterprises such as drugs and human trafficking. The points of origin and destination of smuggling activities have dispersed all over the map and involve a large constellation of actors dispersed across the world, making scales fuzzy.

According to Rumford, bordering is not always a business of the State; non-State actors are more and more engaged in this (see Rumford in Johnson et al., 2011). For instance, vigilantes or militia type organizations such as the "Minutemen" on the U.S.–Mexico border have asserted for themselves border patrolling functions. One extreme argument is that a "borderless" world meant the end of the State as we knew it in a post-Westphalian world. Another more moderate argument is that the State had never disappeared; it has just transferred some of its sovereign power to non-State actors to adapt to the new realities of the emergence of a transnational or global class (Sassen, 2007, pp.164–189) to manage the global network of capital accumulation. Simultaneously, with the emergence of a global class that often is associated with bankers, accountants, software developers, etc., there is also a global marginalized class that lives in global cities and keeps trying to cross the border (physical and economic) seeking a better life in more developed nations than their own. As receiving nations "re-border" their homelands, crossing borders has become more difficult for the marginalized class. Therefore, the cost of the journey has increased as has the need to use the services of smugglers who have turned into human traffickers. An important aspect to highlight is that the murky divide between smugglers (transporting goods that can be sold legally without coercion in the transaction) and traffickers (performing proscribed illegal activities and coercion exists) has disappeared. Smuggling as an enterprise has also undergone an organizational reconfiguration, becoming a transnational actor that controls large amounts of assets ($2.1 trillion) and a wide network of operators who have diversified their economic portfolio (drug trafficking and human trafficking often are controlled by the same criminal organizations) (Andreas, 2002). Drug cartels are one example of how powerful these organizations have become, with substantial financial and war power that can challenge the State authority and its sovereignty over territory – including border points that are crucial to their enterprise. For example, some media outlets estimated that "El Chapo" Guzman, the most famous Mexican drug lord and head of the Sinaloa Cartel, now in prison in the U.S., has assets worth $12.6 billion. As smuggling and trafficking become more profitable and wars among criminal organizations or terrorist acts have become more common, the notion of smugglers as folk heroes has been transformed into that of a societal menace and a "global danger" (ÓTuathail, 1998).

Conclusions

This chapter has scrutinized the intersection between borders and smuggling, and it has revealed interesting connections between both. Borders as social constructs help us understand better the triad of smuggling practice, space, and society. The chapter shows that instead of looking at smuggling as a "deviant" or "subversive" practice that challenges the State authority and sovereignty over its territory, it is more fruitful and insightful to look at smuggling in relational terms which reveal how social relations and networks operate at the border to facilitate enforcement in a more selective way, mediating between local and national interests. Another relevant aspect reveals that smuggling as a social practice is not static but dynamic. Smuggling has adapted, for better or worse, not only in its "products and services," but also its organizational spatial structure linking border and non-border locations in a functional way. Smuggling and trafficking have taken advantage of globalization and transnational networks, some have become global criminal organizations capable of challenging the State and its control of borders. The conceptualization of borders spatially helps us to unpack and explain a variety of smuggling practices, providing a more complex and complete picture of the phenomenon.

Notes

1 Foucault studies the relationship power-space. The main argument is that space is one dimension where power is deployed with the objective of discipline and punishing subjects; spaces instead of being a utopia (imagined paradise) are transformed in heterotopias (existing, real, and nightmarish). Also, Foucault developed the term "governmentality" as an example of a power technology aimed to govern bodies, population, spaces, and movement.
2 Beck's central argument is that there is a break in history, and we are moving from modernity towards the risk society. The modern world shared the view that economic growth and prosperity were good for humankind, thus social values had some cohesiveness around these ideas. However, the risk society challenges the basic notion that growth is good and therefore social cohesion breaks down since risk, risk assessment and perception become central themes of political communities. Smuggling practice (e.g., drugs) and borders are often view as a risk or threat to the local population.

References

Abraham, Itty and van Schendel, Willem. (2005). Introduction: The Making of Illicitness. Willem van Schendel and Itty Abraham (Eds.), *Illicit Flows and Criminal Things: States, Borders, and the Other Side of Globalization*, 1–37. Bloomington, IN: Indiana University Press.

Agnew, John. (1994). The Territorial Trap: The Geographical Assumptions of International Relations Theory. *Review of International Political Economy*, 1:1, 53–80.

Agnew, John. (2008). Borders on the Mind: Re-framing Border Thinking. *Ethics & Global Politics*, 1:4, 175–191.

Amilhat-Szary, Anne-Laure and Giraut, Frédéric. (2015). Borderities: The Politics of Contemporary Mobile Borders. Anne-Laure Amilhat-Szary and Frédéric Giraut (Eds.), *Borderities and the Politics of Contemporary Mobile Borders*. New York: Palgrave Macmillan, 1–22.

Anderson, James and O'Dowd, Liam. (1999). Borders, Border Regions and Territoriality: Contradictory Meanings, Changing Significance. *Regional Studies*, 33:7, 593–604, DOI: 10.1080/0034340995 0078648.

Andreas, Peter. (2002). Transnational Crime and Economic Globalization. Mats Berdal and Monica Serrano (Eds.), *Transnational Organized Crime and International Security: Business as Usual?* Boulder: Lynne Rienner Publishers, 37–52.

Andreas, Peter. (2003). Redrawing the Line: Borders and Security in the Twenty-First Century. *International Security*, 28:2, 78–111.

Balibar, Etienne and Williams, Erin M. (2002). World Borders, Political Borders. *Publication of the Modern Language Association of America*, 117:1, 68–78.

Basu, Gautam. (2014). Concealment, Corruption, and Evasion: A transaction Cost and Case Analysis of Illicit Supply Chain Activity. *Journal of Transportation Security*, 7:3, 209–226.

Baud, Michiel and van Schendel, Willem. (1997). Toward a Comparative History of Borderlands. *Journal of World History*, 8:2, 211–242.

Beck, Ulrich. (1992). *Risk Society: Towards a New Modernity*. Los Angeles: Sage.

Boehmer, Charles and Peña, Sergio. (2012). The Determinants of Open and Closed Borders. *Journal of Borderlands Studies*, 27:3, 273–285.

Brambilla, Chiara. (2015). Exploring the Critical Potential of the Borderscapes Concept. *Geopolitics*, 20:1, 14–34, DOI: 10.1080/14650045.2014.884561.

Brambilla, Chiara and Jones, Reece. (2020). Rethinking Borders, Violence, and Conflict: From Sovereign Power to Borderscapes as Sites of Struggle. *Environment and Planning D: Society and Space*, 38:2, 287–305.

Brunet-Jailly, Emmanuel. (2005). Theorizing Borders: An Interdisciplinary Perspective. *Geopolitics*, 10:4, 633–649, DOI: 10.1080/14650040500318449.

Cooper, Anthony, Perkins, Chris and Rumford, Chris. (2016). The Vernacularization of Borders. R. Jones and C. Johnson (Eds.), *Placing the Border in Everyday Life*, 15–32, New York: Routledge.

Gereffi, Gary, Spener, David and Bair, Jennifer. eds. (2009). *Free Trade and Uneven Development: The North American Apparel Industry After NAFTA*. Philadelphia: Temple University Press.

Heyman, Josiah. (1994). The Mexico-United States Border in Anthropology: A Critique and Reformulation. *Journal of Political Ecology*, 1:1, 43–66.

Heyman, Josiah. (1995). Putting Power in the Anthropology of Bureaucracy: The Immigration and Naturalization Service at the Mexico-United States Border. *Current Anthropology*, 36:2, 261–287.

House, John W. (1980). The Frontier Zone: A Conceptual Problem for Policy Makers. *International Political Science Review*, 1:4, 456–477.

Jessop, Bob. (2002). The Political Economy of Scale. Markus Perkmann and Ngai-Ling Sum (Eds.),*Globalization, Regionalization and Cross-border Regions*, 25–49. London: Palgrave Macmillan.

Johnson, Corey, Jones, Reece, Paasi, Ansi, Amoore, Louise, Mountz, Alison, Salter, Mark and Rumford, Chris. (2011). Interventions on Rethinking 'the Border' in Border Studies. *Political Geography*, 30:2, 61–69.

Kolossov, Vladimir. (2005). Border Studies: Changing Perspectives and Theoretical Approaches. *Geopolitics*, 10:4, 606–632.

Kraudzun, Tobias. (2012). From the Pamir Frontier to International Borders: Exchange Relations of the Borderland Population. Bettina Bruns Judith Miggelbrink (Eds.), *Subverting Borders Doing Research on Smuggling and Small-Scale Trade*, 171–191. Wiesbaden: Springer.

Lapid, Yosef. (2001). Introduction Identities, Borders, Orders: Nudging International Relations Theory in a New Direction. Mathias Albert, David Jacobson, and Yosef Lapid (Eds). *Identities Borders Orders: Rethinking International Relations Theory*, 1–20. Minneapolis: University of Minnesota Press.

Lyon, David. (2005). The Border is Everywhere: ID Cards, Surveillance and the Other. Elia Zureik and Mark B. Salter (Eds.), *Global Surveillance and Policing: Borders, Security, Identity*, 66–82. Portland: Willan Publishing.

Martinez, Oscar J. (1994). *Border People: Life and Society in the US–Mexico Borderlands*. Tucson: University of Arizona Press.

Massey, Doreen (2005). *For Space*. London; Thousand Oaks: Sage.

Newman, David and Anssi Paasi. (1998). Fences and Neighbours in the Postmodern World: Boundary Narratives in Political Geography. *Progress in Human Geography*, 22:2, 186–207.

Newman, David. (2001). Boundaries, Borders and Barriers: Changing Geographic Perspectives on Territorial Lines. Mathias Albert, David Jacobson, and Yosef Lapid (Eds.), *Identities Borders Orders: Rethinking International Relations Theory*, 137–151. Minneapolis: University of Minnesota Press.

Newman, David. (2006a). Borders and Bordering Towards an Interdisciplinary Dialogue. *European Journal of Social Theory*, 9:2, 171–186.

Newman, David. (2006b). The Lines that Continue to Separate Us: Borders in Our Borderless' World. *Progress in Human Geography*, 30:2, 143–161.

Newman, David. (2016). Contemporary Research Agendas in Border Studies: An Overview. *The Routledge Research Companion to Border Studies*, 55–70. London: Routledge.

ÓTuathail, Gearóid (Gerard Toal). (1998). De-Territorialised Threats and Global Dangers: Geopolitics and Risk Society. *Geopolitics*, 3:1, 17–31, DOI: 10.1080/14650049808407605

ÓTuathail, Gearóid (Gerard Toal). (1999). Borderless Worlds? Problematising Discourses of Deterritorialization. *Geopolitics*, 4:2, 139–154, DOI: 10.1080/14650049908407644

Paasi, Anssi. (2012). Border Studies Reanimated: Going Beyond the Territorial/Relational Divide. *Environment and Planning A*, 44:10, 2303–2309.

Paasi, Anssi. (2014). The Shifting Landscape of Border Studies and the Challenge of Relational Thinking. Milan Bufon et al. (Ed.), *The New European Frontiers: Social and Spatial (Re) integration Issues in Multicultural and Border Regions*, 361–379. Newcastle: Cambridge Scholars Publishing.

Rumford, Chris. (2006). Theorizing Borders. *European Journal of Social Theory*, 9:2, 155–169.

Sassen, Saskia. (2007). *A Sociology of Globalization*. New York: W.W. Norton & Co.

Soja, Edward. (1996). *Thirdspace: Journey to Los Angeles and Other Real-and-Imagined Places*. Cambridge, MA: Blackwell Publishing.

Stoddard, Ellwyn R. (1991). Frontiers, Borders and Border Segmentation: Toward a Conceptual Clarification. *Journal of Borderlands Studies*, 6:1, 1–22.

Swyngedouw, Erik. (1997). Neither Global nor Local: Glocalization and the Politics of Scale. Kevin R. Cox (Ed.), *Spaces of Globalization: Reasserting the Power of the Local*, 137–166. New York/London: The Guilford Press.

van Houtum, Henk and van Naerssen, Ton. (2002). Bordering, Ordering, and Othering. *Tijdschrift voor Economische en Sociale Geografie*, 93:2, 125–136.

van Schendel, Willem. (2005). Spaces of Engagement: How Borderlands, Illegal Flows, and Territorial States Interlock. W. van Schendel, and I. Abraham (Eds.), *Illicit Flows and Criminal Things: States, Borders, and the Other Side of Globalization*, 38–68. Bloomington: Indiana University Press.

Weber, Max. (2009). *From Max Weber: Essays in Sociology*. New York: Routledge.

World Economic Forum (WEF). (October 2016). State of the Illicit Economy: *Briefing Paper. REF* 290915, Geneva, Switzerland.

9

TRADING SPACES

Afghan borderland brokers and the transformation of the margins[1]

Jonathan Goodhand, Jan Koehler, and Jasmine Bhatia

Introduction

This chapter focuses on brokers and brokerage in the context of cross border smuggling or illicit trade. Drawing on illustrative case study material from the borderscapes of eastern and western Afghanistan, we shine a light on the lives of two brokers who act as go-betweens and gate-keepers in these complex and often conflictual transnational trading networks. One is a tribal broker in Nangarhar province on the Pakistan border, and another is an illicit trader in Nimroz province on the Iranian border. By focusing on their lives we aim to achieve two things: firstly, to present new empirical evidence on brokers, so as to better understand their lives, motivations, roles and effects – and in particular, how they adapted to border hardening and closures. Specifically, we explore the *positionality* of brokers in terms of their personal backgrounds, their ability to straddle lifeworlds, the 'deal spaces' they occupy, the resources and commodities they move, and the key pathways, corridors and choke points that channel and direct trade flows. We also examine the *dynamics* of brokerage, including the ways that brokers find solutions or 'fixes' to problems but rarely resolve them, and how brokers adapt to (or fail to adapt to) moments of rupture in fluid trading environments. Finally, we reveal the *effects* of brokerage in terms of how brokers cumulatively shape the ways in which states and markets function in marginal frontier and borderland environments. Though their agency is circumscribed, brokers are not merely mediators; they play a role in transforming and reconfiguring connections and relationships within political and market systems.

Secondly, we aim to contribute to wider theoretical debates about brokerage as a lens for conceptualising and analysing the dynamics of illicit trade in borderland environments. We show that paying careful attention to the edges tells us important things about the whole; the lives of seemingly marginal borderland brokers provide a privileged vantage point for understanding the wider political economy of (licit and illicit) trading systems, how they change over time and their distributional effects within and across borders.

In the next section we introduce key terms and provide a brief overview of the emerging literature on brokers and brokerage. We then set out our analytical approach to this phenomenon, which is followed by illustrative case studies of political and trading brokers in Afghanistan. We conclude with some reflections on the theoretical and empirical implications of this analysis.

118   DOI: 10.4324/9781003043645-9

Frontiers and borderlands: spaces of innovation and transformation

In this chapter our focus is on a particular kind of trading space: borderlands and frontier regions that straddle the margins of one or more states. Borderlands are classically understood as zones straddling an international border, whilst frontiers are more fuzzy political spaces, marking zones of transition between different centres of power and regulation. Both are liminal spaces of cultural overlap and hybridity.

Many of today's borderlands bear the traces of earlier frontier dynamics and the legacies of empires, and these dynamics persist beneath the mosaic of nation states (O'Dowd, 2012). Rather than disappearing, frontiers tend to wax and wane in boom and bust cycles, linked to an amalgam of factors including the retreat and expansion of states and markets, the shifting dynamics of conflict, crises of accumulation in metropolitan centers, the building of infrastructure, and shifts in global and regional commodity markets (licit and illicit). 'Frontier effects' and 'border effects' may coexist and interact in the same marginal spaces, with the salience of each shifting over time, as shown in our case studies below.

Trading routes are often grafted onto longstanding regional networks and connections that preceded statebuilding, for example the Silk Route in Central Asia and the ancient trade routes crisscrossing the Sahara (McDougal & Scheele, 2012). Border delineation did not so much interrupt these regional networks of interdependence as restructure them, leading to smuggling networks and semi-licit trade and new regional power centres that were dependent on borders.

Border zones are often 'sensitive spaces' (Cons, 2016), absorbing a disproportionate amount of the time and attention of central state elites. They are frequently places where state authority and sovereignty are contested, access to the means of violence is fragmented and the existence of cross border networks and flows create a centrifugal dynamic that counters the centripetal forces of statebuilding.

Therefore, in studying the margins of the state, we are not looking at disconnected or lagging regions, but often spaces that are central to processes of statebuilding and development. We are interested here in developing a relational approach, which moves beyond methodological nationalism, recognizing transnational and subnational processes that are often rendered invisible in state-centric analysis. This approach reveals borderlands as places of radical uncertainty and rapid change, where peripheral elites and borderland populations are constantly improvising and innovating in order to survive and sometimes prosper.

Borderlands as trading spaces

Borders generate a 'spatial discount' for those who are buying, selling or employing to derive profits by exploiting differences between regulatory regimes on both sides of a border. In this sense, rather than acting as constraints, borders are fields of opportunity. The intensity of economic flows and relations may be greater across the border than with the metropolitan centre within a state. Although smugglers may resist or subvert the state's regulatory efforts, they are rarely revolutionaries. The relationship between smugglers and state officials is more symbiotic in nature, often involving a high degree of collusion (Goodhand, 2020; Nugent, 2002; Taggliacozza, 2005).

Border regimes can be understood as *interactive orders* involving movement and counter movement on the part of those who police and those who transgress various border controls (Goodhand & Meehan, 2018). This takes place not only at the border itself. The policing and enforcement of border regimes can occur through multiple agents in various locations – from the border guards, customs officials, and drones situated at airports, ports, and land borders, to financial regulators and migration officials based in capital cities.

Borderlands have their own particular ecosystems of constraint and opportunity, linked to their specific histories and geographies. Two factors are critical in structuring the dynamics of borderland trade: first, the type and level of state presence at the border; and second, the depth or degree of inequality at the border (Zartman, 2010). According to More (2011), 'extreme borders,' characterized by large economic asymmetries, exhibit particular 'pathologies' – including heightened levels of militarization and violence, illicit drug trafficking, and people smuggling. Rather than promoting convergence and integration that might help alleviate inequalities, the more powerful state typically does the opposite, which has the paradoxical effect of steepening these pathologies further, thus increasing the stakes, incentives and risk premiums associated with illicit cross-border smuggling, as shown in our case studies below.

The distinction between formal/legal and informal/illicit trade may carry little meaning in the borderlands; indeed, in border zones we see ambivalent and unstable encounters between legal and illegal, state and non-state, smugglers and state agents. Legal and illegal forms of trade can be understood as a continuum of possibilities that traders can flexibly use as part of a trading portfolio.

Both smugglers and state agents have an economic interest in controlling lucrative cross-border trading corridors and choke points, especially when there are asymmetric regulatory regimes on both sides. For example, as an unregulated, high-risk, high-opportunity environment, Goma is a crucial node in the network of East African trading corridors (Lamarque, 2014). Profits generated from this business, however, are invested on the other side of the border, where Congolese businessmen build their houses in the more secure and regulated Rwandese state space (*ibid*). As such, government positions at the border, such as police chiefs, customs officials, and border guards are extremely lucrative and cost significant sums to purchase. In order to recoup the initial outlay, officials often rely on rents extracted from the movement of commodities and people across the border. This in turn incentivises the proliferation of smuggling routes away from formal border crossings; for instance, on the Guatemala-Honduras border there are 15 formal crossing points but more than 100 informal ones. These 'blind spots' (*puntos ciegos*) are unofficial border crossings that central government officials have little capacity to control (ICG, 2014).

Traders, brokers and borderland brokerage

Protracted conflict, illicit economies, and the presence of an international border alongside multiple internal borders demarcated by social, political, religious cleavages create a demand for brokers in borderland and frontier regions.

A broker can be defined as someone who acts as an intermediary, playing the role of a go-between or fixer. Brokers occupy a space 'between handshakes and contracts,' where formal institutions cannot be trusted and where informality and social capital are key to getting things done – for example, processing conflicts, distributing resources, and accessing rights and entitlements. Brokers are 'network specialists' whose ability to straddle multiple knowledge systems and life-worlds enables them to act as gatekeepers across various social 'synapses' or 'choke points' (James, 2011; Wolf, 1956) and in doing so "transmit, direct, filter, receive, code, decode, and interpret messages" across these interstitial spaces (Meehan & Plonski, 2017, p. 5).

The term 'broker' is rarely used self-referentially, as most people prefer not to define themselves as such (Bierschenk et al., 2002). In fact, in many contexts it is a pejorative term; for example, in South Asia brokers or 'dalals' are seen as self interested, extractive, dissembling figures (Goodhand & Walton, 2020). Notwithstanding this perception, brokers are ubiquitous in many contexts, particularly borderland regions. They are ambiguous and Janus-faced figures who serve different constituencies, linking national and subnational political systems, or trading networks on two sides of a border. As Wolf (1956) notes, they stand guard over key synapses, or points of friction, acting as both the lubricant and the grit in the political or market system.

To develop further this broad characterisation of brokerage, three points about the positionality, dynamics and effects of brokerage can be highlighted.

First, in terms of their **positionality**, brokers aim to occupy 'deal spaces' or points of friction within political, economic or social systems that require and create opportunities for some form of intermediation and negotiation. In contexts marked by liminality and illegality, brokers fill a void created by the absence of formal regulatory mechanisms to allocate resources, process disputes and make claims. Brokers can play the role of connecting otherwise inaccessible spaces and performing tasks that formal actors are unwilling or unable to do.

Borderlands are places where the local and global collide and become entangled in complex ways. Brokers can be understood as 'friction specialists' who mediate, and reconfigure, relationships among communities, armed groups, state entities and businesses, regional patrons, and legal and illegal activities (Meehan & Plonski, 2017). Particular communities have historically played outsized brokerage roles – for example the Pashtuns of eastern Afghanistan and the Baluch on the borders of Afghanistan, Pakistan and Iran. These groups are both highly local and transregional at the same time. They are adept at facilitating border crossings and gatekeeping. Their identities are bound up with notions and practices of flexible citizenship and operating among different normative orders.

The positionality of brokers varies according to where the demand for brokerage comes from – the extent to which brokers are beholden to the central state or societal groups in the borderlands – and their location within wider systems of governance and markets. *Apex brokers* occupy key synapses that shape the overall balance of power or distribution of resources within political settlements. This tends to be the case in the most salient borderland regions, connecting 'elites that matter' in the centre and the periphery. *Tertiary brokers* sit further down the political system or value chain – either within more marginalised borderlands or between less salient and lucrative internal border regions, rather than the critical interfaces between centre and periphery or across an international border (Goodhand & Walton, 2020).

Second, in terms of the **dynamics** of brokerage, the ambiguity and contradictions of brokers is bound up with their role as fixers who address problems, but rarely fully resolve them. Meehan and Plonski (2017) use the term 'brokerage fix' to describe the dynamic through which brokers perpetually engineer solutions to problems that are always temporary and provisional, and lead to new sets of contradictions and challenges, which in turn require new brokerage fixes. Successful brokers are able to reinvent themselves continually in order to occupy and monopolise deal spaces and to remain relevant. Some experience temporary success in this role but are unable to adapt and are marginalised, whilst others may graduate from being a broker to becoming a key decision-maker at the centre of power. This leads to questions, when looking at individual lives, about whether brokerage can be understood as a long-term career or a short-term transitional phase.

Third, in terms of the **effects** of brokerage, there is a tendency to view brokers as ephemeral, shadowy characters who adapt to change, but are rarely presented as the agents of change. Yet they are more than simply 'intermediaries' facilitating linkages and flows; they are also 'mediators,' with a degree of autonomy, agency and power, enabling them to shape, regulate, and filter flows (Bierschenk et al., 2002; Latour, 2005; Mosse & Lewis, 2006). They enable – and rework – deals among communities, companies and state entities, between peripheries and centres within nations and across international borders (Meehan & Plonski, 2017). Therefore brokerage may have cumulatively structural effects on wider systems of state and market power. Trajectories of change in the borderlands are rarely gradual and linear, but marked by moments of rupture or 'punctuated equilibrium' in which there are major shifts in the dynamics of brokerage and underlying political settlements. The agency of brokers may be inflated during such moments of flux. As we explore further below, apex brokers can reshape political settlements, whilst trade brokers can set in motion new rounds of investment and development in frontier boomtowns.

The political economy of borderland trading and brokerage networks

Borderland trade brokers mediate, filter and channel flows of commodities and resources across borders. Their power is derived from occupying key choke points or places of friction in transnational trading systems. This allows them to generate economic rents, which can in turn be translated into political power. Where high trade profits combine with inconsistent state control, cross-border networks can become alternative systems of power (Dobler, 2016). In Afghanistan for example, when the Taliban came to power in the mid-1990s, they were backed by powerful Afghan traders based in Peshawar, Pakistan, whose interests were undermined by the instability of warlord-dominated Afghanistan.

Border zone economies involve a multitude of actors (traders, transporters, brokers, drivers, loaders, processors, harvesters, farmers, miners, hotel and warehouse owners, government officials – customs officials, border police, military, intelligence agencies – commanders, rebel groups, militias), and complex assemblages and brokerage arrangements, which bring together transport, warehousing and logistics, labour regimes, financing and credit relations, technological innovation and market adaptation, information collection, data analysis and market research. Trading networks are highly adaptive and innovative, having been 'stress tested' by years of conflict, political fluidity and frequent economic shocks in contexts of radical uncertainty.

Trading routes or corridors – understood here as connected and coordinated bundles of transport, logistics, infrastructure, and services that connect centres of economic activity (Hagman & Steppatat, 2016) – are continually shifting. These trading routes vary in terms of their political and economic salience, the actors involved and the governance and brokering relations in which they are embedded. Building on Dobler (2016) a tentative taxonomy of trading corridors or pathways is presented in Table 9.1, each being associated with different types of brokers and brokering dynamics.

A number of observations flow out of this typology, which are developed further in the empirical material below.

First, across this typology of corridors there is a need to unpack and analyse power relations within trade networks, how governance relations and forms of rent extraction and taxation occur at different points in the value chain and the role of brokers in these processes. For example, containerised goods on major roads across official crossing points (Type 4) are likely to have more formal state involvement, more hierarchical relations, higher barriers to entry and greater involvement of apex brokers. In contrast, informal/illicit/semi-licit trade across unofficial crossings along unpaved roads and tracks is likely to involve more players, lower barriers to entry, greater involvement of tertiary brokers, less formal involvement of the state, particularly central state actors – and perhaps may also be more egalitarian and redistributive than containerized, formal trade (Mansfield, 2020a, 2020b). Therefore, we can analyse trading networks in terms of whether they enforce strong hierarchical ties, or rather whether they function through horizontal, diffuse and weak ties.

Trading spaces

Table 9.1 Typology of trading corridors

Pathway type	Description	Key actors, beneficiaries and brokers
Type 1	**Small-scale informal crossings** on tracks in mountain passes and deserts; informal trading in maritime spaces (e.g., drug smuggling in dhows along the Makran coast of Pakistan).	Local communities, local elites, and non-state actors' small-scale markets, hotels, and tea shops, small-scale brokers, women involved in petty trade.
Type 2	**Large-scale informal/illegal crossings:** large-scale movement of goods along unofficial routes/border crossings that are not formally regulated or sanctioned (e.g., militarised transhipment of drugs from Afghanistan across the desert spaces of Nimroz).	Armed groups, government officials (unofficially), powerful business leaders and brokers, communities in border areas involved in the production and transportation of goods.
Type 3	**Licit and illicit goods, transported through official crossings on tarmac roads:** movement of goods and people across formally sanctioned border crossings that may involve adhering to regulations governing these crossings (e.g., border checks, paperwork, etc.) or efforts to transgress regulations and checks to move goods illegally by using formal crossings and infrastructure (e.g., smuggling of drugs and gold through Torkham on the Afghan-Pakistan border).	Customs officials, local government actors, local strong men, powerful business leaders and brokers; frontier boomtowns.
Type 4	**Major transnational (in some cases transcontinental) infrastructure corridors:** including trade and energy corridors and maritime and airports connected to infrastructure and logistics hubs in the Gulf (e.g., the China-Pakistan Economic Corridor within China's Belt and Road Initiative; the Chabahar port in Iran; the Iran-Pakistan gas pipeline project).	Foreign capital and national political elites; 'centres' more than 'peripheries'; regional powers (particularly China, Iran, and the Gulf).

Second, the trading networks vary in terms of their level of (in)formality and the role of information. In illicit networks information tends to be highly fragmented and lower-level actors are only partially sighted – they are only aware of their sections of the corridor, and other nodes in the smuggling network may be unknown to them. However, it is likely that apex brokers are able to see the bigger picture and have privileged access to information along different points of the chain; in the terminology of network analysis, they have greater 'betweenness centrality.'

Third, each route is associated with different types and levels of friction. Type 4 aspires to low-friction or frictionless trade, with fewer intermediaries and flows of goods in containers running through official border crossings. Theoretically, where there is frictionless trade, then there is no need for brokers, but in the 'real world' it is difficult to find such situations. In Type 4 corridors there are fewer points of friction and power is likely to be concentrated amongst a small group of apex brokers, often located in metropolitan centres rather than at the border itself. Conversely, Type 1 flows involve multiple points of friction and consequently multiple points of rent extraction and brokerage. In many ways this makes them more redistributive than Type 4 corridors, in which a greater proportion of accumulated profits tend to flow to the centres of power rather than the border regions. Border hardening and the investment in infrastructure and technologies to manage, filter and funnel flows are likely to increase this dynamic of directing the proceeds of trade towards the centre rather than the borderlands. It also shifts the pattern of trade flows across borders from a capillary action to a funnel action, and as explored in the life histories below, this means that tertiary brokers either get pushed out of 'the game' or they need to reinvent themselves as apex brokers.

Fourth, as noted, brokerage relations and dynamics vary across these four corridors. They are associated with different kinds of 'deal spaces' involving differing barriers to entry and different kinds of brokers. We need more information about the extent to which brokers are generalists or specialists – do they focus on particular kinds of commodities and/or in particular types of corridors? How do brokers respond to moments of rupture? How do they reinvent themselves to find new 'brokerage fixes' and what new sets of contradictions do these fixes produce? Studying the complex life histories of individual brokers can help answer these questions.

Case studies – the life histories of brokers[2]

Context

The border between the Afghan province of *Nangarhar* and Pakistan is mountainous and rugged to the east and south (Figure 9.1), with the Pashtun tribes straddling both sides of the Durand line, which marks the international border (Barfield, 2010; Grötzbach, 1990). Nangarhar is a politically salient border province with strong connections to Kabul, as well as across the border with Pakistan. The main border crossing is at Torkham, the gateway to the Khyber Pass, which cuts through the Spin Ghar mountains. Highway A01 is the key transport corridor, running through Torkham and connecting Peshawar in Pakistan with Jalalabad, the provincial centre and Kabul, the national capital – and since the US intervention of 2001 it also became a key transit route for NATO supplies. In addition, there are multiple informal border crossing points, which have historically been key smuggling routes for a range of licit and illicit commodities (Mansfield, 2020a). Trade is central to the Nangarhar's economy and in 2018 imports and exports through Torkham generated $119 million in taxes (*ibid*).

Nimroz, on the other hand, is a remote frontier region of vast deserts with a historically open border with Iran and Pakistan. Unlike Jalalabad, Ziranj (Figure 9.1) was a neglected administrative outpost in a province inhabited mostly by the Baloch, a large but marginalised minority that straddle the borderlands of Iran, Afghanistan and Pakistan (Boedeker, 2012; Larson, 2010, Titus, 1996). Arbitrage has been central to the local economy – trading networks are grafted onto long standing regional circuits of exchange, which were strengthened in the war years, when mostly Afghan Baluch and Hazara communities resettled in larger numbers on the Iranian side, establishing supply lines to support the anti-communist insurgency in Afghanistan as well as flows of remittances to family members remaining in the country (Kutty, 2014). These connections then provided the basis for smuggling narcotics and economic migrants into Iran and beyond, as well as bringing diesel from Iran into Afghanistan (Mansfield, 2020b).

Trading spaces

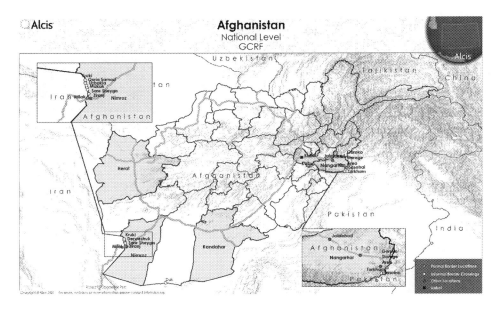

Figure 9.1 Map of Afghanistan, highlighting locations referred to in the case illustrations
Source: Alcis.

Geopolitically, the border region has become more salient as Afghanistan, Iran and India have made investments in infrastructure to increase trade flows including the construction of route 606, which has become a major trading corridor linking Chabahar port in Iran with Ziranj and the Herat-Kandahar highway (*ibid*).

Like many other borderlands, border delineation divided geographically and demographically contiguous spaces and this separation was amplified by statebuilding processes on both sides of the border. The wars of the 1980s and 1990s interrupted these efforts, and Afghanistan's eastern and western borderlands reverted to their historical status as open frontier regions, creating new spaces and opportunities for trading networks with low barriers to entry and multiple flows.

However, since 2001 neighbouring states, and to some extent the Afghan state, have sought to impose stronger border controls linked to concerns about terrorism and illicit narcotics, and a desire to increase official trade flows. This has led to investments in border security including fencing and border walls and infrastructure such as road building, customs posts and warehousing facilities. The 'infrastructural power' of the state (Mann, 1984) now reaches up to the borderline and both borderlands have become more regulated, closing off the multitude of informal crossing points along the borderline and channelling trade flows and movements of people through official crossing points. According to our typology of pathways, the main purpose of border hardening was to enhance licit trade flows along Type 3 and 4 pathways and to close off Type 1 and 2 flows – through enhanced border regulation and policing. These changes drastically reduced informal, largely open-access trade, professionalising and vertically integrating both legal and illegal access to the cross-border trading economy (Koehler et al, 2021; Mansfield, 2020a, 2020b). As explored further below, the dynamics of brokerage shifted accordingly.

The case studies below are drawn from a series of life history interviews with borderland brokers and their associates conducted in Nangarhar and Nimroz between August and

November 2020. They illustrate the *positionality*, *dynamics* and *effects* of brokerage: the process by which apex brokers come to dominate trading networks, what functions they serve, and how their positions as brokers spilled over into other aspects of conflict resolution and mediation. To protect the safety of these individuals, their names have been changed. Where appropriate, minor details have been changed or omitted to obscure their identities.

From insurgent to mediator: emergence of an apex broker in Nangarhar

The first case study looks at the life history of Haji M. Khan, an influential broker and tribal mediator. Haji M. Khan was born and grew up in a small village in a mountainous district bordering Pakistan in the 1950s. The district has limited agricultural land and he, like most people, was employed in the small-scale domestic wood trade with Jalalabad (the provincial centre) and Kabul. His family were also involved in informal cross-border trade in wood, opium, clothes and dry fruit, transported to the Tribal Areas of Pakistan via mules and donkeys, along Type 1 pathways and informal border crossings. Contacts and exchanges across the porous border with Pakistan were more frequent and important to Haji M. Khan and his community than to Kabul or even Jalalabad. While along this part of the border the dominant tribes on the Afghan and Pakistani side were different,[3] they had agreed on mutual protection agreements (*lokhae*). Haji M. Khan enjoyed privileged access since part of his lineage, as well as his eventual in-laws, were from the Afridi tribe on the other side of the border.

Haji M. Khan's cross-border relations provided a lifeline when he, and many other residents of the border district were forced to leave their homes during the initial phase of communist rule and subsequent Soviet occupation. His family settled in relative safety on the Pakistani side of the border while he engaged in *jihad* against the communist government, eventually commanding a front of some 50 armed *mujahids*. Pakistani support and supplies (with US backing) helped the *mujahidin* to secure control over the border districts, and fighters and supplies moved across the border along informal and constantly shifting Type 1 and 2 routes. With the collapse of the communist government in 1991, Haji M. Khan became the commander of a newly established army base close to the Khyber Pass and district administrator for the mujahidin government. Here he became adept at managing and processing conflicts brought to the attention of the district government through tribal elders and their *jirgas* (tribal or community gatherings of elders or 'white beards' who take decisions on issues of collective concern). If *jirga* decisions were not adhered to, Haji M. Khan, as representative of the *mujahedeen* government, provided enforcement.

When the Taliban came to power in 1994, Haji M. Khan fled with his family back across the border to Pakistan. However, the Taliban imprisoned his close relatives and pressured him to surrender his weapons. Eventually, a delegation of tribal elders negotiated his free return and the handover of weapons and vehicles. According to Haji M. Khan, about 100 elders from the Pakistan side and 80 elders from the Afghan side accompanied him when he returned, to guarantee his safety. After being disarmed, the Taliban released Haji M. Khan's kin but continued to monitor his movements. Eventually he decided to return with his family to Pakistan and join the anti-Taliban "Northern Alliance" resistance under one of the main commanders of the Eastern Provinces. When these efforts failed and his commander was arrested, Haji M. Khan settled in Pakistan and focused on building his reputation as a tribal mediator as well as his trade and transportation business between Afghanistan and Peshawar. During this period the drugs trade expanded and the district became a key centre and trading route with the growth of an opium bazaar and many drug processing laboratories.

Trading spaces

After the fall of the Taliban in 2001, Haji M. Khan returned with his family to Afghanistan and continued to gain recognition as an important broker in Nangarhar. Two factors helped him: first, his *jihadi* credentials among the Northern Alliance commanders, who returned to power after the fall of the Taliban. Second, his knowledge of, and high standing with, the tribes on both sides of the Afghan-Pakistan border. Between 2002 and 2019 he was appointed district governor (*woliswol*) multiple times across Nangarhar, many of them key border districts. His *modus operandi* was to work with, and help support, an often fragmented system of tribal representation, decision-making and law enforcement. He played the role of mediator and regulator of conflicts that could not be resolved at a lower level through *jirgas*. He was viewed as an honest broker, who could authorize lower-level mediators to intervene on his behalf. Brokerage involved navigating hybrid forms of authority among multiple sovereigns, including various levels of government, the Taliban, local strongmen, militias, and in recent years, the Islamic State.

As a district governor, Haji M. Khan attempted to engineer a system of tribal representation that – as he saw it – re-connected to a traditional form of tribal governance based on *jirgas*, a system that had been broken by civil war and anti-tribal policies of Taliban rule, and needed proactive 'fixing.' He selected four elders from each tribe to liaise with the government. In some districts he managed to set up tribal counter-insurgency militias and secured state funding for them. He also used the re-invented tribal structure to agree and enforce rules on how to prevent and sanction collaboration with insurgents and finally how to deal with social, political and economic conflicts within and between tribal segments.

> I established a tribal committee and decided that we won't let the enemies of Afghanistan such as Talib, ISIS, thieves, and criminals come to the district, and they accepted and signed the treaty that if anyone provides shelter to above insurgents or enemies, we will burn his house and he will be fined 10 Lakhs Rs. We made this decision with consensus. (Paraphrased from interview)

As a foundation for this strategy, Haji M. Khan leveraged economic wealth to build social capital through networks of personalised trust. This was converted into political power and patronage, which further enhanced his economic standing. He understood that political success and longevity in a violent and competitive environment depended upon building social standing as a just and effective mediator. A reputation for hospitality was underpinned by an 'infrastructure' of high-profile guesthouses across the province where he housed and fed people seeking his advice (*langar khana*). Furthermore, he provided mediation and conflict solving services – including delegating issues to other reliable bodies or individuals, without charge (e.g., to *jirgas* specialising in smuggling-related conflicts).[4] Finally, Haji M. Khan used his influence and official positions to facilitate the illicit re-export of goods imported from Pakistan as transit goods back into Pakistan via major and well-organised smuggling routes.

> Thousands of people used to be engaged in the transit business. When I was district governor, I arranged these transit commodities very well. This trade was arranged by cross-border communities [that] cooperate with us. When there was a problem, we were jointly solving the trade problems on both sides of the border. Now the transit commodities import and export pathway is blocked by Pakistan. [...] I gathered the tribal elders, youth and influential individuals. Thousands of people are now unemployed and the way is still blocked. (Paraphrased from interview).

127

Haji M. Khan showed considerable skills in diversifying income and risks, and in securing his long-term interests by building social, political and material capital. For example, he managed to secure elected positions for two of his immediate kin in the national and provincial councils. A third close relative is thought to play a key role in the cross-border trade business, aided by the political cover of the other two.

Eventually, Haji M. Khan was successful in re-establishing tribal representation in his home district, earning a widespread reputation and some recognition even in Kabul. He continued to play a significant role even after falling out with Kabul appointees in the province and losing his job as district governor. At the time of the fieldwork, he was still regarded as an apex broker and problem solver in his district; tribal militias loyal to him manned checkpoints and informally controlled access to the district undisturbed by the Afghan National Police. The researchers found a mostly idle district administration, while the guesthouses of the broker were over-crowded with people seeking the mediation, support and advice of Haji M. Khan to solve their problems.[5] However, his position was less stable and according to one of his allies interviewed, his interference in Kabul politics had caused him to lose his political backing there, leaving him in a now more precarious position.

A small-scale fuel trader strikes it big: brokerage opportunities in Nimroz

We turn now to a cross-border fuel smuggler in the South-West of Afghanistan. This is a story about how a small fuel trader from a minority group uses his cross-cutting networks to leverage new opportunities in a fast changing border zone, working his way up from being a tertiary broker to becoming a key apex broker in regional trading networks.

Haji Aziz, now in his forties, comes from a modest family of shopkeepers and craftsmen, with a multi-ethnic background, presenting himself as a mixture of "Hazara, Pashtun, Tajik, and Baloch." When the Taliban were in power, his family moved to Nimroz and he worked in shops at the main provincial bazaar of Ghor Ghori, refilling and cleaning fuel barrels smuggled across the border from Iran, earning extra money by filtering and selling excess or waste diesel on the side. Policing of the Iranian border was patchy and uneven at this time, but conversely the demand for fuel and trading infrastructure was low. However, whilst working in the main bazaar, Haji Aziz developed relationships with a range of traders and smugglers, including drug traders connected to the Taliban, who were concentrated in Ghor Ghori bazaar. According to one source, Haji Aziz made his initial capital from drug smuggling; in 2001, when a Coalition air raid destroyed the market and forced the Taliban to abandon the area, Haji Aziz was one of the few local traders who reportedly stayed behind and appropriated sizable amounts of abandoned opium stores.

During the first decade after the fall of the Taliban government, licit and illicit cross-border trade via Nimroz province increased dramatically and Ziranj became a frontier boom town (Drugs & (Dis)order, 2020). Haji Aziz became one of the main importers of fuel, and subse-quently cars, into the province. His business grew rapidly as he started importing fuel directly from Iran. He developed friendly and mutually beneficial relations with government and border officials and capitalised on his existing inter-tribal and cross-border contacts. A former business contact, and later competitor, explained in an interview that Haji Aziz's business activities extended to Kandahar, where he forged strong relations with some of the most influential people in Southern Afghanistan, including indirect access to one of the former President's half-brothers, Ahmed Wali Karzai (then head of the Provincial Council).

However, over the past ten years, trade relations with Iran changed and Haji Aziz was forced to adapt his business. First, Iran tightened its grip on the border and brought the many informal crossings under control. Second, international sanctions sent the Iranian Rial into free fall, introducing high inflationary risks to cross-border trade. Finally, a significant part of the fuel business shifted to other provinces further north, where Iran established large fuel storage facilities as a new hub to distribute fuel across Afghanistan.

Haji Aziz diversified his cross-border business, investing more in domestic trade infrastructure, such as car showrooms and pump stations, in a number of provinces. He also leveraged connections with the provincial government and customs services so as to keep importing fuel and cars at reduced custom rates. In addition, he established himself as a service provider for other cross-border traders, facilitating and mediating their relations with both government offices and the parallel Taliban administration. He provides office space for some 170 licenced *commissionkars* at the official border crossing in Milak, who facilitate official as well as informal customs declarations for traders crossing the border (legal goods flow for the most part from Iran into Afghanistan). Haji Aziz's subordinates provide reduced rates in return for informal service fees. He also controls the main scales that weigh incoming cargo, and reduced net weights are regularly negotiated and certified against a fee. For a time, Haji Aziz was also authorised by Taliban and traders' unions to collect the unofficial but consistently enforced Taliban tax on goods crossing the province, exchanging the official customs tax slip with a tax slip recognized by the Taliban. He had negotiated this unofficial but formalised agreement to streamline official and informal taxation issues and make cross-border trade more predictable for the traders.

However, balancing commercial imperatives with the interests of powerful governmental and shadow-governmental actors involved serious risks and difficult setbacks. First, he lost his access to political protection in Kandahar when his link to the presidential family was killed and the newly appointed police chief demanded his share in undeclared profits made from the car business. Around 2019, Haji Aziz lost his main patron within the provincial Taliban leadership of Nimroz in a drone attack and was almost immediately summoned by his successor, who suspected him of not disclosing fully the profits made from tax collection on behalf of the Taliban. In both cases, he was forced to pay a hefty fine – revealing that even the most influential brokers must cope with a high degree of uncertainty and unexpected rent extraction. Ultimately the power of the armed executive (of both the state and shadow state) trumped the financial power of traders and business people.

Despite these setbacks, there remains a high demand for the mediation skills of Haji Aziz from traders and their associates. According to Haji Aziz, he stays out of politics: "I solve almost 80–100 conflicts per month and I don't want any money from anyone." He says that, "people trust me, so I should serve them." He also invests profits into numerous public welfare activities in Nimroz, evidence of his significant and enduring influence in the province.

Conclusions

This chapter has focused on the role of brokers and brokerage in the context of cross-border smuggling and trading networks. By looking at two personal biographies, we aimed to illuminate the details and complexity of individual lives, whilst revealing wider processes of change linked to border hardening and shifting regional trading systems and political networks.

Firstly, in terms of their positionality, the two brokers have very different backgrounds and biographies, though they share some common characteristics. Both have become significant political and economic brokers, starting off as tertiary brokers, but over time graduating into apex brokers – though neither is sufficiently influential to be involved in brokering trade along Type 4 corridors, and both have been adversely affected and had to adapt to border closures.

Though their career trajectories follow a similar arc, their sources of legitimacy and power are quite different. Haji M. Khan is embedded in the tribal systems of the borderlands; he melded his tribal credentials and 'architecture' of hospitality with his *jihadi* history and his ongoing relationship with 'men of violence' so as to become a credible broker mediating and managing conflicts.

Haji Aziz, in contrast, is neither embedded in a tribal system, nor self-identifies as a particular ethnicity; instead, he positions himself as someone with a hybrid identity who can mediate across and among different social and political groupings. Unlike Haji M. Khan, he is primarily an economic player who lacks a *jihadi* history or 'violence credentials.' Although this can make him vulnerable – as for example when he was arrested in Kandahar – it also means he is able to act as a credible mediator with the Taliban, unlike Haji M. Khan. Like Khan, however, he is attuned to the importance of social standing and the redistributive role of brokers, as shown by his support of social works and welfare in Ziranj.

Secondly, there are similarities as well as differences in the *brokerage dynamics* revealed in the two life histories. Both are living and operating in contexts of radical uncertainty – like all borderlanders living in contexts of fluidity and flux, marked by moments of rupture – including the shifts in conflict dynamics linked to different phases of the war, shifting political regimes, changes in border security and management, and economic shocks.

What marks them out from the wider population is their ability to adapt and improvise so that they come to occupy key 'deal spaces.' These spaces differ and so do the brokerage fixes that they offer. Haji M. Khan is an 'embedded broker' (Meehan & Plonski, 2017) in the sense that his value as a broker lies in his 'betweenness centrality' within the tribal system. Haji Aziz is a 'liaison broker' (ibid) whose value lies in his ability to straddle social as well as territorial borders and boundaries. The fixes that Haji M. Khan provides are primarily related to localized conflicts and state-society relations. Haji Aziz's brokerage fixes are primarily concerned with the management and flows of trade, and this depends on an ability to position himself above, or at a distance from, the political fray. Both embody the agency and ingenuity of borderland brokers, but they are also vulnerable characters, only as powerful as their last 'fix.' The power of Haji M. Khan, for example, appears to be on the decline, linked perhaps to the growing strength of the Taliban, shifts in political coalitions in Kabul and Jalalabad, and the effects of border hardening on local trade networks.

Thirdly, as the last point indicates, *brokerage effects* may be transitory and ephemeral, when viewed from the perspective of one broker or one brokerage fix. However, if we see brokerage in more systematic terms, as central to the way that states and markets are managed and 'performed' in the borderlands, then we can see how brokers may over time – certainly within the lifetimes of our two brokers – have significant structural effects. Haji Aziz, for example, is one of many traders and brokers in Nimroz who has contributed to a remarkable transformation of Ziranj from a frontier outpost to a boom town that has attracted internal investment, significant in-migration and increased governmental interventions and programmes. Brokerage has been central to this process of unruly frontier development, based on agglomerations of illegality, including drugs and people trafficking, drug use and processing, and other forms of illicit trade. In Nangarhar, brokers like Haji M. Khan have been central to the post-2001 statebuilding (and counterinsurgency) project – embedded brokers have played a critical role in extending the footprint of the state, managing coalitions and distributing rents amongst national and local political elites. As a major trading and political hub, Nangarhar is a prize fought over with particular intensity, leading to a constant process of political unsettlement and churning politics. Brokerage has in many ways entered the DNA of states and markets and is central to they way both function and their distributional consequences.

Trading spaces

This brings us to our final point, that studying brokers on the margins can tell us much about how the markets and the wider political system works. The personal biographies of Haji M. Khan and Haji Aziz are inseparable from the wider spatial and political biographies of the frontier regions. Studying the lives of these individuals brings out the complex temporalities, socio-spatial relations and power dynamics of border zones, and it powerfully demonstrates how these regions are far from marginal or lagging zones; instead, they are best understood as transformative spaces and laboratories of change. Studying borders and brokers brings into focus the webs of connections, the points of friction and the fluid relations within trading systems. Our case studies hint at these processes and dynamics, but there is scope, and an urgent need, for further comparative research on this 'missing middle' level of analysis that explores the roles, dynamics and effects of borderland brokers. We have provided a tentative comparison of borderland brokers within different borderland spaces. there is further exciting work to be done, however, which develops in more systematic ways this comparative approach across regions, historical periods and types of licit/illicit flows. This opens up a range of questions yet to be addressed fully about the agency of brokers, how smuggling networks adapt to moments of rupture, the distributional effects of these shifts, and the impacts of peripheral trading economies on power relations and economic development within metropolitan centres.

Notes

1   This chapter draws from fieldwork funded by UKRI Global Challenges Research Fund [Award Reference: ES/P011543/1: 'Drugs & (dis)order: building sustainable peacetime economies in the aftermath of war'] and conducted by the Afghan NGO Organisation for Sustainable Development and Research (OSDR). The project seeks to generate new evidence on how to transform illicit drug economies into peace economies. The chapter also draws upon material and writing derived from an ESRC-funded research project 'Borderlands, Brokers and Peacebuilding in Sri Lanka and Nepal: War to Peace Transitions viewed from the margins' (Ref: ES/M011046/1). We are grateful to our field researchers in OSDR who conducted the interviews underpinning the case studies in this chapter, as well as to the editors Florian Weigand and Max Gallien for their invaluable comments.
2   The case studies are based on 24 in-depth life history interviews in both provinces as well as 740 more focused guideline interviews on licit and illicit economic activities (cf. Drugs and (Dis)order, 2020). Specifically on brokerage, our partner OSDR conducted three interviews with the broker and two of his associates in Nangarhar in August 2020 and seven interviews with the broker and his associates in Nimroz in October and November 2020. In Nangarhar, the associates were tribal elders who have known the broker over a long period of time; one of them was a former sub-commander of the broker. In Nimroz the associates were former business partners and competitors as well as people providing or receiving services of the broker in the context of cross-border trade.
3   The Afghan-Pakistan border often separates the same tribes or sub-tribes, but not in this particular location.
4   According to one interviewee:

> Haji M. Khan has a lot of resources like he has 26 houses and guest houses in his village [...], the province and Kabul. [... H]e has lorries, trucks and agricultural lands. His sons also make a lot of money as they have high-paying jobs. [...] Haji M. Khan represents local communities and derives his power from [the tribes in various districts]. [... The tribes] rely on Haji M. Khan to put an end to their disputes. Many people gather at his home [every day] and it seems like there is wedding party. The reason why people count on him so much is because people are respected at his home. He has been doing mediation since when he was a sincere *Jihadi* commander and he keeps doing it.

5   Typically, people assemble during office hours at the district administration with all sorts of official and informal requests. Here, access to services was clearly dominated by the broker as a one-stop-shop.

References

Barfield, T. J. (2010). *Afghanistan: A Cultural and Political History*. Princeton: Princeton University Press.

Bierschenk, T., J-P. Chaveau and J.-P. O. De Sardan (2002). 'Local development brokers in Africa: The rise of a new social category,' *Working Paper No. 13 Department of Anthropology and African Studies*. Mainz, Germany: Johannes Gutenberg University.

Boedeker, J. (2012). 'Cross border trade and identity in the Afghan-Iranian border region.' In Betina, B. and J. Mieggelbrink (eds), *Subverting Borders. Doing Research on Smuggling and Small-Scale Trade*. V S Verlag, pp. 35–54. https://doi.org/10.1007/978-3-531-93273-6_3

Cons, J. (2016). *Sensitive Space: Fragmented Territory at the India-Bangladesh Border*. Seattle and London: University of Washington Press.

Dobler, J. (2016). 'The green, the grey and the blue: A typology of cross-border trade in Africa,' *The Journal of Modern African Studies*, 54(1), 145–169.

Drugs and (Dis)order. (2020). *Voices from the borderlands 2020: Illicit drugs, de- velopment and peacebuilding. GCRF Drugs and (Dis)Order: Building sustainable peacetime economies in the aftermath of war*. SOAS, University of London. https://drugs-and-disorder.org/voices-from-the-borderlands-2020/

Goodhand, J. and P. Meehan (2018). 'Spatialising political settlements.' In Plonski, S. and Y. Zahbia (eds), *Accord Insight 4: Borderlands and peacebuilding: A view from the margins*. Conciliation Resources, pp. 14–19. https://www.c-r.org/accord/borderlands-and-peacebuilding/spatialising-political-settlements

Goodhand, J. (2020). 'Fragility and Resilience Analysis: The Political Economy of Development in Borderlands.' In World Bank (ed), *From Isolation to Integration: The Borderlands of the Horn of Africa*. Washington, DC: World Bank.

Goodhand, J. and O. Walton (2020). 'Fixes and flux: frontier brokers and post-war politics in Nepal and Sri Lanka.' Draft paper, unpublished.

Grötzbach, E. (1990). *Afghanistan: Eine geographische Landeskunde*. Darmstadt, Wissenschaftliche Buchgesellschaft.

Hagman, T. and F. Steppatat (2016). *Corridors of trade and power: economy and state formation in Somali East Africa DIIs*. Working Paper 2016:8. Copenhagen: DIIS.

ICG (2014). 'Corridor of Violence: The Guatemala – Honduras border,' International Crisis Group, Latin America Report no 52, Brussels, Belgium.

James, D. (2011). 'The return of the broker: Consensus, hierarchy, and choice in South African land reform,' *Journal of the Royal Anthropological Institute*, 17, 318–338.

Koehler, J., G. Rasool, and A. Ibrahimkhel (2021). 'Dynamic borderlands – the challenge of adapting to hardening borders in Nangarhar and Nimroz,' *International Journal of Drug Policy*, 89, 103117.

Kutty, S. N. (2014). 'Iran's Continuing Interests in Afghanistan,' *The Washington Quarterly*, 37(2), 139–156

Lamarque, H. (2014). 'The DR.Congo/Rwanda Border at Goma and Gisenyi: A borderlands perspective,' Draft Paper prepared for the World Bank, GPSURR.

Larson, A. (2010). 'Governance Structures in Nimroz Province.' Kabul, Afghanistan. Research and Evaluation Unit. https://areu.org.af/wp-content/areu_publications/2016/02/1042E-Governance-Structures-in-Nimroz-CS-2010-Web.pdf

Latour, B. (2005). *Reassembling the Social: An Introduction to Actor-Network-Theory*. Oxford: Oxford University Press.

Mann, M. (1984). 'The autonomous power of the state: its origins, mechanisms and results,' *European Journal of Sociology/Archives Européennes de Sociologie*, 25(2), 185–213.

Mansfield, D. (2020a). 'Mules, pick-ups and container traffic: Cross border production and trade and the shaping of Nangarhar's political economy,' Research paper, GCRF Drugs&(Dis)Order.

Mansfield, D. (2020b). 'Catapults, pickups and tankers: Cross border production and trade and how it shapes the political economy of the borderland of Nimroz' (15.01.2020), Research paper, GCRF Drugs & (Dis)Order.

McDougal, J. and J. Scheele (eds) (2012). *Saharan Frontiers: Space and Mobility in Northwest Africa*. Bloomington: Indiana University Press.

Meehan, P. and S. Plonski (2017). *Brokering the Margins: A Review of Concepts and Methods*, Working Paper 1. ESRC Borderlands, Brokers and Peacebuilding Project.

More, I. (2011). *The Borders of Inequality: Where Wealth and Poverty Collide*. Tucson: University of Arizona Press.

Trading spaces

Mosse, D. and L. David (2006). 'Theoretical approaches to brokerage and translation in Development.' In L. David and D. Mosse (eds), *Development Brokers and Translators*. Kumarian: Bloomfield.

Nugent, P. (2002). *Smugglers, Secessionists & Loyal Citizens on the Ghana-Toga Frontier: The Life of the Borderlands Since 1914*. Athens: Ohio University Press.

O'Dowd, L. (2012). 'Contested states, frontiers and cities.' In Wilson, T. and H. Donnan (eds), *A Companion to Border Studies*. Chichester, UK: Wiley-Blackwell, pp. 139–157.

Taggliacozza, E. (2005). *Secret Trades, Porous Borders: Smuggling and States Along a Southeast Asian Frontier, 1865–1915*. New Haven: Yale University Press.

Titus, P. (1996). *Marginality and Modernity: Ethnicity and Change in Post Colonial Baluchistan*. Oxford: Oxford University Press.

Wolf, E. (1956). 'Aspects of group relations in a complex society: Mexico,' *American Anthropologist*, 58(6), 1065–1078.

Zartman, W. (ed) (2010). *Understanding Life in the Borderlands: Boundaries in Depth and Motion*. Athens: University of Georgia Press.

10

SCALES OF GREY

The complex geography of transnational cross-border trade in the African Great Lakes region

Timothy Raeymaekers

Border economies

Borderlands are productive of social spaces at multiple scales.[1] This productiveness results from a particular power-geometry of territorial borders: in border spaces, the difference between what is considered inside and outside, above and below, bottom-up and top-down, legitimate and illegitimate is object of a constant negotiation among agencies placed in multiple geographic locations. Think, for example, of the complex infrastructures that channel and regulate the transnational trade in commodities across boundaries every day: it is easy to imagine that these are not fixed in place but span vast networks of policies, and of human and non- (or more-than-human) relations. At the same time, the assertion of state territoriality has important consequences for the manner in which such infrastructures take shape on the border (wherever we imagine this border to be located), because it is exactly here that claims about national belonging, about power and legitimacy are actively being written into political space. This insight is important for our understanding of the practices of smuggling, or, more widely, of the vast volumes of informal and illegal trade that remain unrecorded in state records, because, apart from taking place in the shadow of official state regulations, such practices have been observed to be capable of subverting, moulding and even transforming state power in the margins. A good example of the latter is the drug economy, which has been shown to transform power relations across the globe's borderlands (for a discussion see Goodhand, 2020). The transformative effects of transborder exchange are not limited to such illicit commodities, however, but they also include the more common aspects of our mobile the global economy. Rather than considering state sovereignty at the border as a legal state of exception, which draws a sharp boundary between what lies outside and inside, on bottom and on top, within or beyond the realm of legitimate agency and interaction (Ferguson and Gupta, 2002; Agamben, 2003; Chatterjee, 2004), this chapter takes a slightly different viewpoint towards the relation between smuggling and state territoriality. It considers the territorial border rather as a grey zone, a space that actively partakes in *making* territorial rule operational in a larger web of interconnections. In this sense, I insist once again on the productiveness of smuggling and contraband, rather than merely highlighting their "illegal" or "criminal" character. In sum, this chapter invites scholars to take serious the concrete ways in which unrecorded trade activities contribute to state territoriality across borders; in other words, how unrecorded trade practices recalibrate political

134   DOI: 10.4324/9781003043645-10

Scales of grey

authority through their operations in the margins of sovereign state laws. After a short overview of the dominant schools of thought on smuggling in the borderlands I will illustrate my view with a case study from Central Africa.

A dominant perspective on borderlands is to depict these as spaces of anti-state resistance. Inspired by the work of James Scott, who rewrites the history of Southeast Asia's border areas as "shatter zones," or "zones of refuge" inhabited by people who have been fleeing historical waves of state oppression (Baud and van Schendel, 1997; for a critique see Lieberman, 2010; Brass, 2012), for example, scholars of Asia and Africa have been able to point out persistent frictions among populations whose freedom of movement and subsistence are constantly threatened by the centralizing projects of modern states (e.g., De Bruijn et al., 2001; Dereje and Hoehne, 2010; Graetz, 2010; Turner, 2010, 2013; Doevenspeck, 2011; Ryzhova, 2018; Brenner, 2019). From this perspective, cross-border trade assumes the aura of a silent rebellion against state regulations that are considered to be intrusive, illegitimate and oppressive (Shelley and Metz, 2017; Endres, 2019).

Other scholars emphasize instead the creative and innovative potential of economic activities that are officially designated as informal, clandestine or criminal in the borderlands. While they may be formally casted as a corruption of institutional norms, their hybrid relationality may in fact become a platform for radically transforming public authority – particularly in so-called weak states or contexts where state sovereignty is fundamentally contested, like zones of protracted armed conflict (Menkhaus, 2007; Raeymaekers et al., 2008; Boege et al., 2009; Bagayoko et al., 2016; Rolandsen, 2019; Goodhand, 2020).

Without denying the important political and economic inequalities that these borderland economies evidently entail at different scales (for a discussion see Meagher, 2014), one needs to be careful to recognize the proximity between economic entrepreneurship and state-making projects at territorial borders. Rather than stealing away resources and legitimacy, in many instances, cross-border trade, even if clandestine, has been observed to contribute significantly to state treasuries and vice versa, be it not through the established legal, official channels. The very meaning of smuggling or contraband, therefore – which may range from informal trade in household commodities to outright illegal trade in drugs and arms – should be viewed from the perspective of a frontier: an oscillating, dynamic space, in which what can be considered as legal and legitimate wealth is the outcome of a complex and active "border work" (Reeves, 2014) across multiple geographic scales (Cunningham and Heyman, 2004; Roitman, 2005; Raeymaekers, 2009, 2014; Chalfin, 2010; Chu, 2010; Goodhand, 2012; Titeca, 2012; Korf and Raeymaekers, 2013; Wilson, 2017; Kean, 2018).

In other words: geography matters, particularly in the way in which capitalist supply chains interconnect with territorial authority across borders. Rather than assuming their marginality, criminality or illegality, we should consider the potential contribution of borderland economies to capitalist development more broadly.

In my own research in the Congolese-Ugandan borderland between 2003 and 2008, I have been trying to find out how the political economy of borderland trade is at once productive of the territorial state, but at the same time redefines and repurposes political order through direct everyday connections and relations across geographic scales. My ethnography of contraband trade in this area builds at once on the excellent work of several colleagues (e.g., Meagher, 1990, 2003; Roitman, 1998, 2005; Titeca, 2012), as well as border studies (e.g., Newman and Paasi, 1998; Donnan and Wilson, 1999; Wilson and Donnan, 1998) and political anthropology (Nugent, 2002; Lund, 2006; Klute and Bellagamba, 2008; Arnaut, Hojbjerg, and Raeymaekers 2008; Hagmann and Péclard, 2010).

Timothy Raeymaekers

For a long time, the African Rift Valley, which runs through the current Cong-Ugandan borderscape, figured as a shifting African frontier among several, adjacent communities like the BaYira and BaHema, whose trade in salt, fish, ivory and artefacts constituted the foundations of intense interactions (particularly between Bunyoro and Kasese and the Congolese Mitumba Mountains: Kopytoff, 1987; Packard, 1987). These pre-colonial trade patterns contributed to an intense cross-border trade in post-colonial times: in a context of rampant economic decline and institutional crisis in the 1970s and 1980s, the smuggling of minerals and commodities formed an alternative livelihood opportunity there where previous occupations in plantation agriculture and mining had been gradually ruined (Mirembe, 2005; Kaparay, 2006; Raeymaekers, 2014). In this context, an emerging class of BaNande (BaYira) entrepreneurs was able to transmit some of its capital and knowledge into this transboundary economy. In Kisangani, for example, around a thousand kilometres from the border, Janet MacGaffey dis-covered a "thriving business centre," where "all sorts of people are running successful and substantial enterprises, despite the shortages of goods, the deterioration of infrastructure and the rampant bribery and corruption so amply documented in the social science literature and the local press." Echoing the predominant optimism about informal entrepreneurship at the time, she concluded that "in the midst of irrationality and unpredictability," some people were capable to make things work in an organized and efficient way and engage in "rational" economic enterprise (MacGaffey, 1987, p. 1). Yet it would be wrong to assume the BaNande's political autonomy: tradesman and -women maintained close connections with exponents of the Zairian and Ugandan state. During the 1990s, these connections intensified in a lucrative commodities trade: while producers in North Kivu and Ituri exported almost all their timber and mineral resources into Uganda, Ugandan army generals, exported US$ millions worth of timber, gold and other valuable resources from Congo during the two Congolese wars of 1996–1997 and 1998–2003 with the tacit support of President Museveni (Reno, 2000; Fahey, 2009). During this period, traders also maintained close relations with non-state armed forces, whose activities contributed significantly to transboundary economic developments.

My case study shows that when we study unrecorded trade in borderlands, globally, it makes sense to differentiate more carefully between what is meant by "legal" and "illegal," "formal," and "informal," rather than assuming such categories as a given. Unofficial transborder trade is by definition difficult to detect, and what is usually described as "informal," "hidden," "parallel," or "underground" economic activity may indeed involve a wide range of degrees of formality and illegality. According to Ellis and MacGaffey (1996), a useful way to distinguish between trade patterns is between trade that is explained as wholly or partially legal on the one hand, and wholly illegal on the other hand. Of the second type on the Congo-Uganda border, one could mention for example the trade in *marijuana* from plantations in South Lubero to Uganda and Kenya, or the smuggling of protected animal species and ivory from the Congolese bush to Western consumers. Although it is formally prohibited by Congolese law, the drug is com-monly tolerated even though it potentially finances violent militia activity. A similar permissive regime applies to the trade in ivory which, although formally illegal, can be found openly outside Congo's national parks: when strolling the streets of Goma and Kinshasa, it is not unusual to meet businessmen offering carved ivory statues or entire tusks to buyers in plain daylight. Next to ivory, one can find a whole range of forest produce openly or less openly on sale on regional markets, going from tropical charcoal, to protected animal species (birds, monkeys), bush meat and occasionally also "traditional" medicine.

Different degrees of (il)legality reveal the hybrid norms and relations that have characterized this trade since colonial independence. While considering this heterogeneity, it becomes clear that very little transboundary trade in this African borderland can actually be characterized as entirely illegal (Englebert and Mungongo, 2016). Rather than assuming their anti-state resistance or complicity with public authorities, it is important to consider its contribution to mediated state authority, not only at a local but at different geographic scales. Many of the border entrepreneurs owe their position and prestige to the simultaneous connections they are able to forge to both anti-state forces and to exponents of state administrations (Raeymaekers, 2014; Titeca, 2012). As I argued elsewhere (Raeymaekers, 2009), the political authority that emerges from one's involvement in this borderland economy cannot simply be categorized along a binary axis of engagement and disengagement with the state. Instead, one needs to consider the intricate networks of relations between legal state authorities and de facto sovereign bodies that determine the concrete ways in which norms and rules are implemented along commercial value chains. Whereas state administrations are continuously engaged in the attempt to govern citizens within predefined territorial limits, de facto sovereignty in the borderland remains characterized by a continuous pattern of negotiation and mediation of regulatory authority along a hierarchy of scales (see also Hansen and Stepputat, 2001; Humphrey, 2004).

Over the years I have observed how cross-border traders have been able to "jump scales" (Swyngedouw, 1997) while they mediate the regulation of their activities with multiple sovereign bodies along established commodity chains. Controlling the nodes of an increasingly globalized trade in commodities has given such mobile actors a comparative advantage over state agencies with less space of manoeuvre.[2] While they still need the state to smoothen cross-border connections, this transboundary engagement has contributed to a growing political legitimacy of Congolese and Ugandan border entrepreneurs, as they assure beneficiaries low import prices and capital gains. Deliberately highlighting the contributions of cross-border trade to local "development" has thus become a central strategy for maintaining and consolidating power in the borderlands: in a context where state authority remains evidently contested, the ideology of marginal development has probably been a key factor of success of these border traders as political power brokers.[3]

What determines the regulation of this Central African cross border economy is not necessarily the level of engagement or disengagement from the state, therefore, but the complex relational infrastructures that underpin public authority over current trade arrangements. These arrangements appear to produce a specific power-geometry (Massey, 1992) that not necessarily *inverts* global-local relations but is able to *subvert* existing webs of domination and subordination, solidarity and cooperation in a wider regional environment. Through their operations, borderland entrepreneurs show that, far from being passive victims and receivers of development, they are also capable of creating their life worlds "as places" (Escobar, 2001, p. 15), with possibly far-reaching consequences for the definition of public authority across borders. Rather than being passively crushed by the anonymous forces of capitalism and globalisation, they demonstrate a capability to actively mould the political space in which their operations take place. This observation confirms the argument that transboundary markets constitute more than a simple economic mechanism; they are a political arena that regulates important facets of social life (Roitman, 1998). Following this line of argument, I opt for a more contingent notion of political power in the borderlands that emerges in concentric circles and in intersecting geographical scales. What distinguishes this perspective is its insistence on the *immanence* and *simultaneity* of social relations on the border and the way these relations come to actively construct the space of public authority across borders.

Timothy Raeymaekers

Concentric circles

More concretely, I imagine the system of relationships that regulates cross border trade in the Congo-Ugandan border space in three specific, interconnected scales. In the largest, transregional orbit, the trade is organized along a more or less stable commodity chain that connects some of the world's leading markets to remote villages in the rural areas of Uganda and Eastern DRC. Commonly, goods are imported by container from China or the Far East through big shipping companies such CMC and AGETRAV. Previous to such transports, Congolese traders have spent months and years looking for the right business contacts on the Asian continent. Though some firms work through direct business representations (Coloma, 2010) most commercial transactions take place orally, without contracts and on the simple basis of trust. Chinese and Congolese small businesses have a lot in common form this perspective, traders told me, as they commonly value such trust more than contractual backing and the respect for legal requirements (Raeymaekers, 2014).

Once commodities arrive in Africa (usually in some of East Africa's big ports like Mombassa), a number of private agencies immediately transform their label to goods with a lower tax regime (for example, if one sends electric generators, they become "bicycle parts," clothes become "rags" and so on). Customs agents refer to such infrastructures as 'laboratoires' or 'agences pirates,' because they "fabricate" false labels to transit commodities across territorial borders. The legitimacy of such agencies is not so straightforward as it may seem though, because their insertion into official state records depends on an active negotiation with the state. Lists of private customs intermediaries circulate frequently in the Ministries, therefore, as clients are included and excluded from such government favours. At the next node in the commercial network, Malaba (on the Kenya-Uganda border) functions as an offload and re-loadpoint for commodities from standard containers onto several, smaller trucks with canvas sheeting (called '*bachiers*'), which can carry 1½ containers each. Not unsurprisingly, traders use this transit to obfuscate customs control: a '*déclarant*' – the agent who declares transiting goods in name of the private businessman – will do all he can to mix goods of several owners together and benefit from the complex paper trails and lack of facilities that customs agencies have to deal with on the border. Most commonly, therefore, this negotiation results in an unwritten agreement: in return for a small fee, Ugandan and Congolese customs agree to facilitate the crossing of goods and adapt the declaration form according to the notification of the *declarant*. On the Congoles side, a '*vérificateur*' then inspects this declaration form and sometimes does a virtual check "to avoid being completely arbitrary" (interview with customs agent, January 2008). Goods are never controlled physically though, because there is neither the time nor a designated place to do this. If the '*déclarant*' agrees on this virtual check d, the goods pass onto the provincial authorities who demand a supplementary tax of a few hundred dollars to settle the final import. Next to these official services, different agencies intervene in this taxation "informally" (without legal backing). They include the Congolese civil and military intelligence (ANR and DEMIAP), hygiene and environmental services, national police (PNC), several customs brigades, and a range of territorial and provincial agencies and authorities. Besides these "informal" taxes, the official customs board may charge up to US$15000 per truck. The final import document ('*déclaration d'importantion définitive*') then gets delivered at the point of arrival after yet another virtual check by the agencies in the administrative centres of Beni or Butembo.

In the "core" of the borderland, finally, a parallel, interconnected pattern develops across the river Lubiriha that divides Congo from Uganda. Particularly on market days, one can observe lines of people crossing the river either on foot or bathing through the water with various goods on their heads. These porters or '*trafiquants*' offer the service of trafficking undeclared goods once they have been unloaded on the other side in Mpondwe. After furtively crossing the river, they run to the '*bombeurs*' who re-load the goods on a truck directed to a nearby Congolese town or transit centre. Given the nature of their job, the ability of these '*trafiquants*' is to pass covertly (Swahili: '*kofichika*') in order to make a living and avoid troubles with the Ugandan 'Red Mamba' (custom police) and Congolese police (during the COVID emergency, such Red Mamba arguably have been replaced by army officials). In the border towns, this petty contraband trade is often the activity of female farmers and disabled men and women, who in this way supplement their daily incomes. Benefiting from their double (Congolese and Ugandan) ID-cards which immigration authorities are willing to deliver for a small bribe (*kidogo kidogo*), the function of these smugglers in the cross-border economy is crucial, as they literally outsource the risk associated with the illegal aspects of this transnational trade. Participants in the border economy refer to this risk as '*la coop*,' '*match*,' '*la lutte*,' or '*punguza*' (*Swahili*: to reduce, get one's share).

Rather than brushing aside such cross-border economic practices as yet another example of Africa's "criminal" economies, a deeper social analysis of these activities may reveal a number of normative and social logics that go beyond legalistic interpretations. The commodity trade between Central Africa and the Far East shows how economic relationships flow through an organized system of relationships that is at once local, regional and global in character. Thanks to this system, for example, traders are able to connect important commercial nodes in China and South-East Asia to rural Africa. Once imported goods arrive in the border towns of Congo and Uganda, they continue their trajectories deep into Congolese territory on the backs of porters, (motor)cyclists and the occasional airplane that travels to the mining areas. As important as this complex economic infrastructure is for local and transboundary development, it depends on a fragile negotiation between public authority and private business that is nonetheless crucial for maintaining the relations of capitalist supply chains in balance in this transboundary context.

The politics of scale

One concept that becomes interesting to explain this process of constantly inverting power relations at the border is that of geographical scale. The concept of scale, which is widely discussed among human geographers, indicates how social relations are themselves productive of geographic spaces; in other words, the scope, speed and reach of relational connections has an impact on the ways power materializes in space (for a discussion see Marston, 2000; Marston et al., 2005; Cox, 2013; Jones et al., 2017). Some geographers use scale to highlight how power relations in contemporary capitalist supply chains has indeed become a highly contingent matter, as there exists no predefined pattern that determines how capital, resources and labour should flow from the centre to the periphery, from top to bottom, or from left to right. In a world where everything is connected permanently, the crux of the problem is not whether the local or the global has theoretical and empirical priority in shaping the conditions of daily life, but rather how the local, the global, and other relevant (although perpetually shifting) geographical scale levels are the result (the product of processes) of sociospatial change. In this sense, it is useful to distinguish between agents who remain fixated in place and others who are able to "jump" scales along such networked connections. Think, for example, of the transnational smugglers-traders and their simultaneous relations to multiple authorities in different geographic locations that I described in detail above. At the same time, the complex geography of their operations also hints at the immanence of political authority along such spatio-temporal scales. Paraphrasing Robert Cox, one could argue that the ultimate interest of participants in the borderland economy appears to lie in mobilizing centers of social power whose power is partially territorial in character, but whose goal is to control the actions and interactions of others" through complex social relations (Cox, 1998, p. 23).

In the case of Congo-Uganda, the system of regulations that is constantly redefined and negotiated at the border has generated important scalar effects that go beyond a simple imposition of global or national processes on local actors. Parallel to the concentric circles described in the first section of this paper, it is illustrative to see the growing dependency of national centres of power on this transboundary complex of relations in terms of taxes and the control over cross-border populations. One can see clearly how the mediation of authority at the border is pushing forward a gradual transformation of regulatory norms pertaining to taxes, economic resources and national revenue at both sides of the territorial border. Starting with the inverted role of local administrative practice, to the "fabrication" of labels and documentation that are projected across regional flows, the border is able temporarily to reverse power relationships between the "national" state and various local agencies as they are performed on a daily, localized basis. In this process, power is not univocally transferred from the state to its perceived anti-form (of anti-systemic resistance, of private agents or of social networks), but its successful mobilization depends on the tactical agency participants' ability to develop in this constantly shifting network of relations.

Authoritative power is to an important extent a social construction that is produced and transformed through everyday relations. This is not to say that power is completely independent of social hierarchies. Whenever state agents have tried to block transboundary trade, for whatever reason, on the Congo-Ugandan border, this invariably resulted in violent protests. Such happened in November-December 2007, for example, when an Ebola outbreak in the Ugandan district of Bundibugyo led custom authorities from Congo and Uganda temporarily to close the border crossing at Mpondwe-Kasindi. In protest, people (petty traders, peasants, angry businessmen, but also 'déclarants' and local customs officers) threatened to employ local rebel forces until the crossing was re-opened. They did this because, they explained, they depended on the border for their daily living (Raeymaekers, 2009). Rather than assuming a neat boundary between the state and 'social' or 'economic' actors, therefore, it makes more sense to investigate the social hegemony that emerges in the context of cross-border interaction, or the capacity of a dominant group to impose a series of practices that are to its advantage (Swyngedouw, 1997; Gramsci, 2007). One could argue that the process of negotiation between state and non-state, factual and official authorities in the Congo-Ugandan borderland has *itself* become productive of a political order that is capable of imposing an ideology of capitalist development based on transboundary connectivities and of "making do" (for a deeper discussion see Raeymaekers, 2014).

A future reflection on borderland economies as contingent power assemblages, I argue, therefore, can potentially reveal new modes to tackle their contribution to local development as outcomes of complex patterns of interaction among geographic scales, rather than linear histories of either resistance or liberal self-reliance. One the one hand, this would require a thorough rethinking of the ways participants in such border economies are capable of negotiating authority across complex relational geographies. On the other hand, it would require us to study more deeply the role of transboundary economies in brokering local authority and development. To focus exclusively on the supposedly resistant or liberal character of transnational contraband trade, at least in the Central African context, has proven largely counterproductive, because both perspectives gloss over the intricate relational geographies that set the terms of its regulation across geographic scales. Highlighting the scope, speed, and reach of these geographies instead has the potential to reveal how capitalist operations across borders continue to depend on active linkages among agencies, norms and institutions that may be ontologically depicted as standing in contrast and opposition, but as a matter of fact remain bound through crucial mediations.

Scales of grey

Notes

1　My definition of borderlands draws on Willem Van Schendel and Michiel Baud, who describe borderlands as "broad scenes of intense interactions in which people from both sides work out everyday accommodations based on face-to-face relationships" (Baud and van Schendel, 1997, p. 216).
2　One important factor that contributes to the weakness of customs agents is their lack of local embeddedness. Jostling their local political influence, important cross-border traders encourage customs agents to be "flexible" and "cooperative," and they do not hesitate to threaten the latter in case of unproductive collaborations. Several agents I interviewed had received death threats during their career, and some decided to change jobs because of these. These dynamics show once again to what an extent cross-border entrepreneurs are able to maintain a certain regime of violence which at once ensures their central role as local capitalists, while keeping together a network of state and non-state agencies involved in cross-border fraud.
3　That said, one must not underestimate the regional solidarities that arise from these daily interactions on the border as they take shape in partial opposition to centralizing states. Recent claims to greater autonomy in terms of local development have included demands for a more adequate partition of customs revenues. The issue of local development has also taken centre stage in ongoing debates about state decentralisation and democratic institutional reform – including debates about the role of "traditional" authorities such as the Rwenzururu Kingdom (Raeymaekers, 2009; Titeca and Fahey, 2016). With Paul Nugent, therefore, one could argue that such ethnic affiliations between Congolese and Ugandan communities increasingly serve to *constitute* power on the border, notably by working on state institutions, community relations, and basic concepts of political space (Nugent 2002, p. 232).

References

Agamben, G. (2003) *Stato di eccezione*, Torino: Bollati Boringhieri.
Arnaut, K. Hojbjerg, C. & Raeymaekers, T. (2008) 'Gouverner entre guerre et paix', *Politique africaine*, (111), pp. 5–21.
Bagayoko, N., Hutchful, E. & Luckham, R. (2016) 'Hybrid security governance in Africa: rethinking the foundations of security, justice and legitimate public authority,' *Conflict, Security & Development*, 16(1), pp. 1–32.
Baud, M. & van Schendel, M. (1997) 'Toward a comparative study of borderlands', *Journal of World History*, 8(2), pp. 211–242.
Boege, V., Brown, A., Clements, K. & Nolan, A. (2009) 'Building peace and political community in hybrid political orders,' *International Peacekeeping*, 16(5), pp. 599–615.
Brass, T. (2012) 'Scott's Zomia, or a Populist post-modern history of nowhere', *Journal of Contemporary Asia*, 42(1), pp. 123–133.
Brenner, D. (2019) *Rebel politics: a political sociology of armed struggle in Myanmar's borderlands*, Ithaca: Cornell University Press.
Chalfin, B. (2010) *Neoliberal frontiers: an ethnography of sovereignty in West Africa*, Chicago: Chicago University Press.
Chatterjee, J. (2004) *The politics of the governed*, New York: Columbia University Press.
Chu, J. Y. (2010) *Cosmologies of credit: transnational mobility and the politics of destination in China*, Durham, NC: Duke University Press.
Coloma, T. (2010) 'L'improbable saga des Africains en Chine', *Le Monde Diplomatique*, 57(674), p. 12.
Cox, K. R. (1998) 'Spaces of dependence, spaces of engagement and the politics of scale, or: looking for local politics', *Political Geography*, 17(1), pp. 1–23.
Cox, K. R. (2013) 'Territory, scale, and why capitalism matters', *Territory, Politics, Governance*, 1(1), pp. 46–61.
Cunningham, H. & Heyman, J. (2004) 'Introduction: mobilities and enclosures at borders', *Identities*, 11(3), pp. 289–302.
De Bruijn M. E., Van Dijk R. A. & Foeken D. W. J. (2001) *Mobile Africa: changing patterns of movement in Africa and beyond African dynamics*, Leiden: Brill.
Dereje, F. & Hoehne, M. V. (2010) *Borders & borderlands as resources in the Horn of Africa*, New York: James Currey.

Doevenspeck, M. (2011) 'Constructing the border from below: narratives from the Congolese–Rwandan state boundary', *Political Geography*, 30(3), pp. 129–142.

Donnan, H. & Wilson, T.M. (1999) *Borders: frontiers of identity, nation and state*, Oxford/New York: Berg.

Ellis, S. and MacGaffey, J. (1996) 'Research on Sub-Saharan Africa's unrecorded international trade: some methodological and conceptual problems', *African Studies Review*, 39(2), pp. 19–41.

Endres, K.W. (2019) *Market frictions: trade and urbanization at the Vietnam-China border*, New York, Oxford: Berghahn.

Englebert, P., & Mungongo, E. (2016) 'Misguided and misdiagnosed: The failure of decentralization reforms in the DR Congo', *African Studies Review*, 59(1), pp. 5–32.

Escobar, A. (2001) 'Culture sits in places: reflections on globalism and subaltern strategies of localization', *Political Geography*, 20(2/1), pp. 139–174.

Fahey, D., (2009) *Explaining Uganda's involvement in the DR Congo, 1996-2008*, Paper prepared for the International Studies Association conference, New York, 15 February.

Ferguson, J. & Gupta, A. (2002) 'Spatializing states: toward an ethnography of neoliberal governmentality', *American Ethnologist*, 29(4), pp. 981–1002.

Goodhand, J. (2012) 'Bandits, borderlands and opium wars: Afghan statebuilding viewed from the margins,' Wilson, T. and Hastings, D., eds. *A companion to border Studies*, London: Wiley-Blackwell, pp. 332–353.

Goodhand, J. (2020) 'Beyond the narco frontier: rethinking an imaginary of the margins', *International Journal of Drug Policy*, 89, pp. 1030–1045.

Graetz, T. (2010) *Mobility, transnationalism and contemporary African societies*, Newcastle: Cambridge Scholars Publishing.

Gramsci, A. (2007) *Quaderni del Carcere, edizione critica dell'Istituto Gramsci a cura di Valentino Gerratana*, Torino: Einaudi

Hagmann, T. & Péclard, D. (2010) 'Negotiating statehood: dynamics of power and domination in post-colonial Africa', *Development and Change*, 41(4) (special issue).

Hansen, T.B. & Stepputat, F. (2001) '*States of imagination: ethnographic explorations of the postcolonial state'*, Durham, NC: Duke University Press.

Humphrey, C., Nugent, D., & Vincent, J. (2004), '*Sovereignty': a companion to the anthropology of politics*, Malden, Oxford & Carlton: Blackwell Publishing, pp. 418–436.

Jones, J. P., Leitner, H., Marston, S. A., & Sheppard, E. (2017) 'Neil Smith's scale', *Antipode*, 49, pp. 138–152.

Kaparay, C. K. (2006) *Finance populaire et développement durable en Afrique au sud du Sahara. Application à la région Nord-Est de la République démocratique du Congo*, PhD Thesis, Université catholique de Louvain.

Kean C. K. Ng (2018) 'Ugandan borders: theatre of life and death', *Journal of Borderlands Studies*, 33(3), pp. 465–486

Klute, G. & Bellagamba, A. (2008) *Beside the state: emergent powers in contemporary Africa*, Cologne: Rüdiger Köppe Verlag.

Kopytoff, I., ed. (1987) *The African frontier: the reproduction of traditional African societies*, Bloomington and Indianapolis: Indiana University Press.

Korf, B. & Raeymaekers, T., eds. (2013) *Violence on the margins: states, conflicts, and borderlands*, New York: Palgrave.

Lieberman, V. (2010) 'A Zone of Refuge in Southeast Asia? Reconceptualizing Interior Spaces', *Journal of Global History*, 5, pp. 333–346.

Lund, C. (2006) 'Twilight institutions: public authority and local politics in Africa', *Development and Change*, 37(4), pp. 685–705.

MacGaffey, J. (1987) *Entrepreneurs and parasites: the struggle for indigenous capitalism in Zaire*, Cambridge: Cambridge University Press.

Marston, S. (2000) 'The social construction of scale', *Progress in Human Geography*, 24(2), pp. 219–242.

Marston, S., Jones, J.P., & Woodward, K. (2005) 'Human Geography without Scale', *Transactions of the Institute of British Geographers*, 30(4), pp. 416–432.

Massey, D. (1992) 'Politics and Space/Time', *Marxist Left Review*, 196, pp. 65–84.

Meagher, K. (1990) 'The hidden economy: informal and parallel trade in Northwestern Uganda', *Review of African Political Economy*, 47, pp. 64–83.

Meagher, K. (2003) 'A back door to globalisation? Structural adjustment, globalisation & transborder trade in West Africa', *Review of African Political Economy*, 95, pp. 57–75.

Meagher, K. (2014) 'Smuggling ideologies: From criminalization to hybrid governance in African clandestine economies', *African Affairs*, 113(453), pp. 497–517.

Menkhaus, K. (2007) 'Governance without government in Somalia: spoilers, state building, and the politics of coping,' *International Security*, 31(3), pp. 74–106.

Mirembe, O.K. (2005) *Echanges transnationaux, réseaux informels et développement local: une étude au Nord-est de la République démocratique de Congo*, PhD Thesis, Université catholique de Louvain.

Newman, D. & Paasi, A. (1998) 'Fences and neighbours in the postmodern world: boundary narratives and political geography', *Progress in Human Geography*, 22(2), pp. 186–207.

Nugent, P. (2002) *Smugglers, secessionists and loyal citizens on the Ghana-Togo frontier: the lie of the borderlands since 1914*, Oxford: James Currey.

Packard, R. (1987) 'Debating in a common idiom: variant traditions of genesis among the BaShu of Eastern Zaire', Kopytoff, I., ed. *The African frontier: the reproduction of traditional African societies*, Bloomington and Indianapolis: Indiana University Press, pp. 148–161.

Raeymaekers, T. (2009) 'The silent encroachment of the frontier: a politics of transborder trade in the Semliki Valley (Congo-Uganda)', *Political Geography*, 28, pp. 55–65.

Raeymaekers, T. (2014) *Violent capitalism and hybrid identity in Eastern Congo: power to the margins*, Cambridge and New York: Cambridge University Press.

Raeymaekers, T., Menkhaus, K. & Vlassenroot, K. (2008) 'State and non-state regulation in African protracted crises', *Afrika Focus*, 21(2), pp. 7–21.

Reeves, M. (2014) *Border work: spatial lives of the state in rural Central Asia*, Ithaca, NY: Cornell University Press.

Reno, W. (2000) 'War, debt and the role of pretending in Uganda's international relations', *Occasional Paper*, Copenhagen: University of Copenhagen, Centre of African Studies.

Roitman, J. (1998) 'The garrison-entrepot' *Cahiers d'etudes Africaines*, 150–152, XXXVIII, 4(2), pp. 297–329.

Roitman, J. (2005) *Fiscal disobedience: An anthropology of economic regulation in Central Africa*, Princeton and Oxford: Princeton University Press.

Rolandsen O.H. (2019) 'Trade, peace-building and hybrid governance in the Sudan-South Sudan borderlands', *Conflict, Security & Development*, 19(1), pp. 79–97.

Ryzhova, N. (2018) 'Invisible trade: sovereign decisions on the Sino-Russian border', Saxer, M., Horstmann, A., Rippa, A., eds., *Routledge handbook of Asian borderlands*. London: Routledge.

Shelley, F.M. & Metz, R. (2017) *Geography of trafficking: from drug smuggling to modern-day slavery*, Santa Barbara, CA: ABC-CLIO.

Swyngedouw, E. (1997) 'Neither global nor local: 'glocalization' and the politics of scale', Cox, K. ed., *Spaces of globalization: reasserting the power of the local*, New York: The Guilford Press.

Titeca, K. (2012) 'Tycoons and contraband: informal cross-border trade in West Nile, north-western Uganda', *Journal of Eastern African Studies*, 6(1), pp. 47–63.

Titeca, K. & Fahey, D. (2016) 'The many faces of a rebel group: the Allied Democratic Forces in the Democratic Republic of Congo', *International Affairs*, 92(5), pp. 1189–1206.

Turner, S. (2010) 'Borderlands and border narratives: a longitudinal study of challenges and opportunities for local traders shaped by the Sino-Vietnamese border', *Journal of Global History*, 5, pp. 265–287.

Turner, S. (2013) 'Under the state's gaze: upland trading-scapes on the Sino-Vietnamese border', *Singapore Journal of Tropical Geography*, 34, pp. 9–24.

Wilson, T. M., & Donnan, H. (1998) *Border identities: nation and state at international boundaries*, Cambridge: Cambridge University Press.

Wilson, A. (2017) 'Ambivalences of mobility: rival state authorities and mobile strategies in a Saharan Conflict', *American Ethnologist*, 44(1), pp. 77–90.

11

SMUGGLING AS A LEGITIMATE ACTIVITY?

The OPEC Boys as social bandits in Northern Uganda

Kristof Titeca

Introduction

The term smuggling often brings strongly negative connotations, and is often associated with criminality and violence. For example, the Wikipedia page[1] on smuggling mostly focusses on the trafficking of adults, children and wildlife. Indeed, in discussing these phenomena, the page highlights how smugglers use coercive tactics such as 'deception, fraud, intimidation, isolation, physical threats and use of force, debt bondage or even force-feeding drugs to control their victims.'[2] Are smugglers always associated with these negative connotations, though – in particular by the communities in which they are embedded?

In their influential edited volume on 'illicit flows,' Abraham and van Schendel (2005: 4) highlight the important differentiation between what states consider legitimate ('legal'), and what people involved in these practices consider to be legitimate or 'licit.' In other words, smuggling – an illegal activity – can also be considered legitimate by the wider population. This chapter further unpacks the ways in which smuggling can be considered legitimate by the local communities. It does so by relying on three concepts and sets of literature: (i) of smugglers as 'social bandits' (Hobsbawm 1959, 1981); (ii) of smuggling as a central concept in local social imaginaries (Taylor 2004; Grant 2014); and (iii) of smugglers as (un)civil society (Bayat 1997a, 1997b). These three concept intersect and overlap, but each highlight a particular aspect in explaining their legitimacy.

Empirically, these concepts will be illustrated by discussing smuggling activities in North-Western Uganda, in particular by focussing on the 'OPEC boys,' a group of smugglers active in the region, smuggling fuel into the country from the nearby Democratic Republic of Congo (DRC) and Southern Sudan. Importantly, these smuggling activities are considered socially legitimate in the wider region. In doing so, this case-study shows how smugglers can be seen as a politically, socially and economically legitimate: as actors who successfully emerge out of poverty and legitimately fend for themselves in a situation of state neglect. Moreover, they are also perceived to be acting in the interest of the population – for example by defending informal traders when threatened by the local government.

144   DOI: 10.4324/9781003043645-11

Social bandits, social imaginaries and uncivil society

How do smugglers relate with the local population, and how are they understood by the latter? In order to answer this question – and understand the ways in which smuggling can be considered legitimate – it is useful to look outside of the smuggling literature stricto sensu. Strikingly similar questions have been asked by other sets of literature, discussing the (potential) legitimacy of illegal activities (which are broader than smuggling). The absolute starting point, and reference, in this literature is Eric Hobsbawm's concept of 'social banditry.'

Hobsbawm first coined the term social bandits in his 1959 book *Primitive Rebels*, in which he discussed 'primitive' or 'archaic' forms of organized social protest. One of the these was the 'social bandit,' most famously known by its archetype such as Robin Hood in England or Diego Corrientes in Andalusia: bandits who are regarded as the champion of the poor, protected and idealized by them (Hobsbawm 1959: 13). The idea was further developed in his book *Bandits*, first published in 1969, and consequently republished in a series of other editions (such as Hobsbawm 1981).

While social bandits are regarded as criminals by the state, the population regards them as 'heroes, as champions, avengers, fighters for justice, perhaps even leaders of liberation, and in any case as men to be admired, helped and supported' (Hobsbawm 1981: 17). This is what makes the bandits 'social,' the link they have with the general population. In this situation, the bandits are not only seen as the population's champions, they are also idealised, and turned into a 'myth' or a 'symbol' (Hobsbawm 1959: 13; 1981: 127). They are associated with 'freedom, heroism, and the dream of justice' (Hobsbawm 1981: 132). Key is their invulnerability to authority, and their championing of the weak, oppressed and cheated. In doing so, social bandits aim to re-establish the social order to how it 'should be:' rights must be wronged and corrected, and cases of injustice must be avenged – particularly in relations between the rich and the poor, or the strong and the weak. Social banditry is therefore a form of self-help to correct perceived wrongs and cases of injustice (Hobsbawm 1981: 26).

Those most prone to joining social banditry are those in a particular social position: male youth between puberty and marriage – when they do not have family responsibilities yet; or those who are not fully integrated into society yet, and are easily drawn into marginality or outlawry. They are 'marginals, soldiers, deserters and ex-servicemen' and are 'natural material for banditry' (Hobsbawm 1981: 31–34).

According to Hobsbawm, social banditry is something of the past, which is no longer possible in (post) capitalist societies – the phenomenon being a product of traditional peasant societies (Hobsbawm 1981: 19–24). Nevertheless, the social bandits idea has been applied to contemporary cases such as the kidnapping of oil workers (Oriola 2013); street leaders in Seoul (Mobrand 2016); urban violence in Trinidad (Pawelz 2018); TV series (Sartore 2017); Colombian Bandits (Rehm 2016), and so on.

The 'social banditry' concept is also useful to look at the ways smuggling is understood by various actors. Similar to social bandits, the idea of smuggling has been described as a 'weapon of the weak' – an economic and political act of resistance against colonial borders, against an exploitative state, and oppressive economic policies (Azarya and Chazan 1987; Titeca 2012). Smuggling constitutes an act of resistance and redistribution, acting in the defense of marginalized sections of society, the 'powerless' (Meagher 2003). This for example was influentially shown by Janet MacGaffey (1987), who showed how the second economy in Zaire was also a political option, allowing the population to 'fend for itself' in the light of a state which was both absent and oppressive. As argued above by Abraham and van Schendel (2005), it is necessary to look beyond official statist discourses on smuggling (which are part of particular power configurations).

These ideas– of smuggling as socially and politically 'legitimate' – do have significant overlap with the concept of social banditry. Yet, what is lacking in these perspectives is an explicit focus on particular actors – the social bandits themselves: how does the 'myth'-making around them happen, and how do they relate with the surrounding community?

In better understanding this, two further sets of literature are useful. First, underdeveloped in the idea of social bandits is that these are formed through profoundly moral understandings of what constitutes 'good' and 'bad.'

Helpful here is the concept of 'social imaginaries,' which constitute a 'collective moral orientation (Grant 2014: 413); a 'largely unstructured and inarticulate understanding of our whole situation, within which particular features of our world show up for us in the sense they have' (Taylor 2004: 25). Social imaginaries are not only a passive 'background' to particular situation, they also offer 'detailed articulations of our own personal circumstances' (Grant 2014: 412). In doing so, they are the common understanding, a collective imagining, which allow collective practices to happen, and offer a 'widely shared sense of legitimacy' for these (political, social and economic) practices (Taylor 2002: 106; Grant 2014: 411). In other words, they explain practices – they offer a purpose and significance – and in doing so make these practices possible (Grant 2014: 412). These social imaginaries are widely shared among the population: they are "carried in images, stories and legends" (Taylor 2002: 106), and are further magnified, but also transformed, through social practices. In other words, social imaginaries are the background against which social bandits occur –the moral basis on which norms of legitimate behavior are evaluated and acted upon. To come back to van Schendel and Abraham's reference from the intro: illegal actions such as smuggling can be considered legitimate because they tap into particular social imaginaries – something which will be explored in the case study.

Second, further deepening the understanding of the above issues is the literature on 'uncivil society,' and in particular the work of Ayad Bayat (1997a, 1997b). Whereas Hobsbawm's social bandits clearly focusses on resistance in rural areas (Hobsbawm 1959: 23), Bayat's idea of uncivil society is very much focused on similar processes urban areas. Ayad Bayat's work argues how debates on 'civil society,' should not only focus on conventional associations, but also, or even particularly on what he calls 'uninstitutionalised and hybrid social activities which have dominated urban politics in many developing countries' (Bayat 1997a: 55). In doing so, he focusses on the urban poor, which largely live in informality, and are weary of formal procedures attempting to regulate their lives and the discipline which the state tries to enforce on their daily lives – such as formal bills and taxes (Bayat 1997a, 1997b). While they don't have institutional power, they are able to take direct action. These actions are more than 'Scottian' forms of resistance, which are hidden, individual and defensive. Instead, they are also offensive, involving collective, open and highly visible actions (Bayat 1997a: 56, 1997b: 4–7).

Autonomy and redistribution are key here, and are key aspects of the uncivil society: acting autonomously from the state, and in doing so obtaining public goods such as illegal land, or shelter, which are unable to be attained through legal and institutional mechanisms (Bayat 1997a: 59–61). In these actions, particular sites – such as the street or illegal land – serve as the main 'locus of collective expression' for those who lack an institutional setting to express their voice (Bayat 1997a: 63).

In the next section, we apply these perspectives to smuggling in Northwestern Uganda, in particular by looking at the OPEC boys.

Smuggling as a legitimate activity?

Smuggling in Northwestern Uganda: the OPEC boys

The West Nile region is located in north-western Uganda, and borders the Democratic Republic of Congo (DRC) and Southern Sudan. The region has characteristics similar to many other borderlands: borders which were introduced during colonial times, separating ethnic groups living on both sides of the borders; and located on the peripheries of their respective national states, with limited possibilities for economic development. In this context, smuggling is a popular source of livelihood, providing not only a livelihood for traders and their families, but also by supplying goods (food and non-food). Its importance therefore transcends the local, by not only providing goods for the border towns, but also at a national and regional level – on the different sides of the border. Studies from the Bank of Uganda for example show how this trade has strongly intensified, from USD 143.2 million in 2010 to USD 269.8 million in 2018.[3]

The most visible and prominent actor within this field are the 'OPEC boys,' a group of fuel smugglers. From the mid-1980s onwards, the OPEC boys were selling smuggled fuel in jerrycans on street-corners in Arua, and in the wider region: there was a general shortage of petrol stations in the area, and their fuel was cheaper. The OPEC boys got their smuggled fuel in different ways: some smuggled it themselves from Congo, others used 'transporters,' which mostly were young(er) boys on bicycles, smuggling the fuel across the border on *'panya roads'* (smuggler roads), avoiding security officials. Others bought their fuel from truck-drivers, who equally smuggled their fuel into Uganda (Titeca 2006; Lecoutere and Titeca 2007).[4]

The OPEC boys were the most important supplier of fuel in the area until the late 2000s. Around this time, the increased number of fuel stations, and the changing tax regime in the DR Congo pushed many of them out of business. While they still exist, their activities are less prominent; contrary to earlier times, they no longer are present on (almost) every corner of the major urban centres in the region.

Throughout their existence, their smuggling activities were generally tolerated by the state authorities; while occasional confiscations would take place, these were rather rare, and the smuggled fuel was sold openly. Why was this the case? In this section, we will unpack their activities, by drawing on the above conceptual toolbox. I start by showing how they are a central part of the social imaginary, to then show how they can be considered social bandits, and a central part of uncivil society.

Field research among the OPEC boys was carried out from 2004 onwards, in Arua. The most intense period of field research was between 2004 and 2010, first as part of my PhD research, and later as part of my postdoctoral work, during which period I spent around a year in the town (Titeca 2006, 2008, 2012; Titeca et al. 2011). In the years after that, research was less intensive, but I kept following up on, and interacting with these actors (Titeca 2018a, 2018b). The main research method was semi- or unstructured interviews and non-participant observation, not only with the OPEC boys, but also with other actors such as (informal) traders, civil society actors, local government representatives, customs officials, and a variety of actors active in the smuggling business (fixers, transporters, and so on).

Before we discuss the OPEC boys, it is important to discuss the 'background' – the way in which smuggling is understood in the social imaginary in the region. After doing so, we are better able to understand the role of the OPEC boys as social bandits and uncivil society.

Smuggling as an important social imaginary in West Nile

In the region of West Nile, smuggling is very much looked at as a legitimate activity. A number of reasons account for this. First, smuggling in West Nile has long historical roots (Meagher

1990; Titeca 2009). When the colonial powers introduced colonial borders, these did not stop the interaction among ethnic groups. While members of the same ethnic group were now living on different sides of the (colonial) borders, and hence became subject to state regulation, untaxed trade – smuggling – continued being considered legitimate (Titeca and De Herdt 2010). Second, smuggling has always been seen as a legitimate way of survival in circumstances in which the population felt marginalized at best, and oppressed at worst. For example, during the successive wars and rebellions affecting the region, many people fled into neighboring (southern) Sudan and Zaire. Smuggling constituted an important livelihood for many during these times (particularly in the late 1970s and early 1980s). Moreover, smuggling acquired an explicitly political meaning when President Museveni came to power. The West Nile region feels marginalized by the Museveni regime. They feel that – contrary to earlier regimes – they are not allowed into positions of power, which (amongst other things) translates itself in limited services and infrastructure (Titeca and De Herdt 2010). This context gave rise to a number of rebel groups which were translating these grievances (Leopold 2005: 46). Smuggling has to be understood in this context: as a way of making ends meet, in circumstances beyond their control – war and displacement, or a regime which is marginalizing them. The following quotes are an illustration of these feelings:

> Smuggling really is the food of the people! Us, women, we have no jobs here. The only thing we can do is to get a small profit out of smuggling. And what we get across, really is for the family![5]

According to security officers, this argument is for example used upon arrest 'When we arrest them, smugglers often say: but I'm not an idler, I'm a smuggler! What else do you want me to do? How should I find something to eat?'[6]

In sum, smuggling acts as an important social imaginary in the West Nile region: In the light of a lack of limited socio-economic opportunities, smuggling is regarded as a legitimate employment.

Adding to this social imaginary are different sets of stories and practices which are widely shared and recounted, and which further feed into the understanding that smuggling is the only way to survive. Among the OPEC boys, many share how smuggling was a way to finance their (secondary) school or university. Inversely, a number of unemployed university graduates are now working as OPEC boys.

Particularly important is the story of the 'Arua boys,' which can be considered as the predecessors to the OPEC boys. In brief, these are smugglers from – as their name suggests – Arua town, which emerged in the 1970s. They emerged in a time of conflict and displacement, and primarily engaged themselves in the trade of gold. They were able to smuggle it from Zaire, and sell it at a high profit in Kampala. They were known for their flashy clothes and extravagant lifestyles. As recounted by a market trader:

> The Arua boys, they used to dress smartly. They would have a tie. Or they would dress in jeans. American jeans were very popular! And they would have a saloon car, mostly a Sunny. If not a car, a motorcycle: Honda or Yamaha. And they would play loud Lingala Music. They used to be very extravagant. They were spending lots of money – because they were very rich, because of the gold trade. They were powerful financially. The Blue Room lodge [in Kampala] was famous these days. But they wouldn't sleep there! They would just go in the morning with the plane, and come back in the evening.[7]

Similar variations were told by many other actors, but they are all variations on the above. Importantly, many of them have transformed over the years into influential businessmen in the region, which are still active in smuggling, but have expanded their activities, including real estate, transport, and so on.

Magnified through these actors and stories, smuggling is seen as a local version of the 'American dream,' the most important form of social mobility, a rags-to-riches, from-zero-to-hero story, present in the wider social imaginary of the border population in West Nile. As one trader summarized this: "From hero to zero: it's not an American dream, it's the Arua dream lived by the OPEC boys!".[8] An anecdotal, but telling, example of this is how a youngster explained an elaborated movie scenario about the Arua boys, portraying the Arua boys, as James Bond-style superheroes, going on adventures in Congo, smuggling goods across the border, and fighting villains of the custom authorities and the Ugandan government.[9] A young Arua cartoonist had a similar idea, and developed a movie poster along these lines, containing the same references – as depicted below (Figure 11.1).

Striking here are the Arua, and OPEC boys, posing as successful personae, in aesthetics referring to successful US gangsta-rappers: cool clothes and names, and an even cooler car. The 'Life is a beautiful struggle' quote refers to the 'from-zero-to-hero' mentality with which they are ascribed – being successful in the light of difficult circumstances. The OPEC boys need to be understood in this context: similar to the Arua boys, their activities are seen as way in which the marginalised population is able to survive.

In sum, smuggling is a clear social imaginary, a collective moral orientation (Grant 2014) for the West Nile region, offering a 'widely shared sense of legitimacy' (Taylor 2002: 106; Grant 2014: 411) to the activity – for those participating it, and for the wider community. This is shared through stories, which center around specific actors – such as for example the ways in which the Arua boys and the OPEC boys are acting, and narrated about. It also is reflected in the day-to-day usage of the term 'smuggling.' It is used literally, without negative connotations. In the words of a local analyst 'different from the way many others use it. It is seen in a positive light, as a survival strategy.'[10]

In the next sections, I will explain how the OPEC boys can be considered as social bandits, and 'uncivil society.'

The OPEC boys as social bandits

The historical roots of the OPEC boys can also found in a period of conflict and displacement. Much of the population was forced out of West Nile after the overthrow of the Amin regime (as Amin hailed from this region and had an important power base in it). People settled in Congo and Sudan in late 1979 and the early 1980s. During this time, a number of exiled young men tried gain an income by smuggling fuel. They did not stop doing so upon return to Uganda, and they started an organization which came to be known as the 'OPEC boys.' Many other young men returning to their home areas, with no education or assets, were easily drawn into his fuel business. They started attracting members from neighboring districts in West-Nile (such as Nebbi or Moyo), to which the OPEC boys from Arua supplied fuel.

The OPEC boys were considered an important social-economic force, in a number of ways. First, and in line with the above, they were an important source of employment for young men. As one OPEC boy argued: 'All of us are looking for survival! This is a marginalized area, and this [smuggling] is our only way of doing this.'[11] In other words, the OPEC boys are very much a product of the above described context producing this particular imaginary, in which

Figure 11.1 Poster of a (fictional) film on the Arua Boys smugglers'.
Source: Edward Aikobua

smuggling is considered a source of livelihood, and legitimate. This would also be reflected in its relation with the local population – and the actions of the latter, which generally would support the OPEC boys in several ways. They would, for example, warn the smugglers in case security agencies were approaching to confiscate fuel, or if something would go wrong.

The OPEC boys also tapped into this imaginary in a different way: they were not only providing employment for a particularly marginalized, and potentially dangerous group, i.e., former rebels and security officers. In the first ten years of group, it was estimated that 40% of the Opec Boys were ex-rebels from the many rebel movements which had been active in the area (UNRF, UNRFII, WNBF, FUNA, LRA) (Gersony 1997), while others were defected government soldiers (the Ugandan government army UPDF or the Local Defense Units, in which the government armed civilians against these rebel forces). After receiving amnesty, the ex-rebels, often without education, land or other assets, were easily drawn into the smuggling business.

Smuggling as a legitimate activity?

This adds another layer to the OPEC boys: they were not only providing a source of survival, they also were providing employment to, and absorbing, a potentially dangerous group, hence providing stability. Certainly in the beginning of the movement, it seemed as this big group of low-skilled, landless, young men had two attractive choices: joining any of the rebel groups in the area[12] or joining the informal economy by becoming an OPEC boy. As the Mayor of Arua town stated: 'These Boys can be tough; they are former soldiers and rebels. They are dangerous and could go back to the bush if not treated carefully.'[13] With few or no assets available, there would be few opportunity costs for the OPEC boys to join a rebellion. Moreover, many ex-combatants have not handed over their weapons to the authorities (CERFORD 2002), in an area in which decades of armed conflict already resulted in an abundance of available light weapons.

In this situation, the OPEC boys very much fed into the social imaginary lined out above: they were seen as a source of survival and employment, which therefore was a legitimate source of livelihood. Interestingly, the agenda of the rebel groups which had been, and were active in the region also drew on this imagery of a region which was neglected by the state, and was fighting to undo this marginalization through violent means. Similarly, smuggling was perceived as a way to protest this marginalization, but in providing more stability.

The above shows how the OPEC boys very much fulfil the idea of social bandits: they are seen as 'fighters for justice' (Hobsbawm 1981: 17), finding an income and creating development in a region which feels abandoned by the national government. Similar to Hobsbawm's ideas on social banditry, their activities are seen as highly legitimate, and as invulnerable to state authority – as they are able to conduct their activities more or less undisturbed. It also is a specific demographic which was part of Hobsbawm's social bandits: young, unemployed men, among which many ex-rebels – which, as also Hobsbawm saw it – were 'natural material for banditry' (Hobsbawm 1981: 31–34).

A last idea which deserves further illustration is the 'social' aspect of social bandits: the ways in which smugglers – in this case, the OPEC boys – are linked with the general population. Bayat's (1997a, b) ideas on uncivil society are particularly useful in doing so.

The OPEC boys as 'uncivil society'

The OPEC boys would use their power to the defense of actors within the urban informal sector, such as market vendors or boys working in the transport sector (motorcycle taxi drivers and others). They would use their power to mediate with the government, or block particular governmental initiatives. Many examples illustrate how they would act as the (above described) 'uncivil society.' For example, they intervened when law enforcement officers confiscated goods from roadside sellers refusing to pay tax (by taking back these goods and creating a riot). They intervened in instances where the urban authorities wanted to remove streetside kiosks, by blocking the roads, and staging protests – ultimately stopping this removal. They also intervened on occasions when the local authorities tried to remove women who were cooking in the different markets in town (as they were accused of contributing to the spread of diseases such as cholera). When the municipal authorities came to remove the women by force, the OPEC boys intervened and made this intervention impossible. They also negotiated with the municipal authorities to find a solution, in which the women were allowed to stay in the end.

While a number of factors contributed to this influence of the OPEC boys (such as the fact that they were particularly well-organized – in sub-groups, with a general leadership), it particularly was their potentially 'rebellious' character which played an important role in this. In the words of an OPEC boy 'they come to us because we are aggressive, we don't fear anyone and are organized.' Moreover, through their close contact and respect by other urban informal groups, they can easily organize protest and chaos within town.

Interrelated with this, the OPEC boys were considered 'political kingmakers.' During a number of consequent elections, the OPEC boys actively campaigned for opposition candidates – all of which won the elections. Out of their 'respected' status, they have a strong impact on public opinion. Politicians confirm how they can easily spread messages about which politicians deserve popular support, or inversely, about which politician has been doing a bad job. They also act as a campaign force – driving in the rallies of the politicians. In return, politicians do provide several services to the OPEC boys. They have been linking them with donors or have helped them to write project proposals through which the OPEC boys have accessed additional funding, for example to start a savings and credit association. They also provide them with material assistance; many OPEC boys consult politicians in case of financial problems such as sickness or problems with school fees for their children.

It is important not to romanticize the activities of the OPEC boys, in particular their use of violence. This was not only a passive background, i.e., a threat constituted by their existence as former rebels; it also played an active role. This was, for example, the case during riots against the governmental authorities, or when intimidating political opponents during electoral periods. Most visibly, there also were instances in which it was used against informers: those caught with, or suspected of, leaking to the customs agents were beaten up seriously. In other words, the flip-side of a social imaginary legitimizing smuggling is that leaking this to the government is considered illegitimate. The OPEC boys did act upon this, often through the actual use of violence.

In sum, the OPEC boys have clear links with the population (the 'social' in social bandits), by whom they are seen as fighters for social justice. In doing so, they function very much how Bayat (1997a, b) described 'uncivil society,' operating through direct, open and visible actions, using the city's streets as their main locus to resist enforced state discipline, such as taxation or other forms regulation. Their actions are not institutionalized, but ad hoc, and in the interests of the urban poor.

Lastly, it is worth mentioning that since around 2010, the influence of the OPEC boys has reduced significantly. It wasn't only that their economic significance declined. Through changing taxation policies, and an increasing number of petrol stations, smuggling fuel became less attractive, leading to a reduced number of OPEC boys. Also their political and social importance reduced. Before, they had quite a tight structure, with an overall leadership – including a charismatic leader, Kaku – and sub-divisions, which were based on street-corners (Titeca 2006). This allowed them to be tapped into the broader urban informal economy, as well as to act swiftly for social and political reasons – as illustrated above. Similar to smuggling activities worldwide, they had an ambiguous relation with government officials. While they had to fear confiscation by customs officials, they also collaborated with government officials in a number of ways. Individual officials (civil servants and/or politicians) would participate in smuggling activities (e.g., through financing it) and/or protect these activities, for example, against the actions of customs officials. Army officials played a particular role in this (again mirroring the important role of security officials in smuggling activities worldwide). After 2010, their reduced economic role also had a cascade effect in these other fields: they no longer had a tight structure or a charismatic leader, with a lesser social and political role – being reduced to one actor in the urban informal economy, rather than being the leading actor.

Conclusions

> For the law, anyone belonging to a group of men who attack and rob with violence is a bandit, from those who snatch payrolls at an urban street corner to organized insurgents or guerrillas who happen not to be officially recognized as such. Historians and sociologists cannot use so crude a definition. In this book we shall be dealing only with some kinds of robbers, namely those who are *not* regarded as simple criminals by public opinion. (Hobsbawm 1981: 17; emphasis in original)

This is how Hobsbawm's book *Bandits* starts: by introducing an important difference between how criminality and (il)legitimacy is looked at by the state, and how it is perceived by local conventions. While Hobsbawm brings in petty thieves and insurgents as examples of social bandits, this chapter aimed to show smugglers also can be added to this: while formally, smuggling is illegal and criminal, it is not regarded as such by local conventions. In unpacking this idea, the chapter first showed the importance of social imaginaries, which are more than 'myth-making:' they lay out importance normative associations, constituting the 'background' in which actions are evaluated, but also authorising concrete actions. It showed how smuggling constitutes a rags-to-riches, from-zero-to-hero story in the region, inspiring many dreams of what is considered one of the few (or even only) form(s) of socio-economic mobility.

The chapter then sets out to show how smuggling constitutes a form of social banditry, showing how smugglers – and in particular the OPEC boys – have important links with the local population: their actions are defending the local population in different ways. They are an important form of local employment, and they often intervene to the advantage of the poor. Different from Hobsbawm's idea of social banditry, the OPEC boys largely operate in urban contexts. Further helping to unpack their 'social' character is Bayat's (1997a, 1997b) idea of 'uncivil society:' they can be considered an unconventional, uninstitutionalised, form of civil society. Through ad hoc, direct and sporadic action, they are an important form of collective action representing the interests of those working in the informal sector, against a state which is seen as neglecting the population at best, and harassing and attacking the population at worst.

A critique on Hobsbawm's idea of social bandits was that he was not relying as much on the actual deeds of the bandits or on what the relevant population thought them to be, but rather on how these were reproduced in myths (Chandler 1978: 241). In doing so, he was accused of exaggerating the link between peasants and bandits – the very link which makes banditry 'social' (Slatta 2004: 29). Also for the OPEC boys, attention should be given not to romanticise their actions. While they definitely performed these social functions, also their 'darker' side should be taken seriously: their passive and active use of the threat of violence.

In sum, smuggling is not only something which is perceived as something negative, both in the functional and normative sense, i.e., as respectively an aberration and contravention of state rules, and something 'bad,' involving deception, fraud and intimidation – as the Wikipedia definition suggests. As this chapter has shown, smuggling can carry a very different meaning in local social contexts, where it can be perceived as a legitimate activity, and play a much-respected social role.

The importance of these findings is not limited to West Nile, or the OPEC boys. It illustrates the importance of taking local understandings of smuggling into account. This does not only help us understand the persistence of smuggling and its widespread nature, but also shows its profoundly social character – in the sense which Hobsbawm suggested: by having close links with the population. Smuggling should therefore be looked at as more than a strictly economic activity, but as a social, and also a political activity: as was demonstrated above, in local social imaginaries, it is seen as an act of resistance, a way to fend for oneself in the light of an absent and oppressive government. Similar to bandits, smugglers such as the OPEC boys can be considered a 'symbol' (Hobsbawm 1981: 127) of this resistance.

Lastly, while further research is needed on the exact conditions in which smuggling can be considered socially legitimate, this chapter brings a number of important pointers. In particular, it highlights the importance of the relation between smugglers and the broader population, and (interrelated with this) the relation between smugglers and the national state. Do smugglers defend the broader poor and/or offer opportunities for this latter group? Do they rather serve as an instrument for elites entrenching existing structural power inequalities? In other words, and linking with earlier (and abovementioned) debates on smuggling: does smuggling constitute a 'weapon of the weak' or a 'weapon of the strong' (Titeca 2012)? It is unlikely that in the latter case, smuggling will be considered socially legitimate – instead being perceived as a manifestation of the criminalization of the state, or a general warlord economy. In other words, understandings and analyses of the nature of smuggling – and in particular on its relation with the local population – are not only conceptual discussions, but also have important implications on the ways in which they are locally perceived and seen as socially legitimate.

Notes

1 Wikipedia, 'Smuggling,' https://en.wikipedia.org/wiki/Smuggling, consulted on 5 September 2020.
2 Wikipedia, 'Smuggling,' https://en.wikipedia.org/wiki/Smuggling, consulted on 5 September 2020.
3 The Bank of Uganda and Uganda Bureau of Statistics keep statistics on Informal Cross-Border Trade or smuggling. As explained elsewhere (Titeca 2020), these figures remain an underestimation.
4 Concretely, the trucks come from Kenya (Mombasa), and are in theory destined for Congo or (South) Sudan: as they are on transit, they don't have to pay taxes. Yet, the trucks either do not reach Congo or (South Sudan), or the fuel is immediately smuggled back into Uganda.
5 Interview women smuggler, 3 February 2010.
6 Interview security officer, 9 April 2007.
7 Interview market trader, 11 April 2007
8 Interview, trader, Arua, 14 October 2008.
9 Interview, 15 October 2008, Arua.
10 Interview analyst, 15 April 2021.
11 Interview OPEC boy, 1 February 2010.
12 The West Nile region has a long history of rebel groups (Leopold 2005); and although the rebel groups have ceased to exist, these ex-rebels still have deep-rooted feelings of marginalization. A factor which is enhanced by the fact that the government is not fulfilling its promises on the amnesty (in particular for the WNBF).
13 Interview Mayor Arua 11-04-07. This view is confirmed by various other actors, such as the URA Customs Enforcement Unit officer 21-11-05, sub-county chairpersons 01-05-07, local trader 11-04-07 and so on (cf. Titeca, 2006).

Bibliography

Abraham, I. and W. van Schendel (2005) 'Introduction: the making of illicitness,' in I. Abraham and W. van Schendel (eds), *Illicit Flows and Criminal Things*. Bloomington and Indianapolis: Indiana University Press, 1–37.
Azarya, V. and N. Chazan (1987) 'Disengagement from the state in Africa: reflections on the experience of Ghana and Guinea,' *Comparative Studies in Society and History*, 29: 106–131.
Bayat, A. (1997a) 'Un-civil society: The politics of the 'informal people,' *Third World Quarterly*, 18(1): 53–72.
Bayat, A. (1997b) *Street Politics. Poor People's Movements in Iran*. New York: Columbia University Press.

Smuggling as a legitimate activity?

Blok, A. (1972) 'The peasant and the brigand: social banditry reconsidered,' *Comparative Studies in Society and History*, 14(4).

CERFORD (2002) 'Small Arms Research in the Border Areas of Uganda. A case study of West Nile districts of Arua, Yumbe, Moyo and Nebbi.' Arua: CERFORD. Unpublished.

Chandler, B.J. (1978) *The Bandit King: Lampiao of Brazil*. College Station, TX: Texas A&M Press.

Gersony, R. (1997) 'The Anguish of Northern Uganda,' report submitted to the US Embassy, Kampala and USAID mission, Kampala.

Grant, J. (2014) 'On the critique of political imaginaries,' *European Journal of Political Theory*, 13(4): 408–426.

Hobsbawm, E.J. (1959) *Primitive Rebels*. Manchester: The University Press.

Hobsbawm, E.J. (1981) *Bandits* (revised edition). New York: Pantheon Books.

Kelty, C. (2008) 'Geeks, social imaginaries, and recursive publics,' *Cultural Anthropology*, 20(2): 185–214.

Lecoutere, E. and K. Titeca (2007) 'The OPEC boys and the political economy of smuggling in northern Uganda.' *Household in Conflict Network Working Paper*, 36.

Leopold, M. (2005) *Inside West Nile*. Oxford: James Currey.

MacGaffey, J. (1987) *Entrepreneurs and Parasites: The Struggle for indigenous capitalism in Zaire*. Cambridge: Cambridge University Press.

Meagher, K. (1990) 'The hidden economy: informal and parallel trade in Northwestern Uganda,' *Review of African Political Economy*, 17(4): 64–83.

Meagher, K. (2003) 'A back door to globalisation? Structural adjustment, globalisation and transborder trade in West Africa,' *Review of African Political Economy*, 30(95): 57–75.

Mobrand, E. (2016) 'The street leaders of Seoul and the foundations of the South Korean Political Order,' *Modern Asian Studies*, 50(2): 636–674.

Oriola, T.B. (2013) *Criminal Resistance? The Politics of Kidnapping Oil Workers*. New York: Routledge.

Pawelz, J. (2018) 'Hobsbawm in Trinidad: understanding contemporary modalities of urban violence,' *Conflict, Security and Development*, 18(5): 409–432.

Rehm, L. (2016) 'Doing politics with violent means: the threshold bandits of the Violencia Tardia in Tolima (Colombia),' *Chronica Mundi*, 11(1): 198–230.

Sartore, M. (2017) 'Robin Hood goes to Neptune: the collective social bandit in *Veronica Mars*,' *Studies in Popular Culture*, 40(1): 53–77.

Slatta, R.W. (2004) 'Eric J. Hobsbawm's social bandit: a critique and revision,' *Contracorriente, A Journal on Social History and Literature in Latin America*, 1(2): 22–30.

Taylor, C. (2002) 'Modern Social Imaginaries,' *Public Culture*, 14(1): 91–124.

Taylor, C. (2004) *Modern Social Imaginaries*. Durham and London: Duke University Press.

Titeca, K. (2006) 'Les OPEC boys en Ouganda, trafiquants de pétrole et acteurs politiques (The OPEC Boys in Uganda: petrol smugglers and political actors),' *Politique Africaine*, (103): 143–159.

Titeca, K. (2009) 'The Changing Cross-border Trade Dynamics Between North-western Uganda, North-eastern Congo and Southern Sudan,' Crisis States Working Paper 63 Series 2, London: London School of Economics and Political Science, Crisis States Research Centre.

Titeca, K. (2012) 'Tycoons and contraband: informal cross-border trade in West Nile, north-western Uganda,' *Journal of Eastern African Studies*, 6(1): 47–63.

Titeca, K., T. De Herdt (2010) 'Regulation, cross-border trade and practical norms in West Nile, north-western Uganda,' *Africa*, 80(4): 573–594.

Titeca, K., L. Joossens, M. Raw (2011) 'Cigarette smuggling and war economies in central and eastern Africa,' *Tobacco Control*, 20(3): 226–232.

Titeca, K. (2018a) 'Illegal ivory trade as transnational organized crime? An empirical study into ivory traders in Uganda,' *British Journal of Criminology*, Online first.

Titeca, K. (2018b) 'Understanding the illegal ivory trade and traders: evidence from Uganda,' *International Affairs*, 94(5): 1077–1099.

Titeca, K. (2020) 'Informal cross-border trade along the Uganda-DRC Border,' Policy Brief Series No 2, Nairobi: UNDP United Nations Development Programme.

12

TALL TALES AND BORDERLINE CASES

Narratives as meaningful contraband

Mareike Schomerus and Lotje de Vries

Introduction

In the early hours of the morning of 24 May 2013, a group of South Sudanese vigilantes attacked the town of Obo in the Central African Republic (CAR), having covered the distance of 100 km from the South Sudan/CAR border to Obo on foot. An unprovoked international attack in violation of CAR's sovereignty could be interpreted as an act of aggression under international law. At the least, one would expect subsequent diplomatic frostiness between the two countries. This attack, however, neither achieved the status of an international incident, nor did it lead to repercussions. Instead, what happened is remembered only as narratives – narratives about the attack and the motivations that drove a few dozen assailants to march on a foreign town. How events unfolded became subject to wild interpretation and mostly locally-anchored forms of meaning making.

In many ways, interpretations of the attack and its aftermath mirror the three ways in which the border between South Sudan and CAR is marked. First, there is the only official demarcation of this international border: a border stone, positioned in the shrubs of the bushland, shown in Figure 12.1. The boundary marker is neither fixed to the ground and nor very heavy. Two people could lift it, making its reliability as official border demarcation questionable.

Second, there is the border itself, which is marked primarily by its lack of definability: a vast area of bush and forest in which the exact location of the border is subject to speculation, moveable, and exists only in people's minds. Where precisely the border is understood to run on any given day depends less on international boundary negotiations and more on the luck of hunters, who want to believe that they are still on home grounds – rather than having veered off into the neighbouring nation – whenever they manage to catch an antelope that can feed the family in addition to fetching some money on the market.

Third, there are the 10 km of road that connect the villages of Ri Yubu on the South Sudanese side and Bambouti in CAR. While it is narrow, built by usage rather than road engineering, full of potholes and barely passable after rain, what is called 'Route Nationale 2' on a map of CAR is the sole officially-named road connection between the two countries. Travelling along it is the only option that offers certainty about moving from one country to the next in a linear way. The villages it connects are some way from the next bigger towns; South Sudan's Tambura, a town of about 10.000 people, lies 40 km east of Ri Yubu, and 600

156

DOI: 10.4324/9781003043645-12

Figure 12.1 The border stone that is the only official demarcation of the border between South Sudan and CAR.

km from South Sudan's capital Juba. If one were to travel by road, the trip from CAR's Bambouti to the nearest bigger town of Obo (which is about the same size as Tambura) would cover 100 km westwards through unoccupied countryside. To reach CAR's capital Bangui from here requires another drive of 1200 km.

Three types of border marking, three characteristics that describe this border: an official border point that projects authority and definition, but does not live up to this solid promise; a non-descript area that captures vastness, changeability and ambiguity depending on needs and experiences; and a road that allows defining the border through hindsight as it affirms upon arrival in the next village that the border has been crossed.

These three characteristics interact in different ways with three types of travellers that cross this border: people; goods; and stories. What turns any movement of people and goods into smuggling are legal frameworks, the mode of travel (in this case, often on the back of military trucks that are not subject to search or declaration on either side of the border), and the fact that the travelling goods or people change value as they cross a boundary, usually gaining in market price in comparison to the worth they had on the territory left behind.

This chapter uses a case study of the particular violent incident of crossing this border to unpack how the three characteristics of the border – the official demarcation, the vast and ambiguous territory, and the road that passes through and offers certainty through hindsight – bestow upon stories, narratives and explanations the characteristics of smuggled goods. Considering how stories and narratives are shaped by crossing a border is new and crucial territory for scholarship on smuggling for two reasons: it highlights the importance of stories and narratives in how people experience and make sense of a situation; and, it embeds emerging research on the power of narratives on people's behaviour within the broader discourse of socially constructed spaces. Borders, the crucial ingredient that smugglers need, are constructed sites of formality as well as informality. Both borders and how they create smuggled goods are great examples of how social construction develops meaning around particular sites or activities. Smuggling is also about the significance that is ascribed to a set of goods or people. Significance or meaning are always created through narratives and stories, so smuggling and meaning are inseparably intertwined.

Contribution to the field: stories as smuggled goods

The relationship between narratives and smuggling is bidirectional. Narratives help create the possibility of smuggling, while the notion of smuggling can form the characteristics of a narrative. When stories travel across borders, stories, too, can become contraband. These borders, however, are often created in the first place through narratives. When on the road, tales, narratives, accounts or anecdotes display all the characteristics of smuggled goods. Their meaning and importance – in short, what they are worth – can be transformed by having crossed an international border. A narrative shape-shifts as it moves into a different value territory; its meaning and power are bestowed upon it by existing in the borderlands and its ability to traverse these. When stories cross borders, their characteristics and interpretations change along with the narrator's position and how the narrator presents the actors in the story. Meaning and behaviour are altered due to real or imagined constraints or opportunities on either side of the border.

Just as smuggled goods are held back until the market is right, information and rumours may increase or decrease in their valuation and impact depending on when they are deployed. However, what a story is worth will ultimately depend on the context of the border crossed. Even in borderlands where shifting sovereignties play a marginal role in people's lives, how desirable a good or a story is on either side of a border remains separated by the border. The border thus acts as a modifier of the value of the story; it can amplify it. Borders can transform the story, and the story can make the borderlands – just like a border of active smuggling will be shaped by its smugglers. This is how the bidirectional relationship between borders and narratives continues to create the context in which smugglers operate.

For smugglers, information from across the border is critical. It is the basis of their decisions on when to smuggle and at what price to sell their wares. How stories are shaped across borders is thus critical to a livelihood and the power to influence the shape of stories is akin to a smuggler's hard currency. If they are able to transmit a story of scarcity across a border, they are able to increase the value of their goods and their reputation as service deliverers to counter shortages.

There are other shared characteristics between goods and narratives. Just like smuggled objects that are hidden from plain sight or transported on packed motorbikes via backroads in the early morning hours, stories can be whispered, told only after dark, or under embargo. In fact, they are perfect material for smuggling as – unlike goods and people – there are no control mechanisms that could even attempt to control their movement.

Tall tales and borderline cases

Current scholarship mostly focuses on how borders are shaped by the goods and people that move across it licit and illicit ways; these are interpreted by assessing their intended economic, social or military purpose and how the border changes that purpose (Frahm, 2015, Schomerus et al., 2013, De Vries, 2011, Feyissa, 2010, Newman, 2010, Brunet-Jailly, 2005). The study of smuggling is currently rooted in a material approach, which emphasises perspectives on the value of goods and the value of power that actors derive from being in control of how particular exchanges of goods happen at the border. Such emphasis overlooks the role of borders as important transport carriers for sensemaking. In addition to understanding borders as socially-produced demarcations, the imagination of the existence of a border invites us to treat borderlands as a space that shapes narratives and gives meaning to events. For the field of border studies and the attempts to understand the nature, role and impact of smuggling, viewing narratives as tradeable artefacts and part of how people experience the border is a departure from how borders are usually utilised as analytical tools.

Borders are often presented or imagined as intensely securitised and governed spaces. In many cases, however, large swaths of borders are in reality non-existent because they are not governed as a border or marked as such. There can be different reasons for this. People living on either side of the border share the same language, culture and livelihoods, so they rarely experience a border as division. Another reason might be that a border area is just too under-populated and thus offers little commercial incentive to gain control of the border (Dobler, 2016). In such cases, states may take calculated risks in leaving border management to non-state actors (Schomerus and De Vries, 2014). Even in these seemingly uncontrolled and open spaces, however, stories exist about the meaning of the border – so even where a border does not in fact exist as a governed space, it does exist as a created and actively used concept to support whatever activity is important to the narrator of the border. In addition to circulating stories about the border, simply crossing the border can change a story, an identity, a narrative – or the value of any of these, just like the value of a good changes when it is smuggled across a line.

A deeper understanding of the 'mental landscape' of border residents is currently a blind spot in the study of smuggling. A mental landscape perspective offers a deeper appreciation of the fact that all human sensemaking of everyday life is shaped by

> memories and narratives of incidents and history … Individual emotions, feelings, beliefs, cognitions, as well as the experience of success and disappointment, intermingle with community experiences. The mental landscape also influences decisions and behaviour, highlighting that both are shaped by context. (Schomerus, 2021b, p. 1, see also Amanela et al., 2020b)

People living near borders use them as perspective or interpretative devices to make sense of events they observe and to create narratives of their lives. Stories, ideologies and meaning are shaped by the presence of the border, often creating different interpretations on either side of it. Particularly in contexts of violent conflict, people, stories and ideas can thus take on the hallmarks of 'smuggled' objects. Narratives used to make sense of acts of violence, for instance, can become a story of 'the other side' when moving from one country to the next, particularly if those narratives include people that behave differently depending on if they are on their home turf or on foreign territory.

Perceiving narratives as contraband helps in understanding the implications of the presence of a border to the people living in its vicinity or those operating it. It also offers a helpful reading of national dynamics as perceived from a nation's borderlands. Stories and narratives as smuggled goods shift from seemingly factual accounts to tall tales or anything in between. The presence of an international border – however vaguely enforced – adds an additional layer of meaning and complexity to stories that are told on both sides. The social act of remembering produces narratives that explain and shape the present in similar ways to how an economic act of illicit trading shapes markets. They create actions, behaviour, memories – and the next narrative.

When the Arrow Boys crossed the border to march to Obo

The border between Ri Yubu and Bambouti, between South Sudan and CAR, offers an insightful case study into how the border and the narratives that are carried across it change both a situation and the meaning ascribed to it. From 2008 onwards, this borderland had seen violent attacks by the Ugandan Lord's Resistance Army (LRA), dispersed after the Ugandan forces launched an airstrike on Congolese territory to punish the LRA for failed peacetalks (Schomerus, 2021a, Atkinson et al., 2012). The LRA spread across Western Equatoria State in South Sudan, Haut Mbomou prefecture in the CAR and the Haut Uélé Province in the Democratic Republic of the Congo. Civilians across three countries suffered this insecurity, as well as further negative impacts from the intense army presence of an African Union (AU) Mission with the aim of finding the LRA leader Joseph Kony. The AU mission was manned by the Ugandan People's Defense Forces (UPDF), supported by military advisors from the United States (US), and to a lesser extent the national armies of the three countries (Rigterink and Schomerus, 2017, Rigterink et al., 2014).

The presence of foreign armies offered little protection for civilians; instead it added its own strain to people's perceptions about the LRA and those who said they came to find them (Schomerus, 2012). On the South Sudanese side, the situation led to the formation of an initially dispersed vigilante militia (Schomerus and Tumutegyereize, 2009). These 'Arrow Boys' patrolled the bush along the border, particularly when there were reports of possible movement of armed groups. This meant criss-crossing the unmarked borderline in pursuit of armed rebels, sometimes walking deep – 5 or 10 km – into the CAR.

The Arrow Boys helped US forces with intelligence reports and were sought-after informants by the nearby-stationed UN forces. These international interactions created both a feeling of being informally validated in their work as a protection force, while supporting a growing grievance about the lack of pay or any other form of official recognition (Schomerus and Rigterink, 2015). Years later, in 2020, after many turns of violence, shifting loyalties and betrayal in which the lack of recognition for the Arrow Boys had played a part, one former Arrow Boy was given the governor position for the area (Braak, 2020 (September 7). The broader fall-out from South Sudan's civil war – which started in December 2013, just two years after South Sudan had gained independence – and the politicisation of the Arrow Boys was posing complex challenges to the reintegration of what had then become a collection of armed groups that were posing a danger to civilians and broader peace (McCrone, 2020).

In May 2013, many of these events were still in the future, and the communities affected by insecurity in this border area experienced the Arrow Boys as their deeply-committed protectors. They were seen to provide a service necessary for survival that the national and international armies had failed to deliver. The Arrow Boys carried the narrative of selfless and competent community protection with pride, particularly when they efficiently liaised with international forces and suffered hardship during challenging weeks of patrolling the bush. Across the border, some youth and hunters from Obo tried to replicate the Arrow Boys model by organizing into a local 'auto-defense' that, while offering security to the area's residents, never achieved the widespread legitimacy that the Arrow Boys enjoyed in the early days.

Tall tales and borderline cases

And then, at 5.45 am on 24 May 2013, everything changed when the group of 40–80 Arrow Boys from South Sudan's Tambura attacked Obo (Ndelet, 2013). The attackers were swiftly arrested by AU soldiers and the local authorities. Twenty-nine of the South Sudanese Arrow Boys were taken to the Obo Gendarmerie; seven of them did not survive the night behind the locked doors of the Gendarmerie.

In the social act of remembering the attack of Tambura's Arrow Boys on Obo, narratives emerged that explained the present and shaped the future in similar ways to how an economic act of illicit trading shapes markets. If we look at narratives as we would at tradable goods that are moving through transport corridors (with the ability to take on the same characteristics that smuggled goods can take on) the shift in value explains the mental landscape of border residents and broader security dynamics. It brings out the role of border crossing as an act of meaning-making, leaving constraints behind and pursuing opportunities.

Official demarcations

Why did the Arrow Boys march for days to use their make-shift weapons to attack a town in a foreign country, known to everyone to be full of armed soldiers from three armies? Moreover, why did seven of the assailants die that night?

The various narratives that exist around this event offer vastly differing explanations, yet they all have two things in common. First, the role of the border and how it changes a person's value, constraints, and opportunities as they cross it. Second, that it is impossible to establish and verify one indisputable, ground-truthed explanation. It may well be the case that there are official explanations on both sides of the border. It seems likely, however, that, similar to the movable boundary marker, the exact meaning of such official explanation shifts between the two national authorities and is as unreliable as an official border stone that can be hauled around by two people. Such authoritative narrative might explain what seems like an overly laborious expression of sheer hubris, naivety or criminal energy. This official narrative has not been shared by either South Sudanese or CAR authorities – despite the involvement of governmental and non-governmental actors on either side of this border in the aftermath of the attack.

That aftermath developed at least some resemblance to an official explanation in the ilk of a movable border-stone. A government delegation from Bangui came to talk to the Arrow Boys who were by then referred to as 'the rebels.' CAR authorities decided to skip formal international follow up and to 'pardon everything,' according to the head of the Gendarmerie in Obo.[1] This move might have been driven by the hope that if CAR did not kick up a fuss about the attack, the South Sudanese authorities would not question further why seven of its citizens died in custody in the CAR. The national chapters of the International Committee of the Red Cross in CAR and South Sudan were charged with the repatriation of both survivors and bodies.

This involvement of national authorities simply suggests the attempt at a narrative of the matter having been dealt with by the authorities, much like the border stone is an attempt of official demarcation. From there on, it gets complicated. Without an official or even logical explanation, the act of sensemaking and situating the story becomes the domain of whoever tells it. Much like smuggled goods, the value of that story and its rationalities differ vastly on both sides of the border, expanding the official demarcation of the story into its vast and ambiguous surrounding territory of bushland, just like the official borderstone sits in undefined territory as seen in Figure 12.2.

Figure 12.2 The South Sudan/CAR borderstone in the vast bushland.

Vast and ambiguous territory: the many versions of the Arrow Boys attack on Obo

That the Arrow Boys walked across an invisible line of shifting sovereignties with the purpose to attack a town across the border has been rationalized along the lines of three broad narrative characterisations. These built upon each other and are told in many variations: rewards and jobs; using territorial expansion to behave in ways that bring gain but are not possible at home; or the pursuit of power.

The first narrative seems like the most rational one, but at the same time displays meaning-making as contraband: the promise of rewards and jobs. Versions of this explanation are that the Arrow Boys were seeking bounty by arresting the leader of the LRA, Joseph Kony. Others claimed that they were guns for hire that had been brought into the interlaced conflict complexities of the South Sudan and the CAR, with possible paymasters being CAR's former president François Bozize, who had been removed from power by the Séléka rebels just a few months prior. Other paymasters on offer were then-Sudanese president Omar al Bashir, South Sudan's president Salva Kiir or vice president Riek Machar respectively (as proxies for their own fight with each other). Some people in South Sudan's Western Equatoria suggested that the Arrow Boys had been hired by South Sudan's notorious National Security to capitalise on the Arrow Boys' skills as spies, offering intel on the situation in the CAR as the country was just becoming embroiled in wide-spread conflict. Proxy wars across borders are common in this region where 'the fluid geographical reach also highlights the blurred boundaries of ideology' (Schomerus, 2021a).

A second set of narratives also looks at material gain, but with a stronger emphasis on how crossing the border increased the possibility and agency of the Arrow Boys' significance and identity. Their violent behaviour and pursuit of material gain would not have been possible within their own communities, so that they had to take their skills gained in serving their communities to get a reward elsewhere for being an Arrow Boy. This narrative suggests that they were fighting their own poverty or even seeking revenge against the various military forces who had treated them with disrespect on their own South Sudanese territory or had not re-numerated them for their intelligence services. Within Obo, too, the individual motivations of these young men were of lesser concern than the overall motivation of their collective action. Compared to explanations in South Sudan, all narratives circulating across the border were firmly situated in the context of Central African politics, which at that moment in time was in great turmoil.

A third and final variation of narratives in which the border becomes an empowering connector is the explanation that the Arrow Boys were seeking to re-establish forcefully an Azande Kingdom that was to traverse the division of the Azande People created by colonial borders. This kingdom was only possibly with the support of the Azande community around Obo in the CAR; since this support for a South Sudanese-led kingdom was not forthcoming, they sought it by force (Schomerus and Rigterink, 2016, Schomerus, 2014). In Obo, too, some residents championed the idea of an independent Azande kingdom, while others hinted at the ambition to march the 1200 km towards Bangui to depose the Séléka rebels from their newly gained power. This narrative echoes arguments from scholarship on this part of Africa, that posits that land, identity and citizenship are inseparable (Laudati, 2011). As Pécaut argues, despite the fact that borders are a shared space, establishing ownership of it or across it remains important and is best achieved by narrating such ownership (Pécaut, 2000).

The story about the deaths of seven men in custody created a separate and autonomous collection of rumours. In Obo the stories of what caused their deaths range from lack of oxygen in the police cell, internal fighting among the assailants, to poisoning by people in Obo (some accusing the Muslim community, others the Ugandan army as poisoners). While sensemaking in Obo revolved around community tensions and suspicion and the conflicts in the wider country, the rumours of the causes of death were also smuggled back across the vast and ambiguous territory, into South Sudan in ways that offered meaning to the relatives of those who lost their lives.

The road that offers hindsight

Narratives are virtuosos of retrofitting; they explain how people – in retrospect – rationalise or even justify their actions and their starting points. Structuration theory has broken down the seemingly bifurcated relationship between structure and agency (Giddens, 1984), while behavioural economists uncovered the decision-making mechanisms that people employ to make quick assessments of a situation (Kahneman and Tversky, 1974). In some sense, the concept of a narrative is itself retrofitted. 'Narrative' is often used as a catch-all term to lump together memory, beliefs, experience, sense-making, social norms or simply the stories that people tell each other about the world in which they live. The personal narrative, following McAdams and McLean, is an internal and evolving life story that integrates an individual's reconstructed past and imagined future to provide life with some degree of unity and purpose (McAdams and McLean, 2013). The collective memory, or the shared pool of knowledge and information among members of a social group creates the emotional 'deep story,' as Hochschild calls it, that binds together a group (Hochschild, 2016, Talarico and Rubin, 2003, Bower et al., 1978).

There does not exist one shared narrative of the border residents – or even amongst Arrow Boys who participated in the ill-fated raid – of why they did what they did. There are some collective semantic memories; these are facts, concepts, and knowledge. Nobody disputes that the raid happened, that the participants used their shared identity as Arrow Boys to attack, or that the Arrow Boys were taken into custody and that seven of them died. This semantic memory mixes with episodic memory – the mosaic of experiences or autobiographical events everyone collects to create an individual or communal 'deep story' of meaning (Hochschild, 2016), which covers the possibilities of motivations and reasons outlined above.

Often, research can implicitly assume that people's semantic, episodic and collective memories are a reliable source of information that is stable and consistent – or at least this can be projected too easily in findings. Such research seemingly offers clarity on causality, human behaviour and politics and how these all intersect – without taking into account its own limited framework that produced such clear knowledge (Bliesemann de Guevara and Kostić, 2017). Overconfident findings derived from using people's narratives as hard data has been rightly challenged as continuing to simplify – sometimes with the best of intentions – situations that cannot be simplified (Perera, 2017) and to offer a single catchy image that suggests a linearity that does not exist (Schomerus, forthcoming).

In many ways, stories that become vaguer the more one tries to clarify them have been one of the defining features of our research projects in the borderlands of South Sudan. Much like George Orwell's account of how, as a colonial police officer in British Burma, he shot an elephant, there is never one story to tell about a scene of events. The meaning and interpretations that can be ascribed to the observable facts irrevocably change depending on who narrates and from what perspective. 'A story always sound clear enough at a distance, but the nearer you get to the scene of events the vaguer it becomes,' Orwell observed in 1936 (Orwell, 1968). There is a further complication to an already difficult factual landscape: Almost inevitably, research in contested geographical, political and identity spaces fails to express the ambiguities and changeability of the 'mental landscape,' which is the core of how all events are experienced and interpreted (Schomerus, forthcoming, Trogisch, 2021).

Border studies have alerted us to the power of the border as an interpretative tool. The inconsistencies in sensemaking are amplified by the fluid environment that a border can provide and the power a border has to change the value of something that crosses it. The border offers also a guard rail – within the fluidity it provides, it structures how humans can make sense of their actions on either side of it. The narratives are deeply embedded in the geography of a borderscape that acts less as a physical, and more as a conceptual demarcation line between behaviour at home and behaviour abroad – which in this case means protection of civilians at home and attacks against them abroad.

Different explanatory narratives for the event emerged and the difference can be explained by the exact role assigned to the border in the narrative. When the border is imagined as separating the Arrow Boys from their communities, it gives them permission to pursue material gain with violence in ways they would not employ at home. In other narratives of the event, the border is conceptualised as a connector that allows the Arrow Boys to walk away and across a border in order to reconnect to the bigger politics at their home. In this narrative, the Arrow Boys are said to have gone into CAR to attack Obo as guns for hire for Central African, Sudanese or South Sudanese politicians. The border in this version is akin to a stage, needed for a performance that offers a different meaning on either side of it (Walker et al., 2011). Playing out the narrative of guns for hire for big men could thus offer 'a stage from which to be seen by others,' as Lund argues in his description of 'fruitful misunderstandings' in the performance of research and presenting grievances (Lund, 2014). The narrative of leaving to influence forces back home allows the border to play an identifiable, if complex part. Crossing the border changes the value of the story from the Arrow Boys as an effective civilian protection militia that accepted being overlooked when it comes to receiving official recognition or payment as part of their service to community to a story of a transactional militia seeking rewards. Imagining the border as the gate to proxy wars and engagement means that this narrative combines the social construction of how the border is imagined and the social construction of who the Arrow Boys are with the social act of remembering the specific event of the Arrow Boys attack on Obo.

That these changes in meaning happen is perhaps not surprising. Moving from one familiar place to another unfamiliar one changes the mind, as Clark and Chalmers argue while establishing that the environment plays an 'active role … in driving cognitive processes' (Clark and Chalmers, 1998). In this interpretation, the border is a tool deployed to become part of the cognitive tools of sensemaking – an artifact that, as Heersmink outlines, can be used to create memories (Heersmink, 2018). These memories are shaped by the artifact on offer, which is deployed in a liminal space of change, where one environment is left behind before another is conquered (Thomas, 2020, 17 March). In that perspective, carrying a narrative across a border and letting it be changed by its environment and social remembering that then creates behaviour and people's actions is not dissimilar to the way the economic act of illicit trading shapes markets on either side of a border.

Narratives as contraband: a future research agenda

With growing scholarship on the meaning of narratives and the influence of information on people's decision-making and behaviour, the perspective of stories as contraband offers untapped potential for understanding how geographical, social and political boundaries intersect with narratives and actions. Often, the analysis of narratives remains limited to perception surveys, which are used to gauge primarily if a policy or programme is perceived to be working. Integrating a lens that treats narratives as goods that can be altered by identifiable factors offers an additional analytical tool to understand human behaviour.

The current material gaze that guides most scholarship on smuggling is too narrow in how it thinks about value, neglecting too easily that value is a social construct that can only be created through storytelling. There are challenges, however, in looking at narratives too myopically through the smuggling lens, always asking how crossing a border changes them. Analysis of the origin and dynamics of narratives is required also without a look across an imagined or demarcated line to understand how stories of value are created within communities and not just by stepping out of their origin context.

This concern does not dampen the need for interdisciplinary research that combines considerations of smuggling and narratives. As smuggling often happens in intensely securitised spaces, the stories of how, exactly, military presence influences people's lives need to be told. The perspective on people's lives requires a much deeper insight into how narratives are constructed and how they shape behaviour, which calls for tighter interdisciplinary work that combines storytelling with behavioural analysis (Amanela et al., 2020a). This is a challenging field, not just in its data collection and analysis, but also in how crossing the disciplinary boundaries to understand better how stories of boundary crossings influence people's actions is communicated and utilised within academia and policy. A smuggling perspective on stories and a story perspective on smuggling potentially offer great insights once more work is done in this field. What it already offers now is the realisation that – just as with the many versions of the Arrow Boy attack on Obo – there is no single policy to recommend and no single story to tell.

Note

1   Interview with Commander of the Gendarmerie, March 17, 2015, Obo.

References

Amanela, S., Flora Ayee, T., Buell, S., Escande, A., Quinlan, T., Rigterink, A. S., Schomerus, M., Sharp, S. & Swanson, S. 2020a. *Part 2: The Mental Landscape of Post-conflict Life in Northern Uganda: Research on Behaviour and Post-conflict Life in Northern Uganda: The Research Design*, London, Secure Livelihoods Research Consortium (SLRC), ODI.

Amanela, S., Flora Ayee, T., Buell, S., Escande, A., Quinlan, T., Rigterink, A. S., Schomerus, M., Sharp, S. & Swanson, S. 2020b. *Parts 1–7: The Mental Landscape of Post-conflict Life in Northern Uganda (report series)*, London, Secure Livelihoods Research Consortium (SLRC), ODI.

Atkinson, R. R., Lancaster, P., Cakaj, L. & Lacaille, G. 2012. Do no harm: assessing a military approach to the Lord's Resistance Army. *Journal of Eastern African Studies*, 6, 371–382.

Bliesemann de Guevara, B. & Kostić, R. 2017. Knowledge production in/about conflict and intervention: finding 'facts,' telling 'truth.' *Journal of Intervention and Statebuilding*, 11, 1–20.

Bower, G., Monteiro, K. & Gilligan, S. 1978. Emotional mood as a context for learning and recall. *Journal of Verbal Learning and Verbal Behavior*, 17, 573–585.

Braak, B. 2020, September 7. 'Warlord politics' guides peace in South Sudan. *Africa at LSE* [Online]. Available from: https://blogs.lse.ac.uk/africaatlse/2020/09/07/warlord-politics-guides-peace-in-south-sudan/.

Brunet-Jailly, E. 2005. Theorizing borders: an interdisciplinary perspective. *Geopolitics*, 10, 633–649.

Clark, A. & Chalmers, D. 1998. The extended mind. *Analysis*, 58, 7–19.

De Vries, L. 2011. Négocier l'autorité. Les micro-pratiques étatiques à la frontière du Sud-Soudan et de la République Démocratique du Congo. *Politique Africaine*, 122, 41–58.

Dobler, G. 2016. The green, the grey and the blue: a typology of cross-border trade in Africa. *The Journal of Modern African Studies*, 54, 145–169.

Feyeissa, D. 2010. The cultural construction of state borders: the view from Gambella. *Journal of Eastern African Studies*, 4, 314–330.

Frahm, O. 2015. Making borders and identities in South Sudan. *Journal of Contemporary African Studies*, 33, 1–17.

Giddens, A. 1984. *The Constitution of Society: Outline of the Theory of Structuration*, Cambridge, Polity Press.

Heersmink, R. 2018. The narrative self, distributed memory, and evocative objects. *Philosophical Studies*, 175, 1829–1849.

Hochschild, A. R. 2016. *Strangers in Their Own Land: Anger and Mourning on the American Right*, New York, NY, New Press.

Kahneman, D. & Tversky, A. 1974. Judgment under uncertainty: heuristics and biases. *Science*, 185, 1124–1131.

Laudati, A. 2011. Victims of discourse: Mobilizing narratives of fear and insecurity in post-conflict South Sudan-the case of Jonglei State. *African Geographical Review*, 30, 15–32.

Lund, C. 2014. The ethics of fruitful misunderstanding. *Journal of Research Practice*, 10(2).

McAdams, D. & McLean, K. 2013. Narrative identity. *Current Directions in Psychological Science*, 22, 233–238.

McCrone, F. 2020. *Hollow Promises: The Risks of Military Integration in Western Equatoria*, Geneva, Small Arms Survey.

Ndelet, J.-B. 2013. Daily report du 24 Mai 2013-OBO: Tentative d'envahissement de la ville d'Obo par un groupe armée en provenance du Sud-Soudan, UN Obo.

Newman, D. 2010. Territory, compartments and borders: avoiding the trap of the territorial trap. *Geopolitics*, 15, 773–778.

Orwell, G. 1968. *Shooting an Elephant and Other Essays by George Orwell*, Ottawa, Distributed Proofreaders Canada.

Pécaut, D. 2000. Configurations of space, time, and subjectivity in a context of terror: the Colombian example. *International Journal of Politics, Culture, and Society*, 14, 129–150.

Perera, S. 2017. Bermuda triangulation: embracing the messiness of researching in conflict. *Journal of Intervention and Statebuilding*, 11, 42–57.

Rigterink, A. S., Kenyi, J. J. & Schomerus, M. 2014. Report of the Justice and Security Research Programme Survey in Western Equatoria State, South Sudan (first round May 2013), London, London School of Economics and Political Science.

Rigterink, A. S. & Schomerus, M. 2017. The fear factor is a main thing: how radio influences anxiety and political attitudes *Journal of Development Studies*, 53, 1123–1146.

Schomerus, M. 2012. They forget what they came for: Uganda's Army in Sudan. *Journal of Eastern African Studies*, 6, 124–153.

Schomerus, M. 2014. Policy of Government and Policy of Culture: Understanding the Rules of Law in the "Context" of South Sudan's Western Equatoria State. In: Marshall, D. & Rosenbaum, M. (eds.) *The International Rule of Law Movement: A Crisis of Legitimacy and the Way Forward*, Cambridge, MA, Harvard Law School Human Rights Programme/Harvard University Press.

Schomerus, M. 2021a. *The Lord's Resistance Army: Violence and Peacemaking in Africa*, Cambridge, Cambridge University Press.

Schomerus, M. 2021b. *The Mental Landscape of Lives in Conflict: Policy Implications*, London, Secure Livelihoods Research Consortium (SLRC)/ ODI.

Schomerus, M. (2021). *Lives and Violence (Revised)*, London, I.B.Tauris/Bloomsbury.

Schomerus, M. & De Vries, L. 2014. Improvising border security: 'A Situation of Security Pluralism' along South Sudan's Borders with the Democratic Republic of Congo. *Security Dialogue*, 45, 1–16.

Schomerus, M., De Vries, L. & Vaughan, C. 2013. Introduction: Negotiating borders, defining South Sudan. In: Vaughan, C., Schomerus, M. & De Vries, L. (eds.) *The Borderlands of South Sudan: Authority and identity in contemporary and historical perspectives*, New York, Palgrave Macmillan.

Schomerus, M. & Rigterink, A. 2016. *Non-State Security Providers and Political Formation in South Sudan: The Case of Western Equatorias Arrow Boys*, Waterloo, Center for Security Governance.

Schomerus, M. & Rigterink, A. S. 2015. 'And then he switched off the phone': mobile phones, participation and political accountability in South Sudan's Western Equatoria State. *Stability: International Journal of Security and Development*, 4, 10.

Schomerus, M. & Tumutegyereize, K. 2009. *After Operation Lightning Thunder: Protecting Communities and Building Peace*. London, Conciliation Resources.

Talarico, J. M. & Rubin, D. C. 2003. Confidence, not consistency, characterizes flashbulb memories. *Psychological Science*, 14, 455–461.

Thomas, E. 2020. Why does travelling change us? *The New Statesman*, 17 March.

Trogisch, L. 2021. Geographies of fear – The everyday (geo) politics of 'green' violence and militarization in the intended transboundary Virunga Conservation Area. *Geoforum*, 122, 92–102.

Walker, R., Simmons, C., Aldrich, S., Perz, S., Arima, E. & Caldas, M. 2011. The Amazonian theater of cruelty. *Annals of the Association of American Geographers*, 101, 1156–1170.

13

GENDER AND SMUGGLING

Caroline E. Schuster

The dominant approach to gender and smuggling in criminological debates has been premised on the notion of women's progressive "emancipation" from restrictive and patriarchal gender roles (Selmini, 2020; Siegel, 2014: 56). It was understood that feminist political struggles the world over would shatter glass ceilings and lead to gender parity, including parity in the illicit labour of smuggling and organised crime. Summarising this thinking, Siegel (2014: 56) writes that, according to this approach, the role of women in criminal families was previously limited to being a passive, obedient and silent wife, mother and sister whose task was to take care of the household, raise the children, participate in funerals and weddings and promote the image of the male family member as 'men of honour.'

These social restrictions were expected to be erased by changing gender norms and women's liberation. Early – and controversial – feminist theories (e.g., Adler, 1975; Simon, 1975) emerged from the Second Wave of Feminism in the 1970s and posited that patterns revealing women's comparative absence from criminal activity would evolve once women were included as active and independent participants in the labour market and public sphere (Selmini, 2020: 347).

In the decades after feminist debates focused attention on women's liberation – including gender parity when it came to criminal profits – the 'emancipation' hypothesis has been critically re-evaluated along two axes. First, feminist theory has taken a much more nuanced approach to gender justice, particularly through wider explorations of subjectivity (Bourgois, 1996; Hautzinger, 2007), gender relations (Connell and Messerschmidt, 2005), and multiple intersecting forms of inequality (Thomas and Galemba, 2013). Second, the emancipation hypothesis was revealed to be a fallacy based on "a lack of in-depth historical research [that] has resulted in the misleading observation that in the past only very few women occupied top positions in organized crime" (Siegel, 2014: 63). The rejection of progressive narratives of women's empowerment was paired with a burgeoning research agenda tracking the global flows of information, economic opportunity, media representations, and communication channels that position women in complex ways vis-à-vis illegal markets (Kleemans et al., 2014; Zhang et al., 2007).

Despite feminist scholarship challenging the traditional view and documenting women's multifaceted role in illicit economies, both popular and scholarly accounts reproduce and

168   DOI: 10.4324/9781003043645-13

Gender and smuggling

reinforce commonly held perceptions about crime generally: men are highly over-represented. As scholarship on masculinity and the drug trade attests, this perception is often held by people within illicit economies themselves: "these male representations reinforce, reproduce, and reconstruct masculinity. Like most masculinities, men are defined as powerful and competent, violent and bold; women as weak and inept," even whilst male drug robbers rely on highly proficient female accomplices to shake down drug dealers (Contreras, 2009: 482). Two issues are at stake. First, there is an empirical question about whether women have been active participants all along, even while their work has been minimised or ignored. Second, there is a normative question about equality, and whether this could be achieved by empowering women to rise through the ranks of smuggling organisations. The focus of this chapter will be on the first question, while addressing the normative implications in the conclusion.

This chapter unpacks gendered tropes that have shaped both popular and scholarly approaches to illicit economies, and their cultural associations with masculine bravado. Using an in-depth ethnographic analysis of the role of smuggling in everyday life, particularly in household provisioning and the sexual division of labour within domestic settings, the chapter develops a broader feminist analysis of the household as a key nexus in contraband economies, and not simply a site of women's oppression. Understanding that nexus offers a better understanding of contraband as it is experienced in everyday life, as well as novel understandings of the fundamental ways gender relations constitute smuggling economies. Focusing on gender in this chapter does not amount to denying that illicit markets are still largely controlled by and benefit men. However, this approach challenges us to rethink the pervasive stereotypes about gendered roles and economic practices by highlighting women's complex positions in the smuggling trade.

Unmarked categories of smuggling

The scant literature on women and girls in smuggling economies is itself telling. As sociologist Sudhir Venkatesh noted in his classic essay on "Gender and Outlaw Capitalism," the moniker *girl gangs* exposes the longstanding subordination of women's experience in street gangs to that of men, such that "male deviant collectives have (unsurprisingly) been given the unmarked category 'gang'" (Venkatesh, 1998: 683). There is a deeply held assumption that men are the agents of gangs, and that women are either epiphenomenal to the social structure of criminal groups, or their passive victims (cf Anderson, 2005 for a critique).[1] This observation – that men occupy the unmarked category of smuggler, narco, gang, mafioso, and so on, while women's participation must always be marked and qualified – applies for illicit economies more generally.

An attempt to document women's participation in smuggling economies also calls for a rethink of how we track illicit economies over the twentieth century. Scholars of globalization have noted a major shift since the 1980s, such that the retreat of the welfare state and deregulation of many industries has put an emphasis on flexible, entrepreneurial, and informal labour. Illicit economies have concomitantly boomed. Women have been considered relatively insulated from the effects of neoliberal restructuring and global shift towards economic precarity that has been associated with the rise of informal and illicit economies in the Global South (Sassen, 2007; Young, 2007). This is

> based on the common assumption that female identity is *generally* not as contested as male identity ... [and] the notion that female identity is rooted almost entirely in the family and the family is somehow less volatile than economic institutions
>
> (Moore, 2007: 190)

Caroline E. Schuster

These assumptions about female identity led to an overemphasis on women's participation in informal but *licit* economies. The feminized attributes of flexibility and care towards the family have been the primary justification for the boom in both not-for-profit and commercial microfinance lending, which sought to harness these apparently "natural" traits and put them in service of micro-enterprises (Kar and Schuster, 2016; Schuster, 2014, 2015). Being able to absorb economic shocks and provide the intimate care work to protect the family from the retreat of welfare states and harsh reality of privatisation has been seen as a testament to women's supposedly inherent 'resilience' (Fraser, 2009). While the effects of microfinance are subject to considerable debate, the findings of both advocates as well as critics cast doubt on the presumption that women are "naturally" bound to the home, and that their economic practices are relatively protected from global economic transformations.

While women's uptick in participation in informal economies has been well documented, evidence points to profound social dislocations for women as well as for men brought on by global political and economic shifts in the twentieth century. Feminist criminologists suggest that the less-well-studied phenomenon of women's participation in illicit economies further challenges us to rethink women's rootedness in the domestic sphere. Joan W. Moore's research on female gangs suggests that migration further dislocates young women from intergenerational socialisation, such that each adolescent group "sets its own norms for sexuality, aggressiveness, and self-control vis-à-vis drug and alcohol use" (Moore, 2007: 192). There is a disconnect, then, between stereotyped portrayals of women as "victims of organized crime or as 'mean girls,' girlfriends, wives, lovers or brides of notorious gangsters and mobsters" (Hübschle, 2014: 31), and the wider (though too often invisible and ignored) reality of women's participation in illicit markets.

This disconnect can be attributed to some widely held beliefs – both among the wider public as well as gang members themselves – about the figures that populate the smuggling trade, whether contraband, organised crime, money laundering, the drug trade, and so on. As criminologist Annette Hübschle has noted in her review of women in organised crime in Southern Africa, women are often ignored because of broader assumptions about a clandestine criminal underworld. This association with violent crime erases the fact that "politicians, law enforcement agents, government officials and businesspersons facilitate illegal market exchanges and collaborate with organized crime networks" (Hübschle, 2014: 33). The reality of everyday economic practices suggests that, while stereotyped representations of violent and powerful men prevail in the media and in criminology treatments of illegal markets, qualitative research indicates a complex interpenetration of licit and illicit economies (Chalfin, 2008; Roitman, 2005), sustained by a diversity of economic projects and livelihood aspirations. This work on the wider social landscapes of contraband challenges the presumption of professional hyper-macho underground gangsters preying on a passive feminized upper world (Hübschle, 2014: 33).

One way to address these limitations is to rethink the familiar dichotomies that separate men's roles from women's roles. Feminist scholars denominate this a "relational approach" to gendered economic life that addresses the connections among social categories rather than focusing on each pole of the binary in isolation. For example, this has led some feminist scholars to suggest women have an important supporting role in apparently masculine illicit economies (Anderson, 2005). Cases such as ethnic Albanian women supporting their husbands while not acting as 'independent bosses' themselves (Arsovska and Begum, 2014), or the elevated position of women in the Italian mafia as groups become more professional and less homicidal (Selmini, 2020), suggest that these supporting roles carry pervasive gendered expectations about care, kinship, and appropriate femininity, and that these are constituted within wider systems of gender and sexuality. I turn now to the gendered roles that shape both smuggling and domestic life at their intersection.

Smuggling and domestic provisioning

What would a relational approach to gendered economic life look like if it were applied to households involved in the smuggling trade? While the market has usually been understood as public, and opposed to domestic family life, a closer inspection of gender relations requires a more nuanced methodology. These interconnections between market and home were the focus of my ethnographic research (2006–2017) on debt and development in Ciudad del Este, the prosperous 'special customs zone' and notorious contraband hub on the Paraguayan side of the Tri-Border Area (TBA) with Argentina and Brazil (Schuster, 2015). Famous in the region as a re-export bottleneck for both licit and illicit commodities, the city is widely stereotyped as the unplanned and chaotic apogee of freewheeling frontier capitalism, driven by the needs of commerce and speculation. Even illicit commodities are re-exported. This is not driven by the quest for lower tariffs, but rather to harness the logistics, transportation, and financing networks that animate *all* trade in the region. Tellingly, "local state actors actively foster spatial disorder and legal uncertainty as part of planning practice" (Tucker, 2017: 74) especially to encourage speculative deals that benefit elites. The initial planning for the city in the late 1950s proceeded along just such lines. Urban development was immediately outsourced to a private conglomerate led by a close associate and sometimes-business-partner of Paraguay's longtime authoritarian regime of President Alfredo Stroessner (1954–1989). For a city designed and developed to channel flows of dark finance, citizens' prosperity and well-being was inextricably linked to the fortunes of commerce, and often bundled up in the smuggling trade.

Since private commercial profits were the only robust social safety net in Ciudad del Este, my research with women who took on small-scale microcredit loans focused attention on their many complex investments. More often than not, seeking out credit from a variety of finance companies, including anti-poverty microcredit loans, was part of an ongoing effort to invest in deals that would buoy them along with the rising tide of commercial fortunes in the city. For poor women making do in the margins of Ciudad del Este's commercial boom, their investments – and the social security they were hoped to engender – were most often fuelled by mounting debts (see Han, 2011, 2012). By the early 2000s, the economy sagged under pressure from Brazilian customs enforcement and the slow-moving effects of regularizing regional customs laws through the Mercosur Southern Common Market (Dent, 2017; Rabossi, 2012; Schuster, 2019a). Seeking social security through commercial windfalls was ever more untenable for low-income families (Schuster, 2019b). The net effect was ever-more desperate investments linked to ever-more desperate loan payments.

One of the most striking encounters with smuggling during my ethnographic fieldwork in Ciudad del Este occurred in a family home surrounded by chickens and pigs, not the glitzy shopping malls and hectic traffic that have made the Paraguayan city a famous contraband hub. We were in the poor peri-urban outskirts of the city, in a settlement at the end of a winding dirt road, sitting around a plastic card table on the front patio in front of a small weatherboard home painted a cheerful salmon pink. I had arrived with the financing team from Fundación Paraguaya, a non-profit microcredit organisation that offered small loans to unlock women's "entrepreneurial potential." We were at this particular house to negotiate the terms of a new line of credit. The three generations of women sitting at the negotiating table – grandmother, mother and daughter – were smugglers. Tellingly, nobody at the gathering was willing to disclose the goods involved.

The disagreement with Josefina, the loan officer in charge of managing the family's line of credit, had nothing to do with moral or legal qualms with the women's dubious line of work. Rather, she was concerned about the paperwork. For the loan to be approved by her own

Caroline E. Schuster

managers in the organisation's head office, Josefina was required to provide some proof of income to guarantee the viability of the business venture, such as purchase orders, sales receipts, and so on. The office was under intense scrutiny due to the wider macrostructural issues: the year was 2009 and we were in the middle of the global financial crisis, and the crash of credit markets around the world. At the microsocial level this left Josefina with a problem. Her folio of documents only contained a contract with the exporter. The hastily prepared agreement contained scant information: the equivalent of a handshake agreement, which would not stand up to scrutiny at the head office. The women insisted that they were planning on traveling across the border between Paraguay and Argentina via Brazil to "do the deal" (*hacer negocio*), but that it simply was not possible to get a formal receipt. They added that their aunt did the same thing and had even introduced them to the smuggling network. Trying to sway Josefina, they argued that their aunt was even a client of Fundación Paraguaya. By their telling, their kins-woman had presented exactly the same information to secure her own approval for a line of credit. However, the whole family business was emphatically off the books, as were so many in Ciudad del Este. Despite being fully aware of what that implied, Josefina was adamant. She wanted a receipt, "something to prove what [she] was buying, some way to demonstrate commercial movement (*movimiento comercial*)."

In the end, the grandmother came to the rescue. She sold the smuggled merchandise at an informal shop in the city centre, and also had a side business selling Avon cosmetics through a multi-level marketing arrangement. While the cosmetics business was financed independently from the smuggling, she offered to use the sales receipts and purchase orders to collateralise the loan her daughter was negotiating with Josefina, which in turn would ensure her own sales venture remained viable. All parties to the deal were satisfied: Josefina understood that the loan would be repaid but was circumspect with her questions, the family secured its line of credit and provided some valid documents for the finance company, and the observing ethnographer got a brief glimpse into Ciudad del Este's smuggling economy.

At the time, I found the encounter quite confronting. I was taken aback with the micro-finance organization's cavalier treatment of smuggling. The loan officer appeared to be much more concerned with getting the proper documentation than with what I perceived to be the more obvious scandal whereby development monies were fuelling the contraband trade. As I came to appreciate later, the complex intermingling of domestic economies with smuggling suggested that contraband also sustained what I call an *economy of gender*. That is, the social categories and scripts available to actors working within the smuggling trade were also relations of gender.

A framework based on an economy of gender is not satisfied with comparing men and women. Instead, we must ask deeper questions about what being a woman actually *means* in Paraguay's smuggling economy, and how womanhood is shaped by illicit trade. Women drew on these gender relations resourcefully to make a living in Paraguay's dangerous and lucrative borderland. The microcredit deal was only possible because the family laundered the loan contract through the perfectly acceptable and feminine Avon business, which offered a veneer of respectability to the endeavour. The reason that the whole thing was believable was that it fit neatly with the microcredit narrative of feminine economic behaviour. The deal was endorsed by the NGO because it sustained the image of "women entrepreneurs" – gender expectations that kept Josefina and the NGO in business. While the NGO clung to the pristine image of the independent businesswoman, actual gendered interdependencies such as intergenerational matriarchal kinship obligations were the life blood of Ciudad del Este's smuggling trade, were minimized by the lender. All of these economic behaviours were organised around specific expressions of feminine subjectivity. Crucially, these specific gendered identities (grandmother,

Gender and smuggling

"hard woman" smuggler (Schuster, 2015), efficient financial professional specialising in women's loans) stuck together in the social network through which Ciudad del Este's commercial monies flowed. It only 'worked' because of the specific gendered performances of its principal actors.

In her research on the spatial logics of "accumulation by transgression" in Paraguay's Tri-Border Area, urban studies scholar Jennifer Tucker (2020: 1465) suggests that a local term, *blindaje*,[2] is used to assess the differential visibility of illicit economic practices in Ciudad del Este. Used as vernacular to describe mutually beneficial arrangements between judges and politicians in the merchant bloc, *blindaje* promises impunity in exchange for kickbacks. This contextual invisibility was powerfully at work in the negotiations between Josefina and the intergenerational family of women smugglers. It was what allowed innocuous and feminised Avon sales receipts situationally to conceal the family's contraband business, and allowed the smugglers to fly under the radar of state surveillance at the border. Tucker suggests that these practices of obfuscation often benefit powerful elites, since investigative journalism and political inquests demand evidence connecting particular individuals to specific criminal acts (Tucker 2020: 1466; see also Schuster 2019a). Notorious contraband kingpins such as former President Horacio Cartes, who sits at the apex of a multi-million-dollar cigarette smuggling empire, rely on this obfuscation. For the ex-President, "raced and gendered performances of (im)plausible deniability also hide accumulation by transgression … [embodying] the alchemy by which transgression transmutes into legitimised political authority" (Tucker, 2020: 1466).

My ethnographic analysis of the economy of gender in Ciudad del Este's marginal low-income neighbourhoods suggests that powerful modes of feminine concealment work alongside elite obfuscation through *blindaje*. Women smugglers are relatively disregarded both by scholars assessing smuggling economies as well as by local narratives valorising masculine success and profits in the contraband trade. This worked to their benefit, as they evaded detection and moved freely in spaces where men were subject to higher scrutiny. However, flipping the script and re-reading the encounter detailed above draws out some unexpected convergences between the position of the former President and the family of smugglers. For the women, powerful family ties exceed the domestic context and connect them to valuable networks of accomplices, savvy negotiations make use of local cultural frameworks of visibility and concealment, and the home is reconceptualised as a key site for financial speculation: these are all economic practices that should make us question whether women are really passive subjects of smuggling. However, even while we centre women in Ciudad del Este's smuggling economy, we must not lose sight of the double disadvantage of gender and poverty. Smuggling offered up a pathway for marginalised women to make ends meet, but not an opportunity for accumulation. Their multiple forms of disadvantage call into question the normative empowerment framework that views women's greater participation as a good thing.

Gendered labour as opportunity and vulnerability

The women smugglers I encountered in Ciudad del Este participated in a type of trade that is very common in border zones and contraband economies throughout Latin America. Often denominated "ant contraband" (*contrabando de hormigas, comercio hormiga*), borderlanders historically moved small quantities of goods through repetitive small trips across a porous border (Galemba, 2017: 6; Schuster, 2015). In Ciudad del Este, locals smuggle household items like cooking oil, petrol, Tupperware, tomatoes, and frozen chickens in order to provision their domestic economies. Women also work for hire, moving small consumer electronics like cell phones and laptops for Brazilian and Argentinean buyers, often slipping these in between the folds of blankets and clothing that are seen as more traditionally feminine purchases. *Contrabando de hormigas* works because women do not fit the expected template of a smuggler, and can thus slip past border guards and checkpoints. This is "everyday petty smuggling in which most local residents are implicated" (Ferradás, 2013: 266). As Rebecca Galemba has noted, based on her ethnography of contraband on the Guatemala-Mexico border, "most of these goods were considered illegal only because they used the unmonitored route to enter and exit the country; otherwise they were mundane items such as corn, coffee, and clothing" (Galemba, 2017: 15), belying the historic interconnection of border zones as well as the role of the border as a politico-legal phenomenon that *creates* smuggling (i.e., redefining local exchange networks and provisioning strategies as extra-legal).

Scholars of Latin American border zones have noted that "local residents have long pursued illegal routes to acquire commodities for their households and workplaces" (Jusionyte, 2013: 244, 2015a), and frequently justify their unlawful – but licit and locally sanctioned – exchanges by critiquing unfair trade regimes and laws emanating from a remote political centre, and benefitting elites (ibid; Schuster 2019a). Through an analysis of the economy of gender in the smuggling trade, it is apparent that phenomenon such as 'ant contraband' are key modes of smuggling, and deeply bound up with wider political and legal dynamics. I argue that a feminist analysis can recast the domestic and the household as key sites within contraband economies, and not simply a characteristic mode of oppression for women bound (and limited by) their reproductive function (Leacock, 1979; Yanagisako, 2015).

Rethinking the domestic and its relation to smuggling economies opens up two further lines of inquiry. First, the interpenetration of intimate and domestic activities such as self-styling and consumption with the flows of global trade and travel, forces us to rethink the boundaries, composition, and scale of "the household." This is particularly important as global manufacturing has moved South, and relies heavily on a feminine labour force. Second, the fact that in many settings women continue to be bound to household and family duties means that violence is especially likely to affect them when drugs and money move through domestic spaces.

Carla Freeman's classic work, "Is Local: Global as Feminine: Masculine? Rethinking the Gender of Globalization" (2001) tracks women who practice "higglering" (market intermediaries) in the Caribbean. Historically, they moved agricultural commodities from the hinterlands, and in turn brought urban commodities back to the countryside. In the context of plantation slavery, "she also came to embody a figure of womanhood in which physical movement, travel, and business acumen were defining characteristics" (ibid: 1019). Today, women travel between Barbados and Miami to make overseas purchases, "reselling these in an active (and illegal) informal market at home" (Freeman, 2001: 1021). Denominated "suitcase traders" due to their iconic travel accoutrements, these women range from airline flight attendants, to middle class women shopping for friends, to specialists who make a business in a particular niche market like baby clothes. Despite the state's attempts to crack down on the "suitcase trade," this practice of illegally importing goods remains an important supplement to the income of unemployed and low-wage workers across the region (see also Ulysse, 2007).

The practice of higglering is especially important for the low-income informatics employees who work as data-entry specialists at multinational companies in the free trade zone. These women come to rely on smuggled fashion accessories as both a supplement to their income as well as a crucial class-marker that helps define their upward social mobility. Rather than a vocation, this involvement in the "suitcase trade" is a supplement to the low wages they earn in offshore informatics *and* a consequence of the globalised work they perform in the corporate workplace.[3] Their desire for the expensive foreign brand-name fashions that mark their

Gender and smuggling

'workplace professionalism' and compliance with the company dress code was reinforced by a system of productivity rewards for high-achieving employees that included travel vouchers on American Airlines, which was owned by the same parent company as the informatics firm. Women went to great lengths to "purchase new clothes and accessories that mark their non-factory [pink collar] status," (ibid: 2024) working as smugglers in order to be perceived as disciplined and productive in their informatics jobs. Their informatics work in turn provided the resources like travel vouchers and incentives like professional recognition, both of which fueled their suitcase trade. Their personal self-styling and domestic provisioning was part and parcel with their public professional ambitions, and both relied on and enabled illicit commercial importation.

Conversely, scholars studying the narco-economy suggest that the regional and transnational drug trade perforates the boundaries of the household and expose women to heightened vulnerabilities in intimate settings. Shaylih Muehlmann's poignant and finely detailed study of the drug war on the US-Mexico border focuses on several interrelated feminine identity categories that shape – and, importantly, constrain – women's options for relating to the narco-economy. Through the figures of "narco-wives, beauty queens, and mother's bribes," she underscores the fact that while "media representations of the drug cartels and the war on drugs [focus] almost exclusively on men [and] chronicle the exploits of macho drug capos, hit men, and smugglers" (Muehlmann, 2013: 30), the templates for feminine comportment are configured around women styled as either mothers or the beautiful and sexualised girlfriends of powerful men. Women feel powerfully attracted to the role of "narco-wife," exemplified by one research participant's story of love at first sight when she saw a local youth sporting alligator-skin boots (symbolically coded for success in the narco business) (see also Arsovska and Begum, 2014). The feminized role of the narco-wife accrues a certain symbolic status of its own, and is empowering for women who attain wealth and can evoke the power to bring punitive violence to bear against rivals. However, the status of narco-wife is even more vulnerable than their powerful macho husbands. Not only are they targets of violence, torture, and murder as vengeance or retaliation against their spouse, but furthermore, "while narcos are still narcos when imprisoned, the luxurious life of a narco-wife is compromised beyond recognition" (Muehlmann, 2013: 47).

Women find themselves limited by the templates of appropriate femininity available within Mexico's narco-economy. At the same time, many low-income women are rendered vulnerable by their husband's or son's work in narco-trafficking through their presence in the home. Muehlemann observes that,

> Because many women in rural Mexico work from home, they tend to be at greater risk of exposure. They are in the places where the police and military are most likely to search first. On the other hand, women's position in their homes also makes them vulnerable to cartel coercion. It is not uncommon in the rural north to intimidate people into allowing their homes to serve as 'stash houses' for drugs between deliveries or sales. In this case, someone knocks on the door and asks the woman at home to take care of something, a package, a vehicle, a box. She knows from their clothes and vehicles they are driving that it would be unwise to refuse. (Muehlmann, 2013: 41)

Thus, women are left with few options, since their implication in the narco-economy is hardly a choice aimed at profiting from the smuggling trade. Instead, it is a feature of the interpenetration of the home and the drug economy, effectively collapsing the distinction between domestic and public spheres (Comaroff, 1987; Helliwell, 2018).

Importantly, women are no less vulnerable when they seek legal and licit work outside of the home. Indeed, as Galemba argues, "The criminalization of contraband moralizes the limited options of the poor by blaming them for their own plight while allowing more powerful entities to claim and protect legitimate profits and determine who can sell and have access to goods" (Galemba, 2017: 20, 2012). This is powerfully illustrated by the role of *maquiladora* manufacturing in Mexican "special customs zones," which demand women's labour and explicitly are geared towards feminized workers who are stereotyped as having "nimble" hands and "docile" attitudes (Salzinger, 2004). Again, there is not a sharp divide between the legal domain of factory work and the illegal world of the drug trade. The North American Free Trade Agreement (NAFTA), which establishes the legal and economic basis for *maquila* manufacturing, is also implicated in the transnational financing flows whereby profits from the drug trade are absorbed by hedge funds in the United States: a process of "moving the money when the bank accounts get full" (Muehlmann, 2013: 134–151).

So why wouldn't women choose the licit option of working at the manufacturing plants rather than remaining at home, exposed to the vulnerabilities of the narco-economy? The short answer is that these are hardly safe themselves.

> The maquiladoras have been associated with another terrifying surge of violence that has specifically targeted women in the region. The femicide that since 2000 has claimed the lives of more than 3,800 women and girls particularly in and around Ciudad Juárez (with another 3,000 still reported missing. (Muehlmann, 2013: 49; Wright, 2001, 2011, 2013)

Tellingly, investigation of the murders – or making any effort at all, for that matter, to find the perpetrators and establish their motives – was never pursued by police. The governor went so far as to declare that the murdering and dumping of dozens of young women was "normal" for a rapidly expanding and impoverished border city such as Ciudad Juárez, and assured Mexican families that "there was nothing to fear as long as they knew where their female family members were" (Wright, 2011: 713). Thus, rather than policing their violent attackers, the authorities preferred to police women's behaviour, using patriarchal norms to suggest "private women safely at home had nothing to worry about" (ibid), and further insinuating that women and girls who had gone missing might have lived "double lives" a sex workers. The effort on the part of public officials to weaken public sympathy for victims led to a culture of impunity, such that victims were blamed for 'transgressing' norms of appropriate femininity. Despite growing activism from feminist organisations, femicide was rarely investigated. Thus, while women's vulnerability to the narco-economy came about indirectly because of their work within the home, women were specifically targeted with violence for working within outside of the home in the *maquila* factories. The targeting of factory workers challenges the moral distinction between legal and illegal, and upends pervasive assumptions about the relatively safety or danger of legal "free trade" versus illegal work in the narco-economy.

Conclusion

Studies thematizing gender in illicit economies and criminal networks have commented pointedly on the "paucity in literature [and] limited number of cases available" (Anderson, 2005: 92; see also Moore, 2007). This is due in part to challenges of taking quantitative approaches to studying smuggling, which provide only a very superficial view of secretive and clandestine practices. Stereotyped assumptions about masculinity, criminality, and violence

Gender and smuggling

further contribute to the limited field of research. Women's smuggling is doubly concealed, as it is invisible to our social science data and also relatively devalued compared to men's work.

A new research agenda focused on the "economy of gender" in smuggling has a number of advantages. Foremost is the empirical benefit of documenting a hitherto invisible and misunderstood area of social life and economic practice. The ethnographic studies surveyed here are beginning to open a window into the dynamics of illicit economies as they are experienced in the everyday. However, localizing analyses of smuggling and providing a detailed account of women's economic practices helps answer one set of problems while leaving another intact. That is, dominant theories of illicit economies as a transnational and macrosocial phenomenon still refer to unmarked categories to produce the guiding concepts and debates that drive scholarship on smuggling. As Carla Freeman warned us in her critique of globalization theory, this is a wider problem for feminist theories of capitalism: "the turn to gender on local terrain has inadvertently been the slippery slope on which the equation between local and feminine gets reinscribed" (Freeman, 2001: 1012). This equation has the consequence of eclipsing women/gender from macro-structural models of political economy. Not only does this limit our theory-building around smuggling, it has real effects on the professional advancement and scholarly accolades of researchers focused on economies of gender, as they find themselves shut out of making high-impact contributions to social theory (Driscoll and Schuster, 2018). Perversely, detailed and novel research on gender and smuggling can open significant new lines of research while also torpedoing a research career.

Alternative avenues are available. In this chapter I advocate for a feminist reconceptualization of smuggling that repositions gendered practices not merely as local or particular effects but also as a constitutive element in these economic systems. We can begin to see how this might take shape in feminist retheorisation of the household as a complex, multiscalar and thoroughly financialised cultural logic, rather than an innate or sub-social unit to which women are bound by their reproductive function (see e.g., MacCormack and Strathern, 1980). Feminist social science across a number of disciplines has a vital role to play by bringing together new theoretical approached to smuggling with granular empirical study of specific contraband economies.

Notes

1   The considerable literature on human trafficking and modern slavery paints a different picture, suggesting that in 30% of the countries that provided data to the United Nations global report on trafficking in persons, women make up the largest proportion of traffickers. The report adds that "in some parts of the world, women trafficking women is the norm" (United Nations Office on Drugs and Crimes (UNDOC), 2009). My review of smuggling focuses on the production and circulation of illicit commodities rather than enslavement. For a feminist approach to human trafficking, see (Ticktin, 2011; Tripp et al., 2013).
2   The term has a double meaning deriving from its military usage to denote a protective screen. See also Jusionyte's discussion of *convivencia* (co-existence and collaboration) as a local idiom on the Argentinean side of the border (Jusionyte, 2015b: 129).
3   In Barbados, this was highly feminized work, where women between the ages of 18–35 entered electronic data from airlines, insurance claims, legal briefs, and so on. Freeman suggests that informatics employers directly encourage the smuggling trips through a matrix of strict dress codes, free airline tickets as a reward for productivity, and women's own desire for fashions that support their self-image of professionalism (Freeman, 2001: 1023–1024).

Caroline E. Schuster

Bibliography

Adler F. (1975) *Sisters in Crime: The Rise of the New Female Criminal.* New York, NY: McGraw-Hill.

Anderson T. L. (2005) Dimensions of women's power in the illicit drug economy. *Theoretical Criminology* 9(4): 371–400.

Arsovska J. and Begum P. (2014) From West Africa to the Balkans: Exploring women's roles in transnational organized crime. *Trends in Organized Crime* 17(1–2): 89–109. https://doi.org/10.1007/s12117-013-9209-1.

Bourgois P. (1996) In search of masculinity: Violence, respect and sexuality among Puerto Rican crack dealers in East Harlem. *The British Journal of Criminology* 36(3): 412–427.

Chalfin B. (2008) Cars, the customs service, and sumptuary rule in neoliberal Ghana. *Comparative Studies in Society and History* 50(02): 424–453. https://doi.org/10.1017/S0010417508000194.

Comaroff J. L. (1987) Sui genderis: Feminism, Kinship Theory, and Structural 'Domains.' In: J. F. Collier and S. J. Yanagisako (eds) *Gender and Kinship: Essays toward a Unified Analysis.* Stanford: Stanford University Press, pp. 53–85.

Connell R. W. and Messerschmidt J. W. (2005) Hegemonic masculinity: Rethinking the concept. *Gender & Society* 19(6): 829–859.

Contreras R. (2009) "Damn, Yo—Who's that girl?" An ethnographic analysis of masculinity in drug robberies. *Journal of Contemporary Ethnography* 38(4). Sage Publications Sage CA: Los Angeles, CA: 465–492.

Dent A. S. (2017) Paraguayan horses: The entailments of internet policy and law in Brazil. *Current Anthropology* 58(S15): S113–S122. https://doi.org/10.1086/688953.

Driscoll J. and Schuster C. E. (2018) Spies like us. *Ethnography* 19(3): 411–430.

Ferradás C. A. (2013) The Nature of illegality under neoliberalism and post-neoliberalism. *PoLAR: Political and Legal Anthropology Review* 36(2): 266–273. https://doi.org/10.1111/plar.12026.

Fraser N. (2009) Feminism, capitalism and the cunning of history. *New Left Review* 56: 97–117.

Freeman C. (2001) Is local: Global as feminine: masculine? rethinking the gender of globalization. *Signs* 26(4): 1007–1037.

Galemba R. B. (2012) "Corn is food, not contraband": The right to "free trade" at the Mexico–Guatemala border. *American Ethnologist* 39(4): 716–734.

Galemba R. B. (2017) *Contraband Corridor: Making a Living at the Mexico–Guatemala Border.* Stanford, CA: Stanford University Press.

Han C. (2011) Symptoms of another life: Time, possibility, and domestic relations in Chile's credit economy. *Cultural Anthropology* 26(1): 7–32.

Han C. (2012) *Life in Debt: Times of Care and Violence in Neoliberal Chile.* Berkeley, CA: University of California Press.

Hautzinger S. J. (2007) *Violence in the City of Women: Police and Batterers in Bahia, Brazil.* Berkeley, CA: University of California Press.

Helliwell C. (2018) Domestic/public distinction. *The International Encyclopedia of Anthropology*: 1–6. https://doi.org/10.1002/9781118924396.wbiea2296.

Hübschle A. (2014) Of bogus hunters, queenpins and mules: The varied roles of women in transnational organized crime in Southern Africa. *Trends in Organized Crime* 17(1–2): 31–51. https://doi.org/10.1007/s12117-013-9202-8.

Jusionyte I. (2013) On and off the record: The production of legitimacy in an Argentine Border Town. *PoLAR: Political and Legal Anthropology Review* 36(2): 231–248. https://doi.org/10.1111/plar.12024.

Jusionyte I. (2015a) *Savage Frontier: Making News and Security on the Argentine Border.* Berkeley, CA: University of California Press.

Jusionyte I. (2015b) States of camouflage. *Cultural Anthropology* 30(1): 113–138.

Kar S. and Schuster C. (2016) Comparative projects and the limits of choice: ethnography and microfinance in India and Paraguay. *Journal of Cultural Economy* 9(4): 347–363. DOI: 10.1080/17530350.2016.1180632.

Kleemans E. R., Kruisbergen E. W. and Kouwenberg R. F. (2014) Women, brokerage and transnational organized crime: Empirical results from the Dutch Organized Crime Monitor. *Trends in Organized Crime* 17(1–2): 16–30. https://doi.org/10.1007/s12117-013-9203-7.

Leacock E. (1979) Class, Commodity, and Status of Women. In: Diamond S. (ed.) *Toward a Marxist Anthropology: Problems and Perspectives.* The Hague: Mouton Publishers, pp. 185–199.

MacCormack C. and Strathern M. (1980) *Nature, Culture and Gender.* Cambridge, UK: Cambridge University Press.

Moore J. W. (2007) Female Gangs: Gender and Globalization. In: Hagedorn J. (ed.) *Gangs in the Global City: Alternatives to Traditional Criminology.* Champaign, IL: University of Illinois Press, pp. 187–203.

Gender and smuggling

Muehlmann S. (2013) *When I Wear My Alligator Boots: Narco-Trafficking in the US–Mexico Borderlands.* Berkeley, CA: University of California Press.

Rabossi F. (2012) Ciudad del Este and Brazilian circuits of commercial distribution. In: G. Mathews, G. L. Ribeiro and C. Alba Vega (eds) *Globalization from Below: The World's Other Economy.* London: Routledge, pp. 54–68.

Roitman J. L. (2005) *Fiscal Disobedience: An Anthropology of Economic Regulation in Central Africa.* Princeton, NJ: Princeton University Press.

Salzinger L. (2004) From gender as object to gender as verb: Rethinking how global restructuring happens. *Critical Sociology* 30(1): 43–62.

Sassen S. (2007) The Global City: One Setting for New Types of Gang Work and Political Culture. In: Hagedorn J. (ed.) *Gangs in the Global City: Alternatives to Traditional Criminology.* Champaign, IL: University of Illinois Press, pp. 97–119.

Schuster C. E. (2014) The social unit of debt: Gender and creditworthiness in Paraguayan microfinance. *American Ethnologist* 41(3): 563–578.

Schuster C. E. (2015) *Social Collateral: Women and Microfinance in Paraguay's Smuggling Economy.* Berkeley, CA: University of California Press.

Schuster C. E. (2019a) The bottlenecks of free trade: Paraguay's Mau cars and contraband markets in the Triple Frontier. *The Journal of Latin American and Caribbean Anthropology* 24(2): 498–517.

Schuster C. E. (2019b) The indebted wage: Putting financial products to work in Paraguay's Tri-Border Area. *Anthropological Quarterly* 92(3): 729–756.

Selmini R. (2020) Women in Organized Crime. *Crime and Justice* 49. Organizing Crime: Mafia, Markets, and Networks: 339–383. https://doi.org/10.1086/708622.

Siegel D. (2014) Women in transnational organized crime. *Trends in Organized Crime* 17(1–2): 52–65. https://doi.org/10.1007/s12117-013-9206-4.

Simon R. J. (1975) *Women and Crime.* Lanham, MD: Lexington Books.

Thomas K. and Galemba R. B. (2013) Illegal anthropology: An introduction. *Political and Legal Anthropology Review* 36(2): 211–214.

Ticktin M. (2011) The gendered human of humanitarianism: Medicalising and politicising sexual violence. *Gender & History* 23(2): 250–265.

Tripp A. M., Ferree M. M. and Ewig C. (2013) *Gender, Violence, and Human Security: Critical Feminist Perspectives.* New York, NY: NYU Press.

Tucker J. (2020) Outlaw capital: Accumulation by transgression on the Paraguay–Brazil Border. *Antipode* 52(5): 1455–1474. https://doi.org/10.1111/anti.12656.

Tucker J. L. (2017) City-stories: Narrative as diagnostic and strategic resource in Ciudad del Este, Paraguay. *Planning Theory* 16(1): 74–98. https://doi.org/10.1177/1473095215598176.

Ulysse G. (2007) *Downtown Ladies: Informal Commercial Importers, a Haitian Anthropologist, and Self-Making in Jamaica.* Chicago, IL: University Of Chicago Press.

United Nations Office on Drugs and Crimes (UNDOC) (2009) *Global Report on Trafficking in Persons.* UN.GIFT Global Initiative to Fight Human Trafficking, February. Available at: //www.unodc.org/unodc/en/human-trafficking/global-report-on-trafficking-in-persons.html (accessed 14 September 2020).

Venkatesh S. A. (1998) Gender and outlaw capitalism: A historical account of the Black Sisters United 'Girl Gang.' *Signs* 23(3). University of Chicago Press: 683–709.

Wright M. W. (2001) Feminine villains, masculine heroes, and the reproduction of Ciudad Juárez. *Social Text* 19(4): 93–113.

Wright M. W. (2011) Necropolitics, narcopolitics, and femicide: Gendered violence on the Mexico-US border. *Signs: Journal of Women in Culture and Society* 36(3): 707–731.

Wright M. W. (2013) Feminicidio, narcoviolence, and gentrification in Ciudad Juárez: The feminist fight. *Environment and Planning D: Society and Space* 31(5): 830–845.

Yanagisako S. J. (2015) Households in Anthropology. In: *International Encyclopedia of the Social & Behavioral Sciences.* Elsevier, pp. 228–232. https://doi.org/10.1016/B978-0-08-097086-8.12088-4.

Young J. (2007) Globalization and social exclusion: The sociology of vindictiveness and the criminology of transgression. In: Hagedorn J. (ed.) *Gangs in the global city: Alternatives to traditional criminology.* Urbana/Chicago, IL: University of Illinois Press: 54–93.

Zhang S. X., Chin K.-L. and Miller J. (2007) Women's participation in Chinese transnational human smuggling: A gendered market perspective. *Criminology* 45(3): 699–733.

PART III

Smuggling goods

14

COCAINE SMUGGLING

Between geopolitics and domestic power struggles

Angélica Durán-Martínez

In 2016 the Government of Colombia signed a peace agreement that ended its 60-year confrontation with the Revolutionary Armed Forces of Colombia (FARC), one of the world's oldest insurgencies. The lengthy agreement, one of the most detailed peace agreements ever signed, included a chapter on the "Solution to the Problem of Illicit Drugs" detailing a plan to eliminate coca crops through an alternative development and crop substitution program, and the depenalization of the lowest level of the cocaine supply chain (coca cultivators). This proposal, though caught in contradictions driven by the idea that coca crops could be completely eliminated, provided a comprehensive plan to address the economic marginalization that underlies the coca economy in Colombia. Yet, four years after signing the agreement the implementation got stalled, constrained by domestic and international challenges. Domestically, budget limitations, lack of political support, the inability to address socio-economic challenges, and the persistence of armed actors undermined the plan's implementation. Internationally, steady cocaine demand, pressures from the United States to fumigate coca crops, and pressures from criminal organizations to maintain cocaine flows, undermined the potential for weakening the illicit cocaine trade while providing sustainable incentives for coca farmers to move into other licit, but less profitable economies. These difficulties in implementing the coca crop substitution programs in Colombia highlight the interplay between local and domestic factors that characterizes cocaine smuggling, and that this chapter will analyze.

The chapter first revisits the most notable power imbalance in the cocaine trade, the geopolitical one, determined by the power disparity between producers and consumers of cocaine, which has been well recognized in the literature. Then the chapter addresses other dimensions of power imbalance that have started to be more recognized recently, and that still lag behind in informing public policy. Lastly, the chapter explores transformations in cocaine supply chains in the twenty-first century and discusses how they have affected cocaine smuggling and the policies aimed to control it.

From coca to cocaine: the geopolitics of cocaine smuggling

The history of cocaine is a just over a century old, yet the history of coca, the plant from which cocaine is extracted, dates back more than 4,000 years. The coca plant has ancestral ceremonial, ritual, and secular uses for indigenous tribes in the Andean region of Latin America, and its uses

DOI: 10.4324/9781003043645-14

and psychoactive potential are very different from cocaine, yet the modern regime of drug control created throughout the twentieth century has treated these substances as roughly the same. Important scholarship on the cocaine trade emerged in the 1980s, highlighting how foreign power imbalances and the US–Latin America relationship during and after the Cold War shaped cocaine trade and policies (Bagley 1988, Lee 1991), but this scholarship tended to be policy oriented and focused on material power considerations. Over the 2010s, the scholarship has expanded theoretically and connected a focus on material power with the analysis of discourses and ideas, exploring intricate power relationships back to colonial times when coca use first became known to the world, passing through the discovery of cocaine and the first efforts to regulate or diminish its use, to the more complicated politics emerging after the entire cocaine commodity chain became globally prohibited in 1961 (Durán-Martínez 2018, Gootenberg 2008).

From colonial regulation of coca to restrictions on cocaine legal trade

The power imbalances associated with coca leaf during colonial times mimic in some ways the disparities that characterize cocaine smuggling since the second half of the twentieth century. The Spanish empire used the stimulating effects of coca leaves to increase productivity in mineral exploitation, but relegated traditional forms of coca chewing and exchange, which were deemed immoral by the Catholic church. When cocaine was first synthesized in 1860, and a legal economy emerged, coca cultivation was concentrated in Peru, which developed a solid legal industry (Gootenberg 2008). Through the late 1800s and early 1900s regulations over the legal commerce tightened progressively, creating the initial opportunities for illicit markets to emerge. Before the legal cocaine trade was outlawed globally in 1961, power imbalances that demonized traditional indigenous practices had already motivated campaigns to eradicate coca crops, blurring the distinction between the plant and the synthetized drug. Such campaigns were promoted both by international crusaders and an array of domestic actors including doctors and lawyers who, without solid scientific evidence, blamed coca chewing for the illnesses and difficulties faced by indigenous communities (Davis 2020).

Cocaine smuggling networks appeared in the early twentieth century in the cracks of the initial quotas on legal commerce but were not as sharply characterized by geopolitical power imbalances, and emerged in response to a combination of temperance campaigns in the United States, and a growing, though still small, market for illegal recreational cocaine use. The appearance of evidence of addiction, and growing cocaine use in the underworld of the United States and some European nations, set the stage for attempts to limit the legal industry. This is turn generated opportunities of diversion from the legal market involving countries where pharmaceutical companies synthetized cocaine, such as Germany or the Netherlands, less known players such as Japan, which maintained coca plantations in Taiwan, and other countries which rivaled Andean coca production at the time, such as Java (Courtwright 2001, Farber 2019, 15–30). World War II disrupted these networks, but then in the 1960s cocaine use started to grow again in the US, setting the stage for a new wave of smuggling.

Historian Paul Gootenberg (2008) documents how as restrictions on the legal cocaine industry grew, the illegal market expanded responding to growing demand. By the 1950s, the oldest legal cocaine industry, Peru's, had decreased in size first because there was competition from other producers in the world (such as Dutch Java) but then because restrictions on non-medical use, and then on medical use, grew, particularly in the United States. After World War II, cocaine use expanded and more sophisticated transnational smuggling networks emerged. These networks, involving mostly traffickers of Cuban and Chilean origin, were relocated to other parts of South America and the United States after the 1959 Cuban Revolution and Augusto Pinochet's 1973 military coup in Chile[1] put pressure on dismantling these networks. The market was mostly seized in the 1970s by emerging Colombian drug trafficking organizations, which became nodes of cocaine smuggling networks and of the war against them. These events shaped a geography of cocaine production that has persisted for decades, with Bolivia, Colombia, and Peru constituting the world's major coca and cocaine producers, and North America, particularly the United States, remaining the largest cocaine consumer in the world. Compared to other illicit drugs (opioids, opiates and, cannabis), as of 2018, cocaine had the lowest reported prevalence rate for the world as a whole (0.38% of the population compared to 3.86 for cannabis or 0.61 for opiates) (UNODC 2020) and consumption was concentrated in the Americas and Oceania, followed by Europe. While power asymmetries characterize all forms of smuggling, it is thus feasible to argue that the influence of the United States in cocaine policy and in its smuggling dynamics is stronger than for other drugs because it is tightly connected to the geopolitical power dynamic between Latin America and the United States.

The US and the war against cocaine

Some historians suggest that the analytical emphasis on the US War on Drugs sometimes overlooks how other superpowers contributed to shaping the international drug control system (Collins 2018). It is undeniable, however, that the United States' influence made cocaine the subject of one of the most militarized antidrug campaigns in history (Andreas 2019). Unlike opioids, for example, legal cocaine trade is marginal and confined to small markets regulated domestically. As Bewley-Taylor (2016) argues, when the first international legal instruments of drug control emerged, the concern with regulating coca and cocaine was weaker compared to concern over opium. The 1912 Hague International Opium Convention, the first multilateral legal instrument for drug control, for example, only contains a minor mention of cocaine, and up to the late 1940s, neither Bolivia or Peru (the main producers of coca leaf at the time) nor countries with pharmaceutical interests in legal cocaine like Germany, supported an international crusade against coca or cocaine. This changed after World War II, when the United States' growing concern with cocaine use aligned more closely with government interests in Bolivia and Peru to eliminate "backward Indian behavior" materialized in coca chewing.

Since mid-twentieth century, US interests have prevailed in coca and cocaine regulation, as reflected in the framing and enforcement of the three major international treaties that make up modern international drug control: the 1961 Single Convention on Narcotic Drugs; the 1971 Convention on Psychotropic Substances; and the 1988 Convention Against Illicit Traffic in Narcotic Drugs. In 1948, the Commission of Narcotic Drugs (CND), dominated by the United States during the early post-war years (Bewley-Taylor 2016), launched the Commission of Enquiry into the Coca Leaf, which with feeble scientific evidence declared that coca leaf was deleterious for health and equated it with cocaine. The US lobby was crucial for the framing of the 1961 Single Convention on Narcotic Drugs, which equated coca and cocaine, did not recognize traditional, legal, and medical uses of coca leaves, and only included an exception that allowed Coca-Cola to procure raw materials for its popular drink. In the 1980s Peruvian and Bolivian delegations at the United Nations, motivated by changing domestic coalitions which now included indigenous groups, lobbied to include language recognizing traditional uses of coca in the 1988 Convention which complemented the 1961 treaty by expanding the policing and sanctions of illicit drug trade. The lobbying was partially successful, but did not change the spirit of the Convention, creating a gray area in the legal status of coca chewing and cultivation for licit purposes. In 1995, US delegates prevented the publication of a study by the United Nations Interregional Crime and Justice Research Institute (UNICRI) which concluded that most coca leaf use had no negative health effects. In 2008 the United States delegation opposed a proposal by Bolivia to reform an article of the 1961 Convention that prohibited and aimed to abolish coca leaf chewing, on the grounds that coca leave production increased cocaine production potential (Bewley-Taylor 2016).

US influence in policing the international cocaine trade has also been manifested in the funding of, and pressure for, militarized campaigns against cocaine trafficking that have led to human rights violations and disproportional policing (Youngers and Rosin 2005). During the Cold War, such campaigns merged with, and reinforced anti-communist efforts, though in many cases the latter took precedence, as became evident in the infamous Iran-Contra scandal (Dale and Marshal 1991). After the end of the Cold War, the emphasis on militarized drug control expanded, with notable campaigns such as Plan Colombia, a controversial antinarcotics plan that since 2000 deployed US$10 billion in US assistance to combat cocaine production and reestablish security in Colombia. Plan Colombia is officially touted as a success story given an initial reduction of coca crops and an improvement in some security indicators, but it also caused human rights violations, extreme militarization, and ignored the expansion of paramilitary groups (Tate 2015). Besides its cost in human lives, militarized campaigns have also been jeopardized when US domestic allies, often touted as drug control champions, engage in drug trafficking themselves, as occurred with the Chief of Intelligence in Peru in the 1990s, Vladimiro Montesinos (Rojas 2005).

The focus of US-influenced policies has been the reduction of supply, rather than demand, which in turn, has put the burden of militarized drug control on drug-producing rather than drug-consuming countries. Yet within the US, cocaine policies have deeply impacted marginalized sectors of the US population, particularly African Americans. As Michelle Alexander argues, in the 1980s as crack use increased, the policies aimed to control it repressed and marginalized black populations, in what she terms The New Jim Crow, a form of maintaining racial segregation through mass incarceration (Alexander 2010). Both the trafficking and use of crack cocaine were concentrated among black populations, because crack provided an escape valve to lives of hardship, and the involvement in trafficking represented an avenue for economic and cultural integration (Farber 2019, Reinarman and Levine 1997). Racialized patterns of use and trafficking fed exaggerated depictions of crack's effects and its "contagious" potential, which were used to legitimize disproportional laws. In 1986, at the peak of the anti-crack euphoria the Reagan Administration introduced mandatory minimum sentences posing radically different penalties for cocaine and crack: a five-year minimum sentence was associated with possession of five grams of crack as opposed to 500 grams in the case of cocaine. The Anti-Drug laws of 1988 deepened this disproportionality by imposing high level trafficking sentences to any member of a drug trafficking conspiracy, regardless of the level of responsibility. Consequently, many low-level dealers lacking resources for private defense lawyers who can negotiate sentences, heavy users, and innocent people lacking legal protection, ended up with long sentences, feeding the mass incarceration problem of the United States. Zero-tolerance policies and sentencing procedures deepened racial biases and systemic inequalities, and hyper-policing also made the trafficking disputes more violent, constituting one factor behind the so-called crime epidemic in the United States between the 1970s and 1980s (Blumstein, Wallman and Farrington 2006, Goldstein et al. 1989).

In sum, the influence of the United States in cocaine control efforts is evident. A focus on the geopolitics of cocaine, however, may have minimized the importance of domestic processes, and other forms of power imbalance, which are explored next.

Domestic processes: state power, development, and violence

Recent literature has recognized how complex domestic power dynamics shape cocaine smuggling as much as international forces (Durán-Martínez 2018, Gootenberg and Dávalos 2018), though debates persist on whether domestic or international forces are more important. Methodological, theoretical, and empirical innovations emphasizing the importance of disentangling micro-processes and the lived experience of all actors involved in smuggling and its policing in specific geographical spaces, have complemented and expanded an earlier focus of the literature on broad descriptions and archival analysis, partially rooted in the idea that qualitative studies of the illicit were impossible. I focus on three issues examined in recent literature illustrating crucial connections between domestic politics and cocaine markets. First, the variation in power and profits along the cocaine supply chain creates inequalities which are either downplayed or reinforced by drug policies. Second, differences in the organization of state power and in the business organization of cocaine trafficking, shape variations in violence associated with the cocaine trade. Lastly, complex relationships with developmental projects make cocaine smuggling both a result of state power, and a reflection of cracks within it, rather than just a simple result of state weakness.

Supply chain divergence

Iconic characters like Pablo Escobar, the infamous leader of the so-called Medellín cartel in Colombia, who has inspired numerous movies and TV shows, have dominated popular images of the cocaine trade. These images emphasize large profits and powerful organizations, but often ignore complicated realities and power imbalances between the lowest levels in the supply chain and powerful criminal leaders.

Cocaine, like heroin, has a long supply chain, from production to distribution, and is characterized by disproportional profits among its stages, reflecting characteristics of the drug (the psychoactive potential of cocaine emerges through a complicated process that adds many chemicals to the coca leaf), the geography of the markets, and the policing of the illegal trade. All of which add large profits to the final product, and most importantly create incentives for criminal organizations to emerge to manage the international trade. For example, the farm gate value of the coca leaves required to produce a kilogram of cocaine in Colombia is less than US$1,000, but the typical retail price of one kilogram in the United States is about US$78,000 (Reuter 2014). More importantly, the connections among individuals involved in the production of raw material (coca growing), and those in the distribution level are tenuous. In Colombia for example, by 2017 the United Nations Office of Drugs and Crime estimated that 44% of coca growers transformed coca leaves into cocaine base, and then sold it to the organizations controlling exports and wholesale. The remaining farmers sell untransformed leaves, but even those selling cocaine base receive a relatively small profit (SIMCI-UNODC Sistema Integrado de Monitoreo de Cultivos Ilícitos – Oficina de Naciones Unidas contra las Drogas y el Crimen 2018, 17).

Recent scholarship based on careful case studies shows how the operation of smuggling networks varies across and within countries (Kenney 2007). For instance, in Peru, drug trafficking organizations are often decentralized and limited to intermediation in the distribution for export (Van Dun 2014). In Colombia, by contrast, various armed groups engage in different aspects of drug trafficking as discussed by Idler in this volume, and consequently, exert more control over lower production levels, although coca growers and distributors remain independent and rarely belong to a trafficking organization. Across the transit regions of the

Caribbean and Central America, many organizations participate in the cocaine trade. While Central American street gangs are increasingly seen as central actors in drug trafficking, and their involvement in the cocaine trade has increased over the years, it is not always direct or predominant, and varies across countries (Dudley 2010). In El Salvador, gangs profit more from extortion than from the drug trade, and remain independent from drug traffickers, whereas in Honduras drug trafficking organizations, colluded with elite politicians, are more powerful and capable of controlling gangs and engaging them in trafficking. In Guatemala, traditional drug trafficking families and organized crime networks engage more prominently in drug trafficking than gangs (Cruz et al. 2012).

Drug policies often fail to recognize such diverse incentives, connections, organizations and profits along cocaine supply chains. For example, in Colombia and Peru in the 1980s and 1990s, the communist guerrillas FARC (Revolutionary Armed Forces of Colombia) and Sendero Luminoso (Shining Path) taxed coca growing and acted as intermediaries of coca growers. Both national and US authorities interpreted this engagement as an attempt to control and profit from the international drug trade, ignoring that cocaine trade was a source of profits but also a strategy to create social support bases among coca farmers (Felbab-Brown 2009). As a result, policies that attacked crops to weaken insurgencies (such as forced eradication) backfired. In Peru, in the 1990s the government mounted a more effective campaign against the Shining Path precisely when it stopped focusing on coca eradication.

Violence

Cocaine markets are often depicted as extremely violent, minimizing the variation that exists within the cocaine trade (Angrist and Kugler 2008, Naim 2006). To be clear, violence is prominent, and a cursory comparison shows higher homicide rates across countries along the cocaine trafficking routes than in those along opiate trafficking routes (UNODC [United Nations Office on Drugs and Crime] 2016). Violence is also evident in prominent examples: the war that Pablo Escobar declared against the government to stop the extradition of Colombian nationals to the United States in the late 1980s; the extreme violence that between 2007 and 2020 has caused more than 300,000 deaths in Mexico; or the role of cocaine trafficking in funding non-state armed actors (paramilitaries and guerrillas) in the Colombian civil war. However, within and across cocaine producing and transit countries violence varies due to factors that the scholarship is only starting to explore, such as the nature of the organizations involved and the level of competition among them, the relations among state power, electoral competition, and criminal groups (Durán-Martínez 2018a, Trejo and Ley 2020) the design of enforcement policies (Lessing 2017), and the less explored civilian interactions with traffickers (Blume 2021).

The violent consequences of transnational illicit markets like cocaine are thus mediated by local power dynamics. Violence tends to increase where competition among criminal groups is higher and declines whenever a group controls the market. The scale of the violence, however, also depends on the nature of the actors involved. Colombia experiences higher violence because more sophisticated trafficking groups participate in all the aspects of the supply chain and connect in intricate ways to a long-standing civil war. In Bolivia by contrast, most actors work in the initial links of the supply chain (cultivation and harvesting of coca leaves, and production of coca paste), thus reducing the economic stakes when market conflicts do emerge (Grisaffi 2019). Additionally, Bolivian cocaleros (coca cultivators) have mobilized through unions and indigenous communities to protect and advocate for legal and traditional uses of coca. As a result, violence in Bolivia is low, though, notably, cocaine fueled elite violence and authoritarian rule in the 1950s and 1980s. In Peru, indigenous movements also exist but they are weaker and were delegitimized due to the connection between coca cultivation and the Shining Path guerrilla group in the 1980s. As a result, weaker grass roots mobilization may have made trafficking networks more prominent and organized than in Bolivia, but more fragmented and decentralized than in Colombia. In Colombia, indigenous traditions related to coca, and indigenous mobilization, are more limited than in Bolivia or Peru. In the 1990s, coca-growing peasants (campesinos cocaleros) mobilized in opposition to the government's forced eradication and militarization policies (Ramírez 2011). The stigmatization and victimization derived from the engagement of armed groups and cocaine trafficking organizations made it difficult for these social movements to advocate for legal coca production. For example, in 1999 indigenous communities founded a company producing coca-derived products, but the institution regulating agricultural and food production prohibited commercialization outside of indigenous communities (Ramírez 2020).

Scholarship on violence also highlights the significance of unpacking state power and its influence on the cocaine trade. States combat crime, but they can also protect and benefit from illicit trades, and changes in state power and in electoral dynamics have contributed to changing violence in cocaine markets. The history of Mexico since the mid-2000s illustrates this dynamic, as the breakdown of the hierarchical political structure created around the decades-old semi-authoritarian rule of the PRI (Revolutionary Institutional Party) was crucial for the spiraling violence the country has experienced since 2007 (Durán-Martínez 2018a, Trejo and Ley 2020). As other contributions in this volume highlight, the relation between state power and smuggling is multifaceted, sometimes highlighting state absence and weakness and others making evident its power and centrality. Thus, rather than assuming unidirectional interactions between states and cocaine markets, the scholarship has advanced in uncovering how forms of organizing state power, and state policies, shape smuggling dynamics. This is also evident in recent studies of the relationship between cocaine smuggling and development (Gootenberg and Dávalos 2018).

Coca, cocaine, and development

The earnings of coca growers and low-level workers are often essential for survival in coca-growing communities and in marginalized distribution hubs with high poverty and limited infrastructure (Grisaffi and Ledebur 2016). The fact that most coca-producing regions are located in poor areas reflects how state weakness, and sometimes absence, are key drivers of illegal economies. Studying the cocaine trade only through the lens of state weakness, however, obscures how state power shapes and even strengthens it, or how cocaine has created alternate paths to accessing state power and economic circuits.

For example, state developmental projects have shaped the geography of cocaine. Gootenberg and Dávalos (2018) document how centers of coca production for the cocaine trade in the 1980s, in the Amazonian frontiers of Bolivia (the Chapare region), Colombia (the Putumayo region), and Peru (the Huallaga Valley), were the subject of state-promoted colonization and agricultural expansion projects in the 1960s. These projects, aimed at expanding agricultural frontiers, attracted migrants with promises of land and employment, but when projects failed or were abandoned, an idle and impoverished work force found an alternative in the illicit cocaine trade (Paredes and Manrique 2021). The cocaine trade then became the main connection of these areas to capitalism; for example, according to UNODC, in 2017 the value of cocaine production in ten municipalities concentrating 44% of total coca crops in Colombia represented almost double the amount of the municipal budget (SIMCI-UNODC Sistema

Integrado de Monitoreo de Cultivos Ilícitos – Oficina de Naciones Unidas contra las Drogas y el Crimen 2018). In some regions, coca leaf trade provides the cash flow that drives local economies, creating complicated relationships between licit and illicit activities (Ramírez 2014). For coca cultivators, the differential profits between coca and other licit crops are not as high as sometimes assumed but are appealing because they are reliable even in difficult-to-access areas (Zevallos 2017).

Understanding that illicit cocaine's history can be traced to failed developmentalist projects adds complexity to the scholarly view of cocaine trade as resulting from state weakness and absence (Bunck and Fowler 2012, Thoumi 1992). Through its drug policies, failed developmentalist projects, and collusion with organized crime, state presence shapes the history of cocaine smuggling. This nuanced understanding of the relation among state, development, and the cocaine trade also provides crucial policy lessons.

For decades, international organizations and governments have implemented alternative development projects aimed at providing sustainable livelihoods that can replace coca cultivation. These projects have more effectively reduced coca crops than other repression and forced eradication models, but they still show mixed results, among other things, because they fail to recognize how coca production and the cocaine trade transform communities, or how crop replacement needs to occur in tandem with the creation of reliable markets for alternative products. More importantly, alternative development often clashes with parallel repressive policies that make state presence ambivalent, while combining strong militarized operations with extremely weak social service provision and legitimacy. To come full circle, these local efforts are complicated by persistent transnational demand for cocaine, which given its illegality, is more profitable than other markets. These tensions are evident in the evolution of attempts to innovate cocaine-related policies, discussed below, which have partly derived from changing supply chains and geopolitical dynamics.

Changing supply chains and geopolitics

The literature on cocaine smuggling has recognized well how the power imbalances discussed so far, and the policies implemented to eliminate cocaine flows and routes, have shaped, rather than eliminated, cocaine flows (Clawson and Lee 1996, Eddy, Sabogal and Walden 1988, Zepeda and Rosen 2014). In the best cases, successful anti-narcotics operations have dispersed smuggling routes to many more locations across the Americas and Africa, and in the worst cases, they have increased levels of violence, as has occurred in Mexico since the government started a militarized campaign to dismantle drug trafficking organizations in 2006. Scholarly debates remain, however, and further research is still necessary to determine the extent to which new policies can emerge and reduce cocaine smuggling, or at least its most destabilizing consequences. This section briefly discusses the connection between anti-narcotic policies and smuggling dynamics, and how, paradoxically, geographic changes partially brought up by anti-narcotic policies have created space for new policies. It also shows how the transformative potential of new policies is hindered by complex economic and social realities and the illegality of the trade.

The distribution of coca and cocaine production among the three Andean countries has varied over time, partially in response to enforcement actions. In the early 1990s, offensives against coca cultivation in Peru and Bolivia prompted crop surges in Colombia. According to the United Nations Office on Drugs and Crime (UNODC 2010, 2014), in 1990, Bolivia and Peru concentrated 87% of the cocaine production potential worldwide; by 2000, Colombia concentrated 79%. This pattern was again reversed between 2000 and 2012, when the coca-cultivated area decreased by 52% in Colombia while it increased by 37% in Peru.[2] After 2014, cultivation increased rapidly in Colombia, reaching a historic high in 2017. In Peru and Bolivia, cultivation declined partially as a result of new policies to control coca cultivation, though both countries also experienced increases in 2016 and 2017, driven by multiple factors including an upward demand trend in the U.S, and a decline in gold prices, as illegal gold mining is an alternative economy to coca, especially in Colombia and Peru.

Enforcement operations and changing market dynamics contributed to multiply cocaine transit points in the 2010s. While in the 1970s and 1980s, most cocaine transited into the United States via maritime routes in the Caribbean, in the new millennium smuggling routes included several inland points in Central America and Mexico, and complicated paths through West Africa into Europe. Countries in the Southern Cone of the Americas became more important, although still minor, transit points for trafficking routes bound for Europe; Venezuela and Brazil became transit points for cocaine routes through South and West Africa. Cocaine processing laboratories, and facilities for processing intermediate and low-quality forms of cocaine base aimed for intraregional markets, have appeared in new countries including Argentina, Chile, Ecuador, and Venezuela (UNODC 2020). The geography of cocaine flows in the 2010s was thus more diverse than in prior decades.

Diversified cocaine supply chains are also linked to new consumption markets. By the late 2010s, the cocaine market in Brazil became the world's second largest, representing 18% of the global market in terms of users, mainly supplied by Bolivia. In the 2010s, local drug use became more widespread and noticeable to governments and citizens across the Americas, though it was not entirely new and often reflected prior inattention to complex long-term consumption trends. In 2015, UNODC estimated an annual cocaine prevalence rate of 0.8% for South America, higher than the 0.7 reported in 2004–2005, but lower than the 1.3% reported in 2013 (UNODC [United Nations Office on Drugs and Crime] 2016). Although increasing rates of cocaine use in countries that are traditionally seen as producing and transit countries have to be analyzed with caution – in no small part because of difficulties in finding reliable data – they indicate that supply chains have dispersed due to the effects of enforcement over cocaine transit routes and production nodes, and a growing cocaine use outside of the United States and Western Europe. The expansion of illicit activity portfolios by criminal groups, though not entirely new, also drives the diversification of cocaine supply chains, as some protagonists of the cocaine trade increasingly engage in other illicit markets, as occurs in Colombia, Mexico, and Venezuela.

It seems appropriate to ask whether these changes can transform the geopolitical imbalance that has characterized policy making regarding cocaine control. This is a question that deserves to be more systematically researched, but an initial look suggests that the effect is mixed. On one hand, in the early 2010s, producing countries' efforts to challenge the militarized war on cocaine, though not welcomed, were not completely boycotted by the United States, perhaps reflecting the political preferences of the Obama administration, and the policy priority given to the opioid epidemic, as cocaine use stabilized and became less of a concern for domestic security in the United States. On the other hand, the United States remains the world's largest cocaine market, and the policy focus on cocaine supply reduction increased again as some statistics indicated growing cocaine use after 2014,[3] and Donald Trump's government reinforced more repressive drug control policies. Beyond the US, cocaine's transnational markets and the difficulty of forging a consensus to reform international conventions, complicate the implementation of alternative supply control policies, as evident in Bolivia and Colombia.

This chapter highlighted that cocaine smuggling has been characterized by a power imbalance between producers and consumers, which has translated into policy making, but at the same time, policy making is still mediated locally. In Bolivia, for example the United States sponsored highly militarized drug operations such as the Triennial Plan, Operation Blast Furnace (1986), and Plan Dignidad (1997),[4] and influenced the drafting of its main drug law – Law 1008 of 1988 (Grisaffi 2019). Some coca cultivation for legal purposes, however, has been allowed, and Presidents like Jaime Paz Zamora or Gonzalo Sanchez de Lozada, who were aligned with US interests, compensated growers for eradication or slowed down eradication campaigns. When Evo Morales, a former leader of the cocalero movement critical of the United States, was elected President in 2006, in a context of growing debate around drug policy and changing supply chains, Bolivia left the international drug conventions re-joining with an exception that excluded coca leaf chewing from the list of controlled substances. Morales also implemented a policy expanding the legal coca production limit set in 1988 from 12,000 to 20,000 hectares, and authorizing legal cultivation in the Chapare, a region traditionally excluded from legal production quotas. To prevent diversion for illegal markets, the government set a cultivation limit of 1,600 square meters per family. The most interesting aspect of the policy, and the main reason for its success in controlling coca crops was that monitoring and implementation were responsibilities of grassroot organizations (Grisaffi 2019).

Morales' policies successfully reduced the hectares of coca cultivated[5] and were dubbed by some analysts as the world's first supply-side harm reduction approach (Farthing and Kohl 2010). As Grisaffi (2019) has documented, success has been caught in contradictions that derive from the persistence and profitability of the international cocaine trade. Morales navigated conflicting demands among his supporters' expectations that he could eliminate restrictions on coca cultivation, and international commitments to deter illegal cocaine. While Bolivia has a successful legal market, the illegal market still sustains the livelihoods of many campesinos who also despise the international restrictions imposed on a market where the demand is generated outside of their country.

Similar contradictions have limited Colombia's efforts to eliminate aerial fumigations of coca crops with toxic chemicals like glyphosate. Colombia has faithfully followed US-driven cocaine control policies, and is the only coca producing country that has allowed glyphosate use, fumigating over 1,800,000 hectares of coca between 1995 and 2015. Fumigations were suspended in 2015, in the midst of the peace negotiations with the FARC, and because of then President Juan Manuel Santos' vocal support for drug policy reform. In 2008, the election of a new President who did not support the reforms proposed in the peace agreement, such as the crop substitution program, alongside increasing cocaine demand in the United States, and a spike in coca cultivation, led the Colombian and United States governments to demand the reactivation of aerial fumigation, using simplistic arguments that connected the growth in crops to the suspension of fumigation, and the growth in demand, to the growth in supply (Durán-Martínez 2018a). While fumigations have not been re-initiated at the time of writing this chapter due to restrictions imposed by the Colombian Constitutional court, the crop substitution and voluntary eradication programs have been undermined, reflecting both the persisting pressure coming from the United States, and the complex internal and external factors that make illicit cocaine smuggling a resilient market.

Conclusion

Cocaine smuggling has been shaped by sharp geopolitical power imbalances which are partially determined by the drug's characteristics: it requires a long process of transformation from the raw material (coca leaf) to the synthetized alkaloid; the coca bush requires particular geographic conditions not widely available across the globe; and once synthetized, the ratio of weight to

Cocaine Smuggling

profit is very high. These characteristics, however, cannot account fully for the particularities of cocaine history, and are not inevitable; for example, both in the late 1800s, when the legal cocaine commerce emerged, and in the twenty-first century, when the illegal cocaine supply chain diversified, the market's geography was much more diverse. In any case, one distinct characteristic of cocaine smuggling, and its policing for most of the twentieth century, is the influence of the US, both as the largest consumer, and the largest enemy, of the drug. As in the case of other smuggled goods, local social, economic, and political dynamics, and a complex set of actors, perceptions, and ideas explain the evolution and changes of cocaine trade.

As other chapters in this volume highlight, both the weakness of state services and the centrality of state power and actions, shape cocaine's history. The 2010s brought changes to the global cocaine supply chain that opened opportunities to rethink cocaine control policies both at the supply and demand side. The effectiveness of those policies, though, is limited by the profitability and extension of cocaine demand in the context of an international drug control regime that restricts legal markets. The future of cocaine control and scholarship on cocaine smuggling require recognizing simultaneously the transnational connections that incentivize the market, and the localized politics that shape the lives of the actors involved in it, from coca cultivators to distributors and users, to law enforcement officials and politicians. This demands, among other things, greater dialogue among scholars of drug use, and those of drug production and trafficking. It also requires nuanced perspectives that question simplistic narratives such as those that exaggerate the dangers and analyze cocaine smuggling only through a security lens, or that alternatively fail to recognize practical and moral conundrums that surround its protagonists.

Notes

1 Not all trafficking networks from Chile disappeared, as those connected to sectors of military and government elites survived (Vergara 2017).
2 The exact size of the changes remains controversial because the measurement of coca crops and cocaine production potential varies over time and between institutions. Statistics can be politicized as reflected in assessments of cocaine production potential in Bolivia (Washington Office on Latin America 2012, Fox 2012).
3 This increase, however, appears in some indicators of use (monthly prevalence, and cocaine deaths, especially those involving opioids) but not in others (overdoses and treatment admissions) (Kilmer and Midgette 2018).
4 The Triennial Plan and Plan Dignidad focused on forced eradication and interdiction operations, and Blast Furnace provided military assistance and counterinsurgency training to search and destroy drug processing operations. These operations generated violence against communities that were vehemently opposed to them.
5 This reduction is reported in UNODC statistics but not in statistics from the Office of National Drug Control Policy of the United States, which has not supported Morales' approach.

References

Alexander, M., 2010. *The new Jim Crow: Mass incarceration in the age of colorblindness.* New York: The New Press.

Andreas, P., 2019. *Killer High: The history of war in five drugs.* New York: Oxford University Press.

Angrist, J. D. and Kugler, A. D., 2008. Rural windfall or a new resource curse? Coca, income, and civil conflict in Colombia. *The Review of Economics and Statistics*, 90(2), pp. 191–215.

Bagley, B. M., 1988. The new hundred years war? US National security and the war on drugs in Latin America. *Journal of InterAmerican Studies and World Affairs*, 30(1), pp. 161–182.

Bewley-Taylor, D. R., 2016. Coca and cocaine: The evolution of international control. In Feilding, A., ed., *Roadmaps to regulation: Coca, cocaine, and derivatives*. The Beckley Foundation.

Blume, L. R., 2021. Narco Robin Hoods: Community support for illicit economies and violence in rural Central America. *World Development*, 143, pp. 105464.

Blumstein, A., Wallman, J. and Farrington, D. eds., 2006. *The crime drop in America*. New York: Cambridge University Press.

Bunck, J. M. and Fowler, M. R., 2012. *Bribes, bullets, and intimidation: Drug trafficking and the law in Central America*. University Park, PA: Penn State Press.

Clawson, P. and Lee, R., 1996. *The Andean cocaine industry*. New York: Springer.

Collins, J., 2018. Rethinking 'flexibilities' in the international drug control system—potential, precedents and models for reforms. *International Journal of Drug Policy*, 60, pp. 107–114.

Courtwright, D. T., 2001. *Forces of habit: Drugs and the making of the modern world*. Cambridge: MA: Harvard University Press.

Cruz, J., Fernández, R. and Santamaría, B., 2012. Political transition, social violence, and gangs: Cases in Central America and Mexico. In Arson, C., ed., *In the wake of war. Democratization and internal armed conflict in Latin America*. Washington, DC: Woodrow Wilson Center Press, pp. 317–349.

Dale, P., and Marshal, J., 1991. *Cocaine Politics: Drugs, armies, and the CIA in Central America*. Berkeley: University of California Press.

Davis, W. 2020. Sobre la coca y la cocaína. In Boletin 17, Observatorio del Patrimonio Cultural y Arqueológico. Bogotá, Facultad de Ciencias Sociales, Departmento de Antropología, Universidad de los Andes.

Dudley, S. 2010. Drug trafficking organizations in Central America: transportistas, Mexican cartels and maras. In Olson, E., Shirk, D. and Seele, A., eds., *Shared responsibility*. Washington, DC: Wilson Center.

Durán-Martínez, A., 2018. *The politics of drug violence: Criminals, cops and politicians in Colombia and Mexico*. Oxford University Press.

Durán-Martínez, A. 2018a. Colombia: nuevo panorama de la guerra contra las drogas. *Razón Pública* 2 July, available from https://razonpublica.com/colombia-nuevo-panorama-de-la-guerra-contra-las-drogas/ [Accessed 30 October 2020].

Eddy, P., Sabogal, H. and Walden, S., 1988. *The cocaine wars*. New York: Norton.

Farber, D., 2019. *Crack: Rock cocaine, street capitalism, and the decade of greed*. New York: Cambridge University Press.

Farthing, L. and Kohl, B., 2010. Social control: Bolivia's new approach to coca reduction. *Latin American Perspectives*, 37(4), pp. 197–213.

Felbab-Brown, V., 2009. *Shooting up: Counterinsurgency and the war on drugs*. Washington, DC: Brookings Institution Press.

Fox, E., 2012. US Report on Colombia cocaine raises more questions than answers. *Insight Crime*, 1 Aug., Available from http://www.insightcrime.org/news-analysis/us-report-on-colombia-cocaine-production-raises-more-questions-than-answers [accessed 18 June 2015].

Goldstein, P. J., Brownstein, H. H., Ryan, P. J. and Bellucci, P. A., 1989. Crack and homicide in New York City, 1988: A conceptually based event analysis. *Contemporary Drug Problems*, 16, p. 651.

Gootenberg, P. 2008. *Andean cocaine: The making of a global drug*. Chapel Hill, NC: University of North Carolina Press.

Gootenberg, P. and Dávalos, L. M., eds., 2018. *The origins of cocaine: Colonization and failed development in the Amazon Andes*. London: Routledge.

Grisaffi, T. and Ledebur, K., 2016. Citizenship or repression? Coca, eradication and development in the Andes. *Stability: International Journal of Security and Development*, 5(1), pp. 1–19.

Grisaffi, T., 2019. *Coca yes, cocaine no: How Bolivia's coca growers reshaped democracy*. Durham: Duke University Press.

Kenney, M., 2007. *From Pablo to Osama: Trafficking and terrorist networks, government bureaucracies, and competitive adaptation*. University Park, Pennsylvania: Penn State Press.

Kilmer, B. and Midgette, G. 2018. Mixed messages: is cocaine consumption in the US going up or down? Available from: https://www.rand.org/blog/2017/04/mixed-messages-is-cocaine-consumption-in-the-us-going.html [accessed 28 Nov. 2018]

Lee, R. W., 1991. *The white labyrinth: Cocaine and political power*. New Brunswick (NJ): Transaction Publishers.

Lessing, B. 2017. *Making peace in drug wars: crackdowns and cartels in Latin America*. New York: Cambridge University Press.

Naim, M., 2006. *Illicit: How smugglers, traffickers and copycats are hijacking the global Economy*. New York: Anchor.

Paredes, M. and H. Manrique. 2021. The state's developmentalist illusion and the origins of illegal cultivation in Peru's Upper Huallaga Valley 1960-1980. *Journal of Latin American Studies*, 53(2), 245–267.

Ramírez, M. C., 2011. *Between the guerrillas and the state: the cocalero movement, citizenship, and identity in the Colombian Amazon*. Durham: Duke University Press.

Ramírez, M. C., 2014. Legitimidad, complicidad y conspiración: la emergencia de una nueva forma económica en los márgenes del estado en Colombia. *Antípoda. Revista de Antropología y Arqueología*, (18), pp. 29–59. http://dx.doi.org/10.7440/antipoda18.2014.03

Ramírez, M. C. 2020. Interculturalidad y replanteamiento del uso de la hoja de coca. In Boletin 17, Observatorio del Patrimonio Cultural y Arqueológico. Bogotá, Facultad de Ciencias Sociales, Departmento de Antropología, Universidad de los Andes.

Reinarman, C. and Levine, H. eds., 1997. *Crack in America: Demon drugs and social justice*. Berkeley: University of California Press.

Reuter, P., 2014. Drug markets and organized crime. In E. Paoli, ed., *The Oxford Handbook of Organized Crime*, pp. 359–381. New York: Oxford University Press.

Rojas, I., 2005. Peru: Drug control policy, human rights and democracy. In C. Youngers and E. Rosin eds., *Drugs and democracy in Latin America: The impact of US Policy*, pp. 185–230. Boulder: Lynne Rienner Publishers.

SIMCI-UNODC Sistema Integrado de Monitoreo de Cultivos Ilícitos – Oficina de Naciones Unidas contra las Drogas y el Crimen. 2018. *Colombia, monitoreo de territorios afectados por cultivos ilícitos 2017*. Bogotá: UNODC-SIMCI.

Tate, W., 2015. *Drugs, thugs, and diplomats: US policymaking in Colombia*. Stanford, CA: Stanford University Press.

Thoumi, F. E., 1992. Why the illegal psychoactive drugs industry grew in Colombia. *Journal of Interamerican Studies and World Affairs*, 34(3), pp. 37–63.

Trejo, G. and Ley, S., 2020. *Votes, drugs, and violence: The political logic of criminal wars in Mexico*. Cambridge University Press.

UNODC (United Nations Office on Drugs and Crime), 2010. *World Drug Report 2010*. Vienna: United Nations.

UNODC (United Nations Office on Drugs and Crime), 2014. *World Drug Report 2014*. Vienna: United Nations.

UNODC (United Nations Office on Drugs and Crime), 2016. *World Drug Report 2016*. Vienna: United Nations.

UNODC (United Nations Office on Drugs and Crime), 2020. *World Drug Report 2020*. Vienna: United Nations.

Van Dun, M., 2014. Exploring narco-sovereignty/violence: analyzing illegal networks, crime, violence, and legitimation in a Peruvian cocaine enclave (2003–2007). *Journal of Contemporary Ethnography*, 43(4), pp. 395–418.

Vergara, E., 2017. *Chile y las Drogas: Una revisión sistemática mirando al futuro*. Santiago: Editorial Cuarto Propio.

Washington Office on Latin America, 2012. UN and US Cocaine Estimates Contradict Each Other, Available from http://www.wola.org/commentary/un_and_us_estimates_for_cocaine_production_contradict_each_other [Accessed 18 June, 2015]

Youngers, C. and Rosin, E. eds., 2005. *Drugs and democracy in Latin America: The impact of US policy*. London: Lynne Rienner Publishers.

Zepeda, R., and Rosen, J., eds., 2014. *Cooperation and drug policies in the Americas: Trends in the twenty-first century*. Lanham: Lexington Books.

Zevallos, N., 2017. Dinámicas locales en torno al cultivo de hoja de coca: elementos para el estudio desde el mercado ilegal de la cocaína. *Revista de Ciencia Política y Gobierno*, 4(7), pp. 9–29.

15

SHARING THE LOAD[1]

The distributive nature of the opium trade in, and from, Afghanistan

David Mansfield

1. Introduction

Smuggling opium has distinct advantages. As a low-weight and relatively high value product it is more remunerative to smuggle opium than other drugs, like cannabis, and it presents fewer logistical challenges than the smuggling of bulky legal goods that are so often ferried across national borders in an attempt to bypass regulation and duties, such as fuel and consumer items. Once dried, it is also easier to transport than fresh or "wet" opium, with a lower weight and a notably less pungent smell, and therefore harder to detect by law enforcement. While clearly converting opium into morphine base, heroin base or heroin hydrochloride offers further financial benefits, as well as additional advantages with regard to reduced weight-to-value ratio and detectability, this is not an activity that everyone can, or wishes to, pursue. The cost of inputs, and access to know-how, markets and official protection, as well as social mores, restrict the number of opium traders that make the move up the value chain into the processing of opiates (Mansfield, 1998, p. 21).

Opium has long been smuggled from those nations where cultivation has been concentrated, such as Afghanistan, Pakistan, India, and Iran in south Asia, and Myanmar, Vietnam, Thailand and Laos in Southeast Asia, to consumers within each region and further afield. Currently, the vast majority of opium seizures are made in Iran, marking Afghanistan's primacy as producer of almost 90% of global opiates, the role Iran plays as a consumer nation of opium, and its position as a major conduit for opiates travelling to Europe, as well as to the efforts the Government of the Islamic Republic of Iran (GIRI) to stem the trade (UNODC, 2020a, pp. 9 & 12). For example, in 2018, GIRI seized 644 metric tons of opium, 91% of global opium seizures. It also interdicted 21 metric tons of morphine, and 25 metric tons of heroin, the equivalent of 53% of global opiate seizures once converted into common heroin equivalents (UNODC, 2020a, p. 13). After Afghanistan – whose authorities seized 27 metric tons of opium in 2018 – the next largest seizures were made in Pakistan where 19 metric tons of opium were seized the same year, almost 50% more than the seizures made by all other countries combined. As such, these three nations – Afghanistan, Iran and Pakistan – constitute 98% of all opium seizures.

Perhaps, it should be of little surprise given some of the risks to researcher and the researched that there has been little empirical work done directly with those that smuggle opium. Instead, much of

196 DOI: 10.4324/9781003043645-15

the scholarly work in this field focuses on the reports of drug control organizations, claims of what has been seized, and estimates of the revenues generated by the drug trafficking groups involved.

For those of us who have spent some time conducting research in drug producing and transit countries, the kind of aggregate statistics and generalisations used to describe the drugs trade prove frustrating. Economic reductionist arguments about high prices and the insurmountable profitability of opium poppy cultivation dominate policy discussions on the motivations for opium poppy growth in Afghanistan, and drug crop cultivation globally. These figures prove misleading, offering inaccurate estimates of the income earned from opium production, ignoring the cost of inputs, as well as the fact that different land tenure and credit arrangements significantly alter the net returns earned by a rural household growing poppy. By failing to document and understand the diverse livelihoods of those cultivating poppy – the different kind of crops grown, the role of livestock and the range of other incomes generated by the household – and how the income earned from opium poppy cultivation is distributed amongst the multiple actors involved, organisations like United Nations Office on Drugs and Crime grossly (UNODC) overestimate the amount earned by those cultivating opium poppy in Afghanistan.

Consequently, either by design or default these estimates imply that those cultivating opium poppy earn significantly more than they do and argue that the most effective way to tackle production is through a limited set of drug control tools: (i) crop eradication as a way of increasing losses, compelling farmers to look for alternatives; and (ii) more restrictive rural development efforts known as "alternative development" that offer farmers inputs to cultivate a limited set of alternative legal crops. These are the very same policies advocated and implemented by drug control organisations like UNODC, and the United States Government's Bureau of International Narcotics and Law Enforcement Affairs in the State Department (INL).

We can see the very same broad-brush descriptions used when discussing "poppy farmers" in the narratives about opium smugglers and traders. Profit, and normative terms such as "greed" are implied in discussions about their motives, when outlining the price differentials as opiates move from one country to another or in discussions about gross profits.

In fact, official and scholarly literature on illicit drugs is littered with statistics highlighting the high value of the trade. Estimates offered of the gross value of the trade typically register in the hundreds of billions, and the UNODC calculates that the value of the opiate trade alone stood at US$55 billion in 2009 (UNODC, 2012, p. 127). In the media and scholarly works, the narrative of the high value and profitability of the trade is often exemplified with a comparison of relative prices for a kilogram of heroin as it moves from one country to another, making its way from source in the global south from Afghanistan, through transit nations, and into what are seen as the consumer nations in the global north, in Europe and North America (Babor et al., 2010, p. 21). References are also made to the manifold increase between the price of opium purchased at the farmgate in Afghanistan and the equivalent weight of heroin sold in the streets of the United Kingdom (Inkster and Comolli, 2012, p. 19). None of these estimates, however, talk of profit – defined here in terms of total revenue minus total costs – of the drugs trade, or what the individuals involved get paid; the costs of doing business are not considered, and profit is only implied, not calculated.

There is some more detailed analysis that offers calculations of the gross profits earned on trade in opiates, which, for example, differentiates by each of the countries involved in upstream trafficking along the Balkan route or through central Asia (Paoli et al., 2009, p. 278; UNODC, 2015). However, here again the costs of smuggling – transport, bribes, storage and investments in innovation – are not factored in; the only costs considered are the price of opiates at the point of purchase in one country and this is compared with the price when sold across the border. As such, we remain largely unsighted on the structure of the drugs trade in the very countries where it is produced and smuggled, and how these gross profits are distributed amongst the population involved (OAS, 2012, p. 24; UNODC, 2020, p. 31). While some scholars like Barbor et al. (2010: 63) refer to "networks rather than organizations or firms," suggesting "long chains of participants," and estimate that "heroin may be bought and sold ten times in the chain connecting opium production in Afghanistan to retail sales in Rome," drug policy makers and analysts are often left wondering whether this is an accurate account of the number of actors involved in the chain. Other questions are "What are the benefits accrued by the different participants?" and ultimately, "How profitable is the trade in drugs to those directly involved – and therefore are the current policies of interdiction, arrest and imprisonment the most effective response?" The narratives of the "warlord," the "drugs baron," "the Taliban," and other nomenclature denoting power and implying market dominance thrive in this analytical vacuum. We have to look for more nuanced and detailed case studies on the smuggling of other goods – such as the ones discussed in this book – to understand better that "smugglers are ordinary people, not profit driven criminals, who hope to improve the quality of their lives and that of their families" (Weigand, 2020, p. 7).

This chapter takes a closer look at those involved in the trade and smuggling of opiates in Afghanistan to understand just how embedded this economy is in local communities and their surroundings: how many people are employed; what costs they incur; how much they are paid; and how interdiction, conflict, and border infrastructure impact on those involved and the money they earn. The chapter consists of three further sections. The next section documents the trade and smuggling of opium with a particular focus on the border provinces of Nangarhar and Nimroz. It draws on in-depth interviews with 96 individuals directly involved in the opium trade and charts how traders, smugglers and others benefitting from the trade have responded to what have been quite dramatic changes in the environment for the purchase, transportation and sale of opium within and on the borders of Afghanistan. The third section distils the lessons learned from these case studies and provides an assessment of some of the wider economic effects of the trade in opium, including estimates of the incomes earned and levels of employment. Finally, there is a conclusion that argues that the business model in the opium trade in Afghanistan is one largely made up of loosely affiliated independent traders and service providers looking to make the most of one of the few remunerative income earning opportunities that exist. This model stands in stark contrast to the narratives of vertical integration, control and vast profits that often dominate discussions about the drugs trade in Afghanistan, its neighbours, and other nations where drugs are sourced.

2. Smuggling opiates: the cost of doing business in Afghanistan

This section examines the cost of smuggling opiates within and from Afghanistan. It draws on in-depth interviews with those directly involved in the purchase and smuggling of opium in two border provinces, Nimroz and Nangarhar, as well as a body of research conducted over more than two decades in other opium producing provinces of Afghanistan, including Badakhshan, Ghor, Helmand and Kandahar. Nangarhar and Nimroz are of particular interest because both provinces have a long history of opium production and cross-border smuggling in a range of different commodities besides drugs. Both have also experienced profound socio-economic and political change due to the Afghan reconstruction effort following the fall of the Taliban in 2001. However, while the eastern province of Nangarhar saw a concentrated international presence and high levels of reconstruction funding between 2001 and 2014, it is the once remote province of Nimroz that experienced the more dramatic change: it was transformed into a major gateway for international trade by investments from neighbouring Iran and its trade partner, India. This section looks at how investments in both provinces and the conflict impacted the opium trade. In the context of this research, the term opium "trader" denotes the person that owns the opium, buying and selling it to other parties for an income; a "smuggler" or "transporter" refers to the person moving opium from one place to another for the trader, in return for an agreed fee, usually at a fixed price per weight.

2.1 Coping with the increase in the cost and risk of cross-border smuggling in Nimroz

The province of Nimroz lies in the southwest of Afghanistan and borders both Pakistan and Iran (see Figure 15.1). Levels of opium poppy cultivation have always been relatively low in Nimroz, particularly compared to other southern provinces like Helmand and Kandahar. With a harsh desert climate and salinated ground water, cultivation is limited to the more fertile district of Khash Rud bordering Bakwa in Farah Province. Instead, the comparative advantage of Nimroz lies in its location, situated between the primary opium growing provinces of the southwest and cross-border markets in Iran and Pakistan.

Once a remote desert area with a relatively small population, the province has recently been transformed by two significant investments in infrastructure that have expanded and canalised the trade of licit commodities like fuel, construction material and other transit goods through the provincial capital of Ziranj and restructured and redirected the movement of illicit goods, including drugs. These important investments in physical infrastructure have been made largely by Iran and aimed at increasing the volumes of trade. For example, in 2005 the GIRI funded

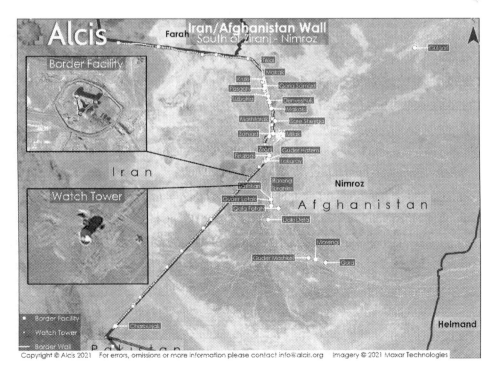

Figure 15.1 Map showing southwest Afghanistan and the province of Nimroz bordering Iran and Pakistan.

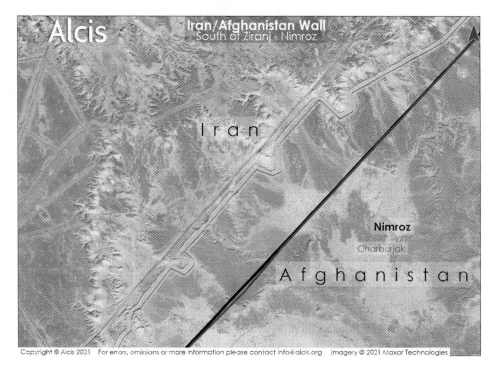

Figure 15.2 Imagery of the Iranian border wall south of the provincial capital Ziranj, Nimroz.

the building of the Pol-e Abrisham bridge across the Helmand river on the outskirts of Ziranj, thereby creating an official border crossing where none had existed before. Then between 2005 and 2009, the Government of India (GoI) provided US$100 million for the construction of a highway from Ziranj to Delaram, connecting the border crossing at Ziranj to Highway One and onward to facilitate travel to Afghanistan's major cities. Along with further construction within Iran, these infrastructural investments are part of the wider geopolitical rivalry between Pakistan and China on one hand, and India and Iran on the other, aimed at realigning trade away from Pakistan towards Iran's deep seaport in Chabahar. Alongside those investments encouraging trade through Ziranj, there were further investments designed to reduce smuggling. The most significant investment was the GIRI's improvements in its border infrastructure, in particular the construction of a border fence along the length of the Iranian border with Afghanistan, and a wall five meters in height and 70 miles in length centred on the areas around Ziranj (see Figure 15.2).

Prior to the start of this major construction project in 2007, the border between Afghanistan and Iran was bounded by a series of berms and ditches built in the late 1990s. While more restrictive than in the 1980s and 1990s when the Baloch people that straddle both sides of the border could move across the border relatively freely by foot, donkey and in some places by pickup, these barriers did little to deter the movement of people and goods. In fact, with limited agricultural land, the economic survival of many of the Afghan villages along the border depended on their ability to trade across the border smuggling everything from diesel and electrical goods to drugs and people.

With the completion of the border wall in 2013, opportunities for smuggling were dramatically curtailed. The formalisation of cross-border movements, including visa requirements for

Afghans, at a price of US$430 per person per trip, further limited who could move easily across the border and accrue the economic benefits of cross-border smuggling (Mansfield, 2020, p. 46). Moreover, along with the border fencing and wall, the GIRI also located military bases at regular intervals along the border. Mobile Units were also established in the Iranian Border Guards (IBG) Command. Typically, its personnel were not from the border area, or posted in a single location, so these mobile units were harder to bribe, and more likely to fire upon those trying to breach the border infrastructure. Some drug smugglers talked of how predictable the accommodations they reached with the more permanent local IBG were, but claimed senior officers and the mobile units would often press for arrests and seizures. One smuggler in Makaki, in the district of Kang, concluded that the mobile units had made smuggling "very dangerous work."

As such, the opportunities for small-scale decentralised smuggling diminished to such an extent that villages reported a significant outflow of the number of young men – some by up to 70%. For example, villages like Kruki in Kang, once a major smuggling hub in the late 1990s/early 2000s is now all but abandoned, in part due to flooding in 2004, but largely due to the Iranian border fortifications restricting the amount of smuggling (see Figure 15.3). Many other villages have suffered the same fate.

The challenges and dangers drug traders and smugglers faced are put into even greater context when we consider the monies earned. On the face of it, gross profits per kilogram look relatively attractive. They could purchase a kilogram of opium in Bakwa in neighboring Farah for between US$50 and US$70, depending on quality, and sell it for anything from US$103 to US$121 in a village across the border in Iran, or for between US$155 and US$187 in more distant locations like Zabul or Zahedan. However, when the actual costs of smuggling are calculated, the net profits on drug smuggling are much less rewarding – around US$30 per kilogram.

Figure 15.3 Imagery of the abandoned border village of Kruki in Kang district, Nimroz.

Table 15.1 Costs incurred by an opium trader of transporting 1 kg of opium from Bakwa to Iran

Category of payment	Recipient	Low		High	
		USD/kg	% of costs	USD/kg	% of costs
"Tax"	Taliban	0.18	1	0.18	0.5
Fee	Smuggler (Bakwa to Afghan Border)	3.91	20.4	6.51	18
Bribe	Afghan Border Police	1.69	8.8	3.26	9
Bribe	Iranian Border Guard	3.18	16.6	4.56	12.6
Fee	Landowner	0.65	3.4	0.65	1.8
Bribe	Afghan National Police	1.73	9	2.21	6.1
Fee	Smuggler (cross-border	7.82	40.8	18.89	52.1
Total		19.17	100	36.27	100

As Table 15.1 shows, the far greater part of the cost of smuggling, approximately two thirds, is absorbed by those paid to transport the opium, the smugglers themselves. "Bribes" to government officials and "taxes" to the Taliban represent a smaller part of the overall cost, absorbing the remaining one third. However, arrangements with law enforcement officials on both sides of the border can be rather precarious and involve multiple individuals. In the journey from Bakwa in Farah to the border with Iran, the Taliban, the Afghan Border Police (ABP) and the Afghan National Police (ANP) all take tribute. On the Iranian side of the border there are payments to be made to the IBG. While none of these payments are particularly high, each reduces the net profits of the opium trader requires time to arrange and are subject to renegotiation and vulnerable to breach.

While the payments made to smugglers makes up the larger part of the costs of the drugs trade, costs remain relatively low within Afghanistan at between US$4.00 to US$6.5, depending on the distance travelled. Payments mount for those responsible for transporting opium over the border. Here a smuggler from the Iranian side will receive around US$8 to take a kilogram of opium from the border crossing, and transport it to the Afghan trader's nominated contact in a village in Iran, a potential distance of between 1 and 4 kilometers. Where these contacts are further afield, in places like Zahedan or Zabul, the smuggler will receive a higher level of payment, up to US$19 per kilogram for a journey that may be as far as 200 kilometers. As such, although transportation costs rise as the distance travelled increases, these costs can be offset by the higher price the trader will receive for their kilogram of opium.

With many of these cross-border opium traders in Afghanistan reporting that they trade anything from 40 to 65 kilograms per month into Iran, net incomes can vary from US$1,200 to US$2,000 per month. However, many feel vulnerable and cite examples of friends or family members who have been arrested, and some cite the consequences. For example, one trader from Charburjak district talked of his brother who lived on the Iranian side of the border having been imprisoned for 11 years in Zahedan after being caught with 60 kilograms of opium. The trader talked of his own involvement in opium smuggling: "I do this work to find money to release my brother."

In the context of better management of both costs and risks, a number of traders report how susceptible their income is to fluctuations in the price of opium in Iran: so much so that a fall in the price of opium on the other side of the border will prompt Afghan traders to cease cross-border smuggling and store their opium, rather than take a loss. Fearful that an inventory leaves

Sharing the load

them even more vulnerable to arrest, seizures, and greater extortion by the authorities, some pay other villagers – those not known for their involvement in the trade – to store their opium at a flat rate of US$0.25 per kilogram.

Since 2018, traders have adopted strategies to manage risks and reduce costs more effectively, including the building of large catapults, known locally as *wolloks*, to propel drugs over the Iranian border wall. Made of steel and rubber strapping left behind by "foreign military forces," these catapults stand at around 1.5 meters in height, and can fire one kilogram between two hundred and three hundred meters. Bypassing the need to pay the IBG, as well as targeting the load directly at contacts across the border, this saves traders up to US$4.5 per kilogram in bribes as well as a fee of around US$ 4.00 per kilogram for those carrying the opium across the border. Traders report that on a "good night" six to eight people can propel 50 kilograms of opium across the border into Iran, resulting in a reduction of almost US$500 in costs.

These developments show that with net profits of less than US$30 per kilogram, and significant risk of arrest, injury and even death, opium smugglers have had to adapt or abandon their trade. Many smaller traders have chosen the latter, conscious that opportunities for smuggling have diminished dramatically with the fortification of the border, not just for opium, but also for the other commodities, including fuel and people. In the absence of the extra income household members earn from these goods across the border, livelihoods have proven unsustainable, hence the outmigration of family members, many moving across the border to Sistan and Baluchestan in Iran. Those that persist do so in the absence of other viable opportunities. Deprived of the chance of moving across the border without a passport and visa to find work, and in the face of a rapidly devaluing currency and fewer work opportunities in the construction trade in Iran, many find themselves on the border with little to do.

Those that have remained have had to adapt to the new circumstances where the costs of smuggling have increased and net profits fallen. As such, volume has proven critical to profitability. For those that remain, there is a limit to how much they can move, and many complain that the trade in opium has become concentrated amongst those with access to the necessary capital and patronage networks, especially those with links to government officials. Indeed, those looking to move more significant volumes across the border have looked at other ways than to scale the Iranian border structures, by either passing through the official crossing at Milak, drawing on more sophisticated concealments and the involvement of officials, or re-routing their cargos south to the Afghanistan/Pakistan border, and the town of Baramchar in Helmand. This latter route entails much larger shipments consisting of convoys of up to 16 cars: ten Toyota Landcruisers containing up to 600 kg of drugs each, and six Datsun pick-ups, four at the front two at the back, all carrying armed men. Carrying up to six tons of drugs, the cost of shipment via this kind of convoy is around US$15.00 per kilogram, cutting even further into net profits.

2.2 The impact of violence and conflict on opium smuggling in Nangarhar, in eastern Afghanistan

The eastern province of Nangarhar has long been one of the major opium growing areas in Afghanistan. Traditionally, cultivation has been concentrated in the mountainous districts to the south of the province bordering Pakistan; areas that have a long history of resisting the writ of the provincial authorities in Jalalabad and have periodically engaged in violent resistance to those that rule in Kabul (see Figure 15.4). These are the same areas in which cross-border smuggling of licit as well as illicit goods has been an economic mainstay and where heroin, and more recently, methamphetamine, processing is concentrated.

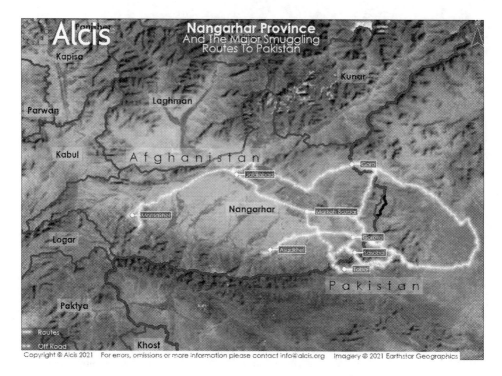

Figure 15.4 Map of Nangarhar, showing the main smuggling routes into Pakistan.

As in Nimroz, the gross profits on opium look relatively attractive with the price fluctuating between US$68 and US$78 per kilogram over much of the period between mid-2014 and late 2018, when purchased fresh in the villages of Sherzad, selling in intermediate markets in Markikhel and Markho for a few dollars mark up, or for between US$103 to US$122 per kilogram on the mountain pass at Tabai or across the border in the Tirah valley. However, since 2015 Nangarhar has seen some rather dramatic shifts in drug smuggling routes, largely due to the conflict that has beleaguered many of the southern districts in the Spinghar that have led to a rise in the cost of smuggling. The Afghan government's efforts to ban opium cultivation in Nangarhar, as well as law enforcement interventions, have played some role in disrupting the flow of opiates through Nangarhar but only on a temporary basis. Far more enduring shifts have been a function of the conflict between the Afghan government and the US military, with – on occasion – the support of Taliban forces, and the Islamic State- Khorasan Province (ISKP), and subsequently the GoP building a border fence along much of its border with Nangarhar.

ISKP moved into Achin in early 2015. Initially, these were thought to be just Orakzai families fleeing[2] the fighting between Pakistani military forces and Tehrak i Taliban militants in the nearby Tirah valley in Pakistan. Within four months, however, these "guests" had declared themselves ISKP and overrun the strategic Mahmand valley in Achin, expelling the Taliban along with most of the residents who resisted their brutal rule (Mansfield, 2016, pp. 12–13). Upon taking control of the valley in July of 2015, ISKP banned cannabis cultivation and gave the drug traders in Shadal bazaar – a major trading hub for opiates and hashish in the province – one month to leave the area. The subsequent winter season opium poppy cultivation was also prohibited by ISKP in the upper parts of Achin. By late 2015, ISKP had gained further ground in Nangarhar, overpowering the Taliban in some of its strongholds in the southern districts of

Sharing the load

Nangarhar and subsequently penetrating parts of Shinwar and Khogiani. Fearful of ISKP gaining a dominant position in Nangarhar, an unlikely alliance formed among the forces of the Afghan government, the Taliban and the US. The campaign culminated in the USG dropping the Massive Ordinance Air Blast (MoAB) – or "Mother of All Bombs" – on the ISKP's stronghold some 3 kilometers from Shadal bazaar in April 2017, and a significant US military presence in the area until as late as July 2020.

The fighting across the Spinghar – but particularly in Achin – from July 2015 had a profound effect on drugs smuggling across the province and beyond. The well-trodden routes through the mountains that had been used by travellers and smugglers en route to Pakistan were no longer secure. In particular the bazaar in Shadal, a focal point of the fighting, had to be abandoned as the major entrepot for opiates and hashish en route to Tirah in Pakistan, first due to ISKP, then due to the presence of US and Afghan government forces. In response, the hub of the drugs trade in the eastern region moved to Markoh, in Shinwar, located on the main Jalalabad to Torkham highway. Although far less remote than Shadal, the move to Markoh was accompanied by a significant rise in the cost of smuggling drugs to Pakistan, particularly for those in the southwestern districts of Sherzad, Khogiani and Pachir wa Agam. Traders and transporters from these districts found themselves unable to take the direct route southeast through Khogiani, and Kot to Achin, and had to reroute north to the area around Jalalabad and along backroads to Markoh, where the drugs are sometimes stored before being handed off to other smugglers and routed through Tabai in Durbaba.

This shift led to a significant increase in smuggling costs incurred by traders (see Table 15.2). For example, in early 2015, the direct route from Sherzad to Durbaba – although quite time consuming given the three to four day journey by mule – cost only US$3.40 per kilogram. However, by 2018, a more circuitous route via Markoh emerged, involving multiple vehicles and a journey by foot from Shinwar to the pass at Tabai in Durbaba, increasing the cost of transportation to US$13.10 per kilogram. There were further additional costs incurred as a result of storage in the area around Markoh (US$0.50/kg), where, as in the borders of Nimroz, villagers were asked to maintain the inventory of traders and smugglers fearful that the authorities would raid their shops or homes around the main bazaar. Even those opium traders in Shinwar who did not need to reroute their opium due to the fighting across much of the Spinghar were subject to an increase in transport costs over this same period, from US$4.9 to US$8.1, due to prevailing levels of insecurity and uncertainty.

If the rise in transport costs within Afghanistan were not significant enough, developments on the border with Pakistan further cut into trader net profits. As with Nimroz, smugglers in Nangarhar transport opium through areas where different armed actors demand a small payment. In return, they allow goods to pass and offer some protection against interdiction. These payments are made by the smugglers and passed on to the trader. While some of these payments may be to members of the ANP or ABP[5] on the journey between Sherzad and Markoh – or to local Taliban commanders[6] – they are relatively small, and do not appear to be part of a coherent system. On the other hand, payments to the Taliban in Shinwar district, the local authorities in Durbaba, and the Amman Committee in Tirah are understood as "rules" that are paid by all those involved in the opium trade.

Within Afghanistan, the payments to both the Taliban and the local authorities remained consistent between 2014 and 2018 despite the ensuing violence in Achin and across much of the Spinghar. However, the cross-border fee – the payment to the peace committee in Tirah, Pakistan – increased more than five-fold from US$1.52 to US$7.60 per kilogram. This rise in costs is directly attributed to the border fence built by the Government of Pakistan (GoP), to restrict the movement of fighters and drugs, as well as to demark Pakistan sovereignty over a

Table 15.2 Costs incurred by an opium trader from transporting 1 kg of from Sherzad to Pakistan

Category of payment	Recipient	2014		2018	
		USD/kg	% of costs	USD/kg	% of costs
Fee	Smuggler (Sherzad to Tabai)	3.40	68.7		
Fee	Smuggler (Sherzad to Markoh)			5.1	23.8
	(Tax to Taliban)[3]	(0.51)		(0.49)	
	(Bribe to Authorities)	(1.52)[4]		(1.47)	
Fee	Storage Villager			0.5	2.4
Fee	Smuggler Markoh to Tabai			8.14	38.1
Bribe	Amman Committee, Tirah	1.52	30.9	7.6	35.7
Total		4.90	100	21.2	100

border that has been contested for centuries. As the Iranian border infrastructure redirected and restructured the drugs trade in Nimroz, so this border fence restructured the drugs business on Nangarhar's border with Pakistan (Mansfield, 2020, pp. 44–45). Initially built along the Mohmand districts of Lalpur and Goshta, along Nangarhar's northern border with Pakistan the GoP fence canalized trade through the official crossing at Torkham, and the smuggling routes in the southern district of Durbaba (see Figure 15.5). Creating a virtual monopoly route through Tirah, the Amman committee took the opportunity to charge greater amounts for those moving any goods – including opium – through their area of influence.

The result is that, with opium prices at both the level of farmgate and trader in the east remaining relatively stable between 2014 and 2018, net profits on the cross-border trade in opium fell by as much as US$16 per kilogram, from between US$30 to US$40 per kilogram in 2014 to between US$14 and US$22 per kilogram in 2018. As with Nimroz, with traders reporting sales of between 40 kilograms and 100 kilograms per month, incomes could be between US$560 to US$2,200 per month (the equivalent of between US$6,720 and US $26,400 per annum). While markedly higher than a national average income of the equivalent of US$500 per annum, with an average of 15 household members – significantly larger than the average household size of eight in Afghanistan – the daily income per person for those trading opium in Afghanistan could be as low as US$1.20 in 2018. While smugglers may receive as much as US$90 for their journey from Markoh to Tabai, and do this journey four times a month,[7] that money is shared amongst an average household of 17 family members. As such, for both trader and smuggler, the opium business is a valuable source of income, but is not enough for a family to prosper; like for those that cultivate opium poppy, it is only one source of income in a much wider portfolio of activities.

3. What do these case studies tell us about opium smuggling in and from Afghanistan?

There are a number of salient points that can be drawn from this more detailed analysis of the changing conditions under which opium is traded and smuggled in Nangarhar and Nimroz, each of which have wider implications for the study of smuggling and the effects of prohibition more generally.

The first is that while undoubtedly the smuggling and trade in opium offers higher levels of income than many other livelihood options, particularly given that the vast majority are

Sharing the load

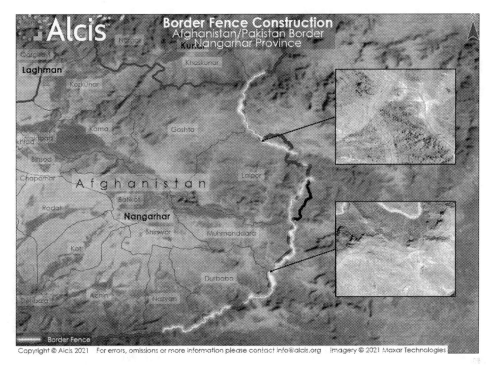

Figure 15.5 Mapping of the border fence built by the GoP with an initial focus on the Mohmand tribal areas north of Torkham

illiterate and without other marketable skills,[8] net profits are much lower than commonly assumed. As these provincial examples show, when the costs of the cross-border trade are included, net profits rarely exceed US$40 per kilogram of opium and are often considerably less. Earlier in-depth fieldwork on the production of heroin base and methamphetamine production indicate low net profit margins, at US$45 per kilogram and US$23 per kilogram, countering many of the more generalised claims about excess profits (Mansfield, 2019, p. 46; EMCDDA, 2020, p. 15).

The reality is that the costs of smuggling opium are high. In contrast to the movement of legal goods across secure terrain, illicit drugs in Afghanistan are smuggled through conflict affected areas where a multitude of armed actors operate. In the context of Afghanistan, these armed actors do not just take the form of the state and its adversaries in the Taliban, but numerous other groups that may have loose affiliations with either or both sides, often operating somewhat independently. Often these groups are backed by the local population as well as having strong connections with criminal and political groups in neighbouring countries.

Each of these entities typically will require a tribute for not interfering with the movement of drugs across their territories or for the security they provide in the area – "safe passage" – but do not have such a dominant position that they can close down the trade without experiencing significant pushback from the population. This suggests a relationship between armed actors– including state actors and insurgents – and the local population involved in the production and trade in opiates that is much more negotiated than current narratives argue. Violence, including efforts at interdiction or banning production, is often used as a bargaining mechanism, deployed to improve rent extraction, as well as performative, designed to show the key donors and international agencies that the authorities are "committed" to counternarcotics efforts – what Mansfield (2018) refers to as the "theater of counternarcotics" – rather than concerted attempts at prohibition.

The case studies also show that the more a route is divided among different armed groups and the more fragmented these groups might be, the greater the costs incurred by traders en route. The conflict in the Spinghar region of Nangarhar, as well as the newly established border infrastructure along the Afghanistan/Pakistan border and Afghanistan/Iranian border, served further to segment these journeys bringing yet more actors – in the form of both smugglers and rent seekers – and further increase the costs for opium traders.

When opium prices are rising, it might be possible for traders to absorb these extra costs, but the conflict in Achin and the construction of the border walls first by the GIRI and then by the GoP occurred at a time when opium poppy cultivation in Afghanistan was exceeding all previous records and opium prices were falling. The collapse of the Iranian rial due to the imposition of US sanctions not only lowered the prices Afghan traders received for their opium but dampened market demand in Iran. In fact, with repeated devaluations, and opium prices in Nimroz traditionally denominated in Iranian toman (the equivalent of ten rial), many Afghan traders were reluctant to be paid in a currency that was fast losing value and, erring on the side of caution, refrained from trade, and pressed to fix prices in US dollar equivalents (Mansfield, 2018, pp. 12–13).

The second salient point these case studies raise is related to the first, and it is just how critical effective risk management is in the opium economy given the low profit margins. In fact, some traders were found to limit their business interests to a small area; for example, trading only in Markikhel in Sherzad where they were familiar with the farmers, traders, and armed actors they transact with. These individuals worked at the very margins of the trade, buying opium at as low a price as possible, negotiating for more generous volumes and selling maybe one or two days later when prices might be higher. Without capital or contacts, these traders were unable to carry the challenges of delayed cash flow or the risk of being caught and having their drugs seized. Even with those that trade further afield, there is a distinct preference for working with those that are already known, and many traders and transporters look to purchase and sell opium and move it along routes where they are familiar with those that they encounter. They believe their ability to draw on familial connections or patronage networks important to negotiate reductions in "taxes," "gifts" or "charity" and to avoid arrest and/or seizure (UNODC, 2020, p. 12). The segmentation of journeys into "familiar" routes allows traders and smugglers to manage risk even if it does increase costs. These examples further highlight how managing risk is more important to those involved in opium smuggling than maximising revenues, further countering the narratives that dominate discussions on transnational and organized crime that emanate from organizations like UNODC.

The example of the multicar convoys operating out of Bakwa travelling to Baramchar in Helmand, highlights how those traders with more capital and powerful connections might be able to avoid the truncated nature of the journeys that other smaller and less influential opium traders engage in. No doubt similar examples could be found were it possible to obtain details from those smuggling large amounts of opiates through the official borders at Torkham or Ziranj, drawing on the support of officials. However, as the convoy example shows the cost implications are significant, with transport costs, and no doubt bribes and fees markedly higher, resulting in significantly lower profit margins per kilogram, and even greater emphasis on the need to move significant volume to maximise income, hence the scale of the shipments moved via Baramchar.

Sharing the load

The third salient point from these case studies is the large number of different actors involved in the movement of drugs from within Afghanistan and its borders, and how much employment and income it generates. The same can be seen with the smuggling of other commodities within Afghanistan with the trade in undeclared fuel, transit goods and minerals creating employment, income and rents for armed actors that is measured in the millions (Mansfield, OSDR and Alcis 2021). As the example for Nangarhar shows, the movement of a kilogram of opium from a farm in upper Sherzad to the Afghan border at Tabai can involve as many as three different smugglers and just as many traders buying and selling the crop. There are other payments to those who consider themselves service providers, the Taliban and the local authorities, who offer security in return for the "taxes," "gifts" and "bribes." This journey within Afghanistan entails three separate journeys and payments to as many as nine different actors, of which seven are directly employed in the opium business, the other two extracting rent. A further journey from the pass in Tabai to the valley in Tirah entails payments to the Amman Committee. While the journey from Nimroz to Iran is not quite as segmented, it still entails payments to two smugglers, a possible fee for storage, and four further payments for the different armed actors en route. As such, both the Nangarhar and Nimroz cases highlight just how much Babor et al. (2010: 63) underestimated the number of transactions made, in their suggestion that "heroin may be bought and sold ten times in the chain connecting opium production in Afghanistan to retail sales in Rome;" in the case of Nangarhar, opium changes hands three times before it even leaves Afghanistan, four times if we are to include the farmer cultivating it.

It is of course difficult to put a precise figure on how many people overall might be involved in cross-border smuggling of opium in Afghanistan, but even if only half the amount of the 482 metric tonnes UNODC (2018) estimate of opium grown in Nangarhar in 2018 were handled by the kind of opium traders and smugglers interviewed for this research – with the rest either processed into opiate derivatives, or transported through Torkham or other borders by more influential traders trading much larger amounts – then it is likely that the shipment would involve a minimum of 600 traders and smugglers and possibly more than 1,500 (see Table 15.3). It would also involve over US$250,000 in payments to the Taliban per annum and almost US $880,000 in fees to the local authorities. Along with those storing opium in their household compounds for a small fee, so that traders can minimise the risks of arrest and seizure, and other service providers such as guards, labourers and those purchasing opium at the farmgate for the trader – *commissionkars* – the opium trade is likely to employ thousands of people in Nangarhar alone, and possibly tens of thousands across the country.

Table 15.3 Estimate of the number of traders and smugglers in Nangarhar

District to Hub[8]	No. of Traders	If 40 kg/ month	223	No. of Traders	If 100 kg/ month	89
	No. of Smugglers	If 30 kg/ month	287	No of Smugglers	If 80 kg/ month	111
Hub to Border	No. of Traders	If 40 kg/ month	446	No. of Traders	If 100 kg/ month	178
	No. of Smugglers	If 30 kg/ month	594	No. of smugglers	If 80 kg/ month	223
Total			1550			601

David Mansfield

Combined with a labour-intensive opium crop, that is estimated to create jobs for hundreds of thousands of people, and in-country heroin production, as well as flourishing supply chains in both cannabis-hashish and now ephedra-ephedrine- methamphetamine, it is highly probable that the drugs economy is by far the largest employer in Afghanistan. Once the multiplier effect is also factored in, the economic effects of the drugs economy become almost impossible to ignore by development donors and International Monetary Institutions, like the World Bank. In fact, there is perhaps something to be said for the distributive nature of the opium trade in its current form. A more dominant vertically integrated business model – such the one found in the opium convoys from Bakwa, or across the official borders in places like Ziranj and Torkham – is likely to be much less distributive, supporting the accumulation of profit, wealth and influence in the hands of a few. As such, it is clear that tackling the opium trade cannot be simply a matter of law enforcement, but requires a sustained long-term development effort.

4. Conclusion

The current literature on the global drugs trade and trafficking offers little when it comes to how costs and benefits are distributed along the supply chain beyond generalised estimates of gross profits at a country level and the calculations that show the bulk of the revenue accrued is in the global north. There is an absence of data as to how these profits, estimated for different nations, are distributed amongst the various actors involved in drug producing and transit nations. We learn little to nothing of the structure of the trade within these countries where the opium economy is likely to make up the greatest proportion of its gross domestic product.

In this analytical vacuum, the narratives that often dominate are those where it is the "warlords," "drug barons," "cartels" and other violent actors that exert control over the opium economy and absorb the bulk of the profits made. In Afghanistan, this has typically manifested in accounts in the media and official reports that it is the Taliban that profits most from the drugs trade, generating revenues measured in the hundreds of millions and controlling the supply chain from farm through to processing and final sale at the border (Brownfield cited in AFP, 2017; Department of Defense, 2017).

This chapter has drawn on empirical evidence and documented the multiplicity of actors involved in the opium trade in two provinces of Afghanistan. It has shown the large number of actors and transactions involved in the purchase, transportation and sale of opium within Afghanistan and on its borders and has documented the more decentralised and negotiated nature of the trade, one in which armed actors like the Taliban, and those working for the government, are not controlling or directing the trade but are service providers, providing "safe passage" for a fee. It has shown just how embedded the trade and smuggling of opium is in the local economy of these two provinces, providing income and direct employment for a large number of people, as well as indirect jobs for a wide range of service providers. Alongside other smuggled goods such as the cross-border value chains in fuel, minerals and transit goods, these economies employ more people, and generate far greater income and rent for border communities than any other industry.

By drawing on the experiences of those directly involved in the drugs trade, this chapter has also documented the high costs associated with the segmented nature of the opium trade in Afghanistan, the low profit margins and the strategies adopted to manage risk and move large volumes. This chapter points to a business model for the opium trade that sits in contrast to narratives of vertical integration, control and vast profits, and points to a supply chain in Afghanistan that consists of loosely affiliated independent traders and service providers looking to make the most of one of the few remunerative income earning opportunities that exist.

Sharing the load

Former drivers, mechanics, farmers and soldiers, residing in conflict affected areas where the cost of living is so high and the quality of welfare services so poor, engage in an illicit trade that is one of the only ways to make sufficient monies for them and their families to prosper.

Notes

1   This chapter draws on fieldwork funded by the UKRI Global Research Challenge Fund project "Drugs and (dis)order", as well as research funded by the Afghan Research and Evaluation Unit, Natural Resources Management project funded by the European Union. The work was conducted in partnership with the Organization of Sustainable Development & Research and Alcis Ltd.
2   Initially, around 100 families from the Orakzai tribe arrived in the Mahmand valley from Pakistan in March 2015, fleeing the GoP's counter insurgency initiatives targeting the TTP in the Tirah valley. These were joined by families from other parts of Pakistan. In July 2015 these refugees had taken control of the valley and raised a black ISIS flag at Shadal bazaar. For more details see David Mansfield, "The devil is in the detail: Nangarhar's continued decline into insurgency, violence and widespread drug production" AREU, February 2016.
3   Paid from the smugglers fee.
4   Paid from the smugglers fee.
5   These payments rarely exceeded US$1.20 – but often less than US$0.30 – per kilogram and were intermittent not regular.
6   Payments to local Taliban commanders would be referred to as "komak," [komak is usually translated as "help"] gifts, and be made of any one of wealth, not just opium traders. Commanders claimed that these payments were for food, clothes and other items for the commander and his soldiers, for their "jihad." Requests for these payments would be sporadic, often timed after each agricultural season, and while demands would initially start at around US$500 to US$600, the amount ultimately paid by the opium trader would rarely exceed a total of US$120.
7   This journey is initially by car and then a four hour walk to the border.
8   Of the 96 interviewed, 69 (72%) were reported being illiterate, 10 (8%) claimed to have finished school up to 6th grade, 8 (8%) up to 9th grade, 4 (4%) up to 10th grade and 5 (5%) up to 12th grade.
9   The District to Hub figure excludes a further 25% of the yield on the basis that the crop in districts such as Achin, Shinwar, Deh Bala and Kot will be transported directly to the border at Tabai and will not be first routed to Markoh.

References

Agence France Press, 2017. From Poppy to Heroin: Taliban Moves into Afghan Drug Production, 8 August 2017. http://newsinfo.inquirer.net/921189/from-poppy-to-heroin-taliban-moves-intoafghan-drug-production#ixzz54uADqs75
Babor, T. et al., 2010. *Drug Policy and the Public Good*. Oxford: Oxford University Press.
European Monitoring Centre for Drugs and Drug Addiction, 2020. Is Afghanistan Emerging as a Globally Important Supplier of ephedrine and methamphetamine, EU4MD Special Report, November. https://www.emcdda.europa.eu/system/files/publications/13410/emcdda-methamphetamine-in-Afghanistan-report.pdf
Inkster, N. and Comolli, V., 2012. *Drugs, Insecurity and Failed States: The Problems of Prohibition*. London: International Institute for Strategic Studies.
Mansfield, D. 1998. The Dynamics of the Farmgate Opium Trade and the Coping Strategies of Opium Traders. Strategic Study #2, Final Report for UNDCP, October.
Mansfield, D. 2016. The Devil Is in the Detail: Nangarhar's Continued Decline into Insurgency, Violence and Widespread Drug Production, AREU, February. https://areu.org.af/publication/1602/
Mansfield, D., 2018. Stirring up the Hornet's Nest: How the Population of Rural Helmand View the Current Counterinsurgency Campaign, AREU, October. https://areu.org.af/publication/1814/
Mansfield, D., 2018a. Bombing Heroin Labs in Afghanistan: The Latest Act in in the Theater of Counternarcotics, LSE International Drug Policy Unit, January. https://www.lse.ac.uk/united-states/Assets/Documents/Heroin-Labs-in-Afghanistan-Mansfield.pdf

Mansfield, D., 2019. Denying Revenue or Wasting Money? Assessing the impact of the Air Campaign against 'Drugs Labs' in Afghanistan, LSE International Drug Policy Unit, April https://www.lse.ac.uk/united-states/Assets/Documents/mansfield-april-update.pdf

Mansfield, D., 2020. Mules, Pick-ups and Container Traffic: Cross-Border Production and the Shaping of the Political Economy of Nangarhar, AREU, June. https://areu.org.af/wp-content/uploads/2020/07/2008E-Mules-Pick-ups-and-Container-Traffic.pdf/

Mansfield, D., 2020. Catapults, Pick-Ups and Tankers: Cross-Border Production and the Shaping of the Political Economy of Nimroz, AREU, August. https://areu.org.af/wp-content/uploads/2020/09/2013E-Catapults-Pickups-and-Tankers.pdf/

Mansfield, D., 2021. Managing Local Resources and Conflict: The Undeclared Economy-Value Chain Mapping and Visualisation of the Talc, Fuel, and Transit Trade in Afghanistan. An unpublished report for the Office of Transitional Initiatives, OTI, Kabul (forthcoming).

Organization of American States, 2012. The Economics of Drug Trafficking, in *The Drug Problem in the Americas: Studies*, Washington DC: OAS.

Paoli, L., Greenfield, V., and Reuter, P., 2009. *The World Heroin Market: Can Supply be Cut?* Oxford: Oxford University Press.

UNODC, 2012. *The World Drug Report*. UNODC: Vienna.

UNODC, 2015. *Drug Money: The Illicit Proceeds of Opiates Trafficked on the Balkan Route*, UNODC, Vienna.

UNODC, 2018. *Afghanistan Opium Survey 2018: Cultivation and Production*, November, UNODC, Kabul.

UNODC, 2020. Voices of the Quchagbar - Understanding Opiate Trafficking in Afghanistan from the Perspective of Drug Traffickers. UNODC Research, AOTP Update, Special Edition, Vienna.

UNODC, 2020a. *World Drug Report: 3 Drug Supply*. UNODC Research, Vienna.

Weigand, F., 2020. *Conflict and Transnational Crime: Borders, Bullets and Business in Southeast Asia*. Cheltenham: Elgar Publishing.

16

ARMS TRAFFICKING

Nicholas Marsh and Lauren Pinson

The primary significance of arms trafficking lies in the ability of a trafficker to increase the destructive potential of a recipient of illicit weapons.[1,2] In contrast to illicit trades in commodities such as narcotics or counterfeit goods, arms trafficking usually involves comparatively little money and few individuals or groups are involved as purchasers or traffickers. Nevertheless, arms trafficking can have a profound political and societal impact when groups involved in political violence or organized crime obtain weapons. As has been shown again and again, massacres can be carried out by small groups or even individuals using powerful firearms.

Various campaigning organizations have often presented what Bourne (2007) describes as the 'amorphous image' of easy access to illicit arms throughout the world, sometimes illustrated with tales of Kalashnikovs being traded for the price of a chicken (see also Chivers 2011, p. 381, Jackson 2010, Marsh 2015). This amorphous image is used by politicians and campaigning NGOs to draw attention to arms trafficking by presenting 'supermarkets for terrorists' or criminals (Marsh 2017, p. 79). Empirical research on arms trafficking, however, paints a very different picture (Bourne 2007, Markowski et al. 2009, Karp et al. 2015, Marsh 2020). Instead, supply and demand for illicitly trafficked arms varies considerably geographically and temporally. Arms trafficking is usually local, and closely linked to regional economies of conflict or organized violence.

The legal production, transfer, and possession of arms is controlled via a complex web of multi-level governance (Greene and Marsh 2012a). At the societal level, weapons are governed via norms, customs, and informal authority (Ashkenazi 2012, Buscemi 2019). Customs or traditional authority figures may dictate who is entitled to own and carry weapons, and under what circumstances they can be used. In areas where state authority is weak or non-existent (such as in borderlands) weapons are usually still governed via other forms of authority (Bartolucci and Kannewarff 2012, Buscemi 2019). Practices and networks can be more important than formal or informal institutions (Buscemi 2021).

At the level of the state, a core function of governance is to regulate weapons present within a jurisdiction (Marsh 2018, Tar and Adejoh 2021). National governments regulate the production, trade, and possession of weapons, though national laws differ (e.g., see Parker 2011a on firearm regulations). In most states, people can lawfully obtain firearms and other weapons used for recreation or hunting. Weapons designed for use by military forces are generally heavily restricted, with civilian possession usually limited to entities such as museums or film

DOI: 10.4324/9781003043645-16

production companies that own deactivated weapons.[3] In particular, states typically have transfer control regulations which govern the international trade in arms. Normally, a party requires authorization from a government to export, transit, or import arms across borders.

At the international level, regional organizations (such as the European Union or the Economic Community of West African States) and the UN Security Council play a role in regulating the arms trade. States have also negotiated agreements, in particular the Arms Trade Treaty. There is considerable interaction between these three levels of governance (Greene and Marsh 2012a), and rules formulated at one level may be unacceptable at another. Successful attempts to control illicit trafficking require concurrence at all three levels (Ashkenazi 2012).

This chapter proceeds as follows: first, we illustrate the implicit scholarly debates on arms trafficking. Next, we detail the four categories of the arms trade. Then, we explain the supply and demand for illicit arms, the extent of arms trafficking, and the national pool of recirculating illicit arms. Finally, we elucidate state- and international-level responses to arms trafficking. We conclude with implications for the study of other types of smuggling.

Academic debates

While it is axiomatic that weapons play a vital role in conflict and violent crime, there has been little specifically academic research into illicit arms trafficking (Marsh 2020: 21–25). The substantial majority of scholarship has taken place outside of peer-reviewed journals, and mostly can be found in reports published by think tanks and research centres (such as Small Arms Survey), international organizations (especially various parts of the UN), NGOs (such as Amnesty International), and consultancy firms (such as Conflict Armament Research). Investigative journalism is another rich source of information.

Research in academic journals similarly focuses upon describing specific illicit flows without engaging in theory building or wider academic debates, for example, McDougal et al. (2015) on total illicit firearm flows from the USA to Mexico, or McDougal et al. (2019) on detection of illicit military–civilian flows of ammunition in Haiti. The one larger body of academic work which engages with other fields is research on illicit arms markets in the United States (e.g., Zimring 1976, Moore 1981, Cook and Braga 2001), though given its unique level of lawful firearms availability and focus upon US gun control debates, research on the US has limited applicability elsewhere. Only a handful of authors have attempted to go beyond geographically limited case studies and descriptions of data collection in order to examine arms trafficking as a phenomenon (Kinsella 2006, Killicoat 2007, Markowski et al. 2009, Marsh 2015).

As such, the great majority of the existing research comprises disparate case studies and data collection that are fragmented geographically, temporally, and methodologically. This body of work is atheoretical and there has often been little engagement between researchers working on arms trafficking and relevant academic fields such as the micro-foundations of conflict. The lack of interest in arms trafficking can be explained partly by the general failure of arms researchers to go beyond case studies and produce datasets or theories that can be used readily by other social scientists (Marsh 2007, Greene and Marsh 2012b). Lacking engagement with experts, social scientists sometimes hold implicit assumptions about arms trafficking which preclude further examination of the subject.

There are two notable areas of *implicit* theory concerning arms availability which can be found in academic research. Firstly, some scholars, many of whom wrote from the 1990s onwards about the so-called 'New Wars' (e.g., Kaldor 2013), have assumed that the world is awash with vast quantities of illicit arms (for summaries see Bourne 2007, pp. 34–39, Jackson

2010, pp. 133–137, Marsh 2012, pp. 23–24). This view, described by Bourne (2007) as an 'amorphous image' of ubiquitous easy availability can be summed up by Klare (1999, p. 16) who writes that "the outbreak of conflict in weak and divided societies is fostered by an immense worldwide abundance of small arms and light weapons." The amorphous image, while drawing attention to arms trafficking, precludes further research. So long as availability is assumed to be constant it cannot be used to explain variation in the outbreak or intensity of violence, nor is there any point in examining the relationship between violence and different means of illicit supply. The amorphous image has been explicitly challenged by scholars who emphasize that arms trafficking is usually local, and closely linked to regional economies of conflict or organized violence (see Bourne 2007, Jackson 2010, Marsh 2012). Many more scholars have implicitly criticized the amorphous image simply by describing the extent to which illicit arms are frequently scarce and the local nature of arms trafficking (e.g., Strazzari and Tholens 2010, Gilgen 2012, Schroeder 2013, Karp et al. 2015).

An implicit consequence of the amorphous image is scholars who do not consider arms supply to be a factor worth considering. For example, Krause (2017, pp. 42, 70–73) lists three factors which he claims encompass the strength of all rebel movements: "members, wealth, and popular support," and he explicitly excludes other forms of resources such as arms (2017, p. 353). Krause does not assume that rebels don't need arms to fight, but that if they have enough people, money, and support they can get all the arms they need. Such an assumption implicitly assumes that resources are fungible (Hazen 2013, pp. 6–15). However, other scholars have argued that illicit arms and other conflict goods are not fungible. Rebels or organized crime groups that are well financed still need to expend considerable effort to develop sources of illicit arms supply (Bourne 2007, Marsh 2007, Hazen 2013). The ease or difficulty in obtaining arms varies considerably depending upon closeness to sources of supply (such as arms obtained from military depots after state collapse). There are logistical challenges even in areas where it is apparently easy for individuals to obtain military-style weapons. High intensity violence uses up vast quantities of ammunition that constantly need to be resupplied, something which is much more difficult if fighters are equipped with a wide variety of weapons.

Secondly, scholars studying conflict or crime have often made two basic and usually implicit assumptions about arms which Bourne (2012) terms *substantive* or *instrumentalist*. The substantive view is that the presence of weapons determines social phenomena. For example, concerning trafficking, Greene and Macaspac Penetrante (2012, p. 142) summarize a "framework of understanding" that a "malign synergy" of uncontrolled flows of weapons and the presence of armed groups will "drive the affected country down a spiral of decline toward state failure." This view has been criticized by scholars who point out that societies are able to govern weapons use and inflows of illicit arms may not result in their use in acts of violence (see, e.g., Greene and Macaspac Penetrante 2012, pp. 154–159, Greene and Marsh 2012c, pp. 258–260, Sagawa 2010, 2018). Conversely, the instrumentalist assumptions view weapons as being irrelevant, something that can be summed up by the phrase made popular by advocacy groups such as the National Rifle Association: "Guns don't kill people, people do." Such an instrumentalist view can be found among scholars who assume that motivation to use violence is an adequate explanation for the incidence and intensity of violence. For example, Booth (2007, pp. 120–1) argues that "politically or racially motivated slaughter, regardless of the perpetrator, is committed with the technology at hand" and so crimes like genocide will still occur whether the perpetrator is armed with clubs or with high-tech weapons. Instead of the substantive or instrumentalist dualism, authors such as Marsh (2020) and Sislin and Pearson (2001) argue instead that arms provide opportunities for violence, which may or may not be used.

Arms trafficking is a usually unseen but necessary condition for armed conflict and organized crime. Scholars make assumptions about it even if they haven't actively thought about arms trafficking or consulted the empirical research. It is therefore useful to provide a summary of how it usually occurs, something which can be found in the following sections.

Types of illicit arms transfers

Researchers and practitioners classify the forms of arms trafficking and drivers of illicit supply and demand. This provides a starting point for understanding how illicit arms markets operate.

The arms trade can be divided into four categories[4]:

1. The *authorized trade* in which transfers are fully in compliance with national and international laws and regulations.
   The following three categories comprise different forms of illicit arms trafficking.
2. The *semi-legal trade* in which different aspects of a transfer may be authorized or unauthorized.[5] For example, a transfer may involve an authorization from the exporting state, but not one from the importing state. Parties involved in arranging arms transfers which break national or international laws may be adept at exploiting loopholes to provide the appearance that their activities are lawful.
3. The *state-sanctioned illicit trade* involves direct complicity of government officials who have political approval for their actions.[6] State-sanctioned trafficking occurs when arms transfers are used as a foreign policy tool and usually involves transfers to non-state parties that have not been authorized to receive weapons by the state where they are located.
4. In the *wholly illicit trade,* all aspects of an arms transfer are unlawful and unauthorized (such as if weapons were sold by one organized crime group to another).

There are often blurred boundaries between the latter three categories. For example, the semi-legal trade and state-sanctioned illicit trade may at times use similar methods; the difference is the level of government complicity. Arms transfer regulations can be complex, and can be broken inadvertently by exporting companies. Even if they are involved in breaking national laws, military or intelligence personnel involved in state-sanctioned trafficking may not be prosecuted if doing so is not in the national interest (Marsh 2002). National laws and regulations may be unclear or non-existent in contexts of state collapse or where there is contested sovereignty between different sides involved in civil wars.

In the absence of marketing and advertising, there is usually little price competition between illicit suppliers. Instead, in areas with effective law enforcement, weapons transfers are arranged through trusted networks (in general, see Morselli 2009, pp. 63–71, or for examples concerning arms trafficking see Duquet and Goris 2018). Such a reliance on networks limits the potential market for trafficked weapons.

Supply and demand of illicitly trafficked arms

The main sources of arms used by illicit traffickers include (Marsh 2018):

- Illicit production of often low-quality firearms.
- Theft or illicit sale from private firearm owners.
- Theft or illicit sale from government stockpiles.

Arms trafficking

- Use of deception in the semi-legal trade to obtain arms from government stocks or from arms-producing firms.
- Donations via the government-sanctioned trade, or from supporters.

The limited illicit production of arms is one constraint on the supply of arms to illicit markets. Weapons need to be made to exacting specifications or they may malfunction and possibly injure the user. Due to economies of scale, mass producing weapons in factories is more efficient than craftsman individually making them to similar specifications in workshops. Arms that are illicitly trafficked were usually lawfully produced in a factory.

Most trafficked weapons are diverted to the illicit market after they have been lawfully produced and transferred (Marsh and Dube 2014, Marsh 2019). Diversion occurs when authorized holdings are transferred to unauthorized end users – for example, when weapons are stolen from a government stockpile.

The most widely used sources of arms differ over time and across regions. In general, armed groups seek to diversify their sources of supply (Bourne 2007). Government stocks are most attractive as they contain large quantities and powerful weapons, but outside state collapse they can be a difficult source for an armed group to access (Marsh 2007, Jackson 2010).

Simply put, people demand illicitly trafficked arms because they wish to obtain weapons that they could not easily obtain lawfully. Normally, users of trafficked arms lack the ability to use or maintain the most sophisticated arms. The only users of illicit fighter aircraft or warships are embargoed states, or quasi-states which may lack diplomatic recognition but control large territories, populations, and resources. The non-state groups and individuals who usually demand trafficked weapons wish to obtain arms that are easy to use and maintain, and that can be transported and concealed from government forces. In practice, illicit arms trafficking usually involves what is known as small arms and light weapons, such as assault rifles, machine guns, grenades, and portable rocket launchers (Greene and Marsh 2012d).

Trafficked arms offer the following three advantages. First, individuals who would otherwise be prohibited can obtain arms. In particular, national regulations may prevent lawful acquisition by people convicted of violent crimes or members of extremist groups. Second, people can obtain prohibited types of weapons, especially powerful arms designed for military use, such as grenades or fully automatic firearms. Third, illicitly trafficked arms may be difficult or impossible to trace by law enforcement officials.

There are three basic forms of demand for illicitly trafficked arms: instrumental need; symbolic role; and collection (Marsh 2015). These are linked to the different forms of illicit trade which are described below. The first is instrumental – weapons may be needed for a specific task. For instance, a group planning a bank robbery will obtain arms used to subdue the staff and customers. Secondly, trafficked weapons may serve a symbolic role. As examples, the Kalashnikov has become a symbol of revolution globally, and groups may prize weapons captured from enemy government forces. Finally, in developed countries, some collectors have obtained significant quantities of illicit arms. While those arms may not have been purchased with aggressive intent, in some cases illicitly acquired collections can involve tens or even hundreds of weapons.

Different forms of demand tie to the three forms of trafficking mentioned earlier. First, the semi-legal trade is typically used to supply larger groups that are involved in political violence or organized crime and often involves complex arrangements designed to obtain weapons under state control. Transaction costs are high and frequently involve rare skills such document forgery. Second, state-sanctioned illicit trade is a policy tool usually used to supply groups involved in political violence. Third, the wholly illicit trade is the most pervasive and can be found in all countries. It most commonly involves demand by individuals or smaller groups (Marsh 2015).

Violence drives most of the demand for illicit arms. In developed countries with low levels of internal violence, demand for illicit arms is limited to small numbers of criminal groups and some collectors. For example, in 2013, UK police officials stated that ballistic tests indicated that most gun crime could be traced back to fewer than 1,000 illicit firearms still in circulation (Fiola 2013). In contrast, in the same year in Colombia – a country that experienced very high levels of organized violence – authorities reported the seizure of 38,236 guns (which were likely a small proportion of the pool of illicit arms in the country) (Karp et al. 2015).

Development also interacts with supply and demand. Firstly, developed states usually have more effective law enforcement agencies and so are better able to prevent illicit trafficking. Secondly, partly as a result of better law enforcement, the most developed states almost always have low levels of lethal violence, resulting in lower demand (the United States is an exception). Finally, higher average incomes entail more resources that can be used to acquire illicit arms. Some middle-income states and some of the least-developed countries may have comparable levels of illicit trafficking.

Extent of arms trafficking

There are large differences in the scale of the different types of arms trafficking noted above.

The semi-legal trade usually involves complex transactions involving several actors. Large quantities of arms may be transported under a veil of apparent legality; for example, shipments crossing borders facilitated by a mixture of forged and genuine documentation. The semi-legal trade has been featured in Hollywood movies such as *Lord of War* but in practice it is rare, and its heyday was in the 1990s and early 2000s. Then, it was possible for dealers and brokers to obtain large quantities of weapons from post-Soviet arsenals with few questions asked. Those practices have declined as stocks were sold off and countries improved their arms trade controls upon joining the EU and NATO.

The largest single transactions can be found in the state-sanctioned trade. Ministries of defence can obtain arms from government stocks or procure them directly from companies. They can also obtain powerful sophisticated weapons such as guided anti-aircraft or anti-tank missiles that are usually difficult to source in illicit markets. Governments can ensure that customs and other officials ignore transfers that may not comply with regulations. The largest contemporary example of the state-sanctioned illicit trade was the CIA-led supply of arms and training to anti-Assad groups in Syria ('Timber Sycamore'), lasting from 2013 to 2017.[7] Precise details of the programme are not publicly stated, but it reportedly cost the US about USD 1 billion per year (Miller and DeYoung 2015). In addition, Timber Sycamore also received financing and weapons from Saudi Arabia claimed to be worth billions of dollars (Mazzetti and Apuzzo 2016), along with further support from other states including Qatar and Turkey.

Trafficking in the wholly illicit trade is usually small scale, moving small numbers of weapons (Marsh 2015). If traffickers cross borders, it is most commonly between neighbouring countries. Arms are bulky and heavy, so it is usually not feasible to try to traffic large quantities in areas where states have effective law enforcement agencies. A trafficker might be able to conceal five firearms in a car, but, in much of the world, they would find it difficult to secretly transport five thousand.

Many small-scale transfers can add up to large numbers of weapons. The 1994 Zapatista uprising in the Mexican state of Chiapas popularized the term the 'ant trade' to describe how many individuals would purchase arms in the United States to smuggle over the border

Arms trafficking

(Ross 1995). Later, it was estimated that between 2010 and 2012 about 200,000 firearms had been trafficked over the US border into Mexico (McDougal et al. 2015).

Differences between trafficking weapons and their ammunition become apparent when violence is more intense. Battlefields use up vast quantities of ammunition, and rebel armies constantly need to be resupplied, whereas they do not need significant numbers of new weapons every day. For less intense violence, a gun and its ammunition can be supplied together.

Illicit prices

Analysis of geographical and temporal differences in illicit prices has been used to describe arms trafficking (e.g., Killicoat 2007, Florquin 2014, McDougal et al. 2019). Recent research provides some insights into the nature of arms trafficking (Marsh 2020, Marsh and McDougal 2020):

- Illicit arms are expensive. Globally, among 727 price observations, the average price of an illicit assault rifle in constant 2010 US dollars is USD1489 (Marsh 2020). When one considers that almost all conflicts are fought in low- or middle-income countries, purchasing illicit arms constitutes a considerable investment for an individual fighter or group.
- There is considerable variation in illicit prices, even in geographically close areas. For example, in 2004, the average reported price for an illicit assault rifle in Iraq was approximately USD160, while in Israel/Palestine it was approximately USD2200 (Marsh 2020).
- Arms prices tend to rise after increases in violence (Marsh 2020). Higher prices suggest that supply is not able to meet demand, and this may limit the intensity of violence and the ability of parties to achieve their aims.
- Prices paid by governments in the authorized trade are usually much lower than illicit prices for similar weapons. Compared to the thousands often paid by insurgents, governments could obtain new Kalashnikovs for about USD200 each, and used ones for as little as USD65 (Marsh 2020).

Analysis of illicit prices suggests that illicit arms are a 'partially tradable' good (Killicoat 2007). Arms trafficking clearly occurs, but anti-trafficking measures by governments and international organizations are able to restrict the illicit trade in most places. Indeed, exceptionally low prices are associated with places where state authority has collapsed (most notably in Iraq during and after 2003).

Recirculation of illicit arms

Illicit arms are durable goods and can be transferred from one owner to another (in some circumstances guns may be rented out by the hour). If properly stored and maintained, weapons can remain in working order for decades, even hundreds of years. Ammunition has a shorter life, as explosives become unstable over time. In practice, though, arms will degrade mechanically if they are allowed to corrode, are damaged while in use, or are not properly maintained. In time, the number of working weapons will slowly decline unless losses due to attrition are replaced with new production.

Because arms are durable and tradable goods, there is a pool of illicit weapons which can be drawn upon, as illustrated in Figure 16.1. As described later in this chapter, a key aim of

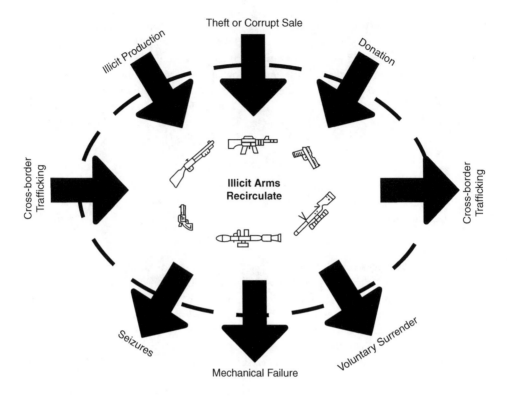

Figure 16.1 An illustration of the national pool of illicit arms

government and multilateral anti-trafficking measures is to shrink the size of the pool – by restricting inflows and extracting arms via seizures and amnesties.

How states counter arms trafficking

States must regulate the manufacture, transfer, state storage, civilian possession, and disposal of weapons in order to prevent the diversion of conventional arms to the national pool of illicit arms (see Figure 16.1). During manufacture and later transfers, marking the weapon can record unique information on its production and ownership and a serial number. Transfer controls require the authorization of the export, transit, and import of weapons. Having a mechanism for information exchange and using end-user certificates (designating the final recipient) helps mitigate the risk of weapon diversion. Export may also necessitate a risk assessment of diversion and/or violating international law. Robust controls on arms transfers also regulate brokering – when an intermediary links interested parties and facilitates the transaction. The government must also oversee the physical security and management of its own storage and stockpiles of law enforcement weapons and military weapons. Control of civilian weapons ownership varies extensively across states, partly due to the lack of international instruments addressing civilian possession.

Due to resource constraints and prioritization, governments vary widely in their ability to effectively monitor and analyze illicit arms flows. Many governments – in both developed and developing countries – do not effectively collect and analyze data on firearms trafficking, and the least developed countries often lack the necessary capacity (Karp et al. 2015, Marsh 2015).

Without intelligence on illicit arms flows, in the short term, governments cannot develop sufficient policies and law enforcement responses, and, in the long term, governments may assume that in the absence of information there is no problem (Marsh 2015).

There are two main political challenges in preventing arms trafficking. First, some states are simultaneously involved in promoting anti-trafficking measures and directly engaged in state-sanctioned arms trafficking (or at least allowing it to occur in their jurisdiction).[8] Some states, especially permanent members of the UN Security Council, perceive arms trafficking as a useful foreign policy tool, and so undermine wider attempts to prevent illicit arms proliferation.[9] Second, attempts to prevent arms trafficking are frequently stymied by official inaction and indifference.[10] Often, arms trafficking is 'someone else's problem.' Law enforcement officers may correctly perceive that diversion occurred in another jurisdiction, but attempts to uncover traffickers will involve lengthy and perhaps fruitless attempts to cooperate with other agencies.

States vary in both interest in countering arms trafficking and available financial and human resources. The transnational nature of illicit trafficking makes international cooperation imperative, since weak-link actors can otherwise allow arms trafficking to endure. With resources, technical ability, willingness, and international collaboration, a government can limit access to arms for criminals, terrorists, and actors involved in conflict.

International assistance and cooperation to counter arms trafficking

Many states are unwilling and/or lack the capacity to counter illicit arms trafficking; as a result, other states contribute international assistance to build capacity to control illicit arms. Anti-trafficking assistance includes aid to augment technical skills and resources, reduce corruption, and strengthen institutions. The provision of assistance to limit the movement of illicit arms uses several avenues, including:

1. physical efforts (e.g., disarmament, destruction, stockpile security and surplus destruction, and law enforcement) that collect, destroy, secure, or detect arms on behalf of the state;
2. legal efforts (e.g., writing legislation and training for customs and border control) to bolster state-level governance; and,
3. social efforts (e.g., dialogue and public relations campaigns) that target the societal level of governance, aiming to construct norms of arms ownership and use.[11]

Governments may have functional or political reasons to provide international assistance to counter arms trafficking – whether to limit illicit arms within their own borders or to help a foreign region of interest. As a result, access to international assistance is not equal across regions. For instance, capacity-building to counter arms trafficking in Central and Eastern Europe is able to access significantly more donor resources and specialist implementing organizations compared with Latin America and the Caribbean, even though the latter region includes states dealing with significant violence carried out with illegal weapons.

Effective international assistance requires matching a state's needs to offers of assistance. In the best-case scenario, international assistance and cooperation involve providing resources alongside sharing technical assistance and other experience-informed solutions to common challenges. Complicating matters for donors, recipient governments sometimes have incentives to reject assistance projects, since receiving resources may entail more external oversight or additional transparency in a politically sensitive area (Pinson 2020).

Several primarily Western states and regional organizations provide international assistance to help control the use and spread of illicit weapons. Major donor states include the United States, the United Kingdom, Germany, and France (Pinson 2020). While some states provide bilateral assistance, states often supply assistance through regional organizations (e.g., EU or NATO) and specialist assistance programs (e.g., South Eastern and Eastern Europe Clearinghouse for the Control of Small Arms and Light Weapons or Regional Approach to Stockpile Reduction).

Historically, donor states and organizations have focused the majority of their international assistance on destroying arms and ammunition, securing state stockpiles, and, to a lesser extent, funding disarmament campaigns. Destroying surplus and insecure weapons eliminates a potential source of weapons to divert. If local law enforcement or military are trained in effective destruction techniques, it also builds local capacity to manage the state stockpile. Physical security and stockpile management measures help to secure state-owned weapons from being diverted to the illicit market. Successful civilian disarmament campaigns remove weapons held by the population. All of these capacity-building measures focus on helping limit the number of weapons that could potentially be diverted to the national pool of illicit arms through theft, corrupt sale, or donation.

Donor states and organizations strategically provide such capacity-building assistance to states and regions as a result of spillover avoidance, responsibility ties, or acute need. First, states with stricter gun control sometimes try to avoid the consequences of illegal guns smuggled over their borders or disrupting regions of interest (spillover avoidance) by focusing assistance toward potential sources of illicit arms (Pinson 2020). For instance, partially in response to terrorist attacks in Western Europe perpetrated with illegal arms, some major donor states, including Germany and France, have shifted funding towards more dynamic aspects of illicit arms trafficking in recent years, such as training for law enforcement and border patrols. Much of this assistance funds capacity building projects in Central and Eastern Europe, making the region a destination for more concentrated assistance even compared with areas experiencing immediate violence. Second, donor states tend to be more involved with former colonies or areas where they were directly involved in a conflict (responsibility ties), sometimes funding stockpile security, arms destruction, or disarmament. Third, though a recipient state's acute need to control potential sources of illicit arms is sometimes matched with resources, donor states tend to target aid to reduce smuggling across their own borders, stabilize a region of interest, or have some historic responsibility (Pinson 2020). While the United States is a major donor state in this issue area, it rarely funds capacity-building measures to counter arms trafficking in its own region, tends to focus on physical security and stockpile management, and domestic political constraints somewhat limit the types of assistance provided. As noted above, some states may bargain over or reject offered assistance, reducing the amount of control held by a donor state or organization. Some of the international instruments discussed in the following section attempt to match needs with resources but often requests remain unfunded.

International and regional agreements and regulations

While international assistance provides resources and expertise aiming to build capacity at the national or regional level, limiting arms trafficking requires international coordination and agreements. International and various regional communities have attempted to set forth guidelines and commitments to capacity-building measures in order to counter arms trafficking.

The main international instruments relevant to countering arms trafficking require different responsibilities from governments:

1. Firearms Protocol – 2001: All State Parties of the Firearms Protocol[12] that supplements the UN Convention Against Transnational Organized Crime have an obligation to implement

Arms trafficking

legislation to counter firearms trafficking, exchange information on legal and illegal participants in the trade, and provide technical assistance to other states. While legally binding, several major arms-exporting states have not ratified the protocol (UN General Assembly 2001).

2. UN Programme of Action to Prevent, Combat and Eradicate the Illicit Trade in Small Arms and Light Weapons in All Its Aspects (PoA) – 2001: All UN Member States are committed to enhance national SALW laws, import and export controls, and stockpile management, in addition to engage in cooperation and assistance to help meet those goals more broadly. The PoA lacks an enforcement mechanism, limiting its utility (United Nations 2001).[13]

3. International Tracing Instrument (ITI) – 2005: The ITI supplements the PoA by establishing international standards on marking, record-keeping, and tracing for small arms and light weapons (UN General Assembly 2005).

4. Arms Trade Treaty (ATT) – 2013: State Parties to the ATT seek to thwart and eliminate the illicit trade in conventional arms, pursuant to their national laws and regulations. The ATT regulates the legal conventional arms trade. However, several major arms-exporting and -importing states are not State Parties to the ATT (UN General Assembly 2013).[14]

5. UN Sustainable Development Goal (SDG) Target 16.4 – 2015: In the SDGs, UN Member States made the commitment to significantly reduce illicit arms flows. Due to the clandestine nature of firearms trafficking, directly measuring these flows is not possible. As a result, SDG Indicator 16.4.2 focuses on how efficient the international community is in tracking origin of illicit firearms in a State (UN General Assembly 2015).

These different international instruments include various provisions to control the legal trade while preventing, detecting, and countering the three variants of the illicit trade.[15] In addition to state obligations and commitments to international instruments, many states have similar obligations under regional organizations of which they are members.

While many of these international and regional agreements require national legislation, those laws are not always passed consistently. Often, international instruments provide general commitments but not specific guidelines to implement. The patchwork of laws, regulations, and enforcement globally provides loopholes and pathways that allow for trafficking. As a complex issue, challenges to enhancing arms controls include the outsized role of major producers and exporters, norms of state sovereignty, and legitimate use of conventional arms for some purposes (Stohl 2017).

Comparison to other types of smuggling

Arms remain unique compared to many other smuggled items. As durable goods, weapons can be sold, trafficked, and used by multiple actors over decades. Ammunition is the one element which is rapidly consumed in an economic sense. At a global level, profits from arms trafficking are likely to be much lower than for other forms of smuggling described in this volume. Instead, weapons are often trafficked in order to facilitate other activities. Trafficked arms are needed by individuals or groups involved in committing crimes (including other forms of smuggling) or acts of political violence. Unlike other forms of smuggling, some governments actively traffic weapons in the pursuit of political objectives.

Notes

1 We use the terms *arms* and *weapons* interchangeably – defined here as specialized instruments which have been designed to cause injury or destruction. Unless explicitly stated, discussion on these terms also includes associated ammunition, parts, and accessories.

  The authorized trade and different forms of arms trafficking involve weapons transfers. A *transfer* occurs when there is a change in the possession or control of a weapon – through sale or donation – from one party to another. A transfer may involve arms crossing borders, or may occur within a state.

  This chapter does not cover improvised objects that may be used to injure, such as kitchen knives, or the trade in nuclear, chemical or biological (NBC) weapons. Fortunately, the illicit trade in finished NBC arms is very limited and potentially distinct from conventional arms trafficking, making it beyond the range of this chapter's limited length.

2 We use the terms *trafficking* and *smuggling* interchangeably, tending to use 'trafficking' more frequently as the term is used more often in the field.

3 There is some blurring in the line between civilian and military weapons, particularly with some types of firearms that are not designed for fully automatic fire which may be used by both military forces and civilians (e.g., pistols and sniper rifles).

4 This categorization builds upon Haug (2001) and Marsh (2002).

5 This trade is elsewhere known as the 'grey market' (Marsh 2002).

6 This form of trade is elsewhere known as 'covert arms supplies.' This term is not used here as such transfers are often carried out openly, and other forms of illicit trade are conducted covertly.

7 However, one considers the ethics of the arms supplies, the shipments were not authorized by the government of Syria and so are included in the definition of illicit used in this chapter.

8 Relatedly, Erickson (2015) shows commitment to the Arms Trade Treaty and similar policies is influenced by states' concerns about upholding or improving their international reputation; yet, shifts to comply with international arms control policies and avoid exporting arms to states that violate human rights may be constrained to keep foreign policy autonomy and protect the defense industry.

9 For a recent addition to the long list of works examining the use of arms transfers surrogates by great powers to proxies see Krieg and Rickli (2020).

10 See Marsh (2015) on the widespread lack of capacity to monitor illicit trafficking. Comments on indifference are based upon authors' conversations with officials in a large number of states and international organizations.

11 Pinson (2020), also see Maze and Parker (2006), Maze (2009), Parker (2011b), Parker and Green (2012) for in-depth assessments of types of assistance provision.

12 Protocol against the Illicit Manufacturing of and Trafficking in Firearms, Their Parts and Components and Ammunition.

13 Various reports have assessed state progress in implementing the PoA, such as Parker and Green (2012).

14 Garcia (2014) surveys the background and potential significance of the ATT. Reports such as Spano and Alpers (2017) detail recommendations on implementing the ATT and PoA. Stohl and Dick (2021) provide an overview of issues related to diversion in the ATT and a recent update on ATT initiatives.

15 Parker (2016) gives more information on each of these instruments, along with a helpful map of where these instruments apply within the lifecycle of a firearm.

References

Ashkenazi, M., 2012. What do the natives know? Societal mechanisms for controlling small arms. *In*: O. Greene and N. Marsh, eds. *Small arms crime and conflict global governance and the threat of armed violence.* London: Routledge, 228–247.

Bartolucci, V. and Kannewarff, A., 2012. Armed violence taking place within societies: SALW and armed violence in urban areas. *In*: O. Greene and N. Marsh, eds. *Small arms crime and conflict global governance and the threat of armed violence.* London: Routledge, 122–137.

Booth, K., 2007. *Theory of world security.* Cambridge; New York: Cambridge University Press.

Bourne, M., 2007. *Arming conflict: the proliferation of small arms.* New York: Palgrave Macmillan.

Bourne, M., 2012. Small arms and light weapons spread and conflict. *In*: O. Greene and N. Marsh, eds. *Small arms, crime and conflict: global governance and the threat of armed violence.* London and New York: Routledge, 29–42.

Arms trafficking

Buscemi, F., 2019. Armed political orders through the prism of arms: relations between weapons and insurgencies in Myanmar and Ukraine. *Interdisciplinary Political Studies*, 5(1), 189–231.

Buscemi, F., 2021. The art of arms (not) being governed: means of violence and shifting territories in the borderworlds of Myanmar. *Geopolitics*, 1–28. https://doi.org/10.1080/14650045.2021.1901083

Chivers, C., 2011. *The gun*. New York: Simon & Schuster.

Cook, P.J. and Braga, A.A., 2001. Comprehensive firearms tracing: strategic and investigative uses of new data on firearms market. *Arizona Law Review*, 43, 277–309.

Duquet, N. and Goris, K., 2018. *Firearms acquisition by terrorists in Europe: Research findings and policy recommendations of Project SAFTE*. Brussels: Flemish Peace Institute.

Erickson, J.L., 2015. *Dangerous trade: arms exports, human rights, and international reputation*. New York: Columbia University Press.

Fiola, A., 2013. After shooting tragedies, Britain went after guns. *Washington Post*, 1 Feb.

Florquin, N., 2014. Arms prices and conflict onset: insights from Lebanon and Syria. *European Journal on Criminal Policy and Research*, 20(3), 323–341.

Garcia, D., 2014. Global norms on arms: The significance of the arms trade treaty for global security in world politics. *Global Policy*, 5(4), 425–432.

Gilgen, E., 2012. A fatal relationship: guns and deaths in Latin America and the Caribbean. In: *Small arms survey 2012: moving targets*. Cambridge: Cambridge University Press, 8–39.

Greene, O. and Macaspac Penetrante, A., 2012. Arms, private militias and fragile state dynamics. *In*: O. Greene and N. Marsh, eds. *Small arms, crime and conflict: global governance and the threat of armed violence*. London and New York: Routledge, 138–160.

Greene, O. and Marsh, N., 2012a. Governance and small arms and light weapons. *In*: O. Greene and N. Marsh, eds. *Small arms crime and conflict global governance and the threat of armed violence*. London: Routledge, 163–182.

Greene, O. and Marsh, N., 2012b. Armed violence within societies. *In*: O. Greene and N. Marsh, eds. *Small arms crime and conflict global governance and the threat of armed violence*. London: Routledge, 79–104.

Greene, O. and Marsh, N., 2012c. Conclusion and priorities for further research. *In*: O. Greene and N. Marsh, eds. *Small arms crime and conflict global governance and the threat of armed violence*. London: Routledge, 248–262.

Greene, O. and Marsh, N., 2012d. Introduction. *In*: O. Greene and N. Marsh, eds. *Small arms crime and conflict global governance and the threat of armed violence*. London: Routledge, 1–10.

Haug, M., 2001. Crime, conflict, corruption: global illicit small arms transfers. *In*: P. Bachelor and K. Krause, eds. *The small arms survey 2001: profiling the problem*. Oxford: Oxford University Press, 165–195.

Hazen, J.M., 2013. *What rebels want: resources and supply networks in wartime*. Ithaca: Cornell University Press.

Jackson, T., 2010. From under their noses: rebel groups' arms acquisition and the importance of leakages from state stockpiles. *International Studies Perspectives*, 11(2), 131–147.

Kaldor, M., 2013. In defence of new wars. *Stability: International Journal of Security and Development*, 2(1), 1–16.

Karp, A., Marsh, N., and Ravalgi, G., 2015. *UNODC study on firearms 2015*. Vienna: United Nations Office on Drugs and Crime.

Killicoat, P., 2007. What price the Kalashnikov? The economics of small arms. *In*: E.G. Berman, K. Krause, E. LeBrun, and G. McDonald, eds. *Small arms survey 2007: guns and the city*. Cambridge: Cambridge Univ. Press, 257–287.

Kinsella, D., 2006. The black market in small arms: examining a social network. *Contemporary Security Policy*, 27(1), 100–117.

Klare, M.T., 1999. The international trade in light weapons: what have we learned? *In*: J. Boutwell and M.T. Klare, eds. *Light weapons and civil conflict: controlling the tools*. Lanham, MD: Rowman and Littlefield.

Krause, P., 2017. *Rebel power: why national movements compete, fight, and win*. Ithaca: Cornell University Press.

Krieg, A. and Rickli, J.-M., 2020. *Surrogate warfare: the transformation of war in the twenty-first century*. Washington, DC: Georgetown University Press.

Markowski, S., Koorey, S., Hall, P., and Brauer, J., 2009. Multi-channel supply chain for illicit small arms. *Defence and Peace Economics*, 20(3), 171–191.

Marsh, N., 2002. Two sides of the same coin? The legal and illegal trade in small arms. *Brown Journal of World Affairs*, 9(1), 217–228.

Marsh, N., 2007. Conflict specific capital: the role of weapons acquisition in civil war. *International Studies Perspectives*, 8(1), 54–72.

Marsh, N., 2012. The tools of insurgency: a review of the role of small arms and light weapons in warfare. *In*: O. Greene and N. Marsh, eds. *Small arms, crime and conflict: global governance and the threat of armed violence*. London and New York: Routledge, 13–28.

Marsh, N., 2015. Firearms seizures and trafficking: a "local" phenomenon. *The Strategic Trade Review*, 1(1), 73–87.

Marsh, N., 2017. Brothers came back with weapons: the effects of arms proliferation from Libya. *PRISM*, 6(4), 79–96.

Marsh, N., 2018. The availability puzzle: considering the relationship between arms and violence taking place within states. *History of Global Arms Transfer*, 6(2), 3–21.

Marsh, N., 2019. Preventing diversion: a challenge for Arms Trade Treaty states parties.' *History of Global Arms Transfer*, 8, 55–66.

Marsh, N., 2020. Because we have the Maxim gun: the relationship between arms acquisition by non-state groups and violence. Doctoral Dissertation. University of Oslo, Oslo.

Marsh, N. and Dube, G., 2014. *Preventing diversion: the importance of stockpile management*. Oslo: Peace Research Institute Oslo, PRIO Paper.

Marsh, N.J. and McDougal, T.L., 2020. Illicit small arms prices: introducing two new datasets. *Defence and Peace Economics*, 1–22. https://doi.org/10.1080/10242694.2020.1757348

Maze, K., 2009. *Implementing the UN Programme of Action: a checklist for matching needs and resources*. Geneva, Switzerland: United Nations Institute for Disarmament Research.

Maze, K. and Parker, S., 2006. *International assistance for implementing the Programme of Action to Prevent, Combat and Eradicate the Illicit Trade in Small Arms and Light Weapons in All Its Aspects: findings of a global survey*. Geneva, Switzerland: United Nations Institute for Disarmament Research.

Mazzetti, M. and Apuzzo, M., 2016. U.S. relies heavily on Saudi money to support Syrian rebels. *New York Times*, 23 Jan.

McDougal, T.L., Kolbe, A., Muggah, R., and Marsh, N., 2019. Ammunition leakage from military to civilian markets: market price evidence from Haiti, 2004–2012. *Defence and Peace Economics*, 30(7), 799–812.

McDougal, T.L., Shirk, D.A., Muggah, R., and Patterson, J.H., 2015. The way of the gun: estimating firearms trafficking across the US–Mexico border. *Journal of Economic Geography*, 15(2), 297–327.

Miller, G. and DeYoung, K., 2015. Secret CIA effort in Syria faces large funding cut. *Washington Post*, 13 Jun.

Moore, M.H., 1981. Keeping handguns from criminal offenders. *ANNALS of the American Academy of Political and Social Science*, 455, 92–109.

Morselli, C., 2009. *Inside criminal networks*. New York: Springer.

Parker, S., 2011a. Balancing act regulation of civilian firearm possession. *In*: E. Berman, K. Krause, E. LeBrun, and G. McDonald, eds. *Small arms survey 2011: states of security*. Cambridge: Cambridge University Press, 261–309.

Parker, S., 2011b. *Improving the effectiveness of the Programme of Action on Small Arms: implementation challenges and opportunities*. Geneva, Switzerland: United Nations Institute for Disarmament Research.

Parker, S., 2016. *A guide to the UN small arms process: 2016 update*. Geneva: Small Arms Survey.

Parker, S. and Green, K., 2012. *A decade of implementing the United Nations Programme of Action on Small Arms and Light Weapons: Analysis of national reports*. Geneva and New York: United Nations Institute for Disarmament Research.

Pinson, L., 2020. Blood or money? Why states allow illicit economies. Doctoral Dissertation. Yale University, New Haven, CT.

Ross, J., 1995. *Rebellion from the roots: Indian uprising in Chiapas*. Monroe, ME: Common Courage Press.

Sagawa, T., 2010. Automatic rifles and social order amongst the Daasanach of conflictridden East Africa. *Nomadic Peoples*, 14(1), 87–109.

Sagawa, T., 2018. Arms availability and violence in the Ethiopia-Kenya-South Sudan borderland. *History of Global Arms Transfer*, 6, 39–44.

Schroeder, M., 2013. Captured and counted illicit weapons in Mexico and the Philippines. *In*: E. LeBrun, G. McDonald, A. Alvazzi del Frate, E.G. Berman, and K. Krause, eds. *Small arms survey 2013: everybody dangers*. Cambridge: Cambridge Univ. Press, 282–317.

Sislin, J. and Pearson, F.S., 2001. *Arms and ethnic conflict*. Lanham, Md: Rowman & Littlefield Publishers.

Arms trafficking

Spano, L. and Alpers, P., 2017. *Implementing the Arms Trade Treaty and the UNPoA*. Sydney: Center for Armed Violence Reduction.

Stohl, R., 2017. Understanding the conventional arms trade. Presented at the Nuclear weapons and related security issues, Washington, DC, USA, 030005.

Stohl, R. and Dick, S., 2021. *Diversion and the Arms Trade Treaty: Identifying good practice and opportunities for progress*. Washington, DC: Stimson Center.

Strazzari, F. and Tholens, S., 2010. Another Nakba: weapons availability and the transformation of the Palestinian national struggle, 1987–2007. *International Studies Perspectives*, 11(2), 112–130.

Tar, U. and Adejoh, S., 2021. The theoretical parameters of the proliferation and regulation of small arms and light weapons in Africa. *In*: U. Tar and C. Onwurah, eds. *The Palgrave handbook of small arms and conflicts in Africa*. Cham, Switzerland: Springer.

UN General Assembly, 2001. *UN protocol against the illicit manufacturing of and trafficking in firearms, their parts and components and ammunition*. https://treaties.un.org/Pages/ViewDetails.aspx?src=TREATY& mtdsg_no=XVIII-12-c&chapter=18&clang=_en

UN General Assembly, 2005. *International instrument to enable states to identify and trace, in a timely and reliable manner, illicit small arms and light weapons*. https://www.unodc.org/documents/organized-crime/ Firearms/ITI.pdf

UN General Assembly, 2013. *Arms Trade Treaty*. Academy Briefing No. 3. https://www.geneva-academy.ch/joomlatools-files/docman-files/Publications/Academy%20Briefings/ATT%20Briefing %203%20web.pdf

UN General Assembly, 2015. *Transforming our world: the 2030 Agenda for Sustainable Development*. https:// sdgs.un.org/2030agenda

United Nations, 2001. *Report of the United Nations Conference on the Illicit Trade in Small Arms and Light Weapons in All Its Aspects*. New York, NY: United Nations.

Zimring, F.E., 1976. Street crime and new guns: Some implications for firearms control. *Journal of Criminal Justice*, 4(2), 95–107.

17

RECONCILING COMPETING POLICIES FOR COMBATTING WILDLIFE TRAFFICKING AND PREVENTING ZOONOTIC PANDEMICS

Vanda Felbab-Brown

Introduction

The planet is currently experiencing alarming levels of species loss caused in large part by intensified poaching, stimulated by a greatly expanding demand for animals, plants, and wildlife products. The rate of species extinction, now as much as 1000 times the historical average and the worst since the dinosaurs died out 65 million years ago, deserves to be seen, gravely exacerbated by climate change, as a global ecological catastrophe meriting high-level policy initiatives to address its human causes. In addition to irretrievable biodiversity loss, wildlife trafficking can also undermine human security of forest-dependent communities, cause local, national, and global economic losses, and even pose threats to national security (Felbab-Brown, 2017).

As the coronavirus pandemic dramatically highlighted, poaching and wildlife trafficking – as well as unmonitored legal trade in wildlife – also pose enormous threats to public health and global economies. As of February 1, 2021, COVID-19 has claimed over 2.2 million lives globally and infected 103 million people (Felbab-Brown, 2021), a number that kept increasing catastrophically throughout the spring of 2021. Twenty years of poverty reduction efforts have been wiped out, with as many as 150 million people pushed into extreme poverty in 2021; both the disease and the economic effects persisted well into 2021 ("COVID-19 to Add as Many as," 2020). Since many have been forced to liquidate their human development assets, they and their children may not be able to recover economically for years or decades. Many have been pushed into participation in illegal economies and thrust into the hands of criminal actors and militants (Felbab-Brown, 2021). Thus, counterproductively, poaching and wildlife trafficking have been also exacerbated, as has deforestation. The cumulative devastation surpasses the scale of destruction many a regional war could inflict.

Even prior to the COVID-19 outbreak, zoonotic diseases (including HIV/AIDS, Ebola, SARS, flu, yellow fever, and others) caused millions of human deaths and a billion cases of human illness per year (Karesh et al., 2012). Seventy-five percent of emerging diseases are zoonotic, the majority originating in wildlife (Taylor et al., 2001).

228

DOI: 10.4324/9781003043645-17

Combatting wildlife trafficking

The loss of human life and economic destruction of pandemic zoonotic diseases, including those linked to poaching and wildlife trafficking, vastly surpass the harms the illegal drug trade (as well as policies to counter it) have generated. The level of resources and policy focus on countering illegal drug production and smuggling, however, dwarfs policy focus on countering poaching and wildlife trafficking. This is all the more inappropriate given that a potentially catastrophic impact of poaching and wildlife trafficking – irretrievable loss of species and biodiversity within a few years and zoonotic pandemics spread through wildlife trafficking in a few months – can be rapid. And unlike illegal drugs, which are non-depletable, wildlife is a quickly depletable commodity.

The global public health and economic devastation caused by the coronavirus (COVID-19) outbreak dramatically reinforces the urgent imperative to minimize the chances of another zoonotic pandemic. Reducing the likelihood of another viral spillover sweeping the world requires a fundamental change in how we interact with nature and how we produce food. COVID-19 is not an isolated, once in a century event. Between 2003 and 2020, a new zoonotic disease threatening at least an epidemic has been identified about once every three years. Reducing the extent of zoonotic disease emergence and spread requires minimizing human interface with wild animals and wild spaces and eliminating transmission points where the likelihood of viral spillover to humans is high, such as unhygienic commercial markets in wild animal meat and live animals. Also needed is better monitoring of the legal trade in wildlife, conservation of natural habitats, and diligent suppression of unsustainable trade in wildlife and *the poaching and wildlife trafficking* – the subject of this chapter. Moving toward such radical changes is difficult in both highly economically developed countries with voracious demands for wildlife, timber, agricultural products and minerals, and poorer countries where wildlife habitats face intense human pressures for land, requiring a radical rethinking of development and global equity issues (Leach et al., 2021) as environmentally destructive policies of one country or even one actor can inflict a devastating pandemic on the entire world.

Conservation policies to preserve species equally can undermine human security when they constrain the access of poor populations to the natural resources on which they depend for basic livelihoods. Thus, there is little consensus on what the best ways are to suppress wildlife trafficking and what steps are necessary to maximize the prevention of zoonosis; i.e., the viral spiral from animals to humans. At least three schools of thought as to how deal with poaching and wildlife trafficking exist and their preferred policy recommendations are at times directly contradictory.

- One school of thought, often embraced by many environmental NGOs but also some conservation biologists, argues for intensified, even militarized law enforcement, increased penalties for poachers, and bans on legal trade in wildlife.
- Another school, comprising many economists of wildlife trade as well as some conservation biologists, maintains that bans will result in greater poaching and emphasizes allowing legal trade.
- A third school of thought, those who promote so-called community based natural-resource management, maintains that local communities should be the authority to decide how local natural resources are treated, including whether animals are hunted and traded or protected.

Their disagreements and contradictory approaches are all the more amplified by the COVID-19 pandemic and the inescapable imperative to respond to it and minimize the chances of another rapidly emerging zoonotic pandemic.

Apart from ideology and emotions, one of the reasons that these debates persist with great vehemence and without prospect for a quick resolution or consensus some 15 years into yet another intense poaching and wildlife trafficking wave is that the outcomes of each approach have been enormously varied, often with more failures than successes registered for each. What that crucially means is that, as uncomfortable as it is for each school of thought, policy experimentation, flexibility, and adjustments are fundamental. One policy approach does not fit all.

The global poaching and wildlife trafficking crisis

Elephants, rhinoceros, tigers, giraffes, parrots, jaguars, giant otters, snakes, reptiles, and many other animals are captured, slaughtered, and trafficked for trinkets, or for Traditional Chinese Medicine. Others are smuggled live for the global pet trade. In combination with habitat destruction and global warming, hunting and poaching might eliminate entire genera of species, further undermining remaining ecosystems. Although East Asian countries, particularly China, Vietnam, and Thailand, are some of the key consumption and demand markets, the United States is widely believed to be the country with the second largest consumer market for trafficked wildlife (United Nations Office on Drugs and Crime, 2020). Demand and supply markets also exist in Latin America; some are new, while others have existed for a long time. They include, for example, the illegal trade in parrots in Brazil and the illegal trade in reptile skins that supplies the affluent in Mexico who love boots made of exotic skins. Wildlife demand markets, both sustainable and environmentally-problematic, also exist in other places often ignored in the story of global poaching, including various East and West African countries, which are often characterized as merely source countries (Barnett, 2000).

Poaching numbers are staggering and devastating. Between 2010 and 2012, almost 100,000 elephants were killed for their tusks in Africa, out of an elephant population that is about 435,000 today, but was 1.2 million in 1980 ("The Elephants Fight," 2015; "Wildlife Slaughter," 2015; Wasser et al., 2015; "World Wildlife Crime," 2016).[1]

Rhinos are faring even worse, with poaching dramatically increasing since 2007. In 2013, about 98% of Africa's rhinos roamed free in four countries, South Africa, Namibia, Kenya, and Zimbabwe, with over two thirds concentrated in South Africa. In South Africa alone, 1,215 rhinos were killed for their horns in 2014, up from 13 in 2007. In 2014, a critical tipping point was reached in South Africa where the number of deaths was believed to surpass the number of births per year (a poaching rate that could wipe out all of Africa's rhinos by 2022) (Halter, 2013). Alarmingly consistent with this trend, the total number of poached rhinos in South Africa, where their numbers are largest, and those dying as a result of poaching (such as orphaned babies) was estimated between 1,160 and 1,500 in 2015 (Amin et al., 2006; "South African Group," 2016).

The northern white rhino subspecies has already gone almost extinct in the wild (Jones, 2015), with only two females remaining. Other species of rhinos – the Indian, Sumatran, and Javan – exist in Asia, all critically endangered and poached. In India, 141 rhinoceros were killed by poachers between 2009 and 2014 ("Rhino Poaching," 2018). The Indonesian subspecies of the Javan rhino was extirpated in 2010 when the presumed last specimen was shot for its horn in Vietnam in 2010 (Nuwar, 2013). Both rhino horn and ivory are highly valuable products. A kilo of rhino horn currently fetches some US$65,000 in China (Milliken & Shaw, 2012), and a kilo of ivory between US$3,000 and 6,000 (Nixon, 2015; "South African Group," 2016). Ivory prices have doubled in recent years, both in demand and source counties (Orenstein, 2013; Wittemyer et al., 2011). One hundred and seventy-one tigers were poached in India between

2010 and 2015, while 19 very rare Siberian tigers were known to be killed in Russia between 2012 and 2013 (Nowell, 2007; "WPSI's Tiger," 2021). This disastrous poaching has been taking place despite the commitment of more than US$100 million in five years by tiger range countries to reduce poaching and double tiger populations by 2020 ("Global Tiger," 2012). These numbers may seem comparatively low, but given that the entire population number is in the low thousands, with perhaps hundreds for particular subspecies, such poaching rates are devastating and can drive the species to extinction.

This global poaching crisis and illegal trade in wildlife coexist with a large and equally expanding legal trade in wildlife. Although sometimes the legal wildlife trade enables conservation of habitats and contributes to species recovery, at other times it facilitates illegal trade by enabling "laundering" of illegally-sourced wildlife and boosting demand for wildlife products, including illegal ones, as detailed below.

The trafficking structures and patterns

Understanding the structure of poaching and wildlife trafficking networks is critical for devising effective policy responses. Dominant narratives today often overemphasize organized crime as an aspect of wildlife trafficking and underemphasize the corruption of government institutions and the wildlife industry in many wildlife-supply countries. Equally, inadequate attention is given to the involvement of local communities in poaching, and the intersections among these communities and global organized wildlife trafficking.

The most important characteristic of poaching and smuggling networks is their diversity. Some have become highly organized and vertically integrated. Other wildlife trafficking supplying global demand is organized but dispersed, with no kingpins or top-level traffickers. Other illegal wildlife trade involves the extensive participation of local communities. Sometimes, communities poach merely for their own subsistence, while they also may sell illegally obtained wildlife products to local, regional, and, via middlemen, global markets. Local communities who interact with organized global poaching networks may join them to generate greater revenue, or because they are physically unable to resist them. At other times, they may try to oppose them.

While recognizing these many variations, three basic types of interdependent actors can nonetheless be identified: consumers; suppliers; and middlemen. Each of them crucially structures the way that wildlife trade networks function. The dispersion or concentration of participants along these nodes; i.e., demand, supply, and transshipment, privileges different types of interdiction, alternative livelihoods, or community-based resource management approaches, as well as demand-reduction strategies (Felbab-Brown, 2017).

Consumers

Although China's consumers dominate the global wildlife market, demand for wild plants and animals is increasing throughout Southeast and East Asia, exacerbated by the region's growing population and its increasing affluence. What were previously mainly source and transshipment locales, such as Thailand and Vietnam, have rapidly become important consumer markets. East Asian diaspora communities, including in the United States, are also important consumers of wildlife products.

Demand for wildlife products is present and increasing in other parts of the world as well, including Latin America and Africa. Some of these types of demand, such as for bushmeat in Africa, are traditional and go back centuries or millennia. Even the long presence of these markets does not necessarily mean that they are sustainable. High population growth in some regions, such as West Africa, can lead to such an expansion of demand that it produces unsustainable rates of hunting. Other types of demand for wildlife, including in Africa and Latin America, are newer, emerging, and expanding as a result of the greater affluence and disposable income in those regions.

Suppliers

The primary motivating factor for poachers and traders is economic, ranging from small-scale subsistence needs for some, to major high-profit business for others. At the start of the smuggling chain, are the hunters of animals and collectors of plants and minerals. This group consists of both poor (often subsistence-level) hunters and professional hunters. Beyond need and greed, other motivations include the rejection of colonial or imposed international values, and a form of political rebellion against the imposition of norms that are seen as alien, discriminatory, and against the basic interests of the community (Bell et al., 2007; von Essen and Allen, 2015).

There is a more basic cause: hundreds of millions of people around the world are dependent on forest products for basic livelihoods. In India, for example, at least 50 million people living in and around forests depend on non-timber forest products (NTFPs) directly or indirectly for subsistence (Tejaswi, 2008). For some marginalized communities in Laos, Cambodia, and Myanmar (Burma), the dependence sometimes tops 70% of people's income.

Illegal wildlife trade can reshape traditional hunting and other forms of forest exploitation. Not all indigenous communities nowadays hunt purely for food, but increasingly for global poaching networks. Indeed, the increasingly commercialized trade in bushmeat is believed to be one of the main causes of unsustainable hunting (Bennett and Robinson, 2000).

Sometimes marginalized communities can be pushed into hunting as a negative side effect of other policies, without their necessarily having previously hunted on such a problematic scale. For example, the suppression of poppy cultivation and heroin production in Myanmar borderlands, along with expanding demand for wildlife products in China – drove some to switch to the illegal wildlife trade (Felbab-Brown, 2006).

Professional hunters and middlemen

The arrival of regional or international wildlife traders often triggers a community's participation in wildlife trafficking. With the arrival of middlemen who facilitate marketing, prices for wildlife increase. Middlemen also stimulate the diversification of poaching. Thus, illegal collection expands from orchids to insects, hunting from civets and bears to pangolins, and from langurs to salamanders, with an emptied forest left behind.

As hunting empties forests, wildlife scarcity makes trapping more time consuming and requires greater skills facilitated by sophisticated equipment. Thus, many less-skilled hunters drop out, and the remaining ones become professionalized (Christy, 2010). Highly skilled professional hunters are sought after by trafficking networks, who frequently facilitate their mobility within a country and at times even between countries. This second group of high-tech hunters also includes recreational hunters who violate hunting regulations. Both types are supported by local trackers, guides, and carriers.

Middlemen are also crucial nodes in the international dimensions of the illegal wildlife trade. In addition to being able to organize local poaching, they are connected to global markets and top-level traffickers. Both middlemen and top traffickers can also exploit and exacerbate

Combatting wildlife trafficking

corruption, such as among customs officials, and cultivate political patrons. Some cultivate political protection on the basis of preexisting patronage networks. Prominent political leaders exert pressure on park management and the courts to release apprehended poachers and traffickers.

At the apex of the smuggling chain are sometimes big traders who facilitate wildlife traffic across the globe. One notorious trafficker with a global reach is Wong Keng Liang, better known as Anson Wong. A Malaysian, Wong first established himself in the illegal (and legal) trade in reptiles, selling anything from legal geckos to illegal Komodo dragons, Chinese alligators, and Madagascar ploughshare tortoises, a critically endangered species with less than 100 remaining in the wild (Christy, 2010). Another wildlife kingpin, Sansar Chand, gained notoriety for allegedly organizing the large-scale poaching of India's tigers and sales of their products throughout Asia ("Sansar Chand," 2014). The Poon family from Hong Kong has traded in ivory and shark fins for generations (Hastie et al., 2002). Perhaps Asia's largest known wildlife trafficker has been the Laotian Vixay Keosavang, often dubbed the "Pablo Escobar of wildlife trafficking." Vixay's trading company, Xaysavang Trading, was implicated in the smuggling of ivory from Kenya and rhino horn from South Africa, and a myriad of other animals, including lizards, turtles, and snakes (Davies and Holmes, 2016). Many of these traffickers did not diversify into the wildlife trade from other illegal markets, such as drugs. Many started their criminal careers in wildlife.

That does not mean that contagion effects will not take place and that criminal groups do not learn from each other about business opportunities in other domains, such as wildlife trafficking. Such learning appears to have taken place already in the case of at least some Mexican criminal groups which now also seem to participate in totoaba bladder smuggling from the Gulf of California to China (Mejia Giraldo and Bargent, 2014).

Few drug or wildlife smuggling organizations are tight-knit, hierarchical networks with a big trader at the apex. In Myanmar, one of the world's poaching and smuggling hotspots, much poaching and smuggling is carried out by poor, low-level poachers and smugglers who sell poached animals in Mong La and Tachilek to both low-level traders and middlemen, and often directly to consumers. Similarly in Indonesia, many poachers in Kalimantan, Sulawesi, and Ambon are unorganized, low-level opportunists, not wildlife kingpins with a global reach. Rhino horn smuggling into Yemen, for decades one of the most important markets for the product, was also highly decentralized.

Indeed, the fact that the criminal boss or a particular criminal group rarely controls much of the illegal trade leads to erroneous policy assumptions: namely, that supposedly knock-out blows against key players are possible. Such recommendations vastly overestimate the extent to which such effects can be delivered and whether or not they have ever been effective in the drug trade, wildlife trade, or other illegal economies.

As with other illegal economies, profit mark-ups grow significantly the further downstream the smuggling chain the product has moved and the more law enforcement it has had to overcome. Such mark-ups are not small even within a country. While a poor hunter in Tam Dao National Park, Vietnam, can earn perhaps a few hundred dollars a year, an owner of a restaurant in Tam Dao will be able to make US$1,000 to US$1,500 selling wildlife meat to tourists, while a medium-sized trader in Vinh Yen will earn more than US$15,000 a year (World Bank, 2005). In Hanoi, the trader's income will be greater yet. In Kenya, a kilogram of rhino horn may fetch US$9,000, while in China it will bring upward of US$70,000 ("South African Group," 2016).

Other actors and stakeholders

As with drugs, timber, and gems, "laundering" within the wildlife trade is not only of profits, but also of actual animals and plants. Since captive-bred animals are exempted from CITES prohibitions on trade, breeding farms are used to launder poached animals. Public and private zoos also provide good cover for smugglers since a zoo can claim to have a breeding program for endangered animals, and thus explain the arrival of new animals. The laundering of animals and falsification of certificates have plagued controls on the ivory trade in China, Hong Kong, Japan, and Thailand, where supply, trade, and retail sales are legally permitted to a degree (Stiles, 2009). Such laundering problems also occur with tiger products in China, where sellers claim that their tiger products come from animals raised on tiger farms, not from poached animals in India and Indonesia (Yang, 2010).

Beyond zoos, corrupt wildlife industry officials tasked with issuing licenses and setting hunting quotas, corrupt veterinarians, or taxidermists who can fake a rhino horn trophy to mask illegal hunting for Asian markets are important players in the illegal trade.

Ecolodges, private reserves and parks, and trophy-hunting outfits play critical roles not just in influencing whether the legal wildlife economy can generate enough income to suppress the temptation to poach, but also in disrupting or enabling actual poaching.

Other stakeholders in the regulation of wildlife trade and conservation – who are thereby at least indirectly stakeholders in the development and implementation of responses to poaching and wildlife trafficking – include logging companies, agribusinesses, the fishing industry, local police and enforcement forces, private security forces, and governments.

Local rangers, police, and wildlife law-enforcement officers frequently obtain only small salaries, little prestige, and limited chance of promotion by enforcing regulations against those involved in the wildlife trade. The pressures of corruption that they, as well as top government officials, face are high.

Other private actors are increasingly hired to supplement wildlife law-enforcement authorities, such as private security companies, former soldiers, foreign trainers, intelligence units, technical operators, and anti-poaching militias. Standing militaries, both domestic and foreign, can also be mobilized to supplement wildlife law-enforcement forces, such as in Nepal or in various parts of Africa. They can provide vital anti-poaching or trafficking resistance. However, they have also been implicated in severe human rights abuses (Cavanagh et al., 2015; Devine, 2014; Massé and Lunstrum, 2016).

The policy debates

The struggles over elephant poaching and ivory policy and over trophy hunting are emblematic of a larger policy search for how to mitigate unsustainable hunting, design anti-poaching policies, and suppress wildlife trafficking.

Given the precipitous and irretrievable collapse of species, there is desperation in the conservation community to find policy silver bullets. As detailed in *The Extinction Market* (Felbab-Brown, 2017), the conservation community is increasingly looking at the successes and failures of decades of global drug policies, whether by demanding stronger and more resourced interdiction and law enforcement approaches or arguing that banning wildlife trade is bound to fail, such as drug prohibition has failed. The debates remain highly polarized in wildlife field – as well as the drug field.

Many environmental NGOs advocate strict bans and call for tougher law enforcement – indeed, this is the policy flavor *du jour* ("Bloody Ivory," 2012; Duffy, 2013; "Inconvenient but

True," 2007; Seguya et al., 2016; "Stop Stimulating," 2013; Stiles, 2004; Thorson & Wold, 2010). For some of them, no legal trade in wildlife, particularly if it involves killing wild animals, should be allowed. Others only oppose legal trade under specific circumstances and for specific wildlife commodities, such as rhino horn and ivory sales. Some conservation biologists support the calls for far tougher law enforcement. Law enforcement authorities often also support bans, not merely because that serves their budgets (as is sometimes alleged by opponents of bans), but because the existence of a legal trade alongside an illegal one significantly complicates the law enforcement task of having to sort through what is legal and what is not, and because the legal trade provides loopholes for the illegal one to exploit.

Total bans on legal wildlife trade and hunting are often pervaded by unrealistic expectations of how effective interdiction and law enforcement policies can be. Such approaches often also underestimate how easy it is to coerce willing participants in wildlife poaching, including poor marginalized local communities dependent on natural resource extraction, to abstain from hunting and embrace conservation.

Characterizations of today's poaching and wildlife trafficking often de-emphasize the role of poor communities and focus predominantly on organized criminal and militant groups. These views are usually accompanied by demands for much tougher legislation and penalties. These characterizations, however, are deeply flawed and easily can lead to counterproductive policies. Take, for example, the community-based nature conservancies in Kenya's Laikipia region (Gettleman, 2017) that have long been heralded as some of Africa's greatest conservation successes. The recent land invasions of these nature reserves by pastoralists unable to obtain fodder for their cattle elsewhere are demonstrating once again that poverty, scarcity, drought, and global warming are pitting some communities' preferences against conservation. Notions long held throughout Africa that wildlife conservation is a white-man's imposition on black Africans are being revived again (Carruthers, 1995; MacKenzie, 1988; Neumann, 2004; Ranger, 1999). Such sentiments are echoed throughout Asia and the Americas, where local populations often feel brutalized by conservation policies (Adams, 2004; Burnham, 2000).

Many conservation biologists and conservation economists thus oppose bans and support market-based mechanisms to promote conservation. They point out that bans have often failed and that governments, businesses, and local communities need to be given material stakes in conservation or it will fail and species will be lost. Their adage is: wildlife stays if wildlife pays (Bulte & Damania, 2005; Moyle, 2003; Rabinovich, 2005; Seguya et al., 2016; Wright et al., 2001).

Indeed, under some circumstances, permitting legal trade proved a highly effective conservation tool for a while. Even the recovery of the white rhino throughout the 1990s in southern Africa was crucially underpinned by such market mechanisms (Hutton & Webb, 2003; Jenkins et al., 2006; Leader-Williams, 2003; 't Sas-Rolfes, 2000; 't Sas-Rolfes, 2012).

Allowing legal trade has not always produced such desirable conservation outcomes. A legal trade can, and often does, allow for the laundering of poached animals, such as in the case of ivory in Thailand where ivory trade from domestic elephants is allowed, or through reptile breeding facilities in Indonesia. Moreover, permitting legal trade may also boost overall demand, including demand for poached animals and their products.

Many so-called critical conservationists may also oppose global bans, rejecting that outsiders, such as international institutions or influential global NGOs, should make policies without adequate input from local communities. In particular, however, the critical conservationists are opposed to conservation policies that hurt poor marginalized populations (Adams & Hulme, 2001; Brockington et al, 2005; Moseley, 2001; Koziell, 2001; Roe, 2011; Roe et al., 2009; Swiderska, 2003; Western & Wright, 1994). Thus, they reject law-enforcement-heavy policies and emphasize the historic injustice of colonial conservation policies that forcefully evicted native populations around the world. They lament what they see as the disproportionate and unfair power of international environmental NGOs who argue for bans and the establishment of protected areas which local communities are prohibited to access for resources while many local communities want to hunt, including for commercial reasons. They allege that environmental conservationism is swinging back to the inappropriate discriminatory exclusion, marginalization, and force-based approaches from which it sought to depart in the 1990s (Dressler et al., 2010). Not all critical conservationists endorse market-based mechanisms; i.e., legal trade, as an effective policy tools. Those of neo-Marxist or post-modernist persuasion see the market – as well as law enforcement – as another means of dispossession of local communities (Duffy, 2014; Kelly & Ybarra, 2016; Loperena, 2016; Lunstrum, 2014; Peluso & Vandergeest, 2011; Peluso & Lund, 2011). Most critical conservationists, however – as well as some conservation biologists – call for "community based natural resource management" (CBNRM) approaches that give local communities the rights to local land and its wildlife and empower them to make their own decisions over local resources.

These policy disputes are not only debates among different philosophies and ideologies or along North-South divisions. Different constituencies within a country – whether it is a supply, transshipment, or demand country – support and advocate different policies. Moreover, within the countries in the same part of the production and trade chain, there are differences. Kenya and South Africa are both supply countries for wildlife trafficking and both are experiencing massive poaching rates. They share colonial legacies of environmental conservation often rejected by local populations. Kenya, however, opposes legal trade in ivory and in 1977 banned all hunting in the country, making close to no exceptions, even for subsistence hunting and hunting as a mechanism of community-based natural resource management. South Africa, on the other hand, has repeatedly lobbied for allowing the sales of its ivory and rhino stocks and has made economic incentives for conservation, including trophy hunting and trade in wildlife, a key hallmark of its conservation policies.

In the wildlife trade and conservation domain, the debates are over means. Are bans and enforcement, or the market and legal trade, the best mechanism to assure species survival and biodiversity? Is the state or are local communities the most effective locus of decision-making over environmental policy?

These debates are also about values. For some environmental NGOs, killing animals is unacceptable. Many advocates of local communities hurt by conservation policies, however, point out that this sentiment puts animals ahead of people. Proponents of CBNRM efforts often argue that environmental conservation should not stand in contradiction to efforts to empower local communities and promote their economic development, and in fact that empowering local communities is the best mechanism of advancing environmental conservation.

Sometimes that is the case, but at other times, a local community, just like the state and industries, may not have an interest in conservation. Local people and indigenous communities may want to make money as quickly as possible by participating in logging, conversion of forests into agriculture, or poaching and wildlife trafficking. Maximalist versions of CBNRM hold that even in these circumstances, an affected local community should not be merely one of the environmental policy stakeholders, but in fact *the* authority to decide how local natural resources are managed. Only in this way can it be assured that community security, well-being, and rights are not ignored by the preferences of globalist conservationists.

It is thus not just that different participants in poaching and trafficking and different stakeholders in the conservation communities have different values and interests. Values and

Combatting wildlife trafficking

interests among the same type of actor vary tremendously and can change over time. These different interests and values thus shape policy objectives and assessments of successes or failures.

Policy outcomes

The systematic policy outcomes of the various policy tools are discouraging. All strategies face structural and resource constraints, whether they be bans and interdiction, legalization and licensing, community-based natural resource management, demand reduction, or anti-money-laundering efforts. In addition to these limitations, the strategies also come with direct downsides. All have produced highly varied and inconsistent outcomes, confounding the search for the "right" policy.

Bans and law enforcement

Bans and intensified law enforcement can help in particular circumstances, depending on local cultural and institutional settings and the ecological requirements of the particular species. Wildlife policy enforcement efforts, whether enforcing bans or making sure that poached animals are not laundered through legal wildlife farms and the legal wildlife trade, are often inadequate. They are severely under-resourced and given low priority. A significant increase in the diligence and resources dedicated to the enforcement of wildlife regulations is certainly warranted. There are, however, limitations on how much even greatly intensified law enforcement can halt poaching and wildlife trafficking, create deterrence effects, and suppress supply in the absence of a dramatic reduction in demand.

The objectives of prohibition and interdiction are to prevent or at least restrict illegal supply and discourage use by creating barriers to entry for both sellers and buyers, boosting prices, limiting commercialization, and creating a normative set of values against threats to vulnerable wildlife ecologies. Just because not every user and supplier is deterred by illegality does not mean that removing illegality will avoid increasing supply and consumption. Nonetheless, if consumption is driven by a desire to display status, power, and wealth, such as by wearing ivory bangles or coats made from endangered species, a ban that discourages such ostentatious display may well shrink demand and be highly valuable. Demand-suppression dynamics would be very different if illegal bushmeat were consumed not as an exotic luxury indulgence, but for subsistence. In the latter case, without alternative protein sources being made available, demand may not go down at all. Thus, demand-suppression approaches need to be tailored in a granular way to particular wildlife products and demand markets and sometimes adapted over time.

Implementing interdiction effectively is hard and very resource intensive. Effective interdiction designed not just to incapacitate poachers and traffickers but also to deter them requires knowing specific structures of particular wildlife smuggling networks. Analyses, though, at times exaggerate the extent to which poaching is undertaken by organized criminals and militant groups. While the latter may be involved, such cases often represent only a sliver of poaching activity. In fact, there is a large degree of variation in the structures of poaching and trafficking networks, and there are many atomized small-level traders and poor poachers also in the business. Exaggerated and simplistic characterizations also divert policy attention away from corrupt practices among legal actors, including licensing entities, ecolodges, and top environmental officials.

Poaching and trafficking networks are often far less vertically integrated than many interdiction advocates imagine. Moreover, even top traffickers and entire wildlife trafficking networks are easily replaceable as long as demand stays robust. Nonetheless, knowing what the poaching and smuggling structures actually look like in a particular place, rather than imagining what they might be, is crucial for making law enforcement and other policy interventions effective in that locality.

As laid out in extensive detail in *The Extinction Market*, there are many relevant lessons from the illegal drug trade and efforts to counter it (Felbab-Brown, 2017). Two decades of the author's interviews and policy exchanges with law enforcement officials show, that even with a very large dedication of resources, rarely does drug interdiction surpass a 50% effectiveness rate, often remaining much lower. Such interdiction levels may be insufficient to prevent the collapse of particular species. What crucially facilitates the effectiveness of interdiction, law enforcement, and bans is a reduction in the demand for a commodity – whether as the result of a ban, purposeful demand reduction strategies, or exogenous factors. Paradoxically, the more effective law enforcement becomes, the more the value of a smuggled animal or wildlife product goes up. Perceived scarcity – whether as a result of species depletion or more effective law enforcement – increases the financial benefits of smuggling.

Drug traffickers expect large losses due to eradication of illegal crops and interdiction of smuggled drugs and often welcome them, for law enforcement boosts prices and makes stockpiles more profitable. At least some wildlife traffickers make similar calculations; traffickers of rare parrots from Indonesia, for example, fully expected a 90–95% mortality of the parrots they illegally collected as a result of their smuggling method. They stuffed the parrots into plastic bottles, threw them into the sea to retrieve them on open water later in order to avoid law enforcement (Felbab-Brown, 2013). The fact that less than 10% of the parrots survived was not a deterrent, as profits on the remaining specimens were more than sufficient. In fact, prices can be boosted by scarcity so much that absorbing huge losses and driving a species to extinction is highly profitable and attractive for traffickers. The rarer the species, the greater its value. As discussed earlier in the chapter, paradoxically, such "effective" interdiction that drives greater poaching in order to supply a stable market, or an even more pernicious rarity market where demand increases with rarity and price, can have devastating effects on species. Such seemingly effective interdiction is, in fact, not at all effective and outright counterproductive.

Legal trade and licensing

Allowing a legal supply of animals, plants, and wildlife products is equally fraught with dilemmas and imperfect outcomes. The arguments for legalizing drugs are substantially different from arguments for permitting legal trade in wildlife products. Critics of the war on drugs argue that since drugs cannot be eliminated from the world, criminalizing drugs overburdens law-enforcement and justice systems, empowers criminal groups, severely undermines human rights, compromises public health, and undermines anti-militancy efforts. Legalization advocates promise that legalization will bring resources to the state in the form of taxes and license fees, and that it will undo the above stated negative effects. Yet many critics of drug prohibition dispute whether drug legalization will in fact undo all of the negative effects, and they do not necessarily support outright legalization, preferring decriminalization and differently designed enforcement measures instead. The extent to which legalization will increase problematic use and addiction is also disputed.

The regulatory arguments for permitting legal wildlife trade are fundamentally different. First, farming or ranching of protected species can take pressure off wild resources. Second, allowing some level of trade can give hunters, ranchers, and others close to traded wildlife resources a stake in preserving species and entire ecosystems, and managing them sustainably. Third, regulated trade can also raise money for conservation.

Just as with bans, the effectiveness of licensing, eco-labeling, and creating a legal supply of wildlife depends crucially on the capacity of law-enforcement bodies effectively to monitor and enforce the regulations and restrictions concerning legal trade in all the countries involved in it; additionally, it depends on consumers preferring legally and sustainably produced items, and on their having the capacity to distinguish genuine from fake labels.

As with bans, many of the presumed or hoped for positive outcomes of legal trade do not always materialize fully in reality. A legal supply does not guarantee sustainability, nor does it necessarily take pressure off the wild supply. If a legal supply is expensive (because of heavy taxes to discourage demand) and difficult to produce (because breeding animals in captivity is hard), then poaching will likely persist. Captive-breeding and licensing schemes often do not prevent the leakage of illegally caught wildlife into the supposedly legal supply chain. Frequently, neither customers nor law-enforcement officials have the capacity or motivation to determine whether a wildlife product was obtained from the wild, from a captive-breeding facility, or from a legal supplier. Permitting a legal supply greatly increases the burden for law-enforcement bodies to differentiate between illegally and legally sourced products. However, while total bans on wildlife trade do away with the need for law-enforcement officials to distinguish between the legal and the illegal, they do not necessarily reduce the overall resource requirements. Legal supply can also reduce moral opprobrium surrounding the trade in particular species, thus inadvertently boosting demand for illegally sourced wildlife and white-washing consumer consciousness.

Moreover, the wildlife revenues from a legal supply – such as breeding facilities or trophy hunting – do not necessarily go to local stakeholders and communities. Other actors, including local or national elites, large eco-businesses, or distant breeding facilities can capture them through corruption, problematic regulatory redesign, or natural market dynamics. Local stakeholders may not benefit from conservation as a result.

Despite current characterizations of poaching networks as highly organized criminal enterprises, many poachers are members of marginalized and desperately poor local communities. Sometimes their poaching activities are fully separate from wildlife trafficking. At other times, these local poachers supply global trafficking networks or work for them as hunters, carriers, trackers, and spotters, as corrupt park rangers also sometimes do. Focusing on finding legal livelihoods for them can be an important component of policies to reduce the illegal trade in wildlife and incentivize communities to resist wildlife trafficking. Although creating economic incentives for communities to support conservation does not address the problem of wildlife smugglers and organized criminal groups, it can simplify and focus law-enforcement efforts. It can encourage community co-operation with law-enforcement bodies, enhance the political sustainability of restrictions on wildlife trade, and reduce political conflict.

Involving local communities: alternative livelihoods and CBNRM

Generating economic incentives for the poor to support conservation policies is also important normatively because the marginalized communities dependent on hunting for basic livelihoods have often suffered greatly as a result of environmental conservation. They have been forced off their land in areas designated as protected, and their livelihoods and human security have been compromised. Laws and regulations are easiest to enforce when the vast majority of people accept them as legitimate and internalize them. The devolution of decision-making power to those who have been poor, marginalized, and without rights may be not only politically and economically beneficial, it can also be psychologically rewarding and enabling.

As shown in great detail in *The Extinction Market*, many alternative livelihood schemes have not been effective (Felbab-Brown, 2017). While frequently prescribed as the mechanism for conservation, ecotourism has unfortunately failed to be a consistent remedy against poaching and wildlife trafficking or a reliable tool of economic growth. It rarely generates sufficient income and jobs as a result of both its own internal limitations and resource capture by elites. Thus, the crucial objective that communities at least earn enough to maintain prior subsistence levels, let alone achieve economic and social advancement, from ecotourism, other alternative livelihoods, or the limited hunting of wildlife, is often elusive.

On the Indonesian island of Seram, for example, twenty poachers of rare parrots were converted (through the work of Profauna, one of Indonesia's NGOs most determined to fight against the illegal wildlife trade) into rescue-center staff and wildlife guides for tourists. As a result of this alternative livelihoods effort, poaching dramatically declined. Success depended on a steady flow of eco-tourists whom the newly converted poachers could guide. For that, an international counterpart to the conservation effort helped recruit US birdwatchers to travel to Seram. When that international supply of eco-tourists fell off, the income from wildlife-guiding for the former poachers shrank and the pressure to resume illegal hunting to generate livelihoods intensified once more (Felbab-Brown, 2013).

The Seram story is a micro-example of the conditions on which successful alternative livelihoods depend. If poor poachers have an assured income from other sources, they are often willing to abandon illegal hunting, even though poaching often brings more money. Income from other sources needs to be steady and assured. The problem with many ecotourism alternative livelihoods efforts is that the income fluctuates greatly and tends to be sporadic and seasonal.

Often, for an area to draw a sufficient number of ecotourists to generate income, it needs to contain large mammals that can be seen fairly easily by tourists. Thus, eastern Africa's savannahs tend to attract many more tourists than rainforest areas. Even there, income from ecotourism can be highly seasonal and lodges either have to build up financial reserves to pay the staff during the low season or else, as is frequently done, fire staff during a part of the year, thus incurring the wrath of the community.[2] In addition to having relatively easily-visible animals, for ecotourism to generate sufficient revenues, parks need to have good infrastructure, such as airports, roads, and lodges, as well as good security. Banditry or presence of militant groups scare off tourists, as do other external shocks as such political instability in the country or economic downturns in tourists' home countries.

Moreover, the number of jobs available through ecotourism may be significantly lower than the potential pool of people who may be recruited as poachers. Even if all existing poachers get legal jobs, are there other poor people who may be recruited as poachers in the area or can move into the area, particularly, if the compensation for poaching rises?

There is a large variation of outcomes concerning the effectiveness of alternative livelihoods and local community involvement in managing habitats and wildlife, some of which reveal the detrimental effects of allowing or not allowing local communities to exist in national parks. Many factors can affect these outcomes, including a community's short-term versus long-term economic horizons, income and employment levels, their attitudes toward nature, community cohesion and leadership structures, and the enforcement of property rights. Alternative livelihoods that address all of the structural drivers of illicit economies have the highest chance of being effective.

CBNRM schemes often go beyond alternative livelihoods, ecotourism, compensation, or limited hunting. They seek to transfer rights to local communities and achieve three objectives: political empowerment; poverty alleviation; and environmental protection. They can be based around trophy hunting, ecotourism, or other alternative livelihoods. Sometimes they have worked spectacularly well, but the outcomes have not been uniform. Beyond good implementation, successes are dependent on a steady and large flow of tourists, trophy hunters, and customers, and sufficiently low densities of people compared to wildlife. In general, they have worked better in arid areas where agriculture is not profitable but where iconic wildlife species are present, rather than fertile areas where converting land to agriculture is profitable or tropical forests where animals are difficult to see and where industrial logging brings far greater revenues than ecotourism. In some cases, communities became richer as a result of CBRNM policies, but then intensified unsustainable hunting and logging to further augment their economic resources at the expense of environmental conservation.

In short, there are no silver bullets, nor even universally appropriate ameliorants. Policy outcomes are highly context specific and contingent. All strategies face structural and resource constraints. In addition to these limitations, the strategies also come with direct downsides. Bans on hunting and local resource extraction can reduce sources of income and lower the standard of livelihood among poor local populations. The imposed relocation of communities and other coercive measures can generate deep resentment and a rejection of conservation, as has often happened in Africa, Asia, and Latin America. Licensing legal trade, however, significantly complicates law enforcement and facilitates traffickers' strategies of evasion.

Bans or licensing can help in particular circumstances, depending on local cultural and institutional settings and the ecological requirements and circumstances of particular species. There are, however, limitations on how much even greatly intensified law enforcement can halt poaching and wildlife trafficking, create deterrence effects, and suppress supply in the absence of a dramatic reduction in demand. Licensing and regulating the hunting and wildlife trade only works under some circumstances. Sometimes it gives various participants a stake in conservation that would otherwise be absent, serving to protect not just a species but also its habitat and the broader ecosystem. At other times, a legal supply of a vulnerable species boosts overall demand, including for poached animals, complicates enforcement, and enables the laundering of illegally sourced products. CBNRM can significantly motivate local communities to support conservation and resist poaching and trafficking, but just as with other tools, the outcomes have varied widely. Going after consumer demand is crucial, but demand-reduction measures are complex and take time. Anti-money-laundering (AML) efforts provide an additional tool, but they will not bankrupt the illegal wildlife trade.

Conclusions

Poaching and wildlife trafficking patterns are highly diverse. In their core characteristics – increasing demand and consumers, poor suppliers (poachers) and layers of middlemen and top traffickers, corrupt government officials, and sometimes organized crime groups – the trafficking networks share much with the illegal drug trade. Just like in the illegal drug trade, there is much diversity in organizational patterns of actual poaching and trafficking.

Also like the drug trade, appropriate policies to counter poaching and wildlife trafficking are vigorously contested. Two of the three key conservation schools of thought described in this chapter have strong analogies in the drug policy debates. The policies advocated by the various schools of thought reflect different values and norms. They also highlight the large diversity of interests among participants in poaching and wildlife trafficking and the conservation policy community. Some of those values and order of preferences closely parallel the illegal drug trade. Many poor poachers, like many poor cultivators of drug crops, will say that whatever harm their activity generates pales in comparison to their need to feed starving families, especially if alternative livelihoods are absent or failing, which is all too often the case in both the illegal drug and wildlife trade.

There are, however, two fundamental differences between these illegal economies. Illicit drugs are a nondepletable resource – they can be produced over and over. Wildlife is rapidly depletable. Once a species is gone, it cannot be brought back; the loss of a set of species within an ecosystem can irreparably unravel the entire ecosystem. Thus, the timelines in countering poaching and wildlife trafficking are far tighter – on the order of a few years – than in the case of the illegal drug trade.

A second big difference is the scale of destruction and harm that poaching and wildlife trafficking pose globally. When they unleash zoonotic pandemics, they bring death rates and global economic contractions that even the most severe illicit drug epidemics, such as the current US opioid epidemic (Felbab-Brown, 2020), cannot match. The magnitude of death and impoverishment is higher than that in the illicit drug trade.

Devising effective policies for countering poaching and wildlife trafficking is compounded by another factor, perhaps the most important policy takeaway – namely, that we must expect huge variation in policy outcomes. The same holds true for drug policy. What works well for a species in one locale may not work well for the very same species in a neighboring locale. What works well in suppressing demand at a given time may not work ten years later. How much a legal or illegal market can be shaped or reduced through supply-and-demand measures depends on their elasticities, which can change over time, as well as a host of other factors, such as local institutional and cultural settings. Policy thus should allow for experimentation.

For a detailed set of policy recommendations of how to counter poaching and wildlife trafficking and locale specificity considerations, see chapter 11 in Vanda Felbab-Brown's *The Extinction Market*. For a discussion of how to address those issues as well as smarten up the legal trade in wildlife to prevent zoonotic pandemics, see Vanda Felbab-Brown "Preventing Zoonotic Pandemics through Biodiversity Conservation and Smart Wildlife Trade Regulations" (Felbab-Brown, "Preventing Zoonotic," 2021).

Notes

1 United Nations Office on Drugs and Crime (UNODC) puts the number of elephants poached during that period at 92,000.
2 Author's interviews with lodge owners, Tsavo National Park and Masai Mara, Kenya, May 2013 and Serengeti National Park and Ngorongoro Conservation Area, Tanzania, summer 2003.

References

Adams, W. and Hulme, D. (2001). Conservation and communities: Changing narratives, policies and practices in African conservation. In Hulme, D. and Murphree, M. (Eds.), *African Wildlife and African Livelihoods: The Promise and Performance of Community Conservation* (pp. 9–23). Oxford: James Currey.

Adams, W. (2004). *Against Extinction: A Story of Conservation*. London: Earthscan.

Amin, R., Thomas, K., Emslie, R. H., Foose, T. J. and Van Strien, N. (2006, July). An overview of the conservation status of and threats to rhinoceros species in the wild. *International Zoo Yearbook*, 40(1): 96–117.

Barnett, R. (Ed.). (2000). *Food for thought: Utilization of wild meat in Eastern and Southern Africa*. Nairobi: TRAFFIC East/Southern Africa. Retrieved from www.traffic.org/general-reports/traffic_pub_gen7.pdf

Bell, S. et al. (2007). The political culture of poaching: a case study from Northern Greece. *Biodiversity and Conservation*, 16(2): 399–418.

Combatting wildlife trafficking

Bennett, E. and Robinson, J. (eds.) (2000). *Hunting for Sustainability in Tropical Rainforests*. New York: Columbia University Press.

Bloody ivory: Stop elephant poaching and ivory trade. (2012, December 12). *The Born Free Foundation*.

Brockington, D., Igoe, J. and Schmidt-Soltau, K. (2005, June). Conservation, human rights, and poverty reduction. *Conservation Biology*, 20(1): 250–252.

Bulte, E. and Damania, R. (2005, August). An economic assessment of wildlife farming and conservation. *Conservation Biology*, 19(4): 1222–1233.

Burnham, P. (2000). *Indian Country God's Country: Native Americans and National Parks*. Washington, DC: Island Press.

Carruthers, J. (1995). *The Kruger National Park: A Social and Political* History. Pietermaritzburg: Natal University Press.

Cavanagh, C. et al. (2015). Securitizing REDD+: Problematizing the emerging illegal timber trade and forest carbon interface in East Africa. *Geoforum*, 60: 72–82.

Christy, B. (2010). Asia's wildlife trade. *National Geographic*, 217(1), Retrieved from http://ngm.nationalgeographic.com/2010/01/asian-wildlife/christy-text

Christy, B. (2010). *The Lizard King*. Guilford, CT: Lyons Press.

COVID-19 to add as many as 150 million extreme poor by 2021. (2020, October 7). *The World Bank*. Retrieved from https://www.worldbank.org/en/news/press-release/2020/10/07/covid-19-to-add-as-many-as-150-million-extreme-poor-by-2021

Davies, N. and Holmes, O. (2016, September 26). The crime family at the centre of Asia's animal trafficking network. *Guardian*. Retrieved from www.theguardian.com/environment/2016/sep/26/bach-brothers-elephant-ivory-asias-animal-trafficking-network

Devine, J. (2014). Counterinsurgency ecotourism in Guatemala's Maya biosphere reserve. *Environment and Planning D: Society and Space*, 32(6): 981–1001.

Dressler, W. et al. (2010, March). From hope to crisis and back again? *Environmental Conservation*, 37(1): 5–15.

Duffy, R. (2013). Global environmental governance and North-South dynamics: The case of CITES. *Environment and Planning C: Government and Policy*, 31(2): 222–239.

Duffy, R. (2014, July). Waging a war to save biodiversity: The rise of militarized conservation. *International Affairs*, 90(4): 819–834.

Editorial Board. Wildlife slaughter goes unabated. (2015, February 15). *The New York Times*.

Felbab-Brown, V. (2006, March 20). Asia's role in the illicit trade of wildlife. *Boston Globe*.

Felbab-Brown, V. (2013, March). Indonesia field report IV: The last twitch? Wildlife trafficking, illegal fishing, and lessons from anti-piracy efforts. *The Brookings Institution*. Retrieved from http://www.brookings.edu/research/reports/2013/03/25-indonesia-wildlife-trafficking-felbabbrown

Felbab-Brown, V. (2017). *The Extinction market: Wildlife trafficking and how to counter it*. Oxford: Hurst and Oxford University Press.

Felbab-Brown, V. et al. (2020, June 22). Overview: The US Opioid Crisis in America. The Brookings Institution. Retrieved from https://www.brookings.edu/multi-chapter-report/the-opioid-crisis-in-america-domestic-and-international-dimensions/

Felbab-Brown, V. (2020, July). Fentanyl and geopolitics: Controlling opioid supply from China. *The Brookings Institution*. Retrieved from https://www.brookings.edu/research/fentanyl-and-geopolitics-controlling-opioid-supply-from-china/

Felbab-Brown, V. (2021, January). Preventing zoonotic pandemics through biodiversity conservation and smart wildlife trade regulations. *The Brookings Institution*. Retrieved from https://www.brookings.edu/research/preventing-pandemics-through-biodiversity-conservation-and-smart-wildlife-trade-regulation/

Felbab-Brown, V. (2021, January 15). Key trends to watch this year on nonstate armed actors. *The Brookings Institution*. Retrieved from https://www.brookings.edu/blog/order-from-chaos/2021/01/15/the-key-trends-to-watch-this-year-on-nonstate-armed-actors/

Felbab-Brown, V. (2021, February 1) Coronavirus world map: Tracking the global outbreak. *The New York Times*. Retrieved from https://www.nytimes.com/interactive/2021/world/covid-cases.html

Gettleman, J. (2017, July 29). Vanishing land fuels 'looming crisis' across Africa. *The New York Times*. Retrieved from https://www.nytimes.com/2017/07/29/world/africa/africa-climate-change-kenya-land-disputes.html

Global tiger recovery program 2010–2012. (2012). *The World Bank*. Retrieved from http://globaltigerinitiative.org/news-blog/by-tag/global-tiger-recovery-program/

Going, going, gone … The Illegal trade in wildlife in East and Southeast Asia. (2005). *World Bank*. Retrieved from http://www-wds.worldbank.org/external/default/WDSContentServer/WDSP/IB/2005/09/08/000160016_20050908161459/Rendered/PDF/334670PAPER0Going1going1gone.pdf

Halter, R. (2013, October 6). Insatiable demand for African rhino horn spells extinction. *Huffington Post*. Retrieved from http://www.huffingtonpost.com/dr-reese-halter/insatiable-demand-for-afr_b_4055075.html

Hastie, J. et al. (2002). Back in business: Elephant poaching and the Ivory black markets of Asia. Environmental Investigation Agency. Retrieved from www.eia-international.org/wp-content/uploads/Back-in-Business-2002.pdf

Hutton, J. and Webb, G. (2003). Crocodiles: Legal trade snaps back. In Oldfield, S. (Ed.), *The Trade in Wildlife: Regulation for Conservation* (pp. 108–120). London: Earthscan.

Inconvenient but true: The unrelenting global trade in elephant ivory. (2007, June). *The Born Free Foundation*.

Jenkins, R. et al. (2006). Review of crocodile ranching programs. *Convention on International Trade in Endangered Species of Wild Fauna and Flora (CITES)*. Retrieved from https://cites.org/common/com/ac/22/EFS-AC22-Inf02.pdf

Jones, J. (2015). A picture of loneliness. *The Guardian*. May 12.

Karesh, W. et al. (2012). Ecology of zoonoses: Natural and unnatural histories. *The Lancet*, 380(9857): 1936–1945. https://reader.elsevier.com/reader/sd/pii/S014067361261678X?token=997036DAFECC2F62E28EBBDACAF5845E942F135AD358641C1CD5571113E3FAB48EB4F5C90C4D2E8DFCBB9D304195CD54

Kelly, A. and Ybarra, M. (2016). Introduction to the themed issue: 'Green security in protected areas.' *Geoforum*, 69: 171–175.

Koziell, I. (2001). Diversity, not adversity: Sustaining livelihoods with biodiversity. *International Institute for Environment and Development (IIED)*. Retrieved from http://pubs.iied.org/pdfs/7822IIED.pdf

Leach, M. et al. (February 2021). Post-pandemic transformations: How and why COVID-19 requires us to rethink development. *World Development*. 138.

Leader-Williams, N. (2003). Regulation and protection: Successes and failures in rhinoceros conservation. In Oldfield, S. (Ed.), *The Trade in Wildlife: Regulation for Conservation* (pp. 89–99). London: Earthscan.

Loperena, C. A. (2016). Conservation by radicalized dispossession: The making of an eco-destination on Honduras's North Coast. *Geoforum*, 69: 184–193.

Lunstrum, E. (2014, June). Green militarization: Anti-poaching efforts and the spatial contours of Kruger National Park. *Annals of the Association of American Geographers*, 104(4): 816–832.

MacKenzie, J. (1988). *Empire of Nature: Hunting Conservation and British Imperialism*. Manchester: Manchester University Press.

Massé, F. and Lunstrum, E. (2016). Accumulation by Securitization: Commercial Poaching, Neoliberal Conservation, and the Creation of New Wildlife Frontiers," *Geoforum*, 69: 227–237.

Mejia Giraldo, C. and Bargent, J. (2014, August 6). Are Mexican narcos moving into lucrative Fish bladder market? *InSightCrime*. Retrieved from www.insightcrime.org/news-briefs/mexico-narcos-fish-bladder-market

Milliken, T. and Shaw, J. (2012). The South Africa – Viet Nam rhino horn trade nexus: A deadly combination of institutional lapses, corrupt wildlife industry professionals and Asian crime syndicates. *TRAFFIC*. Retrieved from http://www.worldwildlife.org/publications/the-south-africa-viet-nam-rhino-horn-trade-nexus

Moseley, W. (2001, September). African evidence on relation of poverty, time preference, and the environment. *Ecological Economics*, 38(3): 317–326.

Moyle, B. (2003). Regulation, conservation, and incentives. In Oldfield, S. (Ed.), *The Trade in Wildlife: Regulation for Conservation* (pp. 41–51). London: Earthscan.

Neumann, R. (2004, September). Moral and discursive geographies in the war for biodiversity in Africa. *Political Geography*, 23(7): 813–837.

Nixon, R. (2015, February 11). Obama administration plans to aggressively target wildlife trafficking. *The New York Times*. Retrieved from http://www.nytimes.com/2015/02/12/us/politics/obama-administration-to-target-illegal-wildlife-trafficking.html?_r=0

Nowell, K. (2007). Asian big cat conservation and trade control in selected range states: Evaluating implementation and effectiveness of CITES recommendations. *Traffic*. Retrieved from www.felidae.org/KNOWELLPUBL/abc_report.pdf

Combatting wildlife trafficking

Nuwar, R. (2013, January 2). It's official: Vietnam's javan rhino is extinct. Which species is next? *Take Part*. Retrieved from http://www.takepart.com/article/2012/12/12/its-official-vietnams-javan-rhino-extinct-and-other-species-will-likely-follow

Orenstein, R. (2013). *Ivory, Horn, and Blood: Behind the Elephant and Rhinoceros Poaching Crisis*. New York: Firefly Books.

Peluso, N. L. and Vandergeest, P. (2011, March). Political ecologies of war and forests: Counterinsurgency and the making of national natures. *Annals of the Association of American Geographers*, 101(3): 587–608.

Peluso, N. L. and Lund, C. (2011, September). New frontiers of land control: Introduction. *Journal of Peasant Studies*, 38(4): 667–681.

Rabinovich, J. (2005). Parrots, precaution and project Ele: Management in the face of multiple uncertainties. In Cooney, R. and Dickson, B. (Eds.), *Biodiversity and the Precautionary Principle: Risk and Uncertainty in Conservation and Sustainable Use* (pp. 173–188). London: Earthscan.

Ranger, T. (1999). *Voices from the Rocks: Nature, Culture and History in the Matopos Hills of Zimbabwe*. Oxford: James Currey.

Rhino poaching 2010–2017. (2018). *Wildlife Protection Society of India*. Retrieved from http://www.wpsi-india.org/crime_maps/rhino_poaching.php

Roe, D., Nelson, F. and Sandbrook, C. (Eds.). (2009). Community management of natural resources in Africa. *International Institute for Environment and Development (IIED)*. Retrieved from http://pubs.iied.org/pdfs/17503IIED.pdf.

Roe, D. (2011). Community-based natural resource management: An overview and definitions. In Abensperg-Traun, M., Roe, D. and O'Criodain, C. (Eds.), *CITES and CBNRM: Proceedings of an International Symposium on the Relevance of CBNRM to the Conservation and Sustainable Use of CITES-listed Species in Exporting Countries*. Gland, Switzerland: International Union for Conservation of Nature. London, United Kingdom: International Institute for Environment and Development. Retrieved from http://pubs.iied.org/pdfs/14616IIED.pdf

Sansar Chand, notorious tiger poacher, dead. (2014, March 19). *Times of India*. Retrieved from www.timesofindia.indiatimes.com/city/jaipur/Sansar-Chand-notorious-tiger-poacher-dead/articleshow/32261903.cms

Seguya, A., Martin, R., Sekar, N., Hsiang, S., Di Minin, E. and MacMillan, D. (2016, October 1). Debate: Would a legal ivory trade save elephants or speed up the massacre? *The Guardian*. Retrieved from https://www.theguardian.com/environment/2016/oct/01/debate-can-legal-ivory-trade-save-elephants

South African group reports slight drop in rhino poaching. (2016, January 2). *Associated Press*. Retrieved from http://bigstory.ap.org/article/fadef7f9221c48908636ac0dc731e87f/south-african-group-reports-slight-drop-rhino-poaching

Stiles, D. (2004). The ivory trade and elephant conservation. *Environmental Conservation*, 31(4): 309–321.

Stiles, D. (2009). Elephant and Ivory Trade in Thailand. TRAFFIC, Petaling Jaya, Selangor, Malaysia. Retrieved from www.traffic.org/species-reports/traffic_species_mammals50.pdf

Stop stimulating demand! Let wildlife-trade bans work. (2013). *Environmental Investigation Agency (EIA)*.

Swiderska, K. (2003). Integrating local values in natural resource assessment: A review of assessment tools. *International Institute for Environment and Development (IIED)*. Retrieved from http://pubs.iied.org/pdfs/G01286.pdf.

Taylor, L., Lantham, S. and Woolhouse, M. (2001). Risk factors for human disease emergence. *Philosophical Transaction of the Royal Society*, B, 356(1411): 983–989. https://www.ncbi.nlm.nih.gov/pmc/articles/PMC1088493/pdf/TB010983.pdf

Tejaswi, P.B. (2008). Non-Timber forest products (NTFPs) for food and livelihood security: An Economic study of tribal economy in the Western Ghats of Karnataka, India. MSc thesis (Ghent: University of Ghent).

The elephants fight back. (2015, November 21). *The Economist*.

Thorson, E. and Wold, C. (2010, March 9). Back to basics: An analysis of the object and purposes of CITES and a blueprint for implementation. *International Environmental Law Project*. Retrieved from http://www.lclark.edu/live/files/4620www.awsassets.wwfcn.panda.org/downloads/wwf_state_of_wildlife_trade_report_2010_____1.pdf

't Sas-Rolfes, M. (2000). Assessing CITES: Four case studies. In Hutton, J. and Dikson, B. (Eds.), *Endangered Species: Threatened Convention: The Past, Present, and Future of CITES* (pp. 69–87). London: Earthscan.

't Sas-Rolfes, M. (2012, February). The rhino poaching crisis: A market analysis. Retrieved from http://www.rhinoresourcecenter.com/pdf_files/133/1331370813.pdf

United Nations Office on Drugs and Crime. (2020). *World Wildlife Crime Report: Trafficking in Protected Species*. Retrieved from https://www.unodc.org/documents/data-and-analysis/wildlife/2020/World_Wildlife_Report_2020_9July.pdf

von Essen, E. and Allen, M. (2015). Reconsidering illegal hunting as crime of dissent: Implication for justice and deliberative uptake. *Criminal Law and Philosophy*, 11(2): 213–228.

Wasser, S., Brown, L., Mailand, C., Mondol, S., Clark, W. and Laurie, C. (2015, June). Genetic assignment of large seizures of elephant ivory reveals Africa's major poaching hotspots. *Science*, 349(6243): 1–7.

Western, D. and Wright, M. (Eds.). (1994). *Natural Connections: Perspectives in Community-Based Conservation*. Washington, DC: Island Press.

Wittemyer, G., Daballen, D. and Douglas-Hamilton, I. (2011, August 18). Poaching policy: Rising ivory prices threaten elephants. *Nature*, 476: 282–283.

World wildlife crime report: Trafficking in protected species. (2016, May). *United Nations Office on Drugs and Crime*, 42–43. Retrieved from https://www.unodc.org/documents/data-and-analysis/wildlife/World_Wildlife_Crime_Report_2016_final.pdf

WPSI's tiger poaching statistics. (2021). *Wildlife Protection Society of India*. Retrieved from http://www.wpsi-india.org/statistics/index.php

Wright, T. F. et al. (2001). Nest poaching in neotropical parrots. *Conservation Biology*, 15(3): 710–720.

Yang, X. (2010, March 18). Tiger deaths raise alarms about Chinese zoos, *New York Times*. https://www.nytimes.com/2010/03/19/world/asia/19tigers.html

18

CIGARETTE SMUGGLING

Trends, taxes and big tobacco

Max Gallien

Introduction

From prison cells to the frontlines of wars, from black market barter currency to luxury product, few licit goods are as intimately associated with smuggling in the popular imagination as cigarettes. Tobacco products were one of the central goods smuggled by the legendary French highwayman and smuggler Louis Mandrin in the eighteenth century (Kwass, 2014), and have provided the modern-day Algerian jihadi leader Mokhtar Belmokhtar with the nickname 'Mr Marlboro' for the role that cigarette-smuggling played in funding his operations. Today, the smuggling of tobacco products is a global industry that spans all continents and can be found almost anywhere where borders separate states. Although estimations vary substantially, studies suggest that today over 11% of the global cigarette market is illicit, amounting to over 650 billion cigarettes per year, and making it one of the most smuggled licit goods on the globe (Joossens et al., 2010).

At first, this role of cigarettes in the global smuggling economy can appear somewhat surprising. Tobacco is not an illegal substance in most countries and legal trade routes exist alongside a highly capitalised industry with a substantial global trade infrastructure. Tobacco is not an essential commodity and its consumer market is smaller than that of gasoline, alcohol, or a huge variety of food products. Contrary to more criminalised narcotics such as cocaine or heroin or minerals such as gold or coltan, its monetary value relative to its size is limited, requiring the movement of larger quantities to secure a substantial profit. While it has frequently been claimed that high levels of taxes and tariffs are driving cigarette smuggling, illicit trade in regions with higher average tax rates such as Europe has been lower in recent years compared to regions with lower average rates such as sub-Saharan Africa. Consequently, tobacco products more broadly, and cigarettes in particular, provide an excellent case study of the drivers and dynamics of the smuggling of licit consumer goods in the modern global economy.

After providing a brief introduction to the varieties of cigarette smuggling and sketching global trends and routes, this chapter focuses on two aspects of cigarette smuggling that are particularly instructive in illuminating the smuggling of licit goods more broadly. First, it surveys discussions on the drivers of cigarette smuggling, highlighting that while analyses frequently have focused on prices, taxes and regulatory instruments, drivers are in fact more diverse, and taxes remain a highly effective policy tool in curbing the adverse health effects of

DOI: 10.4324/9781003043645-18

247

tobacco consumption (Chaloupka, Straif and Leon, 2011). Second, it examines the intersection between the global tobacco industry and tobacco smuggling networks, noting that the two are not as separate and adversarial as is frequently assumed, and how industry influence has shaped smuggling research and policy itself. The chapter concludes by highlighting key conclusions and relevant communalities with other smuggled goods discussed in this volume.

The global illicit cigarette trade

The global illicit trade in cigarettes can be sub-divided broadly into at least three categories. The first includes the illegal trade of genuine brand cigarettes such as Marlboro or Benson & Hedges. The second refers to the smuggling of counterfeits of these brand products, which are consequently not only illegal to be traded, but illegal at the point of production, where they are manufactured without the consent of the brand owner. The third category refers to so-called 'cheap whites' or 'illicit whites' – these are cigarettes that are manufactured legally in one country, but then smuggled into a market where they have no legal distribution, and typically are sold without paying tax.[1] The latter are frequently produced in large bulk for this particular purpose – here, free trade zones on the Arabian Peninsula have received increasing attention in recent years.

Cigarettes are the dominant, but not the only tobacco product that is smuggled. Of the total number of seizures of excisable goods globally by customs organisations in 2019, cigarettes made up 55%. Other products include chewing, dipping and waterpipe-tobacco (22%), and cigars and e-cigarettes (about 7%). It's interesting to note, however, that the smuggling of tobacco products, at least by this rather limited metric, dwarfs the smuggling of alcohol products, which made up the remaining 16% (World Customs Organisation, 2019).[2] While small-scale smuggling and bootlegging of limited quantities of cigarettes is familiar to many, they exist alongside a large-scale and wholesale trade of smuggled cigarettes. Consequently, many of these smuggling operations are not limited to one particular region or borderland, but operate in large international supply chains, and are closely interlinked both with the global infrastructure of the international trade system and its legal structures, featuring free trade zones and 'in transit' systems that allow for the suspension of taxes and duties while goods are passing through a defined customs area (FATF, 2012).

Consequently, cigarette smuggling today does not provide a simple global division between production, transit, and consumption regions – it is prevalent across regions, with illegal trade corridors and markets for different products overlapping and intersecting. While Latin America likely has the largest illicit market share as a percentage of retail sales, Asia and the Pacific's high total retail volume in all probability gives it by far the highest volume of illicit trade if measured in sticks of cigarettes (World Health Organization, no date). Broadly, it is worth noting that the illicit market share in low and middle income countries (12.1%) is estimated higher than in high income countries (9.8%), despite the typically higher price of legally traded cigarettes in the latter (Joossens et al., 2010).

This has been accompanied by a global shift in cigarette consumption more broadly. While the prevalence of smoking in Europe, North America, and high-income countries as a group has dropped substantially and consistently across the past four decades, this pattern is less clear in many developing countries. As a result of simultaneous demographic changes, the total number of smokers in much of the developing world has expanded. Africa's youth, in particular, appears overrepresented among new smokers (Ramanandraibe and Ouma, 2011; Blecher and Ross, 2013; Vellios, Ross and Perucic, 2018). With this, the health challenges of smoking have also shifted – it has been projected that by 2030, 6.8 million out of a global total of 8.3 million tobacco-related deaths will occur in low- and middle-income countries (Mathers and Loncar, 2006).

This points to two interconnected aspects about cigarette smuggling that are worth highlighting. The first is that – like other frequently smuggled goods such as cocaine or heroin – tobacco has substantive negative health effects on those who consume it. Consequently, governments have an incentive to impose additional restrictions on the sale of tobacco products in order to limit negative health outcomes or account for their strain on national health systems. At the same time, unlike various other drugs, there exists a sub-stantive, global and highly capitalised legal market for tobacco products. As the remainder of this chapter will highlight, those two aspects in combination have had a substantive impact on how cigarettes are sold, traded and smuggled, but, critically, also on how this smuggling has been studied, understood and reported.

Smuggling of licit goods: beyond price and taxes

As a good that is frequently smuggled despite the existence of legal channels for its production, trade and distribution, the search for the drivers of tobacco smuggling has typically begun with its price.[3] More specifically, the common assumption is that cigarette smuggling is primarily driven by arbitrage that is based on the evasion of taxes, tariffs and similar restrictions on legal trade. In this, many discussions about cigarette smuggling are representative of an extremely prevalent way of thinking about the smuggling of licit goods, especially in economics. Traditional discussions on the welfare effects of smuggling in economic theory (Bhagwati and Hansen, 1975; Martin and Panagariya, 1984; Norton, 1988) primarily treat the smuggling of licit goods as tariff evasion. The World Custom's Organisation's Illicit Trade Report lists to-bacco smuggling in a section entitled "Revenue" (World Customs Organisation, 2019).

The logic underlying this is simple and reflects the intuitive fact that price differences and arbitrage opportunities have a direct effect on the bottom lines of smugglers of licit goods, and a particularly substantive one in the case of highly taxed goods such as tobacco products. The latter aspect, furthermore, makes this relationship particularly sensitive for goods, such as ci-garettes, which carry substantive health effects. Taxes have been found to be the most effective policy tool to reduce overall smoking prevalence, reduce overall deaths caused by smoking, and raise funding to support health systems in combatting the health effects of smoking (Chaloupka, Straif and Leon, 2011). Consequently, if tax and hence price effects were the primary driver of cigarette smuggling, this would raise substantive questions about the overall welfare effects of taxing tobacco.

Fortunately, however, even a cursory look at the global picture of cigarette smuggling suggests that prices are likely substantially overstated as a driver of tobacco smuggling. While high-income countries in Europe and North America have substantially higher cigarette prices, which are largely driven by substantially higher taxes, their illicit cigarette market share is smaller on average than in lower- and middle-income countries. Africa provides a fitting il-lustration, as it features on average substantially lower cigarette prices and tax rates than Europe, but high levels of tobacco smuggling in various regions on the continent.[4]

In recent years, an increasing body of research has supported the view that prices, tax and tariff rates may certainly affect the calculations of smugglers but should not be looked to as the sole or even dominant driver of tobacco smuggling. A recent global report by the World Bank concludes that "contrary to tobacco industry arguments, taxes and prices have only a limited impact on the illicit cigarette market share at country level" (Dutta, 2019). Illustrative case studies can be found across the globe. South Africa, for example, started to employ a deliberate tobacco control policy in the 1990s, which included a large increase in excise taxes, raising the price of cigarettes. As a consequence, cigarette consumption per capita fell by more than 60% by the early 2000s (Walbeek and Shai, 2015). At the same time, however, the market share of smuggled cigarettes seems to have grown only marginally, despite the rapid increase in price (Blecher, 2010).

Crucially, it does not appear to have undermined substantially the desired revenue and health effects of these tax increases. Using a synthetic control method to estimate tobacco consumption trends in South Africa, a 2017 study directly traces the substantial decrease in smoking to tax measures (Chelwa, Walbeek and Blecher, 2017). Even as the relative market share of smuggled cigarettes increased somewhat, actual consumption in both the licit and illicit market decreased. Notably, the tax revenue from higher excise taxes offset the tax losses caused by illicit trade (Blecher 2010).

The United Kingdom in the 1990s at first seemed to illustrate a simplistic relationship between cigarette prices and smuggling. Seeking to reduce the smoking prevalence, the UK had implemented a series of substantive tax hikes. As the price of cigarettes increased, so did tobacco smuggling. Notably, a significant number of cigarettes smuggled were mainstream tobacco industry brands. Their smuggling and sale at a lower price in the UK undermined both the intended health benefit of the tax hike and the tax revenue itself. However, following this, the UK embarked on an ambitious tobacco control policy in the early 2000s, focusing on supply-side measures such as disrupting distribution chains and investing in new operational responses. In the following decade, the estimated illicit cigarette market share fell from 21% to 9%, leading the UK to a new equilibrium of some of the highest cigarette prices in the world and comparatively lower levels of smuggling (ASH, 2012; Tessa Langley et al., 2019).

As recent years have seen research on tobacco smuggling continuously highlight[5] that price-level dynamics are not the only or perhaps the central factor in driving cigarette smuggling, this has two obvious corollaries. The first is an increasing consensus that high rates of taxation provide the most effective tool for combatting the health effects of tobacco consumption, and that it is not necessarily or automatically undermined by smuggling. Consequently, the World Health Organization (WHO) has been recognising the importance of tobacco taxation in Article 6 of its framework convention on tobacco control and recommending a minimum 75% tax share of the retail price of tobacco (World Health Organization, 2014). At the same time, smuggling control alongside taxation has increasingly become a key WHO issue, as reflected in the WHO Framework Convention on Tobacco Control's (FCTC) adoption of the Protocol to Eliminate Illicit Trade in Tobacco in 2012. The second has been an increasing focus, both by researchers and policymakers, on the non-price drivers of tobacco smuggling, and in particular supply side dynamics.

Diverse drivers and dynamics

A wider view of different drivers and dynamics of cigarette smuggling points to at least three additional sets of – interacting – factors: regional cooperation; the involvement of state actors; and the effectiveness of supply-chain control. The first point is a rather simple addendum to the price debate, noting that the absolute price of cigarettes or their price in global comparison is not as crucial a factor as the price in comparison to a country's immediate neighbours. Here, too, the same limits to the price argument noted above still apply, but this consideration has given rise to increasing efforts to coordinate regional-level agreements, for example among the Economic Community of West African States (ECOWAS).

Cigarette smuggling

A larger set of factors relate to the involvement of state actors and can be grouped under the political and governance context of cigarette smuggling. On a basic level, arguments here have often been focused on the idea of corruption. Publications by the WHO and the World Bank have noted that standard corruption indicators by organisations such as Transparency International strongly correlate with levels of tobacco smuggling (The World Bank, 1999), and may indeed provide a stronger predictor of illicit trade than price or tax levels (Jha and Chaloupka, 2000). Needless to say, this represents a very broad relationship. However, the intuition behind it has remained prevalent in more recent indices that have tried to capture the vulnerability of states to organised crime and illicit trade such as the Economist Intelligence Unit's (EUI) 'Illicit Trade Environment Index,' [6] Frequently, the assumption here is that the ability of smugglers to 'pay their way' is a consequence of 'petty corruption' in customs agencies, created by poor pay of low-level bureaucrats, principal-agent problems or poor institutional design, reflecting a broader 'crime-fragility rationale' (Heuser, 2019) in much analysis on smuggling and states. Typical interventions here have included so-called 'anti-corruption trainings' and new managerial techniques or surveillance methods in the interaction with customs agents.

Ethnographic studies of illegal economies more widely, however, have for a long time questioned these rather simplistic assumptions in accounts of 'corruption.' As a full discussion of this literature – particularly well-developed in African borderland studies and highlighted in other entries in this volume – goes beyond this chapter, I focus on the observations most relevant to the drivers of smuggling. One frequent observation here has been that some political actors or state structures may tolerate cigarette smuggling for reasons other than simple monetary pay-offs that can be monitored, disincentivised or cracked down on. Distributive politics can play a crucial role in motivating states to tolerate and structure smuggling in order to provide incomes for politically relevant actors or otherwise economically marginalised regions (Gallien, 2020b). Both tobacco farmers and small-scale smugglers may represent potential constituencies for such arrangements. The connection of cigarette smuggling to war economies in the Sahel or the DRC have further complicated these dynamics (Titeca, Joossens and Raw, 2011; Kehoe Down, Sawadogo and Stocks, 2021). At the same time, as Andreas (2009) has highlighted, more substantive controls on the trade infrastructure that large-scale smugglers utilise may also be politically undesirable if it simultaneously inconveniences other trade flows – both illicit and licit.

The latter provides a further complication to a simplistic view of 'corruption' in this context. As will be discussed below, the past years have also seen extensive and not always transparent attempts by the formal global tobacco industry to influence, lobby and pressure governments, particularly in developing countries (Boseley, 2017). Consequently, a simple separation of the political influences of different actors within global cigarette supply chains into 'corruption' on the one hand and regular business-state relationships on the other, may be neither analytically simple nor politically meaningful.

There is also a need to rethink where relevant instances of 'corruption' are located, and what they look like. Gallien and Weigand (2021) have noted that the types of interactions through which smugglers engage with state agents at borders include not only petty corruption and genuine enforcement, but a whole range of rather structured deals and informal agreements, from complete toleration to 'flatrate' payments that smugglers make to customs personnel on a regular basis. Notably, they highlight that the types of interactions that state structures offer smugglers is a central determinant of how smugglers choose their routes. Dobler (2016) makes a similar observation, noting that different types of cross-border traders prefer different environments and infrastructure depending on the nature of their trade, their capital, scope, political and social connections. He distinguishes between the actors of the 'green' border that trade across the borderlands, the actors of the 'grey' border that trade through roads and border crossings, and the actors of the 'blue' border that trade through the large transport infrastructure of the global trade system. Given the nature of the global illicit cigarette market as described above, with a range of highly capitalised large-scale actors, it therefore appears that the particular corruptibility of low-level customs agents at border checkpoints that is frequently imagined here frequently may not be a crucial factor. More important aspects may be the ability to gain access to large-scale trade infrastructure, the ability to navigate customs at more central nodes such as airports and ports, and the governance of free trade zones.

All this directly connects to the third and perhaps most critical set of drivers here, which centres around supply-chain control. As highlighted in the section above, the effects of price or tax increases on smuggling have been found to be highly dependent on states' ability to control and combat illicit supply chains into their territory. Returning to the example of South Africa provides a useful illustration here. While the illicit market share did not increase substantially during the introduction of higher tax rates, as discussed above, it did spike in the 2010s. Recent scholarship has attributed this to a simultaneous drop in the ability of the South African Revenue Services (SARS) to perform its central functions as a consequence of internal restructuring and the disbanding of specialised units (Vellios, Walbeek and Ross, 2020, p. 240).

In line with the larger global structures of cigarette smuggling, the focus in thinking about supply chain control has shifted from a simplistic focus on border control and towards a larger and more holistic management of cigarette supply chains. This extends from production to import and distribution, transit and free trade zones. Modern supply chain control can be assisted through simple markers like excise stamps,[7] however best practice increasingly points towards more expansive, consistent and comprehensive track and trace measures (Ross, 2017). It furthermore requires a sensibility to the political and social embeddedness of these streams. Critically, this necessarily includes both the licit and illicit supply chains, including specific measures against tobacco industry involvement in supplying illicit trade corridors (Joossens and Raw, 2008). Consequently, this brings supply chain control even more firmly in the sphere of interest of the global tobacco industry.

As this section has noted, a more in-depth and holistic view of the underlying drivers and dynamics of tobacco smuggling beyond price and taxes brings the analysis of cigarette smuggling a little closer to those dynamics that are frequently highlighted for the smuggling of illicit goods as well: interactions with state structures, embeddedness in politics and the challenges in tracking complex international trade flows. It implies that the distinction between the dynamics of smuggling of 'excisable' goods and other goods often may be somewhat overstated. Crucially, however, the factors discussed here begin to point to an elephant in this chapter that needs to be addressed more systematically: the relationship between cigarette smuggling and the global – legal – tobacco industry. This stands at the heart of the following section.

Industry influence and tobacco smuggling

One of the most important insights from research on tobacco smuggling in recent decades is that limiting analyses to the moments and places where cigarettes are crossing borders illegally obscures more of the wider picture than it illuminates. Understanding the global illicit cigarette market requires the recognition that it is influenced critically by the existence, involvement, and interests of the global legal cigarette industry. The global legal tobacco industry is substantive and highly capitalised, totalling approximately US$800 billion (Euromonitor, 2014). While the market has become internationalised, control has increasingly consolidated, with the vast majority of the market controlled by five transnational companies.[8] Spanning vast globally integrated value chains from production to distribution, transnational bulk trade is a critical feature of the global tobacco industry. Alongside rules of trade, the tobacco industry has also become notorious for seeking to influence the legal context in which cigarettes are sold and priced, using a wide range of tactics from lobbying and campaign contributions to financing and influencing research (Yach and Bettcher, 2000; World Health Organization, 2009). The remainder of this section focuses on three dynamics through which the tobacco industry affects tobacco smuggling: its direct involvement in illegal trade; its indirect involvement through affecting government policy; and its influence on research and academic discourse on smuggling.

First, there has been extensive evidence that the global tobacco industry has actively participated in or relied on the smuggling of its products. Smuggling can help cigarette companies evade taxes and tariffs, undermine control measures such as age limits and warning labels, or more cheaply establish its brand in a market before entering it legally. It is worth noting that today, the vast majority of seized smuggled cigarettes are not illicit whites or counterfeits, but recognised tobacco industry brands (Gallagher et al., 2019). Tobacco industry involvement in smuggling became a major public talking point in the early 2000s, when a *Guardian* exposé examined how British American Tobacco was benefitting from and exploiting the smuggling of its products to boost sales (Maguire and Campbell, 2000). "Smuggling, often organised in a furtive and clandestine manner, has been BAT company policy since the late 1960s" one of the reporters involved later testified in front of the Health Select Committee (TobaccoTactics, 2020). In a reply to the allegations, BAT's deputy chairman replied rather candidly, suggesting that legal tobacco firms also see their products as competing on the illicit market:

> Where any government is unwilling to act or their efforts are unsuccessful, we act, completely within the law, on the basis that our brands will be available alongside those of our competitors in the smuggled as well as the legitimate market. (Clarke, 2000)

A few years prior, the smuggling of cigarettes from Andorra into Spain showed a similar dynamic. At the time, smuggling out of Andorra was a major supply channel for the illicit cigarette market across Europe. Particularly notable, however, was not just the smuggling trade out of Andorra, however, but the legal trade into it. Between 1993 and 1997, legal cigarette exports from Britain to Andorra increased by a factor of over 100, and reached a level that would have been sufficient to supply every citizen of Andorra with 60 British cigarettes per day (Joossens and Raw, 2000). Reducing cigarette smuggling into Spain therefore did not only depend on action at the border or on interdicting of street-level distribution, but both a wider approach to supply chains and legal changes within Andorra. Consequently, researchers highlighted that combatting tobacco smuggling and supply chain control need to focus more directly on the role of the legal tobacco industry in illicit trade – 'turn off the tap,' so to say (Joossens and Raw, 2008).

The late 1990s and early 2000s saw an increasing focus on the industry's role in smuggling by policy-makers, particularly in Europe. Following an investigation by the EU Commission regarding American contraband cigarettes on the European market, tobacco industry giants settled their cases in exchange for payments of US$1.25 billion (PMI), US$400 million (JTI), US$300 million (Imperial) and US$200 million (BAT) (Snyckers, 2020, 52). Despite these expensive settlements, there are numerous indicators that, in a wider global context, many of these same dynamics are still prevalent. For example, between 2008 and 2010, a group of tobacco industry companies had to pay a total of US$1.7 billion in fines for their role in tobacco smuggling in Canada (Daudelin, Soiffer, and Willows, 2013). BAT has been fined repeatedly for a variety of inconsistencies around their book-keeping in South Africa (Snyckers, 2020, 39) and has been fined by HMRC for 'oversupplying' cigarettes to Belgium with a high risk of smuggling (BBC News, 2014).

A particularly striking case study has been highlighted in a recent report by the Organised Crime and Corruption Reporting Project (OCCRP) on cigarette smuggling in West Africa. It highlights, like a range of recent scholarship has done, that profits from the expansion of cigarette smuggling have fuelled the violence in northern Mali by providing funds for armed groups. Critically, however, the report also points to the role of formal tobacco industry and state actors in this dynamic. It argues that British American Tobacco has closely monitored the situation and strategically over-supplied Mali with cigarettes, knowing that they would be traded and distributed by traffickers. At the same time, Malian authorities were found largely to turn a blind eye to these proceedings, overlooking obviously 'impossible' reports by BAT's local distributor (Kehoe Down, Sawadogo and Stocks, 2021).

Despite the continuation of these dynamics, the tobacco industry in recent years has sought to re-position itself as a victim rather than a perpetrator of cigarette smuggling – and, crucially, as a partner in fighting it. This has included a range of Memoranda of Understanding of tobacco industry players with customs agencies and international organisations as well as attempts to affect policy more concretely. One of the most critical aspects of this has been in the context of supply chain control. Both the WHO's Framework Convention on Tobacco Control (FCTC) and the Protocol to Eliminate Illicit Trade in Tobacco Products (ITP) have pointed to track and trace systems as centrepieces to combatting the illicit cigarette trade.

Controversially, however, large tobacco industry players have themselves begun to produce and provide track and trace technologies. Notably, PMI both developed and patented its 'Codentify' system and then licenced it for free to its main competitors (Joossens and Gilmore, 2014). Following this, the industry has increasingly pushed for the adoption of Codentify even though its ties to the tobacco industry are in clear contradiction of the terms of the ITP (Ross et al., 2018; Gilmore et al., 2019). Tobacco control scholars have expressed serious scepticism over the effectiveness of Codentify, noting its vulnerability to falsification, the absence of independent audits, its undermining of tax stamps, and its potential to move further control away from tax authorities and toward the tobacco industry itself (Joossens and Gilmore, 2014; Ross, Eads and Yates, 2018).

Tobacco industry influence on cigarette smuggling has not only been limited to specific policy tools, but also affected how smuggling and counter-smuggling policy is discussed more broadly. Even though the connection between price and tobacco smuggling is not straightforward, as discussed above, the tobacco industry has systematically exploited the bogeyman of smuggling in order to argue against cigarette taxation and other tobacco control policies such as standardised packaging (Fooks, Peeters and Evans-Reeves, 2014; Gallien, 2020a). This has included not just targeted lobbying but also the creation of a policy discourse that simplifies the relationship between price and smuggling, overstates the amount of smuggling, overstates the role of 'illicit whites,' and underplays the involvement of the legal industry (Gallagher et al., 2019). Industry players have sought to influence news coverage (Evans-Reeves et al., 2020) and have partnered with academics, think tanks, consultancies and research institutions such as the International Tax and Investment Center (ITIC), the Economist Intelligence Unit (EIU) and KPMG to establish their perspective in respected fora.[9] Especially with respect to tobacco taxation, there is some evidence that this has been successful – not only has the number of countries that have implemented tobacco tax policy that follows the WHO best practices remained below 20%, it has actually fallen since 2014 (Snyckers, 2020, 91).

Critically for the purpose of this volume, these tactics have affected not only public discourse and policy-making on cigarette smuggling, but also the academic and scientific literature on the topic. In rarer cases, this has been through the direct funding of academic studies, such as PMI's funding of research at the Università Cattolica del Sacro Cuore in Milan and the University of Trento (Fooks, Peeters and Evans-Reeves, 2014). Likely more influential has been the funding of 'grey literature,' as well as in particular indices and data sources to drive discourse and be picked up by scholars. However, this has likely shaped the academic work on tobacco smuggling in more complex ways than might have been anticipated. Despite, and arguably in response to, industry influence, the academic community working on tobacco smuggling has developed research centres and initiatives focused in particular on the tactics of the tobacco industry (such as the Tobacco Control project at the University of Bath), on fact-checking its various studies, and consequently refining methodological approaches to studying cigarette smuggling. It has fostered extreme awareness of the ethics of research funding streams across a group of researchers, who, over the past two decades in particular, have produced one of the most well-developed literatures on the intersections between a legal industry and illegal trade. As the final section notes, this has provided critical contributions for our understanding of smuggling more widely.

Conclusion: lessons from cigarette smuggling

This chapter has noted that despite a frequent focus on prices and taxation, the drivers of cigarette smuggling globally are both highly diverse and tied into local politics and the wider infrastructure of globalised trade. Furthermore, it has discussed the role that the tobacco industry has had in influencing smuggling, anti-smuggling policy and even academic discussions on the issue. While cigarette smuggling has some dynamics that are particular to it, it also shares a variety of features with the smuggling of other goods, including some discussed in this volume. Parallels are particularly notable to the smuggling of other licit goods with internationalised industries, such as oil, and other goods with adverse health effects, such as alcohol, but not limited to these. Consequently, both from the discussions outlined here and the wider recent academic literature on cigarette smuggling emerge important contributions to our understanding of smuggling more widely. This chapter concludes by highlighting three particularly salient lessons.

First, recent work on cigarette smuggling has highlighted that while much scholarship on smuggling, and particularly the smuggling of licit goods, has traditionally taken a cost-benefit-focused view on what drives smuggling and smugglers, a wider view at diverse drivers, actors and their interactions are necessary. This not only includes a broader analysis of both the local and transnational politics in which smuggling is embedded but also an unpacking of more simplistic assumptions around the role and logic of 'corruption' in illegal trade. With this have come clear implications for policy. Strategies that solely consider limiting smuggling through 'making it more expensive' or bumping up customs enforcement, are likely both to over-estimate the role of prices themselves and under-estimate more complex cost-driven dynamics, such as costlier routes leading to the consolidation of monopolistic smuggling structures. Lessons from successful attempts to limit cigarette smuggling include the importance of both multi-pronged approaches and a consideration of the role of the legal industry (Ross, 2015). This connects directly to the following point.

Second, recent work on cigarette smuggling provides outstanding case studies on the intersection between illegal trade and legal, highly capitalised global industries. They not only highlight this as a key area of study that is critically under-researched in the context of a range of other goods but also provide a range of tools that can be applied more broadly. These include methodological innovations and insights into an industry playbook of schemes and strategies that are unlikely to be limited to tobacco. In addition, they provide a reminder of the critical importance of ethics, transparency, and industry-independent funding in scholarship on smuggling today. This leads to a final point.

Third, research on cigarette smuggling teaches a critical lesson on the importance for a field of study to examine its own histories, motivations, funding streams and, fundamentally, biases. This issue has been heightened in this area due to the aggressive attempts by the tobacco industry to influence the knowledge industry on cigarette smuggling and taxation, but this does not imply that it is entirely absent in research on the smuggling of other goods, although it may take different forms. Crucially, biases in a field may not only be introduced through outside intervention or funding streams but through political interests, methodological and geographical blind-spots or the dominance of research agendas set in the 'global north.' Solutions to this lie not just in rigorous research and funding ethics but also the critical self-examination of a field of study and the communication among different disciplines, methodologies, and areas of scholarship. This is a project to which both this chapter and this volume as a whole have sought to contribute.

Notes

1   For a more extensive discussion of 'cheap white' cigarettes, see Ross et al. (2016).
2   This metric is calculated by analysing the number of customs seizure cases. This does not account for the quantity or price of the individual seizure, and is necessarily biased by the intensity of enforcement.
3   While this section focuses on price and tax, a parallel set of discussions to the ones examined here exists for quantity restrictions on cigarette trade and other regulatory instruments such as warning labels.
4   I will discuss the role of relative price differences within regions below, but it is worth noting that a focus on neighbouring countries risks understating the role of shipping and trade corridors between regions.
5   For a more qualitative approach, see for example Titeca, Joossens and Raw (2011).
6   Notably, this index has been created with the involvement of tobacco industry funding. I will return to this point below.
7   Excise stamps are a form of stamp attached to excisable goods, such as cigarette packets, in order to indicate that the excise tax has been paid by the manufacturer.
8   Namely the Chinese National Tobacco Corporation (CNTC), Phillip Morris International (PMI), British American Tobacco (BAT), Japan Tobacco Inc (JT), and Imperial Tobacco Group. Source: Euromonitor (2014).
9   The website https://tobaccotactics.org/, hosted by the University of Bath, is not merely an invaluable resource on tobacco industry tactics but also contains updated lists of organisations that have received funding from the tobacco industry.

Bibliography

Andreas, P. (2009) *Border Games: Policing the U.S.–Mexico Divide*. Ithaca, NY: Cornell University Press.
ASH (2012) 'Tobacco industry myths shattered as smuggling rates fall again,' *Action on Smoking and Health*, 18 October. Available at: https://ash.org.uk/media-and-news/press-releases-media-and-news/tobacco-industry-myths-shattered-as-smuggling-rates-fall-again/ (Accessed: 28 September 2020).
Bhagwati, J. N. and Hansen, B. (1975) 'A theoretical analysis of smuggling: a reply,' *The Quarterly Journal of Economics*, 89(4), pp. 651–657. doi: 10.2307/1884699.

Cigarette smuggling

Blecher, E. (2010) 'A mountain or a molehill: is the illicit trade in cigarettes undermining tobacco control policy in South Africa?,' *Trends in Organized Crime*, 13, pp. 299–315. doi: 10.1007/s12117-010-9092-y.

Blecher, E. and Ross, H. (2013) *Tobacco Use in Africa: Tobacco Control through Prevention.* American Cancer Society, p. 16. Available at: https://www.cancer.org/content/dam/cancer-org/cancer-control/en/reports/tobacco-use-in-africa-tobacco-control-through=prevention.pdf (Accessed: 23 March 2020).

Boseley, S. (2017) 'Threats, bullying, lawsuits: tobacco industry's dirty war for the African market,' *The Guardian*, 12 July. Available at: https://www.theguardian.com/world/2017/jul/12/big-tobacco-dirty-war-africa-market (Accessed: 24 September 2020).

Chaloupka, F. J., Straif, K. and Leon, M. E. (2011) 'Effectiveness of tax and price policies in tobacco control,' *Tobacco Control*, 20(3), pp. 235–238. doi: 10.1136/tc.2010.039982.

Chelwa, G., Walbeek, C. van and Blecher, E. (2017) 'Evaluating South Africa's tobacco control policy using a synthetic control method,' *Tobacco Control*, 26(5), pp. 509–517. doi: 10.1136/tobaccocontrol-2016-053011.

Clarke, K. (2000) 'Dilemma of a cigarette exporter,' *The Guardian*, 3 February. Available at: https://www.theguardian.com/bat/article/0,,191288,00.html (Accessed: 27 August 2020).

Daudelin, J., Soiffer, S., and Willows, J. (2013) 'Border integrity, illicit Tobacco and Canada's security,' *National Security Strategy for Canada Series*. Ottawa, Canada: Macdonald-Laurier Institute.

Dobler, G. (2016) 'The green, the grey and the blue: a typology of cross-border trade in Africa,' *The Journal of Modern African Studies*, 54(1), pp. 145–169. doi: 10.1017/S0022278X15000993.

Dutta, S. (2019) *Confronting Illicit Tobacco Trade: A Global Review of Country Experiences.* Washington, DC: The World Bank.

Euromonitor (2014) *Global Tobacco: Key Findings Part 1 – Tobacco Overview, Cigarettes and the Future.* Strategy Briefing. Euromonitor. Available at: https://www.euromonitor.com/global-tobacco-key-findings-part-1-tobacco-overview-cigarettes-and-the-future/report (Accessed: 28 September 2020).

Evans-Reeves, K. et al. (2020) 'Illicit tobacco trade is "booming": UK newspaper coverage of data funded by transnational tobacco companies,' *Tobacco Control*. doi: 10.1136/tobaccocontrol-2018-054902.

FATF (2012) *Illicit Tobacco Trade.* Financial Action Task Force. Available at: https://www.fatf-gafi.org/media/fatf/documents/reports/Illicit%20Tobacco%20Trade.pdf (Accessed: 28 September 2020).

Fooks, G. J., Peeters, S. and Evans-Reeves, K. (2014) 'Illicit trade, tobacco industry-funded studies and policy influence in the EU and UK,' *Tobacco Control*, 23(1), pp. 81–83. doi: 10.1136/tobaccocontrol-2012-050788.

Gallagher, A. W. A. et al. (2019) 'Tobacco industry data on illicit tobacco trade: a systematic review of existing assessments,' *Tobacco Control*, 28(3), pp. 334–345. doi: 10.1136/tobaccocontrol-2018-054295.

Gallien, M. (2020a) *De-Linking Tobacco Taxation and Illicit Trade in Africa.* ICTD Summary Brief 22. Brighton, UK: International Centre for Tax and Development.

Gallien, M. (2020b) *Smugglers and States: Illegal Trade in the Political Settlements of North Africa.* London: London School of Economics.

Gallien, M. and Weigand, F. (2021) 'Channeling contraband - how states shape international smuggling routes,' *Security Studies*. Available at: https://www.tandfonline.com/toc/fsst20/current (Accessed: 28 September 2020).

Gilmore, A. B., Gallagher, A. W. A., and Rowell, A. (2018). 'Tobacco industry's elaborate attempts to control a global track and trace system and fundamentally undermine the Illicit Trade Protocol,' *Tobacco Control*, 28, pp. 127–140. doi: 10.1136/tobaccocontrol-2017-054191.

Heuser, C. (2019) 'The effect of illicit economies in the margins of the state – The VRAEM,' *Journal of Illicit Economies and Development*, 1(1), pp. 23–36. doi: 10.31389/jied.7.

2014 'HMRC Fines Cigarette Maker £650,000.' BBC News, sec. Business. (November 13, 2014) https://www.bbc.com/news/business-30038328.

Jha, P. and Chaloupka, F. J. (2000) 'The economics of global tobacco control,' *BMJ: British Medical Journal*, 321(7257), pp. 358–361.

Joossens, L. et al. (2010) 'The impact of eliminating the global illicit cigarette trade on health and revenue,' *Addiction*, 105(9), pp. 1640–1649. doi: 10.1111/j.1360-0443.2010.03018.x.

Joossens, L. and Gilmore, A. B. (2014) 'The transnational tobacco companies' strategy to promote Codentify, their inadequate tracking and tracing standard,' *Tobacco Control*, 23(e1), pp. e3–e6. doi: 10.1136/tobaccocontrol-2012-050796.

Joossens, L. and Raw, M. (2000) 'How can cigarette smuggling be reduced?,' *BMJ: British Medical Journal*, 321(7266), pp. 947–950.

Joossens, L. and Raw, M. (2008) 'Progress in combating cigarette smuggling: controlling the supply chain,' *Tobacco Control*, 17(6), pp. 399–404. doi: 10.1136/tc.2008.026567.

Kehoe Down, A., Sawadogo, G. and Stocks, T. (2021) 'British American tobacco fights dirty in West Africa,' *Organised Crime and Corruption Reporting Project*, 21 February. Available at: https://www.occrp.org/en/loosetobacco/british-american-tobacco-fights-dirty-in-west-africa (Accessed: 2 March 2021).

Kwass, M. (2014) *Contraband: Louis Mandrin and the Making of a Global Underground*. 1st edition. Cambridge, MA: Harvard University Press.

Langley T. et al. (2019) 'United Kingdom: tackling illicit tobacco,' in Sheila Dutta (ed), *Confronting Illicit Tobacco Trade: A Global Review of Country Experiences*. Washington, DC: The World Bank.

Maguire, K. and Campbell, D. (2000) 'Tobacco giant implicated in global smuggling schemes,' *The Guardian*, 31 January. Available at: https://www.theguardian.com/uk/2000/jan/31/kevinmaguire.duncancampbell (Accessed: 27 August 2020).

Martin, L. and Panagariya, A. (1984) 'Smuggling, trade, and price disparity: A crime-theoretic approach,' *Journal of International Economics*, 17(3), pp. 201–217. doi: 10.1016/0022-1996(84)90020-5.

Mathers, C. D. and Loncar, D. (2006) 'Projections of Global Mortality and Burden of Disease from 2002 to 2030,' *PLOS Medicine*, 3(11), p. e442. doi: 10.1371/journal.pmed.0030442.

Norton, D. A. G. (1988) 'On the Economic Theory of Smuggling,' *Economica*, 55(217), pp. 107–118. doi: 10.2307/2554250.

Ramanandraibe, N. and Ouma, A. E. (2011) *Facts on Tobacco Use in the African Region*. WHO Regional Office for Africa. Available at: https://www.afro.who.int/sites/default/files/2017-06/facts-on-tobacco-use-in-the-african-region.pdf (Accessed: 24 March 2020).

Ross, H. (2015) *Controlling Illicit Tobacco Trade: International Experience*. Tobacconomics/Economics of Tobacco Control Project. Available at: https://tobacconomics.org/wp-content/uploads/2015/05/Ross_International_experience_05.28.15.pdf (Accessed: 28 September 2020).

Ross, H. et al. (2016) 'A closer look at "Cheap White" cigarettes,' *Tobacco Control*, 25(5), pp. 527–531. doi: 10.1136/tobaccocontrol-2015-052540.

Ross, H. (2017) 'Tracking and tracing tobacco products in Kenya,' *Preventive Medicine*, 105, pp. S15–S18. doi: 10.1016/j.ypmed.2017.04.025.

Ross, H., Eads, M. and Yates, M. (2018) 'Why governments cannot afford Codentify to support their track and trace solutions,' *Tobacco Control*, 27(6), pp. 706–708. doi: 10.1136/tobaccocontrol-2017-053970.

Snyckers, T. (2020) *Dirty Tobacco: Spies, Lies and Mega-Profits*. Tafelberg.

Titeca, K., Joossens, L. and Raw, M. (2011) 'Blood cigarettes: cigarette smuggling and war economies in central and eastern Africa,' *Tobacco Control*, 20(3), pp. 226–232. doi: 10.1136/tc.2010.041574.

TobaccoTactics (2020) 'BAT Involvement in Tobacco Smuggling,' *Tobacco Tactics*, 30 January. Available at: https://tobaccotactics.org/wiki/bat-involvement-in-tobacco-smuggling/ (Accessed: 28 September 2020).

Vellios, N., Ross, H. and Perucic, A.-M. (2018) 'Trends in cigarette demand and supply in Africa,' *PLOS ONE*, 13(8), p. e0202467. doi: 10.1371/journal.pone.0202467.

Vellios, N., Walbeek, C. van and Ross, H. (2020) 'Illicit cigarette trade in South Africa: 2002–2017,' *Tobacco Control*, 29(Suppl 4), pp. s234–s242. doi: 10.1136/tobaccocontrol-2018-054798.

Walbeek, C. van and Shai, L. (2015) 'Are the tobacco industry's claims about the size of the illicit cigarette market credible? The case of South Africa,' *Tobacco Control*, 24(e2), pp. e142–e146. doi: 10.1136/tobaccocontrol-2013-051441.

The World Bank (1999) *Curbing the epidemic: governments and the economics of tobacco control*. Washington, DC: The World Bank.

World Customs Organisation (2019) *Illicit Trade Report 2019*. World Customs Organisation. Available at: http://www.wcoomd.org/-/media/wco/public/global/pdf/topics/enforcement-and-compliance/activities-and-programmes/illicit-trade-report/itr_2019_en.pdf?db=web (Accessed: 28 September 2020).

World Health Organization (2009) 'Tobacco Industry Interference with Tobacco Control,' Available at: https://escholarship.org/uc/item/98w687x5#main (Accessed: 26 August 2020).

World Health Organization (2014) *Factsheet – Tobacco Taxation*. Available at: https://www.euro.who.int/__data/assets/pdf_file/0007/250738/140379_Fact-sheet-Tobacco-Taxation-Eng-ver2.pdf (Accessed: 28 September 2019).

Cigarette smuggling

World Health Organization (no date) 'Illicit Trade in Tobacco – A Summary of the Evidence and Country Responses,' Available at: https://www.who.int/tobacco/economics/illicittrade.pdf (Accessed: 28 September 2020).

Yach, D. and Bettcher, D. (2000) 'Globalisation of tobacco industry influence and new global responses,' *Tobacco Control*, 9(2), pp. 206–216. doi: 10.1136/tc.9.2.206.

19

THEFT AND SMUGGLING OF PETROLEUM PRODUCTS

Tim Eaton

The petroleum sector is highly complex. It produces a vast array of products, from cooking gas to heat homes and prepare food, to fuel for commercial vehicles and aviation fuels. Extensive expertise and infrastructure is required to extract, refine, move and store petroleum products. Internationally, the oil market is regulated: sellers not recognised by the international community and/or subject to restrictive measures are prohibited from dealing with buyers and traders, although they may find means to circumnavigate these measures. The sector involves a wide array of stakeholders, from politicians who pass legislation over the governance of the sector, to technocrats and engineers who are responsible for managing and running it, to security guards and truck drivers who may be responsible for safeguarding the products.

The world consumes in the region of 34 billion barrels of petroleum products per annum. The market value of each barrel of crude oil has fluctuated significantly in recent years. At 2017 prices, the market value was estimated to be $1.7 trillion (Oilprice.com: 2017). The size of the oil market creates significant economic incentives to profiteer illicitly from the sector, and such profiteering takes place at all levels of the supply chain. In 2016, illicit trading in oil via under-invoicing, theft, bunkering and corruption was believed to account for nearly $100 billion a year on the continent of Africa alone (African Development Bank: 2016: p. 7). In keeping with the theme of this handbook, this chapter will focus on the smuggling of petroleum products across national borders, but it necessarily will look at the means through which this is facilitated by factors at the national-level. It should be noted that the smuggling of these products is inextricably connected to theft (i.e., the products are diverted from the supply chain via theft and subsequently smuggled) particularly at the upstream and midstream level. Therefore, the modalities of that theft are also covered here.

Drawing on a wide range of case studies in Europe, Africa, the Middle East and the Americas, the chapter will address smuggling of both refined and unrefined products, by working through the levels of the supply chain, first examining how upstream elements, such as the laws and governance of the oil sector, can be used, or abused, to facilitate smuggling. Next, means of smuggling oil products will be explored – the midstream elements of the supply chain – beginning with the tapping and siphoning of unrefined oil. Diversion of refined products from the midstream and downstream elements of the supply chain will then be assessed, through bunkering and trucking.

Theft and smuggling of petroleum products

Analysing the supply chain, the actors that are in control of each element, and the operating environment in which the activities take place, is an effective way of illustrating how different forms of oil and fuel smuggling function. Such an analysis can reveal much about the underlying power relations in the state in question, the capacities of its institutions and the reach of its capacities for enforcement. While it is helpful to identify when and how petroleum products are diverted from the supply chain and smuggled by identifying upstream, midstream and down-stream phases, the reality is that smuggling dynamics tend to be fluid and may be present at all levels. This chapter consequently explores contemporary fuel smuggling dynamics in Libya to illustrate how smuggling can permeate the upstream, midstream and downstream elements of the fuel sector. See Box 19.1 for details of different modalities of fuel smuggling.

The overall takeaway of this analysis is that the challenges associated with preventing smuggling become greater as the degree of penetration of the profiteers of up the supply chain increases. If, for example, smuggling networks have penetrated the governance of the petro-leum sector upstream by cutting deals with officials in positions of authority to limit oversight or to actively facilitate smuggling, then 'fixing' the problem will depend on a more complex array of interventions than smuggling which is limited to activity in the downstream sector.

Greasing the wheels: upstream governance of petroleum production

The environment in which the petroleum sector operates has a critical impact over the nature and degree of fuel smuggling. While the term "upstream" is used within the oil and gas sector to refer to exploration and production, it is used more broadly here to refer to the governance of the petroleum sector (including the political system, the legal framework and the security situation). Actors present in the upstream level include state officials and legislators, and state and non-state enterprises. The ability of political and military representatives of the state to determine who can engage in oil smuggling allows them to profiteer from the smuggling of the state's assets through kickbacks and to cut deals with local actors in return for looking the other way. Moreover, when governments are prevented from selling to formal international markets, fuel smuggling can be state sanctioned as a means of generating revenues through informal and illicit means. The connivance of such officials with smuggling and the failure to ensure robust and transparent governance of the oil sector is a major facilitator of smuggling.

Some of these upstream dynamics are illustrated in Nigeria, where interests in the oil sector have become intimately connected to elite bargaining over political power. Nigeria is estimated to lose $3–8 billion a year from oil theft and smuggling (Katsouris & Sayne: 2013: p. 17). This is the equivalent of around 10–20% of the country's annual production. Oil theft and smuggling in Nigeria developed in the 1970s and 1980s while the country remained under military rule. Oil theft allowed military officers to sustain themselves while also allowing others to engage in the practice as a form of rent, thereby ensuring stability. The return to civilian rule in the 2000s and subsequent steep global rise in oil prices stimulated greater competition over the sector. This led to the involvement by a broader array of actors, making the lucrative sector both a source of political deal making and a source of conflict (Katsouris & Sayne: 2013: pp. 5–6). Under the administrations of Olusegun Obasanjo (1999–2007), Umaru Musa Yar'Adua (2007–2010) and Goodluck Jonathan (2010–2015), powerbrokers with close involvement in smuggling activities were benefactors of the presidents, who in turn shielded their benefactors from being held accountable for their smuggling activity (Burgis: 2015: pp. 73–79). This protection extended beyond the benefactors themselves to those in their networks: oil thieves and smugglers have been repeatedly protected from prosecution by the Nigerian authorities, (Katsouris & Sayne: 2013: pp. 5–6). Numerous modalities of smuggling exist, including the

Box 19.1 Modalities of oil and fuel theft

Retailing: buying at a subsidised rate and selling at an unsubsidised rate, profiting from price differentials between different markets.

Tapping: diverting supplies from oil pipelines and/or wellheads. There are two different types: "hot tapping" or "pressure tapping" is where small amounts are diverted from the pipelines without significantly reducing the pipeline's high pressure. On the other hand, "cold tapping" involves disactivating part of a pipeline and then placing a new tap in while the pipeline is down. When the pipeline is brought back online the new tap is not noticeable.

Siphoning: fuel is siphoned out and the supply is topped up with other products, such as kerosene or water to mask the missing amount.

Adulteration: In cases where fuel is dyed for use by agricultural machinery, the fuel is adulterated by mixing in other products in order to change the colour. This allows the fuel to be sold at higher prices to the broader consumer market. Other more complex processes exist for removing isotope markers (used to identify where the fuel is rebated).

Bunkering: illegally supplying ships with fuel to be sold on the black market or misrepresented on the formal market.

Trucking: illegal trafficking of fuels in specialised vehicles such as oil tankers, pick-up trucks and specially modified cars with significantly expanded fuel tanks.

Source: Adapted from Ralby (2017) 'Downstream Oil Theft: Culprits, Modalities, and Amounts',

Atlantic Council

tapping of oil pipelines and the illicit bunkering of ships, and then the subsequent smuggling of the oil.

In areas of countries that the state is unable to control, local actors can be granted rights to smuggle oil products in return for security guarantees. For example, in the 2000s, the Ugandan government had limited control in some of its territory. In some of these areas where the government had limited influence, the so-called 'Opec boys' smuggled fuel from the Democratic Republic of Congo with the consent of local Ugandan politicians as part of an alliance between the two sets of actors that allowed the politicians to maintain stability and for the Opec boys to sooth their grievances, generate revenues and leverage their capacity to rebel (Lecoutere and Titeca: 2007: pp. 1–37).

In other cases, there are incentives for political leaders to circumnavigate international regulations in order to profit from smuggling. Overland smuggling and maritime smuggling of crude oil in Iraq developed under the guidance of the regime of President Saddam Hussein in the 1990s. Starved of revenues from international oil sales as a result of the international sanctions regime and so-called "Oil for Food" measures, the regime actively found means of diverting crude to the black market to be trucked into neighbouring Jordan, Syria and Turkey (Eaton et al.: 2019: p. 13). This provided a significant revenue stream for Hussein's regime. Other attempts by governments not recognised by the international community to smuggle oil have been less effective. Libya had two rival governments from 2014 to 2021. The government operating in the east of the country, unrecognised by the international community, sought to export crude oil repeatedly. These efforts, which effectively constitute large scale efforts to smuggle oil, have failed owing to the threat of violations of international law being levied at those who purchase the oil.

Midstream diversion and smuggling of unrefined products

For the purposes of this chapter, midstream activities include the processing, storing and transporting of unrefined petroleum products. The distinction between midstream and downstream smuggling, between refined and unrefined products, is an important one. This is because the oil must be refined – or "finished" – to fulfil its function; i.e., for the crude to become diesel or heating oil. As a result, unrefined products are of lesser monetary value, necessitating either the sale of the product to actors that have access to refining capacity or possession of that capacity – and expertise – within the smuggling network.

The actors directly engaged in diversion of petroleum products midstream are those that have physical control over oil and gas infrastructure, the transportation network (usually pipelines), or the territory through which the products must pass. These include corrupt officials, security actors and criminal networks. The two principal means of diversion from the supply chain and subsequent smuggling are the physical capture of oil and gas infrastructure and the tapping of oil pipelines.

Control of oil and gas infrastructure and the sale of unrefined products

Actors that control oil and gas infrastructure but lack the access to technical expertise and facilities to refine fuel face limitations over their ability to sell the product. Following its capture of oil infrastructure in Syria and Iraq, the Islamic State of Syria and al-Sham (ISIS) was making significant profits from the running of oil fields and refineries, and subsequent smuggling of fuel to areas of Syria under the control of President Bashar al-Assad and also through pipelines to Turkey (Eaton et al.: 2019: p. 14). In response, the international coalition to counter the group decided to bomb the refineries under ISIS control. This led to the development of improvised methods to refining the fuel, such as digging a hole in the ground and flaring the oil to refine it in a rudimentary fashion. The fuel obtained through this process was of a significantly poorer quality and consequently sold for a much lower price (Eaton et al.: 2019: 52).

Greater sophistication is noted in the Nigerian smuggling sector to navigate the challenges associated with the theft of unrefined products. In Nigeria, crude oil appears to have been transported to artisanal refineries both within and outside of the country in the Nile Delta. In 2014, a refinery in Ghana was found to have produced five times its anticipated output of refined fuels due to the alleged input of smuggled Nigerian crude. The scheme required the complicity of actors associated with the Ghanaian production industry (Faucon: 2014), demonstrating the need for significant technical expertise for midstream smuggling.

Access without full control: tapping of unrefined products

For those actors who do not control fully territory that houses oil and gas infrastructure, the tapping of well-heads and pipelines is a means of large scale theft and subsequent smuggling. It can be done in two principal ways: "hot tapping" or "pressure tapping" involves fitting a tap to a high-pressure pipeline in order to divert a relatively small amount of the product. Some of these tapping operations, such as those that take place under water in Nigeria require significant expertise and are difficult to detect. The oil that is tapped either goes directly to artisanal refineries or so-called "mother ships" that may deliver the oil to other refineries, transfer it to other ships or unload it into storage (Ralby: 2017: 19). Perhaps as much as 10% of Nigeria's exports are tapped per day (Ralby: 2017: 19), pointing towards the industrial scale of these activities.

A more rudimentary alternative, "cold tapping," involves disabling or blowing up parts of pipelines and then fitting a tap as the pipelines are repaired, leaving the oil company unable to detect the tap. This approach has been used widely in Mexico, where the tapping and siphoning of pipelines carrying refined fuels of state-owned Petróleos Mexicanos (PEMEX) is a major challenge for the authorities (Ralby: 2017: p. 20). Organised crime groups are reported to bribe and coerce PEMEX employees to gain access to facilities where they can fit taps above- and under-ground in order to access fuel for their own purposes and to sell, as the sector has increasingly become controlled by large cartels. The number of illicit taps increased from an estimated 132 in 2001 to 12,582 in 2018, according to Pemex (Jones and Sullivan: 2019: p. 7). The tactics of the cartels have ended in disaster on some occasions. In one incident, 135 people were killed in an explosion as a result of an illegal tap in Tlahuelilpan, Hidalgo (Jones and Sullivan: 2019: p. 7). In 2011, PEMEX sued 11 U.S. companies for buying up to $300 million of stolen fuel that it said was trucked across the U.S.-Mexico border (Rosenberg: 2011).

Liquid cash: downstream smuggling of refined products

Downstream smuggling refers to the smuggling of refined (finished) products, for the purposes of this chapter. As at the midstream, the actors directly engaged in diversion of petroleum products are those that have physical control over oil and gas infrastructure, the transportation network and/or access to the territory through which the products must pass. Unlike the midstream, however, there are fewer barriers to entry in downstream smuggling, which also allows for the participation of smaller networks of smugglers and individual smugglers, particularly in the movement and sale of the product. Unlike the institutional players (such as heads of companies, and leaders of organised criminal networks) who may be making significant profits, the actors actually moving and selling the product on the lowest echelons of the supply chain are likely to be dependent on smuggling for their survival.

Refined products can be sold direct to the public or the private sector for consumption. The principal means of profiting from the sale of smuggled refined fuels is retailing, while profits can also be increased by adulterating smuggled low value products to imitate high value products.

Price differentials: retailing

Retailing does not necessitate theft. For smugglers who are retailing, profit is obtained by selling for a higher price than that at which they bought the fuel. The incentive to smuggle refined fuels such as gasoline across international borders is usually driven by the difference in prices between neighbouring states. Differentials between prices in neighbouring states are exacerbated by subsidy regimes. Large oil producing countries such as Venezuela, Nigeria and Libya use such subsidies to provide low-cost fuel to their populations, creating significant margins for those who move the subsidised fuels across the border. In 2018, it was reported that fuel smuggled into Colombia from Venezuela increased in value 37,000-fold as a result of Venezuela's financial crisis and subsidy regime, generating profits of $3 million a day for organised crime groups (Insight Crime: 2018).

The smuggling of gasoline from Libya to Tunisia in relatively small amounts via modified cars with oversized fuel tanks or via pickups carrying jerry cans of gasoline is long established, and the subject of informal regulation between Libyan and Tunisian counterparts (Gallien: 2020). The subsidised rate of gasoline in Libya was much as seven times cheaper than gasoline at the pump in Tunisia in 2018, offering a significant margin to smugglers (Eaton: 2018: p. 14). Such margins create opportunities for an array of actors, from individual smugglers, and individual criminal networks to state officials.

Theft and smuggling of petroleum products

Adulteration

After being smuggled across borders, low grade fuels are sometimes adulterated to imitate higher value products for onward sale to consumers to increase profits. This can be achieved by mixing other agents, such as ethanol into the fuel, or by mixing it with higher grade fuel. A prominent example of large-scale adulteration of fuel is found in Ireland. Irish fuel prices, particularly for agricultural grade diesel, made it highly profitable for criminal groups to adulterate the fuel and sell it across the border in Northern Ireland, with only very limited technical knowledge required. The practice was prevalent in the period following the 1998 peace agreement between the governments of the United Kingdom and Ireland, when border controls were relaxed. In 2002, the United Kingdom's Customs and Excise authority estimated that 450 of 700 petrol stations in Ireland were selling illicit fuel. Losses to the UK Treasury from fuel duty fraud were estimated at £450 million in 2000 (Irish Times: 2002). However, the margin obtained by the smugglers in the following decade was reduced significantly by the increase of fuel duties in Ireland and the reduction in the exchange rate from Euros, used in Ireland, to Sterling, used in the United Kingdom (Northern Ireland Assembly: 2012).

Anatomy of the fuel smuggling sector in Libya: leaks at all levels in the supply chain

While it is helpful to identify when and how petroleum products are diverted from the supply chain and smuggled by identifying upstream, midstream and downstream phases, the reality is that smuggling dynamics tend to be fluid and may be present at all levels. Contemporary dynamics in Libya illustrate how smuggling can permeate the upstream, midstream and downstream elements of the fuel sector. Since the overthrow of the regime of Muammar Gaddafi in 2011, the fuel smuggling sector has expanded from a cross-border activity to one that also determines the distribution of fuel in many areas *within* the country, as Libyans are less able to access state subsidised fuel.

A series of upstream problems plague Libya's fuel sector. State officials are likely to be profiting directly from smuggling through their official positions. A number of executives employed by state-owned entities also hold positions in private companies that profit from the fuel sector: a clear conflict of interest. In addition, a fractious security environment makes it nearly impossible for the authorities to enforce the law. The idiosyncrasies of the Gaddafi-era system of governance also make it difficult for state institutions to work together effectively. For example, the state electricity provider can requisition fuel from the state fuel company uni-laterally, and payment for consumption is by no means ensured (Pack: 2021). Oversight is limited, as illustrated by the mechanism for calculating market demand, which is based upon the requirements submitted by sellers rather than data on market needs. Sellers are thus incentivised to inflate their requirements. Moreover, many of the sellers exist only on paper. When, in 2018, the National Oil Corporation spot-checked 105 new gasoline stations registered since 2010, it found that 83 of them did not exist (Eaton: 2019). These have come to be known as 'ghost' stations.

These factors have driven a massive increase in the import of refined fuels (needed because Libya can meet only 20% of its fuel needs with its own refineries) since the revolution. Figures obtained from the Libyan National Oil Corporation indicate a 30% increase in the amount of gasoline being imported from 2010 to 2016. These increases are not explicable by market demand, indicating that demand was being exaggerated and the level of diversion in the system was on the rise. In 2017, the Libyan authorities assessed that around one-third of fuels such as gasoline and diesel are diverted to the market each year (Libya Observer: 2017). This is around 1.3 million tonnes, the equivalent of 178 Olympic-sized swimming pools (Eaton: 2019). In truth, though, the scale of diversion is unknown. Record keeping and public disclosure of statistics and figures is limited at best.

The leaks extend into the mid- and downstream of the fuel sector. The largest refinery in Libya is in north-western Libya, in the city of Zawiya. At the time of writing, it remains controlled by an armed group that has its origins in Libya's civil war. The Nasr Brigade, a revolutionary group, was transformed into a unit of the Libyan state's Petroleum Facilities Guard in 2013, placed onto the state payroll, and officially put in control of the Zawiya refinery. The refinery is a centre of smuggling activity. False paperwork is provided to truck drivers to make shipments destined for the black market look legitimate (especially if the destination station is a 'ghost' station) and the absence of accurate production figures makes it very difficult to ascertain how much of the fuel is being diverted. The National Oil Corporation's inability to control the territory its facilities are located in is a major problem. Similar issues exist at storage facilities, where officials and the armed groups guarding them can make significant profits from diverting the fuel to the black market.

Moreover, in the downstream sector, even fuel that is destined for the formal market must be moved over ground, often through areas controlled by armed actors who may hijack or confiscate some or all of the shipment. This is a particular problem in the south of the country, where a checkpoint economy has developed and armed groups apply informal taxes for the movement of goods to bolster their income.

The result of this activity is that Libyans are not benefitting from the fuel subsidies for which the state is paying in excess of $4 billion a year. In many areas of the country, particularly the south, it has become near impossible for locals to obtain fuel at subsidised rates, and they are instead forced to buy from the black market. Black market rates can be up to 15 times that of the official subsidised rates. "I filled my tank for 6.5 dinars (around $4.50) in Tripoli, 44 dinars ($31) in Sebha (southern Libya), and when I reached Ubari (southern Libya) it cost me 75 dinars ($53)," a driver told Chatham House researchers in August 2019 (Eaton: 2019).

These internal Libyan dynamics have led to shifts in the patterns of cross-border smuggling of fuel. Prior to 2011, the cross-border smuggling of fuel to Tunisia was well established, while Libyan fuel is also smuggled across the eastern border to Egypt and across its southern border to Niger, Chad and Sudan. The changes in Libya's smuggling has an impact on overland smuggling to Tunisia. Tunisian smugglers, who have to traverse the difficult operating environment in Libya, find it more difficult to obtain the fuel at low cost. Smugglers report having to deal with armed actors to obtain the fuel, and being charged inflated rates. Moreover, following the 2015 attack on the Tunisian border town of Ben Guerdane, border security has been increased on the Tunisian side. This has made it more difficult for smugglers to move fuel across the border, especially via desert routes. The impact of these shifts has been illustrated in the market, where prices of Libyan fuel increased four-fold between 2015 and 2019 (Eaton: 2019).

The smuggling of gasoil from Libya via maritime routes to Malta offers a greater margin than the aforementioned overland routes, expanding rapidly after the revolution. In 2015, Italy's Guardia di Finanza initiated operation 'Dirty Oil' in Sicily, targeted at fuel smugglers (Trial International: 2020). The operation led to the arrest of suspects in Libya, Malta and Italy. In Libya, the smuggling network was headed by Fahmi Salim Ben Khalifa, a native of the town of Zuwara, until his arrest in 2017. Salim's status in Zuwara was well known. Salim obtained his fuel from the aforementioned Zawiya refinery and then trucked the fuel to Zuwara (approximately 75km) and Abu Kammash (approximately 150 km) before using pumping stations

Theft and smuggling of petroleum products

to bunker fuel to small fishing boats at sea. The use of the gasoil for the fishing boats' motors presents a means of explaining why the gasoil is loaded onto the boats. Those fishing boats would then bunker the fuel to tankers at sea, mixing the Libyan fuel with the existing fuel on the boat.

To evade detection, the boats undertook measures such as deactivating their GPS tracking (a legal requirement to keep active) and undertook complex manoeuvres to mask the products that they collected (Frattini: 2016). In the case of three shipments identified in investigative reports, the tankers were chartered by two Maltese businessmen and subsequently bunkered in Malta in storage tanks leased by a Swiss company. That Swiss company paid the Maltese businessmen for the fuel (Trial International: 2020). The Maltese businessmen in question are currently undergoing prosecution. The prosecutors in the case allege that the fuel was subsequently transported to Italy and adulterated. Approximately $35 million of gasoil has reportedly been identified in the shipments in question (Corriere del Mezzogiorno: 2017). Increased surveillance and international attention on maritime smuggling of fuel has increased as a result of Operation Dirty Oil. Maritime smuggling from Libya seems subsequently to have reduced.

The result of these dynamics is that smuggling dynamics are no longer dependent on cross border movements. Cross-border smuggling of fuel from Libya is likely to have reduced, but diversion from the local Libyan market has significantly increased. Cross-border smuggling was predicated on retailing and generating a margin from one side of the border to another; i.e., buying at the subsidised rate and selling at a profit on the other side of the border in Tunisia, Egypt, Chad, Sudan and Niger. Now, however, the profit is increasingly obtained from Libyans themselves, as more of the fuel is diverted from the supply chain owing to weaknesses at the upstream, midstream and downstream levels. This means that, despite the state's buying greater amounts of fuel, less fuel is reaching the petrol pump at the official subsidised rates. This means that many Libyans are consequently forced to buy at higher, black market rates.

Engaging with fuel smuggling: how to plug the leaks?

The diversion and subsequent smuggling of petroleum products affects petroleum sectors across the world. There are a series of policies designed to combat it, ranging from attempts to reduce profitability, improve surveillance and transparency and rule-of-law centred efforts.

Reduce the incentives

Smugglers of oil products calculate the risk versus reward of their activities in part through the lens of profitability. One simple answer to reduce the prevalence of fuel smuggling is, therefore, to reduce that profitability. In countries with large subsidy regimes for fuels, this means cutting those subsidies. Iran has been implementing reforms to fuel subsidies since 2007. The price of gasoline was trebled by Iranian authorities through the removal of subsidies in 2019. This has concomitantly reduced the scale of smuggling. Studies assessing the price elasticity of gasoline prices in Iran also agree that the removal of subsidies will reduce the amount of gasoline that is smuggled across Iran's borders (Ghoddusi and Rafizadeh: 2019: 1).

The removal of subsidies is, however, not an economic silver bullet and can have negative impacts upon populations. Of course, price differentials can also be generated through other market variations, such as currency exchange rates. This is why the scale of the profits for smuggling fuel from Venezuela to Colombia was so high. Critics of Iran's approach note that hyperinflation in Iran's currency as a result of international sanctions may soon recreate profit margins for fuel smugglers (Mohseni-Cheraghlou: 2019).

There is also an important distinction to be made between those smugglers whose operations are based solely on profiting from margins between different markets and those whose operations are predicated on theft. Those who are diverting oil products from the supply chain through theft will of course be impacted by reduced margins, but a margin is still present as a result of the lack of direct payment for the oil products that they obtain. Removing subsidies on Libyan fuels may even increase the margin available to those in the smuggling sector who are stealing from the supply chain as prices at the pump will increase significantly.

Moreover, while it may stand to reason that those who are retailing fuel through buying it in one state and selling in another will reduce their activities if the margin is reduced, such a calculation also rests upon the assumption that they may have other means of income to adopt. Those operating at the lowest echelon of the smuggling supply chain, like the truckers, may depend on the business for survival. In Ghana, fuel smugglers have responded to diminishing returns by seeking to smuggle in greater volume (Ralby: 2017: 84). Others have diversified. In Iran, levels of diesel smuggling skyrocketed after price increases to gasoline were implemented (Voice of America: 2020).

Improving the transparency of the sector: papering over the cracks

Another key facilitator of oil and fuel smuggling is a lack of transparency within the oil sector of the states that suffer from the problem: poor reporting and entrenched corruption enable the activities of smugglers.

Fuel marking, where isotopes are added to fuel to allow investigators to ascertain where the fuel was intended to be sold, has become an increasingly prominent countermeasure, and is now mandated by law in many countries (Ralby: 2017: p. 87). In Northern Ireland, the 2015 addition of an isotope marker to fuel supplies allows authorities to understand quickly whether the fuel is rebated or unrebated. The standard 'washing' practices of the fuel smugglers do not remove the marker. UK authorities have observed a downward trend in the number of fuel laundering plants uncovered following its introduction. However, it is noteworthy that fuel smugglers have resorted to "sophisticated, and often dangerous" methods to defeat the marker that create toxic waste as a byproduct (Cross Border Organised Crime Threat Assessment: 2018: p. 16). Such waste has been dumped in remote locations, illustrating that the practice of fuel adulteration remains ongoing (Armaghi: 2018). Other contexts have reported successes from fuel marking. Mozambique's authorities reported the recovery of $25 million in lost revenues and $650,000 in asset seizures in the first semester of implementation of its marking programme (Wilcox: 2020).

Further strategies, such as GPS tracking of fuel trucks have been adopted to increase transparency in the system. Yet, such approaches have proven more open to manipulation by smugglers. In a particularly prominent illustration of this in Uganda, the trackers were given to another person on a motorcycle who would drive the route the truck was *supposed* to have taken to imitate the licit route. Meanwhile, the truck was diverted to the black market. In this case, the Ugandan regulators had become dependent on the data provided by a fuel company that was engaging in fuel smuggling. The chief executive of the company was arrested in 2016 after being implicated following the arrest of a motorcyclist who was carrying a GPS tracker (Ralby: 2017: p. 89).

Enforcement, complicity and second-order effects

Countries that have a greater capacity to enforce laws on the ground have demonstrated significant successes in limiting smuggling practices. The aforementioned efforts by the UK to mark fuel, combined with reforms to regulations and stiffened sentencing guidelines have delivered results. The UK authorities estimate that the illicit diesel market share in Northern Ireland fell from an estimated 19% in 2005–2006 to 6% in 2016–2017 (Cross Border Organised Crime Threat Assessment: 2018: p. 16). As noted, however, fuel smugglers have resorted to more sophisticated approaches to maintain their operations, and analysts warn that an increase in arbitrage opportunities for retailing fuels across the Northern Irish-Ireland border following the exit of the UK from the European Union could lead to a resurgence in smuggling practices (TheConversation: 2019).

The complicity of high-level officials, and sometimes their direct involvement in the smuggling of oil products can make countering the activities of smugglers an intractable problem for those committed to clamping down upon the practice. As noted, in countries such as Nigeria and Uganda, distribution of the *rights* to smuggle can be a key part of a political settlement, and therefore a guarantor of stability. In Nigeria, the support of elites profiting from smuggling has been obtained by candidates for the presidency to support their campaigns and then to help them to maintain their authority following their election. In northern Uganda, the case of the Opec Boys illustrates how the authorities can turn a relatively blind eye to the operations of smugglers, provided they did not rebel against the government. Such developments can lead to the deliberate maintenance of loop holes and governance flaws that prevent enforcement of the law.

Political leaders committed to reducing smuggling must contend with the limitations of their authority, particularly in conflict affected states. In operating environments such as Libya and Mexico, those seeking to disrupt fuel smuggling activities have a very difficult task. How can they contend with armed groups/sophisticated organised crime groups that have control of the territory they must operate within or move their goods through, in lieu of effective state forces?

In Mexico, a sustained multi-faceted offensive to reduce fuel theft is ongoing at the time of writing. The administration of Andrés Manuel López Obrador has shut down pipelines, made adjustments to the supply chain, arrested senior PEMEX executives, increased sentencing guidelines for fuel theft, deployed soldiers to guard infrastructure and unveiled a package of development spending to be targeted at the areas of the country where most pipeline theft is taking place. The Obrador Administration claims to have reduced pipeline theft by 90% as a result of the crack down, but analysts note that there are concerns over how long it can be sustained, arguing that organised crime groups are biding their time before striking back (Jones and Sullivan: 2019: pp. 14–15).

Indeed, it should be noted that such forces have the ability to fight back. In Libya, attempts by the National Oil Corporation to oust the Nasr Brigade from the Zawiya refinery led only days later to a mysterious electricity blackout as the electricity generating plant in the city shut down, resulting in 900 km of Libya's coastline being engulfed in darkness (Eaton: 2019). The commander of the Nasr Brigade is also subject to UN Sanctions for human trafficking, but he has retained his position. Here it is important to understand how the practice of fuel smuggling and rights to it operate in the context in question. Seeking to remove lucrative rent streams in the illicit economy without considering the responses of those who profit may stoke violence.

Conclusions

The examples listed above illustrate that fuel smuggling is not simply a practice conducted by small actors at the end of the supply chain through the movement of jerry cans on the back of a pickup. While such practices obviously exist, fuel smuggling operations also comprise complicit international companies, high level representatives of the state – civilian and military – and can take place in tankers at significant scale. Analysis of fuel smuggling activities in different contexts reveals inextricable connections with theft and exposes a range of challenges, from market incentives, to flaws in the governance of the oil sector, limitations to the control of formal state forces, and complicity of state employees in smuggling operations. It also illustrates that, for some segments of populations – particularly those actors who are involved in the downstream elements of the supply chain – smuggling provides income where few alternatives may exist.

The lessons from attempts to curb the smuggling of petroleum products to date indicate that a detailed assessment of the political economy of the sector must be undertaken to understand who profits and how, and to explore how they might respond. The higher the penetration of profiteers up the supply chain, the more complex the solutions become.

Effective strategies therefore need to be multifaceted and sequenced with other policies – such as cash payments to populations in return for the removal of subsidies and private sector development opportunities – to offset the negative impacts of curbing of such activities on key actors and local communities. The latter must also avoid unduly rewarding illicit activity while also developing a pragmatic course of action that has a realistic chance of successful implementation. Finally, the transnational nature of the smuggling networks indicates that there will always be limits to any country-level strategy. International collaboration, and collaboration with neighbouring states in particular, should be made a priority.

References

African Development Bank (2016). Illicit trade in natural resources in Africa. https://www.afdb.org/fileadmin/uploads/afdb/Documents/Events/IFF/Documents_IFF/ANRC_ILLICIT_TRADE_IN_NATURAL_RESOURCES.pdf

Armaghi (2018). Fuel launderers who dumped toxic waste near Keady 'beneath contempt'. https://armaghi.com/news/keady-news/fuel-launderers-who-dumped-toxic-waste-near-keady-beneath-contempt/72176

Assad, A. (2017). Audit bureau: Libya spent $30 billion on fuel subsidies in five years. *Libya Observer*, 19 August 2017, https://www.libyaobserver.ly/economy/audit-bureau-libya-spent-30-billion-fuel-subsidies-five-years

Faucon, B. (2014). Tiny Ghana oil platform's big output sparks scrutiny. *Wall Street Journal*. 28 August 2014. http://www.wsj.com/articles/tiny-ghana-oil-platforms-big-output-sparks-scrutiny-1408669517.

Burgis, T. (2015). *The Looting Machine: Warlords, Tycoons, Smugglers and the Systemic Theft of Africa's Wealth.* William Collins.

Corriere del Mezzogiorno (2017). *Gasolio rubato in Libia da miliziani dell'Isis e rivenduto in Italia ed Europa: 6 arresti.* https://corrieredelmezzogiorno.corriere.it/catania/cronaca/17_ottobre_18/gasolio-rubato-libia-venduto-italia-ed-europa-nove-arresti-73d0b250-b3cb-11e7-a16e-c85a3b50cb84.shtml

Eaton, T. (2018). *Libya's War Economy: Predation, Profiteering and State Weakness.* Chatham House. https://www.chathamhouse.org/publication/libyas-war-economy-predation-profiteering-and-state-weakness

Eaton, T. (2019). *Libya: Rich in Oil, Leaking Fuel.* Chatham House. https://chathamhouse.shorthandstories.com/libya-rich-in-oil-leaking-fuel/index.html

Eaton, T. et al. (2019). *Conflict economies in the Middle East and North Africa.* Chatham House. https://www.chathamhouse.org/sites/default/files/2019-08-13-ConflictEconomies.pdf

Frattini, D. (2016). Quelle petroliere fantasma dalla Libia all'Italia I traffici nel Mediterraneo (e i Big Data per tracciarli) [Ghost Tankers from Libya to Italy: Trades in the Mediterranean (and Big Data to track

Theft and smuggling of petroleum products

them)], Corriere Della Sera, 25 February 2016. http://www.corriere.it/reportage/esteri/2016/quelle-petroliere-fantasma-dalla-libia-allitalia-i-traffici-nel-mediterraneo-e-i-big-data-pertracciarli/?refresh_ce-cp

Gallien, M. (2020). Informal Institutions and the regulation of smuggling in North Africa. *Perspectives on Politics*, 18(2), 492–508. doi:10.1017/S1537592719001026

Ghoddusi, H. and Rafizadeh, N. (2019). *The Effect of Fuel Subsidy Reforms on the Behavior of Gasoline Consumers*. University of Cambridge. http://www.econ.cam.ac.uk/people-files/faculty/km418/IIEA/IIEA_2019_Conference/Papers/Rafizadeh%20-%20The%20Effect%20of%20Fuel%20Subsidy%20Reforms%20on%20the%20Behavior%20of%20Gasoline%20Consumers.pdf

Irish Times (2002). Major fuel smuggling in North, says audit office. 15 February. https://www.irishtimes.com/news/major-fuel-smuggling-in-north-says-audit-office-1.413617

Jones, N.P. and Sullivan, J.P. (2019). Huachicoleros. *Journal of Strategic Security*, 12(4), 1–24. doi: https://www.jstor.org/stable/10.2307/26851258

Katsouris, C. and Sayne, A. (2013). *Nigeria's Criminal Crude: International Options to Combat the Export of Stolen Oil*. Chatham House. https://www.chathamhouse.org/sites/default/files/public/Research/Africa/0913pr_nigeriaoil_es.pdf

Lecoutere E. and Titeca K. (2007). *The Opec Boys and the Political Economy of Smuggling in Northern Uganda*. Brighton: The Institute of Development Studies, University of Brighton.

Lipin, M. et. al. (2020). Iran's November Gas Price Hike Fails to Ease Fuel Smuggling to Pakistan. Voice of America. 15 February 2020. https://www.voanews.com/middle-east/voa-news-iran/irans-november-gas-price-hike-fails-ease-fuel-smuggling-pakistan

Mining.com (2017). Just How Big is the Oil Market? https://oilprice.com/Energy/Crude-Oil/The-Oil-Market-Is-Bigger-Than-All-Metal-Markets-Combined.html

Mohseni-Cheraghlou, A. (2019). Déjà vu all over again: The three "I"s of gasoline subsidies and social unrest in Iran: Middle East Institute. https://www.mei.edu/publications/deja-vu-all-over-again-three-gasoline-subsidies-and-social-unrest-iran

Northern Ireland Assembly (2012). Official Report: 2011-2: Hansard. http://www.niassembly.gov.uk/assembly-business/official-report/committee-minutes-of-evidence/session-2011-2012/october-2011/northern-ireland-organised-crime-strategy-2012-15/

Pack, J. (2021, forthcoming). *Libya and the Global Enduring Disorder*. London: Hurst.

Ralby, I.M. (2017). Downstream oil theft: global modalities, trends, and remedies. Atlantic Council. https://www.atlanticcouncil.org/wp-content/uploads/2017/01/Downstream_Oil_Theft_web_0327.pdf

Rosenberg, M. (2011). Mexico's Pemex sues U.S. firms over fuel smuggling. *Reuters*. https://www.reuters.com/article/us-mexico-pemex-idUSTRE7516S420110602

The Conversation (2019). Smuggling in the Irish borderlands – and why it could get worse after Brexit. https://theconversation.com/smuggling-in-the-irish-borderlands-and-why-it-could-get-worse-after-brexit-111153

Trial International (2020). Smuggling Libyan gasoil: a Swiss trader navigates through troubled waters. https://trialinternational.org/latest-post/smuggling-libyan-gasoil-a-swiss-trader-navigates-through-troubled-waters/

UK Government (2018). Cross Border Organised Crime Assessment. https://www.justice-ni.gov.uk/publications/cross-border-organised-crime-assessment-2018

Wilcox, M. (2020). Will fuel marking spell the end of fuel smuggling in Africa? *Africa Times*. 31 March. https://africatimes.com/2020/03/31/will-fuel-marking-spell-the-end-of-fuel-smuggling-in-africa/

20

OLD ROUTES, NEW RULES

Smuggling rice in the porous borders of the Sulu, Celebes, and South China Sea

Eddie L. Quitoriano

Introduction

This chapter explains the persistent smuggling of rice in Southeast Asia despite continued efforts to strengthen regulation and cross-country cooperation in monitoring and policing the porous borders of the region, especially those in the Sulu and Celebes Seas.[1]

Rice exchanges in the region preceded the creation of international borders and the formation of modern states. It formed part of the economies of the Sulu Zone that divided the Philippines and Malaysia and the Malacca Strait that divided Indonesia from Singapore and Malaysia before the Dutch, British and Spanish colonizers began to impose controls on the movement of people and goods (Saleeby, 1908; Trocki, 1979, 1990; Warren, 1977).

The historical background and the geographical connections among trading posts in the region partly explain why the unregulated trade in rice and other food products persisted even after the end of World War II when the modern states of Indonesia, Philippines and Malaysia were formed and trade pacts were inked and national laws on tariffs and customs were enacted. However, this explanation is not enough.

The chapter will show why rice smuggling continues to possess traction across the various entrepots in the region because of at least two important factors.

One, rice is the staple food in the region and is therefore an important barometer of food security. A severe fluctuation in prices caused by sudden shifts in supply or perceptions of scarcity is a source of instability and pressure that induces governments to consider all means necessary to procure rice. The stability of supply and price of this staple food, or the lack of it can fuel popular unrest, including rioting and targeted attacks against certain ethnic groups who are perceived to be hoarding supplies or involved in price gouging. As a barometer of food security, rice access also becomes a potent signifier of political legitimacy and authority of the State in countries such as the Philippines, Malaysia, and Indonesia

Two, the unregulated trade and exchange in rice is a socially embedded economic practice that has persisted for generations across the South China Sea despite the precariousness of supplies and the presence of highly protected markets.

Rice smuggling is shrouded by references to the longstanding practice of "barter trade," and there are deep social ties (ethnicity, religion, or otherwise) that bind certain groups and identities across the region. These ties were fostered by a vibrant and robust trade that existed

272

DOI: 10.4324/9781003043645-20

Old routes, new rules

long before modern states were formed and continues to exist as one of the few surviving historical relics of the trade in food and other prestige goods among East, Southeast, and South Asia.

The study demonstrates how the smuggling of rice is a strategic tool in ensuring food security and political legitimacy that often compels state and society to engage in actions that place them in alternating positions of cooperation and contestation. For example, states and substates in the region will agree to leverage and prioritize the stopping of terrorist contagion or the illegal trade in narcotic drugs and weapons rather than impose hard rules on the trade of food commodities, such as rice, and other non-lethal goods.

A nuanced approach is needed at the outset when describing rice trading and the people involved in it. The discourse on rice smuggling often paints informal cross-border trade as a site of illicit, illegal, underground, and criminal entrepreneurs (Donnan & Wilson, 1999[2]; Bonnier & Bonnier, 2019[3]; Centeno & Portes, 2006[4]). In many ports where rice is shipped or traded, however, the absence or non-payment of formal duties or taxes is more commonplace than one would expect.

These realities explain why the research looked at rice smuggling from the perspective of those directly involved in it – unearthing the distinct incentives and colorful narratives that lie beneath the often dour and dark explanations used to explain many shadow economies.

This chapter used an institutional and economic sociological approach to explore and examine the formal and informal rule systems and social relationships that surround the trade in rice. It showed how rice smuggling is an "instituted economy," or an economy embedded in social relations, where market prices do not constitute the sole determinant of the commodity's production, consumption, and exchange processes (Polanyi, 1944/1957: 60). The notion that smuggling is merely a disruption of reigning institutions or rule-systems ignores the many political, social, and cultural aspects that shape and are shaped by rice markets in Southeast Asia.

We begin with an assessment of an historically vibrant trade in rice across Southeast Asia, sourced from records and narratives of cross-border trade and the associated benefits, risks, and conflicts surrounding rice smuggling. A case study of cross-border trade between the provinces of Tawi-Tawi, Philippines and Sabah, Malaysia across the Sulu Sea is employed to train the spotlight on the impervious norms and practices that continue to shape the smuggling of food commodities such as rice across regional borders.

The study utilized "trialogues" and in-depth interviews with both formal and shadow authorities, together with scoping visits to various trading posts in the Sulu Sea.[5] Empirical data is also drawn from extended conversations with consumers, traders, seafarers, financiers, local government officials and political elites, policemen and former rebels.

Finally, the author went on maritime scoping visits to numerous ports on a *kumpit* vessel starting from Zamboanga and going to Sulu, Tawi-Tawi and finally Sabah and back, to observe both legal and illegal cross-border activities.[6] These voyages provided the rich and graphic evidence that showed the impervious multi-layered exchanges and ties that stretched across the Muslim-dominated and rice-consuming entrepots of the Philippines, Malaysia, and Indonesia in Southeast Asia.

Rice security as food security and political legitimacy

Scarcities and price spikes promote images of hunger and impoverishment that put into question the government's right to rule. States and societies have been in turmoil every time rice prices spike and domestic supplies dip. The African food riots in 2008 (affecting Mozambique, Egypt and Morocco) were a result of the 2007–2008 international rice price crisis

(Omar et al., 2019). The 1997–1998 food riots in Indonesia were a result of the decline in supply of rice (and soybeans) and debilitating impact of the financial crisis (Mukherjee and Koren, 2019). So too were the large-scale riots in Pakistan in 1986, 2001, 2002 and 2007 (ibid.).

In all these riots, food insecurity became a clarion call to question and resist the incumbent states' right to rule. Governments would respond by quickly distributing reserves if these were available or by hastily importing rice. Sometimes the government would turn violent and find a scapegoat for the miseries facing their population.

In 1998, the Suharto regime tried to deflect blame by scapegoating and helping fan Muslim hatred against the ethnic Chinese. He ultimately failed and fell, but not before instigating bloody attacks and reprisals against ethnic Chinese traders (Indonesia Alert, February 18, 1998).[7] In Pakistan, the Zia-ul-Haq and Musharraf regimes responded with killings and arrests that rallied citizens to the opposition.[8] In the Philippines, the price of rice has been found to be a significant determinant in presidential election results since the 1950s and well into the 2000s, and has led to the ejection of top government officials who were at the helm of agricultural bureaucracies when a rice crisis struck (Intal and Garcia, 2008).

In sum, governments are fearful of the potential tensions and violent flashpoints that may occur if access to rice is hampered by supply shortages and the consequent spikes in prices. This dilemma underscores why the smuggling of rice may be considered politically feasible and expedient if a tightening of supplies emerges.

The dynamics of rice supply and smuggling behavior

Underlying the rhetoric of globalization and a borderless world are tensions and conflicts derived from the rigidity of political borders despite the dynamism of economic cooperation and social interdependence, especially in staple food products such as rice that projects food security across the region.[9]

The global rice market is a thin, segmented, and imperfect market with a limited number of buyers and sellers, with unpredictable levels and sources of demand, leading to instability and uncertainty (Roche, 1992: 1–2). There are an estimated 110 countries that produce rice, but only a few participate in the export market and only 6.3% of global rice production is traded internationally.

Ninety percent of global supply is now produced and consumed in Asia (Hossain and Narciso, 2004). Southeast Asia stands at the center of the global rice economy, contributing 39.9% of global exports in 2016 (Omar et al., 2019: 5). Exporters include Thailand, Vietnam, India, the United States, China, Pakistan, Australia, Italy, Uruguay, Argentina., Egypt and Spain and the first five control 75% of the market (Hossain and Narciso, 2004). Among the five, Thailand controls 30% of the market (ibid.).

Critical studies about the fragility of supplies first emerged in 1992, when 98% of 354.46 million Metric Tons (MT) of global supply was consumed in their respective countries of production. Only about 12.89 million MT (3.6%) was exported, while 12.34 million MT (3.4%) were imported (Roche, 1992: 148).

With fragile supplies, the general tendency of rice-producing countries is to secure domestic output for their own populations and rely on imports to offset deficiencies in domestic supply. Herein lies the challenge: how can this strategy work in a market beset with uncertainty, complexity, and unbridled competition, and in a situation where global rice supplies are unreliable?

Old routes, new rules

The challenge was underlined in the 2007–2008 rice crisis when only 7% of the 432.6 million MT global output was traded in international markets (Manzano and Prado, 2014). The corresponding price shock saw global prices rising from US$335 to US$1,000 per MT between April 2007 and October 2008 (ibid.). It also induced the sort of "beggar thy neighbor policies" that permitted rice to be smuggled under the gaze of national states and substates. In some provinces of the southern Philippines, smuggled rice flooded local markets with very little state intervention and interdiction. In Sabah and other parts of Malaysia, rice that was imported from Vietnam and Thailand found its way into Philippine markets.

The Philippines modified its policies on importation and allocated 200,000 MT for private sector importation from a total of 2.2 million MT imported (Briones and De la Pena, 2015). During the period, Philippine rice imports comprised 7% of the total supply traded in the international market. Meanwhile, Malaysia responded to the 2008 rice crisis with a knee-jerk reaction to increase the national stockpile threefold, from 92,000 MT to 292,000 MT, also by importation (Omar et al., 2019: 150).

Malaysia and the Philippines are net importers of rice. They belong to the top ten countries that are dependent on imports. Their 2019 rice trade deficits were worth US$441.9 million and US$1 billion, respectively.[10] Their import partners from Southeast Asia – Thailand, Vietnam, Myanmar and Cambodia – belong to the top ten highest rice export gainers during the same year.[11] Thailand alone gained US$4.2 billion in rice export revenues during the year.[12]"

A perennial problem on the Philippine side is rice smuggling, with milled rice being the top agricultural product being smuggled (Lantican & Ani, 2020). An estimated US$1.96 billion worth of milled rice was smuggled to the country between 1986 to 2009 (Alano, 1984). The phenomenon is not completely outside the law. Lantican & Ani (ibid.) show consistent discrepancy of exporting country reports and reports of the Philippine Bureau of Customs averaging 23.3% underreporting during the 2004–2016 period.

During the pre-election year rice crisis in 2018, the Philippine Secretary of Agriculture even proposed the "legalization of rice smugglers" to appease angry publics and recover foregone revenues in the form of "*tara*" (bribe money) to corrupt government officials (Business World Online, August 29, 2018). The "*tara*" referred to by the Secretary was generated from an estimated PHP 2 billion (roughly US$40 million) in avoided rice import tariffs in the maritime trade between southern Philippines and Sabah during the third quarter of 2018.

The Philippines and Malaysia offer helpful comparisons in assessing the dynamics of rice supplies and how they shape smuggling behavior. Both countries are net importers of rice. Domestic output is traded in-country and supply is stabilized with strong control measures and devices. Exposure in the international rice market is mainly used to offset shortfalls in domestic supply and ensure availability of buffer stock.

We also need to change our views about the so-called illegality of rice smuggling in this porous border. Traders do not perceive their actions as illegal. When rents are paid, these pay-offs land in the pockets of the same "law enforcers" or customs agents that are supposed to enforce trade laws.

There is a legal loophole that allows customs officials to look the other way. The Philippine Anti-Agricultural Smuggling Act of 2016 declares large-scale smuggling as economic sabotage or a high crime. However, it is lenient on rice smuggling while harsh on other agricultural products. A smuggler of onions, sugar, corn, pork, poultry, carrots or fish could be considered a saboteur if the Customs valuation of the intercepted goods is PHP 1 million (US$19,700). One has to smuggle PHP 10 million worth of rice (US$197,055), or ten times as much, to be considered a saboteur.

Most of the traders involved are thousands of small women merchant-buyers who partake of the income and benefits to be derived from a coping or survival economy. The view that the smuggling of rice is violent and operates below the pale of the law is undermined in the porous borders of the Sulu Sea where rice smugglers often conduct their business aboveground and in an orderly and non-violent manner – under the noses of State regulators who partake of the "taxes" and "duties" paid to them.[13]

These factors point to a critical yet seldom acknowledged fact; i.e., that the porous maritime borders of Southeast Asia represent a de-facto free trade zone in rice.

Rice smuggling in regional and historical perspectives

The maritime border between the Philippines and Malaysia used to be a robust international "free trade zone" in the seventeenth and eighteenth centuries (Warren, 1977; Warren, 2011). Various commodities were traded, including food products and prestige goods that extended as far as Indonesia, Thailand, China, and India. Goods were not "smuggled," because no duties were expected to be paid for selling and buying rice. In fact, the unfettered traditional trade and exchange of goods across the Sulu Sea became bounded only in the post-colonial period when the legal and normative beginnings of the crime of "smuggling" became prominent between the Philippines, Sabah, and the bigger Federation of Malaya and Indonesia.

In 1967, the Philippines and Malaysia signed an anti-smuggling pact specifically to regulate trade in rice and other commodities between the Philippines and Sabah.[14] The agreement provided for the placement of Philippine customs stations in Sandakan, Semporna and Kota Kinabalu and free movement of people residing in border areas.[15] The protocol to the agreement defined the border areas: the Sabah administrative districts of Sandakan, Lahad Datu, Semporna, Kudat and Tawau on the Malaysian side and the Province of Sulu and the Balabac Island Group including Palawan Province on the Philippine side.[16] People living in the border areas could move freely for business, social visits and pleasure with the mere carriage of a two-week border pass and without need of a passport.

However, cooperation against smuggling dwindled less than a year the signing of the anti-smuggling pact. Diplomatic relations between the two countries soured in 1968 when the Philippine government passed Republic Act No. 5446 that referred to Sabah as part of Philippine territory.[17]

Nevertheless, the peoples of Sabah and southern Philippines continued to engage in trade and social visits. The salience of trust and the role of traditional social networks such as the Muslim clans and tribes on both sides of the maritime border, plus the free and robust movement of people and goods is manifest in the fact that cross-border trade in rice has always referred to the centuries-old practice of barter as reference.

Barter as concealment of rice smuggling

The maritime trade exchanges connecting Tawi-Tawi (Philippines) and Sabah (Malaysia) is one such arena where traditional norms governing the exchange of goods and ethnic ties were being reformed in the post-colonial period. The traditional exchange of goods was redefined as smuggling and the nurturing of ethnic ties as illegal immigration. Only the traditional and embedded practice of barter survived the changes in trade rules – remaining as a social practice that is mutually recognized by both the Philippines and Malaysia.[18]

The practice of barter trade is context specific and geographically situated. In Sabah, rice exports to Southern Philippines used the language of barter even when it was enabled by the trans-shipment of rice from Vietnam or Thailand. In short, the incoherence and inconsistency in rules governing barter trade facilitates the illicit trade in rice. The conclusion that one gets is that barter really constitutes just one of many transactions that masks the smuggling of rice into different borders. This thesis is buttressed too by the formidable requirements for regulating frontier areas governed by traditional rules and practices.

The shared maritime borders among the Philippines, Malaysia and Indonesia are two adjacent seas, the Celebes and Sulu seas, that encompass 210,000 square miles. It forms part of the global trade route. It is difficult to control not only because of its size, but also because of the thousands of ocean-going vessels plying the route.[19] The eastern coast of Sabah, particularly, Sandakan, Lahad Datu, Semporna and Tawi – is a maze of coral reefs, sandbars, mudflats, shoals and submerged rocks that is more suitable for small craft of seafarers with local knowledge than large-scale amphibious operations (CIA, 1969).

Although wooden-hull trading vessels are no longer registered for import trading and permitted to cross international waters, they continue to carry rice and other commodities across the Sulu Sea from the ports of Sandakan and Tawau (in Sabah) to the Chinese pier in Bongao and other island municipalities of Tawi-Tawi.[20] Upon docking, Tausug crew watch over Sama laborers climbing up and down the wooden ladders to unload sacks of rice and boxes of cigarettes, cooking oil, sugar, *kari* noodles and other foodstuffs to the backsides of a row of apartments that double up as *bodegas* (small warehouses) and wholesale stores. Most of these are owned by Chinese merchants, for whom the pier is named.

Alongside the trading vessels are passenger liners ready to load people and cargo for travel and distribution to the islands while hundreds of smaller boats carry, retail packs of rice, noodles, gasoline in family-size bottles of soft drinks, sugar, cooking oil and other stuffs for redistribution to retail stores on stilts or in the small islands nearby. On the other side of the piers are public markets where smaller stores and hawkers retail the same goods to consumers.

Rice smuggling as an instituted economy[21]

The rice economy is instituted with cultural symbols and embedded social networks and the smuggling of rice continues to be carried out using the language and practices of traditional barter traders in Sabah and Tawau in Malaysia, Tarakan in Indonesia, and Tawi-Tawi and Sulu in the southern Philippines.

Transactions include reciprocal exchanges and redistributive arrangements, i.e., prices were not solely defined by supply and demand, and arrangements allowed discounts for the poor, the disabled, victims of natural and man-made calamities, and others. Barter trade helped to thicken social capital relations and nurture kinship ties across the seas. It helped establish life-long relationships especially between women traders who were unified by one religion despite their different nationalities and tribes. This agreement held the strongest traction in the case of rice.

For example, the 40-member Karandahan Association of Tawi-Tawi is a group of Sama small traders who are directly involved in the import and retail of rice, oil, fuel, flour and sugar. Their ethnic configuration is designed to secure economic space for the Sama without clashing with the interests of big Tausug and Chinese traders. They helped lubricate the kinship relations of members with those in Sabah and Indonesia without completely isolating themselves from the wider economic field.

Working more broadly with other economic actors motivated Karandahan to become part of the Filipino Muslim Traders Association and the wider and multi-ethnic BIZNET of the Tawi-Tawi Chamber of Commerce and Industry. The wider network enabled them to identity export markets in Sabah and Indonesia. A similar dynamic occurred across the sea in Sabah where the traditional Tausug, Sama and Sabahan traders joined the formal groupings and institutions registered with the Sabah State Ministry of Finance.

Many people from Sulu had relatives living and working in Sabah and other adjacent Malaysian and Indonesian provinces and vice-versa. Inter-marriages among Malaysians, Filipinos, and Indonesians were not uncommon, especially among merchants and traders. Kinship ties and traditions among the Tausug, Sama, and Bajau took root amidst the shared religion and practices of Islam, and especially in the pursuit of customs, celebrations, and festivals that were woven into the trade relationships that bound residents of multiple outposts.

It was clear that the artificial territorial limitations that were imposed following the formation of modern states modified the nature of traditional trading but did not end it. The effort to divide ethnic peoples into different nationalities did not likewise deter traditional links and relationships (Chouvy, 2013: 8, 10, 11).

When Sabah was still part of the Sulu Sultanate, the Tausug and Sama Bajau who crisscrossed the Sulu Sea to barter or engage in various exchange of goods and the maintenance of social and ethnic ties did not consider themselves either Filipinos or Malaysians. Even today, the Bajau, largest ethnic group in Sabah, and the Sama Bajau of Southern Philippines pay no heed to the notion of national borders (Rabasa and Chalk, 2012: 1, 2).

We can better understand the dynamics behind the legal and illegal cross-border trade in rice that is nested in practices and traditions by travelling from Tawi-Tawi to Sabah and back.

Tawi-Tawi to Sabah and back: the cross-border trade in rice

The smuggling of rice between Malaysia and southern Philippines is a mix of small-scale procurements of rice and other foodstuffs from Sabah by barter traders from Tawi-Tawi and Sulu and large-scale rice smuggling by Manila-based big firms. Like the Philippines, the prominent role of Malaysia in rice exporting, despite the shared lack of rice surpluses is cause for serious attention. Both countries appear to function as the providers of international free ports and trans-shipment facilities that bigtime smugglers can use for their Southeast Asian rice trading operations.

Traveling in the Sulu Sea to scope the legal and illegal transit of rice and other commodities gives any observer a front-row seat into the intricacies of the rice trade and an insight into the sophistication of its participants, especially the women-merchant traders coming from all the ports across the Sulu Sea.

Behind the surge of large-scale smuggling and away from the headlines of news dailies is the regularity of cross-border trading between Tawi-Tawi and Sabah. While Zamboanga City serves as a conduit for large-scale smuggling and redistribution to the national capital, Bongao, the capital of Tawi-Tawi, serves as the nexus for the redistribution of smuggled rice into the islands, including those Malaysian islands close to Tawi-Tawi.

Tawi-Tawi traders procure rice from registered barter traders in Sabah and procure supplies from the ports of Sandakan and Tawau. The smuggled rice is then brought to Bongao, which is the locus of a highly organized smuggling supply chain. From Bongao, rice is procured by merchant-traders, many of whom are women entrepreneurs who pool their capital to buy in the barter trade markets for immediate redistribution to local consumers. This system is different from that of large-scale smugglers using the same transhipment node, transferring the smuggled rice to private wharfs and warehouses in Zamboanga City before re-transporting them to large markets in the National Capital Region.

Rice is brought to Tawi-Tawi, not hidden in containers nor mixed with other goods; it is out in the open or brought in with fake invoices. Everyone knows that the legal documents are flawed and that the data on rice volumes and prices are all faked, but everyone joins in performing a charade where people know each other, yet engage each other as if they were strangers in serious negotiation with state officials. The entire scene looked serious enough to secure a sense of formality, but in the end, you knew that each one has done this regularly, like buying and selling rice and other food stuffs next door, as they had done for centuries. Some traders sign the Informal Import Declaration and Entry Form[22] and pay nominal fees while most others do not. No government agency in Tawi-Tawi is monitoring the volume and value of rice imports.

Cross-border rice trading between Sabah and Tawi-Tawi is really about the importation of rice from Sabah, and the export of a few commodities from the Philippines. Other commodities, such as copra, seaweed and fishes are rarely on the list because both ports produce ample supplies of each. Although both are deficient in rice production, Sabah is a beneficiary of leaked trans-shipped rice from Vietnam and Thailand, which in turn is re-exported and smuggled into the Philippines.[23]

As has been in the past, rice insufficiency is a key driver in the cross-border importation to Tawi-Tawi. The nearest and most practical source is Sabah. A trialogue with three smugglers and a discussion with other traders revealed that there were at least 300 wooden-hull vessels operating in the Zamboanga, Sulu and Tawi-Tawi areas.[24] Currently, there are 15 trading vessels operating from Bongao, the capital town of the province that are owned by traders who acquired knowledge and expertise from their parents and the parents before them.[25] The vessel count does not include wooden-hull vessels of lower tonnage that ferry passengers and cargoes of dried seaweed and dried fish between islands.

Wooden-hull boats from Bongao are engaged in passenger line operations to major islands of the province and tramp line freight operations in cross-border trade with Sabah.[26] Traders-shippers from Bongao enter into contractual agreement with barter traders-suppliers in Sabah. Before the Malaysian ban on rice transhipment in late 2018, a hundred boats take off from Sabah each month, exporting rice worth RM 600,000 (roughly, US$140,000) and other supplies such as sugar, flour and cigarettes worth RM 300,000 (roughly US$70,000) per boat (Borneo Post, January 6, 2019).[27] Bongao traders usually mobilize PHP 10 to 12 million of capital (roughly, US$200,000–240,000) for each trading run of break-bulk cargo consisting of rice, noodles, cooking oil, cigarettes and other stuffs.

Cross-border trading is a pooled endeavor involving the vessel owner and his crew, plus the politicians, policemen, teachers, entrepreneurs, and other stakeholders that are either on board the vessel or invested heavily in its cargo. Capital is raised among interested parties who can put up at least PHP 40,000 to PHP 50,000 per trip, for a total of at least PHP3–5 million per trip. Purchase capital is electronically transmitted in advance by pawnshops doubling as remittance centers in Bongao in close coordination with remittance centers in Sabah.

The entire enterprise relies on high levels of trust – in the safety of the vessel, the protection of its passengers, and the guaranteed return on investments. Actual trading is highly capitalized and the risks are shared by everyone on board, in varying scales, according to each one's capacity and resources. Passengers on the vessel are joined by rice resellers in wholesale markets, other small boat owners, and a few port loaders.

All smuggled goods are declared as "barter" goods. In addition to bulk cargo on wooden-hulled freight vessels, small-scale smuggled goods are brought back by passengers on liner vessels or by small traders from outlying islands nearest to Sabah such as Sitangkai and Sibutu (closest to Semporna, Lahad Datu and Tawau) or Cagayan de Sulu (closest to Sandakan). Landed costs and domestic retail prices are low because of avoided tariffs while boat owners and trip organizers shield the "investors" from administrative costs and rents accruing to customs officials.

The entire trip is a chance to witness the longstanding ethnic ties between the Bajaus, largest ethnic group in Sabah, and the Sama Bajau of the Southern Philippines who both pay little heed to national borders. According to a Sama Bajau trader interviewed on board the vessel, the Sama Bajau in the eastern parts of Indonesia, Eastern Sabah and Southern Philippines are really engrossed with rice because it is seen as the most important agricultural crop.[28] *Buwas kuning* (yellow rice[29]) is an indispensable part of the *pag-omboh* (giving food to dead ancestors) and *mag-omboh* (annual rice ritual), which are mandatory and believed to be the means of protecting families from curses (Hussin, 2019). The preparation of *buwas kuning* itself is socially significant and is often accompanied by deeds of sharing and family reunions.

It was also a chance to recognize the unifying force of a single religious identity in the dominant Islamic religion of citizens in both Tawi-Tawi and Sabah. Like other Muslims, the abject conditions brought by natural or man-made calamities, where the hoarding of goods and the monopoly of scarce resources is a kneejerk response, was universally scorned by all the respondents aboard the ship. They claimed that the admonitions in the Qu'ran and the Hadith prevented that kind of behavior. They are jovial and generous and each one partakes of one another's food.

There is indeed some symmetry in the practices of Asian peoples where rice is not only a cereal for basic sustenance but is also woven into social, religious, and cultural fabric of life. In one conversation the author heard of the many different ways to cook and process rice, including the rituals and festivals that accompanied these processes. Rice also played a prominent role in marriage ceremonies in both Sabah and Tawi-Tawi. Finally, for the Ibans of Sarawak, rice is central to their ancestors, and the author was fortunate to have joined a weeklong rice festival when communities from other Rumahs joined the celebration.

Conclusion

The smuggling of rice persists despite continued efforts to strengthen regulation and cross-country cooperation in monitoring and policing the porous borders of the Sulu Sea, because of the convergence of economic and social incentives and motivations among those involved in smuggling – whether as perpetrators or regulators. Rice smuggling, as we have seen, is community driven and founded upon a long-standing tradition of barter trade and reciprocal food security, ring-fenced from criminal activity and contributive to political and economic stability.

Rice smuggling is not only an informal economy, but also an economic arrangement that straddles different sets of institutions: legal and illegal; formal and informal; aboveground and underground. Across the porous borders of Southeast Asia where rice is traded, we see actors wearing different hats – as enforcers and facilitators or as formal and shadow authorities who possess legitimacy and authority.

Illicit cross-border trade of rice and other goods between the Tawi-Tawi, Philippines and Sabah, Malaysia has persisted because it is protected from coercive strategies by multiple layers of stakeholders that benefit from the trade. They include the extended families, clans, and tribes that are settled in the various ports across the Sulu Sea, the women trader-entrepreneurs who travel regularly to Sabah and vice-versa to buy supplies that they can sell, the shadowy authorities involved in the importation and exportation of other illicit goods that can be shipped and disguised as rice shipments, the formal authorities who collect the rents in numerous tollgates, and the armed groups and terror networks, engaged in kidnap-for-ransom and human trafficking, that are able to wreak havoc in this loosely monitored and unguarded part of Southeast Asia.

Old routes, new rules

Finally, there are the traders themselves who want to prevent the same racist idioms and targeted attacks waged by various publics against their families and enterprises in times of rice scarcity and price instability. Food rioting is a frightening experience that has occurred in both Indonesia and Malaysia, and the attacks and looting of granaries are a particular phenomenon in the Philippines. In all these cases, the indigenous Chinese traders have borne the brunt of attacks on their lives and properties.

This continued smuggling of rice is anchored on a paradox: it is a staple food in Malaysia and the Philippines. While both countries have an incentive to ensure stable supplies and the absence of severe price fluctuations, the same rice smuggling can lead to prices that can disrupt incentives for producers in both countries to produce rice sufficiently. This interaction will create perpetual tensions and place both the state and social forces into situations where they will alternately collide or cooperate to avoid a prolonged food crisis where "rice nationalism" may emerge and threaten food security over the long term.

This chapter presented counter-intuitive findings that broke some myths about how this informal economy is viewed. The social networks that operate beneath the radar to sustain smuggling activities underscore the rule-systems that people find important in an economy embedded in their traditions and social relations.

We have seen how food security is a legitimate social aspiration that cannot be barred by restrictions, legal or otherwise. It is crucial for the legitimacy, authority, and the longevity of an existing regime, and will remain an overarching objective that needs to be fulfilled.

We have also seen the impervious nature of the barter system as the language of compromise between rice smugglers and legal authorities on both sides of the Sulu Sea. When barter is evoked, everything falls in place – the tolerance, the higgling and haggling, the settlement, and finally, the payments that illustrate the huge revenues that are lost from government coffers. Because of this institutionalized process, the BIMP-EAGA aim to formalize the barter trade will not work.[30]

In conclusion, it is important to emphasize that the reigning frameworks used in the conduct of informal economy studies must shift from the formal–informal and legal–illegal dichotomies into a new framework that illustrates and reveals the seamlessness between two systems that interact regularly. Rice smuggling is, after all, an economic, social, and political arrangement that straddles different sets of institutions: legal and illegal; formal and informal; and above-ground and underground.

Notes

1 The Sulu and Celebes seas are on the southern tip of the Philippines flanking the Sulu Archipelago on the southwest and southeast. Both seas were the sites of the seventeenth–eighteenth-century robust international trade in what Warren (1977, 2011) called the Sulu Zone. They served as borderless maritime bridges among peoples in the Celebes islands, coastal zones of North Borneo and Sulu Archipelago, engendering evolution of economic, social and political institutions until disrupted by the colonial projects of the Dutch and Portuguese in Indonesia, the British in North Borneo and the Spanish and Americans in the Philippines. Henceforward, new borders were created during the formation of the Malaysian, Indonesian and Philippine states after World War II.

2 Donnan and Wilson (199) argue that smuggling is an act of subversion that defy borders and, therefore, the state.

3 Literature specific to rice smuggling is scarce. Bonnier and Bonnier (2019) cite that organized crime plays a major role in the illicit trade of agri-food products (in general) and that the same trade destabilizes food security, subsidizes wider criminal activity and threaten political and economic stability.

4 Centeno and Portes (2006) argue that the relationship between the state and informal economy actors is theoretically and inevitably conflictive given state assertion of monopoly of authority and, on the

other, propensity of informal economy actors to subvert that authority. However, within that antithesis of state power and informality is the practical devolution of such conflict into various forms of accommodation.

5 Trialogues are mediated dialogues where a third-party participates in an in-depth interview or conversation to build trust and mediate the discussion of delicate and controversial issues that may surface. These are often used in interview sessions where the presence of a third-party trusted by the respondent enables the sharing of confidential information.

6 The kumpit is a seagoing trading vessel that can carry about 500 metric tons of rice and other commodities across the Sulu Sea to various ports in Malaysia and Indonesia.

7 The move echoes the anti-Chinese riots in 1965 when the Indonesian military accused ethnic Chinese as the fifth column of the Chinese Communist Party (Indonesia Alert, ibid.).

8 It is estimated that 1600–2000 people were killed and 15,000 arrested during the violent response of the Zia ul-Haq regime in 1986 (Mukherjee and Koren, 2019).

9 See Hurrell (2003). International Law and the Making and Unmaking of Boundaries, in Moore, M. and A. Buchanan. (eds.). (2003). *States, Nations and Borders: The Ethics of Making Boundaries.* Cambridge, UK: Cambridge University Press, p, 287.

10 See: http://www.worldstopexports.com/rice-exports-country/

11 Ibid.

12 Ibid.

13 In her study on smuggling along the border of Cameroon and Nigeria, Niger-Thomas (2001) found that women traders perceived their activities as legitimate even though they recognized that they were still taking risks.

14 Agreement on anti-smuggling cooperation between the government of Malaysia and the government of the Republic of the Philippines, September 1, 1967; from https://www.officialgazette.gov.ph/1967/09/01/the-philippine-claim-to-a-portion-of-north-borneo-agreement-on-anti-smuggling-cooperation-between-the-government-of-malaysia-and-the-government-of-the-republic-of-the-philippines/.

15 Ibid.

16 Protocol to the agreement on anti-smuggling cooperation between the government of Malaysia and the government of the Republic of the Philippines; from https://www.officialgazette.gov.ph/1967/09/01/the-philippine-claim-to-a-portion-of-north-borneo-protocol-to-the-agreement-on-anti-smuggling-cooperation-between-the-government-of-malaysia-and-the-government-of-the-republic-of-the-philippines/.

17 REPUBLIC ACT NO. 5446, An Act to Amend Section One of Republic Act 1346, entitled: "An Act to define the Baselines of the Territorial Sea of the Philippines". From: https://www.officialgazette.gov.ph/1968/09/18/republic-act-no-5446/.

18 Barter is very similar to what Bevan & Wengrow (2010:22) described as a bazaar economy where transactions involve mobilization of personal networks of loyalty and affiliation.

19 See: Rabasa, A. and Chalk, P. (2012). Non-Traditional Threats and Maritime Domain Awareness in the Tri-border Area of Southeast Asia: The Coast Watch System of the Philippines. Sta. Monica, CA: Rand Corporation. https://www.rand.org/content/dam/rand/pubs/occasional_papers/2012/RAND_OP372.pdf. From December 2010 to July 2011, 55,368 vessels were monitored.

20 Under Philippine Maritime Industry rules (MARINA Memorandum Circular No. 73, series of 1993), wooden-hull vessels below 500 Gross Registered Tons may be given Temporary Special Permit on condition that owners also procure Manning Certificate, Cargo Ship Safety Equipment Certificate, Radio Station License and International Loadline Certificate (Maritime Industry Authority, 1993). The Maritime Industry Authority has, since 2007, suspended registration of newly acquired and newly built wooden-hulled ships. All ships plying overseas should be made of steel (Maritime Industry Authority, 2007).

21 An instituted economy according to Polanyi (1944/1957, 60, 62,64) refers to the human economy as an instituted process, embedded and enmeshed in institutions or rules that may be economic or non-economic. Rice is an instituted economy because it is an enterprise embedded in more than just simple market exchanges, but also norms, motives, and values.

22 This is the Bureau of Customs (BOC) Import Entry and Import Declaration and Entry Form 177 for barter traders. They cannot sign BOC Form 236 (Import Entry and Internal Revenue Declaration Form) because this form is only for registered steel-hulled vessels.

23 In the aftermath of Philippine interception of smuggled rice from Sabah in June 2018, the Malaysian Ministry of Agriculture and Agri-based Industry banned transhipment in July 2018. The ban has been

Old routes, new rules

extended since January 1, 2019 (http://www.olgn.org/wp-content/uploads/2018/12/7.-OL-USA-industry-news.pdf). In a statement to the Malaysian Parliament on 19 March 2020, Chan Foong Hin (MP for Kota Kinabalu) called for the lifting of the ban on the ground that not all rice transhipment involves smuggling ("No to total ban of rice transhipment in Sabah," https://dapmalaysia.org/statements/2019/03/19/28383/). Earlier the BIMP-EAGA Business Council also lobbied for the lifting of the ban (https://www.thestar.com.my/news/nation/2018/08/13/council-lift-rice-transhipment-ban/).

24 See Nikko Fabian, "Plea to allow Kumpits when barter trade resumes," *Daily Express*, July 21, 2019. Retrieved from: http://www.dailyexpress.com.my/news/138163/plea-to-allow-kumpits-when-barter-resumes/.

25 Interview with a local trader based in Bongao, Tawi-Tawi (17 June 2020). Name and location withheld.

26 See Austria, M. (2002). Philippine Domestic Shipping Industry: State of Competition and Market Structure, PASCN Discussion Paper No. 2002-04. Philippine Institute for Development Studies, Makati City. http://pascn.pids.gov.ph/DiscList/d02/s02-04.pdf. The domestic shipping transport industry consists of three sectors: liner, tramp and industrial carriage. New regulations prescribe that vessels used for international shipping should be steel-hulled, among other requirements.

27 Roughly US$138,000 or PHP 6.9 million worth of rice based on US$ to RM and US $ to PHP exchange rate on 22 March 2020.

28 Name and date withheld.

29 White rice becomes yellow rice when mixed with *dulaw* (turmeric) during cooking. The practice is also common among Maranaw and Maguindanao Muslims in the Philippines.

30 BIMP-EAGA stands for Brunei Darussalam-Indonesia-Malaysia-Philippines, an ASEAN sub-regional cooperation system that started in 1994 and encompasses the whole of Brunei Darussalam, the provinces of Kalimantan, Sulawesi, Maluku and West Papua in Indonesia, the states of Sabah, Sarawak and federal territory of Labuan in Malaysia and Mindanao and the province of Palawan in the Philippines. One of the agendas of the sub-regional cooperation system is the revival and formalization of barter trade.

Bibliography

Abraham, I. and van Schendel, W. eds., (2005). *Introduction: The Making of Illicitness*. In: *Illicit Flows and Criminal Things: States, Borders and the Other Side of Globalization*. Bloomington and Indianapolis: Indiana University Press, pp. 1–37.

Ahuja, S.C. and Ahuja, U. (2010). *Rice in Social and Cultural Life of People*. In Sharma, S.D. (ed.). *Rice: Origin, Antiquity and History*. Boca Raton, FL: CRC Press, pp. 39–84.

Alano, B. (1984). Import Smuggling in the Philippines, An Economic Analysis, Journal of Philippine Development, Volume XI, Issue 2, Philippine Institute of Development Studies. Available at: https://dirp4.pids.gov.ph/ris/pjd/pidsjpd84-2smuggling.pdf (Accessed: 16 January 2021).

Amirell, S. E. (2005). The Return to Piracy: Decolonization and International Relations in a Maritime Border Region (the Sulu Sea), 1959-63, *Working Papers in Contemporary Asian Studies* no. 15, Center for East and South-East Asian Studies, Lund University. Available at: http://portal.research.lu.se/ws/files/4564544/3127790.pdf (Accessed 27 April 2018).

Balisacan, A., Sombilla, M. and Dikitanan, R. (2010). Rice Crisis in the Philippines: Why Did It Occur and What Are Its Policy Implications?, In Dawe, D. (ed.). *The Rice Crisis Markets, Policies and Food Security*. London and Washington: Earthscan and FAO.

Bevan, A. and Wengrow, D., eds., (2010). *Cultures of Commodity Branding*. First Edition. Left Coast Press: Left Coast Press.

Bhagwati, J. and Hansen, B. (1973). A Theoretical Analysis of Smuggling, *The Quarterly Journal of Economics*, Volume 87, Issue 2, pp. 172–187. Available at: 10.2307/1882182 (Accessed: 27 April 2021).

Bonnier, U. and Bonnier, L. (2019). *Mapping the Impact of Illicit Trade on the Sustainable Development Goals*. Transnational Alliance to Combat Illicit Trade (TRACIT). [ebook]. Available at: https://unctad.org/meetings/en/Contribution/DITC2019_TRACIT_IllicitTradeandSDGs_fullreport_en.pdf (Accessed: 28 December 2020).

Briones, R. and De la Pena, B. (2015). Competition Reform in the Philippine Rice Sector, Discussion Paper Series No. 2015-04, *Philippine Institute of Development Studies*. Available at: https://pidswebs.pids.gov.ph/CDN/PUBLICATIONS/pidsdps1504.pdf (Accessed: 27 December 2020).

Castells, M. and Portes, A. eds., (1989). *World Underneath: The Origins, Dynamics and Effects of the Informal Economy*. In: *The Informal Economy: Studies in Advanced and Less Developed Countries*. Baltimore and London: The Johns Hopkins University Press, pp. 11–37.

Centeno, M. A. and Portes, A. eds., (2006). *The Informal Economy in the Shadow of the State*. In: *Out of the Shadows: Political Action and Informal Economy in Latin America*. University Park, PA: The Pennsylvania State University Press, pp. 23–48.

Chouvy, P. A. ed., (2013). *An Atlas of Trafficking in Southeast Asia: The Illegal Trade in Arms, Drugs, People, Counterfeit Goods and Natural Resources in Mainland Southeast Asia*. New York, NY: I.B. T Co. Ltd.

Chen, M. A. ed., (2006). *Rethinking the Informal Economy: Linkages with the Formal Economy and the Formal Regulatory Environment*. In: *Linking the Formal and Informal Economy: Concepts and Policies*. Oxford, UK: Oxford University Press, pp. 75–92.

CIA. (1969). *Intelligence Report: Geographic Brief on Sabah*. Available at: https://www.cia.gov/library/readingroom/docs/CIA-RDP84-00825R000100620001-7.pdf (Accessed: 15 December 2020).

Cororaton, C. (2004). Rice Reforms and Poverty in the Philippines: A CGE Analysis, ADB Institute Discussion Paper No.8. Available at: https://www.adb.org/sites/default/files/publication/156759/adbi-dp8.pdf (Accessed: 16 December 2020).

Customs Administrative Order No. 13–2019, Customs Bonded Warehouses. Available at: https://customs.gov.ph/wp-content/uploads/2019/10/cao-13-2019-Customs_Bonded_Warehouses.pdf (Accessed: 24 January 2021).

De la Rosa, N.P. (2014). Porous Peace in Mindanao's Free Trade Area, Policy Brief, April 2014, *International Alert*. Available at: https://www.international-alert.org/sites/default/files/Philippines_PolicyBriefBorderTrade_EN_2014.pdf (Accessed: 13 December 2020).

Granovetter, M. (1985). Economic Action and Social Structure: The Problem of Embeddedness. *American Journal of Sociology*, Volume 91, Issue 3, pp. 481–510.

Granovetter, M. (2017). *Society and Economy: Framework and Principles*. Cambridge, Massachusetts: The Belknap Press of Harvard University Press.

Hedman, E. and Sidel, J. (2000). *Philippine Politics and Society in the Twentieth Century: Colonial Legacies, Post-Colonial Trajectories*. London and New York: Routledge.

Hossain, M. and Narciso, J. (2004). Global Rice Economy: Long-Term Perspectives. In: *FAO Conference Rice in Global Markets and Sustainable Production Systems*. Roe. Available at: http://www.fao.org/rice2004/en/pdf/hossain.pdf (Accessed: 13 December 2020).

Hurrell, A. (2003). International Law and the Making and Unmaking of Boundaries. In: Moore, M. and Buchanan, A., eds. (2003). *States, Nations and Borders: The Ethics of Making Boundaries*. Cambridge, UK: Cambridge University Press.

Hussin, H. (2019). Buwas Kuning (Yellow Rice) and Its Symbolic Functions among Bajaus of Malaysia. *SAGE Open*. Available at: https://journals.sagepub.com/doi/full/10.1177/2158244019885140 (Accessed: 13 December 2020).

Indonesia Alert, Economic Crisis Leads to Scapegoating of Ethnic Chinese, February 18, 1998. Available at: https://www.hrw.org/report/1998/02/18/indonesia-alert/economic-crisis-leads-scapegoating-ethnic-chinese-february-1998

Intal, P. and Garcia, M. (2008). Rice and Philippine Politics. Research Paper Series RPS 2008-01, *Philippine Institute for Development Studies*. Available at: https://pidswebs.pids.gov.ph/CDN/PUBLICATIONS/PIDSRP0801.pdf (Accessed: 17 December 2020).

International Alert. (2014). *Rebellion, Political Violence and Shadow Crimes in the Bangsamoro: The Bangsamoro Conflict Monitoring System (BCMS) 2011–2013*. [ebook]. Available at: https://www.international-alert.org/sites/default/files/Philippines_BangsamoroConflictMonitoringSystem_EN_2014.pdf (Accessed: 21 December 2020).

International Alert-Philippines. (2016). *Violence in the Bangsamoro and Southern Mindanao 2011–2015*. [ebook]. Available at: https://conflictalert.info/publication/ (Accessed: 21 January 2020).

Lantican, T.L.D.C. and Ani, P.A. (2020). *The Philippine Fight against Agricultural Smuggling: Review of Philippine Policies and Initiatives*. [ebook] FFTC Agricultural Policy Platform. Available at: https://ap.fftc.org.tw/article/1867 (Accessed: 16 February 2021).

Manzano, G. and Prado, S.A. (2014). *Distributional Impact of the 2008 rice crisis in the Philippines*. [ebook]. Available at: https://unctad.org/en/PublicationChapters/gds2014d3_02_Philippines_en.pdf (Accessed: 12 February 2021).

Maritime Industry Authority Memorandum Circular No. 73-1993, *Guidelines on the Temporary Utilization of Inter-island/Coastwise Vessels in the Overseas/Trade Operations, including Barter Trade*. Available at: https://marina.gov.ph/wp-content/uploads/2018/07/mc073.pdf (Accessed: 2 February 2021).

Old routes, new rules

Maritime Industry Authority Advisory No. 02-2007, *Prohibition of the Registration of Newly-acquired/Built Wooden Hulled Ships*. Available at: https://marina.gov.ph/wp-content/uploads/2018/07/MA-2007-02.pdf (Accessed: 2 February 2021).

Mukherjee, B. and Koren, O. (2019). *The Politics of Mass Killing in Autocratic Regimes*. Cham, Switzerland: Palgrave Macmillan.

Niger-Thomas, M. (2001). Women and the Arts of Smuggling. *African Studies Review*, Volume 44, pp. 43–70.

OECD/ILO (2019). *Tackling Vulnerability in the Informal Economy, Development Centre Studies*. [ebook] Paris: OECD Publishing. Available at: 10.1787/939b7bcd-en (Accessed: 22 January 2021).

Omar, S.C., Shaharudin, A. and Tumin, S.A. (2019). *The Status of the Paddy and Rice Industry in Malaysia*. [ebook] Kuala Lumpur: Khazanah Research Institute. Available at: http://www.krinstitute.org/assets/contentMS/img/template/editor/20190409_RiceReport_Full%20Report_Final.pdf (Accessed: 16 January 2021).

Polanyi, K. (1957). The Economy as Instituted Process. In: Polanyi, K. Arensberg, C. and Pearson, H., eds. (1957). *Trade and Market in the Early Empires*, New York: The Free Press.

Polanyi, K. (1944/1957). *The Great Transformation: The Political and Economic Origins of Our Time*. Boston: Beacon Press.

Portes, A. (2010). *Economic Sociology: A Systematic Inquiry*. Princeton, NJ: Princeton University Press.

Rabasa, A. and Chalk, P. (2012). *Non-Traditional Threats and Maritime Domain Awareness in the Tri-border Area of Southeast Asia: The Coast Watch System of the Philippines*. [ebook] Rand Corporation. Available at: https://www.rand.org/content/dam/rand/pubs/occasional_papers/2012/RAND_OP372.pdf (Accessed: 13 December 2020).

Roche, J. (1992). *The International Rice Trade*. Cambridge, England: Woodhead Publishing Limited.

Saleeby, N. (1908). *The History of Sulu*. Manila: Bureau of Printing.

Samad, P.A. and Darusalam, A.B. (1992). Malaysia-Philippines Relations: The Issue of Sabah, *Asian Survey*. Volume 32, Issue 6, pp. 554–567. Available at: 10.2307/2645160 (Accessed: 25 January 2021).

Sarris, A. (2010). *Trade Related Policies to Ensure Food (Rice) Security in Asia*. In: Dawe, D., ed. (2010). *The Rice Crisis: Markets, Policies and Food Security*. London and Washington, DC: Earthscan and FAO, pp. 61–87.

Tagliacozzo, Eric. *A Sino-Southeast Asian Circuit: Ethnohistories of the Marine Goods Trade*. In: Tagliacozzo, E. and Chang, W., eds. (2011). *Chinese Circulations: Capital, Commodities, and Networks in Southeast Asia*. Durham and London: Duke University Press, pp. 432–454.

The Asia Foundation (2019). *Trade in the Sulu Archipelago: Informal Economies Amidst Maritime Security Challenges*. [ebook] San Francisco: The Asia Foundation. Available at: https://asiafoundation.org/wp-content/uploads/2019/10/Trade-in-the-Sulu-Archipelago-Informal-Economies-Amidst-Maritime-Security-Challenges.pdf (Accessed: 20 January 2021).

Timmer, P. (2010). Food Security in Asia and the Challenging Role of Rice. *The Asia Foundation*, Occasional Paper No. 4. Available at: https://www.asiafoundation.org/resources/pdfs/OccasionalPaperNo4Food SecurityFinal.pdf (Accessed: 18 December 2020).

Trocki, C. (1979). *Prince of the Pirates: The Temenggongs and the Development of Johor and Singapore, 1784–1885*. Singapore: Singapore University Press.

Trocki, C. (1990). *Opium and Empire*. Ithaca, NY: Cornell University Press.

United States Department of State. (2016). *Country Reports on Terrorism 2015 – Foreign Terrorist Organizations: Abu Sayyaf Group*. Available at: https://www.refworld.org/docid/57518d6f2e.html (Accessed: 1 August 2020).

Van Schendel, W. (2005). *Spaces of Engagement: How Borderlands, Illegal Flows and Territorial States Interlock*. In: Van Schendel, W. and Abraham I., eds. (2005). *Illicit Flows and Criminal Things: States, Borders and the Other Side of Globalization*. Bloomington and Indianapolis: Indiana University Press, pp. 38–68.

Van Schendel, W. and Abraham O., eds. (2005). *Illicit Flows and Criminal Things: States, Borders and the Other Side of Globalization*. Bloomington and Indianapolis: Indiana University Press.

Warren, J. (1977). Sino-Sulu Trade in the Late Eighteenth and Nineteenth Century. *Philippine Studies*, Volume 25, pp. 50–79.

Warren, J. (2011). The Global Economy and the Sulu Zone: Connections, Commodities and Culture. *Crossroads: Studies on the History of Exchange Relations in the East Asian World*, Volume 3, pp. 1–38.

21

THE INTERSECTIONS OF SMUGGLING FLOWS

Annette Idler

Introduction

Across the world, trafficking routes are used for multiple types of goods in various directions. In Libya, people, arms, drugs, and contraband are smuggled on the same routes, in Myanmar, both human trafficking and drug trafficking takes place across the border to Thailand and China at the same crossings, and in Colombia, cocaine is shipped abroad via Venezuela and on that same route gasoline is smuggled from Venezuela into Colombia. To account for this interconnectedness, this chapter conceptualizes smuggling flows as illicit supply chain networks. These networks comprise multiple interconnected forms of transnational organized crime, ranging from the illicit drug trade through arms, human, and wildlife trafficking, to financial flows stemming from money laundering essential to all these forms of organized crime. Of course, not all forms of transnational organized crime have the same underlying logics. In the case of human trafficking, for example, the victims of the crime are not only those who may be forced to help traffickers, or those who are targeted because they are in the traffickers' way, but also the very people that are being trafficked (see, e.g., Chapkis 2003). Similarly, the dimension of illegality varies. Gasoline or oil, for example, in themselves are not illegal, but the practice of smuggling them is. Cocaine, on the other hand, unless for medical use, is illegal in most circumstances already – regardless of whether it is trafficked across borders or not. Still, across these different logics, the networked character largely remains the same: it connects victimless with other types of transnational organized crime, smuggling flows of household goods with those of illicitly used goods, or of people, and local petty smugglers with large-scale global trafficking rings.

The networks include strategic trafficking nodes, that is, illicit business hubs and starting points of international trafficking routes where various illicit flows converge. These intersections are the places where unscrupulous entrepreneurs, such as criminals, rebels, or corrupt military officials, meet to strike business deals. Rivalry over economic profit among these actors entails selective violence against potential and actual betrayers. Demonstrating the relevance of these trafficking nodes in the context of four analytical dimensions of illicit supply chain networks – the input-output structure, the institutional context, territoriality, and the governance structure – this chapter calls for moving beyond the study of individual flows in isolation. It suggests focusing both scholarly and policy attention on the interconnectedness of legally and

The intersections of smuggling flows

illegally used routes in order to grasp the social, economic, and political repercussions on the localities in which the flows are embedded and the people who inhabit them.

In what follows, I briefly contextualize the interconnectedness of illicit flows historically. Subsequently, I conceptualize illicit supply chain networks and demonstrate how and why analyzing the intersections of trafficking flows is important to enhance our overall understanding of the illicit economy and its link to instability.

The interconnectedness of illicit flows in historical perspective

Illegal economic cross-border movements are historic (Friman and Andreas 1999, 1). According to Manuel Castells (2010, 172), "Crime is as old as humankind. Indeed, in the biblical account of our origins, our plight began with the illegal traffic of apples." State formation goes back to illicit flows, as Charles Tilly (1985) showed on European states, and Peter Andreas (2014) on the United States, the "smuggler nation." Likewise, the interconnectedness and multi-directional nature of illicit flows is nothing new. Syria, for example, has long been a transit point for drugs originating from Europe, Turkey, and Lebanon and destined for Jordan, Iraq, and the Persian Gulf. Local cross-border tribes and groups have engaged in trafficking livestock and consumer goods (and to a limited extent, drugs) between Syria and its neighbours since the inception of the state after the fall of the Ottoman Empire. The region also features a long-standing tradition of looting and antiquity smuggling from archaeological sites.

Nonetheless, the interconnectedness of illicit flows, that is, "flows of illicitly used goods or money, or of trafficked people" (Idler 2020, 336),[1] has taken on new forms, characterized by a global network of transactions and exchanges that occur in an ever accelerating speed.

How did we get there? The end of the Cold War entailed a proliferation of states with highly fragile regions and of what some considered "failed states" – convenient hubs for traffickers to operate from (Naím 2007, 26). In countries where state capacities are weak, especially at the geographical margins, borders are hard to control and officials are easily corrupted (Naím 2007, 29). These locations thus become destinations or starting points of individual flows and – especially if they are geostrategically significant – hubs connecting various flows that both enter and leave the country. Nigeria, for example, has turned into a trading hub for heroin from the Middle East to Europe and North America, as well as for ivory and rhino horn trafficking. Similarly, Haiti has become a major transit zone for cocaine trafficked from South America into the US, while also witnessing human trafficking from Haiti into the Dominican Republic.

The Cold War's end, together with the acceleration of globalization in the 1990s, also brought about important changes in the global economy. When the Iron Curtain fell in 1991, both licit and illicit trade expanded across states formerly belonging to the East and West blocs respectively. These economic activities benefitted from more interdependent and expanded markets, fewer border checks, and the privatization of state property in the former East bloc, including military hardware. Economic liberalization and increased financial mobility in an increasingly globalized world further consolidated the interconnectedness of different illicit flows (Andreas 2003; see also Lexico Oxford Dictionary 2020). Enhanced communication and information technologies as well as transportation infrastructures in the 1990s expanded the networks of flows that came to span entire continents. Global illicit networks transformed into less centralized webs of transactions (Naím 2007, 227): just as in the global licit economy, where companies source, formulate, and assemble globally, smugglers exchange and enhance illicit products globally. Financial liberalization allowed smugglers to make their transactions less traceable than ever before. Smugglers can break down large cashless financial flows into different parts with different networks financing each part, sometimes without knowing who else is involved.

In the first two decades of the twenty-first century, the pace at which information spreads accelerated further, which contributed, in part, to three trends that favour the interconnectedness of illicit flows. First, violent non-state groups have proliferated with more new groups having formed in the past ten years or so than over the past six decades together. Second, these groups operate increasingly transnationally. At its height, the so-called Islamic State (IS), for example, declared provinces in ten different countries. Third, relatively easy and instant access to information has changed patterns of mobilization, propaganda, and recruitment with social media quickly reaching individuals far away from the physical location of the respective group. These trends have boosted the interconnectedness of illicit flows because they facilitate dynamic links among groups: in Syria and neighbouring countries, those labelled terrorists such as IS engage in spot sales with arms or ammunition dealers (Solomon 2015); in the Central Mediterranean, human smugglers work with Libyan militias (Micallef and Reitano 2017); in South America, left-wing guerrillas cooperate with Mexican drug cartels (Idler 2019); and, globally, organized criminals subcontract hackers (EUROPOL 2018, 15–24). Overall, through these developments, the scope of the activities belonging to the "Other Side of Globalization" (Abraham and Schendel 2005, 4) has expanded: global networks supersede local smugglers, common criminals join transnational terrorists, and chains of illegal drug, human, or weapons trafficking expand past regions to extend across continents (Deville 2013, 63).

State regulation, law enforcement, and political awareness of illegal economic cross-border activities have changed also (Andreas 2009, 15). Realists stress borders' function of delineating territorial sovereignty, and globalists argue that growing global interdependence has made borders progressively less relevant due to a continuing de-territorialization (Brenner 1999, 60–67) that has led to a "borderless world" (Ōmae 1990). Accordingly, globalization would have transformed borders into "bridges for commercial transactions rather than economic barriers and fortified military lines" (Andreas 2003, 83). However, analyzing the interconnectedness of illicit flows confirms that, rather, "geopolitics is transformed, not transcended" (Andreas 2003, 108). As Clunan and Trinkunas (2010, 9) put it, "asymmetries in states' taxation and regulation in a world of globalized demand create the incentives for engaging in 'jurisdictional arbitrage' in the form of smuggling and trafficking." While border controls have become stricter through sophisticated intelligence and surveillance technologies, these same technologies enable those who evade the law to circumvent controls and adapt to changing market conditions. More border control to curb such activities may be counterproductive: the greater the risk associated with the illegal enterprise, the higher the profits and hence the incentives to engage in it (Schendel 2005, 59).

Against this backdrop, illicit entrepreneurs take advantage of the bureaucratic constraints, if not inertia, of law enforcement authorities to benefit from new technologies. They quietly expand and consolidate global illicit supply chain networks that slowly pervade the entire international system, comprising both state and non-state actors such as non-governmental organizations or the private sector with the international community hardly noticing it. The transformative power of online illicit marketplaces, also called cryptomarkets, illustrates this well. The now defunct Silk Road for example, a website that operated on an encrypted part of the internet, the TOR network, also known as the "Dark Net" or "Dark Web," used to facilitate the illicit trade of drugs (Martin 2014; see also Lusthaus 2013). Both buyers and sellers benefitted from anonymity provided by this "cyber-assisted" crime.[2] By facilitating direct online exchange, global networks become more efficient and harder to trace as intermediaries and traffickers at times become superfluous. These are the actors that may resort to violence to

The intersections of smuggling flows

achieve their ends, hence the decrease in physical transactions can also lower the chance of spectacular violence. While this may seem a positive "side-effect," the consequence is also concerning: being increasingly managed and controlled in non-physical space, these illicit supply chain networks have the potential to erode the international system from within by penetrating its structures without triggering violent conflict that would alert the system's defenders (Idler 2017).

The complexity of these illicit operations makes them less noticeable to the international community than large geopolitical shocks, but in no way less significant. From the corruption of state officials and others due to the lack of control mechanisms to the alienation of communities from central states as a result, the possibility of shifting operations to cyberspace has opened opportunities to actors involved in interconnected illicit flows that we are only beginning to understand.

Illicit supply chain networks – the intersections of illicit flows

Drawing on Idler (2020, 339–42), I now conceptualize interconnected illicit flows as illicit supply chain networks (Deville 2013, 65).[3] A "supply chain, a complex network of organizations and facilities which are mostly settled in a vast geographical area or even the globe, synchronizes a series of interrelated activities through the network" (Govindan, Fattahi, and Keyvanshokooh 2017, 119; see also Christopher 1998). Supply chain networks are commonly analyzed along four dimensions: (i) input-output structure; (ii) territoriality; (iii) institutional context; and (iii) governance structure (Gereffi and Korzeniewicz 1994; Bair 2005). As I show with examples from across the globe, analyzing illicit supply chain networks along these four dimensions sheds light on the nature and implications of the intersections of illicit flows.

i Input-output structure

Illicit supply chain networks that concern goods that need to be processed (as opposed to flows of people for example) can be analyzed according to their input-output structure. "A [supply chain] network converts raw materials into final products and then delivers them to customers. It includes various types of facilities, and each type plays a specific task in the network" (Govindan, Fattahi, and Keyvanshokooh 2017, 112). Given that various illicit supply chains are interconnected, this process manifests a networked character.[4]

In the illicit supply chain networks of cocaine or heroin, for example, the main supply chain begins with production activities: resource extraction (that is, coca or opium poppy cultivation and harvesting), and the processing of the raw material into the final product (processing coca leaves into coca paste and coca paste into cocaine, or processing opium poppy into opium, then morphine, and then heroin). The supply chain continues with three further interrelated activities: the actors involved transport the good domestically, traffic it internationally, and distribute it in markets. This supply chain intersects with supply chains of goods that are added to process the raw material into the final product, including gasoline (in the case of cocaine production) and chemical precursors (such as acetic anhydride to process morphine into heroin) (European Monitoring Centre for Drugs and Drug Addiction and Europol 2019).

The flow of cocaine, heroin, or any other illicitly produced good intersects with flows of other goods. Illicitly used drugs are, for example, exchanged in as drugs-for-arms deals. Such barter agreements have included small and light arms but also advanced military-grade weapons such as surface-to-air missiles (European Monitoring Centre for Drugs and Drug Addiction and Europol 2019). Other types of barter agreements involve ammunitions, counterfeit medicines, or humans; for example, kidnapped hostages or trafficked people may be exchanged for illicit goods through barter agreements. Criminals and other violent non-state groups often strike such business deals via intermediaries. These illicit flows intersects with flows of money (profits from sales of the illicitly produced goods) that the groups launder to redirect it into the licit economy (see e.g., Abraham and Schendel, 2005; Deville 2013). These intersections form the nodes of the trafficking routes. On the market side, international traffickers typically liaise with local dealers who distribute the illicit good among consumers or other types of clients.

Figure 21.1 illustrates the illicit supply chain networks.

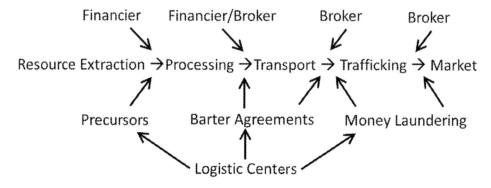

Figure 21.1 Illicit supply chain networks

Analyzing illicit supply chain networks in line with their input-output structure sheds light on the expertise that is necessary to coordinate and connect various flows. The police commander of a Colombian town in a region highly affected by cocaine trafficking and interconnected flows of gasoline, arms, people, and chemical precursors described this the following way to me during one of my fieldwork trips to the region:

> We often hear about the term "route." Delinquents even sell routes. In the criminal sphere, when they say that the Rastrojos [a Colombian right-wing violent non-state group] sell a route, what they really sell is the logistics chain of the business. This includes the know-know, information on how it works, and who is involved. They say: 'Look, I know who is producing, who has land to produce coca. I know how the precursors enter this sector and I have the contact. I know where the laboratories are and who is able to process the coca leaves into coca base and then the coca base into cocaine. It includes the entire procedure. I know where we can store the cocaine. I know with whom and where we can take it out of the country and what means of transport we can use, and I know who will receive it abroad, in Spain or in the US, or in other export countries. And I know how we can transport the money because I have the necessary contacts for that.' This is a route.[5]

Understanding and, ultimately, addressing intersecting smuggling flows, thus starts with grasping the expertise involved in this illicit enterprise, rather than only tracing its physical expressions. The same expertise is often used for various types of flows that operate on the same routes. In the Colombian context, cocaine, gasoline, chemical precursors, money, weapons, and people are linked to the same input-output structure; in Libya, drugs, arms, people, and contraband share the same routes; and in Mali, flows of cigarettes, arms, and drugs interlink.

The intersections of smuggling flows

Such routes are not limited to single countries or regions. In 2018, a case spanning South America, Europe, and West Africa made headlines: a Colombian broker, facilitating cocaine trafficking from South America to the European Union via West Africa, intended to exchange the drugs in a barter agreement with advanced military-grade weapons, including surface-to-air missiles. These weapons were supposedly destined for the militant Islamic group Ansar al-Dine operating in Mali. Given Ansar al-Dine's links with al-Qaeda, this should have allowed the Colombians to use routes passing through al-Qaeda controlled territory in the Sahara Desert. The cocaine-weapons exchange was planned to occur in Croatia. This is not unusual: Colombian traffickers are known to buy protection for their drug shipments from armed actors who control the land routes from West Africa to Europe in the form of drugs, money, or weapons (The Investigative Project on Terrorism 2018; European Monitoring Centre for Drugs and Drug Addiction and Europol 2019, 42; Katersky 2019).

ii Territoriality

The spatial distribution of supply chain networks entails its territoriality.[6] Each locality has a specific function, or role, within the networks. For example, coca or opium poppy cultivation and laboratories are located on production sites of these illicit supply chain networks. Illicit flows intersect and converge in strategic towns, villages, or harbours. These localities function as strategic trafficking nodes, where physical transactions take place or where these transactions are coordinated in logistic centers. They also include starting points of international trafficking routes.

Understanding historical legal trading patterns helps identify the locations where illicit flows intersect. Often, trafficking nodes or starting points of international trafficking routes have been, or still are, trade hubs for legal commerce due to their strategic location. In Libya for example, arms and drugs are trafficked via routes that have been used historically for transporting legal products. Consider Libya's regional capital of Sebha, located in the south west of the country, and known for its historical function in trans-Saharan trade as a strategic node. Three historic trade routes converge in Sebha: first, the route that starts in Algeria and continues to the East; second, the route that begins in Niger and extends to the south; and third, the route that begins in Libya's southern neighbour Chad. It is also located near the Sharara oil field, which further adds economic importance to the town. This position makes it prone to being a hub where illicit trade routes connect too and hence violent non-state groups, such as the Misuratan militias, take interest in controlling the town (Reitano and Shaw 2017).

Geostrategic locations can also impede legal commerce when illicit flows are historic and precede appropriate institutional state presence. The towns of Tumaco and Buenaventura at Colombia's Pacific coast, for instance, are important starting points of international trafficking routes. In Tumaco, numerous different violent non-state groups are present, aiming to get a share of the profit made from cocaine trafficking, gasoline smuggling, and related forms of trafficking. These groups have ranged from the Revolutionary Armed Forces of Colombia-People's Army (FARC-EP) and the National Liberation Army (ELN) as well as the FARC-EP's successor groups, to paramilitary groups and their successors, and Mexican drug cartels (Idler 2019, 180–194). Even though both Tumaco and Buenaventura have the potential to be important legal trading hubs because of their location, the lack of state infrastructure, high militarization, and endemic corruption pose severe obstacles to fulfilling this potential.

These examples – Sebha, Tumaco, and Buenaventura – are trafficking nodes of intersecting flows at the local level, but, due to their geostrategic location, also entire regions are prone to being hubs of various types of illicit flows. Referring to flows of illicitly used drugs, Philip

Robins (2021) calls this "narco-geography." The Middle East, for example, is a recipient of Afghan heroin via Pakistan or Iran; cocaine from the Andean region enters via Brazil; and tramadol (non-medical use of pharmaceutical opioids) comes from China and India (UNODC 2018). Understanding how these flows converge in a single region and where routes – not only in the physical sense, but also in terms of the necessary expertise as discussed above – are shared is an important first step to disrupt them.

Even though over longer periods illicit supply chain networks may shift geographically, from a short-term perspective, the locations for most of the supply chain functions prior to international trafficking are relatively exogenous if they involve natural resources. Coca or opium poppy cultivation, for example, requires adequate climatic conditions, and other raw materials such as gold, diamonds, or coltan are only found in certain regions. Thus, resource extraction sites are relatively fixed. Likewise, laboratories used to process raw materials into the final product are predominantly located in proximity to cultivation or extraction sites.[7] Domestic transport depends on adequate transport infrastructure such as fluvial systems or roads. To some extent, the locations of strategic nodes are also exogenous. Starting points of international routes are located in harbours, or border towns, where illicit goods are shipped abroad.

Intersecting flows of chemical precursors, for instance, typically come from countries where these products are cheaper; weapon flows connect with countries suffering armed conflict or other forms of instability since these weapons sustain the fighting of (non-state) armed groups. Money flows connect with countries whose currency is convenient for money laundering. This is exemplified by money flows from Colombia deriving from the cocaine industry into the dollarized Ecuadorian economy. These last two examples indicate the relevance of demand or convenience in determining the market end of illicit flows; that is, their direction, as part of the territoriality of illicit supply chain networks. The existence of consumers who can afford relatively pricey drugs such as cocaine, as is the case in the United States and in Western Europe, likewise influence the direction of drug flows.

Drug policies and local cultures also inform the territoriality of illicit supply chain networks, including the transit countries. A common cocaine route from South America to Europe transits West Africa, where corruption of state officials facilitates the business. Impunity and inefficient drug policies have also led to a situation in which the region is increasingly becoming a consumption market, in addition to its function as transit zone (Pokoo and Aning 2021). A similar dynamic can be observed in North Africa (27–33 Herbert and Gallien 2020). Flows of human smuggling typically lead from unstable regions into more industrialized regions, whereas illicit flows of, for instance, toxic waste can be traced in the opposite direction: from waste-producing industrialized countries into unstable regions with weak state governance where the waste can be dumped while those in charge remain in impunity (Hägerdal 2019; Andreatta and Favarin 2020).

Illicit supply chain networks operate in physical and non-physical spaces concurrently, with the latter gaining traction. If in the "upperworld," novel technologies have shrunk geography by making the world more connected, in the "underworld," they have allowed illegal actors to side-line geography entirely. In the process of globalization, way stations along trafficking routes have partly moved into cyberspace (Naím 2007), complicating the territoriality of illicit supply chain networks. Warehouses often exist online, which reduces risks because participants in the illicit chains do not meet each other. Internet-based spot sales and barter agreements of drugs, slaves, or weapons, to name just a few "products" in places such as the Dark Web, as mentioned above, and remotely controlled shipments are examples where it may be difficult to determine the territoriality of these flows. Services like TOR do not exist in any particular physical location and yet enable transactions across the globe. As a side-effect of the ability of decentralized networked actors to circumvent laws and regulations, these actors can enhance their comparative advantage of being flexible and resilient to external shocks even more in the non-physical space, while those abiding by the rules are likely, increasingly, to lag behind. At the same time, transactions in cyberspace also help expand and foster territorial, physical networks of flows across borders (Prince 2016). The territorial aspect in physical space thus remains significant and has important social, economic, and political implications, especially in the trafficking nodes where various flows intersect.

iii Institutional context

Typically, weak state governance systems characterize the institutional context of illicit supply chain networks.[8] In many marginalized areas in unstable regions, state representatives are absent. In such contexts, local populations have few legal economic opportunities to sustain their livelihoods. The income that people can gain thanks to various intersecting illicit flows in these regions would not be available otherwise. Even though most of the time, generating income this way is illegal, local community members consider it legitimate. People's involvement can take various forms. First, they participate directly in forms of smuggling. This includes "survival smuggling" of essentials such as food on the one hand, and of illicit commodities on the other (United Nations and World Bank 2018, 70). Survival smuggling is practiced across the globe, ranging from nomadic communities in the Sahel to the indigenous Wayúu across the Colombia-Venezuela border. These forms are typically unconnected from other types of illicit flows.

Second, local community members smuggle goods that are used for daily consumption *and* are part of illicit supply chain networks. Take the gasoline smuggling across the Colombia-Venezuela border. Given that the Venezuelan government used to subsidize gasoline, Colombians and Venezuelans had been smuggling gasoline from Venezuela into Colombia for decades to sell it openly on the streets. Local law enforcement authorities were aware of the illicit practice, but since it was so wide-spread – and alternative economic opportunities were lacking – efforts to tackle it were sparse. At least until the early 2010s, before Venezuela further descended into a downward spiral of political and socio-economic crisis,[9] three types of smuggling were common: the small-scale one of a few litres; the medium one that fills car tanks; and the large-scale one in which entire trucks were filled with gasoline (Idler 2019, 169–174). This third type directly connected with cocaine trafficking in two ways. First, the gasoline was used to process coca leaves into cocaine, as part of the input-output structure. Second, it formed part of gasoline-drugs deals: the same trucks that transported gasoline from Venezuela to Colombia transported cocaine in the opposite direction. As in other smuggling hotspots around the world (see, e.g., Gallien 2020), such deals were highly regulated through informal arrangements, involving the local population. In places such as La Paz, in the Colombian Cesar department, where the gasoline was taken off the trucks, locals for example were (ab)used to help with storage. They had to give their houses or garages, for example, to stockpile the gasoline. They were paid in return, and hence this practice helped them feed their families, but, at the same time, denying their service exposed them to threats of violence and the implementation thereof, as a report by the local Ombudsman's Office confirms (SAT, Sistema de Alertas Tempranas. Defensoría del Pueblo de Colombia 2012). Furthermore, the small-, medium-, and large-scale types of smuggling were closely interlinked. Even if small-scale smugglers, so-called *pimpineros*, were not directly involved in large-scale forms of trafficking, they typically had to pay "taxes" to the violent non-state group that controlled the route for the purpose of large-scale trafficking. This put these smugglers into an extremely vulnerable position: they suffered abuse by the armed actors yet could not turn to the local authorities for help as they themselves were involved in an illegal business.

Gasoline smuggling across the Ecuador-Colombia border is another case in point. Local community members used to smuggle gasoline from Ecuador to Colombia for their vehicles and boats. Even though illegal, they considered smuggling legitimate because alternative livelihood options were scarce. When the Ecuadorian authorities imposed stricter rules and limited the volume of gasoline that can be trafficked per day, the income of many contrabandists no longer sufficed to cover their daily expenses. Furthermore, it led to human rights abuses against those small-scale traffickers by the local authorities while large-scale traffickers linked to the cocaine industry continued business as usual (Idler 2021). As shown in these examples, addressing the links among different types of illicit flows needs to be based on analyzing the transnational political economy of a region, and indeed its moral economy (Arias and Grisaffi 2021).

Syria's oil smuggling business is a similar example. Syrian rebels used to sell a barrel of oil for up to 22 US dollars. Those involved in refining earned 30 cents for each litre of gasoline that was sold. Just as the community members in La Paz that were connected to gasoline smuggling by helping stockpile the product, in Syria, community members were also involved in related forms of business. This included transport and services, such as repairing engines damaged by the fuel of low quality, offering food, fuel, and other goods to smugglers along the road, or helping truckers fit large tanks to their vehicles (Steenkamp 2017). Likewise, one can distinguish among different forms of smuggling. On the one hand, the small-scale form originates in small oil fields controlled by local tribal chiefs who control extraction. The oil is then transported across territories controlled by local militias who charge taxes or protect – against payment – basic refineries. On the other hand, large-scale smuggling has been controlled by more powerful and violent non-state groups, especially IS. The group controlled around 8% of Syria's oil fields and sold the oil in Syria and Iraq via brokers to local and international buyers (Steenkamp 2017).

In situations like the gasoline-cocaine flows across the borders that Colombia shares with Venezuela and Ecuador respectively, or the oil smuggling and interlinked businesses in Syria and across the border to Iraq, the side effects can be severe if the state engages in crackdowns against large-scale traffickers. Given the interconnectedness of flows, these measures may also interrupt survival smuggling or put small-scale smugglers at risk if they are stigmatized as whistle-blowers. Likewise, blocking (physical) routes through border closures, not only diverges (rather than disrupts) large-scale transnational organized criminal operations, but also disrupts local contraband, which is often rooted in the absence of legal livelihood options. As a result, local populations may develop or increase grievances against the state and feel more alienated from it while being drawn to the illicit armed actors because they may provide protection.

A common institutional context of illicit supply chain networks also includes strong state presence but little accountability; for example, when state officials are corrupt and hence decide to be selectively absent by turning a blind eye to the illicit business, or to participate in the illicit business themselves. States participate in illicit supply chain networks in various ways. Jonathan Kelman (2015) distinguishes among four types of participation: direct revenue generation; indirect revenue generation; procurement; and territorial control. With a slightly different emphasis, Gallien and Weigand (2021), distinguish among six types of relationships between states and smugglers, ranging from genuine enforcement to petty corruption. With the very authority designed to curb these flows in many cases becoming their promoter, the effectiveness and resilience of these networks becomes greatly enhanced. In this sense, the territorial state defined by state borders preconditions the institutional context in which illicit supply chain networks are most thriving.

Linked to the role of state officials in facilitating illicit supply chain networks is Williams and Godson (2002)'s argument that at least four political moments are conducive to the prosperity of these networks. The first political moment is when states with strong capacities become weaker because such a weakening process facilitates the corruption of the older elite. The second one concerns the transition from a command economy to a free market: in such cases, criminals in charge of illicit flows easily can gain control over parts of the licit economy, such as banks, as well, and thus operate in a grey zone between the underworld and the upperworld, with both licit and illicit flows operating on the same routes. A third moment are periods of armed conflict or when groups engage in terrorist attacks, armed actors use their expertise as entrepreneurs of violence for criminal ends, contributing to the illicit business. Fourth, after the signing of a ceasefire or a peace agreement, former (state and non-state) military leaders may aim to maintain power via controlling (parts of) illicit supply chain networks, or those armed groups that remain outside the agreement may strive to expand their income basis in the illicit economy.

iv Governance structure

The relationships of the actors involved shapes the governance structure of illicit supply chain networks. One or several (violent) groups – including both state and non-state actors – carry out or control each network activity (e.g., protection of production sites, domestic transport). In many cases, this division of labour yields territorial segmentation (Deville 2013, 65; see also Govindan, Fattahi, and Keyvanshokooh 2017, 112).[10] The groups typically respect territorial limits of influence, within which each group exerts economic, social, and/or political control.[11] Their presence is relatively localized in a particular place or node. This specialization maximizes profits from each supply chain step. These steps are interlinked through the relationships that these groups have with each other. They are also linked through little-known middlemen, so-called financiers, or more powerful brokers. In the case of natural resource extraction, financiers may buy the raw, or only minimally processed, material from the farmers or workers and ensure it reaches laboratories, where it is processed further. Especially in contexts of armed conflict, as is the case with the cocaine business in Colombia, or the heroin and opium business in Afghanistan and Myanmar, they operate where one group, for example an insurgent group, controls cultivation on its own, or where such a group subordinates others and engages at the "fringes" of that territory in stable arrangements with other groups, including state actors (Chouvy 2010; Mansfield 2016; Idler 2019). Powerful brokers negotiate among the parties, including over the final product.

The relatively clear division of labour that characterizes most elements of illicit supply chain networks does not hold at the intersections of trafficking flows. Here, economic interests of various non-state groups converge, but there is also competition, especially if more than two groups are present, or if one non-state group and the state, or state actors, compete. Even though, generally, they mistrust each other as rivals, on these particular occasions they reduce mistrust to be able to strike business deals such as drugs-for-arms barter agreements; they forge short-term arrangements. General mistrust persists however, so trafficking nodes are typically rife with selective violence targeted against actual and potential cheaters and betrayers. Often, the local population gets caught in the crossfire.

Brokers serve to strike deals in the case of more regular transactions. Brokers are perceived to be trustworthy and reliable by all groups involved, and they have networks across sectors in society: typically, they are connected with local political and economic elites, civil society, and

Annette Idler

armed actors. Examples of such brokers include alias Megateo, a former rebel leader who became the main intermediary of illicit supply chain networks centered on cocaine in Colombia. Heading the remaining faction of the otherwise demobilized Popular Liberation Army (EPL), he had links with the left-wing FARC-EP and ELN rebels, but also with right-wing groups. Local community members considered him a role model, as he was originally from the region and was considered to care for the locals. He connected the various links of the supply chain. After the Colombian state forces killed him in 2015, a power struggle around his replacement broke out. Filling that void took rather long because of the unique characteristics such an individual needs to possess (Idler 2020). Some of these brokers resemble a war lord, as did Megateo. Others resemble more closely an entrepreneur, for instance Victor Bout, imprisoned in the United States (Roth 2010, 150). He is known as a Russian arms dealer, supplying among others, multiple rebel groups in Africa and the Colombian FARC rebels with weapons. He is also known to have been involved in money laundering operations and in sales of aircraft and surface-to-air missiles. In brief, he connected various types of illicit flows and thus facilitated the smooth operating of illicit supply chain networks (Farah 2012; Farah and Braun 2010).

Conclusion

This chapter has demonstrated the importance of analyzing the interconnectedness of illicit flows rather than studying them individually in order to better understand how they operate, what their social, economic, and political implications are, and to identify possible entry points to tackle them. Conceptualizing the intersections of smuggling flows as trafficking nodes that form part of illicit supply chain networks shows their unique role in terms of the input-output structure, the institutional context, the territoriality, and the governance structure of these networks. They hold these networks together and, while bringing livelihood opportunities for local communities in locations that function as trafficking nodes, they also make these communities extremely vulnerable to abuse by both non-state and state actors.

The implications for the study of unstable regions where illicit flows intersect and of the illicit economy more broadly are clear. First, this chapter shows the need to challenge state-centric concepts to study the intersections of illicit flows because these flows reach across borders. Academic studies still tend to be organized as country (comparative) case studies, rather than as studies across borders. Considering transnational borderlands as starting points for research rather than adopting national perspectives on smuggling flows is crucial to overcome this bias. This has methodological implications. Students of smuggling face asymmetries in state-centric data sources, such as national statistics. Those who adopt an ethnographic approach across borders, for example through multi-sited fieldwork, deal with further complications, such as securing support networks, visa, and research permits across borders. Future work needs to address both the conceptual shift and discuss ways to address these methodological challenges.[12] Second, we must map the interconnectedness of illicit supply chain networks to identify disruptors rather than focus on individual supply chain links. This includes centering scholarly attention on the mechanisms that link different supply chain networks instead of focusing on individual flows in isolation. Scholarship to date has mostly focused on the most salient or most lucrative type of smuggling in a given region, thereby neglecting how less profitable, or less sensational interconnected flows drive the overall network. Conceptualizing smuggling flows as illicit supply chain networks in which multiple flows of different types of goods are interconnected helps address this issue. For example, rather than focusing on cocaine trafficking only in South America, enhancing understanding of the flows of chemical precursors

The intersections of smuggling flows

that are used to process coca leaves into cocaine is an important entry point to grasp the extension and functioning of the overall cocaine supply chain network. Third, we need to study the *moral* economy of illicit supply chain networks, not just the *political* economy to understand the role that these networks have for people's daily lives. Where legal livelihood opportunities are scarce, what is legitimate does not necessarily map on to what is legal. This has consequences for entire interrelated legal and illegal, and formal and informal markets.

These implications for the study of intersecting smuggling flows yield important practical considerations. "State solutions" may not necessarily work. Scrutinizing local perceptions and experiences of people living in locations of trafficking nodes demonstrates that a law enforcement approach may not only be ineffective, it can also put people at risk. This does not mean that hierarchical state bureaucracies are necessarily ill-equipped to counter illicit cross-border networked organizations that are embedded in local communities. Rather, these characteristics need to be accounted for (Eilstrup-Sangiovanni and Jones 2008). We need to anticipate the implications of disruptions for the moral economy. As the analysis with a view to the institutional context of illicit supply chain networks shows, measures to thwart illicit interlinked networks may undermine people's licit livelihood strategies: discouraging the trafficking of illicit goods via such routes must come along with protecting and promoting legal commerce in order not to jeopardize people's economic and food security. Ultimately, any investment needs to be holistic and inclusive of local communities to drain the support to illicit networks.

Acknowledgements

The author would like to thank Florian Weigand and Max Gallien for helpful comments on earlier drafts of this chapter.

Notes

1 For an overview of various different illicit flows, see Nellemann et al. (2018).
2 For the distinction between cyber-assisted, cyber-enabled, and cyber-dependent crime see Wall (2017, 1081).
3 I borrow from the global commodity chain literature (see, e.g., Gereffi and Korzeniewicz 1994; Bair 2005). For discussions of supply chain networks in the licit economy see for example Govindan, Fattahi, and Keyvanshokooh (2017); Klibi and Martel (2012); Snyder et al. (2006).
4 For interconnectedness see Dicken et al. (2001, 91).
5 Interview by the author with the police commander of a remote, violence-affected town in Colombia, 2012.
6 For the role of locality and place in supply chains see Bair (2005, 159).
7 There is some flexibility, as the existence of mobile cocaine processing laboratories, for instance, demonstrates (Idler 2019, 261).
8 This is not necessarily the case for money laundering and for transactions that take place in cyberspace.
9 Smuggling dynamics have since reversed: it became more common for gasoline to be smuggled from Colombia into Venezuela.
10 In the case of the cocaine industry, in the 1980s and 1990s this spatial division of labour concerned even countries: Bolivia and Peru hosted the cultivation and harvesting of coca leaves, and their processing into coca paste; Colombia hosted further processing, trafficking, and the starting points for international export (Gootenberg 2012, 169).
11 Markers such as graffiti, pamphlets, or flags, or practices such as charging protection money define these limits. The operational territories of violent non-state groups often coincide with an urban–rural divide. See Tickner, García, and Arreza (2011); Laverde and Tapia (2009).
12 See Idler (2019, Appendix A) for ways to address some of these challenges.

297

Annette Idler

References

Abraham, Itty, and Willem van Schendel. 2005. "Introduction: The Making of Illicitness." In *Illicit Flows and Criminal Things: States, Borders, and the Other Side of Globalization*, edited by Willem van and Abraham Schendel, 1–37. Bloomington: Indiana University Press.

Andreas, Peter. 2003. "Redrawing the Line: Borders and Security in the Twenty-First Century." *International Security* 28: 78–111.

Andreas, Peter. 2009. *Border Games: Policing the U.S.-Mexico Divide*. 2nd ed. Ithaca: Cornell University Press.

Andreas, Peter. 2014. *Smuggler Nation: How Illicit Trade Made America*. New York: Oxford University Press.

Andreatta, Daniela, and Serena Favarin. 2020. "Features of Transnational Illicit Waste Trafficking and Crime Prevention Strategies to Tackle It." *Global Crime* 21(2): 130–153. https://doi.org/10.1080/17440572.2020.1719837.

Arias, Enrique Desmond, and Thomas Grisaffi. 2021. "Introduction." In *The Governance of the Global Narcotics Trade*, edited by Enrique Desmond Arias and Thomas Grisaffi.

Bair, Jennifer. 2005. "Global Capitalism and Commodity Chains: Looking Back, Going Forward." *Competition & Change* 9(2): 153–180. https://doi.org/10.1179/102452905X45382.

Brenner, Neil. 1999. "Beyond State-Centrism? Space, Territoriality, and Geographical Scale in Globalization Studies." *Theory and Society* 28(1): 39–78. https://doi.org/10.1023/A:1006996806674.

Castells, Manuel. 2010. *End of Millennium*. 2nd ed. Oxford: Wiley-Blackwell.

Chapkis, Wendy. 2003. "Trafficking, Migration, and the Law: Protecting Innocents, Punishing Immigrants." *Gender & Society* 17(6): 923–937. https://doi.org/10.1177/0891243203257477.

Chouvy, Pierre-Arnaud. 2010. *Opium: Uncovering the Politics of the Poppy*.1st ed. Cambridge, MA: Harvard University Press.

Christopher, Martin. 1998. *Logistics and Supply Chain Management: Strategies for Reducing Cost and Improving Service*. 2nd ed. London: Financial Times/Pitman.

Clunan, Anne L., and Harold A. Trinkunas, eds. 2010. *Ungoverned Spaces: Alternatives to State Authority in an Era of Softened Sovereignty*. Stanford: Stanford University Press.

Deville, Duncan. 2013. "The Illicit Supply Chain." In *Convergence: Illicit Networks and National Security in the Age of Globalization*, edited by Michael Miklaucic and Jacqueline Brewer, 63–74. Washington, DC: National Defense University.

Dicken, Peter, Philip F. Kelly, Kris Olds, and Henry Wai-Chung Yeung. 2001. "Chains and Networks, Territories and Scales: Towards a Relational Framework for Analysing the Global Economy." *Global Networks* 1(2): 89–112. https://doi.org/10.1111/1471-0374.00007.

Eilstrup-Sangiovanni, Mette, and Calvert Jones. 2008. "Assessing the Dangers of Illicit Networks: Why al-Qaida May Be Less Threatening Than Many Think." *International Security* 33(2): 7–44. https://doi.org/10.1162/isec.2008.33.2.7.

European Monitoring Centre for Drugs and Drug Addiction, and Europol. 2019. "EU Drug Markets Report 2019." Luxembourg: Publications Office of the European Union. https://www.emcdda.europa.eu/system/files/publications/12078/20192630_TD0319332ENN_PDF.pdf.

EUROPOL. 2018. "Internet Organised Crime Threat Assessment." EUROPOL. https://www.europol.europa.eu/activities-services/main-reports/internet-organised-crime-threat-assessment-iocta-2018.

Farah, Douglas. 2012. "Fixers, Super Fixers and Shadow Facilitators: How Networks Connect." International Assessment and Strategy Center. https://cco.ndu.edu/Portals/96/Documents/Articles/Fixers_Super-Fixers_and_Shadow_Facilitators_Farah.pdf.

Farah, Douglas, and Stephen Braun. 2010. *Merchant of Death: Money, Guns, Planes, and the Man Who Makes War Possible*. Chichester: Wiley.

Friman, H. Richard, and Peter Andreas. 1999. *The Illicit Global Economy and State Power*. Lanham, MD; Oxford: Rowman & Littlefield Publishers.

Gallien, Max. 2020. "Informal Institutions and the Regulation of Smuggling in North Africa." *Perspectives on Politics* 18(2): 492–508. https://doi.org/10.1017/S1537592719001026.

Gallien, Max, and Florian Weigand. 2021. "Channeling Contraband: How States Shape International Smuggling Routes." *Security Studies* 0(0): 1–28. https://doi.org/10.1080/09636412.2021.1885728.

Gereffi, Gary, and Miguel Korzeniewicz. 1994. *Commodity Chains and Global Capitalism*. Westport, CT; London: Praeger.

The intersections of smuggling flows

Gootenberg, Paul. 2012. "Cocaine's Long March North, 1900–2010." *Latin American Politics and Society* 54(1): 159–180. https://doi.org/10.1111/j.1548-2456.2012.00146.x.

Govindan, Kannan, Mohammad Fattahi, and Esmaeil Keyvanshokooh. 2017. "Supply Chain Network Design under Uncertainty: A Comprehensive Review and Future Research Directions." *European Journal of Operational Research* 263(1): 108–141. https://doi.org/10.1016/j.ejor.2017.04.009.

Hägerdal, Nils. 2019. "Toxic Waste Dumping in Conflict Zones: Evidence from 1980s Lebanon." *Mediterranean Politics* 26(2): 198–218. https://doi.org/10.1080/13629395.2019.1693124.

Herbert, Matt, and Max Gallien. 2020. "A Rising Tide: Trends in Production, Trafficking and Consumption of Drugs in North Africa." Global Initiative against Transnational Organized Crime. https://globalinitiative.net/wp-content/uploads/2020/06/A-rising-tide-trends-in-production-trafficking-and-consumption-of-drugs-in-North-Africa-GITOC.pdf.

Idler, Annette. 2017. "The Future of International Security: Challenges for Responses to the World's Changing Security Landscape." Discussion Paper. World Economic Forum's Global Future Council on International Security. https://conflictplatform.ox.ac.uk/cccp/research/the-future-of-international-security-challenges-for-responses-to-the-worlds-changing-security-landscape.

Idler, Annette. 2019. *Borderland Battles: Violence, Crime, and Governance at the Edges of Colombia's War*. New York: Oxford University Press.

Idler, Annette. 2020. "The Logic of Illicit Flows in Armed Conflict: Explaining Variation in Violent Nonstate Group Interactions in Colombia." *World Politics* 72(3): 335–376. https://doi.org/10.1017/S0043887120000040.

Idler, Annette. 2021. "Warriors, Victims, and Vulnerable Regions: A Critical Perspective on the War on Drugs." In *Transforming the War on Drugs*, edited by Annette Idler and Juan Carlos Garzón Vergara. London: Hurst Publishers. https://www.hurstpublishers.com/book/transforming-the-war-on-drugs/.

The Investigative Project on Terrorism. 2018. "US v. Cardona-Cardona, et Al.:" The Investigative Project on Terrorism. https://www.investigativeproject.org/case/881/us-v-cardona-cardona-et-al.

Katersky, Aaron. 2019. "Man Charged in Alleged Drugs-for-Weapons Deal with al-Qaeda-Linked Group." *ABC News*, January 18, 2019. https://abcnews.go.com/US/man-charged-alleged-drugs-weapons-deal-al-qaeda/story?id=60471639.

Kelman, Jonathan H. C. 2015. "States Can Play, Too: Constructing a Typology of State Participation in Illicit Flows." *Crime, Law and Social Change* 64(1): 37–55. https://doi.org/10.1007/s10611-015-9568-4.

Klibi, Walid, and Alain Martel. 2012. "Scenario-Based Supply Chain Network Risk Modeling." *European Journal of Operational Research* 223(3): 644–658. https://doi.org/10.1016/j.ejor.2012.06.027.

Laverde, Zully, and Edwin Tapia. 2009. *Tensión En Las Fronteras*. Bogotá, Colombia: CODHES.

Lexico Oxford Dictionary. 2020. "Meaning of Globalization in English." 2020. https://www.lexico.com/definition/globalization.

Lusthaus, Jonathan. 2013. "How Organised Is Organised Cybercrime?" *Global Crime* 14(1): 52–60. https://doi.org/10.1080/17440572.2012.759508.

Mansfield, David. 2016. *A State Built on Sand: How Opium Undermined Afghanistan [Electronic Resource]*. Ebook Central. New York, New York: Oxford University Press. https://ezproxy-prd.bodleian.ox.ac.uk/login?url=https://ebookcentral.proquest.com/lib/oxford/detail.action?docID=4803072.

Martin, James. 2014. "Lost on the Silk Road: Online Drug Distribution and the 'Cryptomarket.'" *Criminology & Criminal Justice* 14(3): 351–367. https://doi.org/10.1177/1748895813505234.

Micallef, Mark, and Tuesday Reitano. 2017. "The Anti-Human Smuggling Business and Libya's Political End Game." *Global Initiative against Transnational Organized Crime, Institute for Security Studies*, North Africa Report, 2 (December): 24.

Naím, Moisés. 2007. *Illicit*. London: Arrow.

Nellemann, Christian, Jürgen Stock, Mark Shaw, International Criminal Police Organization, RHIPTO, and Global Initiative Against Transnational Organized Crime. 2018. *World Atlas of Illicit Flows*. http://globalinitiative.net/wp-content/uploads/2018/09/Atlas-Illicit-Flows-FINAL-WEB-VERSION-copia-compressed.pdf.

Ōmae, Ken'ichi. 1990. *The Borderless World: Power and Strategy in the Interlinked Economy*. London: Collins.

Pokoo, John M., and Kwesi Aning. 2021. "West Africa—Securitized Drugs as an Existential Threat." In *Transforming the War on Drugs | Hurst Publishers*, edited by Annette Idler and Juan Carlos Garzón Vergara. London: Hurst Publishers. https://www.hurstpublishers.com/book/transforming-the-war-on-drugs/.

Prince, Daniel. 2016. "The Dark Web: What It Is and How It Works." *World Economic Forum* (blog). 2016. https://www.weforum.org/agenda/2016/10/the-dark-web-what-it-is-and-how-it-works/.

Reitano, Tuesday, and Mark Shaw. 2017. "The Politics of Power, Protection, Identity and Illicit Trade." Crime-Conflict Nexus Series 3. United Nations University Centre for Policy Research.

Robins, Philip. 2021. "The Crescent Three States—Which Way to Go?" In *Transforming the War on Drugs | Hurst Publishers*, edited by Annette Idler and Juan Carlos Garzón Vergara. London: Hurst Publishers. https://www.hurstpublishers.com/book/transforming-the-war-on-drugs/.

Roth, Mitchel P. 2010. *Global Organized Crime: A Reference Handbook*. ABC-Clio.

SAT, Sistema de Alertas Tempranas. Defensoría del Pueblo de Colombia. 2012. "Informe de Riesgo N° 024-12." Bogotá, Colombia: Defensoría del Pueblo de Colombia.

Schendel, Willem van. 2005. "Spaces of Engagement: How Borderlands, Illicit Flows, and Territorial States Interlock." in Schendel, Willem van, and Itty Abraham, eds. 2005. *Illicit Flows and Criminal Things: States, Borders, and the Other Side of Globalization*. Bloomington: Indiana University Press, 38–68.

Schendel, Willem van, and Itty Abraham, eds. 2005. *Illicit Flows and Criminal Things: States, Borders, and the Other Side of Globalization*. Bloomington: Indiana University Press.

Snyder, Lawrence V., Maria P. Scaparra, Mark S. Daskin, and Richard L. Church. 2006. "Planning for Disruptions in Supply Chain Networks." In *Models, Methods, and Applications for Innovative Decision Making*, 234–257. INFORMS TutORials in Operations Research. INFORMS. https://doi.org/10.12 87/educ.1063.0025.

Solomon, Erika. 2015. "Isis: The Munitions Trail." *Financial Times*, November 30, 2015. https://www.ft.com/content/baad34e4-973c-11e5-9228-87e603d47bdc.

Steenkamp, Christina. 2017. "The Crime-Conflict Nexus and the Civil War in Syria." *Stability: International Journal of Security and Development* 6(1): 11. https://doi.org/10.5334/sta.522.

Tickner, Arlene B., Diego García, and Catalina Arrezea. 2011. "Actores Violentos No Estatales y Narcotráfico En Colombia." In *Políticas Antidroga En Colombia: Éxitos, Fracasos y Extravíos*, 1. ed, 413–445. Bogotá, DC, Colombia: Universidad de los Andes.

Tilly, Charles. 1985. "War Making and State Making as Organized Crime." In *Bringing the State Back In*, edited by Peter B. Evans, Dietrich Rueschemeyer, Theda Skocpol, Structures Social Science Research Council. Committee on States and Social, Studies Joint Committee on Latin American, and Europe Joint Committee on Western, 169–191. Cambridge: Cambridge University Press.

United Nations, and World Bank. 2018. "Pathways for Peace: Inclusive Approaches to Preventing Violent Conflict." Washington, DC: World Bank. http://hdl.handle.net/10986/28337.

UNODC. 2018. "World Drug Report 2018." Vienna: UNODC.

Wall, David S. 2017. "Crime, Security, and Information Communication Technologies." *The Oxford Handbook of Law, Regulation and Technology*. July 20, 2017. https://doi.org/10.1093/oxfordhb/97801 99680832.013.65.

Williams, Phil, and Roy Godson. 2002. "Anticipating Organized and Transnational Crime." *Crime, Law and Social Change* 37(June): 311–355. https://doi.org/10.1023/A:1016095317864.

PART IV

Smuggling and mobility

22

HUMANITARIAN SMUGGLING IN A TIME OF RESTRICTING AND CRIMINALIZING MOBILITY

Ilse van Liempt

Introduction

If we are to win the fight against the smugglers, Europe needs to be ready to take action in order to seize the boats, destroy them and arrest the smugglers and bring them to justice.

European Commissioner for Migration, Home Affairs and Citizenship, Dimitris Avramopoulos, 23 April 2015

On 23 April 2015, the European Commissioner for Migration, Home Affairs and Citizenship, Dimitris Avramopoulos, and the EU Council expressed their determination to come to grips with people smuggling in the Mediterranean. It is nothing new to blame smugglers for the increase of unexpected arrivals of migrants, but in the current refugee 'crisis,' the issue of migrant smuggling has become very much the center of attention. Fighting against smuggling is most often proposed as the 'solution' to the refugee 'crisis' by politicians in the public arena.

In principle, there are two main reasons why states may be willing to counter human smuggling. The first reason has to do with the fact that smuggling is linked to irregular immigration: although it should be clear that not all smuggled migrants are irregular in the proper sense (many of them being refugees and asylum seekers), smuggling is nonetheless one of the most eye-catching ways (at least for the mass media) by which irregular immigration takes place; fighting it can thus be a way of fighting irregular immigration itself. This line of reasoning fits in the criminological framing that is linked to an increasing demand for migration in poorer parts of the world (van Liempt & Sersli 2012). Smugglers are in this frame referred to as the 'dark side' or the 'underbelly' of globalization (Moises 2005) who facilitate irregular migration. Smuggled migrants are given an unclear role under this approach: while, on the one hand, they are not necessarily to be criminalized for the mere fact of having been smuggled, on the other hand, it is clear that their rights and needs are not what states are fighting for when they adopt this perspective.

The second reason states may be concerned with human smuggling stems, instead, from the need to protect the migrants themselves from the many risks they may face if smuggled:

DOI: 10.4324/9781003043645-22

303

economic exploitation; deception; degrading treatment along the way; and even death. Under this approach, smuggled migrants are perceived as victims of the smugglers who thrive on their aspiration to go abroad. An important assumption behind this logic is that stopping smugglers will result in such pain and misery for irregular migrants that news will get back to potential migrants and they will stop coming. Smugglers are seen as having created migration possibilities for those immigrants that states have defined as unwanted. This is also the logic behind the British government's refusal to support large-scale rescue of irregular migrants in the Mediterranean (Collyer 2016).

The paradox between this 'control and care' reasoning is illustrated very well if we look at how the UN approach to human smuggling differs from the EU approach. Even though it does not formally qualify smuggled migrants as *victims*, the protection of their rights is among the UN Protocol's main concerns, as is explicitly stated, for example, in Art. 2: "The purpose of this Protocol is to prevent and combat the smuggling of migrants, as well as to promote cooperation among states Parties to that end, *while protecting the rights of smuggled migrants.*" The EU Facilitation Directive, however, describes the role of the smuggled migrant by using verbs ("assisting someone *to enter,*" "*to transit,*" "*to stay*"), thus revealing that the person is seen as someone actively contributing to the whole deed. The UN Protocol, on the contrary, uses – at least in Art. 3(a) – a noun ("procuring *the entry* of someone"), thus describing the migrant's position more as the result of another person's action than as an action itself.

Regardless of these differences in how smuggled migrants are seen, in both the UN Protocol and the Facilitation Directive the smuggler's conduct is recognized to have a wrongness of its own: a wrongness that is not a mere reflection of irregular migration, but derives directly from its being a commodification of human beings, an exploitation of the migrant's vulnerability as a source of enrichment, of money-making.

In the sideline of both the Protocol as well as the Directive it is mentioned that it excludes from the scope of the criminalisation "the activities of those who provided support to migrants for humanitarian reasons or on the basis of close family ties." In this chapter, we will focus on this broader perspective on human smuggling. Even though the assumption inherent in many of the policy initiatives around fighting human smuggling and studies around human smuggling is that organized crime is involved (van Liempt & Sersli 2012, Baird & van Liempt 2015), it is equally important to bear in mind that smuggling is not perceived as a crime everywhere, always, and by everybody. Academic literature on human smuggling points to evidence that it likely has existed as long as borders have, as there have always been people who, for all sorts of reasons, were unable to travel via ordinary legal routes (Fittko 2000, Siener 2008, Mar 2010).

This chapter puts a broader perspective on human smuggling to illustrate the various reasons migrants might need smugglers and the different ways smuggling can evolve. The category of the 'humanitarian smuggler' is put central in this chapter to challenge the purely criminological discourse around human smuggling that is dominant, and to provide a more complex, diverse picture of the practice.

What do we know about the facilitators behind human smuggling?

The earliest academic conceptualization of human smuggling comes from Salt and Stein (1997), who framed human smuggling as a 'business.' As geographers, they made important distinctions among the various types of services offered in countries of origin, in transit, and at the destination, as well as the interconnections among these places. They also differentiated between legitimate and illegitimate markets in which actors pursue profit and commercial gain around human smuggling, which has been important in understanding its embeddedness. Despite these

Humanitarian smuggling

nuances, human smuggling was tied directly and solely into questions of organized crime, which has been central to discussions of migrant smuggling from early studies until now (Salt and Stein 1997, Chin 1999, Lazcko and Thompson 2000, Salt 2000). Defining the exact role of organised crime in human smuggling organizations generated a lasting debate in smuggling studies (Heckmann 2004, Neske 2006, Colucello and Massey 2007, Kaizen and Nonneman 2007, Kyle and Koslowski 2011, Soudijn and Kleemans 2009, UNODC 2011).

It is not surprising that when the UN Protocol against the Smuggling of Migrants by Land, Air and Sea came into being in 2000, migrant smuggling was officially included in the definition of organized crime. This event marked the framing of human smuggling as a global criminal business (Gallagher and David 2014). In 2000, the strengthening of the penal framework of smuggling was also put high on the European Council's agenda. Its delegations, however, had very different views on the various types of smuggling that exist and what constitutes 'humanitarian' grounds for the smuggling of asylum seekers.

The discussion on a continuum of types of smuggling links to a whole field of academic research that shows that the criminal discourse is helpful for understanding different actors involved in the process of human smuggling and the stages of the process, but it lacks a wider perspective. By following a narrow track dictated by a purely economic perspective, the complexity behind human smuggling is denied. It, for example, does not give any indication of the reasons smuggling begins or continues in a certain context other than making profit (Kyle 2011, van Liempt 2007, Spener 2009; Kyle and Dale 2001) and underestimates the role of personal networks in the migration process (Staring 2004, Herman, 2006).

Studies that take a wider perspectives show that it is often local people living in border regions involved in the smuggling business for whom profiting from smuggling goods and/or people is a low-profile way of making a living without necessarily being connected to international organized criminal organisations (Chin 1999, Icduygu and Toktas 2000, Mabrouk 2003, Spener 2009, Missbach 2015, Sanchez 2015). These studies also show the complexity around the fact that smuggling is sometimes organized by family members of migrants, who may profit from and exploit relatives, but who are also inclined to act out of humanitarian reasons (Koser 1997, Staring 2004, Buchen, 2014).

Smuggling through social networks

The role of personal networks has been underestimated in the human smuggling process (Herman 2006) and research on the transnational scope of familial networks has added an important theoretical dimension to the study of human smuggling (Staring 2004). One of the main findings of studies that look into the role of networks is that smuggling depends on unique network characteristics coupled with individual agency, and that trust plays a key role (Koser 2008). Herman (2006) argues for incorporating 'the social non-profit factor' into the study of human smuggling to bring the role of personal and familial ties into the foreground (Herman 2006: 217).

Stefan Buchen (2014) followed a case in Essen (Germany) where in January 2013 'an international people-smuggling gang' was identified as part of a Europe-wide operation. It was reported that suspects were arrested in 37 places across Germany and some arrests were made in Greece and Poland. The 'head of the gang' was a 58-year-old Syrian man from Essen. The authorities estimated that he had made a €300,000 profit out of smuggling activities, although they did not find any cash. Buchen discovered the 'head of the gang' was not a professional smuggler but an engineer who went to work every day and had not smuggled anything or anyone before the war broke out in Syria. He turned out to be part of a group of Syrians who came together at the beginning of the war to help Syrian refugees escape their country. None of their 'customers' had felt threatened, poorly treated, or exploited, and relatively small amounts of money had been paid for the services. This example stands for many smuggling cases and shows that the smuggling market is complex, with highly differentiated services (Icduygu and Toktas 2000, Zhang and Chin 2002, Sanchez 2015). Some earn substantial amounts of money, but many individuals in the smuggling process receive little or no compensation for their services (Kyle and Dale, 2001, 50).

Smuggled migrants' perspectives

Only few studies have centered around smuggled migrants' perspectives (Koser 1997, Efionayi-Mader et al. 2001, Bilger et al. 2006, van Liempt 2007, Spener 2009). These studies add an interesting dimension to the debate by pointing out that there is often remarkably little stigma attached to the smuggling business from migrants' points of view. Migrants who have used the services of smugglers rarely view them as dangerous criminals who should be imprisoned, but often describe them as 'the people who most helped them' (Sharma 2003, 60), as life savers, or as a necessary evil in a world with many restrictions on mobility (van Liempt 2007). The fact that there are few migrants willing to testify against their smugglers supports this view of smugglers as helpers. Nevertheless, the prices charged can be very high, and some suffer from exploitation or poor treatment. The important context of helping people escape war, poverty, and misery makes smugglers necessary.

In a quantitative survey carried out with migrants who had enlisted the services of smugglers to cross from Mexico into the USA, 75% of the 655 interviewees declared that they were satisfied with the service provided by their smuggler, and 45% would recommend their smuggler to a family member or a friend (Slack and Martínez 2018, p. 162). An additional important reason not to testify against smugglers is that friends/family members who are still back home might one day need these services too. Labeling human smugglers as evil is too simple and does not take into account the political reality that people need to cross borders to find protection.

Smuggling for humanitarian reasons under current EU Law

Activities of those who provided support to migrants for humanitarian reasons or on the basis of close family ties were previously excluded from the scope of criminalization. The EU Facilitation Directive also has an optional safeguard known as *the humanitarian clause* which provides EU Member States with the possibility to exempt cases of smuggling from crim-inalization. Both the UN Protocol and the EU Facilitation Directive risk suppressing genuinely humanitarian acts of assistance, as they give states discretion to criminalize a broad range of acts of assistance to irregular migrants. Carrera and Guild (2016) argue that the Facilitative Directive suffers from an implementation gap in several areas, including the threshold of what constitutes an act of smuggling and the possibility of a humanitarian defense.

The decision to include an optional 'humanitarian clause' was not without discussion and internal disagreements within the EU. Its wording is ultimately the product of a compromise amongst the drafters put forth by the Swedish presidency (Council of the European Union 2001). For example, Austria was entirely opposed to Article 1.2 (the optional humanitarian clause) and the UK submitted several reservations (Council of the European Union 2001). By contrast, Germany proposed that the humanitarian clause should be 'compulsory' (Council of the European Union 2001). Whilst the product of compromise, the optional humanitarian exemption ultimately permits the criminalization of humanitarian acts of smuggling because the

Humanitarian smuggling

Directive does not oblige EU member states to impose sanctions when humanitarian motives are involved in smuggling.

As such, countries have varied in how they have transposed this Directive into national legal frameworks. According to Art. 1 (2),

> Any member state may decide not to impose sanctions with regard to the behavior defined in paragraph 1 (a) by applying its national law and practice for cases where the aim of the behavior is to provide humanitarian assistance to the person concerned.

Behind this provision lies a clue to the fact that humanitarian concerns are not a key worry for EU laws against smuggling. The meaning of Art. 1 (2) is, indeed, that member states are not obliged, but merely permitted to grant 'facilitators' a humanitarian defense for their conduct, which unavoidably makes helping immigrants more risky for potential helpers, thereby indirectly impinging upon the chances migrants have to be helped when they find themselves in need of humanitarian assistance. Currently, facilitating irregular entry is punished in all 28 EU member states and the EU Actions to fight against smuggling have run in parallel with an incremental use of sanctions in the EU against individuals directly or indirectly involved in helping and/or providing humanitarian assistance to irregular migrants.

A recent report by the EU Fundamental Rights Agency (Fundamental Rights Agency FRA 2014) reveals that only a quarter of member states "have national legislation that reflects, at least in some form, the safeguards in Article 1 (2), allowing states not to impose sanctions when irregular entry is facilitated for humanitarian purposes." The optional humanitarian clause had been explicitly transposed at the national level in only eight Member States. The same FRA report similarly notes that "more than a quarter of member states fail in their national legislation to exempt non-profit acts or humanitarian assistance from the rules of facilitation of stay" (Fundamental Rights Agency FRA 2014). In the autumn of 2015, during which substantial numbers of refugees in desperate situations travelled through both EU and Schengen states, some of the EU's measures against facilitation of irregular migration were instrumentalised by some political leaders to warn their citizens and the citizens of neighbouring states against assisting refugees on the move. EU law, of course, does not disregard completely the rights of smuggled migrants; it could not do so, since many of these rights are either recognised in the EU Charter of the Fundamental Rights or are the object of international obligations for the member states. Two examples. According to Art. 1(2),

> Any member state may decide not to impose sanctions with regard to the behaviour defined in paragraph 1(a) by applying its national law and practice for cases where the aim of the behaviour is to provide humanitarian assistance to the person concerned.

The meaning of Art. 1(2) is that member states are not obliged, but merely permitted to grant "facilitators" a humanitarian defence for their conduct, which unavoidably makes helping immigrants more risky for potential helpers, thereby indirectly impinging upon the chances migrants have to be helped when they find themselves in need of humanitarian assistance.

Examples of humanitarian smuggling

Apart from refugees involved in smuggling countrymen who are in need of help to escape war tarn countries, civil society in Europe has also increasingly become involved in helping refugees with their often difficult border crossing processes. One famous recent example is that of Salam

Ilse van Liempt

Aldeen who helped save lives in the Agean Sea, but was later accused of human smuggling. Aldeen, a 34-year-old man from Denmark, was never trained as a lifeguard but when he saw an overcrowded dinghy sinking off the coast of the Greek island of Lesbos in the summer of 2016 he started to rescue the people. The boat came from Turkey and was haphazardly constructed. It had lasted most of the short (10 kilometer) journey across the Agean Sea but the motor began to dislodge only a few hundred meters off the coast of Lesbos. As the boat started to sank Salam told the people to get off, hold onto the boat and paddle to shore. He helped them push and steer the boat from the back. There were women and children on board and a picture of Salam holding a baby made it all over the news. Back in Denmark, Salam Aldeen decided to go back to Lesbos and see if he could help. He started Team Humanity in September 2015 and he became an 'island legend.' As an almost native Arabic speaker (his father is originally from Iraq) he rescued many migrants. Aldeen had responded to distress calls from more than 200 boats with an estimated total of more than 10,000 refugees on board, seeking to uphold the duty to rescue at sea.

In January 2016 Aldeen was arrested on charges of human smuggling. As the driver and owner of the boat, Aldeen faced harsher punishment than the other rescuers. Four rescuers were given a bail set at 5000 Euros, while Aldeen's bail was set at 10,000 Euros. He faced up to ten years in prison. Also, Aldeen was barred from leaving the country, whereas the others were not. He has to check into a police station every week and is not allowed to leave Greece, just like so many immigrants today who are stuck in Greece. He continued his charity work helping refugees stuck on the Greek islands despite the charges. In May 2018 he faced the Geek court with four co-volunteers and was cleared of charges of bringing migrants into Greece illegally.

Large organizations like Save the Children and Médecins Sans Frontiers (MSF) recently also have been accused of collaborating with human smugglers with their rescue operations in the Central as well as Eastern Mediterranean sea. It is important to contextualize these accusations. The Mare Nostrum Operation, which was initiated after the large shipwreck in 2014 off the coast of Lampedusa, was framed in the discourse of humanitarianism. In late 2014, because of a lack of support from the European Union the Italian state retreated from their Mare Nostrum Operation, leaving thousands to die at sea; it was criticized for a nine-fold increase in deaths between 2014 and 2015.[1] NGOs such as MSF then stepped in to fill this gap as a response to this danger to life (Pallister-Wilkins 2018). MSF launched its own SAR operations in 2015, initially by providing medical assistance on-board the MOAS' (Migrant Offshore Aid Station) boat. Soon MSF was running boats of its own: the Bourbon Argos; the Dignity 1; and lately the Prudence, while also joining forces with SOS Mediterranean on their the Aquarius (Pallister-Wilkins 2018). MSF's objective is to save human lives in full respect of its independent mandate as a medical humanitarian organization. SAR efforts produce a mobile humanitarianism that cannot be fixed easily in time or space. It occurs where rescue is needed. The types of care that can be offered and the conditions under which the care is offered depend hugely on politics.

Some politicians and officials in EU member states (for example Italy, Belgium and Austria) now claim that by providing SAR service Mare Nostrum and NGOs have made the journey safer and easier, thereby encouraging migrants and refugees to make the journey, acting thus as a pull factor for migration, or a bridge to Europe, and increasing the numbers. These are claims that are not substantiated with data. A recent assessment compared the before, during and after the Mare Nostrum period showed that the number of arrivals (and deaths) was higher before Mare Nostrum was introduced and during the period that involved NGOs.[2] By only focusing on *who* provides the border crossing, the important discussion of *why* people need to cross borders is left aside, and the complexities involved in migration are overlooked. Human smuggling is increasingly framed as a threat to the state rather than a reaction to restrictions imposed by states (see also Kyle and

Humanitarian smuggling

Dale 2001, Kyle and Siracusa 2005). This narrow focus results in a narrow understanding of what human smuggling is, and has an impact on how it is 'combatted.'

Conclusion

On the European Agenda on Migration the "fight against smugglers and traffickers" has been identified as a key priority. In particular, the Agenda has called for improvements to the current EU legal framework "to tackle migrant smuggling and those who profit from it." However, in the EU Action Plan against Migrant Smuggling adopted in May 2015, the European Commission notes that appropriate criminal sanctions should be in place while avoiding the risks of criminalising those who provide humanitarian assistance to migrants in distress, thus implicitly acknowledging the inherent tension between the criminalisation of smugglers on the one hand and of those providing humanitarian assistance on the other, through a range of behaviours that cover facilitation of not only irregular entry and transit, but also irregular residence and stay.

At present, the overall numbers of investigations and prosecutions leading to effective convictions of migrant smugglers across the entire European Union is low. Several studies have been conducted regarding EU member states' national transposition and implementation of the Facilitators' Package, or more generally, on policies and programmes focused on smuggling across the EU and in cooperation with third countries and the characteristics of the phenomenon. A significant gap exists, however, concerning the actual effects that these laws have on those working at the front line of providing humanitarian assistance, public services and fundamental human rights to irregular migrants, in particular, civil society organisations. What we witness at the borders is that the criminalization of smuggling has affected the willingness of small professional shipmasters to come to the rescue of migrants in distress. Moreover, court cases of convicted individuals have a wider impact on future possible helpers. Suppressing assistance of refugees very well may be the primary aim of criminalization; it is not so much about prosecuting people but much more about warning others not to do this. Criminalization of humanitarian forms of smuggling may thus impact people's willingness to help refugees because it makes helping migrants riskier and indirectly impinges on the chances migrants have to be helped when they find themselves in need of humanitarian assistance.

For the past decade, service providers across several member states have raised concerns that the hardening stance on migrant smuggling at the political level could impact the day-to-day service provision of humanitarian actors. It has been feared that renewed efforts to combat the smuggling of migrants and refugees could affect irregular migrants' access to their fundamental rights, including healthcare, education and housing. As such, it undermines the support for more humane solutions to the refugee crisis.

Protecting the fundamental rights of irregular migrants requires differentiating between smugglers and those providing humanitarian assistance to irregular migrants. This is particularly true as civil societies – NGOs as well as individuals – are often the ones that cover the basic needs of migrants. It is paramount to ensure that those helping migrants are given the legal certainty that they will not be prosecuted for their assistance. It must be acknowledged that family members and friends helping people escape war situations should not be criminalized. More debate is required regarding the significant differences between a citizen's or an NGO's perspective of facilitating irregular entry and transit, and the perspective of the state.

The plight of refugees in dreadful situations has inspired many people in the past and today to reach out and help. Many of these actions could be treated as crimes, under current national rules of the EU against irregular migration. The criminalization of humanitarian acts is evolving without much discussion. Getting a humanitarian exemption clause put in the Facilitation Directive could be a way to solve this dilemma. The clause is currently optional and not used by most EU states. The number of states using it is, in fact, decreasing. A humanitarian exemption has proven not to be sufficient. Humanitarian acts in this context must be more narrowly defined, either by making more explicit the meaning of "humanitarian," or defining more clearly the criminal element. A more explicit definition of what constitutes humanitarian here is needed in order not to put 'helpers' at risk.

Narrowing the smuggling definition to acts of facilitation where the smuggler is doing harm, or risk of harm to the individual could also be an option, as Landry (2016) suggests. In the absence of legal pathways, let us not forget that smuggling is usually essential to the ability of most refugees to claim their right under the Refugee Convention, and that criminalization of smuggling will do more harm to refugees than good. Smuggling is often the only means to enjoy fundamental rights, such as living in unity with one's family or escaping violence. The 'fight' against smuggling will only be successful when it is part of a broader set of measures including more promising attempts for conflict resolution and development in regions of origin. It is difficult to challenge the dominant representation of smuggling at a time when many people die as a result of dangerous border crossings, but it is necessary to stress that criminalization of smuggling will not improve migrant's access to protection at a time when mobility is restricted by governments.

Notes

1 (https://deathbyrescue.org/).
2 (www.law.ox.ac.uk/research-subject-groups/centre-criminology/centreborder-criminologies/blog/2 017/03/border-deaths).

References

Baird, T. and Liempt, I van (2015) 'Scrutinising the double disadvantage: knowledge production in the messy field of migrant smuggling,' *Journal of Ethnic and Migration Studies*, 42(3), pp. 400–417.

Bilger, V., Hofmann, M. and Jandl, M. (2006) 'Human smuggling as a transnational service industry. Evidence from Austria,' *International Migration*, 44(4), pp. 59–93.

Buchen, S. (2014) *Die Neuen Staatsfeinde. Wie die Helfer Syrischer Kriegsfluchtlinge in Deutschland kriminalisiert werden.* Bonn: Dietz-Verlag.

Carrera, S. and Guild, E. (2016) *Irregular Migration, Trafficking and Smuggling of Human Beings: Policy Dilemmas in the EU.* Brussels: Centre for European Policy Studies (CEPS).

Chin, K. L., (1999) *Smuggled Chinese: Clandestine Immigration to the United States.* Philadelphia: Temple University.

Colucello, S. and Massey, S. (2007) 'Out of Africa: the human trade between Libya and Lampedusa,' *Trends in Organized Crime*, 10, pp. 77–90.

Collyer, M., (2016) Cross-border cottage industries and fragmented migration, in Carrera, S. & E. Guild (eds.), *Irregular Migration, Trafficking and Smuggling of Human Beings: Policy Dilemmas in the EU.* Brussels: Centre for European Policy Studies.

Council of the European Union, 6766/01, Brussels, 9 March 2001 (http://data.consilium.europa.eu/doc/document/ST-6766-2001-INIT/en/pdf).

Efionayi-Mader, D., M. Chimienti, J. Dahinden and Piguet, E. (2001) *Asyldestination Europa. Eine Geographie der Asylbewegungen.* Zurich: Seismo.

Fittko, L. (2000) *Escapes Through the Pyrenees.* Illinois: Northwestern University Press.

Fundamental Rights Agency (FRA) (2014) "Criminalisation of migrants in an irregular situation and of persons engaging with them." http://fra.europa.eu/en/publication/2014/criminalisation-migrantsirregular-situation-and-persons-engaging-them

Humanitarian smuggling

Gallagher, A. T. and David, F. (2014) *The International Law of Migrant Smuggling*. Cambridge: Cambridge University Press.

Heckmann, F. (2004) 'Illegal migration: what can we know and what can we explain? The case of Germany,' *International Migration Review*, 38(3), pp. 1103–1125.

Herman, E. (2006) 'Migration as a family business: the role of personal networks in the mobility phase of migration,' *International Migration*, 44(4), pp. 191–230.

Icduygu, A. and Toktas, S. (2000) 'How do smuggling and trafficking operate via irregular border crossings in the Middle East? Evidence from fieldwork in Turkey,' *International Migration*, 40(6), pp. 25–52.

Kaizen, J. and Nonneman, W. (2007) 'Irregular migration in Belgium and organized crime: an overview,' *International Migration*, 45(2), pp. 121–146.

Koser, K., (1997) 'Social networks and the asylum cycle: the case of Iranians in the Netherlands,' *International Migration Review*, 31(3), pp. 591–611.

Koser, K. (2008) 'Why migrant smuggling pays,' *International Migration*, 46(2): pp. 3–26.

Kyle, D. and Dale, J. (2001) Smuggling the state back in: agents of human smuggling reconsidered, in Kyle, D. and R. Koslowski (eds.) *Global Human Smuggling: Comparative Perspectives*. Baltimore: Indiana University Press, pp. 29–57.

Kyle, D. and Siracusa, C. A. (2005) Seeing the state like a migrant: why so many non-criminals break immigration laws, in van Schendel, W. and I. Abraham (eds.) *Illicit Flows and Criminal Things*. Bloomington: Indiana University Press, pp. 153–176.

Kyle, D. and Koslowski, R., (eds.) (2011) *Global Human Smuggling: Comparative Perspectives* (2nd edition). Baltimore: The Johns Hopkins University Press.

Landry, R., (2016) *The 'Humanitarian Smuggling' of Refugees. Criminal Offence or Moral Obligation?*, Oxford: Refugee Studies Centre, Working Paper Series No. 119.

Lazcko, F. and Thompson, D., (eds.) (2000) *Migrant Trafficking and Human Smuggling in Europe: A Review of the Evidence with Case Studies from Hungary Poland and Ukraine*. Geneva: International Organization for Migration (IOM).

Liempt, I. van (2007) *Navigating Borders: Inside Perspectives on the Process of Human Smuggling into the Netherlands*. Amsterdam: Amsterdam University Press.

Liempt, I. van and Sersli, S. (2012) 'State responses and migrant experiences with human smuggling: a reality check,' *Antipode*, 45(5), pp. 1029–1046.

Mabrouk, M. (2003) 'A sociological study of clandestine emigrants and their imaginary,' *Revue Semestrielle Tunisiennes de Sciences Social*. Tunis: CERES.

Mar, L. (2010) *Brokering Belonging: Chinese in Canada's Exclusion Era, 1885–1945*. New York: Oxford University Press.

Missbach, A. (2015) *Troubled Transit: Asylum Seekers Stuck in Indonesia*. Singapore: ISEAS.

Moises N. (2005) *Illicit: How Smugglers, Traffickers, and Copycats are Hijacking the Global Economy*. New York: Doubleday.

Neske, M. (2006) *Menschensmuggel. Deutschland als transit and zielland irregular migration*, PhD thesis, University of Bamberg.

Pallister-Wilkins, P. (2018) 'Médecins Avec Frontières and the making of a humanitarian borderscape,' *Environment and Planning D: Society & Space*, 36(1), pp. 114–138.

Salt, J. (2000) 'Trafficking and human smuggling: a European perspective,' *International Migration*, 38(3), pp. 31–56.

Salt, J. and Stein, J. (1997) 'Migration as a business: the case of trafficking,' *International Migration*, 35(4), pp. 467–494.

Sanchez, G. (2015) *Human Smuggling and Border Crossings*. Routledge.

Sharma, N. (2003). 'Travel agency: A critique of anti-trafficking campaigns,' *Refuge: Canada's Journal on Refugees*, pp. 53–65.

Siener, W. (2008) 'Through the back door: Evading the Chinese Exclusion Act along the Niagara Frontier, 1900 to 1924,' *Journal of American Ethnic History*, 27(4), pp. 34–70.

Slack, J., and Martínez, E. D. (2018) 'What makes a good human smuggler? The difference between satisfaction with and recommendation of coyotes on the U.S.–Mexico border,' *The Annals of the American Academy of Political and Social Sciences*, 676(1), pp. 152–173.

Soudijn, M. R. J. and Kleemans, E. R. (2009) 'Chinese organized crime and situational context: comparing human smuggling and synthetic drugs trafficking,' *Crime Law and Social Change*, 52(5), pp. 457–474.

Spener, D. (2009) *Clandestine Crossings: Migrants and Coyotes on the Texas–Mexico Border*. New York: Cornell University Press.

Staring, R. (2004) 'Facilitating the arrival of illegal immigrants in the Netherlands: irregular chain migration versus smuggling chains,' *Journal of International Migration and Integration*, 5(3), pp. 273–294.

UNODC (2011) *The Role of Organized Crime in the Smuggling of Migrants from West Africa to the European Union*. Vienna: United Nations.

Zhang, S. and Chin, K. L. (2002) *The Social Organisation of Chinese Human Smuggling: A Cross National Study*. San Diego: San Diego State University.

23

MIGRANT SMUGGLING AND THE SOCIAL ORGANISATION OF CROSS-BORDER MOBILITY

Luca Raineri

Introducing migrant smuggling: inaccurate framings, wrong approaches, self-fulfilling prophecies

Although the phenomenon of migrant smuggling has a long history (Wokeck, 1999), the lack of conceptual clarity and methodological rigour have long inhibited the emergence of a scientific field of inquiry on the subject. Since its inception, the criminological perspective has remained dominant (Van Liempt and Sersli, 2012). The theoretical assumptions and normative concerns of law enforcement have shaped the conceptualisations of, and responses to, migrant smuggling. The tendency to look at migrant smuggling more as a pathology than as a social phenomenon has thus long influenced the foundational research questions – and answers – of migrant smuggling research, including about the identities of smugglers and smuggled individuals, their modes of organisation, the drivers of their actions, and the most appropriate policy responses.

This chapter engages in a brief reconstruction of this genealogy. It contrasts early conceptualisations and related popular beliefs on migrant smuggling with recent approaches and findings, which offer a more nuanced and complex view of the phenomenon. It argues that the growing availability of rigorous and empirically-rich studies has contributed to questioning the analytical purchase of institutionalist and neo-institutionalist perspectives on migrant smuggling and crime (Kleemans, 2014), highlighting instead the explanatory value of the network theory, with its emphasis on social capital and ties. Policy approaches built on unconfirmed assumptions may have contributed to rehabilitating past views, making the criminalisation of migrant smuggling a self-fulfilling prophecy.

The predominance of law enforcement concerns and criminological lenses in the apprehension of migrant smuggling transpires from the early studies on the phenomenon commissioned by international organisations (IOM, 1994; UNODC, 2011a) to the more recent iterations of a so-called "crisis" of migrant smuggling and irregular migration in Europe (EUROPOL, 2016). Seminal studies have struggled to disentangle migrant smuggling and its distinctive features from other forms of irregular migration, including most notably human trafficking (ILO, 1975; Salt, 2000; Kyle and Koslowski, 2001; Tailby, 2001). The adoption of the Protocol against the Smuggling of Migrants by Land, Sea and Air – commonly referred to as the Smuggling of Migrants Protocol – supplementing the 2000 UN Convention against

DOI: 10.4324/9781003043645-23

Transnational Organized Crime (UNCTOC), has supplied an authoritative and clear-cut definition of migrant smuggling, enabling the comparative analysis of a phenomenon that by its very nature straddles national borders. It has also contributed, however, to framing, from the outset, migrant smuggling as a matter of law enforcement, associated with transnational organised crime.

As a result, policy and scholarly discourses on migrant smuggling have an in-built tendency to reiterate the analytical grids and normative standpoint of criminological perspectives. This stands out clearly in at least two domains, which the chapter investigates critically: the economic analogy of migrant smuggling's drivers and modes of organisation; and the security emphasis of response strategies.

Migrant smuggling is often framed as an economic activity (a "business," "market," or "industry") where the lack of legal protection enables smugglers to resort to exploitative and predatory practices (Salt and Stein, 1997; Aronowitz, 2001; Schloenhardt, 2002). This stands in contrast with the posited passivity and victimhood of migrants. The neoliberal analogy between transnational smuggling networks and transnational corporations operating in the legal economy has reinforced the understanding that migrant smuggling is carried out by centralised organisations exercising a hierarchical command and control over a variety of profit-making criminal activities, including the trafficking of women, weapons and drugs. Studies informed by this intellectual scaffolding often strive to obtain accurate figures of the cash flows of the criminal organisations allegedly implicated in migrant smuggling, with a view to dissecting their "business model" (Salt and Stein, 1997; UNODC, 2011a; Reitano and Tinti, 2015). This endeavour somehow reproduces the ambition to attach "memorable numbers" to the estimated profits of criminal organisations, so as to catalyse media attention and political action (Andreas, 2010). Engaging in this direction, a comprehensive retrospective report by UNODC (2011a) cited – without much distancing – the figures of migrant smuggling's estimated profits put forward by early scholarship (all of them reported in Salt and Stein, 1997), ranging from $3 billion along the China – US route, to a global annual income of $5-7 billion. Were this economic power converted into political influence and military might, the standard argument goes, criminal organisations emboldened by smuggling profits, including those of migration, could pose an unprecedented challenge to international stability (Naim, 2012).

The sensation of the imminence of a threat has thus contributed to justifying the mobilisation of considerable resources to stem irregular migration and smuggling. With organised crime depicted as the new Evil Empire, the post-Cold war transition from a warfare to a crimefare posture by Western countries (for the US: see Andreas and Price, 2001; for the EU: see Stambol, 2019) has paved the way to the militarisation of the response to migrant smuggling. Illustrations of this are not in short supply, whether at the US-Mexico border (Nuñez-Neto, Siskin and Viña, 2005), in Australia (Schloenhardt, 2003; Weber and Grewcock, 2011), or in the EU (Lutterbeck, 2006; Akkerman, 2017). Fuelling the oft-noticed securitisation of migration and smuggling (Buzan, 1991; Galemba, 2018), declarations of a war against migrant smuggling (Raineri and Strazzari, 2021) have been accompanied by the deployment of the arsenal previously tested on the war on drugs (Horwood, 2019), with its focus on enhanced border controls, law enforcement cooperation, and supply eradication.

In the last years, however, the proliferation of critical perspectives, scientific research designs and empirically-rich studies on migrant smuggling increasingly has questioned the underlying assumptions of the criminological approach, leading to the conclusion that the alleged link between migrant smuggling and organised criminal syndicates is poorly substantiated. The subsequent sections of the chapter build on these research developments to show that the prevailing mode of organisation of irregular cross-border mobility is characterised less by

Migrant smuggling

hierarchical top-down arrangements, than by loose horizontal networks, in which criminal syndicates typically play a marginal role. This leads us to interrogate the conditions that enable the coordination of migrants and smugglers, in the absence of an over-arching regulation and enforcement: mitigating the behaviouralist over-emphasis on profit-maximisation, the network theory highlights that social capital, social ties and social embeddedness help explain the trajectories and choices of the actors involved in migrant smuggling. In this framework, law enforcement measures and securitised approaches appear more effective in reshaping than in disrupting migrant smuggling: by severing cross-border social networks, they paradoxically incentivise the provision of protection by criminal organisations. This observation has led scholars to argue that the criminalisation of migrant smuggling may be seen as a iatrongenic effect of misguided militarised responses.

Emerging evidence on migrant smuggling worldwide: from centralised syndicates to horizontal networks

Focusing on a variety of geographic areas and investigating different smuggling networks, an increasing amount of literature is putting forward the idea that the organisation of migrant smuggling is, in the largest majority of the cases, less akin to a top-down hierarchical pyramid than to a horizontal network characterised by loose and opportunistic affiliations. Rather than orchestrated by a criminal mastermind pulling the strings behind the scenes, as (neo-) institutionalist criminological approaches would have it, migrant smuggling appears to be the result of the complex interactions of large numbers of smaller, flexible actors efficient at organising piecemeal and ad hoc activities while retaining a relative degree of independence and proactiveness (Baird and Van Liempt, 2016). Within this context, solidarity and trust emerge as key features of the relationship between smugglers and smuggled migrants much more often than previously imagined. An overview of the recent findings of migrant smuggling research across the world contributes to corroborating this view.

Migrant smuggling from China to the US has been associated regularly with organised crime and the traditional triad societies (Robertson, 1977). In recent years, however, the growing availability of fine-grained, multi-sited ethnography has enabled a much more granular understanding, suggesting that migrant smuggling from China to the US is largely dominated by small groups of freelance entrepreneurs who build their own networks independently, often on the basis of their previous social interactions. This has prompted the conclusion that Chinese migrant smuggling organisations "are made up of decentralized associations of criminals of diverse backgrounds, and the relationships among core members are mostly horizontal" (Zhang and Chin, 2002, p. 759), with no single organization monopolising or centralising the sector (Chin, 1999; Zhang, 2008; Zhang and Chin, 2003).

Studies looking at the smuggling of migrants into the US from the Mexican border has led to very similar conclusions. Spener (2009) has noted that local smugglers are poorly organised, with no evidence of market monopolisation by a single group. Sanchez reiterates the same observation, arguing that there is no evidence of "the existence of a single, centralised, power providing operational or logistical support in any of the smuggling groups identified" (Sanchez, 2015, p. 44). Izcara Palacios (2014) has highlighted that the resort to violence is infrequent among competing smuggling groups. This may be seen as the result of kinship ties and links of reciprocity shaping the migrant smuggling "market" (Sanchez, 2017).

The research findings about the organisation of migrant smuggling to the EU are consistent with this picture. Examining the role of Chinese organisations in the smuggling of migrants via the Netherlands, Soudijn (2006) and Kleemans (2007; see also Soudijn and Kleemans, 2009) have found no evidence of a centralised organisation, and argue that a plurality of actors coexist, while competition among them is regulated less by the resort to violence than by reputation-building measures. Looking at Belgium, Kaizen and Nonneman (2007) have recognised the importance of kinship and ethnic ties in the articulation of migrant smuggling, arguing that smugglers operate in small groups characterised by cellular structures and opportunistic business partnerships. In Poland, Okolski (2000) has noted that migrant smuggling operations exhibit limited engagement by the Russian mafia.

Studies focusing on migrant smuggling across the Middle East, and especially Turkey, have led to similar observations. Demir, Sever and Kahya (2017) note the absence of an "international umbrella organization" with "branches in several countries," arguing instead that migrant smuggling is based on "loosely connected" groups with limited if any internal hierarchy, that "communicate and cooperate [...] horizontally" across the different stages of the process (Demir Sever and Kahya, 2017, pp. 384–385; see also Campana, 2020). Case studies focusing on Turkey-based organisations smuggling migrants from Syria (Achilli, 2018), Iran and Iraq (Içduygu and Toktas, 2002; Içduygu, 2018) corroborate the same findings, noting that smugglers operate independently along a small part of a larger chain with no centralised organisation or oversight.

Studies focusing on Africa, too, have further confirmed the emerging general conclusion that small-scale coordination on a case-by-case basis, rather than central oversight by hierarchical criminal syndicates, is the prevalent mode of organisation of transnational migrant smuggling. In Libya, this was the case during the Gaddafi regime (Pastore, Monzini and Sciortino, 2006). Interestingly, the fall of the authoritarian ruler and the rise of a patchwork of armed groups and militias does not appear to have changed the picture radically (Campana, 2018; Sanchez, 2020). "The presence of kingpins who can exert monopolistic control over a certain route," while frequently aired in media and policy discourses, remains strongly disputed and poorly corroborated by convincing evidence (Campana, 2018, p. 493). In a similar vein, researches on West Africa have noted that in this region, too, migrant smuggling is fragmented, and depends more on individual initiatives, 'homespun' organisational arrangements, and small-scale negotiations than on an integrated chain of professional services deployed internationally and centralised vertically (UNODC, 2011b; Benattia, Armitano and Robinson, 2015). In Niger, where migratory flows directed to Libya and Europe have soared considerably since 2014, smuggling remains dominated by "small-scale low-investment activities" featuring "rather fragmented and uncoordinated chains of actors" (Brachet, 2018, p. 29), while the dynamics of market competition – essentially non-violent in nature – witness to the absence of a consolidated criminal monopoly (Raineri, 2018).

The migratory route from the Horn of Africa may represent a possible exception to this trend. Here, studies commissioned or carried out by think tanks, international organisations and law enforcement agencies contend that hierarchically structured criminal cartels are able to coordinate the shipping of migrants from Eritrea to Europe via Libya (Sahan/IGAD, 2016; UNHCR, 2019). Recent scholarly work, however, has questioned this view. Emerging evidence from ethnographic immersion (Ayalew Mengiste, 2018) and social network analysis (Campana, 2018) suggests that the modus operandi of migrant smuggling from the Horn of Africa to Europe remains highly fragmented. The resort to sophisticated organisational arrangements, which has also been noted, coexists with a high degree of social embeddedness and permeability of smuggling networks operating along this route.

One could be tempted to argue that the over-reliance on bottom-up research designs may have contributed to distorting these findings. After all, ethnographic methods generally provide access to the perceptions of smuggled migrants and low-level smugglers who, even if

Migrant smuggling

well-intentioned and transparent, may be simply unaware of the functioning of the higher, more secretive echelons of the organisations that empower and shape their activities (a similar position surfaces, for instance, in Malakooti, 2016). The reality seems to be exactly the opposite though. Data access limitations have concurred to cement the hegemony of the criminological approach to the study of migrant smuggling. As a result of the difficulties in observing, measuring, and gathering reliable data on an inherently opaque activity (Koser, 2009; McAuliffe and Laczko, 2016), studies on migrant smuggling have long been shaped by law enforcement who (claim to) have first-hand information, as UNODC has also recognized (UNODC, 2011a). Ethnographic research on migrant smuggling has contributed to eroding this informational bias. Interestingly, subsequent studies drawing on alternative, non-ethnographic methods of data collection and analysis – such as judicial sources, regression analysis of wiretapping metadata, content analysis of wiretapping records and social network analysis (SNA) – have corroborated the same conclusions (Soudijn and Kleemans, 2009; Webb and Burrows, 2009; Leman and Janssens, 2011; Demir, Sever and Kahya, 2017; Campana, 2018). This proliferation points to an emerging consensus that the involvement of hierarchically structured criminal syndicates in the organisation of migrant smuggling is tenuous at best.

Scholars have put forward a plausible explanation of this seeming anomaly. Arguably, traditional criminal organisations excel at those racketeering activities in which territorial control can be exploited, such as gambling, prostitution and protection (Paoli, 2003). Being geographically constrained in their own turf, however, they are ill-equipped to meet the fluid demands of a multi-sited, transnational market, such as migrant smuggling. This is what Zhang and Chin (2002, 2003) call the structural deficiency of traditional criminal cartels. Nevertheless, as the subsequent sections suggest, law enforcement measures to curtail (the supply side of) human smuggling can incentivise the demand for the protection of informal transactions, thereby creating a fertile ground for organised criminal groups to step back in.

Migrant smuggling and network theory

Building on the above, it is safe to conclude that research findings do not uphold the narrative of migrant smuggling as organised by tentacular crime syndicates structured hierarchically and able to generate (criminal) economies of scale by ensuring central oversight to the transnational shipping of migrants from their home village to their countries of destination. To the contrary, migrant smuggling is typically facilitated by networks organised horizontally, featuring multiple affiliations and limited geographic reach. Migrants typically negotiate their shipment through every single leg of their journey with a variety of different providers of smuggling services, who generally act as freelance entrepreneurs and do not report to a higher-level hierarchy belonging to a single, unitary, criminal organisation. This is not to imply that all social organisation and hierarchy is entirely absent from migrant smuggling. Proponents of the network theory acknowledge that smugglers do retain different levels of influence, but this is more the result of their capacity to connect a variety of networks and bridge a diversity of social environments than of any pre-given organisational hierarchy (Kleemans, 2007; Campana, 2018). In other words, it is less a matter of top-down dominance from a vertical perspective, than of central strategic positioning from a horizontal perspective.

Within this framework, the network theory opens up the questions of how migrants and smugglers establish connections, and negotiate their agreements. On the one hand, in fact, the availability of a plurality of providers of smuggling opportunities, rather than of a single violent monopolist, enables migrants to exercise a much greater degree of autonomy and agency (Van Liempt and Doomernik, 2006; Sanchez, 2020). It becomes apparent that in many cases migrants choose their own smugglers, building on the feedback collected from common acquaintances or online (Campana, 2020). While the exploitation of naivety and need make scams far from infrequent, increasing access to social media technology contributes to reducing informational asymmetry. On the other hand, trust between migrants and smugglers is of extreme importance (Kleemans, 2007; Golovko, 2018; Sanchez, 2018). This is in line with the findings of an emerging ethnographic literature on criminal networks in general (Nordstrom, 2007), and contributes to questioning the standard assumption held by an influential tradition of political science – from Hobbes to Weber – arguing that transactions taking place beyond state regulation are bound to generate anarchy, violence and ultimately social disintegration. The observation, often reported, that migrants typically trust smugglers more than the law enforcement apparatuses tasked with fighting them (see for instance Golovko, 2018) highlights that this may not be always the case. In other words, the network theory shifts the focus away from the overemphasis on economic capital – whether that spent by migrants or raised by profit-seeking criminal organisations – to the social capital as a key variable to explain the trajectories, dynamics and organisation of migrant smuggling.

From this perspective, pre-existing bonds between smugglers and migrants often provide an asset to leverage social capital and minimise uncertainty and risk. The literature offers ample illustration of how family networks account for a key enabler of migration, including irregular migration and smuggling (Staring, 2004; Bilger, Hofmann and Jandl, 2006; Zhang, 2008). Increasingly, available scholarship has highlighted that migrant smugglers frequently share the same social and ethnic background as the migrants being smuggled (Neske, 2006; Soudijn, 2006; Majidi, 2018; Stone-Cadena and Álvarez Velasco 2018). Coming from impoverished communities, smugglers choose their "career" less out of greed than lack of alternatives, with migrant smuggling often complementing other sources of income (Sanchez, 2020). As a result, smugglers often share the same milieu and concerns as the migrants, leading to a blurring of the lines between the two categories.

The focus on the motivations and the recognition of the common social and moral standpoint that often ties smugglers and migrants together has also helped debunk the myth of a normative polarisation between, respectively, ruthless predators and naïve victims. To be sure, abuses and scams are not uncommon in migrant smuggling, but their exhibition and media overemphasis – often with sensationalistic tones – has all too often led us to overlook the positive interactions that are frequent between migrants and smugglers. There is no shortage of reports highlighting the "morality" of smugglers, who can come to be seen as "saviours" by migrants left with few alternatives (Pastore, Monzini and Sciortino, 2006; Van Liempt, 2007; Tinti and Reitano, 2016; Achilli, 2018; Ayalew Mengiste, 2018). At the same time, smugglers often see themselves as honest providers of a service that meets an exogenously given social demand of mobility, which is constrained by legislations widely held as unjust and unfair (Golovko, 2018; Mannocchi, 2019). Altruistic motivations often compound profit-seeking, making the interactions between smugglers and migrants irreducible to an economic rationality calculus. As Sanchez (2020, p. 22) has observed, "[smuggling] fees are often dependent of negotiations, community obligations, moral duty and other forms of reciprocity that go beyond financial values or returns, and are hardly ever the same, even for migrants traveling together or following the same trajectory."

These observations highlight that the research on migrant smuggling is in line with the overall conceptualisation of the 'criminal' world that is emerging from recent studies; i.e., that crime is not separate from, but deeply interwoven into the texture of ordinary social life and entangled in everyday intercourses, where criminal contacts intermesh with habitual social patterns (Kleemans and Van de Bunt, 1999; Hudson, 2014; Baird and Van Liempt, 2016). In the same vein, smugglers are in most cases more accurately described as ordinary citizens partially engaging in extralegal activities, than as professional gangsters segregated in a secretive criminal underworld.

Anti-smuggling policies: the iatrogenic effects of disrupting networks

The concept of "criminal iatrogenesis" was introduced to describe cases in which anti-criminal policies ended up fuelling, rather than curbing, criminal activities and organisations, prompting the observation that the cure prescribed to fight crime proved worse than the disease (Cohen, 1988; see also Brenner, 2021, in this volume). In its early iterations, criminal iatrogenesis referred mostly to the 'unintended consequences' or 'collateral damage' produced by the US "war on drugs." The questionable results of the latter have not prevented the revamping of some of its measures in the framework of an emerging war on migrant smuggling (Horwood, 2019), including an almost exclusive focus on (the curtailment of) the supply side of smuggling activities. Concurring with this view, scholars have highlighted the iatrogenic effects of the policies designed to fight migrant smuggling in Australia (Weber and Grewcock, 2011) and Europe (Stambol, 2019), spilling over to, respectively, south-east Asia and Africa.

Across a multiplicity of different country cases, in fact, common features emerge from the analysis of the strategies, policies and measures adopted to respond to, and fight against, migrant smuggling. These typically include: a restriction of the visa regime for unregulated border crossing; a criminalisation of migrant smuggling, including the adoption of harsh penalties for smuggling-related offences; enhanced border protection, often with the use of military assets; the externalisation of border controls to countries of origin and transit of migratory flows, including the creation of buffer zones; the use of transit camps and off-shore processing; the declaration of a war against migrant smuggling and trafficking (often conflated), framed as part of a broader fight against terrorism and transnational organised crime; and the strengthening of law enforcement cooperation with countries of transit and origin of migrants (Weber and Grewcock, 2011).

The extent to which these measures have proved successful in curbing migrant smuggling worldwide remains highly questionable. At the same time, evidence from different regions is piling up to suggest that such anti-smuggling policies have often resulted in the organisational restructuring of migrant smuggling, prompting a progressive replacement of small-scale, 'homespun' networks with larger, more sophisticated criminal organisations (UNODC 2011a, 2018). The latter are in fact better equipped for circumventing stricter border controls and forging the high-level partnerships required to condone illicit activities, owing to their greater economic resources and skilful use of organised violence. The rising entry barrier in the illegal(-ised) market of migrant smuggling is therefore credited for pushing towards greater criminal professionalisation while at the same time driving smaller operators out of the market. Furthermore, the disruption of small-scale migrant smuggling networks that is prompted by anti-smuggling law enforcement measures contributes to severing the "chain of trust" and personalised ties that make the infrastructure of cross-border mobility (Van Liempt, 2007). This can fuel a demand for the protection and enforcement (armed, if need be) of risky but profitable extralegal transactions, which mafia-like organisations present in the territory may be eager to meet with a view to expanding their protection rackets. Key brokers of transnational smuggling networks are thus absorbed, more or less willingly, within organised criminal structures consolidating beyond borders and confined localities (Morselli, 2009).

There is no shortage of reports documenting these dynamics. The rising stakes of well-structured criminal and armed groups in the organisation and protection of migrant smuggling has been noted in a variety of contexts, including the Caribbean (Kyle and Scarcelli, 2009), Libya (Stocker, 2017; Campana, 2018), and Sudan (Tubiana, Warin and Saeneen 2018), to name but a few. As this phenomenon appears correlated to the strengthening of transnational law enforcement efforts against migrant smuggling, critical observers have argued that anti-smuggling policies have counterintuitively contributed to "manufacturing smugglers" (Brachet, 2018).

These observations, however, should not lead one to overlook the important analytical distinction between smuggling and protection providers. Drawing on the ideal-types introduced by Tilly's (1985) historical sociology, smugglers refer to the actors that facilitate the cross-border clandestine shipment of people and goods to make profit. Protection providers, instead, are seldom involved in the actual delivery of smuggling services, and limit themselves to controlling the territory where migrant smuggling takes place. In exchange, they extract (or extort) a cut of the revenues from smugglers operating in 'their' territory – which may be substantial, as Sanchez (2020) suggests. The relationships between smugglers and criminal organisations engaged in the protection of criminal activities can range from cooperation to rivalry. Smugglers can benefit from the weak territorial control that criminal organisations contribute to, but they can also resent a situation of unpredictability and unwanted attention. In some cases, "organised crime groups involved in protection might recruit former smugglers to help them levy the protection tax because of their knowledge of the routes, and their ability to detect other smugglers" (Campana, 2020). In other cases, criminal protectors can coerce smugglers into partnerships through extortion, for instance, by kidnapping migrants in transit and asking a ransom to the smugglers for their liberation, as observed in Libya, Mali and Mexico (Spener, 2009; Izcara Palacios, 2014; Malakooti, 2019).

The entrance of armed criminal organisations into the migrant smuggling "business" frequently leads to an escalation of exploitation and abusive practices vis-à-vis migrants. Numerous reports by UN agencies and NGOs provide ample illustration of this (UNSMIL and OHCHR, 2016; Testa, 2019; UNHCR, 2019). The borders between migrant smuggling and trafficking are thus subject to erosion (Reitano et al. 2018). On the one hand, this further highlights the iatrogenesis of policies that are often designed, at least on paper, to serve humanitarian purposes such as "saving lives": this was, for instance, the stated priority number one of the EU Agenda on Migration issued in the aftermath of the shipwreck off the shore of the island of Lampedusa that killed more than 800 people. On the other hand, there is a surprising – and somewhat disturbing – lack of evidence that safety and risk concerns, even if backed by reliable information, significantly can influence the preferences of migrants and prospective migrants resorting to smuggling. Recent reports (Raineri and Golovko, 2019) note that migrants often leave their countries of origin in spite of being reportedly aware of the risks that await them on the road, suggesting that, with the disruption of smuggling networks and "chains of trust," accessibility, affordability and (poor) law enforcement have become the key determinants of irregular migration's routes, modalities and destinations.

Conclusion

The criminalisation of migrant smuggling may be seen as a self-fulfilling prophecy. The concept of migrant smuggling was immediately incorporated in the semantic field of organised crime when it was originally disentangled from the cognate notions of human trafficking and irregular migration. The growing availability of scholarly works and empirically-informed studies, however, has contributed to dispelling the early image of migrant smuggling as organised by tentacular crime syndicates structured vertically and stretched transnationally. A different theory

Migrant smuggling

has progressively made its way, one that investigates migrant smuggling by stressing the significance of ad-hoc partnerships over rigid affiliations, of social capital over economic capital, of agency over coercion, of social embeddedness over seclusion, of normality over exceptionality, and most importantly, of horizontal networks over top-down hierarchies.

However, the transnational diffusion of measures to combat migrant smuggling has contributed to prompting a transformation of the phenomenon. By disrupting of the "chain of trust" that typically provides the infrastructure of migrant smuggling, unscrupulous law enforcement measures have in many cases paved the way to the entrance of criminal syndicates in a sector where they used to be marginal. The iatrogenic effect of anti-smuggling policies thus turns the arrow of causality between "threat" and response on its head, making organised crime infiltration less the cause of anti-smuggling law enforcement measures, than the consequence. This should not lead one to underwrite the conflation of migrant smuggling and organised crime, that media and policy discourses tend to depict. Criminal and armed cartels are only infrequently involved in the actual organisation of migrants' cross-border journeys. More often, they prey on smugglers and migrants alike by upholding a protection racket of migrant smuggling unfolding in 'their' territories.

For all these reasons, it seems fair to conclude that – in the field of migration – the very notion of "smuggler" is problematic and calls for some degree of critical distancing. Its connotation has become too politically charged to claim a degree of neutrality suitable for scientific investigation. At the same time, its denotation runs the risk of being empirically empty. Ethnographic research has demonstrated that one can hardly encounter "smugglers" on the ground, as both migrants and the facilitators of migrant smuggling use a variety of different concepts, such as *"passeurs"* in francophone West Africa (Brachet, 2018), "connection men" in anglophone Africa (Lucht, 2012), "snakeheads" in China (Chin, 1999; Zhang, 2008), *"coyotes"* in Latin America (Spener, 2009; Stone-Cadena and Álvarez Velasco, 2018), as well as other terms depending on the context. This proliferation points to a research agenda that, aware of its own positioning in a field of struggle, avoids oversimplifying the reality with conceptual shortcuts that are potentially misleading, and engages instead in a careful, detailed, fine-grained mapping of a social phenomenon characterised by a huge degree of variation that it would be unscrupulous to gloss over.

References

Achilli, L. (2018) 'The 'Good' Smuggler: The Ethics and Morals of Human Smuggling among Syrians'. *Annals of the American Academy of Political and Social Sciences* 676(1), pp. 63–77.

Akkerman, M. (2017) 'Militarization of European Border Security' in Karampekios, N., Oikonomou, I. and Carayannis, E. (eds.) *The Emergence of EU Defense Research Policy. From Innovation to Militarization.* Berlin: Springer, pp. 337–355.

Andreas, P. (2010) 'The Politics of Measuring Illicit Flows and Policy Effectiveness' in Andreas, P. and Greenhill, K. (eds.) *Sex, Drugs, and Body Counts, The Politics of Numbers in Global Crime and Conflict.* Ithaca: Cornell University Press, pp. 23–45.

Andreas, P. and Price, R. (2001) 'From War Fighting to Crime Fighting: Transforming the American National Security State'. *International Studies Review* 3(3), pp. 31–52.

Aronowitz, A. (2001) 'Smuggling and Trafficking in Human Beings: The Phenomenon, the Markets That Drive It and the Organizations That Promote It'. *European Journal on Criminal Policy and Research* 9(2), pp. 163–195.

Ayalew Mengiste, T. (2018) 'Refugee Protections from Below: Smuggling in the Eritrea-Ethiopia Context'. *Annals of the American Academy of Political and Social Sciences* 676(1), pp. 57–76.

Baird, T. and Van Liempt, I. (2016) 'Scrutinising the Double Disadvantage: Knowledge Production in the Messy Field of Migrant Smuggling'. *Journal of Ethnic and Migration Studies* 42(3), pp. 400–417.

Benattia, T., Armitano, F. and Robinson, H. (2015) *Irregular Migration between West Africa, North Africa and the Mediterranean*. Abuja-Paris: Altai Consulting.

Bilger, V., Hofmann, M. and Jandl, M. (2006) 'Human Smuggling as a Transnational Service Industry: Evidence From Austria. *International Migration* 44(4), pp. 59–92.

Brachet, J. (2018) 'Manufacturing Smugglers: From Irregular to Clandestine Mobility in Sahara'. *Annals of the American Academy of Political and Social Science* 676(1), pp. 16–35.

Buzan, B. (1991) *People, States and Fear. An Agenda for International Security Studies in the Post-Cold War Era.* London: Rowman and Littlefield.

Campana, P. (2018) 'Out of Africa: The Organisation of Migrant Smuggling across the Mediterranean'. *European Journal of Criminology* 15(4), pp. 481–502.

Campana, P. (2020) 'Human Smuggling: Structure and Mechanisms'. *Crime and Justice* 49(1), DOI: 10.1086/708663

Chin, K. (1999) *Smuggled Chinese: Clandestine Immigration to the United States*. Philadelphia: Temple University Press.

Cohen, S. (1988) 'Western Crime Models in the Third World: Benign or Malignant' in Cohen, S. (ed.) *Against Criminology*. New Brunswick: Transaction Publisher, pp. 172–202.

Demir, O., Sever, M. and Kahya, Y. (2017) 'The Social Organisation of Migrant Smugglers in Turkey: Roles and Functions'. *European Journal of Criminal Policy Research* 23(3), pp. 371–391.

EUROPOL (2016) *Migrant Smuggling in the EU*. The Hague: EUROPOL.

Galemba, R. (2018) "He Used to be a Pollero' The Securitisation of Migration and the Smuggler/migrant Nexus at the Mexico-Guatemala Border'. *Journal of Ethnic and Migration Studies* 44(5), pp. 870–886.

Golovko, E. (2018) *Players of Many Parts: The Evolving Role of Smugglers in West Africa's Migration Economy*. Geneva: Mixed Migration Centre. Available at: https://mixedmigration.org/resource/players-of-many-parts/

Horwood, C. (2019) *The New 'Public Enemy Number One'. Comparing and Contrasting the War on Drugs and the Emerging War on Migrant Smugglers*. Geneva: Mixed Migration Centre. Available at: https://mixedmigration.org/wp-content/uploads/2019/03/060_new-public-enemy-number-1_full-report.pdf

Hudson, R. (2014) 'Thinking through the Relationships between Legal and Illegal Activities and Economies: Spaces, Flows and Pathways'. *Journal of Economic Geography* 14(4), pp. 775–795.

İçduygu, A. (2018) 'Middle East' in Triandafyllidou, A. and McAuliffe, M. (eds.) *Migrant Smuggling Data and Research: A Global Review of the Emerging Evidence Base*. Geneva: IOM, pp. 19–44.

İçduygu, A. and Toktas, S. (2002) 'How Do Smuggling and Trafficking Operate via Irregular Border Crossings in the Middle East? Evidence from Fieldwork in Turkey'. *International Migration* 40(6), pp. 25–54.

ILO (1975) *Migrant Workers (Supplementary Provisions) Convention (No. 143)*. Geneva: ILO.

IOM (1994) 'Trafficking in Migrants: Characteristics and Trends in Different Regions of the World'. *Discussion Paper* No. 1/11th IOM Seminar on Migration. Geneva: IOM.

Izcara Palacios, S. (2014) 'Coyotaje and Drugs: Two Different Businesses'. *Bulletin of Latin American Research* 34(3), pp. 324–339.

Kaizen, J. and Nonneman, W. (2007) 'Irregular Migration in Belgium and Organized Crime: An Overview'. *International Migration* 45(2), pp. 121–146.

Kleemans, E. (2007) 'Organized Crime, Transit Crime, and Racketeering'. *Crime and Justice* 35(1), pp. 163–215.

Kleemans, E. (2014) 'Theoretical Perspectives on Organized Crime' in Paoli, L. (ed.) *Oxford Handbook of Organised Crime*. Oxford: Oxford University Press, DOI: 10.1093/oxfordhb/9780199730445.013.005

Kleemans, E. and Van de Bunt, H. (1999) 'The Social Embeddedness of Organized Crime'. *Transnational Organized Crime* 5(2), pp. 19–36.

Koser, K. (2009) 'Dimensions and Dynamics of Irregular Migration'. *Population, Space and Place* 16(3), pp. 181–193.

Kyle, D. and Koslowski, R. (eds.) (2001) *Global Human Smuggling. Comparative Perspectives*. Baltimore: Johns Hopkins University Press.

Kyle, D. and Scarcelli, M. (2009) 'Migrant Smuggling and the Violence Question: Evolving Illicit Migration Markets for Cuban and Haitian Refugees'. *Crime Law and Social Change* 52(3), pp. 297–311.

Leman, J. and Janssens, S. (2011) 'Albanian Entrepreneurial Practices in Human Smuggling and Trafficking: On the Road to the United Kingdom via Brussels, 1995–2005'. *International Migration* 50(6), pp. 166–179.

Migrant smuggling

Lucht, H. (2012) *Darkness before Daybreak. African Migrants Living on the Margins in Southern Italy Today.* Berkeley: University of California Press.

Lutterbeck, D. (2006) 'Policing Migration in the Mediterranean'. *Mediterranean Politics* 11(1), pp. 59–82.

Majidi, N. (2018) 'Community Dimensions of Smuggling: The Case of Afghanistan and Somalia'. *Annals of the American Academy of Political and Social Sciences* 676(1), pp. 97–113.

Malakooti, A. (2016) 'North Africa' in McAuliffe, M. and Laczko, F. (eds.) *Migrant Smuggling Data and Research: A Global Review of the Emerging Evidence Base.* Geneva: IOM, pp. 85–104.

Malakooti, A. (2019) *The Political Economy of Migrant Detention in Libya: Understanding the Players and the Business Models.* Geneva: Global Initiative Against Transnational Organized Crime. Available at: https://globalinitiative.net/analysis/migrant-detention-libya/

Mannocchi, F. (2019) *Io, Khaled, vendo uomini e sono innocente.* Torino: Einaudi.

McAuliffe, M. and Laczko, F. (eds.) (2016) *Migrant Smuggling Data and Research: A Global Review of the Emerging Evidence Base.* Geneva: IOM.

Morselli, C. (2009) *Inside Criminal Networks.* New York: Springer.

Naim, M. (2012) 'Mafia States, Organized Crime Takes Office'. *Foreign Affairs* 91(3), pp. 100–111.

Neske, M. (2006) 'Human Smuggling to and through Germany'. *International Migration* 44(4), pp. 121–163.

Nordstrom, C. (2007) *Global Outlaws: Crime, Money and Power in the Contemporary World.* Berkeley: University of California Press.

Nuñez-Neto, B., Siskin, A. and Viña, S. (2005) *Border Security: Apprehensions of 'Other than Mexican' aliens.* Washington, DC: Congressional Research Service Report for Congress. Available at: https://trac.syr.edu/immigration/library/P1.pdf

Okolski, M. (2000) 'Illegality of International Population Movements in Poland', *International Migration* 38(3), pp. 57–89.

Paoli, L. (2003) *Mafia Brotherhoods: Organized Crime, Italian Style.* Oxford: Oxford University Press.

Pastore, F., Monzini, P. and Sciortino, G. (2006) 'Schengen's Soft Underbelly? Irregular Migration and Human Smuggling Across Land and Sea Borders to Italy'. *International Migration* 44(4), pp. 95–119.

Raineri, L (2018) 'Human Smuggling across Niger: State-sponsored Protection Rackets and Contradictory Security Imperatives', *Journal of Modern African Studies* 56(1), pp. 63–86.

Raineri, L. and Golovko, E. (2019) *Navigating Borderlands in the Sahel. Border Security Governance and Mixed Migration in Liptako-Gourma.* Geneva: Mixed Migration Centre. Available at: https://mixedmigration.org/resource/navigating-borderlands-in-the-sahel/

Raineri, L., and Strazzari, F., 2021. Dissecting the EU Response to the 'Migration Crisis', in MacGinty, R. (ed.) *Title TBC.* Manchester: Manchester University Press.

Reitano, T. and Tinti, P. (2015) 'Survive and Advance. The Economics of Smuggling Refugees and Migrants into Europe', *ISS Paper* 289. Dakar: Institute for Security Studies. Available at: https://issafrica.org/research/papers/survive-and-advance-the-economics-of-smuggling-refugees-and-migrants-into-europe

Reitano, T., McCormack, S., Micallef, M. and Shaw, M. (2018) *Responding to the Human Trafficking–migrant Smuggling Nexus.* Geneva: The Global Initiative Against Transnational Organized Crime. Available at: https://globalinitiative.net/wp-content/uploads/2018/07/Reitano-McCormack-Trafficking-Smuggling-Nexus-in-Libya-July-2018.pdf

Robertson, F. (1977) *Triangle of Death: The Inside Story of the Triads, the Chinese Mafia.* London: Routledge.

Sahan/IGAD (2016) *Human Trafficking and Smuggling on the Horn of Africa-Central Mediterranean Route.* Nairobi: IGAD. Available at: https://igad.int/attachments/1284_ISSP%20Sahan%20HST%20Report%20%2018ii2016%20FINAL%20FINAL.pdf

Salt, J. (2000) 'Trafficking and Human Smuggling: A European Perspective'. *International Migration* 38(3), pp. 31–56.

Salt, J. and Stein, J. (1997) 'Migration as a Business: The Case of Trafficking'. *International Migration* 35(4), pp. 467–494.

Sanchez, G. (2015) *Human Smuggling and Border Crossing.* Abingdon: Routledge

Sanchez, G. (2017) 'Critical Perspectives on Clandestine Migration Facilitation: An Overview of Migrant Smuggling Research'. *Journal on Migration and Human Security* 5(1), pp. 9–27.

Sanchez, G. (2018) 'Mexico' in Triandafyllidou, A. and McAuliffe, M. (eds.) *Migrant Smuggling Data and Research: A Global Review of the Emerging Evidence Base, vol. 2.* Geneva: IOM, pp. 143–166.

Sanchez, G. (2020) 'Beyond Militias and Tribes: The Facilitation of Migration in Libya', *EUI Working Paper RSCAS* 2020/09. Available at: https://cadmus.eui.eu/bitstream/handle/1814/66186/RSCAS_2020_09.pdf?sequence=1&isAllowed=y

Schloenhardt, A. (2002) *Organised Crime and Migrant Smuggling: Australia and the Asia-Pacific*, Research and Public Policy Series No. 44. Canberra: Australian Institute of Criminology. Available at: https://www.aic.gov.au/publications/rpp/rpp44

Schloenhardt, A. (2003) *Migrant Smuggling: Illegal Migration and Organised Crime in Australia and the Asia Pacific Region*. Leiden: Brill.

Soudijn, M. (2006) *Chinese Human Smuggling in Transit*. Leiden: Netherlands Institute for the Study of Crime and Law Enforcement.

Soudijn, M. and Kleemans, E. (2009) 'Chinese Organized Crime and Situational Context: Comparing Human Smuggling and Synthetic Drugs Trafficking'. *Crime, Law and Social Change* 52(5), pp. 457–474.

Spener, D. (2009) *Clandestine Crossings: Migrants and Coyotes on the Texas-Mexico Border*. New York: Cornell University Press.

Stambol, E.M. (2019) 'The Rise of Crimefare Europe: Fighting Migrant Smuggling in West Africa'. *European Foreign Affairs Review* 24(3), pp. 287–308.

Staring, R. (2004) 'Facilitating the Arrival of Illegal Immigrants in the Netherlands: Irregular Chain Migration Versus Smuggling Chains'. *Journal of International Migration and Integration* 5(3), pp. 273–294.

Stocker, V. (2017) *Leaving Libya. Rapid Assessment of Municipalities of Departures of Migrants in Libya*. Tunis: Altai Consulting. Available at: http://www.altaiconsulting.com/wp-content/uploads/2017/08/2017_Altai-Consulting_Leaving-Libya-Rapid-Assessment-of-Municipalities-of-Departure-of-Migrants-in-Libya.pdf

Stone-Cadena, V. and Álvarez Velasco, S. (2018) 'Historicizing mobility: coyoterismo in the indigenous Ecuadorian migration industry'. *Annals of the American Academy of Political and Social Sciences* 676(1), pp. 194–211.

Tailby, R. (2001) 'Organised Crime and People Smuggling: Trafficking to Australia'. *Trends and Issues in Crime and Criminal Justice* 208. Available at: https://www.aic.gov.au/publications/tandi/tandi208

Testa, G. (2019) *Waning Welcome: The Growing Challenges Facing Mixed Migration Flows from Venezuela*. Geneva: Mixed Migration Centre. Available at: https://mixedmigration.org/resource/waning-welcome-the-growing-challenges-facing-mixed-migration-flows-from-venezuela/

Tilly, C. (1985) 'War Making and State Making as Organized Crime' in Evans, P., Rueschemeyer, D. and Skocpol, T. (eds.) *Bringing the State Back In*. Cambridge: Cambridge University Press, pp. 169–191.

Tinti, P. and Reitano, T. (2016) *Migrant, Refugee, Smuggler, Saviour*. New York: Hurst Publisher.

Tubiana, J., Warin, C. and Saeneen, G. (2018) *Multilateral Damage. The Impact of EU Migration Policies on Central Saharan Routes*. The Hague: Clingendael CRU Report. Available at: https://www.clingendael.org/pub/2018/multilateral-damage/

UNHCR (2019) *From Hand to Hand: The Migratory Experience of Refugees and Migrants from East Africa across Libya*. Geneva: UNHCR.

UNODC (2011a) *Smuggling of Migrants: A Global Review and Annotated Bibliography of Recent Publications*. Vienna: UNODC.

UNODC (2011b) *The Role of Organized Crime in the Smuggling of Migrants from West Africa to the European Union*. Vienna: UNODC.

UNODC (2018) *Global Study on Smuggling of Migrants*. Vienna: UNODC.

UNSMIL and OHCHR (2016) *Detained and Dehumanized. Report on Human Rights Abuses against Migrants in Libya*. Geneva: OHCHR.

Van Liempt, I. (2007) *Navigating Borders: Inside Perspectives on the Process of Human Smuggling into the Netherlands*. Amsterdam: Amsterdam University Press.

Van Liempt, I. and Doomernik, J. (2006) 'Migrant's Agency in the Smuggling Process: The Perspectives of Smuggled Migrants in the Netherlands'. *International Migration* 44(4), pp. 165–190.

Van Liempt, I. and Sersli, S. (2012) State Responses and Migrant Experiences with Human Smuggling: A Reality Check. *Antipode* 45(4), pp. 1029–1046.

Webb, S. and Burrows, J. (2009) 'Organised Immigration Crime: A Post-conviction Study', *Research Report* 15. London: Home Office. Available at: https://assets.publishing.service.gov.uk/government/uploads/system/uploads/attachment_data/file/116629/horr15-report.pdf

Weber, L. and Grewcock, M. (2011) 'Criminalizing People Smuggling: Preventing Or Globalizing Harm?' in Allum, F. and Gilmour, S. (eds.) *The Routledge Handbook of Transnational Organized Crime*. London: Routledge, pp. 379–390.

Migrant smuggling

Wokeck, M. (1999) *Trade in Strangers: The Beginnings of Mass Migration to North America.* University Park: Pennsylvania State University Press.

Zhang, S. (2008) *Chinese Human Smuggling Organizations: Families, Social Networks, and Cultural Imperatives.* Stanford: Stanford University Press.

Zhang, S. and Chin, K. (2002) 'Enter the Dragon: Inside Chinese Human Smuggling Organizations'. *Criminology* 40(4), pp. 737–767.

Zhang, S. and Chin, K. (2003) 'The Declining Significance of Triad Societies in Transnational Illegal Activities: A Structural Deficiency Perspective'. *British Journal of Criminology* 43(3), pp. 469–488.

24
HUMAN SMUGGLING, GENDER AND LABOUR CIRCULATION IN THE GLOBAL SOUTH

Priya Deshingkar

Introduction

Irregular[1] migration[2] facilitation, or human smuggling, has been made hyper-visible in the context of tightening border controls in Europe, North America and other prosperous parts of the world. The focus of this discourse is predominantly on South-North clandestine journeys, especially from Africa in the case of Europe (ENACT 2020), based on data on interceptions in the Mediterranean. This narrative has eclipsed South-South human smuggling, which is equally if not more significant in terms of the numbers it involves; however, research on it remains thin (see for example Ayalew et al. (2018), Lindquist (2012), Lindquist et al. (2012) and Afsar (2009)). South-South smuggling may involve being smuggled across a border between two neighbouring countries or to a distant country. Every day, millions of irregular border crossings take place between countries in the Global South that share borders, such as Myanmar and Thailand or Bangladesh and India.

There are also clear "corridors" of smuggling among non-contiguous countries, some separated by considerable distances and on separate continents, such as Bangladesh and South Africa (Momen unpublished), Myanmar and Malaysia (Deshingkar et al., 2019), and Ethiopia and Saudi Arabia (Adugna et al., 2021). These corridors have evolved with the emergence of relatively lucrative work options in manufacturing and processing, care work and a variety of jobs in cities. Corridors are strengthened as transnational networks of migration are established, leading to further migration to particular destinations where migrants can draw on the support of their networks in integrating and making a life for themselves.

Irregularity in migration encompasses a range of scenarios – overstaying visas (Momen and Deshingkar et al., 2019), delinking from tied work permits (Deshingkar et al., 2019; Jureidini, 2017), irregular border crossings (Ayalew et al., 2018; Triandafyllidou 2020; Triandafyllidou and Bartolini, 2020), rejected asylum seekers and the children of undocumented parents (Triandafyllidou and Bartolini, 2020). Here we are concerned mainly with the actors and processes involved in irregular border crossings which involve entering a country without complying with the necessary requirements for legal entry, such as possessing a valid visa, work permit or health certificate, or entering at points not designated as ports of entry.

Smuggling processes in West Africa are deeply connected to the geopolitics of migration management, as many of the policies that shape it are driven by interests in the North. In South

326

DOI: 10.4324/9781003043645-24

and South East Asia, they are shaped by the immigration regimes and labour circulation policies in receiving countries, but in different ways, as discussed in the following pages.

In order to provide a thick account of smuggling operations on the ground, only three contrasting countries are discussed in detail below, namely Ghana, Bangladesh and Myanmar.[3] They share similarities – all have more than 70% of the population depending on agriculture and between 68% and 77% living in rural areas.[4] They also have key differences which provide fertile opportunities for exploring how the intersection between culture, the geopolitics of migration control, globalised patterns of labour circulation, and the state, shape human smuggling patterns.

In the three countries under consideration, migration for low-paid and informal work is most common and as such, the focus of this chapter is on smuggling as it relates to the broad category of labour migration. While labour circulation from poor countries towards rich countries has now become an established part of key sectors including care work and construction work, restrictions on mobility are also mounting at the same time. For many, being smuggled across borders is often the only realistic option to access remunerative work opportunities. Even this, though, has become difficult and expensive since the act of human smuggling itself was criminalised with the launch of the UN Convention against Transnational Organized Crime in 2000 and its Protocol against the Smuggling of Migrants by Land, Sea and Air, which came into force in 2004. Its sister Protocol to Prevent, Suppress and Punish Trafficking in Persons Especially Women and Children was introduced at the same time. Smuggling always involves crossing a border and may be voluntary, whereas trafficking can occur in the same country and always involves the exploitation of a person for profit.[5]

Southern countries in irregular migration "hot spots" have taken a range of steps to implement the Protocol and limit human smuggling, often with the aid of rich countries in the North that seek to contain migrants before they reach their shores. These measures include imprisoning and fining smugglers, awareness creation campaigns about the costs and risks of irregular migration and smuggling, and physical policing along known routes (Ayalew Mengiste, 2018; Ayalew et al., 2018; Carling, 2016; Sanchez, 2017). The justification for the increased policing of smuggling activities is to protect migrants, who are characterised as gullible and vulnerable, against smugglers, who are constructed as unscrupulous criminals and traders in human beings (Adugna et al., 2019; Sanchez, 2018). The process of smuggling is constructed in this imagination as beginning with an unsuspecting migrant entering the process voluntarily, only to be subjected to physical torture, execution and extortion further along the journey (Aronowitz, 2001). These messages are repeatedly reinforced through international media agencies such as AFP and Reuters (Adugna et al., 2021). While such outcomes are seen in a few cases, growing empirical evidence shows they are not representative of the experience of all migrants who use the services of smugglers.

Smuggling and gendered circuits of labour circulation

The extant literature indicates that there are often diverse infrastructures of human smuggling in the same geographical location for different kinds of destinations, occupations, and often quite separate infrastructures for men and women. For example, there are separate smuggling networks for feminised occupations and for those that are typically the reserve of men: in Ghana (Awumbila et al., 2019b, 2019a); Bangladesh (Abrar et al., 2017; Afsar, 2009; Rahman, 2020); Indonesia (Lindquist, 2012); and Myanmar (Franck et al., 2018).

Gender plays out in other ways in landscapes of smuggling. Women in patriarchal societies are subjected to additional barriers to mobility as they are seen as the weaker sex in need of protection, especially if they choose to migrate with the help of a smuggler. Here the UN Protocol on Human Trafficking with its explicit emphasis on 'women and children' is often invoked, ostensibly to protect women who are regarded as more vulnerable to abuse. Developing country governments are under intense pressure to comply with this international agenda through the influential US government's Trafficking in Persons (TIP) report (Palmary and de Gruchy, 2016).

There are also moral anxieties in many cultures about the sexual encounters that female migrants may have which pose a threat to their purity and the honour of the family. Traditional notions of masculinity in many societies construct the risks and dangers of migration experienced by men as strengthening of their character and making them into brave adult men. The opposite is true in these discourses on female migration, as women are seen as inherently more vulnerable and in need of constant surveillance, accompaniment and protection by men or the state (Deshingkar, 2021; Huijsmans, 2014; Platt et al., 2018) Consequently, female migrants have been subjected to migration bans in several countries – Ethiopia, Ghana, Nigeria, Myanmar, Bangladesh and Indonesia. This includes bans on certain kinds of feminised migration and low-paid work or bans on migration to certain destinations or both, some of which are discussed under the case studies below.

A deeper look at the intersections between human smuggling, global restrictions on mobility, immigration regimes and particular gendered occupations, yields important insights into how the state, smuggling networks, and employers in destination countries relate to each other. The analysis in the remainder of the chapter unpicks the dynamics of smuggling related to construction work and domestic work that are two of the most accessible occupations for migrants all over the world. Both are highly gendered occupations due to cultural notions and gendered stereotypes in both sending and receiving countries about the inherent capabilities of men and women and the work that is appropriate for them (Deshingkar and Zeitlyn, 2015; Zeitlyn et al., 2014). Domestic work is feminised and employs mainly women along certain migration corridors such as Ethiopia to Saudi Arabia and Sri Lanka to the Middle East (Fernandez, 2019; Gamburd, 2000). Additionally, domestic work is also racialised, wherein women from certain nationalities and ethnic groups are constructed as suited to servitude in the home based on their appearance and skin colour (Anderson and Anderson, 2000). Domestic and care work is important for female migrants with few formal qualifications. ILO estimates suggest that there are roughly 67 million domestic workers over the age of 15 worldwide, 80% of whom are women. Migrants are heavily represented in "global care chains," of domestic and care work with workers drawn mainly from poorer countries in the Global South (Parreñas, 2015; Yeates, 2012), into rich countries where more women are entering the workforce and the social reproduction of the family is passed on to domestic workers (Fong et al., 2020). Construction work is an accessible source of employment for male migrants (BWI, 2006), employing nearly 110 million people worldwide (ILO, 2001). Globally, the construction sector is heavily dependent on migrant labour (Buckley et al., 2016) and it is also a sector where irregular migrants are concentrated.

While the demand for migrant construction and domestic workers has grown, immigration regimes in receiving countries have become more exclusionary with complicated bureaucratic processes that are difficult for those who are located in remote locations away from government offices and the numerous agencies that provide health certificates and identity documents. Smugglers have become more important in migration for both occupations, for example, for the migration of domestic workers from Ethiopia to the Middle East (Fernandez, 2013) which is an important destination for migrants smuggled in for domestic work (Mahdavi, 2013). Similarly, Large numbers of Rohingya and other impoverished or persecuted people are

Human smuggling in the Global South

smuggled into Malaysia for work in a range of informal labouring jobs, including construction (Wahab, 2018).

There are important differences in the way that smuggling for construction work and domestic work are organised; this depends on the policy context in both sending and receiving countries, the economic circumstances of the family, gendered policies, and norms within the family and wider society. Entangled with these structural factors are processes related to the financing of smuggling and the materialities of travel such as documents and transport vehicles.

Not just at the border

A key observation of this chapter is that human smuggling cannot be seen as a process that happens only at the border. Rather, it is shaped by a variety of spatially dispersed actors who fulfil different but complementary functions. This is especially characteristic of brokerage and smuggling, which are linked to placement at destination. In such instances, there is usually a continuum from the first point of contact between a migrant and a local broker to the end destination which is facilitated by interconnected intermediaries, including the actual border smugglers (Awumbila et al., 2019b; Deshingkar et al., 2019). Village level brokers in the migrant's own community may have established relations with recruitment agents in towns and cities who in turn are linked to travel operators, passport authorities, passport photo units, health testing centres, immigration officials and border police, and smugglers at the border, then finally placement agencies in the destination country. However, this is not the case for all forms of human smuggling and in some corridors where policing is intense, there is no discernible chain or network. Here smugglers and other intermediaries may come together more opportunistically as they have to navigate new controls and chart different pathways to overcome those. An example of this is human smuggling through Niger, where new and different smuggling routes around Agadez, an important hub for irregular migration in West Africa (Molenaar, 2017), are in a constant state of flux (Bredeloup and Pliez, 2011). A similar situation is seen in clandestine journeys between Ethiopia and Saudi Arabia, where smugglers are exploring new routes and linking up with new intermediaries all the time (Adugna et al., 2021).

In both kinds of scenarios, the village-level broker is often a key figure in remote and poorly connected societies, as they are critical for brokering contacts with the outside world and providing up-to-date intelligence on the best destination, modes of transport, official procedures and the required documentation. Brokers are either ex-migrants belonging to the same community or people with connections, knowledge of the outside world and the ability to communicate across different worlds and social rules (Abrar et al., 2017; Lindquist, 2012). Such is the cultural and linguistic divide between migrants and city-based officials and bureaucrats, that a broker is needed to interpret and communicate between the two parties. Brokers are also well connected beyond the villages that they operate in and are able to access key personnel and negotiate on behalf of the migrant to obtain documents and permissions.

Therefore, in order to understand the workings of human smuggling and the ways in which it shapes migration and labour markets, it is important to consider it in its entirety, and not just at the border. Smugglers can be conceptualised as one part of the broader infrastructure that facilitates irregular migration. Xiang and Lindquist's (2012) concept of the "infrastructures of migration" that emerged from their research on low-skilled migration from China and Indonesia examines the interconnected actors, technologies and institutions that together facilitate mobility, offers a useful framework of analysis. They argue that all of these components must be considered together with intersectionality as an operational logic to understand how they work together to make migration happen. The concept of migration infrastructures lends itself well to analysing human smuggling and irregular migration for low-paid occupations as it dwells on both the social aspects of human smuggling as well as is materialities, including documents, physical barriers at border crossings, makeshift accommodation structures, boats, desert vehicles and mobile phones. It provides the tools to interrogate how gender, immigration regimes, transport networks and the structure of employment intersect in different ways. I use it below to reveal the everyday manifestations of globalised labour circulation that depend on cheap foreign labour and the range of actors, and institutions that mediate it.

A socially embedded process

While considering the breadth of different actors and institutions involved in smuggling, it is also important to note that smuggling processes are deeply rooted within communities at points of origin and transit. These communities are comprised of actors with diverse interests whose search for work and business and social relations with migrants and smugglers continuously shapes and constitutes the spaces of brokerage and smuggling (Adugna et al., 2019; Bredeloup and Pliez, 2011; Deshingkar, 2021; Huijsmans, 2014). In poor communities with few sources of paid work, smuggling offers a critical source of income, albeit a modest one. These kickbacks from smuggling and the visible improvement in the standard of living of migrants' families has earned smugglers a reputation akin to that of heroes (Adugna et al., 2019). In fact, smugglers are able to operate precisely because local communities endorse their operations and perceive them as bringing benefits to everyone and not just the migrants and their families. In southern Ethiopia, where irregular migration to South Africa is widespread, those who facilitate it are called *Berri Kefach* or door openers (Adugna et al., 2019). These findings are corroborated in the wider literature; extended immersive research by Osella (Osella, 2014) among migrant communities in Kerala travelling to the Gulf, as well as research by Akesson and Alpes in Cape Verde and Cameroon (Åkesson and Alpes, 2019; Alpes, 2017) juxtapose the perceptions of local communities of brokers as critical to realising their migration project, notwithstanding their criminalisation by the state. Such narratives of smugglers being benefactors should not detract from the extremely high risk faced by migrants embarking on long and dangerous clandestine journeys, such as over-land crossings through the Sahara. The likelihood of coming to serious harm is very real; whether and to what extent they are able to escape and overcome adverse experiences to achieve their ultimate goal depends on a host of factors that are unpicked through empirical evidence of smuggling in the three countries under consideration.

Against this backdrop, the chapter draws attention to two implications of human smuggling. First, it shows how human smuggling and irregular migrants are critical to sustaining circuits of labour circulation of cheap and disposable workers. Heavily restricted immigration regimes such as the *Kafala* system in the Middle East[6] create ideal conditions for human smuggling and irregularity. In turn, the irregular status of migrants allows employers and placement agencies to exploit them, with fewer obligations to protect their rights. Migrant construction workers and domestic workers are thus placed in a hyperprecarious situation (Lewis et al., 2015) that governments in receiving countries are complicit in producing. Second, the examples discussed below illustrate that human smuggling can open up opportunities for people from poor and marginalised backgrounds by enabling them to access work that holds the potential for making life-changing investments back home. The objective of the chapter is to draw attention to the complexity of the phenomenon and provide a nuanced understanding of South-South human smuggling. The three country cases are presented next to highlight these differences.

Human smuggling in the Global South

Ghana

Ghana has a long history of migration within the country and internationally (Akyeampong, 2000) and is now an important source country for irregular migrants in the Libyan construction industry (Kandilige and Hamidou, 2011). Migration to Libya began in the 1990s when Gaddafi actively wooed sub-Saharan migrants (Bredeloup and Pliez, 2011). In recent years the country has been less welcoming to migrants both because of growing anti-migration sentiment in the context of a deteriorating economy and also introduction of the EU-Libya Migration treaty which sought to limit migration into Europe and targeted West African migrants in particular (Tonah and Codjoe, 2020).

Libya is the chosen destination here, not because migrants are unable to travel to Europe but because the Libyan labour market offers relatively high earning opportunities, albeit full of risk and uncertainty. In the current geopolitical context of ever-increasing controls on mobility and shrinking opportunities for legal migration, being smuggled across several countries northwards towards Libya has become the norm (Awumbila et al., 2019b; Kandilige and Hamidou, 2019). Nkoranza in the Brong Ahafo region and the border towns of Bawku and Tamale in Northern Ghana and are key points of origin and crossing the border out of Ghana. Policy barriers to movement within West Africa combined with differences in currency and language among the countries make the assistance of smugglers critical, especially for organising long and treacherous journeys through the Sahara Desert, traversing several international borders.

This kind of high risk and dangerous migration is male dominated due to cultural norms and the place of migration in men's strategies to achieve wealth and prove their manhood. Male migration in Ghanaian society is embedded in traditional notions of masculinity; among young men it is inextricably linked to establishing themselves as 'independent, respectable and marriageable adults' (Kleist, 2017), while older men migrate to provide for their families and invest in land, housing and business (Awumbila et al., 2019b). International migrants or "Borgas" as they are known locally, are admired for their material wealth, lifestyle, and ability to support their family members (Kleist, 2017). Women's migration from this area for low-paid work to Libya is rare, as there are fewer manual jobs for women there, so it is assumed that any woman who migrates, for sex work; this stigmatisation impacts on her marriage chances back home (Darkwah et al., 2019). However, migration for domestic work to the Gulf states is on the rise from the capital city and its adjacent areas, as discussed below.

Nkoranza in Brong Ahafo is well known for its "connection men" who facilitate journeys to Libya as well as European destinations. They have connections in the transit towns of Bawku, Niamey, and Agadez whom they can recommend to the migrant or communicate with themselves if they deem it necessary. Connection men are preferred over legal channels because they are more accessible, deals with them can be struck up immediately without paperwork, and they offer the promise of delivering the migrant to Libya, as they have successfully organised numerous irregular crossings before. They offer a package at one service point: organising the trip through the desert; and obtaining passports and other documents without the need for official documents (Awumbila et al., 2019b; Lucht, 2013).

Returned and deported migrants recount harrowing details of journeys by road in a variety of overcrowded trucks, buses and pick up vans through Togo, Benin and Niger all the way up to Libya with the constant threat of being robbed, beaten and imprisoned or deported (Awumbila et al., 2019b).

A majority of male migrants who have been smuggled into Libya are employed in construction as well as other artisanal jobs, such as electricians and tailors (Tonah and Codjoe, 2020). Irregular migrants are preferred by small construction companies as they are cheaper to employ and more exploitable. Propelling this stream of irregular migration from rural Ghana was the desire to earn better among those who wanted more than agriculture could offer. The average cost of being smuggled into Libya in 2017 was around $6000, and only those who could sell assets or borrow to finance the journey were able to migrate (Awumbila and Torvikeh, 2018; Teye et al., 2015). The high cost did not guarantee a smooth journey and most migrants recounted horrific accounts being robbed at gunpoint, seeing other migrants die on the way, and being beaten. The suffering did not end after entering Libya either; migrants recalled being randomly robbed by militias, and being kept in overcrowded illegal detention without clean drinking water or washing facilities until they were bailed out by a relative. Deportations were common where migrants lost everything, including their money and their reputation as successful men back home.

Libya, nonetheless, continued to be seen as a place where money could be made, and lives could be transformed. Returned migrants mentioned that if they managed to stay in Libya without being deported for two years, the earnings from construction work there would be more than they would earn back home in a decade and this allowed them to buy land, pay off debts and invest in small businesses. This was one reason for deported and returned migrants planning to remigrate to Libya once again. Another reason for men's remigration was to rescue their masculine identity of being family providers (Kleist, 2017).

For women, the routes to international migration and finding work in achieving such transformations are more complex. Ghana passed the 2005 Human Trafficking Act, amended in 2009, which criminalized sex and labour trafficking. Well-known brokers, trusted by communities, were arrested and imprisoned, leaving smuggling to less accountable fly by night operators (Deshingkar, 2018). Women aspiring to leave the country for low paid work in the Gulf must negotiate social structures at home to depart culturally ascribed life trajectories and structural factors at destination. These propel them towards certain feminised niches in the job market. Domestic work is an important avenue of employment for women and girls from poor backgrounds within Ghana; some may attempt international migration after gaining experience and saving enough to pay brokers.

Ghana is a relatively new entrant to the globalised circuits of labour that supply domestic and care workers to the Gulf countries. Ghanaians are now found in significant numbers in the UAE, Kuwait and Saudi Arabia together with workers from Ethiopia, Eritrea, Uganda, Kenya and Nigeria (Bisong, 2021). The number of Ghanaians seems to be on the rise and Saudi Arabia is the most popular destination (GAATW, undated) despite a ban on migration to the Gulf countries for domestic work in 2017. The ban was introduced to safeguard women against abuse after there were reports of abuse at the hands of brokers and employers (GAATW, undated).

While the ban halted the operations of licensed recruitment agencies, informal brokers and smugglers continued to operate and facilitated the migration of Ghanaians to the Gulf States through neighbouring countries (Deshingkar, 2018). The Accra-Tema area has become a hub for the recruitment and irregular migration of women to the Gulf and is known for connection men who have "successfully" sent women abroad. Prior to the ban the Ghanaian Labour Department arranged exit permits, pre-departure preparation and monitoring of workers after they had reached their destination. During the ban, none of these processes was followed, as most of the migration for domestic work to the Gulf was irregular (GAATW, undated).

Awumbila's (Awumbila et al., 2019b) study was able to reach a very small number of female returnees from the Gulf who had all come back before expected, as they found the work too demanding and the behaviour of the employers unacceptable. Both in this study and the research reported in the GAATW report, it was mainly women who were not married or

Human smuggling in the Global South

supported by a husband who decided to migrate. It is not clear how many of the women who migrate from Ghana are remaining in the Gulf for extended periods of time as research is scarce, but the numbers quoted by GAATW suggest that more and more women are deciding to migrate there: smugglers are key to enabling them to fulfil their aspirations.

Myanmar

Myanmar is now the largest exporter of low-skilled labour in Southeast Asia (Testaverde et al., 2017). Decades of chronic underdevelopment and conflict, as well as the long border with Thailand, have created opportunities for human smuggling and irregular migration. There are an estimated five million Myanmar migrants in Thailand, with many entering through migrant smugglers (Carden, 2014). In fact, irregular migrants are a critical component of the profit model of Thai firms that is based on cheap and exploitable labour (Pearson and Kusakabe, 2012).

A significant proportion of this cheap labour is from the bordering states of Mon and Kayin (Deshingkar et al., 2019). For young men and women, migration to Thailand has become an important way of repaying family debts and supporting younger siblings.

Notwithstanding the proximity of Mon and Kayin to Thailand, the journey is nearly always undertaken with the help of transport providers known as "Carry" who smuggle them across the border. There are several reasons for this, includinghigh costs and complicated and time-consuming migrant registration processes in Thailand (Buckley et al., 2016). In addition, migrants prefer to remain irregular, as this gives them more options for staying in the country longer and switching employers (Deshingkar et al., 2019). Another reason is that migrants say they feel better protected by a smuggler, who handles all the bribes and complicated transport arrangements along the way (Deshingkar et al., 2019). It is seen that even highly experienced migrants who have been migrating to Thailand for several years use the services of Carry to enter Thailand either through the dedicated ports of the Three Pagoda pass or along other points in the porous border. On average, migrants from Mon paid 30,000 kyat in 2018 (1 USD = 1000 kyat) to village-level brokers who linked with their Carry to cross the border to Thailand and then another 1,200 baht (1 USD = 30 Thai baht) for onward journeys that were paid to local transporters and informal placement agencies. These costs were usually financed through borrowing from relatives and paid off gradually after finding work. Nearly all crossed the border illegally without any documents, but then regularised their status after a period of time. In fact, despite a series of measures introduced by the Thai government to control irregular migration and the bilateral Memorandum of Understanding, nearly all migration from Myanmar to Thailand is irregular (Balcaite, 2019; Thu and Ko, 2015).

The cultural context of irregular migration and human smuggling for construction work is altogether different in Myanmar compared with Bangladesh and Ghana. Those migrating from Mon and Kayin are young, often in their early 20s, with low levels of education and belonging to very poor families (Deshingkar et al., 2019). Masculinities and femininities play out in this smuggling landscape too, but in a less polarised way, perhaps because the migration is over a shorter distance and involves fewer risks compared to trans-Sahara migration in West Africa. While women are still socially constructed as the weaker sex and in need of protection and their identities constructed as daughters, wives and mothers, changing attitudes to migration have meant there are now options for them to travel abroad and work in a sector that is male dominated in other parts of the world. Female migrant construction workers were mainly from the poorest families without older male siblings who could migrate to support the family. Many women in the study by (Deshingkar et al., 2019) provided culturally accepted reasons for their

333

migration and justified it as a way of fulfilling their duty to provide for their parents in their old age, their younger sibling's education, or monk ceremonies.

Kayin is known for the migration of domestic workers to Thailand, and this pattern has resulted from social networks and established migration streams. As was seen in the case of Mon construction workers, the prevalence of informal brokers and Carry was widespread in this kind of migration. The journeys of female domestic workers were much longer and far more hazardous than those of male construction workers because most of them were being delivered all the way to the homes of informal brokers in the heart of Bangkok. One respondent in Deshingkar et al. (2019) study said the 500 km journey from her home to Bangkok took ten days with several stops in hideouts along the way. Although none of the women reported sexual harassment or abuse by the brokers, deception and physical confinement was common.

While the exploitation and deceit experienced by migrants travelling with the assistance of a Carry have been documented by Meyer et al. (2015), there is insufficient discussion in the literature on the other aspects of the relationship between migrants and smugglers. Those travelling to construction sites just across the border in Thailand were unequivocal in saying that migrating with Carry was the easiest and surest way of reaching their destination, if a bit expensive. Many said they felt protected by the brokers and Carry, in contrast to the policy discourse on smugglers, which portrays them as ruthless criminals (Deshingkar et al., 2019). Women migrating for domestic work also felt it was best to migrate with the help of known smugglers, in spite of the difficulties they experienced, as they understood that the steps they took were necessary to evade detection at the border. They preferred the Carry to handle everything, paying border officials and other brokers, instead of negotiating their passage with unknown people all by themselves.

The poorest families, who were not able to finance the migration of their daughters, entered debt-migration, which is widespread in domestic work across Asia (Deshingkar, 2021; Platt et al., 2017). In Myanmar it was encountered more frequently in the poorest families where aspiring migrants could not mobilise capital to finance the migration (Griffiths and Ito, 2016). The costs of migration (transport, obtaining papers, permits and visas) and job placement are borne by the broker and/or employer, and the migrant repays through salary deductions over a period ranging from four months to a year. The interviews carried out by (Deshingkar et al., 2019) suggested that migrants were remitting substantial amounts of money back to their families; this corroborates the findings of (Kusakabe and Pearson, 2015).

Bangladesh

There are multiple circuits of transnational irregular migration originating in Bangladesh, with smuggling networks extending across the globe all the way to Libya in the West (Siddiqui and Bhuiyan, 2013) and Malaysia in the east (Rahman, 2020). Bangladesh has emerged as an important source country for irregular migrants who are employed in construction labour in the Gulf countries, as well as rich countries in Southeast Asia. Such workers are critical to the success of construction projects such as the FIFA stadium in Qatar, and smuggling and brokerage is intertwined with entering the country and finding work under the *Kafala* system (Renkiewicz, 2016). The infrastructure of smuggling stretches all the way from the villages of migrants right up to companies in the destination country. It encompasses a range of formal and informal institutions and individuals, including village-level brokers, recruitment agencies, travel agents, medical testing centres, training centres, border officials and airline staff (Abrar et al., 2017; Deshingkar et al., 2019).

Human smuggling in the Global South

Village-level brokers fulfil several functions; they may act as a guarantor for money lenders so that migrants can obtain loans to finance their migration (Rahman, 2012), which are offered at usurious interest rates of between 30–60% (Jureidini, 2014). Others borrow from relatives or sell family assets. Brokers may also help the migrant choose an appropriate destination based on their market intelligence. Abrar et al.'s (2017) research shows that brokers also select and channel migrants into particular jobs and help them choose a "bhalo" or good visa which could be an irregular "azad" or free visa. An Azad visa is one that is bought from a legally registered kafeel, or sponsor, by a broker to sell on to a migrant, their family, or another intermediary. Such a visa allows a migrant to enter the country as a worker tied to this particular kafeel, but in practice they can work for anybody. Such kafeels can include companies in Qatar that have unused visas which they sell to agents. There are an estimated 400,000 irregular Bangladeshi migrants in Qatar, and most have entered the country on these so called *azad* or free visas (Momen and Deshingkar, 2020; Jureidini, 2014: 87).

The free visa system is widespread in the Qatari construction industry. The process of recruiting workers starts with the village-level dalal or broker who takes a large lump sum from the migrant and offers them a "package." This consists of help with obtaining a passport, checking the authenticity of the visa, helping them to mobilise any other documents that are needed, and linking them up to their chosen registered recruitment agency (RA) in a major city like Dhaka. Brokers play a role in both official migration as well as irregular migration. In the former, they help the migrant to complete the formalities, and in the latter they manage the process with an *azad* visa, which involves linking up known RAs who have bribed contacts in key institutions like medical testing centres and passport offices as well as aviation personnel and border officials. The average price of a free visa in 2017 was QAR 25,000 (about USD 6867).

The context of female irregular migration in Bangladesh is similar to Ghana and Myanmar: the country had introduced a series of restrictions on women's migration, but these were progressively relaxed, resulting in an increase in the number of female migrants. However, women's ability to migrate internationally continues to be shaped by numerous religious, cultural and political barriers that they must negotiate, and this can explain why their numbers have remained low (Belanger and Rahman, 2013). Afsar's study among Gulf returnees in Bangladesh noted that there were no female migrants from the conservative Noakhali and Sylhet areas. Like Ghana, international migration among women is higher in the capital city of Dhaka and its surrounding areas where gender norms are more relaxed (Afsar, 2009; Siddiqui, 2002). Migration to the Gulf is an important route out of a socially constrained situation for divorced, separated and widowed women. In Afsar's sample, half the women were divorced, abandoned or widowed. Others belonged to extremely poor families with no cultivable land and were migrating to escape debt and domestic abuse.

Even there are no restrictions on women's migration, there is evidence of irregular border crossings and the prevalence of the *azad* visa system in this kind of migration too. Up to 45,000 Bangladeshi women had migrated to the Gulf countries between 1998 and 2011 (Rahman, 2012). Nasra Shah and Lubna Al-Kazi's research on irregular migration in Kuwait shows that relatives can buy *azad* visas from Kafeels and send them directly to women in Bangladesh (Shah and Al-Kazi, 2017). Another route was fake or "*gala kata*" visas (Afsar, 2009). In Afsar's study of brokerage in Bangladesh, a majority of women used the services of brokers to complete travel formalities (e.g., medical check-up, visa processing and flight arrangements). The broker would procure "*gala kata*" visas and forged passports with the help of local government officials and printing machine operators. Passage for the migrant in possession of the fake documents would be assured through the broker's network with airline staff both in Bangladesh and the destination country (Afsar, 2009).

There is no doubt that the Kafala system was important in creating the conditions for smuggling and irregularity to flourish. However, there is also evidence of irregularity being mobilised by migrants for their own ends. Some of the women in Shah and Al-Kazi's study did not renew their work permits and remained irregularly in Kuwait for years, even decades. During their stay, they remitted significant sums back to dependents in Bangladesh, and some succeeded in paying for the higher education of their children (Shah and Al-Kazi, 2017).

Conclusion

The research synthesised in this chapter shows that smuggling arrangements are far more complex than policy narratives suggest. A multitude of arrangements can exist even in the same geographical region: often there are separate infrastructures of smuggling for men and women because they are heading to different destinations and occupations. Human smugglers offer a wide range of services for migrants including advice on routes and destinations, protection during the journey, documentation and transportation across borders.

The hardship that migrants experience while being smuggled needs to be understood with an appreciation of their goals for the advancement of their families and themselves. Smuggled migrants can and do remit significant amounts of money which is critical for improving the family's standard of living, educating siblings, investing in durable assets and repaying family debts.

In today's globalised world, interconnected by new technologies and modes of travel, the demand for cheap labour in rich countries has drawn migrants from poor countries with limited opportunities. These globalised labour regimes intersect with infrastructures of smuggling which perpetuate power asymmetries and gender inequalities by channeling particular ethnicities and nationalities into certain kinds of work. These processes contribute to the production of highly gendered and racialised patterns of migration and labour circulation.

Conversely, the infrastructures of smuggling help to expand migrant agency by giving people more choices. However, the process remains arbitrary, as there is an unpredictable mix of how "good" the smuggler is, how bribeable the border officials and police are, how much money the migrant can mobilise and, crucially, luck and chance. As human smuggling is by definition outside the purview of the law, there is no way of enforcing standards related to the treatment of migrants, costs, modes of transport, housing of migrants along the way and their reception in destination countries. In such a lawless and arbitrary process where migrants are away from their usual support networks, the smuggler has a great degree of power over migrants.

The experiences described here show that migrants' relationship with smugglers is complex. Smugglers play an ambiguous role as they are embedded in processes that reproduce structural inequalities such as the employment of undocumented migrants in highly exploitative work; at the same time, they are instrumental in opening up opportunities for marginalised communities who would otherwise have no access to international labour markets and higher wages that can be transformative for the individuals involved and the families left behind. It must be borne in mind, however, that common to all scenarios was the prevalence of informal employment arrangements without official contracts. Furthermore, the combination of state policies to combat human smuggling, trafficking and irregular migration with the constant threat of criminalisation and deportation creates insecure working and living conditions where migrant workers must accept exploitative work in order to survive, save and remit money.

In sum, this chapter provides a much-needed nuanced picture of what migration actually involves for millions of people who have been denied the right to legal and free mobility within the developing world. Smugglers transcend political borders and provide a critical link that connects those who have been excluded by global development with some of its gains, albeit in a highly unequal fashion. These studies on South-South smuggling are important for gaining an understanding of the relationship between poverty and the ability to migrate. Smugglers can make migration a possibility even for the very poor and those without formal educational qualifications, and help them to access international migration which is usually the preserve of the rich.

Notes

1 Migration becomes "undocumented" or "irregular" in policy parlance, when it occurs outside the legal and regulatory frameworks of the sending, transit, and destination countries. Irregular migration includes other possibilities such as remaining in the country without a visa; working in contravention of work restrictions and remaining in the country after the visa expires. Human smuggling facilitates one form of irregular migration which is crossing a border illegally with the use of falsified documents or without documents or entering a country at points other than officially sanctioned ports of entry. The term smuggling as it is used here encompasses processes that enable the illegal crossing of borders including the use of clandestine routes, bribing border officials and the falsification of travel and identity documents.
2 I use the term "migration" as an all-encompassing term to indicate mixed migration flows including economic migrants, refugees and other categories of forced migrants as their journeys may change from one form to another over the course of the journey.
3 The material is drawn heavily from research carried out under the DFID funded Migrating out of Poverty Consortium (MOOP), a ten-year programme of multidisciplinary research across Asia, Africa and the Middle East with a focus on the migration industry in the Global South.
4 http://documents1.worldbank.org/curated/en/336541505459269020/pdf/119753-PN-P133833-PUBLIC-Ghana-Policy-Note-Ag-Sector-Review.pdf.
   http://documents1.worldbank.org/curated/en/829581512375610375/pdf/121822-REVISED-PovertyReport PartEng.pdf.
   https://www.worldbank.org/en/results/2016/10/07/bangladesh-growing-economy-through-advances-in-agriculture#:~:text=More%20than%2070%20percent%20of,least%20part%20of%20their%20income.
5 For other differences please refer to https://www.unodc.org/e4j/en/tip-and-som/module-11/key-issues/differences-and-commonalities.html.
6 The Kafala system is now being reformed but the effects of that were not evident at the time of data collection.

References

Abrar, C., Deshingkar, P., Taslima Sultana, M., Haque, K.N.H., Reza, M., 2017. Emic perspectives on brokering international migration for construction from Bangladesh to Qatar. Working paper 49, Migrating Out of Poverty. University of Sussex, U.K.

Adugna, F., Deshingkar, P., Atnafu, A., 2021. Human smuggling from Wollo, Ethiopia to Saudi Arabia: Askoblay criminals or enablers of dreams? *Public Anthropol.* 3, 32–55.

Adugna, F., Deshingkar, P., Ayalew, T., 2019. Brokers, migrants and the state: Berri Kefach "door openers" in Ethiopian clandestine migration to South Africa. Working paper 56. Migrating Out of Poverty. University of Sussex, U.K.

Afsar, R., 2009. *Unravelling the vicious cycle of recruitment: Labour migration from Bangladesh to the Gulf States.* ILO.

Åkesson, L., Alpes, J., 2019. What is a legitimate mobility manager? Juxtaposing migration brokers with the EU. *J. Ethn. Migr. Stud.* 45, 2689–2705.

Akyeampong, E., 2000. Africans in the diaspora: The diaspora and Africa. *Afr. Affairs.* 99(395), 183–215.

Alpes, M.J., 2017. Why aspiring migrants trust migration brokers: The moral economy of departure in Anglophone Cameroon. *J. Int. Afr. Inst.* 87, 304–321.

Anderson, B., Anderson, B.L., 2000. *Doing the dirty work?: The global politics of domestic labour.* Palgrave Macmillan.

Aronowitz, A.A., 2001. Smuggling and trafficking in human beings: The phenomenon, the markets that drive it and the organisations that promote it. *Eur. J. Crim. Policy Res.* 9, 163–195.

Awumbila, M., Deshingkar, P., Kandilige, L., Teye, J.K., Setrana, M., 2019a. Please, thank you and sorry–brokering migration and constructing identities for domestic work in Ghana. *J. Ethn. Migr. Stud.* 45, 2655–2671.

Awumbila, M., Teye, J.K., Kandilige, L., Nikoi, E., Deshingkar, P., 2019b. Connection men, pushers and migrant trajectories: Examining the dynamics of the migration industry in Ghana and along routes into Europe and the Gulf States. Working paper 65. Migrating Out of Poverty. University of Sussex, U.K.

Awumbila, M., Torvikeh, G.D., 2018. Women on the move: A historical analysis of female migration in Ghana, in: *Migration in a Globalizing World: Perspectives from Ghana.* Sub-Saharan Publishers, pp. 171–189.

Ayalew Mengiste, T., 2018. Refugee protections from below: Smuggling in the Eritrea-Ethiopia context. *Ann. Am. Acad. Pol. Soc. Sci.* 676, 57–76.

Ayalew, T., Adugna, F., Deshingkar, P., 2018. Social embeddedness of human smuggling in East Africa: Brokering Ethiopian migration to Sudan. *Afr. Hum. Mobil. Rev.* 4, 1333–1358.

Balcaite, I., 2019. Brokered (Il) legality: Co-producing the Status of Migrants from Myanmar to Thailand, in: The Migration Industry in Asia: Brokerage, Gender and Precarity. Palgrave Macmillan, pp. 33–58.

Belanger, D., Rahman, M., 2013. Migrating against all the odds: International labour migration of Bangladeshi women. *Curr. Sociol.* 61, 356–373.

Bredeloup, S., Pliez, O., 2011. The Libyan migration corridor. Improving EU and Us Immigration Systems. Paper prepared for the European project. European University Institute.

Bisong, A., 2020. Regional solutions: Regulating recruitment and protection of African migrant workers in the gulf and the middle east. The European Centre for Development Policy Management.

Buckley, M., Zendel, A., Biggar, J., Frederiksen, L., Wells, J., 2016. *Migrant work & employment in the construction sector.* International Labour Organisation.

BWI, 2006. *Defending workers rights in construction.* Building and Woodworkers International.

Carden, M.R.J., 2014. Smuggling of Female Migrant Workers from Myanmar to Thailand. Master of Arts thesis, Chulalongkorn University. https://cuir.car.chula.ac.th/dspace/bitstream/123456789/44685/1/5681215924.pdf

Carling, J., 2016. West and Central Africa. *Migrant smuggling data and research: A global review of the emerging evidence base.* International Organization for Migration. 25–53.

Darkwah, A.K., Thorsen, D., Boateng, D.A., Teye, J.K., 2019. Good for Parents but Bad for Wives: Migration as a Contested Model of Success in Contemporary Ghana. Working paper 61. Migrating Out of Poverty. University of Sussex, U.K.

Deshingkar, P., 2021. Criminalisation of migration for domestic work from Myanmar to Singapore—need for a radical policy shift. *Eur. J. Crim. Policy Res.* 1–15. https://doi.org/10.1007/s10610-020-09477-w

Deshingkar, P., Awumbila, M., Teye, J.K., 2019. Victims of trafficking and modern slavery or agents of change? Migrants, brokers, and the state in Ghana and Myanmar. *J. Br. Acad.* 7, 77–106.

Deshingkar, P., Zeitlyn, B., 2015. South-South migration for domestic work and poverty. *Geogr. Compass.* 9, 169–179.

Fernandez, B., 2019. *Ethiopian migrant domestic workers: migrant agency and social change.* Springer.

Fernandez, B., 2013. Traffickers, brokers, employment agents, and social networks: The regulation of intermediaries in the migration of Ethiopian domestic workers to the Middle East. *Int. Migr. Rev.* 47, 814–843.

Fong, E., Yeoh, B. S. A., 2020. Migrant domestic workers: disadvantaged work, social support, and collective strategies in East Asia. *Am. Behav. Sci. 64*, 703–708.

Franck, A.K., Arellano, E.B., Anderson, J.T., 2018. Navigating migrant trajectories through private actors: Burmese labour migration to Malaysia. *Eur. J. East Asian Stud.* 17, 55–82.

Gamburd, M.R., 2000. *The kitchen spoon's handle: Transnationalism and Sri Lanka's migrant housemaids.* Cornell University Press.

Griffiths, M., Ito, M., 2016. *Migration in Myanmar: Perspectives from current research.* Social policy and Poverty Research Group.

Huijsmans, R., 2014. 19 Gender, masculinity, and safety in the changing Lao-Thai migration landscape, in: *Migration, Gender and Social Justice.* Springer, pp. 333–349.

ILO, 2001. *The construction industry in the twenty-first century: Its image, employment prospects and skill requirements.* International Labour Organisation.

Jureidini, R., 2017. Irregular migration in Qatar: The role of legislation, policies, and practices. *Ski. Surviv. Irregul. Migr. Gulf.* 135.

Jureidini, R., 2014. *Migrant labour recruitment to Qatar.* Bloomsbury Qatar Foundation Journals.

Kandilige, L., Hamidou, M.N., 2019. Migrants in countries in crisis: The Experiences of Ghanaian and Nigerien migrants during the Libyan Crisis of 2011. *Afr. Human Mob. Rev.* 5(2).

Kleist, N., 2017. Disrupted migration projects: The moral economy of involuntary return to Ghana from Libya. *Africa.* 87(2), 322–342.

Kusakabe, K., Pearson, R., 2015. Remittances and women's agency: Managing networks of obligation among Burmese migrant workers in Thailand, in: *Transnational Labour Migration, Remittances and the Changing Family in Asia.* Springer, pp. 50–81.

Lewis, H., Dwyer, P., Hodkinson, S., Waite, L., 2015. Hyper-precarious lives: Migrants, work and forced labour in the Global North. *Prog. Hum. Geogr.* 39, 580–600.

Lindquist, J., 2012. The elementary school teacher, the thug and his grandmother: Informal brokers and transnational migration from Indonesia. *Pac. Aff.* 85, 69–89.

Lindquist, J., Xiang, B., Yeoh, B.S., 2012. Opening the black box of migration: Brokers, the organization of transnational mobility and the changing political economy in Asia. *Pac. Aff.* 85, 7–19.

Mahdavi, P., 2013. Gender, labour and the law: The nexus of domestic work, human trafficking and the informal economy in the United Arab Emirates. *Glob. Netw.* 13, 425–440.

Meyer, S.R., Robinson, W.C., Abshir, N., Mar, A.A., Decker, M.R., 2015. Trafficking, exploitation and migration on the Thailand-Burma border: A qualitative study. *Int. Migr.* 53, 37–50.

Molenaar, F., 2017. *Irregular migration and human smuggling networks in Niger.* Clingendael CRU Rep. Febr.

Momen, L., Deshingkar, P., 2020. Hyper-precarious lives: Bangladeshi migrants on Azad visas in Qatar during the COVID-19 pandemic. https://www.routedmagazine.com/bangladeshi-azad-qatar

Osella, F., 2014. The (im) morality of mediation and patronage in south India 16 and the Gulf, in: *Patronage as Politics in South Asia.* Cambridge University Press. pp. 365–394.

Palmary, I., de Gruchy, T., 2016. How unpopular policies are made: Policy making for migrant women in South Africa, Bangladesh and Singapore. Working Paper 45, Migrating Out of Poverty. University of Sussex, U.K.

Parreñas, R., 2015. *Servants of globalization: Migration and domestic work.* Stanford University Press.

Pearson, D.R., Kusakabe, K., 2012. *Thailand's hidden workforce: Burmese migrant women factory workers.* Zed Books Ltd.

Platt, M., Baey, G., Yeoh, B.S., Khoo, C.Y., Lam, T., 2017. Debt, precarity and gender: Male and female temporary labour migrants in Singapore. *J. Ethn. Migr. Stud.* 43, 119–136.

Platt, M., Davies, S.G., Bennett, L.R., 2018. Contestations of gender, sexuality and morality in contemporary Indonesia. *Asian Studies Review.* Special Issue 1, 1–15.

Rahman, A., 2020. A Study on irregular migration from Bangladesh to Malaysia through the Bay of Bengal and the Andaman Sea. *Otoritas J. Ilmu Pemerintah.* 10, 120–131.

Rahman, M.M., 2012. Bangladeshi labour migration to the Gulf States: Patterns of recruitment and processes. *Can. J. Dev. Stud. Can. Détudes Dév.* 33, 214–230.

Renkiewicz, P., 2016. Sweat makes the green grass grow: The precarious future of quatar's migrant workers in the run up to the 2022 FIFA World Cup Under the Kafala System and recommendations for effective reform. *Am. Univ. Law Rev.* 65, 8.

Sanchez, G., 2018. Five misconceptions about migrant smuggling. Policy Brief, European University Institute, Issue 07.

Sanchez, G., 2017. Critical perspectives on clandestine migration facilitation: An overview of migrant smuggling research. *J. Migr. Hum. Secur.* 5, 9–27.

Shah, N.M., Al-Kazi, L., 2017. Irregular migration to and within Kuwait: Enabling and sustaining factors, in: *Skilful Survivals: Irregular Migration to the Gulf.* European University Institute.

Siddiqui, T., Bhuiyan, R.A., 2013. Emergency return of Bangladeshi migrants from Libya. S. Rajaratnam School of International Studies, NTS Working Paper Series, 9.

Strauss, K., McGrath, S., 2017. Temporary migration, precarious employment and unfree labour relations: Exploring the 'continuum of exploitation' in Canada's Temporary Foreign Worker Program. *Geoforum.* 78, 199–208.

Teye, J.K., Awumbila, M., Benneh, Y., 2015. Intra-regional migration in the ECOWAS region: Trends and emerging challenges. *Migration and Civil Society as Development Drivers - a Regional Perspective.* Centre for European Integration Studies. 97–123.

Testaverde, M., Moroz, H., Hollweg, C.H., Schmillen, A., 2017. *Migrating to opportunity: Overcoming barriers to labor mobility in Southeast Asia*. World Bank.

Thu, S., Ko, K., 2015. Myth and reality in irregular migration from Myanmar. MA dissertation. Victoria University of Wellington.

Tonah, S., Codjoe, E., 2020. Risking it all: Irregular migration from Ghana through Libya to Europe and its impact on the left-behind family members. *Global Processes of Flight and Migration*. Göttingen University Press. 25–40.

Triandafyllidou, A., Bartolini, L., 2020. Irregular migration and irregular work: A chicken and egg dilemma, in: *Migrants with Irregular Status in Europe*. Springer, pp. 139–163.

Wahab, A.A., 2018. The colours of exploitation: Smuggling of Rohingyas from Myanmar to Malaysia (Warna-Warni Eksploitasi: Penyeludupan Rohingya dari Myanmar ke Malaysia). *Akademika*. 88, 5–16.

Yeates, N., 2012. Global care chains: A state-of-the-art review and future directions in care transnationalization research. *Glob. Netw*. 12, 135–154.

Zeitlyn, B., Deshingkar, P., Holtom, B., 2014. Internal and Regional Migration for Construction Work: A Research Agenda. Working paper 14, Migrating Out of Poverty, University of Sussex. U.K.

25

HUMAN SMUGGLING IN THE TIME OF COVID-19

Lessons from a pandemic

Lucia Bird Ruiz-Benitez de Lugo

Introduction

The unprecedented restrictions on human movement imposed around the world to curb the spread of COVID-19 in the spring of 2020 posed new challenges and protection risks for migrants and refugees. They also cast into sharp relief the impacts of responses to irregular migration, and human smuggling, that are centred on border control, particularly on the protection risks faced by migrants and refugees on their journeys.

Political discourse construing the fight against COVID-19 as a 'war' quickly gained significant momentum. Restricting or halting human movement – COVID-19's key transmission 'tactic' – became a key part of the 'battle,' with epidemiological contact tracing another crucial 'weapon.' Irregular and clandestine movement erodes the efficacy of these measures, making it difficult to establish a comprehensive picture of exposure or contain the spread of the virus.

In this context, it is no surprise that the military was quickly deployed in many countries to restrict the domestic movement of individuals and strengthen border controls. Migration policy and discourse, shaped by the need to control an unprecedented global pandemic, increasingly became framed through the lens of national security, accelerating pre-existing trends. In line with this, untracked human movement became the enemy of states fighting this public health disaster.

Exploring how pandemic response measures have shaped the human smuggling industry, and consequent migrant protection risks, offers an unparalleled opportunity to scrutinise the unintended consequences of responses to irregular migration and human smuggling, which are principally based on border control and interdiction of smugglers. In the wake of the most significant global shock experienced for decades, it also presents a unique chance to move away from extant response paradigms.

'Shocks,' or 'critical junctures' (often significant economic or political crises), can expand the 'reform space' available to policy-makers, enabling adoption of innovative approaches, and offering an opportunity to 'do things differently' (Capoccia, 2016; Fritz, Levy, Ort, 2014). The COVID-19 pandemic presents a shock of unprecedented geographic scope and scale, triggering calls by political commentators for policy-makers 'not [to] let a good crisis go to waste' (Marquette, 2020).

DOI: 10.4324/9781003043645-25

In the context of human smuggling, a rethink is certainly required. While human smuggling has been a policy priority across states of transit and destination since the turn of the century, the global response remains fragmented and of questionable effectiveness (Bird, 2019). The responses to human smuggling available and implemented by policy-makers have stagnated; COVID-19 could create space for innovation.

At the time of writing, this opportunity had not been acted upon. Instead, responses to human smuggling in the context of the pandemic have largely constituted an acceleration of pre-existing approaches which seek to block movement through the militarisation of borders, and reduce the supply of smugglers through interdiction.

Prior to the pandemic, the growing securitisation of the migration landscape was shown to drive migrants' reliance on smuggling networks and increase protection risks on the migrant trail. Evidence collected across 2020 points to the exacerbation of these trends by COVID-19-driven shifts in policy.[1]

The pandemic has deepened economic strain in many regions, increasing drivers for migration, while the parallel closure of legal migration routes has ensured a growing proportion of migration is irregular, and smuggler facilitated. In order to understand why, it is key to delineate accurately the mechanics underpinning the smuggling market. Human smuggling is best understood as a services industry, where smugglers are service providers who, for a fee, help migrants to cross boundaries and overcome barriers, which may be geographic, political or cultural.[2] The harder an obstacle in migration journeys is to cross independently, the greater the demand for human smugglers. As borders became newly securitised, and human movement further restricted due to COVID-19, smugglers become yet more essential.

The COVID-19 crisis also looks set to have long-term consequences for both the perception of and protections afforded to migrants. Migrants have been stigmatised in some areas as potential carriers of the virus, with some communities actively opposing their presence. Such stigmatisation could harden into longer-lasting antipathy towards migrants that persists beyond the end of the COVID-19 crisis, potentially eroding the raft of protections afforded to migrants and refugees under international and domestic laws.

This chapter explores the impacts of COVID-19 responses on the human smuggling market, including on the vulnerabilities of migrants and refugees. This underscores the medium–term consequences for those on the move, but also shines a spotlight on the flaws in current response frameworks, and analyses whether a shift away from the blanket application of criminal justice approaches is needed.

The closure of legal migration pathways

Between March and September 2020 an unprecedented number of countries around the world sought to close, or partially close, their borders to the entry of non-nationals, rendering all cross-border human movement illegal (with narrow exceptions, in some states, for movement deemed 'essential'). Pursuant to the Pew Research Centre, as of 1 April, 91% of the global population lived in states with restrictions on international arrivals, 39% with completely closed borders (Connor, 2020).

Countries around the world, ranging from Algeria to Greece, and El Salvador to the United States, funnelled further resources into border control, enhancing the hardware and official, often military, patrolling of borders (Snow, 2020). The widespread deployment of military to prevent irregular border crossings further militarised the broader migration landscape, as well as COVID-19 emergency responses, which in some cases arguably breached extant humanitarian practises and international law. The closure of Maltese and Italian ports to irregular arrivals,

Human smuggling in the time of COVID-19

including to NGO vessels (Reidi, 2020; Reuters, 2020), and Malaysia's turning away boats of Rohingya refugees are merely two of many such incidents (Loy, 2020).

State imposed restrictions, together with widespread fear of infection, made migrant and refugee journeys far more difficult, including for the vast numbers seeking to return home – a response tracked in previous pandemics, including Ebola (Betancourt et al., 2016). Where border closures prevented migrants and refugees returning home independently, many used the services of smugglers. Zimbabwe, among other countries, experienced a significant influx of irregular migrants seeking to return to their home countries after losing their livelihoods in South Africa due to the pandemic (Kavhu, 2020).

Restrictions on domestic and cross-border movement temporarily depressed both regular and irregular migration in many regions.[3] Frontex reported that in March 2020 the 'number of detections of illegal border crossings on Europe's main migratory routes fell by nearly half' from February, and by 85% between March and April, reaching record lows.[4]

In the face of increased obstacles to smuggling operations, some networks previously focussing on human movement responded to the higher risk of such activities, as stopping human movement became prioritised at borders, by leveraging their networks to smuggle goods instead. In many contexts, goods became a secondary focus of border control, meaning the risks involved were lower. Smugglers responded to new demands for legal commodities whose supply chain has been disrupted by COVID-19 trade restrictions, or which had been rendered illegal by new state regulation.[5] This has been reported in regions as diverse as Niger, where smugglers have confirmed switching to moving goods and fuel from Libyan cities in the south to goldfields in northern Chad in reaction to heightened interdiction risk, and Thailand, where gemstone traders have used human smugglers to move their wares (Senior organized crime analyst, Personal Communication, 14 April 2020).

However, given that the factors driving demand for human movement had not diminished, the lull was predicted, from the beginning of the pandemic, to be temporary. In line with this, across many regions, irregular migration started to increase, reaching and in some cases exceeding pre-pandemic levels, as soon as restrictions started to ease.

Illustratively, while interceptions of migrants and refugees departing from Algeria and Tunisia in March 2020 were dramatically fewer than January 2020 figures, which had been particularly high for the season, by July interceptions had once again increased (GI-TOC analysis of Algerian Ministry of defense data etc.; 2020). The economic stress caused by COVID-19, compounding the challenges faced by two faltering economies, continues to drive irregular emigration, with nationals of both countries constituting a far higher proportion of arrivals in Italy than in the previous year (UNHCR, 2020; The New Humanitarian, 2020).

Similarly, as movement restrictions in Guatemala eased in late July 2020, irregular migration towards the United States increased sharply, with both detentions of Guatemalan nationals by US Border Force, and deportations experiencing a significant spike (Road, 2020). Overall US Border Patrol apprehensions across the border with Mexico plummeted between March and April 2020, but quickly started increasing again from May onwards, exceeding pre-pandemic figures, and those of the same month of 2019, by September (US Customs, 2020).

4Mi survey data collected by the Mixed Migration Centre (MMC) between April and September 2020 regarding the impact of COVID-19 on refugees and migrants travelling across mixed migration routes in Africa, Asia and Latin America found that, in parallel to the increasing difficulties of migration journeys, 37% of respondents indicated a greater need for smugglers (rising to 44% and 46% respectively in West Africa and Latin America) (Mixed Migration Centre, 2020).

As legal pathways shrink and the obstacles to independent irregular migration grow (due to enhanced border control), a growing proportion of migrants are forced to move irregularly, and require the help of smugglers to so (Reitano and Bird, 2018). Consequently, they will have to endure the heightened protection risks associated with more clandestine modi operandi.

Growing demand for human smuggler services

Smuggling markets react quickly to increased demand. The March 2020 closure of the Benin-Niger border in response to the COVID-19 pandemic significantly increased human smuggling activity in the region. Before March, a small smuggling industry helped irregular migrants refused entry at official border crossings. Following the border closure, the market quickly adapted to cater for increased demand by local Nigerian and Beninese migrants wishing to cross the border. Profits from this expansion have been re-invested in enhancing transport infrastructure, cutting the journey times by adding motors to the pirogues traditionally used for smuggling activity. Similarly, the increase in irregular maritime departures from Algeria noted above was, in late 2020, accompanied by heightened investment in infrastructure (boats with expensive imported engines), and levels of organisation (with simultaneous departures of 30 boats).

The specific context of COVID-19, and in particular the proliferation of domestic movement restrictions, has meant that heightened demand is coupled with difficulties in accessing a smuggler – 43% of refugees and migrants surveyed by the MMC reported increased difficulties accessing smugglers, with Latin America the only region where respondents reported this less frequently (Mixed Migration Centre, 2020). In some contexts, including Niger, heightened focus on interdicting smugglers in the context of the pandemic can also present obstacles to migrants' obtaining their services.

As in any services industry, the price of smuggling services is determined by supply and demand market dynamics. Consequently, as demand for smuggling services grows and supply (or access to supply) is restricted, prices are driven upwards. Further price inflation is triggered by the increased risk faced by smugglers operating in an environment made increasingly hostile to migrants by COVID-19 – the higher price reflects the increased risk of detection and sanction.

These dynamics can be tracked in Northern Mali, where smuggling operations drastically decreased between March 2020 and September 2020. This decrease was in part due to the temporary counter-COVID-19 movement restrictions imposed by the Coordination of Azawad Movements (CMA), a coalition of armed groups which has consolidated support across much of this area, including Timbuktu and Gao, two smuggling transit points on the journey northwards to Algeria and Niger. But predominantly due to the uptick in security at the Mali-Algeria border, where smugglers reported a significant spike in surveillance and patrolling by Police Border Guards, Gendarmerie Gardes Frontières units, and military patrols. When smuggling resumed in September 2020, prices paid by migrants travelling from Timbuktu in Mali to Algeria had doubled, with the increase attributed by those on the ground to the heightened border security. (After a few months prices returned close to pre-pandemic levels, as border restrictions eased, facilitating the smuggling of people, but also fuel, lowering fuel prices and therefore smuggling prices.)

The price increase is in line with global trends tracked by the Mixed Migration Centre, which found that half of migrants and refugees surveyed in September 2020 noted an increase in smuggler fees since the beginning of the pandemic. In line with the supply and demand dynamics outlined above, price increases were most widely reported in areas where respondents had most identified an increased need for smugglers, particularly where this was coupled with reported difficulties in accessing smuggling services.[6]

Increased risk for migrants

Changes to smuggling mechanics

Environments which become more hostile to migration enhance the protection risks faced by migrants and refugees in both transit and destination (Carling, Gallagher and Horwood, 2015; Reitano and Bird, 2018; Tinti and Reitano, 2016). This occurs due to the changing dynamics of the migrant-smuggler relationship, but also because of widespread erosion of migrant and refugee rights enabled by growing anti-migrant sentiment.

While the price increases reported above will in some cases translate into heightened profits for smugglers, it also makes movement financially unfeasible for some migrants. Migrant populations in forced immobility – either as a result of increased law-enforcement efforts, unaffordable smuggler prices, or otherwise – have been found to be at high risk of trafficking (Columb, 2019). Adding another layer of risk, in the context of a pandemic, stationary migrant populations (including the millions of migrants in camps around the world) living in migrant-reception centres and camps characterized by high-density accommodation and poor sanitation are highly vulnerable to contagion.

As more migrants are unable to pay for their journeys at the outset, this engenders growth in pay-as-you go structures, where migrants work along the journey to pay the smuggling fee, increasing their vulnerability to exploitation. Research shows that 'pay as you go,' and particularly 'travel now, pay later schemes,' where migrants work along the journey to pay off debt to smugglers for previous travel, make migrants extremely vulnerable to labour or sexual exploitation, often at the hands of trafficking networks.[7]

The risks associated with the smuggled journey itself also increase in contexts where there is greater state focus on preventing movement. Smugglers moving further underground to evade detection in more hostile operating environments have been repeatedly tracked to take riskier routes or use more dangerous transport mechanics, such as sealed lorry containers, or ever smaller boats, with catastrophic consequences for migrant safety (Reitano and Bird, 2018).

An early harbinger of these consequences was the asphyxiation of 64 Ethiopian men on 24 March 2020 in the container of a goods lorry in which they were being smuggled across the border from Malawi into Mozambique (GI-TOC, 2020). This occurred four days after the Mozambican government imposed strict border controls to prevent any unnecessary movement of people in response to the pandemic (Agence de Presse Africaine, 2020). It is believed that the migrants and refugees were being smuggled along the popular southern route towards South Africa, and that the enhanced border security measures will drive other smugglers moving significant numbers of migrants and refugees across the border to adopt similar, extremely risky, approaches.[8]

Similarly, following the border closure with Libya, and in order to avoid enhanced presence of Nigerien military and Tebu militia, smugglers in Niger reported using more clandestine routes to enter Libya, which carry greater protection risks for migrants and refugees. This includes the route taken through Chad, usually used only as a last resort given the myriad risks presented by military, bandits and traffickers. This heralds further increase in fatalities – in May the bodies of 20 Nigerien migrants believed to have been returning home from Libya were found in the desert kilometres from Madama, a border settlement on the north-eastern frontier of Niger, after the smugglers' vehicle had broken down. The smuggler had reportedly taken the more circuitous route due to the growing number of interceptions of smugglers by Nigerien military.[9]

Embedding this incident in a wider global picture, 61% of migrants and refugees surveyed by MMC in September 2020 reported a shift to riskier routes by smugglers since the start of the pandemic; notably this was even higher (over 70% in Niger), in states focussing on smuggler interdiction.

Compounding the risks of the journey, the increasingly hostile environments faced by migrants and refugees in transit – driven by fear of contagion among communities and anti-migrant rhetoric – means that those who have engaged smuggling services will find themselves more reliant on their smugglers. Evidence shows that in contexts where migrants do not feel safe, they are under tighter control of their smugglers, who become their de facto protectors. Such migrants are consequently more vulnerable to abuse at the hands of their smugglers (Reitano and Bird, 2018).

Vulnerabilities due to increased anti-migrant sentiment

Smugglers, however, are only one of myriad actors which pose protection risks to migrants and refugees in transit and destination. Anti-migrant sentiment, fuelled by public discourse characterising migrants as carriers of COVID-19,[10] increases the threat posed by this broader set of actors, including community attacks fuelled by fear and xenophobia, and abuse at the hand of state officials, the latter a group repeatedly identified as one of the key perpetrators of abuse against migrants and refugees.

Further, the growth in anti-migrant sentiment enables measures which breach refugee and migrant rights enshrined in international law,[11] leaving few avenues for recourse in the face of abuse. Prior to the pandemic, record forced displacement levels – reaching 79.5 million by the end of 2019 – were already putting significant pressure on international legal frameworks and commitments in place to protect the rights of those on the move, in particular of refugees (UNHCR, 2020). Myriad states, arguably in breach of their obligations to interpret their commitments under international treaties 'in good faith' were already responding to such displacement levels by implementing a range of measures to impede access to asylum, and subjected irregular migration to a wide range of criminal and repressive sanctions (Corten and Klein, 2011; Fitzmaurice, 2014). The pandemic has offered an opportunity for policy-makers seeking to limit extant protections to push through controversial measures, masked in emergency rhetoric.

To provide one case study, before the COVID-19 outbreak in March 2020, President Trump made several attempts to erode the rights of migrants and refugees accorded by international law, but such attempts were often met by fierce criticism and subsequently reversed or watered down. With COVID-19 widely recognised to constitute a national security threat, emergency anti-contagion measures that similarly ride roughshod over migrant rights were subject to little public scrutiny.

In line with this, on 23 March 2020, the US Department of Homeland Security stated it would 'return ... aliens [seeking to enter the US] to the country they entered from ... Where such a return is not possible, CBP [US Customs and Border Protection] will return these aliens to their country of origin' (US Homeland Security, 2020). Although the measures came into effect on 21 March for an initial 30-day period, despite widespread condemnation of the order, including by UNHCR, (Lakhani, 2020) the Center for Disease Control and prevention introduced an indefinite order in October 2020 (Center for Disease Control and Prevention, 2020). Human rights organisations have repeatedly highlighted that such orders are not aligned with the rights of refugees to seek asylum, and risk potentially catastrophic harms to expelled individuals (Sawyer, 2020). Reports of irregular migrants being ejected back into Mexico only

96 minutes (on average) after entering the US also suggests that obligations to assess whether migrants can return safely are being ignored (Miroff, 2020).

Research by Freedom House, a US thinktank, found that in 80 of 192 countries surveyed, the condition of human rights had deteriorated since the start of the pandemic (Freedom House, 2020). The decline is particularly acute in struggling democracies, or repressive states, and is expected to continue as the pandemic fades. The erosion of human rights during emergencies is notoriously difficult to reverse.

The commitments made by states to respect the human rights of migrants and refugees in the 2018 Global Compacts look to be in danger of quickly being forgotten (UNGA, 2019). International and national frameworks protecting migrant and refugee rights, already under strain, may suffer long-lasting damage.

If migrants, refugees and asylum seekers lose hope that their rights will be respected and that their claims will be dealt with fairly and lawfully, fewer will engage with authorities to regularize their status. Instead, a greater proportion will remain in host countries with tenuous irregular status, forming a shadowy parallel society that is highly vulnerable to exploitation by organized crime, including trafficking networks. This trend has already been identified in countries whose asylum systems quickly became more hostile, such as Sweden which reacted to the 2015/16 'migrant crisis' by amending its legal frameworks surrounding migration and asylum (Larsson, 2017).

The erosion of frameworks in place to protect the rights of migrants and refugees therefore increases the vulnerability of those on the move not only at the hands of the smugglers facilitating their movement, but to a range of criminal operators in transit and destination, most commonly human trafficking networks.

Rethinking the response?

Responses to the smuggling industry can be divided broadly into two categories – those focusing on supply, and those addressing demand.

Policy-makers have typically prioritised the former, and the COVID-19 pandemic appears to have tipped the balance yet more firmly in their favour.[12] The focus of these supply-side responses is on deterring smugglers from operating by heightening enforcement and increasing the risk of interdiction and prosecution. These are underpinned by the criminalisation of human smuggling, and consequent adoption of a criminal justice response.

A more nuanced understanding of the human smuggling marketplace recognises both the operation of criminal networks with a high degree of organisation, and of structures more accurately perceived as community enterprises with low organisation in contexts where alternative livelihoods are limited. This broad range of operators calls into question whether criminal justice measures are always appropriate.

Human smuggling was criminalised under international law by the UN Protocol against the Smuggling of Migrants by Land, Sea and Air which came into force in 2004, and constitutes one of three Protocols supplementing the United National Convention on Organized Crime (UNODC, 2000). The Smuggling Protocol is inherently attached to the UNTOC, and should not be read – as it often is – in isolation. One key danger of doing so is that it dilutes the focus of the Protocol on organised crime.

This is misleading, and instead the Smuggling Protocol should be understood as a criminal justice instrument intended to have a limited scope: namely, to shape the response to organised crime networks involved in human smuggling. The UNTOC definition of 'organised crime group' is notoriously expansive:

a structured group of three or more persons, existing for a period of time and acting in concert with the aim of committing one or more serious crimes or offences established in accordance with this Convention, in order to obtain, directly or indirectly, a financial or other material benefit. (UNODC, 2004)

However, even taking this into account, research into human smuggling has pointed increasingly towards a market which is dominated by loosely affiliated individuals, or organisations with limited hierarchy. It is arguable that many of these would not meet the criteria of the UNTOC definition, and should therefore fall beyond the scope of the criminalisation obligations in the Smuggling Protocol, and consequently under national legislative frameworks. This is not an approach which has gained significant traction to date, yet deserves greater exploration and analysis.

Conclusion

COVID-19, and state responses to the virus, bring two long-recognised correlations into sharp relief: firstly, that between shrinking legal pathways for migration and the growing need to migrate irregularly; and secondly, that between increasing investment in border control to restrict irregular migration, and the increased demand for smugglers.

These linked phenomena call into question the efficacy of existing response frameworks, and highlight that they can be counterproductive, because they may heighten demand for smugglers, and drastically increase the vulnerabilities of those on the move.

As the evidence base surrounding the structure of human smuggling operations grows, there is a growing argument that some smuggling dynamics should not be treated as forms of organized crime, rendering criminal justice responses inappropriate and calling for a fundamental pivot in responses (Achilli, Sanchez and Zhang, 2018; McAuliffe and Laczko, 2016).

Such a pivot would instead focus more on strands of responses which address the structural underpinnings of the human smuggling market, including policies and interventions which focus on the demand for help to move irregularly. These include enhancing legal avenues for movement, seeking to render smuggling services unnecessary, and addressing the original drivers for migration and displacement (Carling, 2017).

It is crucial to ensure that the pandemic does not mark a sharp decline in the protections granted to migrants and refugees in law and policy across the world, but instead that policymakers take the opportunity to address flaws in extant counter-smuggling responses.

The widespread decimation of livelihoods and unprecedented unemployment caused by the pandemic across many regions has heightened the underlying drivers for migration, triggering increased outflows of irregular migrants as internal controls imposed at the beginning of the pandemic are relaxed.

Considering a wider array of response tools, and moving away from knee-jerk reliance on the two-pronged formula of border control and interdiction, are urgently needed in order to avoid responding to pandemic-enhanced outflows in ways that drastically increase the harms faced by the growing numbers of those on the move.

Notes

1 This chapter draws on data collected by the Global Initiative Against Transnational Organized Crime through its networks and civil-society partners in the field around the world.

Human smuggling in the time of COVID-19

2 It is key to distinguish human smuggling from human trafficking, as they are distinct phenomena and different crimes under international law. While trafficking broadly constitutes the recruitment or harbouring of persons through coercion or deceit for the purpose of exploitation, smuggling takes places on the basis of a willing transaction between migrant and smuggler – in effect, a bilateral contract for services. Although in some cases smuggling arrangements may end in trafficking, the vast majority will not. For further discussion see: Tuesday Reitano and Lucia Bird, Understanding contemporary human smuggling as a vector in migration, Global Initiative Against Transnational Organized Crime, May 2018, https://globalinitiative.net/wp-content/uploads/2018/05/TGIATOC-understanding-Contemporary-Human-Smuggling-1936-hi-res.pdf.

3 4Mi survey data collected by the Mixed Migration Centre between April and September 2010 about the impact of COVID-19 on refugees and migrants travelling across mixed migration routes in Africa, Asia and Latin America found that 47% of surveyed refugees and migrants cited increased difficulty crossing borders as an impact of the coronavirus crisis on their migration journey. Mixed Migration Centre, update COVID-19 Global Thematic Update #1, 1 September 2020.
Impact of COVID-19 on migrant smuggling, https://reliefweb.int/sites/reliefweb.int/files/resources/126_Covid_Snapshot_Global_smuggling.pdf.

4 When analysing Frontex figures, it is key to note that a growing number of migrants are likely stuck in transit on their journeys further away from Europe's borders. Frontex, Situation at EU external borders in March – Detections halved from previous month, 16 April 2020, https://frontex.europa.eu/media-centre/news-release/situation-at-eu-external-borders-in-march-detections-halved-from-previous-month-mZrikq; Frontex Situation at EU external borders in April – Detections lowest since 2009, 12 May 2020, news release, https://frontex.europa.eu/media-centre/news-release/situation-at-eu-external-borders-in-april-detections-lowest-since-2009-mJE5Uv.

5 The rapid emergence of cigarette smuggling markets into South Africa, and alcohol smuggling markets into Namibia, following the states' banning of such products during the pandemic is one example of illicit smuggling dynamics quickly emerging to meet new demand. See: Defence Web, Smuggling of alcohol, cigarettes on the rise, 20 April 2020, https://www.defenceweb.co.za/featured/smuggling-of-alcohol-cigarettes-on-the-rise/; IOL, Spike in people smuggling beer, whisky into Namibia amid coronavirus crackdown, 28 April 2020, https://www.iol.co.za/news/africa/spike-in-people-smuggling-beer-whisky-into-namibia-amid-coronavirus-crackdown-47308917.

6 The proportion of respondents reporting higher smuggling fees was especially high in Malaysia (74%), Niger (68%) and Libya (65%), all countries in which it was frequently noted that access to smugglers had become more difficult (74%, 56% and 66% respectively). Mixed Migration Centre, update COVID-19 Global Thematic Update #1, 1 September 2020.
Impact of COVID-19 on migrant smuggling, https://reliefweb.int/sites/reliefweb.int/files/resources/126_Covid_Snapshot_Global_smuggling.pdf.

7 Recent research tracking the vulnerabilities to trafficking of irregular migrants travelling across the Sahel on their journeys towards Europe found that 83% of migrants who reported paying smugglers through 'travel now, pay later' structures were trafficked, compared to the average rate of 60% across the rest of the migrants surveyed. Arezo Malakooti, The Intersection of Irregular Migration and Trafficking in West Africa and the Sahel: Understanding the Patterns of Vulnerability, Global Initiative Against Transnational Organized Crime, forthcoming. These percentages are from a quantitative survey of 1689 randomly selected migrants across two countries (Niger and Mali).

8 This is not the case for the far northeast of Mozambique. This region is significantly impacted by heavy rain and a failure to maintain bridges, a situation which has cut almost all road traffic from Tanzania. It is also impacted by insurgency, particularly as the insurgents are trying to take control of Macomia and Quissanga districts. Email exchange with Joe Hanlon, academic, journalist, and editor of weekly newsletter on Mozambique, 31 March 2020; email submissions by Mozambican journalist, 1 April 2020. Email exchange with Joe Hanlon, academic, journalist, and editor of weekly newsletter on Mozambique, 31 March 2020.

9 This specific incident is reported in: https://www.facebook.com/498168007057993/posts/1352274041647381/?d=n%0D. Ongoing monitoring of human smuggling by The Global Initiative Against Transnational Organized Crime in the Sahel.

10 Suhret Fazlic, the mayor of Bihać, Bosnia, reportedly told the press that migrants could be dangerous as potential carriers of COVID-19. See Lorenzo Tondo, Bosnia crams thousands of migrants into tent camp to 'halt COVID-19 spread,' *The Guardian*, 27 March 2020, https://www.theguardian.com/global-development/2020/mar/27/bosnia-crams-thousands-of-migrants-into-tent-camp-to-halt-covid-19-spread.

11 Refugees, and to a lesser extent migrants, are ascribed rights both within standalone instruments, including the 1951 Refugee Convention, and in the broader international human-rights legal framework, including the Universal Declaration of Human Rights.

12 For example, throughout the first quarter of 2021 the UK Home Secretary, Priti Patel, has sought to push through legislative reform to prescribe life sentences for human smugglers, and the Home Office has scaled up the practice of charging migrants steering boats with criminal offences. Although COVID-19 is likely only one of the factors driving this, it is certainly a pivotal backdrop shaping this response. Jamie Grierson, Priti Patel has not secured deals with European countries over UK asylum overhaul, *The Guardian*, 24 March 2021, https://www.theguardian.com/politics/2021/mar/24/priti-patel-has-not-secured-deals-with-european-countries-over-uk-asylum-overhaul.

References

Achilli, Luigi, Sanchez, Gabriella, and Zhang, Sheldon X. (eds), Migrant smuggling as a collective strategy and insurance policy: views from the margins, Special issue of The Annals of the American Academy of Political and Social Science, 676, 1, 2018, http://hdl.handle.net/1814/51944.

Agence de Presse Africaine, COVID-19: Mozambique closes schools, tightens border controls, 20 March 2020, http://apanews.net/en/pays/mozambique/news/covid-19-mozambique-closes-schools-tightens-border-controls.

Article 2, UNTOC, https://www.unodc.org/documents/middleeastandnorthafrica/organised-crime/UNITED_NATIONS_CONVENTION_AGAINST_TRANSNATIONAL_ORGANIZED_CRIME_AND_THE_PROTOCOLS_THERETO.pdf.

Betancourt, Theresa S., Brennan, Robert T., Vinck, Patrick, Vander Weele, Tyler J. et al., Associations between mental health and Ebola-related health behaviors: a regionally representative cross-sectional survey in post-conflict Sierra Leone conflict Sierra Leone, *PLoS Medicine*, 13, 8, 2016, doi: 10.1371/journal.pmed.1002073.

Bird, Lucia, Human smuggling in Africa: The creation of a new criminalised economy?, 4 July 2019, ENACT, https://enact-africa.s3.amazonaws.com/site/uploads/2020-07-27-human-smuggling-continental-report-web.pdf.

Capoccia, Giovanni, Critical junctures, in Orfeo Fioretos, Tulia Falleti, Adam Sheingate (ed), *The Oxford Handbook of Historical Institutionalism*, Oxford Handbooks Online, 2016, https://www.oxfordhandbooks.com/view/10.1093/oxfordhb/9780199662814.001.0001/oxfordhb-9780199662814-e-5.

Carling, Jørgen, Gallagher, Anne and Horwood, Christopher, Beyond definitions: global migration and the smuggling- trafficking nexus, Regional Mixed Migration Secretariat, PRIO, 2015, www.mixedmigration.org/resource/beyond-definitions/.

Carling, Jørgen, How should migrant smuggling be confronted?, in M. McAuliffe and M. K. Solomon, (ed). *Conveners Ideas to Inform International Cooperation on Safe, Orderly and Regular Migration*, Geneva: IOM, 2017, https://publications.iom.int/books/how-should-migrant-smuggling-be-confronted.

Center for Disease Control and Prevention, Order suspending introduction of certain persons from countries where a communicable disease exists, 13 October 2020, https://www.cdc.gov/coronavirus/2019-ncov/order-suspending-introduction-certain-persons.html.

Columb, Seán, Organ trafficking in Egypt: 'They locked me in and took my kidney,' *The Guardian*, 2019, https://www.theguardian.com/global-development/2019/feb/09/trafficking-people-smugglers-organs-egypt-mediterranean-refugees-migrants.

Connor, Phillip, More than nine-in-ten people worldwide live in countries with travel restrictions amid COVID-19, 1 April 2020, Pew Research Center, https://www.pewresearch.org/fact-tank/2020/04/01/more-than-nine-in-ten-people-worldwide-live-in-countries-with-travel-restrictions-amid-COVID-19/.

Corten, Olivier and Klein, Pierre, *The Vienna Conventions on the Law of Treaties: A Commentary*, Oxford: OUP, 2011.

Fitzmaurice, Malgosia, The practical working of the law of treaties, in Malcolm D. Evans (ed), *International Law* (4th edn, Oxford: OUP, 2014).

Freedom House, Democracy under lockdown, October 2020, https://freedomhouse.org/sites/default/files/2020-10/COVID-19_Special_Report_Final_.pdf.

Human smuggling in the time of COVID-19

Fritz, Verena, Levy, Brian, and Ort, Rachel, Problem-driven political economy analysis, The World Bank's Experience, 2014, https://openknowledge.worldbank.org/bitstream/handle/10986/16389/9781464801211.pdf.

GI-TOC compilation and analysis of Algerian Ministry of Defense, Tunisian Ministry of Defense, and Tunisian Ministry of Interior media releases, 1 January–July 2020.

Global Initiative Against Transnational Organized Crime, 64 migrant deaths in Mozambique is a 'sickening and needless waste of human life,' 25 March 2020, https://globalinitiative.net/pr-migrants-mozambique/.

Kavhu, Sharon, Porous borders pose new COVID-19 threat to Southern Africa, 23 May 2020, *Southern Times*, https://southerntimesafrica.com/site/news/porous-borders-pose-new-covid-19-threat-to-southern-africa.

Lakhani, N., US using coronavirus pandemic to unlawfully expel asylum seekers, says UN, 17 April 2020, *The Guardian*, https://www.theguardian.com/world/2020/apr/17/us-asylum-seekers-coronavirus-law-un

Larsson, Milene, Sweden's Hidden People, Vice, 27 July 2017, https://www.vice.com/en_uk/article/kzadbw/watch-our-new-documentary-swedens-hidden-people.

Loy, I., Rohingya boat rescued after weeks at sea, 16 April 2020, *The New Humanitarian*, https://www.thenewhumanitarian.org/news/2020/04/16/Bangladesh-Rohingya-boat-rescued.

Marquette, Heather, On COVID-19 social science can save lives: Where do we start?, 22 April 2020, Oxfam, https://oxfamblogs.org/fp2p/on-covid-19-social-science-can-save-lives-where-do-we-start/.

McAuliffe, Marie, and Laczko, Frank (eds), Migrant smuggling data and research: a global review of the emerging evidence base, 2016, International Organisation for Migration, https://publications.iom.int/system/files/smuggling_report.pdf.

Miroff, Nick, Under coronavirus immigration measures, U.S. is expelling border-crossers to Mexico in an average of 96 minutes, *The Washington Post*, 31 March 2020, https://www.washingtonpost.com/immigration/coronavirus-immigration-border-96-minutes/2020/03/30/13af805c-72c5-11ea-ae50-7148009252e3_story.html.

Mixed Migration Centre, Update COVID-19 global thematic update #1, 1 September 2020, https://reliefweb.int/sites/reliefweb.int/files/resources/126_Covid_Snapshot_Global_smuggling.pdf.

Morales, Sergio, En agosto se disparó la migración a Estados Unidos debido a las medidas relajadas, 9 September 2020, Prensa Libre, https://www.prensalibre.com/guatemala/migrantes/en-agosto-se-disp.aro-la-migracion-a-estados-unidos-debido-a-las-medidas-relajadas/.

Reidy, E. The COVID-19 excuse? How migration policies are hardening around the globe, 17 April 2020, *The New Humanitarian*, https://www.thenewhumanitarian.org/analysis/2020/04/17/coronavirus-global-migration- policies-exploited.

Reitano, Tuesday and Bird, Lucia, Understanding contemporary human smuggling as a vector in migration, global initiative against transnational organized crime, May 2018, https://globalinitiative.net/wp-content/uploads/2018/05/TGIATOC- understanding-Contemporary-Human-Smuggling-1936-hi-res.pdf.

Reuters, Malta rescues 140 migrants but holds them on tourist boats offshore, 22 May 2020, https://www.reuters.com/article/us-malta-migrants-idUSKBN22Y2Q5.

Sawyer, Ariana, CDC director doubles down on endangering asylum seekers, 15 October 2020, Human Rights Watch, https://www.hrw.org/news/2020/10/15/cdc-director-doubles-down-endangering-asylum-seekers.

Snow, S., 540 additional troops to deploy to U.S.-Mexico border over COVID-19 concerns, 1 April 2020, *Military Times*, https://www.militarytimes.com/news/coronavirus/2020/04/01/540-additional-troops-to-deploy-to-us-mexico-border-over-COVID-19-concerns/.

Tinti, P. and Reitano, T., *Migrant, Refugee, Smuggler, Saviour*, New York: Hurst & Co Publishers, 6 October 2016.

UN General Assembly, Global compact for safe, orderly, and regular migration, 11 January 2019, un https://www.un.org/en/ga/search/view_doc.asp?symbol=A/RES/73/195; UN Report of the United Nations High Commissioner for Refugees, Global compact on refugees, reissued 13 September 2018, https://www.unhcr.org/gcr/GCR_English.pdf.

UNHCR, Figures at a Glance, 18 June 2020, https://www.unhcr.org/uk/figures-at-a-glance.html.

UNHCR, Italy, Sea arrivals dashboard, July 2020; Layli Fooudi, COVID-19 fallout drives Tunisians to Italy despite deportations, 1 September 2020, *The New Humanitarian*, https://www.thenewhumanitarian.org/news-feature/2020/09/01/Italy-Tunisia-migration-deportations-coronavirus.

UNODC, Protocol against the smuggling of migrants by land, sea and air, 2000, https://www.unodc.org/documents/middleeastandnorthafrica/smuggling-migrants/SoM_Protocol_English.pdf.

US Customs and Border Protection, Southwest border migration FY, 2020, https://www.cbp.gov/newsroom/stats/sw-border-migration.

US Homeland Security, Fact sheet: DHS measures on the border to limit the further spread of coronavirus, 23 March 2020, https://www.dhs.gov/news/2020/03/23/fact-sheet-dhs-measures-border-limit-further-spread-coronavirus.

PART V

Smuggling and conflict

26

THE ILLICIT TRADE AND CONFLICT CONNECTION

Insight from US history

Peter Andreas

Introduction

Scholars and policy analysts have devoted considerable attention to contemporary "war economies," particularly the relationship between illicit trade and armed conflict in the post-Cold War era (Pugh, Cooper and Goodhand 2004). Much of the focus has been on how violent non-state actors have increasingly exploited illicit commerce to fund rebellion (Arnson and Zartman 2005). It is commonly asserted that this alleged convergence between war-making and illicit profiteering is a distinctly post-Cold War phenomenon facilitated by globalization and a radically changed geopolitical context – even a defining characteristic of so-called "new wars" (Jung 2003; Munkler 2005; Kaldor 2012).[1] A frequent argument, for example, is that in the absence of formal external sponsorship from the United States or the former Soviet Union, insurgents have turned increasingly to alternative forms of material support and taken advantage of the same revolutions in transportation and communication that have facilitated licit trade. This includes illicit exports dubbed "conflict commodities," such as drugs, timber, ivory, and precious stones (Winer 2005). Partly thanks to the campaigns of international NGOs such as Global Witness, therefore, diamonds from conflict zones in West Africa have been labeled "blood diamonds" and have been the target of an ambitious international certification system for rough diamonds known as the Kimberly Process (Smillie 2005).

Illegal drugs such as opium and cocaine have come to be associated especially with armed conflict, given their role in insurgencies in places such as Colombia and Afghanistan (Kan 2009; Felbab-Brown 2010). Government officials charge that insurgents in drug-producing zones – often labeled "narco-terrorists" or "narco-guerrillas" – have been driven increasingly by drug profits rather than political grievance. As the "greed and grievance" debate in the scholarly literature has underscored, it is important to differentiate between commodities causing and those facilitating conflict (Berdal and Malone 2000; Ballentine and Sherman 2003). It should be remembered, moreover, that the FARC, for example, dates back to the 1960s, long before Colombia even became a cocaine exporter (Andreas 2020, 229).

Much of the attention on the illicit political economy dimensions of conflict is welcome and long overdue – all armed conflicts, after all, have a political economy, and this includes an illicit side. In various ways and to varying degrees, they use smuggling networks and criminal actors to create and sustain the material basis for warfare. Such conflicts are partly made possible by

DOI: 10.4324/9781003043645-26

"taxing" and diverting humanitarian aid, diaspora remittances, illicit exports, clandestine trading across front lines, and black-market sale of looted goods. The importance of smuggling practices and criminal actors becomes even more apparent in the context of evading international economic sanctions and arms embargoes imposed to discourage conflict (Andreas 2005; Naylor 2008). In this respect, external intervention contributes to the criminalization of a conflict, creating an economic opportunity structure for clandestine commerce and making the competing sides more reliant on cross-border smuggling channels. Under these conditions, war is a continuation of business by clandestine means: military success on the battlefield may hinge on entrepreneurial success in the murky underworld of smuggling. Moreover, the smuggling networks and embargo-busting infrastructure built up during wartime can leave a lasting legacy for the post-war reconstruction period.[2]

Too often, however, the end result of this greater attention on war economies and the "crime-conflict nexus" has been to distort and exaggerate more than to explain and inform. The contemporary novelty of the illicit trade and conflict connection tends to be simply asserted rather than empirically demonstrated. As a partial corrective, what is needed is a more historically informed, nuanced and critical examination of the complex relationship between illicit trade and warfare.

In this chapter, I offer a brief historical reality check for contemporary debates about illicit trade and conflict by examining critically the early American experience, arguing that illicit commerce and its connection to armed conflict played an essential role in the very making of the nation, and that the distinction between a patriot and profiteer was often a blurry one. I focus on three cases: the American War of Independence; the War of 1812; and the American Civil War. In all three cases, illicit trade profoundly shaped the nature, duration, and outcome of the conflict. In the case of the War of Independence, illicit trade successfully supplied the rebellion against Britain, but also complicated postwar reconstruction. In the case of the War of 1812, illicit trade in the form of "trading with the enemy" extended the conflict, helped to turn it into a stalemate, and subverted US efforts to annex Canada. In the case of the Civil War, southern illicit cotton exports via blockade running helped to prolong the conflict, allowing the Confederacy to persist far longer than would otherwise have been the case. Together, these cases illustrate not only the crucial importance of the illicit trade-conflict connection in the making of America, but also the utility of a more historical lens in understanding the dynamics of cross-border smuggling.[3]

The smuggling war of Independence and its aftermath

By definition, the rebels in Britain's distant American colonies attempting to break away from the Crown in the 1770s were illicit non-state armed actors. Their political grievances against the imperial authorities and proclaimed pursuit of "liberty and freedom" – celebrated in American history books as the nation's founding story – are well known. Less widely recognized, however, is the central role of illicit non-state armed actors clandestinely supplying George Washington's Continental Army with smuggled arms and other war materials.

A rag-tag force of colonial rebels went to war against the world's greatest military power. As American General William Moultrie wrote in his memoirs of the Revolution, the colonists rebelled "without money; without arms; without ammunition; no generals; no armies; no admirals; and no fleets; this was our situation when the contest began" (Moultrie 1802, I:63–54). No wonder, then, that the British expressed such smug confidence that their overwhelming military superiority quickly and easily would put down the American rebellion. Indeed, at first glance, the insurgency should have been short lived.

The illicit trade and conflict connection

It did not turn out that way. Why not? Smuggling is a crucial part of the answer, and was especially important in sustaining the rebellion before the French finally intervened and tipped the military balance on the ground. The British lost the war in the American colonies for many reasons, including geographic disadvantage and French intervention. Losing the war on smuggling – failing to deter and interdict desperately needed clandestine shipments of arms and other war supplies to George Washington's forces – played no small role. While at times subverting the Revolution by prioritizing profits over patriotism, illicit traders defying Britain's wartime embargo ultimately proved to be essential to its success. Colonial smugglers put their clandestine transportation methods, skills, and networks to good use supplying the insurgency. Part of this simply involved building on previously well-established illicit trading relationships, such as in the West Indies. It also involved fostering new commercial connections directly with Northern Europe, such as France and Sweden – no easy task in wartime (Nuxoll 1985, 283–286).

From the very start, the Continental Army was in desperate need of clothes, arms, ammunition, food, and other supplies – and with the single exception of food, all of these required large-scale imports from abroad, in violation of the British blockade. This was especially important in the years before France formally entered the war in 1778 (followed by Spain in 1779, and Holland in 1781), tipping the military balance. Most crucial was gunpowder: "the want of powder was a very serious consideration for us;" recounted General Moultrie, "we knew there was none to be had upon the continent of America" (Moultrie 1802, I:78). Indeed, there were no powder mills operating in the colonies when the war started (York 1979, 27). Virtually all of the gunpowder used by the colonists in the first two and a half years of the war had to be smuggled in – mostly from France via the West Indies (Herring 2008, 18; Stephenson 1925, 277–279). Most of these military supplies were exchanged for colonial products, including cod, lumber, flour, tobacco, and indigo. Victory on the battlefield hinged on success in the world of smuggling. Over one hundred different ships reportedly smuggled in supplies during this time period, evading the British warships attempting to blockade the Atlantic coast (Stephenson 1925, 279).

Smuggled gunpowder trickled in ever so slowly. The situation was especially bleak by the end of 1775. On Christmas Day 1775, George Washington wrote: "Our want of powder is inconceivable. A daily waste and no supply administers a gloomy prospect" (Chauncey 2009, 3:299). Some have argued that if in mid-January 1776 the British had known about the extreme scarcity of gunpowder, they "could have marched out to Cambridge and crushed the newly recruited colonial army" and "thus the revolution would have ended" (Stephenson 1925, 274). The British withdrew from Boston in March 1776, unaware of the anemic condition of the colonial forces. At one point, a 13-mile long chain of colonial sentries around Boston did not have even an ounce of gunpowder (Huston 1991, 111). There was also a shortage of arms, including muskets, cannon, pistols, and bayonets. Unlike gunpowder, however, which had to be replenished perpetually, the arms supply was cumulative, and thus dependence on smuggling channels declined over time. The same was not true of other military-related supplies, however, such as tent materials, clothing, shoes, and blankets, which wore out more quickly, creating chronic shortages throughout the war (Nuxoll 1985, 8–9).

Wartime smuggling blurred the line between patriot and profiteer. Smuggling was both essential to the revolutionary war effort and profitable for the well placed and well connected. Some illicit traders sold smuggled gunpowder and other supplies at highly inflated prices to the Continental Army. The Brown brothers in Providence, for instance, were especially well positioned to profit from the war. Their wartime business ventures included organizing "powder voyages" to France, Holland, and Spain (Patton 2008, 16). One account of the Brown family history describes the Revolution as a "personal bonanza" for John Brown, who allegedly emerged from the war as the richest man in Rhode Island (Rappleye 2006, 210–211). In one deal, he offered a shipment of smuggled pistol powder to colonial forces at a substantial mark up. Desperate for the supplies, Stephen Moylan replied on behalf of George Washington: "The General will take it, though it is a most exorbitant price" (Force 1840, 3:1688).

General Washington denounced widespread war profiteering, at one point declaring, "There is such a thirst for gain, and such infamous advantages taken to forestall, and engross those Articles which the Army cannot do without, thereby enhancing the cost of them to the public fifty or a hundred pr. Ct., that it is enough to make one curse their own Species, for possessing so little virtue and patriotism" (Fitzpatrick 1936, 13:335). He urged that merchants should "not take an undue advantage of the Distresses of their Country, so as to exact an unreasonable Price" (Fitzpatrick 1931, 3:459). Nevertheless, with the colonies sometimes competing with each other for scarce provisions, smugglers could not resist inflating prices and selling to the highest bidder (York 1979, 27). For instance, Elias Hasket Derby of Salem acknowledged in 1776 that one hundred percent profits could be made on imported items such as gunpowder, cotton, cocoa, and sugar, and that one hundred and fifty percent above normal prices was "more than common" on linens and paper (Fairburn 1955, 1:379).[4]

Thus, for all the patriotic fervor of the American Revolution, more base economic opportunism was also at work in keeping both civilians and rebel soldiers supplied. While supplying the Continental Army, smugglers also used this as a cover and opportunity to bring in high-value civilian goods such as silks and chinaware: private trade "piggy backed" on supply ships restricted by contract only for military purposes (Patton 2008, 17), This was a form of "smuggling within smuggling," often involving clandestinely importing consumer goods that served little or no military purpose but were in high demand.

Moreover, the very smuggling interests and practices that kept the Continental Army supplied during the War of Independence would prove to be a daunting challenge for the new republic. Smugglers, who had subverted British rule in the American colonies, would now also subvert government authority in the very nation they helped to create. For some merchants, the popular rallying cry of "no taxation without representation" really meant "no taxation even with representation." Old smuggling habits and attitudes would prove hard to change. As Massachusetts Representative Fisher Ames described the smuggling challenge in his address to the first US Congress in May 1789, "The habit of smuggling pervades our country. We were taught it when it was considered rather as meritorious than criminal; …"[5]

Illicit trade today also often is blamed for impeding and complicating post-war reconstruction in places such as Bosnia and Kosovo.[6] Long forgotten, though, is that this was also true for the United States in the aftermath of the Revolutionary War. The very smuggling practices that aided the War of Independence turned into an obstacle for the newborn American state. The powerful legacy of colonial smuggling contributed to merchant resistance to centralized state authority and regulation of commerce. Smuggling now undermined American rather than British revenue collection and greatly complicated US border management and foreign relations. This was a particularly serious problem for the nascent federal government, given that virtually all of its revenue derived from duties imposed on imports.

Illicit trade was therefore a major challenge to early American state making – just as it is for state-making efforts across the globe today. Indeed, this is an often-overlooked part of America's early "strong society, weak state" profile. At the same time, concerns about smuggling stimulated government expansion and the creation of a border management infrastructure, notably the establishment of the customs service as one of the first pillars of the federal government. Indeed, in a highly fragmented country deeply suspicious of centralized state

The illicit trade and conflict connection

authority, inhibiting illicit trade and collecting duties on imports through a federal customs service was the main rationale for a uniform system of government in the early years of the republic (Shapiro 2009). Efforts to combat maritime piracy and embargo busting also stimulated the early development of the navy. In other words, illicit trade and related activities were double-edged, both challenging and building up the new American state. The same is true today – witness the enormous growth of criminal law enforcement in the face of massive drug law evasion in recent decades – suggesting more continuity with the past than is typically recognized. While we should be careful not to overstate or misinterpret the historical parallels, neither should they be glossed over.

Trading with the enemy in the War of 1812

The War of 1812 between the United States and Great Britain was supposed to be quick and short lived. Instead, it turned into a stalemate that dragged on for two and a half years, with British forces kept well fed and supplied with the help of American smugglers pursuing illicit profits over patriotism. The Enemy Trade Act of 1812 outlawed trade with America's enemies and only permitted American vessels in US ports. This was followed by the sweeping but short-lived embargo of 1813 (outlawing all exports and giving officials more invasive powers), and the Enemy Trade Act of 1815, passed shortly before the conclusion of the war. These restrictions included a further militarization of customs enforcement, as naval and other military forces were increasingly tasked with not only fighting British troops but also smugglers.

Despite these efforts, trade with the enemy flourished, and mushroomed with the heightened demand generated by the influx of British forces in 1814 (Hickey 1989, 225). "We have been feeding and supplying the enemy," bemoaned a Republican newspaper, "both on our coast and in Canada, ever since the war began." (Hickey 1989, 168). Indeed, much to Madison's dismay, America's trading spirit often seemed stronger than its fighting spirit. "Self, the great ruling principle, [is] more powerful with Yankees than any people I ever saw," one British officer commented disparagingly (Hickey 1989, 216).

Nowhere was this more apparent than in the US-Canada borderlands, where Americans proved more enthused about illicitly trading with their northern neighbors than conquering them. This diverted scarce supplies to the enemy, increased the costs of feeding US soldiers, and undermined popular support for the war (Taylor 2011, 290–292). Even as some state militia units simply refused orders to march into Canada (Herring 2008, 128). American smugglers were far less inhibited in their border crossings and engagements with the enemy. Indeed, some militia members deployed to secure the border instead colluded in border smuggling. Military intelligence also covertly flowed across the border. "The turpitude of many of our citizens in this part of the country," commented navy Lieutenant Thomas Macdonough in dismay, "furnishes the Enemy with every information he wants" (Hickey 1989, 226). Colonel Zebulon Montgomery Pike, commander of the 15th Infantry based in Burlington, described soldiers and civilians on the border as "void of all sense of honor or love of country" due to their cross-border dealings (Muller 1976, 90–91).

The US-Canada border became the most important backdoor for wartime trading, building on the illicit trade routes and networks that flourished during the embargo era. Smuggling was not only good business for border communities, but good for relieving cross-border tensions in a time of war. Vermonters in the Lake Champlain Valley, for instance, remained largely unprotected from a British invasion and had good reason to maintain peaceful relations with their immediate neighbors in Lower Canada. Smuggling fostered an informal form of local

Peter Andreas

cross-border interdependence that had a pacifying effect. Smuggling thus became a peculiar mode of peacemaking (Alcock 1995).

Some illicit trade across the US-Canada line was seasonal. During the winter months, one wartime smuggler from Orleans County, Vermont, later recalled, "the goods and merchandise which came from Canada were smuggled in winter when the swamps and rivers were frozen and when the deep snows could be made into a hard road over the roughest ground" (Little 2008, 46). He noted that the main threat in the Vermont countryside was not confiscations by the authorities but rather the armed gangs who used the cover of patriotism as an excuse to rob smugglers. Meanwhile, during the summer, entire herds of cattle were smuggled through the forests of Vermont, New Hampshire, Maine, and New York into Canada to feed the Royal Army (Brandes 1997, 56). With the largest herds of cattle in the northeast, Vermonters were especially well placed to take advantage of a tripling of the price of beef during the war (Muller 1976, 90).

In late July 1813, an exasperated American General George Izard complained, "On the eastern side of Lake Champlain, the high roads are found insufficient for the supplies of cattle which are pouring into Canada. Like herds of buffaloes, they press through the forest, making paths for themselves…Nothing but a cordon of troops, from the French Mills [in northern New York] to Lake Memphramagog [in northern Vermont] could effectively check the evil. – Were it not for these supplies, the British forces in Canada would soon be suffering from famine, or their government subjected to enormous expense for their maintenance" (Dobson 1816, 57). Two years into the war, the British governor-general in Canada reported to the Foreign Office that, "Two-thirds of the army in Canada are at this moment eating beef provided by American contractors, drawn principally from the States of Vermont and New York" (Whitehead 1963, 44). Some New England cattle smugglers never even had to step foot into Canada: after marching their livestock to the border, their Canadian counterparts would woo the animals across with a basket of corn (Hickey 1989, 227).[7]

The border was equally porous further east, with the major smuggling hot spots changing with the shifting geography of the war (Strum 1983). When the British invaded and then occupied part of eastern Maine in the summer of 1814, British merchants flocked to the town of Castine to exploit wartime trading opportunities for the next eight months. The British authorities fully encouraged the brisk cross-border illicit trade to compensate for the severe shortage of foodstuffs and other supplies in Canada (Smith 2001). Wartime smuggling was about everyday survival, but it was also about profits. Take the case of William King, a successful Maine merchant who also headed the local militia: he supplied the British military with provisions, and the British supplied him with blankets, which he then sold at a profit to the American military (Nagel 2002). King went on to be elected the first governor of Maine in 1820, and later served as the collector of customs at Bath from 1830 to 1834 (Taylor 1977).

Early on in the war, the British government even sold trading licenses to American merchants that exempted them from seizure by British privateers and the Royal Navy. American naval officers had an especially difficult time identifying US merchant ships operating with these licenses, since the captain would keep the license hidden unless boarded by a British ship. To dupe the captain into voluntarily producing the incriminating license, American naval officers would at times masquerade as British when boarding the vessel, wearing British uniforms and showing the British flag. These ruses sometimes worked, but smugglers became less gullible and more wary of such deceptions over time. The owners of a licensed American merchant ship smuggling goods into Canada warned the master that

The illicit trade and conflict connection

you must be aware of the facility with which American cruisers may pass as English ...
When in with any of the B.[ritish] B.[lockading] squadron, come forward with your
Ex.[port] Li.[cense] which will safely pass you ... If you have any suspicions destroy all
at once ... (Crawford 1986, 167).

The British favored New England shippers in allocating trading licenses, since the
commercially-oriented northeast was most opposed to the war.[8] Britain's blockade of the
eastern seaboard initially did not extend to New England, a strategy meant to secure illicit
supplies but also create division and discord between the anti-war Federalist northeast and the
Republican administration in Washington. It was certainly politically awkward that New
Englanders were supplying British vessels blockading the rest of the American seaboard. Even
after the Royal Navy extended its blockade to include New England in April 1814, the British
continued to facilitate and encourage illicit American trade (especially to Canada) as long as it
aided their subjects and military forces (Hickey 1989, 533). Rhode Islanders on Block Island,
for instance, regularly brought both supplies and intelligence to British ships off the coast
(Brandes 1997, 56). The British openly used the harbor at Provincetown, Massachusetts, to
resupply their ships: small American vessels reportedly brought "[f]resh beef, vegetables, and in
fact all Kind of supplies" to these ships on a regular basis (Hickey 1989, 537). "The fact is
notorious," announced the Lexington *Reporter*, "that the very squadrons of the enemy now
annoying our coast ... derive their supplies from the very country which is the theatre of their
atrocities" (Hickey 1989, 171).

At the same time as American smugglers supplied enemy forces, the battle against smuggling
distracted US troops from their war-fighting mission. In October 1813, General Wade
Hampton even ordered military raids into Canada from the Lake Champlain region of Vermont
to try to disrupt the "shameful and corrupt neutrality of the lines, for the purpose of gain"
(Cruikshank 1905, 3:194). Similarly, the following March, Colonel Clark headed a detachment
toward Missisquoi Bay, Vermont,

with a view to cut up by the roots the smuggling intercourse which had been carried
on to a great extent; besides it was necessary to prevent the constant supply of provisions which were daily passing to the enemy from this state.[9]

"Blood cotton" and blockade running in the American Civil War

Few of today's illicit exports from conflict zones rival the importance of Confederate cotton –
we could call it "blood cotton" – in fueling a war that cost more US lives than any other
conflict in American history. Well over 600,000 soldiers lost their lives, and hundreds of
thousands more were injured. Illicitly exchanging cotton for arms contributed to this heavy
human toll by supplying Confederate forces and enabling the war to drag on much longer than
would otherwise have been possible. The illicit flow of arms and other materials, funded by
contraband Confederate cotton, could not in the end shift the military balance on the ground
and change the ultimate outcome of the war, but it did profoundly shape its character and
longevity. Although attracting far less attention than the Civil War's famous battles, southern
success on the battlefield depended on commercial success in the underworld of smuggling.

The North attempted to impede such clandestine commerce by imposing an ambitious naval
blockade on southern ports. On April 19 1861, President Lincoln announced a naval blockade
on the South – soon dubbed the "Anaconda Plan" – with the aim of squeezing the Confederacy

361

Peter Andreas

into submission by blocking contraband of war. Although it was an impossible task to police with patrolling the 3,549 mile-long Confederate coastline, blockaders could focus primarily on the handful of major southern ports with the requisite infrastructure and transportation links to handle large volumes of external supplies. During the course of the war, the Union's four blockading squadrons captured 136 blockade-runners and 85 more were destroyed (Wise 1988, 221).

The runners, though, usually outmaneuvered the blockaders. Historian Stephen Wise calculates that almost 300 steamships were involved in blockade running between the fall of 1861 and spring 1865, and out of an estimated 1,300 runs, more than 1,000 succeeded (Wise 1988, 221). Blockade runners managed to smuggle out roughly half a million bales of cotton, and smuggle in a thousand tons of gunpowder, half a million rifles, and several hundred cannon (McPherson 1988, 380). Wise estimates that blockade runners provided the South with 60% of its weapons, one-third of the lead for its bullets and the ingredients for three-fourths of its powder, and most of the cloth for its uniforms (Wise 1988, 7). Clearly, the Confederacy could not have survived without this clandestine lifeline to the outside world.

Successful blockade running sometimes meant that Confederate soldiers were better supplied than their Union counterparts. At one point, General Ulysses S. Grant replaced his own rifles with captured southern weapons:

> At Vicksburg 31,600 prisoners were surrendered, together with 172 cannon, about 60,000 muskets with a large amount of ammunition. The small-arms of the enemy were far superior to ours ... The enemy had generally new arms which had run the blockade and were of uniform caliber. After the surrender I authorized all colonels whose regiments were armed with inferior muskets, to place them in the stack of captured arms and replace them with the latter (Dattel 2009, 198).

In the first year of the war, the blockade was so thin that it scarcely deserved to be labeled as such. The Confederate government dismissively called it a "paper blockade." Over time, though, the blockade tightened and thickened considerably, targeting the relatively small number of key southern ports, especially Charleston and Wilmington, that remained in Confederate hands (New Orleans, the largest southern port, was captured and occupied by the Union early on in the war, and by 1863 blockade-runners were largely restricted to the ports of Wilmington, Charleston, Mobile, and Galveston). The blockade typically had multiple layers, with a layer of smaller ships patrolling closer to shore able to signal to warships several miles out when a blockade-runner was leaving port.

Blockade-runners adapted to these Union tactics by deploying faster, more agile and lower-profile British-made steamer vessels, painted gray or bluish green and burning smokeless anthracite coal for added stealth. Under the cover of fog and darkness, these blockade-runners could sneak by a Union warship in close proximity without being detected. When detected, many blockade-runners could simply outmaneuver and outrun their would-be captors. Despite the wartime context, the blockade enforcement-evasion game was mostly nonviolent: blockade running ships were typically not armed (to save weight but also to avoid being classified as an armed pirate ship, which brought much harsher penalties), and Union warships preferred to capture rather than destroy them in order to seize the cargo and receive the prize money.

Two British island ports, Bermuda and Nassau, served as the main hubs for blockade-runners, not unlike the transshipment role that the Dutch island of St. Eustatius played during the American Revolution. Bermuda and Nassau became bustling island warehouses for Europe-bound cotton and southern-bound contraband. Cotton – "white gold" – served as the de facto

The illicit trade and conflict connection

currency for purchasing European war materials and other supplies. One blockade-runner described the wartime scene at Nassau's port: "Cotton, cotton, everywhere! Blockade-runners discharging it into lighters, tier upon tier of it, piled high upon the wharves, and merchant vessels, chiefly under the British flag, loading with it" (Underwood 2008, 55).

Nassau, with a sympathetic governor and local population, was the favored transshipment point given its proximity to southern ports. In 1863, some 164 steamers departed Nassau for southern ports, while only 53 cleared for Bermuda (Wise 1988, 132). From Nassau, blockade-runners could reach Wilmington (570 miles) or Charleston (515 miles) in just three days. This not only saved time but also coal, and less space devoted to coal meant more space devoted to profitable cargo. Secretary of the Navy Welles complained about Nassau's complicity:

> Almost all of the aid which the Rebels have received in arms, munitions, and articles contraband have gone to them through the professedly neutral British port of Nassau. From them the Rebels have derived constant encouragement and support ... It is there that vessels are prepared to run the blockade and violate our laws, by the connivance and with the knowledge of the colonial, and, I apprehend, the parent, government (Mahin 1999, 170).

Mexico also served as a backdoor for smuggling cotton out, bringing in war supplies, and getting around the blockade (Irby 1977). As the only neutral country sharing a land border with Confederate territory, Mexico enjoyed a special niche in wartime trading. The Mexican border town of Matamoros became a smuggling depot, where war supplies could be ferried across the Rio Grande to Brownsville, Texas, and exchanged for southern cotton. A Union general lamented that "Matamoros is to the rebellion west of the Mississippi what the port of New York is to the United States. It is a great commercial center, feeding and clothing the rebellion, arming and equipping, furnishing the materials of war" (Underwood 2008, 72). One historian describes the area as resembling the California gold rush of 1849, with entrepreneurs, speculators, agents, and brokers drawn to it like a magnet (Meiners 1977). According to one estimate, more than 20,000 speculators from the Union, Confederacy, England, France, and Germany arrived in four years (Delaney 1955).

The tiny Mexican coastal hamlet of Bagdad, at the mouth of the Rio Grande some thirty miles from Matamoros, experienced an equally dramatic growth spurt, mushrooming in size from a handful of huts to a town of some 15,000 residents virtually overnight. In April 1863, the commander of the Eastern Gulf Blockading Squadron was informed that there were as many as 200 ships waiting to unload their cargoes and load cotton at Bagdad. During this same period, the commander of the Confederate raider *Alabama* reported that business was booming in Bagdad: "The beach was piled with cotton bales going out, and goods coming in. The stores were numerous and crowded with wares" (Underwood 2008, 71).

There was little that Union naval authorities could do about the use of Mexico to circumvent the blockade. As stipulated in the 1848 treaty of Guadalupe Hidalgo, the Rio Grande was neutral and therefore could not be blockaded by Mexico or the United States within a mile north or south of its entrance. Union warships slowed the trade down through harassment (by constantly boarding and inspecting vessels), but could not stymie it completely (Wise 1988, 88). This supply line was crucial in sustaining the Confederate war effort West of the Mississippi. Due to geographic distance and a poor transportation system, however, the Mexico connection was far less consequential than blockade running for supplying Confederate forces elsewhere.

Blockade running officers and crews were well rewarded for their risk-taking. This is illustrated by the pay scale of the commercial blockade runner the *Venus*. The captain received

$5,000, the first officer $1,250, the second and third officers $750 each, the chief engineer $2,500, the pilot $3,500, and each crewmember $250. These wages were paid in gold, half up front and the other half after the successful round-trip run (Wise 1988, 110–111). Crews and officers also greatly supplemented their income on the inbound trip by carrying scarce necessities and luxury items in their personal belongings, ranging from toothbrushes to corsets, which they could sell for many times their original value. On the outbound trip, they were allowed to carry personal supplies of cheap cotton, which they similarly sold at greatly inflated prices.

Confederate cotton exports were much reduced from pre-war levels, but reduced supply also meant highly inflated prices – assuring substantial profits for those who managed to evade the blockade. Cotton prices in Europe soared to as much as ten times their prewar levels. At such prices, the incentives to run the blockade remained high even as the risks increased over time – with the chances of being caught one in three by 1864 and one in two by 1865 (McPherson 1988, 380). Blockade-running cotton traders were challenged by the blockade but also enriched by it. A popular toast captured this dynamic:

> Here's to the Southern planters who grow the cotton; to the Limeys who buy the cotton; to the Yankees that maintain the blockade and keep up the price of cotton. So, three cheers for a long continuance of the war, and success to the blockade-runners (Dattel 2009, 195).

Relying on private commercial shippers for desperately needed war materials, however, had a serious downside for the Confederate government. Transportation costs were extremely high, accounting for much of the increase in cotton prices. These high transportation costs also decreased the incentives to ship bulky items, notably much needed machinery and railroad iron (Surdam 2001, 6). Moreover, commercial blockade-runners motivated more by profits than patriotism – or in the case of Rhett Butler, "for profit only," as he told Scarlet O'Hara in *Gone With the Wind* – devoted scarce cargo space to high-value luxury goods and civilian items, ranging from books to booze, rather than strictly military necessities.[10]

Confederate officials had little choice but to outsource most blockade running to private shippers. The Confederacy simply lacked the administrative capacity and apparatus to impose centralized control over the business of blockade running, even had it wanted to. Moreover, doing so would reduce the profit incentives that sustained the blockade running system – as was evident when the Confederacy banned the importation of luxury goods. Even as it attempted to impose greater regulation, therefore, the Confederate government remained dependent upon appealing to the profit motives of foreign merchants (Mahin 1999, 91).[11]

Blockade-runners fed, armed, and clothed the Confederacy until Union forces sacked the ports of Charleston and Wilmington. In late 1864, General Lee's army in Virginia depended almost entirely on imported food from Europe. The supply lines to Europe were severed when the last Confederate port on the Atlantic was shut down in the first months of 1865. With the Wilmington supply line cut, Lee's army was starving when he surrendered at Appomattox in April (Mahin 1999, 173).

In the end, the northern blockade can be seen as both a failure and a success. Its porosity suggests it was a failure, as evidenced by the repeated success of blockade-runners throughout the war years. Historians tend to agree that the war would have ended much sooner if the North had been able to seal off southern ports. As historian James McPherson points out, though, in evaluating the effectiveness of the blockade we must also ask: what would the supplying of the South have looked like in the absence of the blockade? He notes that the

The illicit trade and conflict connection

South's pre-war seaborne trade levels were significantly higher than wartime levels despite much higher supply needs during the war years. Wartime seaborne trade was less than one-third of its pre-war level. Importantly, the blockade forced the Confederacy to rely on ships built to maximize speed and stealth at the expense of cargo capacity. He concludes that the blockade succeeded in significantly reducing southern supplies, even if it did not cut them off entirely (McPherson 1988, 381–382). The blockade also forced the Confederacy to rely on less convenient ports, including Matamoros, which was far from the war's main battlefields (Surdam 2001, 6).

The Union blockade also appears relatively more successful when compared with blockades during earlier American wars. The British Royal Navy attempted to blockade American ports during the Revolutionary War and the War of 1812. As we saw early on in our story, the British lost the American War of Independence partly because they failed adequately to interdict smuggled European gunpowder and other war supplies to the colonial rebels. The Royal Navy's blockade of the eastern seaboard had more success in the War of 1812, contributing to a stalemated outcome. Fast forward to the American Civil War, where for the first time the side imposing the blockade was the victor. On balance, it seems that the Union naval blockade was porous enough to help prolong the war and provide an enormously lucrative opportunity for contraband traders, yet was also sufficiently effective ultimately to constrain Confederate fighting capacity.

Conclusion: Historical déjà vu

What is really new and different about the connection between illicit trade and conflict in the contemporary era? Not nearly as much as we are often led to believe, and indeed there may be more continuity with the past than is typically recognized. The historical parallels should not, of course, be overstated or misinterpreted, but neither should they be glossed over – as is too often the case in contemporary accounts of the illicit trade-conflict nexus. While the links between illicit trade and conflict have received considerable attention in scholarly and policy debates in recent years, it is certainly not a post-Cold War invention. It goes back not just decades (the drugs-conflict connection was an important feature of the Cold War, from Southeast Asia to South Asia and Central America (McCoy 2003)), but centuries. This has been strikingly evident by looking at America's own early history. Much to the dismay of the British imperial authorities, transatlantic smuggling kept George Washington's Continental Army supplied during the American War of Independence. Much to the delight of the British however, American colonial merchants illicitly traded with the enemy and helped keep English forces supplied during the War of 1812. No contemporary "conflict commodity," whether diamonds, ivory, or cocaine, has been more important in shaping war than was the case of smuggled Confederate cotton during the American Civil War.

Then, as now, smuggling provoked anti-smuggling initiatives that built up state policing capacities. Then, as now, it was often difficult to differentiate clearly between financial gain and political grievance in motivating and sustaining rebellion. There is certainly no evidence to suggest that today's insurgents are much more profit driven than some of their American predecessors. The grievances were real, but so too were the fortunes made from war.

Notes

1 For a critique of the "new wars" label, see Stathis Kalyvas (2001).
2 For a more detailed case study of the criminal aftermath of war, see Peter Andreas (2008).

3 For a more detailed account, from which this chapter partly draws on, see Peter Andreas (2013). Some notable historical works beyond the American case include Michael Kwass (2014); Philip Thai (2018); Eric Tagliacozzo (2005).
4 Derby wrote this letter to his ship captain, Nathaniel Silsbee, stationed at Hispaniola.
5 *Annals of Congress*, 1st Cong., 1st sess., 311.
6 On post-conflict reconstruction and the criminalized legacies of war in the western Balkans, see especially the special issue of *Problems of Post-Communism*, May–June 2004.
7 This illicit trade sometimes also included use of counterfeit American bank notes forged in Lower Canada. The problem of counterfeit American bank notes coming in from Canada predated the war, but the Canadian government only cracked down on the forgers in December 1813 when a substantial amount of bogus Lower Canadian army bills manufactured in Boston was about to be introduced via northern Vermont. See Little, *Loyalties in Conflict*, 48–49. For a more detailed discussion of counterfeiting in early America, see Stephen Mihm (2007).
8 When Madison was informed of this British favoritism toward New England in the license trade, he told Congress in February 1813 that this was an "insulting attempt on the virtue, the honor, the patriotism, and the fidelity of our brethren of the Eastern States" (Hickey 1989, 528).
9 Quoted in the *Vermont Republican* 18 April, 1814, available in, *Records of the Governor and Council of the State of Vermont*, ed. E. P. Walton (Montpelier: J. & J.M. Poland, 1878), 6:497-498.
10 Some scholars argue that the importation of luxury items actually helped the South, since it made blockade running profitable. See Robert B. Ekelund Jr. et al. (2004).
11 The most important exception to this was the handful of ships operated by the Ordinance Bureau, the only Confederate agency that directly carried out its own blockade running.

References

Alcock, Donald G. "The Best Defense is … Smuggling? Vermonters During the War of 1812," *Canadian Review of American Studies*, 25, no. 1 (Winter 1995): 73–91.
Andreas, Peter. "Criminalizing Consequences of Sanctions: Embargo Busting and It's Legacy," *International Studies Quarterly*, 49, no. 2 (June 2005).
Andreas, Peter. *Border Games: Policing the U.S.-Mexico Divide* (Ithaca: Cornell University Press, 2000).
Andreas, Peter. *Blue Helmets and Black Markets: The Business of Survival in the Siege of Sarajevo* (Ithaca: Cornell University Press, 2008), chapter 6.
Andreas, Peter. *Smuggler Nation: How Illicit Trade Made America* (New York: Oxford University Press, 2013).
Andreas, Peter. *Killer High: A History of War in Six Drugs* (New York: Oxford University Press, 2020).
Annals of Congress, 1st Cong., 1st sess., 311.
Arnson, Cynthia and William Zartman, eds, *Rethinking the Economics of War: The Intersection of Need, Creed, and Greed* (Baltimore: Johns Hopkins University Press, 2005).
Ballentine, Karen and Jake Sherman, eds., *The Political Economy of Armed Conflict: Beyond Greed and Grievance* (Boulder: Lynne Rienner, 2003).
Berdal, Mats and David M. Malone, eds. *Greed and Grievance: Economic Agendas in Civil Wars* (Boulder: Lynne Rienner, 2000).
Brandes, Stuart D. *Warhogs: A History of War Profits in America* (Lexington: University of Kentucky Press, 1997).
Crawford, Michael J. "The Navy's Campaign Against the Licensed Trade in the War of 1812," *American Neptune*, 46, no. 3 (1986).
Chauncey Ford, Washington. *The Writings of George Washington: Collected and Ed. By Worthington Chauncey Ford* (Ithaca: Cornell University Library, 2009).
Dattel, Gene. *Cotton and Race in the Making of America* (Chicago: Ivan R. Dee, 2009).
Delaney, Robert W. "Matamoros, Port of Texas During the Civil War," *Southwestern Historical Quarterly*, 58, no. 4 (April 1955): 473–474.
Ekelund, Robert B. Jr. et al. "The Unintended Consequences of Confederate Trade Legislation," *Eastern Economic Journal*, 30, no. 2 (Spring 2004): 187–205.
Fairburn, Armstrong. *Merchant Sail* (Center Lovell, ME: Fairburn Marine Educational Foundation, 1955).

The illicit trade and conflict connection

Fitzpatrick, John. *Writings of George Washington* (Washington, D: United States Government Printing Office, 1931).

Felbab-Brown, Vanda. *Shooting Up: Counterinsurgency and the War on Drugs* (Washington, DC: Brookings, 2010).

Force, Peter. *American Archives: Fourth Series, Containing a Documentary History of the English Colonies in North America from the King's Message to Parliament of March 7, 1774 to the Declaration of Independence of the United States*, ed. Peter Force (Washington, DC: Published by M. St. Clair Clarke and Peter Force, 1840), 3:1688.

Hamilton, Alexander. "Federalist No. 12," *The Federalist Papers: Alexander Hamilton, James Madison, and John Jay*, ed. Ian Shapiro (New Haven: Yale University Press, 2009).

Herring, George C. *From Colony to Superpower: US Foreign Relations since 1776* (New York: Oxford University Press, 2008).

Hickey, Donald R. *The War of 1812: A Forgotten Conflict* (Urbana: University of Illinois Press, 1989).

Huston, James A. *Logistics of Liberty: American Services of Supply in the Revolutionary War and After* (Newark: University of Delaware Press, 1991).

Irby, James A. *Backdoor at Bagdad: The Civil War on the Rio Grande* (El Paso: Texas Western Press, 1977).

Izard, George. *Official Correspondence with the Department of War: Relative to the Military Operations of the American Army under the Command of Major General Izard, on the Northern Frontier of the United States in the Years 1814 and 1815* (Philadelphia: Thomas Dobson, 1816).

Jung, Dietrich, ed. *Shadow Globalization, Ethnic Conflicts and New Wars* (London: Routledge, 2003).

Kaldor, Mary. *New and Old Wars: Organized Violence in a Global Era* (Stanford: Stanford University Press, 3rd ed. 2012).

Kalyvas, Stathis. "New and Old Civil Wars: A Valid Distinction?" *World Politics*, 54, No. 1 (October 2001).

Kan, Paul Rexton. *Drugs and Contemporary Warfare* (Washington, DC: Potomac Books, 2009).

Kwass, Michael. *Contraband: Louis Mandarin and the Making of a Global Underground* (Cambridge: Harvard University Press, 2014).

Little, John I. *Loyalties in Conflict* (Toronto: University of Toronto Press, 2008).

Mahin, Dean B. *One War at a Time: The International Dimensions of the American Civil War* (Washington, DC: Brassey's Inc., 1999).

McCoy, Alfred. *The Politics of Heroin* (Chicago: Lawrence Hill Books, 2003, revised edition).

McPherson, James M. *Battle Cry of Freedom: The Civil War Era* (New York: Oxford University Press, 1988).

Meiners, Fredericka. "The Texas Border Cotton Trade, 1862-1863," *Civil War History*, 13, no. 9 (December 1977): 293–294.

Mihm, Stephen. *A Nation of Counterfeiters: Capitalists, Con Men, and the Making of the United States* (Cambridge: Harvard University Press, 2007).

Moultrie, William. *Memoirs of the American Revolution, so far as it Related to the States of North and South Carolina, and Georgia* (New York: D. Longworth, 1802), I: 63–64.

Muller III, H.N. "A 'Traitorous and Diabolical Traffic:' The Commerce of the Champlain-Richelieu Corridor During the War of 1812," *Vermont History*, 44, no. 2 (Spring 1976).

Munkler, Herfried. *The New Wars* (Cambridge: Polity Press, 2005).

Nagle, Margaret. "The Golden Era of Smuggling," *Today Magazine* (University of Maine), December 2001/January 2002.

Naylor, R.T. *Patriots and Profiteers: Economic Warfare, Embargo Busting, and State-Sponsored Crime* (Montreal: McGill-Queens University Press, 2008, 2nd ed.).

Nuxoll, Elizabeth Miles. *Congress and the Munitions Merchants: The Secret Committee of Trade during the American Revolution, 1775–1777* (New York: Garland Publishing, 1985).

Patton, Robert H. *Patriot Pirates: The Privateer War for Freedom and Fortune in the American Revolution* (New York: Pantheon, 2008).

Pugh, Michael and Neil Cooper with Jonathan Goodhand, *War Economies in a Regional Context* (Boulder: Lynne Rienner, 2004).

Rappleye, Charles. *Sons of Providence: The Brown Brothers, the Slave Trade, and the American Revolution* (New York: Simon & Schuster, 2006).

Smillie, Ian. "What Lessons from the Kimberly Process Certification Scheme?" in Karen Ballentine and Heiko Nitzsche, eds. *Profiting from Peace: Managing the Resource Dimensions of Civil War* (Boulder: Lynne Rienner, 2005).

Smith, Joshua. "Patterns of Northern New England Smuggling, 1782–1820," in *The Early Republic and the Sea: Essays on the Naval and Maritime History of the Early United States* (Washington, DC: Brassey's, 2001).

Stephenson, Orlando W. "The Supply of Gunpowder in 1776," *American Historical Review*, 30, no. 2 (January 1925).

Strum, Harvey. "Smuggling in Maine during the Embargo and the War of 1812," *Colby Library Quarterly*, XIX, no. 2 (June 1983): 90–97.

Surdam, David G. *Northern Naval Superiority and the Economics of the American Civil War* (Columbia: University of South Carolina Press, 2001).

Tagliacozzo, Eric. *Secret Trades, Porous Borders: Smuggling and States Along a Southern Asian Frontier, 1865–1915* (New Haven: Yale University Press, 2005).

Taylor, Alan S. "The smuggling career of William King," *Maine Historical Society Quarterly*, 17 (Summer 1977): 19–38.

Taylor, Alan. *The Civil War of 1812: American Citizens, British Subjects, Irish Rebels, and Indian Allies* (New York: Vintage, 2011).

Thai, Philip. *China's War on Smuggling: Law, Economic Life, and the Making of the Modern State, 1842–1965* (New York: Columbia University Press, 2018).

The Documentary History of the Campaign upon the Niagara Frontier in the Year 1813, ed. E. Cruikshank (Welland: Tribune Office, 1905), 3: 194.

The Vermont Republican 18 April, 1814, available in, *Records of the Governor and Council of the State of Vermont*, ed. E. P. Walton (Montpelier: J. & J.M. Poland, 1878), 6: 497–498.

The Writings of George Washington from the Original Manuscript Sources, 1745–1799, ed. John C Fitzpatrick, (Washington, DC: United States Government Printing Office, 1936), 13:335.

The Writings of George Washington: 1775–1776, ed. Worthington Chauncey Ford (New York: G.P. Putnam's Sons, 1889), 3: 299.

Underwood, Rodman L. *Waters of Discord: The Union Blockade of Texas During the Civil War* (Jefferson, NC: McFarland, 2008).

Winer, Jonathan M. "Tracking Conflict Commodities and Financing," in Karen Ballentine and Heiko Nitzsche, eds. *Profiting from Peace: Managing the Resource Dimensions of Civil War* (Boulder: Lynne Rienner, 2005).

Wise, Stephen R. *Lifeline of the Confederacy* (Columbia: University of South Carolina Press, 1988).

Whitehead, Don. *Border Guard: The Story of the United States Customs Service* (New York: McGraw-Hill Book Co., 1963).

York, Neil L. "Clandestine Aid and the American Revolutionary War Effort: A Re-Examination," *Military Affairs*, 43, no. 1 (February 1979).

27

SMUGGLING, SURVIVAL, AND CIVIL WAR ECONOMIES

Aisha Ahmad

Civil wars create serious consequences for neighbouring states, such as mass displacement, weapons proliferation, and other deadly contagion effects (Lake and Rothchild, 1998; Bourne, 2005; Greenhill, 2008). One of the less obvious spillover effects of civil wars is the militarization and criminalization of economic networks in border regions. In many parts of the world, informal trading economies existed for centuries before the formation of modern state borders; however, when civil wars break out, these conflicts mutate old commercial systems into new criminal networks. In this chapter, I explain why and how civil wars alter pre-existing smuggling economies, turning the informal into the illicit.

To help the reader understand this phenomenon, I present evidence from three key countries where smuggling and civil war intersect: Afghanistan; Somalia; and Mali. An historical and political analysis of contemporary wartime smuggling economies in these three cases is essential to understanding the intersection between criminality and insurgency today. By taking seriously the effects of colonialism and Cold War interference on longstanding informal trade economies, this chapter provides needed context on both contemporary civil wars and the war economies that sustain them.

Afghanistan, Somalia, and Mali are three of the most volatile conflict zones in the world today, and each of these border regions is home to rampant smuggling and criminal activity. Drawing on over a decade of field research, my analysis reveals why these states were pre-disposed to crisis and collapse, resulting in the militarization and criminalization of the informal economies in their borderlands. My empirical observations presented in this chapter draw from the scholarly literature, as well as my own qualitative and quantitative data collected in each of these regions. My field research, conducted as part of larger global projects on civil war economies, was conducted in compliance with strict university research ethics protocols.

The chapter unfolds in the following four parts. In the first section below, I outline the historical and political origins of smuggling, specifically looking at how colonial borders affected existing economic systems in each of these three countries. Second, I show how international interference helped catalyze the eruption of civil war in Afghanistan, Somalia, and Mali. Third, I critically examine the concept of legality in contemporary civil wars, and then outline some of the features of smuggling in civil wars. In the fourth and final part, I conclude with some observations on smuggling and human survival.

DOI: 10.4324/9781003043645-27

Aisha Ahmad

Old trade routes and modern borders

In order to analyze smuggling operations in contemporary civil wars, it is first necessary to unpack the historical origins of these economic networks. Much of the existing literature on civil war economies focuses on how resources can fuel conflict processes (Collier and Hoeffler, 2004; Le Billion, 2006). Scholars such as Ross (2004), Fearon (2004), and Lujala et al. (2005) investigated the relationship between natural resources and civil war onset or duration, and found that having large mineral endowments can worsen conflict in low- and middle-income countries. Building on this core "resource curse" literature, other scholars have investigated how oil or aid resources also may produce similar consequences on conflict duration and severity (Shearer, 2000; Ross, 2006; Cotet and Tsui, 2013).

More recent developments in the civil war economy literature have focused more closely on how rebel groups finance their operations. Specifically, the "rebel governance" literature draws on insights from the resource curse scholarship, but focuses on why insurgent groups often tax and govern communities, much like states do (Hoffmann, Vlassenroot and Marchais, 2016). For example, Weinstein (2007) shows that rebels with natural resource endowments engage in more predatory violence, but insurgents who rely on taxes to stay afloat are more likely to curtail their violence and develop governance relationships with citizens. Building on these insights, Mampilly (2011) draws on years of fieldwork in multiple conflict zones to explain why rebels govern in some cases more than others. Similarly, through her extensive field research in Colombia, Arjona (2016) explains how rebels seek to rule over citizens, resulting in the emergence of an unexpected type of wartime social order.

The civil war economies literature is not, however, limited to the study of natural resources or rebel taxation. A burgeoning body of scholarship has also emerged that examines the role of private businesses in conflict zones. Shelley (2014) uncovers how corruption, organized crime, and terrorism become entangled in conflict zones around the world. Ahmad (2017) explains why and how business elites played a role in jihadist takeovers in Somalia, Afghanistan, Mali, and Iraq. Much has also been written on the relationship between organized crime and terrorism, particularly on the relationships between narcotics trafficking and insurgent or terror groups (Hutchinson and O'malley, 2007; Boeke, 2016).

This chapter builds on, but also diverges from, this literature by uncovering how these economic systems have evolved and mutated over time. The transnational criminal networks that dominate civil war economies today did not materialize out of a void. Rather, these illicit economies are often modern mutations of informal trade and transit networks that existed long before the state. This historical context is essential for understanding what is referred to as smuggling today. As this volume has made clear, smuggling is the clandestine import or export of goods across an international border, which evades the payment of trade taxes and customs duties levied by the state (Forstater, 2018). When traders skirt past government taxes and regulations at a border, we call them smugglers.

Herein lies the problem. For much of the world, the modern state and its borders are a relatively new construct, spread through the violence of colonialism, and with little consideration of social and economic realities on the ground (Griffiths, 1986). When European imperialists drew these borders across Africa, Asia, and the Americas, their goal was to carve up land and steal resources from these civilizations (Rodney, 1972). These colonial lines, often drawn on a map with a ruler, haphazardly divided ancient social and economic systems into separate territories (Asiwaju, 1985).

When postcolonial states inherited these borders decades later after regaining independence, they thus became responsible for regulating movement across these foreign-drawn lines. In

Smuggling and civil war economies

many cases, these boundaries existed on maps, but had no meaning on the ground. It is therefore unsurprising that precolonial social and economic systems often continue to play a more significant role in everyday life than the state itself (Meagher, 2005).

Nonetheless, many of these newly independent states desperately needed revenue, and therefore tried to levy import-export taxes at their borders (Bird, 2012). This move rendered informal precolonial trade networks – a primary source of income for many families – illegal (Meagher, 2014). Of course, in many cases these newly independent governments also lacked mechanisms to enforce the collection of these duties (Prichard et al., 2019). As a result, many people simply ignored these new trade taxes, and continued to move goods as they had for many hundreds of years (Boone, 2014).

The majority of these people do not see themselves as smugglers, nor do they believe their cross-border businesses are illicit or illegitimate (Reitano and Shaw, 2014). Traders and transporters in these borderlands often have centuries-old family connections along ancient trade routes, and believe in the legitimacy and appropriateness of continuing trade in their traditional ways (Bøås, 2012). Rather, it is these new borders, taxes, and regulations that often have no legitimate historical or social basis within these borderland communities.

For example, in the border region between Pakistan and Afghanistan, trade has flowed across these mountain passes for many hundreds of years before the delineation of the so-called Durand Line, drawn by British diplomat Mortimer Durand in 1893 (Omrani, 2009). Durand, who knew nothing of these ground realities, drew this line through an ancient and well-established social and economic community (Omrani, 2009). This line remains politically contentious to present day, and has produced a slew of devastating security crises.

From an economic standpoint, the Durand Line is also the origin point of the contemporary smuggling industry in this border region. In the 1960s, Pakistan's imposition of customs duties on trade inadvertently gave birth to a new smuggling industry that profited off the evasion of these taxes. Of course, traders circumventing these duties insisted that their business dealings were appropriate, rooted in both kinship and history. They argued that these caravan passes were part of the centuries-old Silk Route that connected China, Persia, and Rome, and that their families had transited goods through these mountain routes for generations.[1] For many of these businesspeople, it was not their trade that was illegitimate; it was the border and the duties that were a sham.

The Malian-Algerian border proved equally problematic. This border was drawn by French imperialists, with a ruler, and cut through the middle of the Sahara desert (Lecocq, 2010). Once again, there was no demarcation of this border on the ground, and yet it officially divided Tuareg and Moorish communities and families in the region into separate countries (Hoehne and Feyissa, 2013). This French-drawn line also cut straight through well-established and vital trade networks that had connected the Sahelian and Saharan regions (Scheele, 2012). Tuareg and Moorish traders in this border region have moved goods and gold along these ancient caravan routes for centuries (Lydon, 2009) and continue to rely on these networks to acquire everyday essentials. The French-drawn border arbitrarily cut up these old caravan routes. When the Malian and Algerian states gained independence, the line became an international border, and so the unregulated movement of goods along these routes could now be called smuggling.

Of course, few consider their historic trade to be smuggling. In fact, Tuareg and Moorish communities in this region see their everyday commercial and transport businesses as not only legitimate, but also critical to survival.[2] These communities live in remote and scarce border regions, and have received very little state support for economic development (Lecocq, 2010). In both the colonial and postcolonial periods, their relationship with the state has been distant and fraught (Kone, 2017). Unsurprisingly, the Malian-Algerian border region has also produced a plethora of disastrous security problems.

The same story applies to Somalia's troublesome borders. These modern borders cut through ancient economic networks that connected the Indian Ocean sea trade to the East African interior (Mubarak, 1997a; Ahmad, 2017). Decided by British, French, and Italian colonialists, these lines were once again drawn with a ruler on a map in the middle of a desert (Lewis, 1980). European avarice and competition over lucrative African territories led to the demarcation of these colonial borders in the late nineteenth century, which had serious political and economic consequences for the entire region (Thompson, 2015).

In terms of social and political impact, these lines divided ethnic Somalis into five different colonial polities: French Somaliland; British Somaliland; Italian Somaliland; British-colonized Kenya; and Italian-occupied Ethiopia. These divisions also had serious repercussions for the traditional trade networks that supported livelihoods across the region (Thompson, 2015). For many hundreds of years, Somalia's coastline has housed important seaport entrepôts connecting East Africa to important Indian and Middle Eastern maritime trade networks. French, Italian, and British colonial borders slashed through these well-established economic systems.

These borders carried forward into the postcolonial period, resulting in the formation of modern-day Djibouti, Somalia, Ethiopia, and Kenya (Lewis, 1980). Each of these newly independent countries was responsible for its own trade regulations and customs duties, and for controlling the movement of people and goods across these borders. While this technically turned informal trade into smuggling, in practice, the remote desert regions between these countries remained largely ungoverned. As such, most people living in these peripheral border areas – almost all who are Somalis – simply carried on with their business as usual (Rasmussen, 2017; Majidi, 2018). Like many other countries that inherited colonial borders, Somalia has also had violent and fraught relationships internally and with its neighbours (Bereketeab, 2013).

In each of these three cases, European colonialists created absurd borders that divided and disrupted well established social and economic systems. Ancient trading economies existed in these regions over many centuries, and had no connection to the colonial borders that were forced upon them. This historical context is essential for understanding the origins of smuggling economies, well before the outbreak of modern civil wars.

The road to civil war

Having established where each of these smuggling economies came from, it is necessary next to outline why and how civil wars erupted in the cases examined here, and how these civil wars then further mutated these economic systems, turning the informal into the illicit. This historical political analysis requires an evaluation of the consequences of both inherited colonial borders and aggressive Cold War interference. It is no surprise that the disastrous civil wars in Afghanistan, Somalia, and Mali all occurred after the Cold War. Close examination of these three cases reveals that these civil wars were the result of sustained external interference by foreign powers.

Afghanistan is arguably a quintessential case. The decade-long 1979–1989 Soviet military invasion and American-backed mujahideen rebellion left over a million people dead, and millions more injured or displaced (Edwards, 2002). The Soviets irreparably ruined much of Afghanistan's agricultural land, in an effort to starve the population into submission (Byman, 2015). Meanwhile, the United States colluded with Pakistan to traffic weapons and supplies through the smuggling channels in the mountains (Rubin, 2000). Because the Soviets had scorched orchards and farmlands across Afghanistan, farmers turned to hardy and reliable opium

Smuggling and civil war economies

crops to stay afloat (Kreutzmann, 2007). The smuggling community in the Pakistan-Afghanistan border region soon found itself moving guns into Afghanistan, and drugs out (Ahmad, 2017).

When the Soviets finally withdrew in defeat, the war-ravaged country proved unable to recover from such brutal political and economic devastation (Byman, 2015). Then-President Mohammad Najibullah attempted to steward a transition between 1989 and 1992, but he had remained dependent on Soviet support to stay afloat (Cordovez and Harrison, 1995). This transitional government was also strongly opposed by the mujahideen rebels who resented Najibullah's communist and Soviet affiliations (Rubin, 2013).

The abrupt end of the Cold War catalyzed another wave of conflict. By 1992, Soviet support had dried up, and Najibullah's government went bankrupt. Between 1992 and 1996, Afghanistan descended into a civil war among the former mujahideen rebel factions, many backed by neighbouring Pakistan (Akhtar, 2008). Bodies piled in the streets and rape gangs terrorized women and children from rival ethnic and religious communities. This ethnic civil war was so brutal that it eventually led to the rise of the Taliban, and further exacerbated militarization and radicalization in the Pakistan-Afghanistan border region (Goodson, 2001).

After both the Americans and Soviets lost interest in Afghanistan following the end of the Cold War, Pakistan continued its aggressive, blatant interference via the unruly border (Akhtar, 2008). The Pakistan-Afghanistan border region remained the chief conduit of this interference, and the epicentre of both insurgency and illicit trade. The infiltration of Arab terrorist networks in Afghanistan culminated in the devastating 9/11 attacks, followed by a 20-year American-led occupation. After 40 years and repeated international interventions, Afghanistan has not recovered from this legacy of external interference and internal fragmentation.

Somalia suffered a similar fate. Although Somalia did not suffer a full-scale superpower invasion during the Cold War, it did become dangerously entangled with both the Soviets and the Americans. From 1969 until the late 1970s, dictator and then-President, Siad Barre adopted a socialist political and economic platform in order to win desperately needed foreign support from the Soviet Union (Samatar, 2016). However, Barre was also obsessed with redrawing the ruler-drawn colonial borders that divided ethnic Somalis into different countries (Mukhtar, 2003). In 1977, Barre launched a military offensive to recapture the Ogaden region of Ethiopia, and act that provoked international condemnation, including from the Soviets. This border war not only failed, but the Ogaden War also ended Somalia's relationship with the Soviet Union.

Given his dependence on foreign support, Barre was therefore forced to court an American alliance (Mukhtar, 2003). To prove his new loyalty and secure a desperately needed IMF loan, in the early 1980s Barre implemented a number of drastic economic reforms that reversed his previous socialist policies (Mubarak, 1997b; Samatar, 2008). Fearing disloyalty and opposition, he also began favouring his own clan faction and violently targeting his rivals, which only worsened economic disparity and increased clan conflict (Lewis, 2008).

The end of the Cold War sent Somalia into a tailspin. The combination of dwindling foreign support and haphazard IMF-imposed economic reforms culminated in an economic crisis. With no superpower to bail him out, the Barre government went bankrupt. Hawiye clan militias seized control of Mogadishu, and Barre's Darod-Marehan clan were butchered in the streets. The government dissolved in 1991 and Barre fled. The Somali countryside was overrun by armed groups that created their own fiefdoms, each run by a local clan warlord (Makinda, 1999). An ill-timed drought compounded the crisis; together, civil war and famine produced a devastating humanitarian disaster.

Between 1992 and 1995, the UN launched an intervention in Somalia, which aimed to protect food aid deliveries and restore political order. Instead, these aid convoys unwittingly helped empower the reigning Hawiye-Abgal, while marginalizing the rival Hawiye-Habr-Gidr clan (Ahmad, 2012). In response, the aid convoys were attacked, and the UN was dragged into a clan conflict it did not understand. Food aid became a wartime currency, and traditional traders grew rich by looting and trafficking these sacks of grain. After the UN withdrew in failure in 1995, Somalia descended into a brutal clan-based civil war.

In 2006, a local movement of Islamic courts overthrew the clan warlords, established a new government, and briefly restored peace and security (Barnes and Harun, 2007). By 2007, however, this Islamic government was quickly overthrown by a new US-backed Ethiopian invasion (Samatar, 2007). Not only did this external interference plummet Somalia back into a clan-based civil war, but it also gave birth to a new jihadist insurgency, al-Shabaab, that continues to control large swaths of the countryside (Ahmad, 2017). Despite countless international interventions, or perhaps because of them, Somalia has now been at war for three decades.

The Malian case was, for many years, heralded as a shining example of post-Cold War success, even after suffering years of foreign interference, brutal IMF-imposed structural adjustment policies, economic upheaval, and military dictatorship.[3] Unlike Afghanistan and Somalia, Mali survived the end of the Cold War without a civil war. Despite widespread protests and a military coup in 1991, the country avoided either a return to authoritarianism or a civil war. In the 1990s, analysts were quick to hail Mali as a grand success (Storholt, 2001).

These optimistic observers did not, however, pay close attention to what was happening in the northern border region at these critical time periods. While Mali appeared to be a democratic success, severe conflict processes had already developed in the north of Mali and in Algeria, which would eventually catalyze a devastating civil war. First of all, during the Cold War, then-President Moussa Traoré had clamped down on the restive Tuareg population in northern Mali, leaving them impoverished and marginalized (Lecocq and Klute, 2013). When the Cold War ended, these repressed populations pushed back, once between 1990 and 1995, and again between 2007 and 2009 (Lecocq and Klute, 2013). While the government quelled these Tuareg revolts, these repeated uprisings revealed a systemic failure by the Malian government to control and integrate its northern border region into the country. The French-drawn border between Mali and Algeria and decades of western-backed dictatorship guaranteed conflict with these northern communities.

Second, while Mali was relatively peaceful in the 1990s, neighbouring Algeria was not.[4] In fact, the 1991–2002 civil war in Algeria gave birth to a jihadist movement that had serious implications for Mali. When Algerian government pushed back its jihadists, they retreated into the Saharan hinterland (Bøås, 2015). By 2002, the extremist Salafist Group for Preaching and Combat (GSPC) was the only significant jihadist group left in Algeria, and it had retreated south towards the ungoverned Malian border region. On its heels, the GSPC launched a lucrative kidnapping-for-ransom campaign (Bøås, 2015). With its ransom moneys, these Algerian jihadists then built relationships with both Tuareg rebel leaders and smugglers in the border region. By 2006, the GSPC has transformed into Al-Qaeda in the Islamic Maghreb (AQIM), and emerged as the leading terrorist group in the region, with strong links to smuggling networks in northern Mali. Therefore, while democracy in Bamako appeared politically stable, an unprecedented conflict was fomenting in the restive northern border region.

The third major catalyst of the 2012 Malian crisis came not from neighbouring Algeria, but from nearby Libya. This Libyan-Malian connection had been developing for many decades, as disenfranchised Malian Tuaregs long sought refuge and economic opportunities in oil-rich Libya. Notably, many young Tuareg men from this Malian diaspora had found jobs in Muammar Gaddafi's paramilitary Islamic Legion (Shaw, 2013). As a result, when in 2011

NATO launched a military operation that toppled Gaddafi and plummeted Libya into a devastating civil war, the Malian Tuareg diaspora fled Libya. At this time, many Malian Tuareg who had been living in Libya returned home to northern Mali with advanced weapons and training (Marsh, 2017).

The NATO intervention therefore not only collapsed the Libyan state, but also catalyzed the civil war in Mali (Ronen, 2013; Shaw, 2013). The evidence suggests that returning diaspora fighters from Libya joined forces with Tuareg rebels and their new AQIM allies, and in 2012, launched a countrywide separatist campaign (Boeke and de Valk, 2019). Since this uprising, Mali has become one of the most dangerous and extreme conflict zones in the world today.

Each of these cases reveals an important underlying fact. Civil wars are international phenomena. Not only did these countries inherit problematic colonial borders, but foreign parties also incited and inflamed conflicts inside their already fraught borders. Afghanistan, Somalia, and Mali all collapsed under the weight of these external pressures. The causes of these domestic political crises were international, and so it is not surprising that their ramifications cross borders.

It should now be clear that the sophisticated transnational smuggling networks in contemporary conflict zones do not originate out of the ether at the moment war breaks out. Rather, these are modern mutations of longstanding informal economic systems, many of which have existed and evolved over hundreds of years, and have adapted to survive multiple external shocks. Civil wars, therefore, do not cause smuggling; rather, these conflicts further mutate longstanding informal trading networks into new militarized and criminalized borderland economies.

Legality in lawless lands

Understanding these criminal economies requires a critical analysis of what legality means in a civil war. Law is a manifestation of power. For example, European imperialists created laws that allowed them to steal from and enslave local people. These moral crimes were legal because those in power wrote the laws. Indeed, law and justice are often incongruent. Yet, in all modern states, the government is supposed to define rules and enforce compliance, and this coercive power is the cornerstone of modern political order-making. However, when the power behind that order weakens, or collapses, the law loses its hold over society. When the rule of law is absent, contested, or unenforceable, it can be difficult to determine what is legal or illegal, or whether these terms even make sense.

Of course, most contemporary conflict zones are hubs of both insurgent violence and criminal activity. When rebel groups compete for power and territory, they necessarily require resources and supplies to finance their war effort: guns; bullets; food; and medical supplies. To acquire these supplies, rebels tax, steal, pillage, divert, swindle, mine, and traffic. Much of the existing scholarship on smuggling in civil wars therefore investigates the intersections of criminality, insurgency, and terrorism (Cornell, 2005). When researchers "follow the money," they are investigating how armed groups capture diamond mines (Ross, 2006), divert humanitarian aid (Ahmad, 2012), traffic drugs (Björnehed, 2004), or extort civilians (Sabates-Wheeler and Verwimp, 2014). In order to make sense of these civil war economies, however, it is necessary to reflect critically on the concept of legality.

In each of the three cases in this chapter, state weakness and failure produced legal grey zones in the borderlands. For the smuggler in northern Kidal, the Malian government sitting in southern Bamako has no right to interfere with his longstanding trade relations. The businessman in Spin Boldak has little time for economic policy debates in either Kabul or

Islamabad. The trader in Gedo region is not interested in tariffs and regulations that benefit Somali politicians sitting in Mogadishu. These cases reveal a disparity between what governments declares to be law, and what communities consider to be appropriate.

The outbreak of civil war is an intensification of this disparity. Rebellions usually happen when communities hit a breaking point, turning tensions into violence (Keen, 2000). It is often a justice motive that sparks rebels to take up arm against the government, based on a perceived disparity between benefits and entitlements (Gurr, 1970; Welch, 1993). When rebels challenge the state for the right to rule, not only is there no longer a monopoly on the use of force, there is also an active competition over the system itself. Regardless of which side is officially recognized by the international community, a civil war is evidence of a violent domestic disagreement about who has the right to rule.

This does not mean that the rebel challenger needs to articulate or codify an alternative set of laws. The act of violently contesting power inherently implies a challenge to the rules and regulations of the state. When rebels seize control of territory from the state, they may declare certain contraband goods legal, or government taxes forfeit. They may also impose new taxes and regulations of their own (Mampilly, 2011; Sabates-Wheeler and Verwimp, 2014; Arjona, Kasfir and Mampilly, 2015; Arjona, 2016; Revkin, 2020). Communities that are caught between government and rebel actors in this military contest are often forced to accept whatever version of law is imposed on them.

Of course, it is more likely that rebellions will emerge in regions where the government already has less influence and where its ability to enforce its laws is already weak (Herbst, 2001). Peripheral regions and borderlands that are located far from government centres of control are often more vulnerable, especially if there are pre-existing grievances that insurgents can coopt. As rebel challengers assume control over these territories, they necessarily build new relationships with the informal economic communities in these borderlands, whether through incentives or coercion (Malik and Gallien, 2020).

For the informal traders who have long operated in these borderlands, the outbreak of civil war presents a slew of new challenges and opportunities. There are new forms of rebel extortion and taxation, as well as dramatic shocks to supply and demand in local and regional markets. However, civil wars also often attract new connections to transnational criminal organizations, and greater opportunities in illicit trade (May 2017; Adetiba, 2019).

To start, it is common for cash-strapped rebels to shake down businesses for "taxes," so that they can finance their war effort. For smugglers who have made a living off of tax-free trade, rebel taxes can eliminate their competitive edge. Even more, when there are multiple, competing armed groups operating in a border region, a businessperson can get taxed by each faction along a trade route. These compound rebel taxes dramatically increase the price of goods at point of sale, and can have a crushing effect on an entire smuggling industry (Ahmad, 2017).

Civil wars do not, however, produce only debits. In many cases, rebels also create new opportunities for businesses, especially in illicit trade. Not only can armed groups provide protection for traffickers operating in active conflict zones, but they often also bring forward new investments and connections that can expand business opportunities. As noted earlier, AQIM earned tens of millions of dollars in kidnapping for ransom, which then allowed it to invest in revamping the smuggling industry in the Malian-Algerian border region (Bøås, 2015). Within a few years, the traditional smuggling community in northern Mali had mutated into the hub of the cigarette trafficking across West Africa (Raineri and Strazzari, 2015). This success then drew the attention of even bigger transnational criminal organizations. With AQIM and other armed groups providing cover, the Malian-Algerian border region became a conduit for cocaine trafficking, connecting Latin American drug cartels to European markets (Ellis, 2009).

Smuggling and civil war economies

Of course, it is not only rebels who become entangled in criminal activity. With such lucrative opportunities available, many political actors on the side of the state also become heavily involved in organized crime. In Mali, for example, the leader of the pro-Government *Groupe autodéfense touareg Imghad et alliés* (GATIA) has been heavily implicated in narcotics trafficking (International Crisis Group, 2018). In Afghanistan, former President Hamid Karzai's brother was known for running a massive heroin operation in Kandahar (Risen, 2008). State officials in Guinea Bissau are allegedly heavily involved in narcotics trafficking, allowing Latin American drug cartels to move product into West Africa an onwards to European markets (*BBC News*, 2020).

State officials can also get incredibly rich through a plethora of other corrupt activities, such as looting state coffers and pilfering international aid. Tens of millions of dollars simply went missing in Karzai's government (Epstein, 2011; Rosenberg, 2013; Press, 2019). In Somalia, parliamentary positions were often treated as opportunities to loot foreign aid.[5] When the rule of law functionally has collapsed, it is often players that have access to the halls of power that are the most heavily engaged in criminality and corruption.

When civil war breaks out, state actors, transnational criminal organizations, rebel groups, terrorists, and ordinary citizens all become embroiled in these complex conflict economies (L. Shelley, 2014; Ahmad, 2015). Despite fighting each other on the battlefield, sometimes these actors even make business deals across enemy lines. In Mali, for example, there is evidence that bitterly opposed ethnic factions have forged secret "gentlemen's agreements" to ensure their respective trafficking routes are not disrupted as they go to war against each other.[6] As Andreas (2008) shows, even international peacekeeping forces have found themselves entangled with criminal organizations and predatory militias, even as they try to curtail these pernicious actors on the battlefield (Andreas 2008).

Civil wars not only involve a diverse set of competing actors, but also a messy mix of licit and illicit activities. Not all of the business activities in a civil war economy are dangerous or criminal. People living in a conflict zone still need to buy onions, shoes, gasoline, and cell phone chargers. A trucker may transport sugar and flour on one route, and cocaine and assault rifles on another. Rebels may illegally acquire weapons from states or private suppliers, but then may barter these arms in the marketplace to buy other essential supplies, like blankets or medicine (Adetiba, 2019). Even seemingly obvious illicit activities, like human trafficking, often have a more complex story at ground level. For example, according to ECOWAS regulations, it would be perfectly legal for a Burkinabe citizen to travel through Niger to the Malian-Algerian border without a visa; a bus company taking migrants to this border point would have broken no laws, even though it is part of a transit route connected to human smugglers in Libya (Opanike, Aduloju and Adenipekun, 2015). Similar legal questions can arise with other types of smuggling. Some border points are unregulated, whereas others may be subject to laws that have no enforcement, or that have competing claims of authority and legitimacy.

When civil wars break out, there is a challenge to the authority of the state to create and enforce such laws. Under these conditions, it may be less useful to focus on teasing out what are legal versus illegal activities, especially in places where the rule of law functionally has collapsed. Rather, it makes more sense to examine how the shock of civil war forces local business actors to adapt to survive, including in ways that may create, empower, and enrich transnational criminal cartels. This dynamic adaptation among multiple, interdependent actors better explains the complex civil war economies we see today.

Aisha Ahmad

Smuggling and survival

For most people, civil war brings poverty, loss, and terrible hardships. For savvy traders and transporters, however, war can also bring about new opportunities for wealth generation. To succeed under difficult wartime conditions, smugglers must be able to adapt quickly to new market demands, locally and regionally. They must strike deals with armed groups across multiple turfs, and buy off crooked politicians, police officers, and border control agents. After greasing these wheels, they must hire or negotiate enough muscle to secure their convoys from bandits and other rivals on the roads. Finally, they must push their product and ensure their buyers can and will pay.

The financial rewards of this hustle can be lavish (Ahmad, 2017). Smugglers who demonstrate competence and success in navigating goods through a conflict zone can crush their competition, and quickly grow into wartime tycoons. With their trafficking windfalls, they form monopolies, invest in new business ventures, and build multi-company conglomerates. These powerful mafias are then able to use their economic might to influence conflict dynamics on the ground. They not only forge agreements with armed groups, but also with corrupt government actors on the take.

These business elites also play a critical role in the lives of the ordinary people living in wartime conditions: the truckers, wholesalers, merchants, shopkeepers, and even tea-sellers on the streets. Together, these diverse characters co-create the business ecosystem of the civil war economy, one that is truly interdependent. While relationships among business tycoons, rebel groups, and ordinary citizens are unequal, there is also an overall symbiosis in this business ecosystem that keep goods and cash moving.

Consider, for example, a smuggling tycoon who makes a deal with a rebel coalition to move his product, allowing each rebel faction in the alliance to take a cut in exchange for their "security." With these funds, the commanders pay their foot soldiers, who then buy liquor from their local shopkeeper. The smuggler also pays off a local government official, who distributes a cut to his cronies to ensure their loyalty. These cronies then refurbish their old jeeps at their local garage. When the smuggler finally delivers his convoy and receives his windfall, he refurbishes his home, creating new jobs and construction contracts. Of course, there is coercion and theft throughout this system. There are also everyday business activities that keep the money supply moving. When the tycoon earns and spends, the contractor, liquor store owner, driver, bricklayer, mechanic, shoemaker, and tea-seller all go home with a little extra in their pockets.

If this smuggling tycoon and the armed groups disappeared today, the cash flow would freeze and those people who are dependent on this illicit business ecosystem would go hungry. Nonetheless, narcotics, human, and weapons trafficking have a devastating effect on local and regional security, and these businesses worsen violence and human rights abuses against civilians. From both a moral and security standpoint, this unhealthy economic activity needs to stop. Indeed, the vast majority of people living in these war zones would heartily agree. In fact, even most ordinary traders and transporters who are caught up in these dangerous businesses want to transition to a safer, licit option, if another profitable opportunity was made available.[7] The challenge then becomes supporting safe and sustainable alternative livelihoods for people living in these troubled borderlands.

It would be erroneous, however, to frame the economies of war-torn border regions solely in terms of criminality and corruption. Transnational criminal organizations and trafficking tycoons are not the only businesspeople in these civil war economies. Ordinary people living under wartime conditions also hustle to protect their lives and livelihoods. They respond to

Smuggling and civil war economies

fluctuations in supply and demand, adapt to changing battlefield conditions, and build un-expected alliances to advance their security and prosperity. Even under extraordinarily challenging circumstances, human beings continue to truck, barter, and trade, in a demonstration of human resilience.

This local economic adaptation is also often a response to serious environmental and climate pressures. In each of the three cases outlined in this chapter, threats to agricultural land forced local economies to adapt (Raleigh, 2010; Ogallo et al., 2018; Privara and Privarova, 2019). During the nineteenth century, the British deforested swaths of the Pakistan-Afghanistan border region (Tucker, 1983), causing lasting desertification and soil salinization (Faiza et al., 2017). Climate change now compounds the damage caused by this historic British theft and destruction. Somalia and Mali also suffered colonial theft, and are now both located in deadly climate change red zones. Both of these countries are experiencing rapidly increasing droughts and losses of arable lands (Doucet, 2019). These environmental pressures, caused almost entirely by wealthy foreign powers, have pushed already fragile ecosystems to the brink of collapse. Naturally, human beings living in these regions must adapt their economic activities to adjust to this barrage of externally imposed political, economic, and environmental shocks.

Given this fragility, it would therefore be disastrous for the international community simply to attack wartime business ecosystems that are currently sustaining vulnerable communities. Rather, human beings in these troubled regions need economic and environmental alternatives. This is not a security problem that can be solved with force. The solutions to these problems lie in sustained investment, climate change adaptation, and new seed technologies. Most people living under these difficult conditions would welcome the development of safe and stable economic options.

Finally, it is easy to label drug smugglers and arms traffickers in unruly border regions as nefarious criminals. Yes, these are serious economic and security problems. Nonetheless, this use of language has consequences. It allows decision-makers to call the rich cocaine-sniffing European partygoer a victim, while labeling the 15-year-old Malian truck driver a villain worthy of an air strike. It labels Somali and Afghan shopkeepers arms trafficker, while ignoring the fact that the weapons they are selling were surreptitiously brought into their countries by America, Russia, and other great powers. Indeed, it requires an audacious level of intellectual and moral dishonesty to wax poetic about illegality in fragile border regions, while ignoring the sheer magnitude of colonial theft and illegal interventions these countries have suffered. Any honest conversation about these serious security and economic issues must therefore include a frank discussion about reparations.

Notes

1 Author fieldwork and interviews with traders in Pakistan-Afghanistan border region.
2 Author fieldwork, Mali. See also Bensassi et al. (2016).
3 Political leadership played a role in Mali's transition. In March 1991, the military coup led by Amadou Toumani Toure deposed Traoré. Yet, instead of claiming power for himself, Toure set up a transitional council to usher in a new democratic government. Toure stepped down from power, and in 1991 Alpha Oumar Konaré became Mali's first democratically elected President.
4 The Algerian Civil War began when the ruling National Liberation Front (FLN) party realized it was set to lose the first-ever Algerian election to the popular Islamist Salvation Front (FIS). The FLN cancelled the election and banned the FIS, sparking a new Islamist rebellion.
5 Author's fieldwork, Nairobi, February 2013.
6 Author's fieldwork, Bamako, February 2018.
7 Interviews with arms smugglers in Afghanistan and Somalia.

Aisha Ahmad

Works cited

Adetiba, T. (2019) 'Transnational syndicates and cross-border transfer of small arms and light weapons in West Africa: A threat to regional security', *Journal of African Union Studies*, 8(1), pp. 93–112.

Ahmad, A. (2012) 'Agenda for peace or budget for war? Evaluating the economic impact of international intervention in Somalia', *International Journal*, 67(2), pp. 313–331.

Ahmad, A. (2015) 'The security bazaar: Business interests and Islamist power in Civil War Somalia', *International Security*, 39(3), pp. 89–117. doi: 10.1162/ISEC_a_00187.

Ahmad, A. (2017) *Jihad and Co. Black Markets and Islamist Power*. New York: Oxford University Press.

Akhtar, N. (2008) 'Pakistan, Afghanistan, and the Taliban', *International Journal on World Peace*, 25(4), pp. 49–73.

Andreas, P. (2008) *Blue Helmets and Black Markets: The Business of Survival in the Siege of Sarajevo*. New York: Cornell University Press.

Arjona, A. (2016) *Rebelocracy*. New York: Cambridge University Press.

Arjona, A., Kasfir, N. and Mampilly, Z. (2015) *Rebel Governance in Civil War*. New York: Cambridge University Press.

Asiwaju, A. (1985) *Partitioned Africans: Ethnic Relations Across Africa's International Boundaries, 1884–1984*. London: Hurst.

Barnes, C. and Harun, H. (2007) 'The Rise and Fall of Mogadishu's Islamic Courts Union', *Journal of Eastern African Studies*, 1(2), pp. 151–160.

BBC News (2020) 'Cocaine and Guinea-Bissau: How Africa's "narco-state" is trying to kick its habit', 28 May. Available at: https://www.bbc.com/news/world-africa-52569130 (Accessed: 22 February 2021).

Bensassi, S. et al. (2016) 'Algeria-Mali trade: The normality of informality', *Middle East Development Journal*, 8(2), pp. 161–183.

Bereketeab, R. (ed.) (2013) *The Horn of Africa: Intra-State and Inter-State Conflicts and Security*. London: Uppsala, Sweden: Pluto Press; In cooperation with Nordiska Afrikainstitutet.

Bird, R. (2012) *Taxation and Development: What Have We Learned from Fifty Years of Research?* Working Paper 1. International Centre for Tax and Development.

Björnehed, E. (2004) 'Narco-terrorism: The merger of the war on drugs and the war on terror', *Global Crime*, 6(3/4), pp. 305–324. doi: 10.1080/17440570500273440.

Bøås, M. (2012) 'Castles in the sand: Informal networks and power brokers in the northern Mali periphery', in Utas M. (ed.) *African Conflicts and Informal Power: Big Men and Networks*. New York: Zed Books, pp. 119–136.

Bøås, M. (2015) 'Crime, coping, and resistance in the Mali-Sahel periphery', *African Security*, 8(4), pp. 299–319. doi: 10.1080/19392206.2015.1100506.

Boeke, S. (2016) 'Al Qaeda in the Islamic Maghreb: Terrorism, insurgency, or organized crime?', *Small Wars & Insurgencies*, 27(5), pp. 914–936. doi: 10.1080/09592318.2016.1208280.

Boeke, S. and de Valk, G. (2019) 'The unforeseen 2012 crisis in Mali: the diverging outcomes of risk and threat analyses', *Studies in Conflict & Terrorism*. doi: 10.1080/1057610X.2019.1592356.

Boone, C. (2014) *Property and Political Order in Africa*. Cambridge: Cambridge University Press.

Bourne, M. (2005) 'The proliferation of small arms and light weapons', in Krahmann E. (eds) *New Threats and New Actors in International Security*. New York: Palgrave MacMillan, pp. 155–176.

Byman, D. (2015) *Al Qaeda, the Islamic State, and the Global Jihadist Movement: What Everyone Needs to Know*. New York: Oxford University Press.

Collier, P. and Hoeffler, A. (2004) 'Greed and grievance in civil war', *Oxford Economic Papers*, 56(4), pp. 563–595.

Cordovez, D. and Harrison, S. (1995) *Out of Afghanistan: The Inside Story of the Soviet Withdrawal*. Oxford: Oxford University Press.

Cornell, S. E. (2005) 'The interaction of narcotics and conflict', *Journal of Peace Research*, 42(6), pp. 751–760. doi: 10.1177/0022343305057895.

Cotet, A. M. and Tsui, K. K. (2013) 'Oil and conflict: what does the cross country evidence really show?', *American Economic Journal: Macroeconomics*, 5(1), pp. 49–80.

Doucet, L. (2019) *The Battle on the Frontline of Climate Change in Mali*. BBC. Available at: https://www.bbc.com/news/the-reporters-46921487.

Edwards, D. B. (2002) *Before Taliban: Genealogies of the Afghan Jihad*. Berkeley: University of California Press. Available at: http://link.library.utoronto.ca/eir/EIRdetail.cfm?Resources__ID=39059&T=F (Accessed: 26 June 2016).

Smuggling and civil war economies

Ellis, S. (2009) 'West Africa's international drug trade', *African Affairs*, 108(431), pp. 171–196.

Epstein, J. (2011) *Audit: Karzai Blocking Cash Oversight.* Politico. Available at: https://www.politico.com/story/2011/07/audit-karzai-blocking-cash-oversight-059453.

Faiza, N. et al. (2017) 'Giant deforestation leads to drastic eco-environmental devastating effects since 2000: A case study of Pakistan', *The Journal of Animal & Plant Sciences*, 27(4), pp. 1366–1376.

Fearon, J. D. (2004) 'Why do some civil wars last so much longer than others?' *Journal of Peace Research*, 41, pp. 275–301. doi: 10.1177/0022343304043770.

Forstater, M. (2018) *Illicit financial flows, trade misinvoicing, and multinational tax avoidance: The same or different?* CGD Policy Paper 123. Center for Global Development.

Goodson, L. P. (2001) *Afghanistan's Endless War: State Failure, Regional Politics, and the Rise of the Taliban.* Seattle: University of Washington Press.

Greenhill, K. (2008) 'Strategic engineered migration as a weapon of war', *Civil Wars*, 10(1), pp. 6–21.

Griffiths, I. (1986) 'The scramble for Africa: Inherited political boundaries', *The Geographical Journal*, 152(2), pp. 204–216.

Gurr, T. R. (1970) *Why Men Rebel.* Princeton: Princeton University Press.

Herbst, J. (2001) *States and Power in Africa: Comparative Lessons in Authority and Control.* Princeton: Princeton University Press.

Hoehne, M. V. and Feyissa, D. (2013) 'Centering borders and borderlands: The evidence from Africa', in Korf, B. and Raeymaekers, T. (eds) *Violence on the Margins.* Palgrave Macmillan US (Palgrave Series in African Borderlands Studies), pp. 55–84. doi: 10.1057/9781137333995_3.

Hoffmann, K., Vlassenroot, K. and Marchais, G. (2016) 'Taxation, stateness and armed groups: Public authority and resource extraction in Eastern Congo: Taxation and public authority in Eastern Congo', *Development and Change*, 47(6), pp. 1434–1456. doi: 10.1111/dech.12275.

Hutchinson, S. and O'malley, P. (2007) 'A crime–terror nexus? thinking on some of the links between terrorism and criminality', *Studies in Conflict & Terrorism*, 30(12), pp. 1095–1107. doi: 10.1080/105761 00701670870.

International Crisis Group (2018) *Drug trafficking, violence, and politics in Northern Mali.* Africa No. 267. International Crisis Group.

Keen, D. (2000) 'Incentives and disincentives for violence', in M. Berdal and D. M. Malone (eds) *Greed and Grievance: Economic Agendas in Civil Wars.* Boulder, CO: Lynne Rienner, pp. 19–43.

Kone, K. (2017) 'A southern view on the Tuareg rebellions in Mali', *African Studies Review*, 60(1), pp. 53–75.

Kreutzmann, H. (2007) 'Afghanistan and the opium world market: Poppy production and trade', *Iranian Studies*, 40(5), pp. 605–621. doi: 10.1080/00210860701667688.

Lake, D. A. and Rothchild, D. S. (eds) (1998) *The International Spread of Ethnic Conflict: Fear, Diffusion, and Escalation.* Princeton, NJ: Princeton University Press.

Le Billion, P. (2006) *Fuelling War: Natural Resources and Armed Conflict.* New York: Routledge.

Lecocq, B. (2010) *Disputed Desert: Decolonisation, Competing Nationalisms and Tuareg Rebellions in Northern Mali.* Leiden, The Netherlands: Koninklijke Brill.

Lecocq, B. and Klute, G. (2013) 'Tuareg separatism in Mali', *International Journal: Canada's Journal of Global Policy Analysis*, 68(3), pp. 424–434. doi: 10.1177/0020702013505431.

Lewis, I. M. (1980) *A Modern History of Somalia: Nation and State in the Horn of Africa.* London: Longman.

Lewis, I. M. (2008) *Understanding Somalia and Somaliland: Culture, History, Society.* London: Hurst & Co.

Lujala, P., Gleditsch, N. P. and Gilmore, E. (2005) 'A diamond curse?', *Journal of Conflict Resolution*, 49, pp. 538–562. doi: 10.1177/0022002705277548.

Lydon, G. (2009) *On Trans-Saharan Trails: Islamic Law, Trade Networks, and Cross-cultural Exchange in Nineteenth-Century Western Africa.* Cambridge: Cambridge University Press.

Majidi, N. (2018) 'Community dimensions of smuggling: The case of Afghanistan and Somalia', *The ANNALS of the American Academy of Political and Social Science*, 676(1), pp. 97–113.

Makinda, S. M. (1999) 'Clan conflict and factionalism in Somalia', in Rich P. B. (ed.) *Warlords in International Relations.* London: Palgrave MacMillan, pp. 120–139.

Malik, A. and Gallien, M. (2020) 'Border economies of the Middle East: Why do they matter for political economy?', *Review of International Political Economy*, 27(3), pp. 732–762.

Mampilly, Z. (2011) *Rebel Rulers: Insurgent Governance and Civilian Life During War.* New York: Cornell University Press.

Marsh, N. (2017) 'Brothers came back with weapons: The effects of arms proliferation from Libya', *PRISM*, 6(4), pp. 78–97.

May, C. (2017) *Transnational Crime and the Developing World*. Washington, DC: Global Financial Integrity.

Meagher, K. (2005) 'Social capital or analytical liability? Social networks and African informal economies', *Global Networks*, 5(3).

Meagher, K. (2014) 'Smuggling ideologies: From criminalization to hybrid governance in African clandestine economies', *African Affairs*, 113(453), pp. 497–517.

Mubarak, J. A. (1997a) 'The "hidden hand" behind the resilience of the stateless economy of Somalia', *World Development*, 25(12), pp. 2027–2041.

Mubarak, J. A. (1997b) 'The "hidden hand" behind the resilience of the stateless economy of Somalia', *World Development*, 25(12), pp. 2027–2041.

Mukhtar, M. H. (2003) *Historical Dictionary of Somalia*. Oxford: Scarecrow Press.

Ogallo, L. et al. (2018) 'Climate change projections and the associated potential impacts for Somalia', *American Journal of Climate Change*, 7(2).

Omrani, B. (2009) 'The Durand Line: History and problems of the Afghan-Pakistan border', *Asian Affairs*, 40(2), pp. 177–195. doi: 10.1080/03068370902871508.

Opanike, A., Aduloju, A. and Adenipekun, L. (2015) '*COWAS protocol on free movement and trans-border security in West Africa*', Covenant University Journal of Politics and International Affairs, 3(1). doi:10.41 72/2169-0170.1000154 A

Press, K. G., The Associated (2019) *Afghanistan's Karzai says American cash fed corruption, Military Times*. Available at: https://www.militarytimes.com/flashpoints/2019/12/11/afghanistans-karzai-says-american-cash-fed-corruption/ (Accessed: 22 February 2021).

Prichard, W. et al. (2019) *Innovations in tax compliance: Conceptual framework (Enforcement, Facilitation, and Trust)*. Policy Research Working Paper WPS9032. Washington: The World Bank.

Privara, A. and Privarova, M. (2019) 'Nexus between climate change, displacement, and conflict: Afghanistan Case', *Sustainability*, 11(20).

Raineri, L. and Strazzari, F. (2015) 'State, secession, and Jihad: the micropolitical economy of conflict in Northern Mali', *African Security*, 8(4), pp. 249–271.

Raleigh, C. (2010) 'Political marginalization, climate change, and conflict in African Sahel states', *International Studies Review*, 12(1), pp. 69–86.

Rasmussen, J. (2017) *Sweet secrets: Sugar smuggling and state formation in the Kenya-Somalia borderlands*. DIIS Working Paper 2017: 11. Danish Institute for International Studies.

Reitano, T. and Shaw, M. (2014) 'People's perspectives of organised crime in West Africa and the Sahel', *Institute for Security Studies Papers*, 2014(254).

Revkin, M. R. (2020) 'What explains taxation by resource-rich rebels? Evidence from the Islamic State in Syria', *Journal of Politics*, 82(2), pp.757–764.

Risen, J. (2008) *Reports link Karzai's brother to Afghanistan heroin trade. New York Times*. Available at: https://www.nytimes.com/2008/10/05/world/asia/05afghan.html.

Rodney, W. (1972) *How Europe Underdeveloped Africa*. Washington, DC: Howard University Press.

Ronen, Y. (2013) 'Libya, the Tuareg and Mali on the eve of the "Arab Spring" and in its aftermath: An anatomy of changed relations', *The Journal of North African Studies*, 18(4), pp. 544–559.

Rosenberg, M. (2013) 'With bags of cash, C.I.A. seeks influence in Afghanistan', *The New York Times*, 28 April. Available at: https://www.nytimes.com/2013/04/29/world/asia/cia-delivers-cash-to-afghan-leaders-office.html (Accessed: 22 February 2021).

Ross, Michael L. (2004) 'What do we know about natural resources and civil war?' *Journal of Peace Research*, 41, pp. 337–356. doi: 10.1177/0022343304043773.

Ross, M. (2006) 'A closer look at oil, diamonds, and civil war', *Annual Review of Political Science*, 9, pp. 265–300.

Rubin, B. R. (2000) 'The political economy of war and peace in Afghanistan', *World Development*, 28(10), pp. 1789–1803.

Rubin, B. R. (2013) *Afghanistan in the Post-Cold War Era*. Oxford: OUP USA.

Sabates-Wheeler, R. and Verwimp, P. (2014) 'Extortion with protection: Understanding the effect of rebel taxation on civilian welfare in Burundi', *The Journal of Conflict Resolution*, 58(8), pp. 1474–1499.

Samatar, A. I. (2007) 'Ethiopian invasion of Somalia, US Warlordism & AU Shame', *Review of African Political Economy*, 34(111), pp. 155–165.

Samatar, A. I. (2008) 'Somalia's post-conflict economy: A political economy approach', *Bildhaan: An International Journal of Somali Studies*, 7(1). Available at: https://digitalcommons.macalester.edu/bildhaan/vol7/iss1/8.

Smuggling and civil war economies

Samatar, A. I. (2016) *Africa's First Democrats: Somalia's Aden A. Osman and Abdirazak H. Hussein*. Bloomington: Indiana University Press.

Scheele, J. (2012) *Smugglers and Saints of the Sahara: Regional Connectivity in the Twentieth Century*. Cambridge: Cambridge University Press.

Shaw, S. (2013) 'Fallout in the Sahel: The geographic spread of conflict from Libya to Mali', *Canadian Foreign Policy Journal*, 19(2), pp. 199–210.

Shearer, D. (2000) 'Aiding or abetting? Humanitarian aid and its economic role in Civil War', in Berdal M. and Malone D. M. (eds) *Greed and Grievance: Economic Agendas in Civil War*. Lynne Rienner/IDRC.

Shelley, L. (2014) 'Blood money: How ISIS makes bank', *Foreign Affairs*. Available at: https://www.foreignaffairs.com/articles/iraq/2014-11-30/blood-money (Accessed: 13 February 2016).

Shelley, L. I. (2014) *Dirty Entanglements: Corruption, Crime, and Terrorism*. New York, NY: Cambridge University Press.

Storholt (2001) 'Lessons learned from the 1990-1997 peace process in the North of Mali', *International Negotiation*, 6(3), pp. 331–356.

Thompson, V. B. (2015) *Conflict in the Horn of Africa: The Kenya-Somalia border problem 1941–2014*. Lanham: University Press of America.

Tucker, R. P. (1983) 'The British colonial system and the forests of the western Himalayas, 1815-1914', in *Global Deforestation in the Nineteenth Century World Economy*. Durham, NC: Duke University Press.

Weinstein J. M. (2007) *Inside Rebellion: The Politics of Insurgent Violence*. New York: Cambridge University Press.

Welch, D. A. (1993) *Justice and the Genesis of War*. Cambridge England; New York, NY: Cambridge University Press.

28

CHECKPOST CHESS

Exploring the relationship between insurgents and illicit trade

Shalaka Thakur

> Vehicles pass through our land, it is our duty to receive tax from them.
>
> KNO (non-state armed group) member[1]

Introduction

When you visit the Government of India Land Ports Authority website and check the amount of trade at the official Indo-Myanmar border crossing 'Moreh,' the total import and export presented[2] is INR 0 per year. The truckloads of products – from everyday electronics and medicines to areca nuts and cigarettes – that you see crossing at this buzzing border paint a different picture. When you speak to the traders doing business across this border, their estimate for licit goods is INR 10–15 crores (EUR 1.4–1.7 million) per *day*. Much of the trade that happens across this border, therefore, is 'informal trade,' done without import/export tariffs, commonly understood as smuggling. Illicit goods like drugs carve out a separate space for themselves. Security forces at the border on the Indian side estimate an approximate INR 4,000 crores (EUR 463 million) worth of heroin and meth entering Manipur through Moreh each year.

This border crossing is also dotted with various non-state armed groups, state security forces, and other state actors. This chapter seeks to explain the role that non-state armed groups play in shaping the smuggling economy.[3] While non-state armed groups and smugglers are often instinctively considered natural allies, given the covert nature of their functioning, as evidence from this case shows, their role in the smuggling economy is far more complex than commonly understood. Furthermore, it is often intrinsically tied to their relationship with the state and state actors. By exploring the relationships non-state armed groups have with the state and traders/smugglers,[4] this chapter seeks to elucidate how the three create and mould the informal cross-border economy.

Most literature around insurgents and smuggling has focused on the role smuggling plays in rebel finance and the role of informal economies in sustaining rebel groups. However, the reverse – the role that non-state armed groups play in the wider smuggling economy – has not been explored as much. Predominantly ensconced in literature on 'war economies' (see Berdal

384

DOI: 10.4324/9781003043645-28

and Malone 2000, Keen 1998, Nordstrom 2004), works arguing 'greed' as a key driver of conflict (Collier and Hoeffler 2001), and viewing war economies as a 'malignant form' of economic activity (Ballentine and Sherman 2003) put the role of insurgents in economically viable areas like cross-border trade in a primarily exploitative light. Other accounts speak to the ambiguities of war economies and the livelihoods they create, and the communities that come to depend on them (Duffield 2001, Nordstrom 2004). Moving beyond the lens of war economies, Weigand (2020) finds that the role non-state armed groups play in the smuggling economy depend on and are tempered by the amount of territorial control they enjoy and the extent to which they depend on public legitimacy, offering more nuance to the rebel-smuggler link. As van Schendel and Abraham (2005) postulate, law and crime both emerge from historical and ongoing struggle over legitimacy. Understanding the role that insurgents play, beyond being merely economically driven actors, is hence imperative to understanding their role in the smuggling economy.

Many borderlands, and certainly this one, are a space of overlapping and competing state and non-state authorities, blurring the lines of what the 'state' is in terms of both monopolisation of violence and questions of legitimacy. They are thus, as scholars have argued, places where state authority may be contested or at times even entirely supplanted (van Schendel 2005). Moving beyond the Weberian idea of the state is therefore an imperative step to understanding the functioning of the smuggling economy. It is useful then, to take what Hagmann and Peclard (2010, 46) would call a 'more grounded approach to statehood whose starting point is empirical and not judicial.' The rebel governance and wartime orders literature (see e.g., Arjona 2016; Mampilly 2011; Staniland 2012) looks at rebels as actors with an interest in and ability to control and govern territory, beyond simply engaging in violence against the state, and has much to contribute in this regard. The role of non-state armed groups in this economy, conversely, also allows for a more nuanced and comprehensive understanding of authority and regulation in informal cross-border trade. This trade itself can be viewed as a function of hybrid governance resulting from the interactions of state and non-state actors (Titeca and Flynn 2014), including armed groups, and economic informality viewed, not as a lack of state regulation, but rather as alternative forms of regulation, operating below and beyond the framework of the state (Meagher 2011). Furthermore, this kind of informal regulation may at least in part be based on socially accepted understanding (Raeymaekers 2010).

Drawing on these insights, this chapter sets out to further our understanding of the role of non-state armed groups in informal cross-border trade through the case of Moreh at the Indo-Myanmar border. To explore some of the ways in which non-state armed groups shape the smuggling economy, it firstly investigates the micro-dynamics of the way fees and access of goods and vehicles across the border are negotiated by such groups. This section of the chapter also delves into the logics of taxes, as expressed by them, levied by non-state armed groups. The variations in manner of involvement speak to questions of authority, with professed logics of their involvement in the smuggling economy seemingly state-like in their ambition. This section also illustrates that, contrary to distinct zones of control, with territories clearly demarcated between state and rebel control, there is an intertwining of the state and non-state actors, who operate in the same space and time.

The next section looks into how non-state armed groups incentivise smuggling. On the one hand, it finds that by levying informal fees on traders, non-state armed groups incentivise them to skirt state-imposed tariffs. Traders can often avoid state taxes, but not those of non-state authorities, which speaks to dimensions of how control and authority are exercised in the borderlands. It also finds that rules and taxes levied at the border by non-state armed groups create informal barriers to entry, allowing only certain types of traders and smugglers, who are organised and rich enough to deal with these groups, access to some cross-border trade.

The last section in this chapter looks at the effect of ceasefires and other agreements geared towards reducing violence in the smuggling economy. It finds that groups in agreements with the state play a much bigger and more systematic role in the smuggling economy, and that this, in turn, perpetuates corruption on the side of the state. Creating a type of political order which lies somewhere between coexistence and collusion and occasional confrontation, these agreements, while playing the much-needed role of reducing active fighting and conflict, also perpetuate systems of methodical exploitation and entrench vested interests.

Mapping Moreh: micro-dynamics of informal cross-border trade

Slip kaatne se hi gaadi ja sakti hain

(without their (non-state armed group's) receipt, your truck cannot move).[5]

– Trader, Moreh

In some ways, the relationship that informal traders have with non-state armed groups and with the state are strikingly similar. Many traders interviewed in Moreh do not find the involvement and taxes taken informally from the non-state armed groups any more or less unacceptable than the tariffs levied formally by the state, or the bribes taken informally by state actors. It is amounts and process of involvement that concerns traders, not the legality of the actor involved. For some smugglers dealing in illicit goods, they avoid detection by non-state armed groups and state security with equal determination. For others, the non-state armed groups are akin to 'business partners' who create conditions that are favourable to them and their business. This section will touch upon all three of these relationships.

The actors

The non-state armed groups found in this border region[6] can be divided broadly into three ethnic groups: the Kuki groups like the KNA (Kuki National Army) and UKLF (United Kuki Liberation Front) whose area of influence is (AoI) Moreh town; the Naga group NSCN-IM (Nationalist Socialist Council of Nagaland-Isak Muivah); and various Manipur valley-based groups, who are currently based on the Burmese side of the border, while making the occasional appearance in Moreh. All groups stand on a platform of secession or greater autonomy. The state actors found here are customs and sales tax officers, police, IRB (Indian Reserve Battalion), paramilitary (called Assam Rifles), and the army. The presence of the insurgent groups, in part believed to be covertly supported by China,[7] explains the presence of various Indian security forces. All these actors play a direct or indirect role in the smuggling economy. While some actively get involved in trading of different goods, usually, taxes and bribes in the form of cash or cuts from the shipment are taken by all the non-state armed groups and many of the state actors. Contrary to how the smuggling economy is often envisioned, the areas of state and non-state control are not clearly divided or demarcated; rather, they are all operating in the same space.

While some traders belong to the Meitei communities that are originally from Manipur, many big traders based in Moreh are 'Mayangs' or 'outsiders,'[8] mostly from other parts of India. Though from different communities and dealing in different goods, they speak of 'Mayang unity' while dealing with non-state armed groups. The trader community has formed a

'Chamber of Commerce' in Moreh that not only has to deal with the state, but also negotiates with non-state armed groups. The yearly lump sums to be paid are negotiated with different groups by the whole community so as to get beneficial rates from the non-state armed groups. Their relationship with the non-state armed groups is to a great extent similar to the one with state actors, when paying fees and taxes. In addition to this, the traders also pay a house tax to some Kuki non-state armed groups.[9] As many of the traders do not belong to ethnicities that are originally from the region, and whose non-state armed groups function in this region, friction between the trader communities and non-state armed groups sparks up from time to time. However, the degree of violence has gone down over the past couple of decades. A trader who has been in Moreh since the 1980s described 'They were very violent, they would threaten. Now it has been systemised.'[10] Despite the reduction in violence that long-term traders spoke of, paying the non-state armed groups is not optional.

Informal taxes and unseen roads

Paying non-state armed groups in this region is something that every big trader crossing the border must do. The payments are made in different forms. Some are fixed yearly costs paid as lump sums to different groups in the form of 'godown tax' or 'entry tax' usually ranging between 5000 and 10,000 euros per group per year. In addition, vehicles carrying the goods are taxed along the road to and from the border crossing. Receipts are given by different non-state armed groups. While some have their organisation's name on the receipt, others issue receipts under the names of non-existent transport associations. More recently, receipts have started being issued in the form of text messages.

On average, when crossing from Moreh to Imphal, the capital of Manipur a mere 107 km away, traders pay informal fees at least nine checkpoints on an average ride, as a part of the border crossing process into the main city. A truck carrying cigarettes or betel nuts, for example, would be taxed approximately INR 10000 (around EUR 110) per journey by non-state armed groups. In addition, there are various payoffs the traders have to make to state actors along the way, being stopped at three police checkposts, two customs posts, and occasionally one army post. They pay small bribes, usually less than EUR 10 per stop, although this varies depending on the shipment and its size. Traders at the border put the average of the informal taxes they pay to both state (in the form of bribes) and non-state armed groups at 20% of the value of their shipment, a substantial amount of it attributed to non-state armed groups.

Some goods, particularly illicit ones (teak, drugs, exotic wildlife) are often transported on parallel make-shift roads in the jungle that have been created expressly with the intention of skirting the authorities. In these cases too, they are skirting all authorities – state and non-state – equally, rather than simply avoiding detection by state authorities while actively colluding with insurgents to avoid detection. For example, a teak smuggler explained that he takes other routes, even though they are much slower and inconvenient, as he finds 'fewer UGs (underground groups, local term for non-state armed groups" after "under ground groups" within the brackets)[11] and fewer police' along these routes.[12]

Some non-state armed groups play an active role in smuggling and cross-border trade. For example, the NSCN-IM budget shows 'cement,' 'betel nuts' and 'trade in Moreh' as sources of income,[13] which indicate a more active role in informal cross-border trade. For the most part, however, when it comes to non-state armed groups in the 'informal trade' or illegal smuggling, their involvement is mostly confined to taxation of goods crossing the border. Traders' relationships with state actors is quite similar when it comes to the payment of these fees. As one trader put it, 'We can't just blame the UGs – if they take 10 rupees, government (Indian state) will take 20'.[14] Traders also accuse the state of making legal trade extremely difficult, and wanting to keep their own informal checkpoints, where they collect bribes on crossing the border – a steady source of income.

Drugs and drawing lines

The role of non-state armed groups in the drug economy is a surprising one. According to sources within Moreh and the state security forces on the ground, while a few non-state armed groups in Moreh tax drugs arriving from Myanmar, this is in no way the norm.

Heroin and World is Yours (WY) tablets (methamphetamine mixed with caffeine) come in from Myanmar, while ephiderenes and amphetamines go across from India to Myanmar (Shivananda 2011). These ingredients are then often used to convert opium into heroin, known locally as 'number 4.' At the Assam Rifles checkpoints, cars and people are thoroughly checked. Drug addiction rates in Manipur are very high, with more than 10% of the general population being opioid users (GoI report 2019). According to the Indian Army webpage 'this drug corridor is an easy source of income for insurgents who collaborate with criminal gangs to smuggle drugs across the border' (Indian Army webpage 2019). According to Indian security forces on the field though, non-state armed group involvement is limited. The non-state armed groups that are involved in the movement of drugs do not play a major role and also do not treat drug trafficking as a major source of income for their group. Furthermore, despite the lucrative nature of the drug business at this border, many non-state armed groups do not take a cut on drugs at all, on the basis of ideology, a view claimed not only by them, but reiterated by traders and locals in Moreh. It is often politicians and state security forces that are linked to large movements of drugs, according to traders and media reports.[15] The non-state armed groups of communities (like the Kuki community), that are known traditionally to grow opium are also described by the Indian state security forces as playing a very small role in the drug economy, mostly as runners and small fry. During a meeting I attended of an NGO which has been working with drug addicts and protesting the rise of the drug economy, many of them believed that the drug trade had grown considerably since the valley-based non-state armed groups had been driven out by the Indian security forces. Although it is difficult to triangulate this claim, the perception of these NGOs and civilians that the non-state armed groups keep the drug trade in check is an interesting and unintuitive one.

Another example of the tempering effects legitimacy is seen to have on the type of trade non-state armed groups get involved in can be seen with human trafficking. Despite India's being a lucrative market and a major destination for human smugglers, and despite the very porous nature of the border, non-state armed groups at this border are largely not involved in human trafficking, as per accounts of the local community and traders in Moreh. In 2018, when the trafficking of underage girls was taken up by some businessmen in Moreh, it was condemned by the local community, including the non-state armed groups.[16] The traffickers were, according to locals, outsiders – not a part of the usual trader community or tribal population of Moreh – and were driven out as they were seen as a threat to the 'social fabric' of Moreh.

Narratives of non-state armed groups

A member of the KNA, a major player in the Moreh informal economy, explained why his group took cuts from vehicles crossing the border. He frames this sort of involvement as their 'right towards their mission' as they are fighting for their land and their people. He framed their involvement in cross-border trade as an articulation of their presence, beyond just financing of their group. This authority is backed by evidence from constituents in the group's area of influence. On occasions when the state security forces take action against collections on goods entering and leaving Moreh, they are often faced with violent protests by locals, indicating a degree of legitimacy of the KNA in the area. Similarly, as a minister from the non-state armed group the NSCN-IM proclaimed, 'They can never stop the NSCN from collecting taxes, they cannot stop this contribution to the movement.'[17] While his quote was in reference to all taxes taken by the group in all their areas of influence, the cuts taken from cross-border trade form a substantial amount.[18]"

Making of the smuggler: how non-state armed groups incentivise smuggling

'They (referring to a non-state armed group) will call me and say "Eat well. Today is your last dinner".

– Smuggler, Moreh[19]

Although it is the state that, through legislation, makes an act of trade smuggling, within these established legal bounds the presence of non-state actors often pushes traders dealing in licit goods into trading their products across the border illegally, thereby incentivising smuggling. The presence of non-state armed groups provides a new set of authorities to deal with and pay. Paying multiple sets authorities is unfeasible for many traders, and when having to choose whom to pay, it is often easier (and safer) for traders to avoid paying the state authorities rather than non-state armed groups, thereby leading to more traders dealing in legal goods to choose to avoid state-imposed tariffs and resort to smuggling.

In line with this, non-state armed groups also create systems of informal regulations and barriers to entry on the movement of certain goods, in some cases incentivising certain types of people and smugglers over others. In some cases therefore, the presence of non-state armed groups helps certain smugglers and traders capture a larger share of the market by creating barriers to entry, not unlike what the state does.

Incentivising smuggling

Peter Andreas (2009) postulates that if tariffs are high, smugglers are incentivised to smuggle legal commodities trying to evade these tariffs. The presence of non-state armed groups, in a similar vein, makes the (informal) taxes[20] to be paid by traders high, even if the state is not levying them. At some crossings, where non-state armed groups are the only authority present, they might replace the state and determine the tariff prices. At other places, like in Moreh, where they function alongside the state, it changes the traders' calculation of whether and how much to pay each authority in question.

High state-imposed tariffs are a reason traders give for avoiding formal, legal trade. However, they blame, in equal part, the presence of non-state armed groups and the less avoidable taxes that they charge. Many cite the difficulties of paying non-state armed groups as the reason they cannot afford to pay state tariffs in addition to these informal tariffs. In many cases, if it were just the state taxes they had to pay, they claim they would. However, knowing that they have to pay taxes to various non-state armed groups, often under the threat of violence, makes paying both unfeasible. Since non-payment to non-state armed groups is a dangerous option, having far harsher implications, they instead opt for not paying the official state tariffs, bribing state actors whom they meet along the way instead.

The cycle of increased informal trade at Moreh can thus be attributed to the tariffs by both the state and non-state armed groups. The state often kicks it off with high tariffs. For example, at the Indo-Myanmar border in Moreh, there is an 'Integrated Check Post (ICP).' Equipped with state-of-the-art infrastructure, multiple lanes for trucks to ply and sophisticated screening devices, it is usually, nevertheless, empty. At the time of my last visit in early 2020, it was absolutely desolate. When I met the officer in charge and complimented him on the scale and grandeur of the checkpost, he sheepishly commented on how it would be even nicer if anyone used it.[21] He is referring to how most traders avoid it on account of the official tariffs they would have to pay there. Moving a few hundred meters away from the slick, lonely ICP concrete roads to the blurry dirt paths, trade is abuzz.

Trucks carrying goods from Myanmar stop on the Myanmar side. The goods are then carried as headloads or piled on to motorcycles and carried to trucks on the Indian side, where they are piled onto Indian trucks. Police sit languidly by, watching the trucks load. Their lookout is for drugs and arms, and the movement of the electronics, garments, cigarettes, toys, cement and medicine before them now is not of much interest. They understand, like everyone else here, that this trade is important, and its technically being 'informal' is little reason to stop it. The trucks on the Indian side, having entirely avoided the ICP, then embark on a journey dotted with stops by the state and non-state armed groups.

In some cases, the state tariffs are considered too high to pay, irrespective of non-state armed group taxation and fees. Multiple traders mentioned the example about the remarkably high tariffs on importing betel nuts (40%) under India's new 'Normal Trade' policy from 2015, up from a previous concessionary rate of just 5%. One of the most traded items across the border, traders are now unable to pay this high tariff, and betel nut is traded informally, with reports showing that smuggling surged in the aftermath of the change in these tariffs (see, for example Ambedkar et al. 2019). While customs offices can sometimes be seen overflowing with seized betel nuts, some customs officers in their interviews also admit the counterproductive effect of this tariff on formal trade and the difficulties traders face because of it. Paying state-imposed tariffs can avert the bribes traders pay to the 'uniformed' (state) collectors along the way, but the latter option often proves to be more economical and expedient. Multiple traders complained of how they had tried going down the legal route a couple of times, and how it was made extremely difficult for them. As one trader grumbled 'Instead of telling us (to do formal trade), why don't they change their rules?'[22] However, state officers and customs officials speak to the entrenched vested interests traders have in operating outside the legal system, arguing that they would be unwilling to pay even if official tariffs were reasonable.[23]

As illustrated in the section above, paying non-state armed groups in this region is something that every big trader crossing the border must do. These are costs that traders cannot avoid or forgo, under the threat of violence, and must factor into their expenses. Paying the formal tariff in addition would make no business sense, explained traders. Non-state armed groups on the Indo-Myanmar border thus play no small role in encouraging traders to forgo the payment to the state. They make traders who have been working in these regions 'smugglers' from the Indian state's point of view. As far as the non-state armed groups are concerned though, this is their land, their area of control, and dues have been paid.

Barriers to entry and informal regulation

The presence of non-state armed groups can determine the level of organisation of the smugglers. According to Andreas, the level of organisation in smuggling economies varies considerably, depending especially on a state's 'tough' enforcement practices at a certain border (ibid., p. 20). Non-state armed groups in Moreh and their enforcement of taxes also plays a role in pressurising traders into more organised structures. It creates a sort of barrier-to-entry which only seasoned traders and smugglers are able to cross.

As one teak smuggler candidly declared 'I consider them (the UGs) as business partners.'[24] In his line of work, he explained running a successful business meant keeping others out of it and the non-state armed groups served as partners in making this happen. Since he has been in this industry for a while, he is able to negotiate with the groups and pay their charges. In exchange, the higher tariffs the groups would charge newcomers dissuades competition, giving him a near monopoly.

Peace deal/piece meal: how ceasefires and suspension of operations play a role in the smuggling economy

> Earlier they (referring to a non-state armed group) used to be scared, now as they have an agreement, they take openly. Now they've just set up a gate (to collect money).[25]
>
> – *Trader, Moreh*

De-escalation of violence through ceasefires and other peace deals comes at a price and with the non-state armed groups along the Indo–Myanmar border areas, this price often takes the form of offering a larger piece of the pie in the smuggling economy. Smuggling becomes a larger, more organised part of the ceasefire economy for both non-state armed groups as well as state actors, playing an arguably larger role during halfway peace than it did during the peak of conflict.

Certain features of ceasefires and suspension of operations deals (SoO) at Moreh lead to a degree of impunity from state actions against non-state armed groups, as the trade-off for the state would be a return to active fighting. This leads to increased territorial control, as their territory is no longer actively contested militarily by the Indian state, although they may continue to fight other groups over territory. As territorial control sets the outer limits to which they can involve themselves in the smuggling economy, agreements with the state enhance the possibility of non-state armed groups involving themselves in the smuggling economy in a larger and more systematic way. This, in turn, cements their presence in the area, which entrenches a large presence of state security forces in the region, with quite a substantial slice of the smuggling arranged for themselves. Agreements can also be seen as a form of 'external legitimacy,' or recognition by the Indian state. Non-state armed groups who are (tacitly) allowed to operate may therefore alter their dependence on internal legitimacy from their own constituents, thereby changing the calculus of what sorts of smuggling a group might get involved in.

Restructuring the calculus of territorial control and internal legitimacy

The role that non-state armed groups play in the smuggling economy depends heavily on public legitimacy and territorial control (see Weigand 2020). The sort of state-insurgent relationship can affect directly how much territory a non-state armed group is able to control, as well as the extent to which internal legitimacy factors into its role in informal trade. Confrontation, coexistence or collusion of/with the state is what, to a large extent, determines how much territory a group controls, as well as how dependent they remain on internal legitimacy in their decision making.

While legitimacy and accountability might regulate what types of smuggled goods non-state armed groups get involved in, it is territorial control that sets the external limits to where and how they are able to get involved in smuggling. The extent of territory controlled determines the amount and method of collection and how regularised the taxation is. Non-state armed groups that control territory would be able to set up collection checkpoints, where they take a specific cut based on certain criteria, like vehicle and shipment size and type. Apart from this, they also collect fixed yearly contributions from regular traders. Groups that do not control territory would have a more ad hoc manner of collection, taking as much as they can, when they can. While traders lose a far greater percentage in taxes to the non-state armed groups controlling territory, they can account for it based on regularisation and predictability. Traders interviewed in Moreh were able to map out where they had to pay and an approximation of how much for the non-state armed groups that control territory. From the groups that do not control territory, the monetary pinch is considerably less, but the ad hoc nature of collection makes it harder to prepare for. A trader may or may not have to pay a cut to a non-state armed group not controlling territory, but when he does it is difficult to predict the amount and when it will happen.

To illustrate, let us do a case comparison of non-state armed groups in varying relationships with the state. You see two kinds of groups – the ones who are still actively fighting with/ hiding from the state, and with whom the Indian state currently has no form of a peace deal, are Meitei groups, from the Manipur valley. Groups with which the state is currently in ceasefire or suspension of operations are the NSCN-IM and the Kuki groups. Valley-based groups previously had an allocated spot that they operated out of on the Myanmar side of the border. Multiple traders recalled being called in for meetings to determine rates to be paid, and the valley-based non-state armed groups were considered heavyweights even among the crowded non-state armed group space in this border region. After heavy securitisation/military interventions over the past decade, including a couple of joint operations with the Myanmar army to oust valley-based groups, the usual post they used to function out of remains empty and unused. Constantly being on the run from security forces has pushed them into hiding, and the valley-based groups who now no longer control territory, and their role in the smuggling economy on this border has been reduced to that of an ad-hoc collector. According to traders, the collection from these groups has been reduced to close to nothing[26] over the last two years. The removal of this once big player in the smuggling economy due to militarisation has, however, not drastically reduced the 'cut' of non-state armed groups in the smuggling economy. Despite this, they make ad-hoc payment demands, particularly in the form of the big sums to be paid by smugglers yearly.

Let's compare this type of involvement with that of non-state armed groups that are in some sort of agreement with the state. As per the rules of the ceasefire, which the state has with the Naga group the NSCN-IM, they are not allowed to engage in 'extortion.' Similarly, as per the SoO, which the state has with various Kuki groups, the non-state armed groups are to remain in their camps and suspend all operations (as the name would suggest), including taxation of goods from across the border. However, these arrangements, rather than forcing non-state armed groups to toe this line, tend to offer a degree of tacit permission by the state, who would prefer this buy-out to a resurgence of violence. The NSCN-IM is a Naga group that has been in ceasefire with the Indian state since 1997. The 1990s saw turf wars for the control of Moreh. While the Kukis won this turf war and Moreh is considered their area of influence, traders doing business in Moreh need to factor in the NSCN-IM and negotiate the yearly rate they pay the group on goods coming from across the border. In addition, they have a collection point a few kilometres from Moreh. The ceasefire has increased the income of the NSCN-IM,

Checkpost chess

a sizeable amount of which comes through their cuts and involvement in cross-border trade. For example, the trade of betel nuts is one of the sources of income for the military wing of the NSCN-IM, the Naga army, adding about INR 1275000 (EUR 146,500)[27] to their revenue in the year 2019-2020. The taxes and fees taken by the group are stated as an income source in their budget. Apart from the betel nuts and other major goods, 'Moreh market, transport of goods to and fro' is another entry that can be found in the 'sources of income' part of the NSCN-IM budget. The actual sum collected probably differs substantially from the numbers in the budget, much like the fees taken by state actors in 'informal' ways would not show up in import duties or customs reports of the state. The NSCN-IM also takes onus for many taxes they levy on the goods going through their area of influence/territory. When the IM takes a cut from a shipment, the name of the organisation, as well as a signing authority is on the receipt they issue. The ceasefire further allows them this symbolism, as the tradeoff for taking sustained action against this taxation would tip the precarious balance of the ceasefire. In a way, through the claiming of the taxes they are charging on goods coming from and going into Myanmar, they differentiate themselves from other armed actors who take cuts without attaching their name to it, creating the impression of a proper signing authority that levy taxes on shipments moving through their area.

The role of the state, in many cases, does not remain that of turning a blind eye to the cuts taken by non-state armed groups in order to maintain peace, but a far more active role in this smuggling economy themselves. The murky borderland is in in fact a much-desired posting with rumours of police heads paying up to an equivalent of 1 crore rupees (EUR 113,000) for the postings. In Moreh, non-state armed group collection points that I observed were a stone's throw away from police and security forces along the same route.

David Brenner's chapter, (following this one) compellingly describes the case of economic pacification, geared towards breaking 'rebel-smuggler nexus,' can increase violence, conflict and insecurity. This is not only because economic interventions in contexts of conflict can shift the incentives of warring factions in unforeseen ways. In the context of Moreh, you see how halfway peace is bought by incentivising non-state armed groups to get a larger part of the smuggling economy, while simultaneously incentivising an informal state-smuggler nexus. While reduction of violence and eventual peace is an imperative goal to move towards, as one trader complained in reference to the consequences of the suspension of operations arrangements, 'Agreements with government should not be a mandate for harassing public.'[28]

Conclusion

Dono ka phayda hain, magar public ka phayda nahi hain.[29]

(They both (non-state armed groups and state actors) profit, but the people lose.)

— Trader, Moreh

The relationship among traders, non-state armed groups and the state is a complicated one, and in its many permutations and combinations, is an important factor in shaping the economy of informal and illicit cross-border trade. This chapter attempted to throw some light on this relationship.

The findings in this chapter challenge the idea that smuggling occurs in rebel-controlled borderlands, beyond the purview of the state. On exploring the micro-dynamics of the smuggling economy, it finds that the role of non-state armed groups are in fact often inextricably interwoven with state actors. It demonstrates how non-state armed groups play a large role in incentivising smuggling in a space that they often share with state actors, while at the same time creating parallel informal barriers-to-entry for different goods and types of smugglers. They are not alone though, with state legislation and state actors also encouraging the informal trading of goods across the border. The presence of non-state armed groups leads to the presence of many state security forces in this region, increasing the number of actors in the movement of goods across the border, and determining the calculus of what informal arrangements must be made or what fees must be paid. Finally, the chapter shows that a larger piece of the smuggling economy for non-state armed groups and state actors is often the price for (relative) peace. Traders consider agreements between the state and non-state actors contributing factors to more systematic and larger cuts taken by both. The fear-infested environment of constant conflict was, contrary to popular belief, less fertile a field for smuggling.

The case of Moreh presents useful insights into the role of non-state armed groups, and how their entangled relation with state actors shapes the smuggling economy. These findings speak to an undeniable need to pay closer attention to non-state armed groups while studying the smuggling economy and to the value of using smuggling as a lens through which to understand non-state armed group governance and authority in the borderlands.

Notes

1 Interview, April 2021.
2 In Indian Rupees (INR) crores.
3 Based on research conducted in the border town of Moreh, in the state of Manipur at the Indo-Myanmar border 2019–2021. Interviews were conducted primarily with traders, who deal with both state and non-state armed groups to negotiate cross-border trade and also with members of non-state armed groups, customs officers and state security forces. Alongside this, observations on how cross-border trade takes place were conducted. This choice of methodology takes an empirical rather than legal approach to the actualities of mapping informal trade and governance of border regions.
4 I use the word 'trader' instead of 'smuggler' in many cases as this is term used by the traders themselves and even the customs officials and state security forces in the region for people who trade in licit goods even if they are not paying state tariffs. Interviewees across the board would draw a clear distinction between what they consider 'informal trade' – the trade of electronics, food items, cigarettes, betel and areca nuts, clothes, toys and other licit goods traded – and 'smuggling,' a term that they reserve for drugs, exotic wildlife products, people and arms. Trader, customs officers and security forces, while describing trade in Moreh would use the categories 'formal trade,' 'informal trade' and 'illegal smuggling.' These different understandings of trade do not fit into the neat categories of external observers. In fact, he need for 'informal trade' version of this smuggling economy is considered as necessary, even by actors within the state apparatus. In the state of Manipur alone, more than 50,000 people out of the 2.8 million population are estimated to depend on the smuggling economy for their livelihood, 90% of it attributed to the crossing in Moreh (see Mahadevan 2020).
5 Interview, trader, Moreh January 2020.
6 My findings for this chapter are primarily based on the Indian side of the border, and the different actors traders would encounter at the Moreh-Tamu border.
7 Based on telephonic interviews with army officers in October 2020, also see https://www.efsas.org/commentaries/differences-between-nscn-and-indian-government-raises-suspicions-of-a-chinese-hand/ https://www.business-standard.com/article/current-affairs/china-s-weapon-supply-to-myanmar-terrorists-re-ignites-insurgency-fears-120072500118_1.html.
8 Term used in Manipur for people who are not Meitei, Kuki or Naga but from mainland India.
9 According to interviewees in the community, during the turf wars between Naga and Kuki non-state armed groups, both organised on the basis of tribe and ethnicity, when both groups tried to recruit the then large Tamil trading community to join their non-state armed groups as they had numbers and sizeable resources, an offer which they declined.
10 Interview, trader, Moreh January 2020.
11 term used locally for non-state armed groups.

12 Interview, Manipur February 2021.
13 Based on NSCN-IM budget for the year 2019–2020.
14 Telephonic interview, trader, August 2020.
15 According to local interviewees in Moreh and for example: https://indianexpress.com/article/north-east-india/manipur/imphal-district-council-chairman-arrested-along-with-drugs-worth-over-27-crore-5226048/; https://timesofindia.indiatimes.com/india/Army-officer-five-others-held-with-drugs-worth-Rs-24-cr-in-Manipur/articleshow/18667037.cms.
16 Interview, Moreh, January 2020.
17 Interview, Manipur November 2019.
18 based on the NSCN-IM budget for 2019-20.
19 Interview, Imphal, February 2021.
20 I use the term 'tax' as it the term used by the non-state armed groups and by the traders and often times 'illegal tax' as referred to by state authorities.
21 Interview, Moreh January 2020.
22 Interview, trader, Moreh January 2020.
23 Interview, state official, Manipur August 2020.
24 Interview, Manipur February 2021.
25 Interview, trader Moreh January 2020.
26 Interview, trader, Moreh January 2020.
27 Budget for the NSCN-IM 2019-20.
28 Telephonic Interview, Trader, August 2020.
29 January 2020. While in this quote he is referring to the non-state armed groups and state actors, it should be noted here that the trader community is also amongst those who profit as per local accounts in Moreh and Imphal and as can be seen in the example of the teak smuggler.

References

Andreas, P. (2009) *Border Games: Policing the U.S.–Mexico Divide* (2nd ed). Ithaca, NY and London: Cornell University Press.

Ambedkar, A., Agrawal, A., Rao, R., Mishra, A. K., Khandelwal, S. K. and Chadda, R. K. (2019). Magnitude of Substance Use in India. On behalf of the group of investigators for the National Survey on Extent and Pattern of Substance Use in India New Delhi: *Ministry of Social Justice and Empowerment*, Government of India.

Arjona, A. (2016) *Rebelocracy: Social Order in the Colombian Civil War.* Cambridge: Cambridge University Press.

Ballentine, K. and Sherman, J. (2003) *The Political Economy of Armed Conflict. Beyond Greed and Grievance.* Boulder and London: Lynne Rienner Publishers.

Berdal, M. and Malone, D. (2000) *Greed and Grievance: Economic Agendas in Civil War.* London: Lynne Rienner Publishers.

Collier, P. and Hoeffler, A. (2001) *Greed and Grievance in Civil War.* Washington DC: World Bank.

Duffield, M. (2001) *Global Governance and the New Wars: The Merging of Development and Security.* Zed Books.

Hagmann, T. and Péclard, D. (2010) Negotiating Statehood: Dynamics of Power and Domination in Africa. *Development and Change.* 41. 539–562.

Keen, D. (1998) The Economic Functions of Violence in Civil Wars. Adelphi Papers No.320. Oxford: International Institute for Strategic Studies.

Mahadevan, P. (2020) Crossing the line, *GI-TOC report.* https://globalinitiative.net/analysis/india-myanmar/

Mampilly, Z. (2011) *Rebel Rulers: Insurgent Governance and Civilian Life during War.* Ithaca, London: Cornell University Press.

Meagher, K. (2011) Informal Economies and Urban Governance in Nigeria: Popular Empowerment or Political Exclusion?. *African Studies Review.* 54. 47–72. doi: 10.1353/arw.2011.0026.

Nordstrom, C. (2004) *Shadows of War Violence, Power, and International Profiteering in the Twenty-First Century.* London: University of California Press.

Raeymaekers, T. (2010) Protection for Sale? War and the Transformation of Regulation on the Congo–Uganda Border. *Development and Change*. 41. 563–587.

Staniland, P. (2012) States, Insurgents, and Wartime Political Orders. *Perspectives on Politics*. 10(2). 243–264.

Shivananda, H. (2011) Nexus of Drug Trafficking and Militancy Exposed at New Delhi, *IDSA Comment*, https://idsa.in/idsacommentsNexusofDrugTraffickingandMilitancyExposedatNewDelhshivanandah_130411.

Titeca, K. and Flynn, R. (2014) "Hybrid Governance," Legitimacy, and (Il)legality in the Informal Cross-Border Trade in Panyimur, Northwest Uganda. *African Studies Review*. 57. 71–91. doi: 10.1017/asr.2014.6.

Van Schendel, W. (2005) *The Bengal Borderlands: Beyond State and Nation in South Asia*. London: Anthem Press.

Van Schendel, W. and Abraham, I., eds. (2005) *Illicit Flows and Criminal Things: States, Borders and the Other Side of Globalization*. Bloomington: Indiana University Press.

Weigand, F. (2020) *Conflict and Transnational Crime: Borders, Bullets and Business in Southeast Asia*. Cheltenham and Northampton: Edward Elgar Publishing.

29

REBELS, SMUGGLERS AND (THE PITFALLS OF) ECONOMIC PACIFICATION

David Brenner

Introduction

Rebels and smugglers often make natural bedfellows. This is due to the clandestine and peripatetic nature of both rebel movements and smuggling economies, as well as their borderland geographies. State actors thus seek to dry up smuggling flows in order to erode the revenue streams of armed groups that tax smuggling operators or operate smuggling economies themselves. Economic pacification strategies can pursue breaking up the rebel-smuggler nexus in two different ways.[1] The state can attempt to restrict the flow of goods that are linked to armed group funding by sanctioning the trade of certain commodities. Alternatively, the state can aim to undercut the profit margins of smuggling operations by liberalising restrictive trade regimes, thereby turning smuggling into official trade.

The effect that economic pacification has on the dynamics of conflict are, however, far from straightforward. As this chapter suggests, such strategies can, in fact, increase rather than decrease violence, conflict and insecurity. This is not only because economic interventions in contexts of conflict can shift the incentives of warring factions in unforeseen ways. More importantly, economistic approaches to conflict operate on limited assumptions about the nature of political violence and consequently fail at addressing the underlying political causes of conflict. To explore some of the unintended effects and pitfalls of economic pacification, the following chapter will proceed as follows. It will first discuss the nexus between smuggling and rebellion and contextualise economic pacification policies on the basis of political economy scholarship. It will then explore two different approaches to eroding smuggling revenues through two empirical case studies. The chapter will look to attempts of restricting smuggling economies in the case of US sanctions on so-called conflict minerals in the border areas of the eastern Democratic Republic of the Congo (DRC). It will then turn to eastern Myanmar for an example where state policy sought to undermine rebel revenues by liberalising rather than restricting border trade. In both cases, economic policies to weaken rebel groups have not translated into a decrease of insecurity and violence, let alone in the pacification of armed conflict itself.

DOI: 10.4324/9781003043645-29

David Brenner

Smuggling as a source of rebel revenue

Smuggling makes for a good source of revenue for rebel movements. Taking up arms against the state is costly but illegal. In order to fund a rebel movement, including the purchase of arms and munition, the mobilisation of people, the training and payment of recruits, the provision of services to people in rebel-held territories, among other needs, rebels must generate revenue. As rebels cannot fund themselves through formal economic activities, partaking in illicit economies, including cross-border smuggling, is imperative. Moreover, arms and munition are normally not available for purchase through legal channels and must be acquired on the black market (at least in the absence of other sources).

At the same time, the black market itself often expands in contexts of war as smuggling becomes the lifeline for many people in a context where large parts of the formal economy collapse. From besieged Sarajevo to the Afghan and Myanmar borderlands, during war people often depend on smuggling to make a living while communities depend on smugglers for everyday goods (Goodhand 2004, Andreas 2011, Brenner 2019). From the rebel perspective, the clandestine and peripatetic nature of smuggling economies is compatible with the mobility and surreptitiousness dictated by guerrilla warfare. Most formal economies, including agriculture, manufacturing or resource extraction, are dependent on at least relatively stable territorial control. By contrast, smuggling or taxing smuggling operators is feasible in contexts of lose, fragmented and often mixed control of territory. Even if rebel movements rule territory as a quasi-state within the state, however, smuggling remains key to their economic orders. This is because flows of goods within or across rebel territory avoid official tax and tariffs, by definition turning trade into smuggling. This is most pronounced when rebel territory spans inter-state borders (Weigand 2020, pp. 134–135).

In fact, many rebel groups are located in remote border areas where smugglers operate across international borders. This is due to a mix of factors. Borderlands are geographically distanced from the centre of state power. While borders themselves are mostly highly securitised, borderlands are often less territorialised in terms of the geographic reach and penetration of state power. In many contexts, it is simply more feasible to recruit and mobilise armed resistance to the state (Buhaug and Gates 2002). This lack of state territorialisation in many borderlands is far from coincidental. The drawing of borders itself left many borderland communities disaffected with the nation-states in which they had come to be placed (Korf and Raeymaekers 2013). The contested nature of the state in many borderlands is thus a direct effect of state formation processes. This is particularly important for contemporary conflicts in the Global South, most of which are ethnonational conflicts directly linked to colonial border drawing and state formation (Wimmer 2012, pp. 2–3, Mamdani 2018).

To sum up, the organisational mode and particular geography of smuggling turn it into an ideal source of revenue for rebel groups. This is true for a range of contemporary conflicts: non-state armed groups in the eastern DRC smuggle minerals and marijuana (Seay 2012); rebels in Myanmar are involved in the smuggling of timber and gemstones (Brenner 2019); and insurgents in Syria engage in the smuggling of weapons and everyday goods (Herbert 2014). The reliance of rebels on illicit economies in general and commodity smuggling in particular is anything but new. This is despite the oft-heard notion that many rebel groups were less reliant on illicit economies during the Cold War because they received financial support from one or the other superpower (e.g., Kaldor 2012; Malešević 2008). Despite Cold War alliances, rebel groups often sought financial self-reliance. Notwithstanding US support, the Afghan mujahideen, for instance, financed their struggle against the Soviet Union by smuggling heroin, just as the Angolan UNITA financed its operations through ivory and diamond smuggling (Naylor

Rebels, smuggler and economic pacification

1993). In some cases, the US even aided the smuggling activities of its non-state allies in order to ensure their financial self-reliance. In the Golden Triangle of Southeast Asia (the restive border regions of Myanmar, China, Laos and Thailand), the CIA aided anti-communist forces during the Cold War by providing logistical support for large-scale smuggling of heroine, including transportation in CIA airplanes, in effect turning the region into one of the world's largest exporters of narcotics (McCoy 1972).

Despite this long-standing nexus between smuggling and armed conflict, the issue of armed group financing has only attracted scholarly interests since the political economy turn of Conflict Studies in the 1990s. Grappling with the post-Cold War outbreak of new or thought-to-be frozen conflicts in the Global South, some voices initially forwarded culturalist explanations that stressed ethnic difference as the main driver of civil wars from Yugoslavia, to Rwanda and Sierra Leone (Huntington 1993, Kaplan 1994). Others, however, stressed the economic rationale underlying these armed conflicts, highlighting how elites took an interest in perpetuating violence because they profited from globalised war economies (Collier and Hoeffler 1998, Keen 2008, Kaldor 2012). Political economists dedicated considerable work to disentangling different types and facets of war economies and how they relate to conflict dynamics. They have, for instance, discussed what kind of resources are more or less associated with violent conflicts, given how lootable or transportable they are (Ross 2004, Le Billon 2012, Rigterink 2020). Their findings stress that the state is mostly as deeply implicated in the economic orders that emerge during protracted armed conflict as are non-state actors (Berdal and Keen 1997). Smugglers, for instance, often cooperate with state actors, such as border officials and security forces. This is particularly so for large-scale smuggling operations that need access to the infrastructure of the formal economy, such as ports and airports (Weigand 2020, pp. 123–125). In a similar vein, critical scholars have highlighted the need to analyse war economies in a regional and global perspective rather than simply locating them within one or another seemingly bounded nation-state container (Duffield 1999, Pugh et al. 2004, Keen 2008). Building on this, discussions focused on the implications of war economies on war-to-peace transitions, including conflict resolution, post-war reconstruction, state-and peacebuilding (Goodhand 2004, Turner and Pugh 2006, Le Billon and Nicholls 2007, Wennmann 2009).

Economic pacification and its pitfalls

From an economic perspective, ending armed conflict is about making conflict a) less economically *feasible* by undercutting the revenue base of warring factions and b) less economically *desirable* by decreasing the profitability for conflict entrepreneurs. While political economy scholars of civil war stress the deep involvement of the state in most war economies, economic pacification policies predominantly target non-state armed groups. After all, policies are formulated by states (or state-based international organisations). Economic pacification of the rebel-smuggler nexus thus aims at undercutting the revenues that non-state armed groups generate by smuggling or taxing smuggling operators. Generally speaking, the state can attempt this in two different ways. On the one hand, the state can attempt to restrict the flow of goods linked to armed group funding with targeted sanctions. On the other hand, the state can aim to undercut the profit margins of smuggling operators by liberalising restrictive trade regimes, thereby turning smuggling into official trade.

The remainder of this chapter will explore both approaches through two different contexts: a) international sanctions on so-called conflict minerals smuggled from the eastern DRC; and b) the liberalisation of border trade in eastern Myanmar. Both cases compare and contrast in ways that illuminate different economic pacification attempts as well as their unintended consequences. In the case of the DRC, the US sanctioned the cross-border trade of industrial minerals in an attempt to erode the funding base of non-state armed groups in northern Kivu. In the case of Myanmar, the country's military regime liberalised a highly restrictive border trade regime in order to undercut the funding of rebels that control the main smuggling routes to Thailand. While both policies decreased the immediate smuggling revenues for non-state armed groups, they did not lead to a reduction of conflict, violence or insecurity.

Restricting border trade: the case of the DRC

Economic sanctions are an established tool in contemporary international relations. States, groups of states, and international organisations regularly use sanctions to force governments into political concessions by restricting flows of goods, finance and people (Jones 2014, p. 1). In the context of civil wars, non-state armed groups have also become the target of international sanctions as a means of economic pacification. Such sanctions include the freezing of international assets and capital of non-state combatants and restricting the smuggling of commodities from or to territories controlled by non-state-armed groups. In 1992, the United Nations Security Council (UNSC) has, for instance, imposed an embargo on the export of timber from and the import of petroleum to areas controlled by the Khmer Rouge (resolution 792) (Lapaš 2010). In 1998, the UNSC legislated a ban on the trade of diamonds from UNITA-controlled areas of Angola (resolution 1173). The latter developed into the Kimberley Protocol Certification Scheme, a multi-stakeholder effort to prevent so-called 'blood diamonds' – i.e., diamonds that are mined in conflict areas – from being sold internationally (Ibid.).

Similarly, section 1502 of the Dodd-Frank Act (hereafter Dodd-Frank) seeks to restrict what has come to be known as 'conflict minerals' from entering the global market. The law was passed by US Congress as a wide-ranging legislation on global finance regulation under the Obama administration in 2010. The insertion of the 'conflict minerals section' was due to considerable lobbying efforts by human rights groups. It requires US electronics manufacturers to trace and report the source of minerals from the eastern DRC and certify that they are 'conflict free.' Conflict minerals from the eastern Congo include gold and the '3Ts:' tin; tantalum; and tungsten. These metals are relatively rare but essential for the production of consumer electronics such as mobile phones and computers. The eastern DRC provinces of North and South Kivu, Maniema, Orientale, and Katanga are among the few places in the world where all four metals can be found in relatively large quantities.

Eastern DRC – especially the Kivu provinces – is also home to one of sub-Saharan Africa's most protracted armed conflicts among a variety of non-state armed groups and the Congolese state. Campaigners behind Dodd-Frank – locally known as 'Obama's law' – view the profits from extracting and trading gold and the '3Ts' as the main driver of armed conflict as well as its associated human rights violations (Bafilemba et al. 2014). Armed groups are estimated to have generated $185 million per year from the trade of these minerals before Dodd-Frank by controlling mines and smuggle operations (Ibid.). According to the Enough Project – one of the main organisations behind Dodd-Frank – the act has been highly successful in eroding these revenues by squeezing armed actors out of the mineral business. Following their logic, the act created a certification scheme for conflict-free minerals, which made non-certified minerals realise much lower market prices (30% to 60% less). This, in turn, made mining and trading much less profitable for armed actors (Ibid.).

Independent assessments of Dodd-Frank, however, paint a much more sobering picture. Scholars point to both important regulatory loopholes and unintended consequences of conflict

Rebels, smuggler and economic pacification

and violence (Seay 2012, Cuvelier, Van Bockstael, et al. 2014, Parker and Vadheim 2017, Stoop et al. 2018). In terms of loopholes, it is far from clear whether Dodd-Frank has an actual impact on the funding base of armed groups in the DRC. As the act's co-sponsor Barney Frank put it: 'The purpose is to cut off funding to people who kill people' (Aronson 2011). To be sure, Dodd-Frank worked to reduce the profitability of conflict minerals. This was because Dodd-Frank acted as a de-facto boycott of conflict minerals from eastern DRC. The cheapest way to comply with the new legislation for US manufacturers was not to certify minerals from eastern DRC as 'conflict free' but to avoid sourcing minerals from the country's conflict zone altogether (Parker and Vadheim 2017, p. 9). That said, the most profitable 'conflict mineral' in the region – gold – has been exempted from regulation under Dodd-Frank, which only im-posed certification on the '3Ts.' This is because most of the gold from DRC is exported to the jewellery market rather than the electronics sector, and gold is much less traceable than the '3Ts' for geological reasons (Parker and Vadheim 2017, p. 11). According to a report produced by the Congolese senate in 2009, about \$1.24 billion worth of gold – or 98% of all gold mined in the DRC – was smuggled out of the country per year (de Koning 2010, Bafilemba et al. 2014, p. 5).

Dodd-Frank has not eroded the funding of armed groups in the eastern DRC in a significant way. Besides falling back on revenues from gold mining, armed groups also increased smuggling of other commodities – including beer, cigarettes, cannabis and palm oil – in order to make up for the shortfalls of funds produced from the '3Ts' (Seay 2012, p. 16, Parker and Vadheim 2017, p. 11). Moreover, it is not clear whether Dodd-Frank actually decreased conflict, violence and insecurity or had the contrary effect. Indeed, a variety of studies indicate the latter. Geo-referenced data suggests that fighting among armed groups might have intensified, especially in areas of gold mining sites, as competition over the last unregulated conflict mineral increased due to banning the '3Ts' (Parker and Vadheim 2017, p. 41, Stoop et al. 2018, p. 2). Moreover, armed group violence against civilians might have also increased because some armed groups who governed mining sites before and provided basic protection now fell back on looting to make up for their lost income (Parker and Vadheim 2017, p. 3, Stoop et al. 2018, p. 2). In many communities of eastern DRC, mining moreover constitutes the only paid work available. Despite the deplorable conditions in which many miners work, the ban on minerals has led to large-scale unemployment and loss of livelihoods in the region (Seay 2012, pp. 14–15). After Dodd-Frank came into effect, local researchers estimated that about one to two million artisanal miners in eastern Congo lost their jobs (Ibid.). This had a paralysing effect on the regional economy more generally (Cuvelier, Van Bockstael, et al. 2014). Consequently, human in-security seems to have risen considerably as a result of Dodd-Frank. Infant death rates in policy-affected mining communities, for instance, increased by at least 143% (Parker et al. 2016).

On a more general level, attempting to reduce conflict, violence and insecurity by restricting the smuggle of minerals mistakes the means for the ends of violence. In eastern Congo – as arguably in all contexts of armed conflict – war economies are but one driver of conflict. In fact, the main advocates of Dodd-Frank reduce a protracted conflict rooted in long imperial histories to a monocausal economistic logic of profiteering. To be clear, country experts confirm the importance of violent economies beyond conflict minerals for understanding the dynamics of conflict in the eastern DRC (Laudati 2013, Verweijen 2013). They also, however, highlight the need for understanding and addressing dynamics of ethnic identity, the predatory and exclu-sionary nature of state institutions, as well as competing land claims among different com-munities in a conflict that is bound up with a wider, regional complex of conflicts (Vlassenroot 2002, Van Acker 2005, Autesserre 2006, Prunier 2008). Country experts thus point out that the key problem of economic pacification policies in the DRC is their underlying reductionist assumptions about the relationship between illicit economies and armed conflict, as well as the thin empirical evidence that is used to substantiate these claims (Cuvelier, Vlassenroot, et al. 2014).

Liberalising border trade: the case of Myanmar

Dodd-Frank illustrated some of the pitfalls and unintended consequences of economic interventions that aim at eroding armed group finances by restricting transborder trade in certain commodities. In contrast to restricting border trade with economic sanctions, economic pacification can also aim at eroding armed group revenues by liberalising the trade in commodities from which armed groups benefit. While this is a less common approach in contexts of civil war, it is an established policy debate in the context of organised crime profiting from illegal market activities (Lavezzi 2014). One way of undercutting the profits of organised crime is to decriminalise its trade and the commodities or activities it is based on. Prohibiting commodities and activities does not only push their production, trade and operation into the realm of the illegal. It also increases their profitability. US prohibition of alcohol in the 1920s and 1930s, for instance, gave unprecedented rise to the mafia in America after an 'entire industry – one of the most important in the country – had been gifted by the government to gangsters' (Dash cited as in Mappen 2013, p. 5). Decriminalising activities ranging from narcotics, to gambling and prostitution is often debated as one way of combatting organised crime (Lavezzi 2014). Some scholars and activists thus view the liberalisation of drugs as an alternative, and more effective way of addressing the war economy in contexts like Colombia, especially when compared to highly restrictive and militarised policies such as the US-funded Plan Colombia (Francis and Mauser 2011, Vergara 2014).

In the context of economic pacification, Myanmar is an instructive place to study the effects of government policies aimed at eroding the funding base of armed groups by liberalising border trade. This is because rebel groups in the Southeast Asian country have long profited from one of the least open border trade regimes. Between 1962 and 1988, the military regime in Burma[2] followed a self-isolationist economic policy. Under the so-called 'Burmese Way to Socialism' Burma nationalised all trade and levied heavy tariffs on imports in order to build an independent economy with the effect that people in Burma suffered an immense shortage of everyday goods. At the same time, almost all of the country's borderlands have come under the control of numerous armed groups since the 1950s (Jones 2014, p. 786). Most of these armed groups emerged as ethnonational rebel movements seeking more autonomy or outright independence from an ethnocratic postcolonial state after the failure of post-independence settlement between the country's ethnic majority and its ethnic minorities over questions of equality and power sharing. Other armed groups included the Chinese-backed Communist Party of Burma, itself largely recruited from ethnic minority communities in the country's northern border areas (Smith 1999, pp. 102–110, Brenner 2019, pp. 35–40).

The combination of official trade restriction and de-facto lack of state control over the country's border areas meant that the black market in Burma was booming during much of the Cold War. While everyday goods – such as fuel, medicine, agricultural machinery and textiles – were smuggled into the country in vast quantities, they were paid for with the illicit export of raw materials, including opium, timber, gemstones, rice and cattle. According to estimates, Burma's smuggling economy comprised of about 40% of the country's gross national product in 1988, equivalent to approximately $3 billion (Smith 1999, p. 25). Rebel groups controlling most of the smuggle routes in and out of the country were the main beneficiaries of illicit trade. They taxed smuggling operators between 5% and 10%, so smuggling in fact became the 'armed opposition's lifeblood' (Smith 1999, p. 99). One Karen rebel officer, for instance, recollects that during the 1980s the Karen rebellion made several thousands of US dollars at one smuggle gate between Thailand and Myanmar per day (Ralph and Sheera 2020, p. 83). Consequently, some of the heftiest battles in Myanmar's civil war have been fought over smuggling routes and border gates (Ibid., pp. 83–87).

In fact, this is a dynamic that can be observed even today as large parts of Myanmar's borderlands, including border crossings, remain under the control of non-state armed groups. Since the 1990s, however, smuggling revenues declined steeply for many of the country's rebel movements. Partly this was because Myanmar's armed forces have managed to take control over some of the country's main trading routes. More important was a strategy of economic liberalisation. By abandoning self-isolationist economic policies and legalising most transborder trade with its neighbours, the ratio of smuggling to official trade from 1990 to 2005 fell from 85 to 50% (Jones 2014, p. 794). This was not a purely economic measure, but formed part of a bundle of policy reforms with which the Myanmar state aimed to pacify its restive border areas and consolidate its own presence instead (Jones 2014, Brenner 2019, pp. 40–46). It is important to note, though, that the consolidation of state control over transborder economic flows has been highly uneven. This is dependent on territorial control, state-armed group relations in a given region, and the involvement of military units in smuggling. It also depends on legal status of commodities and amount of protective tariffs on certain economies (Meehan 2011, Woods 2011, Jones 2014). In 2013, for instance, Thai beer, Malaysian palm oil, and second-hand cars from Japan were still smuggled on a large scale from Thailand to Myanmar (Figure 29.1).

Figure 29.1 A palm oil smuggler on the Moei River that marks the border between Myanmar and Thailand
Source: author (David Brenner)

This uneven and contested nature of state consolidation over the country's smuggling economy has not led to the pacification of Myanmar's protracted civil war. Similar to the sanctions on smuggling minerals from the DRC, liberalising border trade has transformed conflict, violence and insecurity. While economic opening up has eroded the revenue base of some armed groups – such as Karen rebellion – it empowered other armed actors, mostly militia groups that emerged as splinter factions of ethnic rebel movements and operate in close co-operation with the state (Buchanan 2016). Many of them benefit from the increased openness of trade in a context where the rule of law remains suspended. This is not least because there is insufficient interest from powerful state authorities in bringing the country's smuggling economy into the formal and legal fold. Military and civilian officials themselves remain invested in some of the country's most lucrative smuggling industries, including the country's jade and narcotics industries, both of which are deeply intertwined with the formal economy (Meehan 2011, Jones 2014, Weigand 2020, pp. 43–74).

Consequently, insecurity and violence for civilians in Myanmar's border areas has not receded in areas where rebel groups themselves were weakened by way of economic pacification. On the contrary, civilians need to navigate an even greater plethora of armed actors today than they had to in the past (Brenner 2019, pp. 56–57). This also holds true for the places where the actual fighting between warring factions has stopped (Hedström and Olivius 2020). In large parts of Myanmar's border areas, the civil war continues unabated. At the time of writing, Myanmar's army is battling various rebellions in the country. As with the DRC, this is mainly because economic pacification policies in Myanmar do not address the root causes of political conflict. While they might have achieved the temporary erosion of rebel revenues or even the partial co-optation of rebel elites, they do not address underlying political demands and grievances among large parts of the country's ethnic minority communities. As a matter of fact, attempts at economic pacification that do not address the political dimensions of conflict are likely to result in the remobilisation of armed resistance, as seen in the country's north (Brenner 2019, pp. 98–102).

Conclusion

Smuggling is a well-suited economic activity for rebel movements to fund their struggle against the state. This is not least because the modus operandi and geography of smuggling operators is often compatible with the guerrilla operations of armed clandestine movements. Unsurprisingly then, pacification strategies aim at undercutting lucrative smuggling operations by restricting illicit trade flows or formalising them through liberalising trade regimes. This chapter explored two cases that shed light on such strategies and their pitfalls. It first traced the effects of section 1502 of the Dodd-Frank Act, a US law that effectively works as a sanction on so-called 'conflict minerals' in the eastern DRC. It then reviewed how Myanmar's military regime liberalised border trade with its neighbours with the aim of eroding smuggling revenues of border-based rebel movements. In both contexts, economic pacification policies ultimately failed to mitigate conflict, violence and insecurity.

While Dodd-Frank succeeded in squeezing armed actors out of the trade of certain minerals in the eastern DRC, it has neither resulted in the erosion of armed group funding nor in reducing the intensity of armed conflict and its ramifications for the civilian population. In fact, armed groups could easily switch to other modes of funding, including the mining and smuggling of gold and the looting of civilians. This, in turn, increased fighting and insecurity in the region. Moreover, the boycott on minerals from the eastern DRC decimated the local economy, having disastrous effects on the human security of local communities. Economic pacification strategies in Myanmar also led to mixed results. Liberalising border trade in the attempt to bring clandestine economies under state control worked to undercut smuggling revenues of some rebel groups. State consolidation, however, has been highly contested and uneven. This is not least because powerful state actors themselves remain deeply invested in the country's smuggling economies. Rather than formalising most border trade completely, the state has thus come to rely more heavily on militias in governing illicit trade, leading to the proliferation of armed actors in the Myanmar's border areas. Shifting economic flows also led to the increased fragmentation and power struggle within armed movements, as well as renewed armed conflict.

Both cases demonstrate that the main problem with economic pacification strategies is not so much that shifting economic incentive structures can have unintended consequences that increase rather than decrease conflict, violence and insecurity. This is part of the story. The main pitfall of economic pacification strategies lies in their limited assumptions. In fact, they are born out of a reductionist understanding that views economic rationale and feasibility rather than political motivations as the main drivers of contemporary armed conflict. This understanding has increasingly underpinned the disciplinary study of civil war and rebel groups in political science, international relations, and development studies ever since these fields have become dominated by the paradigms of neo-positivism and methodological individualism (Cramer 2002; Baczko, Dorronsoro, and Quesnay 2018, pp. 2–18). To be sure, there has been substantial critique against simplistic accounts that reduces human motivation to take up arms to mere economic profiteering (e.g., Cramer 2002; Keen 2008; Malešević 2008). The spectre of economism haunts scholarship on and policy responses to armed conflict up until today, effectively depoliticising the actors, drivers, and the very nature of conflict itself. In fact, rebel groups today are often viewed primarily through the lens of the so-called "conflict-crime nexus," a perspective that has come to be particularly influential in formulating international policy responses (de Boer and Bosetti 2017). Pacification strategies born out of this understanding, such as the Dodd-Frank Act's provision on 'conflict minerals' in the eastern DRC, thus primarily aim at undercutting rebel revenues in order to make conflict less desirable and less feasible. In the case of Myanmar, army generals have not followed Western-led scholarship and policy. Their counterinsurgency strategies, however, are also tied to an economistic understanding of conflict and pacification. Here the state does not try to undercut smuggling revenues of rebel groups only. It also tries to consolidate its presence in restive border areas through co-opting non-state elites by way of economic incentives, and restive populations by way of economic development (Brenner 2019, pp. 110–111). What transpired clearly, though, from both scenarios is that scholars and policy makers need to move beyond an economistic understanding of conflict in order to address the political drivers of conflict, violence and insecurity.

Notes

1   The term *pacification* is chosen deliberately in order to highlight the fuzzy border between counter-insurgency, conflict resolution and peacebuilding practices. Some scholars see this nexus between peacebuilding and counterinsurgency as a pragmatic turn in peacebuilding, which partly stems from the failure of liberal peacebuilding and partly from the increased entanglements between counter-insurgency and peacebuilders in places such as Afghanistan and Iraq, where UN peacebuilding interventions cannot be viewed separately from US counterinsurgency wars (Moe and Stepputat 2018). Critical scholars highlight that analytically liberal peacebuilding has always been 'a form of riot control directed against the unruly parts of the world' to uphold liberal world order (Pugh 2004, p. 41). In

many parts of the world, the technologies of peacebuilding and counterinsurgency are in fact not all too different (Turner 2015).

2 Myanmar's military rulers changed the name of the country from Burma to Myanmar in 1989. Using one or the other name has sometimes been contentious since. In recent years a scholarly consensus emerged to use *Burma* when discussing events prior to 1989 and *Myanmar* for events after 1989. This convention is followed here.

References

Andreas, P., 2011. *Blue Helmets and Black Markets: The Business of Survival in the Siege of Sarajevo*. Ithaca, NY: Cornell University Press.

Aronson, D., 2011. How Congress Devastated Congo. *The New York Times*. August 11.

Autesserre, S., 2006. Local violence, national peace? Postwar "settlement" in the Eastern DR Congo (2003–2006). *African Studies Review*, 49(3), 1–29.

Baczko, A., Dorronsoro, G., and Quesnay, A. 2018. *Civil War in Syria: Mobilization and Competing Social Orders*. Cambridge: Cambridge University Press.

Bafilemba, F., Mueller, T., and Lezhnev, S., 2014. *The Impact of Dodd-frank and Conflict Minerals Reforms On Eastern Congo's Conflict*. Washington, DC: Enough Project.

Berdal, M. and Keen, D., 1997. Violence and economic agendas in civil wars: Some policy implications. *Millennium*, 26(3), 795–818.

Brenner, D., 2019. *Rebel Politics: A Political Sociology of Armed Struggle in Myanmar's Borderlands*. Ithaca, NY: Cornell University Press.

de Boer, J., and Bosetti, L., 2017. *The Crime–Conflict Nexus*. United Nations University Centre for Policy Research. Crime-Conflict Nexus Series: No. 1. Available from: https://collections.unu.edu/eserv/UNU:6429/Crime_conflict_nexus1.pdf [Accessed 2 March 2021].

Buchanan, J., 2016. *Militias in Myanmar*. The Asia Foundation. Available from: https://asiafoundation.org/wp-content/uploads/2016/07/Militias-in-Myanmar.pdf [Accessed 2 March 2021].

Buhaug, H. and Gates, S., 2002. The geography of civil war. *Journal of Peace Research*, 39(4), 417–433.

Collier, P. and Hoeffler, A., 1998. On economic causes of civil war. *Oxford Economic Papers*, 50(4), 563–573.

Cuvelier, J., Van Bockstael, S., Vlassenroot, K., and Iguma, C., 2014. Analyzing the Impact of the Dodd-Frank Act on Congolese livelihoods. Social Science Research Council. doi: https://s3.amazonaws.com/ssrc-cdn1/crmuploads/new_publication_3/analyzing-the-impact-of-the-dodd-frank-act-on-congolese-livelihoods.pdf

Cuvelier, J., Vlassenroot, K., and Olin, N., 2014. Resources, conflict and governance: A critical review. *The Extractive Industries and Society*, 1(2), 340–350.

Cramer, C., 2002. Homo economicus goes to war: Methodological individualism, rational choice and the political economy of war. *World Development*, 30(11), 1845–1864.

Duffield, M., 1999. Globalization and war economies: Promoting order or the return of history. *Fletcher F. World Affairs*, 23, 21.

Francis, J.N. and Mauser, G.A., 2011. Collateral damage: The 'War on Drugs', and the Latin America and Caribbean region: Policy recommendations for the Obama administration. *Policy Studies*, 32(2), 159–177.

Goodhand, J., 2004. From war economy to peace economy? Reconstruction and state building in Afghanistan. *Journal of International Affairs*, 58(1), 155–174.

Hedström, J. and Olivius, E., 2020. Insecurity, dispossession, depletion: Women's experiences of post-war development in Myanmar. *The European Journal of Development Research*, 32(7), 379–403.

Herbert, M., 2014. Partisans, profiteers, and criminals: Syria's illicit economy. *Fletcher F. World Affairs*, 38, 69.

Huntington, S.P., 1993. If not civilizations, what? Paradigms of the post-cold war world. *Foreign Affairs*, 72(5), 186–194.

Jones, L., 2014. Explaining Myanmar's regime transition: The periphery is central. *Democratization*, 21(5), 780–802.

Kaldor, M., 2012. *Kaldor, Mary, New and Old Wars: Organised Violence in a Global Era*. 3rd ed. Cambridge: Polity.

Kaplan, R.D., 1994. The coming anarchy. *Atlantic Monthly*, 273(2), 44–76.

Keen, D., 2008. *Complex Emergencies*. Cambridge: Polity.

de Koning, R., 2010. Conflict minerals in the Democratic Republic of the Congo. *Stockholm International Peace Research Institute Policy Paper*, SIPRI Policy Paper No. 27, Stockholm International Peace Research Institute.

Korf, B. and Raeymaekers, T., 2013. Introduction: Border, Frontier and the Geography of Rule at the Margins of the State. In: B. Korf and T. Raeymaekers, eds. *Violence on the Margins: States, conflict, and borderlands*. New York: Palgrave Macmillan, 3–27.

Lapaš, D., 2010. Sanctioning non-state entities. *Revue internationale de droit pénal*, 81(1), 99–124.

Laudati, A., 2013. Beyond minerals: broadening 'economies of violence' in eastern Democratic Republic of Congo. *Review of African Political Economy*, 40(135), 32–50.

Lavezzi, A.M., 2014. Organised crime and the economy: A framework for policy prescriptions. *Global Crime*, 15(1–2), 164–190.

Le Billon, P., 2012. *Wars of Plunder: Conflicts, Profits and the Politics of Resources*. New York: Columbia University Press.

Le Billon, P. and Nicholls, E., 2007. Ending 'resource wars': Revenue sharing, economic sanction or military intervention? *International Peacekeeping*, 14(5), 613–632.

Malešević, S., 2008. The sociology of new wars? Assessing the causes and objectives of contemporary violent conflicts. *International Political Sociology*, 2(2), 97–112.

Mamdani, M., 2018. *Citizen and Subject: Contemporary Africa and the Legacy of Late Colonialism*. Princeton, NJ: Princeton University Press.

Mappen, M., 2013. *Prohibition Gangsters: The Rise and Fall of a Bad Generation*. New Brunswick, NJ: Rutgers University Press.

McCoy, A.W., 1972. *The Politics of Heroin in Southeast Asia*. New York: Harper & Row.

Meehan, P., 2011. Drugs, insurgency and state-building in Burma: Why the drugs trade is central to Burma's changing political order. *Journal of Southeast Asian Studies*, 42(3), 376–404.

Moe, L.W. and Stepputat, F., 2018. Introduction: Peacebuilding in an era of pragmatism. *International Affairs*, 94(2), 293–299.

Naylor, R.T., 1993. The insurgent economy: Black market operations of guerrilla organizations. *Crime, Law and Social Change*, 20(1), 13–51.

Parker, D.P., Foltz, J.D., and Elsea, D., 2016. Unintended consequences of sanctions for human rights: Conflict minerals and infant mortality. *The Journal of Law and Economics*, 59(4), 731–774.

Parker, D.P. and Vadheim, B., 2017. Resource cursed or policy cursed? US regulation of conflict minerals and violence in the Congo. *Journal of the Association of Environmental and Resource Economists*, 4(1), 1–49.

Prunier, G., 2008. *Africa's world war: Congo, the Rwandan genocide, and the making of a continental catastrophe*. Oxford: Oxford University Press.

Pugh, M., 2004. Peacekeeping and critical theory. *International Peacekeeping*, 11(1), 39–58.

Pugh, M.C., Cooper, N., Pugh, M., and Goodhand, J., 2004. *War economies in a regional context: challenges of transformation*. London: Lynne Rienner Publishers.

Rigterink, A.S., 2020. Diamonds, Rebel's and Farmer's Best Friend: Impact of Variation in the Price of a Lootable, Labor-intensive Natural Resource on the Intensity of Violent Conflict. *Journal of Conflict Resolution*, 64(1), 90–126.

Ross, M.L., 2004. What do we know about natural resources and civil war? *Journal of peace research*, 41(3), 337–356.

Saw Ralph and Naw Sheera, 2020. *Fifty Years in the Karen Revolution in Burma: The Soldier and the Teacher*. Ithaca, NY: Cornell University Press.

Seay, L., 2012. What's wrong with Dodd-Frank 1502? Conflict minerals, civilian livelihoods, and the unintended consequences of western advocacy, Working Paper No. 284, Center for Global Development.

Smith, M., 1999. *Burma: Insurgency and the Politics of Ethnic Conflict*. London: Zed Books.

Stoop, N., Verpoorten, M., and Windt, P. van der, 2018. More legislation, more violence? The impact of Dodd-Frank in the DRC. *PLOS ONE*, 13(8).

Turner, M., 2015. Peacebuilding as counterinsurgency in the occupied Palestinian territory. *Review of international studies*, 41(1), 73.

Turner, M. and Pugh, M., 2006. Towards a new agenda for transforming war economies. *Conflict, Security & Development*, 6(3), 471–479.

Van Acker, F., 2005. Where did all the land go? Enclosure & social struggle in Kivu (DR Congo). *Review of African Political Economy*, 32(103), 79–98.

Vergara, J.C.G., 2014. Modernizing drug law enforcement in Latin America. *Transnational Institute Series on Legislative Reform of Drug Policies*, 29.

Verweijen, J., 2013. Military Business and the Business of the Military in the Kivus. *Review of African Political Economy*, 40(135), 67–82.

Vlassenroot, K., 2002. Citizenship, identity formation & conflict in South Kivu: the case of the Banyamulenge. *Review of African Political Economy*, 29(93–94), 499–516.

Weigand, F., 2020. *Conflict and Transnational Crime: Borders, Bullets & Business in Southeast Asia.* Cheltenham: Edward Elgar Publishing.

Wennmann, A., 2009. Getting Armed Groups to the Table: peace processes, the political economy of conflict and the mediated state. *Third World Quarterly*, 30(6), 1123–1138.

Wimmer, A., 2012. *Waves of War: Nationalism, State Formation, and Ethnic Exclusion in the Modern World.* Cambridge: Cambridge University Press.

Woods, K., 2011. Ceasefire capitalism: military–private partnerships, resource concessions and military–state building in the Burma–China borderlands. *Journal of Peasant Studies*, 38(4), 747–770.

PART VI
Addressing smuggling

30

BLUE FRONTIERS

In pursuit of smugglers at sea

Carina Bruwer

1 Introduction

'Smuggling' refers to the act of intentionally trading in a legal commodity in violation of national or international laws (see, for example, Bruwer, 2020).[1] Smuggling has an economic goal, such as making a profit and evading taxes and sanctions (Basu, 2013). For example, even a small price differential can be an incentive for cross-border fuel smuggling, as has been seen in the waters around places like Venezuela, Iran, Nigeria and Thailand (Ralby & Soud, 2018:9). Central to many smuggling operations, therefore, is the movement of these commodities in a way that is obscured from law enforcement. As criminal networks moving commodities are experts at this clandestine form of transport, they often turn to the oceans where their commodities can either be hidden behind 80% (United Nations Conference on Trade and Development, 2018: 23) – 90% (Hudson, 2018) of global trade, or where they can merely avoid the limited maritime law enforcement and security entities operating across the 70% of earth's surface which is made up of the oceans. It is also at sea and in port where many smuggling attempts are countered.

Although the oceans are often portrayed as lawless (Prada & Roth, 2008; Urbina, 2019; Allott, 2021), such a blanket statement fails to reflect the reality of many state and non-state actors working to counter criminal activities at sea. It also fails to acknowledge that although the maritime domain is used as a vector for trade, the commodities being moved are almost exclusively destined for land. This highlights the importance of also considering territorial, and especially port security in efforts to achieve maritime security. This chapter considers smuggled commodities typically moved by sea and the impact which these commodities have once they reach land. It then turns to the international laws regulating human activity at sea and the challenges in implementing them in efforts to counter smuggling activity at sea and in ports.

2 Commodities smuggled at sea and modes of transportation

Most traded goods have historically been transported by sea, therefore making smuggling arguably as old as maritime trade. As the oceans as transport node benefit licit traders, so too the benefits attract illicit traders. Maritime transport allows for the movement of large quantities of goods, much more so than via land or air. It also allows for less law enforcement scrutiny due to

DOI: 10.4324/9781003043645-30

the vast size of the oceans and the challenges of responding to smuggling activities in waters where states have limited law enforcement assets and are afforded limited law enforcement powers. This is either due to international law limitations, failure to enact sufficient national laws providing for extra-territorial exercise of jurisdiction to counter crimes far from land, or even because states have no desire to exercise any form of control over their vessels at sea.

For these reasons, anything and everything can be moved across the seas. Migrants can be moved in containers or on board migrant smuggling vessels which are nearly certain to sink. Narcotics can be moved in makeshift submarines designed specifically for drug trafficking, or on board container vessels moving legal goods, passing through many transit destinations in-between as states struggle or neglect to secure their borders, and shipping companies ask few questions about their loads. Similarly, going out and illegally catching tons of fish is as easy as faking a fishing license, turning off your Automatic Information System (AIS) or merely plundering the fish stocks of a state which has little capacity to prevent it. To make the journey even more worthwhile, a drug shipment could be added on board.

The vessels used to move illicit goods depend on factors such as the commodity being moved, the region through which the conduit is moved, available resources and technologies, and law enforcement pressure. The modus operandi may change as law enforcement efforts to counter it are successful, sometimes even causing smuggling networks to copy other networks' successful modus operandi. An example is Iran and North Korea which turned to techniques refined by drug traffickers to move sanctioned military equipment in containers on board vessels from states known for lax oversight. This also reflects how, as containers became increasingly used over time, it became a low risk and effective concealment method for many illicit commodities (Griffiths & Jenks, 2012: 35–36). As smuggling networks gain expertise in exploiting transport systems, they may also use these expertise to expand to other commodities (Basu, 2013: 323).

When it comes to smuggling at sea, criminal networks have nearly free reign, especially on the high seas where no State enjoys sovereignty. This does not mean that there isn't an increasing amount of entities responding to such criminal activities at sea, or that there aren't any legal frameworks regulating the seas. It does however reflect that the resources and expertise required to address criminal networks are often outweighed by those smuggling or trafficking illicit commodities at sea. Smugglers are masters of evasion and have adjusted over time to allow them to expand markets and avoid law enforcement. It is also no secret that the transnational nature of contemporary smuggling activity holds many benefits for smugglers, as well as the increasingly large global maritime fleet behind which illicit commodities can be hidden.

3 The potential dangers of smuggled commodities moved at sea

One of the biggest tragedies of 2020 illustrates the potential catastrophe which can result from illicit or dangerous goods shipped by sea. The COVID-19 pandemic has been linked to the consumption of wildlife (Wu, Chen & Chan, 2020). COVID-19 is a zoonotic disease which, though yet to be confirmed, is suspected of originating from the human consumption of illegally traded wildlife like pangolins (Lam et al., 2020), thereby causing the disease to be transmitted from animals to humans. Pangolins are the most trafficked mammal in the world (TRAFFIC, no date) and as Asia's own pangolins numbers have plummeted, the overwhelming majority of pangolins are now moved from Africa to Asia (World Wildlife Foundation, 2016), either alive, dead or stripped of their scales, in multiple tonnes in containers on board commercial shipping vessels (UNODC, 2020: 53). Had such shipments never left Africa for Asia, the pandemic might have been prevented. Multiple tonnes of illegal wildlife products are

Blue frontiers

shipped at sea and have driven many species to the brink of extinction. While the annihilation of species is the primary impact of the illegal wildlife trade, it often also funds conflicts, causes violence and leads to endemic corruption across the globe (see for example, Barron, 2015; Brooks & Hopkins, 2016; CITES, n.d.; EIA, 2018: 32; UNODC, 2020).

Many other commodities are moved in direct violation of national and international laws and trade embargoes, posing a similar security risk. Examples include charcoal smuggled from Somalia and heroin smuggled from the Makran Coast off Iran and Pakistan, both funding terror organizations in Somalia and Afghanistan respectively. Smuggling at sea also holds particular dangers for crewmembers and migrants who pay to be smuggled. Thousands of migrants and refugees armed only with hope and often fearing persecution in their country of origin drown at sea as people smugglers make use of vessels which are unseaworthy, sometimes purposefully relying on the responsibility of other vessels, both law enforcement and merchant, to rescue vessels in distress (Røsæg, 2020).[2] Migrants may also fall victim to human traffickers (Karim, 2020). Crew members of vessels used exclusively for smuggling, such as dhows, are also easily forsaken by vessel owners once they have been intercepted and have failed to deliver their illicit cargo. Smuggling at sea therefore threatens a wide variety of interests, including human life, the environment and security across the globe. In response to this, an increasing number of state and non-state actors are entering the maritime domain in efforts to respond to smuggling activity at sea. State actors include maritime entities like navies and coast guards, while private entities include the shipping and transport industries.

4 The international legal framework regulating responses to smuggling at sea

Despite the oceans being vast and the number of actors able to operate at sea being limited, they are not unregulated. There is a legal framework dedicated exclusively to regulating human activity at sea – the United Nations Convention on the Law of the Sea (UNCLOS). UNCLOS, along with more general international legal frameworks which also apply at sea, is however consistently under-enforced, perhaps especially so when it comes to criminal activity, which was never intended to be the convention's principal focus.

Three key questions determine the response to smuggling activity at sea – which actors may respond, what may they do and do they wish to exercise this right? The answer to the first two questions lies in the international legal frameworks of UNCLOS and the United Nations Convention against Transnational Organized Crime (UNTOC). It is however important to remember that, although international law specifies the rights and obligations of states, it re-mains the responsibility of states to incorporate these international law rights and obligations into their domestic legislation in order to allow them to establish jurisdiction over smuggling activities at sea. This is because states establish jurisdiction in terms of their national laws, not international law. This section covers selected international legal frameworks applicable specifically to smuggling at sea.

United Nations Convention on the Law of the Sea (UNCLOS)

Flag State Jurisdiction

UNCLOS Article 92 provides that a vessel may only sail under the flag of one state and that the primary jurisdiction over the activities of that vessel, when operating on the high seas, lies with that state, also known as the Flag State. A vessel's Flag State is the state in which the vessel is registered or is otherwise entitled to fly its flag, such as through ownership.[3] UNCLOS Article

94 places a duty on Flag States to exercise this jurisdiction over their vessels "in administrative, technical and social matters".[4] Flag State jurisdiction therefore implies that the Flag State holds the primary responsibility to prevent and punish acts of smuggling committed on board its vessels, both on the high seas and in certain Coastal State waters as discussed in the following sections.

Coastal State Jurisdiction

In certain waters nearest to land, Flag State jurisdiction gives way to Coastal State jurisdiction. A Coastal State for the purpose of this chapter is a state which borders the sea and in which waters, known as maritime zones, a vessel is located when it commits an offence. Depending on how far away from a Coastal State a foreign vessel suspected of smuggling is intercepted, the Coastal State has varying powers to respond thereto. The further away from a Coastal State a crime is committed, the weaker the Coastal State's right to respond becomes. Figure 30.1 indicates the different maritime zones and their distance from the coast.

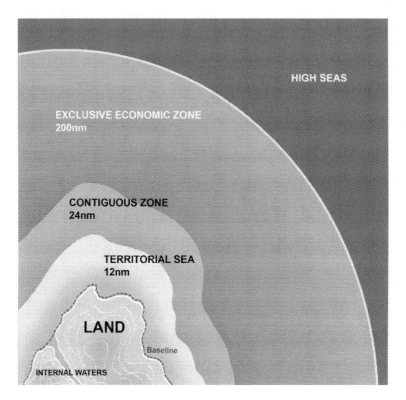

Figure 30.1 Maritime zones
Source: Illustration by Louw and Keyser, 2020

Internal waters

A Coastal State's internal waters,[5] such as river mouths or ports, are sovereign. When a suspected smuggling vessel is identified by a Coastal State within its internal waters, the Coastal State has the right to board that vessel, search for smuggled commodities and arrest and

Blue frontiers

prosecute the crew for that crime, provided the crime has been criminalized and jurisdiction established in terms of the Coastal State's national legislation. No authorization needs to be sought from the Flag State to board its vessel. In this case, it will not matter where the vessels or the crew are from and it will be as if the crime was committed within the Coastal State's land territory. This right to board and respond to smuggling activity in any Coastal State's maritime zones, however, only applies to merchant vessels, not vessels on government service for non-commercial purposes,[6] such as naval vessels. In all Coastal State maritime zones, only authorized vessels on government service, such as warships or law enforcement vessels, may intercept smuggling activity.

Territorial sea and archipelagic waters

Coastal States also have sovereignty in their territorial sea[7] and archipelagic waters.[8] UNCLOS Article 27 allows Coastal States to establish jurisdiction over certain crimes in these maritime zones, which includes smuggling activity:

1. The criminal jurisdiction of the coastal state should not be exercised on board a foreign ship passing through the territorial sea to arrest any person or to conduct any investigation in connection with any crime committed on board the ship during its passage, save only in the following cases:

    a. if the consequences of the crime extend to the coastal state;
    b. if the crime is of a kind to disturb the peace of the country or the good order of the territorial sea;
    c. if the assistance of the local authorities has been requested by the master of the ship or by a diplomatic agent or consular officer of the flag state; or
    d. if such measures are necessary for the suppression of illicit traffic in narcotic drugs or psychotropic substances.[…]

As smuggling activity aimed for the Coastal State's territory will impact on the Coastal State, the Coastal State may board such vessels and prosecute for smuggling activities. In accordance with UNCLOS Article 27(5), the Coastal State may however not establish such criminal jurisdiction for crimes committed before a foreign flagged vessel entered the Coastal State's territorial sea and the vessel is merely passing through its territorial sea without the intentions of entering its internal waters. The only exception to this is for resource related crimes, as discussed under the exclusive economic zone (EEZ) below.

Contiguous zone

The Coastal State must claim a contiguous zone (Guilfoyle, 2009: 13)[9] in its national legislation before being afforded the jurisdiction applicable in that zone. The contiguous zone was in fact established to allow Coastal States to respond to smuggling activity beyond their territorial seas (UNODC, 2019: 40). In this zone, the Coastal State may only establish criminal jurisdiction over activities which violate its fiscal, immigration, sanitary or customs laws. This jurisdiction is twofold and distinguishes between Coastal States' right to *prevent* and *punish* certain crimes (see, for example, Guilfoyle, 2009:13):

1. When encountering a vessel suspected of smuggling activity in this zone and the vessel is heading towards the Coastal State's territorial sea, the Coastal State may only board the vessel and warn it not to proceed into its territorial sea, as doing so will violate its fiscal, immigration, sanitary or customs laws. It may not arrest the vessel or prosecute for any smuggling offence which has not yet taken place in the Coastal State's land territory, territorial sea or internal waters. However, if the commodity being smuggled is a resource, such as fish, in violation of the Coastal State's sovereign rights in its EEZ, the Coastal State may board, arrest and prosecute the vessel and crew.[10]
2. If the vessel is suspected of having already committed smuggling activity within the Coastal States' land territory, internal waters or territorial sea, the Coastal State may stop, board, search and arrest the vessels and crew and prosecute if evidence of smuggling activity is found. This applies only to crimes which have already been committed within the Coastal States' territory.

As smuggling activity will typically breach customs regulations, or, in the case of people smuggling, immigration laws (see, for example, UNODC, 2004: 11), the Coastal State is entitled to establish jurisdiction over vessels which have already committed smuggling offences in its territory, territorial sea or internal waters. This means that up to 24 nautical miles from the Coast, States have the right to arrest and prosecute those suspected of smuggling activities in their territory.

Exclusive economic zone (EEZ)

The Coastal State's powers are much more limited with regard to the crimes it may respond to in its EEZ[11] as these are limited to resource related crimes.[12] If a vessel is therefore suspected of transporting fish caught illegally in the Coastal State's EEZ, criminal jurisdiction may be established over the vessel in this zone. However, if a vessel is suspected of trafficking drugs in the EEZ, criminal jurisdiction over the vessels may only be established once it enters the Coastal State's territorial sea. This is in accordance with UNCLOS Articles 27 and 33. There are however exceptions, such as hot pursuit which applies once a vessel flees from law enforcement after committing an offence in a Coastal State's relevant maritime zones.[13]

High seas

The high seas are all waters which do not form part of internal waters, territorial seas, archipelagic waters or exclusive economic zones. The primary jurisdiction and responsibility to respond to smuggling on the high seas[14] rests with the Flag State.[15] UNCLOS does however contain a few exceptions to this, most notably in Article 110, which allows foreign flagged vessels to be boarded on the high seas under certain conditions in order to confirm their flag.[16] Of these exceptions, none are aimed specifically at smuggling, though some may be used to board suspected smuggling vessels. Article 110(1)(d) allows visitation of vessels suspected of being without nationality, while Article 110(1)(e) allows vessels to be boarded if they, although hiding it, are in fact from the same state as the law enforcement vessel wishing to board. Article 110(b) might also apply, as it allows vessels suspected of engaging in the slave trade to be boarded, but this depends on differing interpretations of whether human trafficking can be considered a modern form of slave trade (See, for example, Davidson, 2015; Davidson, 2010).

Which steps intercepting States may take if illicit activity is indeed found on vessels without nationality, remains debated. Most States argue that there is no legal basis to arrest and prosecute

(Papastavridis, 2013: 208.), while others argue that by virtue of being without nationality vessels attempt to escape any jurisdiction and therefore enjoy the protection of no state (Guilfoyle, 2009: 17–18; 297), therefore they can be prosecuted by the intercepting State in accordance with its national laws.

Additional exceptions to Flag State jurisdiction on the high seas are found in other international legal instruments. For example, in order to allow states to respond to drug trafficking on board foreign vessels on the high seas, the United Nations Convention against Illicit Traffic in Narcotic Drugs and Psychotropic Substances of 1988 allows states to request Flag State permission to board foreign flagged vessels and establish jurisdiction over drug trafficking activity, as discussed below.

United Nations Convention against Illicit Traffic in Narcotic Drugs and Psychotropic Substances (Vienna Convention)

The Vienna Convention was established to promote cooperation among states wishing to counter transnational drug trafficking.[17] It contains a section aimed specifically at drug trafficking at sea which provides an exception to Flag State jurisdiction on the high seas. Article 17(3)[18] allows states to request confirmation of registry from a foreign Flag State upon reasonable suspicion of their vessels being engaged in drug trafficking on the high seas. Only once registry has been confirmed may the vessel request further authorization from the Flag State to board the vessel, conduct a search and take steps should evidence of drug trafficking be found.[19] If the Flag State confirms the Flag, but refuses their vessel to be boarded or searched, the interdicting state may take no further action. If the Flag State allows their vessel to be boarded, they can authorize the interdicting state to take such steps as they deem fit to counter drug trafficking. This could include arrest and prosecution.

United Nations Convention against Transnational Organized Crime of 2000 and Protocols (UNTOC)

UNTOC is the primary international instrument applicable to smuggling activity. Trafficking and smuggling, when conducted by a group, are forms of organized crime, which are typically crimes which have a profit or other material benefit as motive (Varese, 2010; Von Lampe, 2016).[20] While UNCLOS forms the jurisdictional basis for responding to smuggling activity at sea, UNTOC was established with the aim of countering transnational organized crime on land, sea and air by enabling cross-border cooperation. UNTOC has three protocols, namely the Protocol to Prevent, Suppress and Punish Trafficking in Persons, especially Women and Children, the Protocol against the Smuggling of Migrants by Land, Sea and Air (Migrant Smuggling Protocol) and the Protocol against the Illicit Manufacturing of and Trafficking in Firearms, their Parts and Components and Ammunition. From the protocols it is already clear which crimes are typically considered forms of trafficking or smuggling – human trafficking, migrant smuggling and arms trafficking. This list is hardly exhaustive and commodities like fauna and flora, drugs and counterfeit goods can all be added thereto. UNTOC, however, only applies to crimes which are executed by an organized criminal group,[21] which are of a transnational[22] nature and which are punishable by at least 4 years imprisonment.[23]

UNTOC Article 15 reflects Article 94 of UNCLOS, confirming Flag Sate jurisdiction over vessels engaged in smuggling or trafficking activity at sea.[24] UNTOC, being aimed at countering transnational organized crime, has numerous provisions which provide for transnational counter-efforts and investigations. Examples include Articles 16–20 on mutual legal assistance

(MLA), joint investigations and extradition, all providing a useful tool which states can use to conduct cross-border law enforcement operations and investigations. Again, it is important that states must incorporate the provisions of UNTOC into their national legislation in order to exercise their rights to respond to smuggling and trafficking activity at sea in terms of UNTOC.

UNTOC's Migrant Smuggling Protocol, for example, reflects similar provisions to the Vienna Convention. It contains a section aimed specifically at migrant smuggling at sea which also allows foreign flagged vessels to be requested to confirm their registry and once confirmed, to be requested permission to board the vessel on suspicion of migrant smuggling and to take steps as authorized by the Flag State if evidence of migrant smuggling is found.[25] It goes further than the Vienna Convention, however, in that it also allows states to board vessels without nationality if they are suspected of smuggling migrants.[26] Key to the Protocol is therefore that it allows an additional jurisdictional basis to board foreign and stateless vessels on the high seas if suspected of migrant smuggling. The Migrant Smuggling Protocol is aimed at migrant smugglers and not migrants, who must have their rights protected despite their status of attempting to enter another state illegally.[27]

United Nations Security Council Resolutions

Often, international legal frameworks are insufficient to address the contemporary manifestations of threats to security and crime. This has necessitated additional jurisdiction regimes, such as those authorized by the United Nations Security Council (UNSC) in terms of resolutions. Resolution 2240 of 2015 applicable to migrant smuggling in the Mediterranean (See, for example, United Nations Security Council, 2019a) is one such an example, where the UNSC concluded that migrant smuggling between North Africa and Europe is of such serious concern, posing a threat to international peace and security, that it required the authorization of an additional jurisdictional regime than that contained in UNCLOS and UNTOC.

UNSC Resolution 2240 allows for flagged vessels to be boarded by foreign navies on the high seas if they believe the vessel to be engaged in migrant smuggling. While the Resolution notes that attempts must be made to notify the Flag State of such actions, this is not a prerequisite for boarding.[28] Similarly, the UNSC has imposed embargoes on the smuggling of arms and charcoal into and out of Somalia (United Nations Security Council, 2014; United Nations Security Council, 2019b). In terms of UNSC Resolution 2082 of 2014, foreign flagged vessels can be boarded on the high seas and in Somalia's territorial sea if they are suspected of smuggling arms or charcoal. Similar to Resolution 2240 on migrant smuggling, while good faith efforts must be made to gain authorization from the Flag State, this is not a prerequisite for boarding (United Nations Security Council, 2014). These are clear exceptions to Flag State jurisdiction when the existing legal frameworks seem insufficient to address serious threats within a defined region at a certain moment in time.

Bilateral and multilateral treaties

In addition to international laws and UNSC authorizations, states may conclude agreements amongst themselves agreeing to a specific interdiction regime which is perhaps not provided for in existing international legal frameworks. Examples are often found in regional agreements in response to drug trafficking. One example is the 1995 Council of Europe Agreement on Illicit Traffic by Sea, implementing Article 17 of the United Nations Convention against Illicit Traffic in Narcotic Drugs and Psychotropic Substances of the 1988 Convention. In terms of this agreement, Member States of the Council of Europe undertake to exercise jurisdiction over each other's vessels engaged in drug trafficking, but also over vessels without nationality. Where UNCLOS Article 110 is silent on which enforcement actions may be taken against a vessel without nationality once it has been boarded to confirm its flag, the Council of Europe Agreement Article 5 allows Members to establish their jurisdiction over such vessels.[29]

International Ship and Port Facility Security (ISPS) Code

The ISPS Code is the primary international instrument applicable to port security and therefore applies to Coastal State efforts to counter smuggling through ports. The Code is a 2004 amendment to the Safety of Life at Sea (SOLAS) Convention of 1974 and applies to vessels on international voyages. Although the Code was initially established to provide protection against terror activities, its application also benefits efforts to counter smuggling, provided its guidelines are implemented. It establishes minimum standards to which vessels and ports must adhere to ensure safety and security in ports and on board vessels. This is aimed at protecting both vessels entering ports and ports from arriving vessels. Multiple tonnes of smuggled or trafficked goods however continue to pass through ports on vessels across the globe and efforts to counter smuggling through ports are arguably some of the least effective measures due to massive volumes of trade, corruption, concealment of illicit shipments and limited security measures on land.

5 Challenges in responding to smuggling at sea

The previous section has described the options available to those working to combat smuggling activity at sea and in ports. But when it comes to putting these rights and obligations into practice, there are many obstacles. In addition to rough seas, unpredictable weather, dilapidated vessels and the inherent challenges in responding to smuggling at sea, many additional factors come into play for those wishing to respond to smuggling activity at sea. Below are selected examples.

Flags of Convenience

Flags of Convenience (see, for example, Marine Insight, 2019), also known as international or open registries (Watt, & Coles, 2019: 45; Ford & Wilcox, 2019: 98), refer to flagging regimes whereby vessels register in a state to which it does not necessarily have a link, such as the owner being a national of the Flag State or the shipping company being registered there. Once a vessel is registered in a Flag State, it has the nationality of that state.[30] Although UNCLOS Article 91 requires a genuine link between the Flag State and the vessel, a 'genuine link' is not defined. Economic motivations are one of the key factors influencing flagging to an open registry and a 'genuine' link might include such an economic link (Hamad, 2016: 207). Flagging under open registries, can however also be done to evade Flag State jurisdiction when a vessel is purposefully flagged to a state which is known to exercise little control over its vessels. This is when a Flag becomes referred to as 'convenient' (Hamad, 2016: 213-214; Ford & Wilcox, 2019: 298). If a vessel suspected of smuggling is flagged to a known Flag of Convenience, this might raise additional suspicion. A vessel may also be deregistered and reregistered under a Flag of Convenience in order to avoid sanctions (Griffiths & Jenks, 2012: 41), for example.

   If those wishing to smuggle commodities at sea use vessels registered under Flags which are known to exercise little control over its vessels, it allows them the freedom to do as they wish on board the vessel (see, for example, Hamad, 2016: 221). This may include, for example, employing a foreign crew and paying them sub-standard wages or not adhering to ISPS code requirements. Key Flags of Convenience include Panama, Liberia and the Marshall Islands, which have open registries due to the financial benefits it brings. In turn, vessel owners may choose to flag to such States because registration is easy and cheap, and because in doing so they may avoid having to pay income tax (Chapsos, 2018). A Flag is also considered as a Flag of Convenience if a vessel flies more than one flag and switches between them. UNCLOS Article 92 provides that such a vessel shall be assimilated to a vessel without nationality as a vessel may have only one Flag State.[31] One example of how multiple flags are used is of the STS 50, a notorious fishing vessel used to plunder the seas illegally. It claimed to be flagged to eight Flag States, all of whose exercise of Flag State authority leaves much to the imagination (Tory, 2020).

Flags of Convenience pose a particular problem to countering smuggling efforts, especially on the high seas. Not only do Flag States which are unable or unwilling to exercise control over their vessels pose a threat to safety and security at sea (Hamad, 2016: 215), they also limit foreign law enforcement efforts in response thereto as the Flag State has the primary responsibility to respond to smuggling activity on board its vessels. It is only once such a flagged vessel enters Coastal State waters that Coastal States may respond to smuggling activity on board those vessels. The challenge, however, remains when these vessels operate on the high seas and may never even enter Coastal State waters if they instead tranship their illicit cargo to other vessels going to shore.[32] Such at-sea offloads simulate a port without any port state control (Long, 2018). The use of Flags of Convenience may also make it nearly impossible to establish who owns a vessel, as owners may have gone out of their way to conceal their identity (Hamad, 2016: 220–222; Tory, 2020).

Vessels without nationality

The second and perhaps most challenging smuggling vessel to counter, is one without nationality. While no vessel can ever be truly without a nationality, as all vessels belong to someone who is a national from somewhere, and typically returns to one specific state after voyages are complete, a vessel is considered without nationality under the following conditions:

1. UNCLOS Article 92 (2) provides that a vessel is without nationality if it is flying more than one flag and uses them according to convenience;
2. If the Master fails to make a valid claim of registry, such as when it cannot provide the necessary documents as proof of its Flag State upon a request by law enforcement;
3. If the flag which is claimed by the master is denied by the state which has been claimed;
4. If the claimed Flag State cannot confirm or deny that it is their vessel; and
5. If the Flag State being claimed is not recognized by the intercepting state (McLaughlin, 2016: 486–487).

As noted earlier, UNCLOS Article 110 provides exceptions to Flag State jurisdiction on the high seas and allows certain vessels to be boarded in order to confirm their flag. One of these grounds is suspicion of being a vessel without nationality.[33] The UNTOC Migrant Smuggling Protocol also allows the boarding of a vessel suspected of being without nationality and engaging in migrant smuggling.[34]

There is no consensus among states on whether vessels without nationality can be assimilated to a vessel of the state wishing to intercept its smuggling activity, based on the fact that the

Blue frontiers

vessel enjoys the protection of no State. Some states therefore argue that they can establish their national jurisdiction on board that vessel and seize illicit commodities, arrest the vessel and crew and prosecute for that crime as if the vessel is their own. For example, Seychelles, a victim of the Indian Ocean heroin trade, has incorporated the right to try any drug trafficking offences committed outside of Seychelles on board vessels displaying no flag.[35] The US historically also has asserted that it may exercise enforcement jurisdiction over stateless vessels on the high seas because their activities threaten the interests of the US (Guilfoyle, 2009: 80–83).

Most states, however, feel that while they may board such vessels to verify their nationality, they have no further jurisdictional basis to establish their national laws and prosecute the crew for the crimes they have committed on the high seas. Instead, they would require an additional basis, such as a link to a crew member or the victim of a crime (see, for example, Guilfoyle, 2009: 17–18; 297; Gallagher, 2014: 246). As the second approach seems to be most prominent, stateless smuggling vessels enjoy a great deal of impunity when intercepted on the high seas. At best their illicit cargo will be seized, but the crew and vessels are likely to be allowed to continue on their way. This is why vessels without nationality are considered by some as inherently criminal as their main aim may be to avoid any form of jurisdiction (Hamad, 2016: 208).

The trafficking of Afghan heroin from Iran and Pakistan illustrates the challenges posed by vessels without nationality, which heroin trafficking dhows active in the Indian Ocean often are. While these dhows, which show no sign of registry, may be boarded by foreign navies to confirm their flag, few states have enacted national legislation which allows them to establishment enforcement jurisdiction over vessels without nationality engaged in drug trafficking.[36] The current practice is therefore to board these vessels to confirm their flag and if no nationality can be proven and heroin is indeed found on board, the heroin shipment is seized, samples taken and thrown overboard, after which the vessel and crew are let go. This practice has however resulted in the same vessels continuing to ferry heroin up and down the Indian Ocean with little consequence. Only once these vessels enter Coastal State waters may they be intercepted and seized for prosecution, allowing the vessels to be removed from circulation (Bruwer, 2020: 67–68).

Lack of private industry responsibility for vessel actions and illicit cargo

While some vessels used to smuggle goods are without nationality or privately owned and used exclusively to smuggle goods, vast amounts of commodities are smuggled on board commercial shipping vessels moving the overwhelming majority (United Nations Conference on Trade and Development, 2018; Hudson, 2018) of world trade. As the global shipping industry expands, so will its exploitation by smugglers and traffickers. Despite this, the shipping and transport industry has not fully taken responsibility for what is moved on board their vessels. While the primary responsibility for enforcing laws lies with the Flag State, an additional responsibility falls upon vessel owners and shipping companies which need to ensure that they have the necessary measures in place to prevent their vessels being used for smuggling. The ISPS Code aims to achieve this by setting minimum standards to which vessels must adhere to prevent their use for illicit purposes. With sea-borne insecurity threatening all corners of the globe, not only through smuggling, but also terror activity and environmental threats, it is long overdue that shipping companies take more responsibility for their fleet and the cargo they carry. Granted, this is no easy task. The largest container vessels carry over 20,000 twenty-foot equivalent unit containers. There are however few alternatives which are equally likely to prevent the use of cargo vessels for illicit means than those imposed by the shipping and transport industry.

Human rights concerns

Vessels on the high seas are notorious for human rights abuses – from the slave trade, to forced labour on fishing vessels and human trafficking. Another, lesser mentioned manifestation presents itself in response to illicit activities at sea. Smuggling vessels might come from regions where human rights enjoy little protection. This not only threatens the human rights of the crew while at sea, but also once they are returned home after being intercepted by law enforcement. If a smuggling vessel is intercepted in line with international law and smuggling activity is found on board, the vessel and crew's arrest and prosecution might not be considered an option by foreign law enforcement, despite having the necessary jurisdiction to do so. This can be the case when the crew might be subjected to human rights abuses due to their smuggling activity should they be returned to their home state.

Another example illustrating the tension between human rights and law enforcement at sea is migrant smuggling operations which turn into rescue operations. International law places a duty on states to render assistance to vessels in distress.[37] Foreign law enforcement, may however actively avoid rescuing migrant vessels as they do not wish to take responsibility for those migrants (Neuman & Allafort-Duverger, 2018). Not only does this put migrants' lives at risk, but it fails to take action against smugglers. Migrant smuggling is perhaps the most vivid example of states neglecting their international law duties at sea, driven not by the lack of a framework allowing them to assist, but rather by politics and fear (International Chamber of Shipping, 2019). Many European states, for example, do not wish to allow the thousands of migrants who cross the Mediterranean in search of a better life into their states, thereby neglecting their duties towards them at sea. This has caused merchant vessels and non-governmental organizations to shoulder the responsibility of rescuing distressed migrants, rather than navies or coast guards (See, for example, Roche, 2016; Amnesty International, 2019; Tondo, & Stierl, 2020). This, however, does not solve the issue of few states agreeing to disembarkation of migrants at a place of safety and possible violations of the right to non-refoulement.

Some smuggling crews have also turned to setting their vessels alight (Rubira, 2019) or purposefully sinking vessels to avoid detection of illicit activities, thereby destroying evidence, endangering the crew and environment and forcing rescue operations (Bennett, 2012).

Opportunities in responding to smuggling at sea

While international legal frameworks allow states to act against certain smuggling activity at sea, states do not always have the resources or appetite to do so. This is why counter-responses are ideally implemented in partnership, such as by the naval coalitions collectively responding to migrant smuggling in the Mediterranean (Coventry, 2019: 9–10; EUNAVFOR MED Operation Sophia, n.d.) and heroin trafficking in the Western Indian Ocean (Bruwer, 2020: 67–68). Such cooperative efforts are increasingly seen as traditional maritime security threats have made way for non-state threats which individual states and their navies are unable to counter effectively. Where a state fails to respond to smuggling activity around its littoral, either due to an inability to counter it themselves, or perhaps due to other motivations, such as corrupt interests in the smuggling of a commodity, the international community often steps in. The smuggling of charcoal from Somalia is one such an example (see, for example, Rawlence, 2015). This, however, depends on whether the smuggling activity also threatens the interests of the responding states. A more recent, yet successful effort, is the contribution of non-state actors joining the response to smuggling at sea. Examples include NGOs like Global Fishing Watch

Blue frontiers

working on IUU fishing and NGO vessels rescuing migrants. While this illuminates the inability of states to address smuggling alone, it illustrates the success which can be achieved if a whole of society approach is taken to address a scourge which indeed harms all of society.

It must be noted that a typical response to increased law enforcement activity at sea is that criminal networks merely shift their activities to where there is less law enforcement scrutiny (see, for example, West African Commission on Drugs, 2014). Examples of law enforcement displacement are found in the South American cocaine trade. As the market for cocaine in Europe grew and law enforcement pressure on places like Mexico and the Caribbean became increasingly stringent, traffickers began to move cocaine via West Africa (see, for example, UNODC, 2007: 17–18; McGuire, 2010: 16; O'Regan, 2010). This was also seen in the heroin trade off eastern Africa. As traditional heroin trafficking routes across the Balkans became increasingly policed and unstable, traffickers shifted to the sea (Bruwer, 2020: 62).

Law enforcement measures alone, therefore, rarely have the desired effect of combatting smuggling activity. Instead, as with all forms of transnational crime motivated by profit-making, smuggling needs to be addressed at the level of demand, supply and the logistics facilitating the movement of these commodities. However, this is easier said than done. Supply reduction efforts are particularly challenging as supply often serves as a livelihood for people with few licit alternatives. In addition, if demand is not addressed, sources of supply are likely to continue to be found if the demand for an illicit commodity remains high. Demand reduction efforts, however, pose particular challenges, as they are not only neglected, but badly understood.

The need to address demand and supply on land in addition to the movement of illicit commodities at sea, also illustrates the disconnect often found in responding to criminal activity at sea. While seizing smuggled goods at sea indeed prevents large quantities from reaching shore, it does little to address demand apart from perhaps driving up the price of the commodity.

Conclusion

This chapter has illustrated that the oceans are not a lawless void. Instead, states, the shipping industry and criminals interact on the seas daily. Licit and illicit actors therefore compete for the use of the seas and are joined by those working to protect regular shipping and to counter illicit trades. As the traditional response to smuggling activity has been to step up security and law enforcement efforts, smugglers have not only shifted to the sea to evade such efforts on land, but they have also expanded their modus operandi by using a wider variety of vessels, with some even expanding their trade to other commodities in doing so. While these non-state criminal actors entering the maritime domain have given rise to previously unseen forms of inter-state and public–private cooperation, these actors, even when acting in unison, remain ill-equipped to successfully counter these activities at sea as criminal networks typically outsmart and out-resource them. Most importantly, maritime counter-efforts also fail to address demand and supply.

What should perhaps worry states most about smuggling activity is not necessarily the activity itself, but rather the corruption which nearly always facilitates smuggling activity. While the impact of some smuggled commodities might seem harmless, its potential to hollow out state institutions is a very real threat, especially in the developing world. No amount of law enforcement can rid states of endemic corruption and alternatives must therefore be sought to prevent law enforcement efforts from being bypassed by corrupt activities.

Carina Bruwer

Notes

1 There is a difference between trafficking and smuggling, as trafficking refers to the trade in prohibited commodities, such as humans, while smuggling refers to trade in commodities which themselves are not prohibited but their trade in contravention of laws is, such as illegally traded cigarettes. For the purpose of this chapter, any reference to 'smuggling' may be assumed to also refer to 'trafficking' if the commodity being traded is illegal, like humans or narcotics.

2 UNCLOS Article 98; Regulation V-33 of *International Convention on the Safety of Life at Sea of 1974*.

3 UNCLOS Article 2: "1. Ships shall sail under the flag of one state only and, save in exceptional cases expressly provided for in international treaties or in this Convention, shall be subject to its exclusive jurisdiction on the high seas."

4 UNCLOS Article 94: "1. Every state shall effectively exercise its jurisdiction and control in administrative, technical and social matters over ships flying its flag. 2. In particular every state shall: (a) maintain a register of ships containing the names and particulars of ships flying its flag, except those which are excluded from generally accepted international regulations on account of their small size; and (b) assume jurisdiction under its internal law over each ship flying its flag and its master, officers and crew in respect of administrative, technical and social matters concerning the ship. [...] 6. A state which has clear grounds to believe that proper jurisdiction and control with respect to a ship have not been exercised may report the facts to the flag state. Upon receiving such a report, the flag state shall investigate the matter and, if appropriate, take any action necessary to remedy the situation."

5 UNCLOS Article 8: "waters on the landward side of the baseline of the territorial sea form part of the internal waters of the State".

6 UNCLOS Article 32: "With such exceptions as are contained in subsection A and in articles 30 and 31, nothing in this Convention affects the immunities of warships and other government ships operated for non-commercial purposes."

7 UNCLOS Article 2 (1): "The sovereignty of a coastal state extends, beyond its land territory and internal waters and, in the case of an archipelagic state, its archipelagic waters, to an adjacent belt of sea, described as the territorial sea."; UNCLOS Article 3: "Every state has the right to establish the breadth of its territorial sea up to a limit not exceeding 12 nautical miles, measured from baselines determined in accordance with this Convention."

8 UNCLOS Article 46: "'archipelagic state' means a state constituted wholly by one or more archipelagos and may include other islands; (b) 'archipelago' means a group of islands, including parts of islands, interconnecting waters and other natural features which are so closely interrelated that such islands, waters and other natural features form an intrinsic geographical, economic and political entity, or which historically have been regarded as such."; UNCLOS Article 47: "An archipelagic state may draw straight archipelagic baselines joining the outermost points of the outermost islands and drying reefs of the archipelago provided that within such baselines are included the main islands and an area in which the ratio of the area of the water to the area of the land, including atolls, is between 1 to 1 and 9 to 1."; UNCLOS Article 49 (1): "The sovereignty of an archipelagic state extends to the waters enclosed by the archipelagic baselines drawn in accordance with article 47, described as archipelagic waters, regardless of their depth or distance from the coast."

9 UNCLOS Article 33:

   1. In a zone contiguous to its territorial sea, described as the contiguous zone, the coastal state may exercise the control necessary to: (a) prevent infringement of its customs, fiscal, immigration or sanitary laws and regulations within its territory or territorial sea; (b) punish infringement of the above laws and regulations committed within its territory or territorial sea. 2. The contiguous zone may not extend beyond 24 nautical miles from the baselines from which the breadth of the territorial sea is measured.

10 UNCLOS Article 73:

   1. The coastal state may, in the exercise of its sovereign rights to explore, exploit, conserve and manage the living resources in the exclusive economic zone, take such measures, including boarding, inspection, arrest and judicial proceedings, as may be necessary to ensure compliance with the laws and regulations adopted by it in conformity with this Convention. 2. Arrested vessels and their crews shall be promptly released upon the posting of reasonable bond or other

Blue frontiers

security. 3. Coastal state penalties for violations of fisheries laws and regulations in the exclusive economic zone may not include imprisonment, in the absence of agreements to the contrary by the states concerned, or any other form of corporal punishment. 4. In cases of arrest or detention of foreign vessels the coastal state shall promptly notify the flag state, through appropriate channels, of the action taken and of any penalties subsequently imposed.

11 UNCLOS Article 55:

The exclusive economic zone is an area beyond and adjacent to the territorial sea, subject to the specific legal regime established in this Part, under which the rights and jurisdiction of the coastal state and the rights and freedoms of other states are governed by the relevant provisions of this Convention." Article 57: "The exclusive economic zone shall not extend beyond 200 nautical miles from the baselines from which the breadth of the territorial sea is measured.

12 UNCLOS Article 56:

1. In the exclusive economic zone, the coastal state has: (a) sovereign rights for the purpose of exploring and exploiting, conserving and managing the natural resources, whether living or non-living, of the waters superjacent to the seabed and of the seabed and its subsoil, and with regard to other activities for the economic exploitation and exploration of the zone, such as the production of energy from the water, currents and winds; (b) jurisdiction as provided for in the relevant provisions of this Convention with regard to: (i) the establishment and use of artificial islands, installations and structures; (ii) marine scientific research; (iii) the protection and preservation of the marine environment; (c) other rights and duties provided for in this Convention.

13 UNCLOS Article 111:

1. The hot pursuit of a foreign ship may be undertaken when the competent authorities of the coastal state have good reason to believe that the ship has violated the laws and regulations of that state. Such pursuit must be commenced when the foreign ship or one of its boats is within the internal waters, the archipelagic waters, the territorial sea or the contiguous zone of the pursuing state, and may only be continued outside the territorial sea or the contiguous zone if the pursuit has not been interrupted. It is not necessary that, at the time when the foreign ship within the territorial sea or the contiguous zone receives the order to stop, the ship giving the order should likewise be within the territorial sea or the contiguous zone. If the foreign ship is within a contiguous zone, as defined in article 33, the pursuit may only be undertaken if there has been a violation of the rights for the protection of which the zone was established. 2. The right of hot pursuit shall apply *mutatis mutandis* to violations in the exclusive economic zone [...] 3. The right of hot pursuit ceases as soon as the ship pursued enters the territorial sea of its own state or of a third state. 4. Hot pursuit is not deemed to have begun unless the pursuing ship has satisfied itself by such practicable means as may be available that the ship pursued or one of its boats or other craft working as a team and using the ship pursued as a mother ship is within the limits of the territorial sea, or, as the case may be, within the contiguous zone or the exclusive economic zone or above the continental shelf. The pursuit may only be commenced after a visual or auditory signal to stop has been given at a distance which enables it to be seen or heard by the foreign ship.

14 UNCLOS Article 86:

The provisions of this part apply to all parts of the sea that are not included in the exclusive economic zone, in the territorial sea or in the internal waters of a state, or in the archipelagic waters of an archipelagic state. This article does not entail any abridgement of the freedoms enjoyed by all states in the exclusive economic zone in accordance with article 58.

15 UNCLOS Article 94.
16 UNCLOS Article 110:

1. Except where acts of interference derive from powers conferred by treaty, a warship which encounters on the high seas a foreign ship, other than a ship entitled to complete immunity in accordance with articles 95 and 96, is not justified in boarding it unless there is reasonable ground for suspecting that: (a) the ship is engaged in piracy; (b) the ship is engaged in the slave trade; (c) the ship is engaged in unauthorized broadcasting and the flag state of the warship has jurisdiction under article 109; (d) the ship is without nationality; or (e) though flying a foreign flag or refusing to show its flag, the ship is, in reality, of the same nationality as the warship. 2. In the cases provided for in paragraph 1, the warship may proceed to verify the ship's right to fly its flag. To this end, it may send a boat under the command of an officer to the suspected ship. If suspicion remains after the documents have been checked, it may proceed to a further examination on board the ship, which must be carried out with all possible consideration.

17 Vienna Convention Article 2.
18 Vienna Convention Article 17(3):

A Party which has reasonable grounds to suspect that a vessel exercising freedom of navigation in accordance with international law, and flying the flag or displaying marks of registry of another Party is engaged in illicit traffic may so notify the flag state, request confirmation of registry and, if confirmed, request authorization from the flag state to take appropriate measures in regard to that vessel.

19 Vienna Convention Article 17(4):

4. In accordance with paragraph 3 or in accordance with treaties in force between them or in accordance with any agreement or arrangement otherwise reached between those Parties, the flag state may authorize the requesting state to, *inter aria*: a) Board the vessel; b) Search the vessel; c) If evidence of involvement in illicit traffic is found, take appropriate action with respect to the vessel, persons and cargo on board.

20 The term 'organized crime' is debated. See, for example, Varese, F. 2010. What is organized crime? In: F. Varese F, ed. *Organized crime: critical concepts in Criminology.* London: Routledge; Von Lampe, K. 2016. *Organized crime: analysing illegal activities, criminal structures, and extra-legal governance.* Thousand Oaks: Sage.
21 UNTOC Article 2(a): "Organized criminal group" shall mean a structured group of three or more persons, existing for a period of time and acting in concert with the aim of committing one or more serious crimes or offences established in accordance with this Convention, in order to obtain, directly or indirectly, a financial or other material benefit.
22 UNTOC Article 3(2):

An offence is transnational in nature if: *(a)* It is committed in more than one state; *(b)* It is committed in one state but a substantial part of its preparation, planning, direction or control takes place in another state; *(c)* It is committed in one state but involves an organized criminal group that engages in criminal activities in more than one state; or *(d)* It is committed in one state but has substantial effects in another state.

23 UNTOC Article 2 (b).
24 UNCLOS Article 15(1):

Each State Party shall adopt such measures as may be necessary to establish its jurisdiction over the offences established in accordance with articles 5, 6, 8 and 23 of this Convention when: [...]

Blue frontiers

(b) The offence is committed on board a vessel that is flying the flag of that State Party or an aircraft that is registered under the laws of that State Party at the time that the offence is committed.

25 UNTOC Migrant Smuggling Protocol Article 8 (2):
A State Party that has reasonable grounds to suspect that a vessel exercising freedom of navigation in accordance with international law and flying the flag or displaying the marks of registry of another State Party is engaged in the smuggling of migrants by sea may so notify the flag state, request confirmation of registry and, if confirmed, request authorization from the flag state to take appropriate measures with regard to that vessel. The flag State may authorize the requesting state, inter alia: *(a)* To board the vessel; *(b)* To search the vessel; and *(c)* If evidence is found that the vessel is engaged in the smuggling of migrants by sea, to take appropriate measures with respect to the vessel and persons and cargo on board, as authorized by the flag state.

26 UNTOC Migrant Smuggling Protocol Article 8(7):
A State Party that has reasonable grounds to suspect that a vessel is engaged in the smuggling of migrants by sea and is without nationality or may be assimilated to a vessel without nationality may board and search the vessel. If evidence confirming the suspicion is found, that State Party shall take appropriate measures in accordance with relevant domestic and international law.

27 UNTOC Migrant Smuggling Protocol Article 5.
28 UNSC Resolution 2240 Para 7:
Decides, with a view to saving the threatened lives of migrants or of victims of human trafficking on board such vessels as mentioned above, to authorise, in these exceptional and specific circumstances, for a period of one year from the date of the adoption of this resolution, Member States, acting nationally or through regional organisations that are engaged in the fight against migrant smuggling and human trafficking, to inspect on the high seas off the coast of Libya vessels that they have reasonable grounds to suspect are being used for migrant smuggling or human trafficking from Libya, provided that such Member States and regional organisations make good faith efforts to obtain the consent of the vessel's flag state prior to using the authority outlined in this paragraph.

29 Council of Europe Agreement Article 5:
1. A Party which has reasonable grounds to suspect that a vessel without nationality, or assimilated to a vessel without nationality under international law, is engaged in or being used for the commission of a relevant offence, shall inform such other Parties as appear most closely affected and may request the assistance of any such Party in suppressing its use for that purpose. The Party so requested shall render such assistance within the means available to it. 2 Where a Party, having received information in accordance with paragraph 1, takes action it shall be for that Party to determine what actions are appropriate and to exercise its jurisdiction over any relevant offences which may have been committed by any persons on board the vessel. 3 Any Party which has taken action under this article shall communicate as soon as possible to the Party which has provided information, or made a request for assistance, the results of any action taken in respect of the vessel and any persons on board.

30 UNCLOS Article 91.
31 UNCLOS Article 92(2):
A ship which sails under the flags of two or more states, using them according to convenience, may not claim any of the nationalities in question with respect to any other state, and may be assimilated to a ship without nationality.

32 In the case of a mother vessel using smaller vessels to smuggle commodities ashore, constructive presence can form the basis for interception. This however falls outside the limited scope of this chapter.

33 Article 110(1)(d).

34 Article 8(7).

35 Misuse of Drugs Act.

36 Article 52 (1) of the Misuse of Drugs Act of Seychelles, Act 5 of 2016, for example, allows Seychellois courts to prosecute crimes of drug trafficking on board vessels displaying no flag.

37 UNCLOS Article 98; SOLAS Regulation 33; Chapter 2 International Convention on Maritime Search and Rescue, 27 April 1979, 1403 UNTS 27.

References

1995 Council of Europe Agreement on Illicit Traffic by Sea, implementing article 17 of the *1988 Convention*, European Treaty Series, No. 156.

Allott, A. 2021. *'Lawless' high seas undoing New Zealand's seabird conservation efforts.* 4 March. Available from: https://www.stuff.co.nz/environment/124417477/lawless-high-seas-undoing-new-zealands-seabird-conservation-efforts. [Accessed 29 March 2021].

Amnesty International. 2019. *Italy: Sea-Watch 3's captain must not be prosecuted for saving lives.* 2 July. Available from: https://www.amnesty.org/en/latest/news/2019/07/sea-watch-3-captain-must-not-be-prosecuted-for-saving-lives/. [Accessed 30 August 2020].

Barron, D.H. 2015. How the illegal wildlife trade is fuelling armed conflict. *Georgetown Journal of International Affairs.* 16(2). Available from: https://www.jstor.org/stable/43773711.

Basu, G. 2013. The role of transnational smuggling operations in illicit supply chains. *Journal of Transport Security*, 6, 315–316. DOI: 10.1007/s12198-013-0118-y.

Bennett, A. 2012. That sinking feeling: stateless ships, universal jurisdiction, and the Drug Trafficking Vessel Interdiction Act. *Yale Journal of International Law*, 37(2), 433–461. Available from: https://digitalcommons.law.yale.edu/yjil/vol37/iss2/5. [Accessed 30 August 2020].

Brooks, C. & Hopkins, M. 2016. How protecting animals led to allegations of torture and rape. *National Geographic.* 19 September. Available from: https://www.nationalgeographic.com/news/2016/09/wildlife-tanzania-poaching-human-rights-abuses/. [Accessed 5 February 2021].

Bruwer, C. 2020. Smuggling and trafficking of illicit goods by sea. In: L. Otto, ed. *Global challenges in global maritime security: an introduction.* New York: Springer.

Chapsos, I. 2018. Why it's so hard to keep track of ships that get up to no good. *The Conversation.* 4 January. Available from: https://theconversation.com/why-its-so-hard-to-keep-track-of-ships-that-get-up-to-no-good-38323. [Accessed 27 March 2021].

CITES. n.d. *Wildlife crime.* Available from: https://cites.org/eng/prog/iccwc/crime.php. [Accessed 29 March 2021].

Coventry, T. 2019. Appropriate measures at sea: extraterritorial enforcement jurisdiction over stateless migrant smuggling vessels. *Maritime Safety and Security Law Journal*, 2019-20(7).

Davidson, J.O. 2010. New slavery, old binaries: human trafficking and the borders of 'freedom'. *Global Networks*, 10(2), 244–261.

Davidson, J.O. 2015. 'Trafficking' as a modern slave trade? Mobility, slavery and escape. In: J.O. Davidson, ed. *Modern slavery: the margins of freedom.* London: Palgrave Macmillan, 109–132. Available from: 10.1057/9781137297297_5. [Accessed 25August2020].

EIA. 2018. *Taking stock: an assessment of progress under the National Ivory Action Plan process.* London: EIA. Available from: https://eia-international.org/wp-content/uploads/EIA-report-NIAP-2018.pdf. [Accessed 5 February 2021].

EUNAVFOR MED Operation Sophia. n.d. *About us.* Available from: https://www.operationsophia.eu/. [Accessed 30 August 2020].

Ford, J.H. & Wilcox, C. 2019. Shedding light on the dark side of maritime trade: a new approach for identifying countries as flags of convenience. *Marine Policy*, 99(2019).

Gallagher, D. 2014. *The international law of migrant smuggling.* Cambridge: Cambridge University Press.

Griffiths, H. & Jenks, M. 2012. *Trends in maritime trafficking, ship registration and seizures in maritime transport and destabilizing commodity flows.* Sweden: Stockholm International Peace Research Institute.

Guilfoyle, D. 2009. *Intercepting vessels at sea*. New York: Cambridge University Press.

Hamad, H. 2016. Flag of convenience practice: a threat to maritime safety and security. *IJRDO-Journal of Social Science and Humanities Research*, 1(8).

Hudson, A. 2018. *Blue economy: a sustainable ocean economic paradigm [online]*. United Nations Development Programme, November 26. Available from: https://www.undp.org/content/undp/en/home/blog/2018/blue-economysustainable-ocean-economic-paradigm.html. [Accessed 30 August 2020].

International Chamber of Shipping. 2019. *Mediterranean migrant rescue crisis*. Available from: https://www.ics-shipping.org/docs/default-source/key-issues-2019/mediterranean-migrant-rescue-crisis-(june-2019).pdf. [Accessed 30 August 2020].

International Convention for the Safety of Life at Sea, 1 November 1974, London, 1184 UNTS 278.

Karim, N. 2020. Traffickers demand ransoms for Rohingyas held at sea in SE Asia. *Reuters*. Available from: https://www.reuters.com/article/us-bangladesh-malaysia-rohingya-traffick-idUSKBN23M1AC. [Accessed 27 March 2021].

Lam, T.T., Jia, N., Zhang, Y. et al. 2020. Identifying SARS-CoV-2-related coronaviruses in Malayan pangolins. *Nature*, 583, 282–285. Available from: 10.1038/s41586-020-2169-0. [Accessed 5 August 2020].

Long, T. 2018. Investigation into seized toothfish vessel highlights need for transparency. *Global Fishing Watch*, 2 May. Available from: https://globalfishingwatch.org/impacts/investigation-into-seized-toothfish-vessel-highlights-need-for-transparency/. [Accessed 27 August].

Marine Insight. 2019. *7 Dangers of flag states*, 11 October. Available from: https://www.marineinsight.com/maritime-law/7-dangers-of-flags-of-convenience-foc-to-seafarers/. [Accessed 16 August 2020].

McGuire, P.L. 2010. *Narcotics trafficking in West Africa: a governance challenge*. The Pardee Papers No. 9/March 2010. Boston: Boston University.

McLaughlin, R. 2016. Authorizations for maritime law enforcement operations. *International Review of the Red Cross*, 98(2), 486–487. Available from: 10.1017/S1816383117000340. [Accessed 4 August 2020].

Neuman, M. & Allafort-Duverger. T. 2018. NGOs are not in collusion with smugglers. *Medicine sans frontiers*, 7 October. Available: https://www.msf-crash.org/en/publications/humanitarian-actors-and-practices/ngos-are-not-collusion-smugglers [Accessed 27 August 2020].

O'Regan, D. 2010. *Cocaine and instability in Africa: lessons from Latin America and the Caribbean*. Washington: Africa Center for Strategic Studies.

Papastavridis, E. 2013. *The interception of vessels on the high seas: contemporary challenges to the legal order of the oceans*. Oxford: Hart Publishing.

Prada, P. & Roth, A. 2008. On the lawless seas, it's not easy putting Somali pirates in the dock. *Wall Street Journal*. 12 December. Available from: https://www.wsj.com/articles/SB122903542171799663. [Accessed 29 March 2021].

Ralby, I. & Soud, D. 2018. *Oil on the water: illicit hydrocarbons activity in the maritime domain*. Washington: Atlantic Council Global energy Centre.

Rawlence, B. 2015. *Black and white: Kenya's criminal rackets in Somalia*. Nairobi: Journalists for Justice.

Roche, P. 2016. The rescue of migrants at sea: obligations of the shipping industry. *Norton Rose Fullbright*, March. Available from: https://www.nortonrosefulbright.com/en/knowledge/publications/09f857fc/the-rescue-of-migrants-at-sea---obligations-of-the-shipping-industry. [Accessed 30 August 2020].

Røsæg, E. 2020. The duty to rescue refugees and migrants at sea. *Oxford University*, 25 March. Available from: https://www.law.ox.ac.uk/research-subject-groups/centre-criminology/centreborder-criminologies/blog/2020/03/duty-rescue#:~:text=There%20is%20a%20duty%20pursuant,felt%20moral%20obligation%20among%20seafarers.&text=There%20is%20a%20duty%20to,%2C%20Regulation%20V%2D7). [Accessed 29 August 2020].

Rubira, M. 2019. Iranian dhow catching fire in Seychellois waters. *Critical Maritime Routes Programme*, 6 March. Available: https://criticalmaritimeroutes.eu/2019/03/06/iranian-dhow-catching-fire-in-seychellois-waters/. [Accessed 30 August 2020].

Tondo, L. & Stierl, M. 2020. Banksy funds refugee rescue boat operating in Mediterranean. *The Guardian*, 27 August. Available from: https://www.theguardian.com/world/2020/aug/27/banksy-funds-refugee-rescue-boat-operating-in-mediterranean?utm_term=Autofeed&CMP=twt_gu&utm_medium&utm_source=Twitter#Echobox=1598547499. [Accessed 30 August 2020].

Tory, S. 2020. Catch me if you can: the global pursuit of a fugitive ship. *Haiku Magazine*, 3 March. Available from: https://www.hakaimagazine.com/features/catch-me-if-you-can/. [Accessed 30 August 2020].

TRAFFIC. n.d. *Pangolins: working to save the world's most trafficked mammal.* Available from: https://www.traffic.org/what-we-do/species/pangolins/. [Accessed 24 August 2020].

United Nations Conference on Trade and Development. 2018. *Review of maritime transport 2018.* New York: United Nations.

United Nations Convention against Illicit Traffic in Narcotic Drugs and Psychotropic Substances, 20 December 1988, Vienna, 28 ILM 497.

United Nations Convention against Transnational Organized Crime, 15 November 2000, New York, 40 ILM 353.

United Nations Convention on the Law of the Sea, 10 December 1982, Montego Bay, 1833 UNTS 3.

United Nations Security Council. 2014. *Resolution 2182 (2014)*, 24 October, S/RES/2182 (2014). Available from: file:///E:Research/S_RES_2182(2014)_E%20(1).pdf. [Accessed 30 August 2020].

United Nations Security Council. 2019a. *Implementation of resolution 2437 (2018): Report of the Secretary-General*, 5 September, S/2019/711. Available from: https://www.securitycouncilreport.org/atf/cf/%7B65BFCF9B-6D27-4E9C-8CD3-CF6E4FF96FF9%7D/s_2019_711.pdf. [Accessed 30 August 2020].

United Nations Security Council. 2019b. *Resolution 2498 (2019)*, 15 November, S/RES/2498 (2019). Available from: https://undocs.org/en/S/RES/2498(2019). [Accessed 30 August 2020].

UNODC. 2004. *Practical Guide for competent national authorities under Article 17 of the United Nations Convention against Illicit Traffic in Narcotic Drugs and Psychotropic Substances of 1988.* Vienna: UNODC.

UNODC. 2007. *Cocaine trafficking in West Africa: the threat to stability and development.* Vienna: UNODC.

UNODC. 2019. *Maritime crime: a manual for criminal justice practitioners.* Vienna: UNODC.

UNODC. 2020. *World Wildlife Crime Report: trafficking in protected species.* Vienna: UNODC.

Urbina, I. 2019. Lawless ocean: the link between human rights abuses and overfishing. *Yale Environment 360*, 20 November. Available from: https://e360.yale.edu/features/lawless-ocean-the-link-between-human-rights-abuses-and-overfishing. [Accessed 29 March 2021].

Varese, F. 2010. What is organized crime? In: F. Varese F, ed. *Organized crime: critical concepts in Criminology.* London: Routledge.

Von Lampe, K. 2016. *Organized crime: analysing illegal activities, criminal structures, and extra-legal governance.* Thousand Oaks: Sage.

Watt, E.B. & Coles, R. 2019. *Ship registration: law and practice.* 3rd ed. Oxfordshire: Informa Law.

West African Commission on Drugs. 2014. *Not just in transit: drugs, society and the state in West Africa.* Geneva: Kofi Anan Foundation, 8. Available from: http://www.wacommissionondrugs.org/wp-content/uploads/2014/11/WACD-Full-Report-Eng.pdf. [Accessed 30 August 2020].

World Wildlife Foundation. 2016. *Big five at CITES.* Available from: https://wwf.panda.org/our_work/our_focus/wildlife_practice/wildlife_trade/cites_cop17/big_five_at_cites_pangolin/. [Accessed 30 August 2020].

Wu, Y., Chen, C. & Chan, Y. 2020. The outbreak of COVID-19: an overview. *Journal of Chinese Medicine Association*, 83(3), 217–220. Available from: doi: 10.1097/JCMA.0000000000000270. [Accessed 1 August 2020].

31

COMMUNITIES AND CRIME WARS

Adaptation and resilience

Matt Herbert, Tuesday Reitano, and Siria Gastelum Felix

Introduction

Smuggling, as many of the chapters in this volume have underscored, is not inherently perceived or experienced to be a deviant phenomenon for communities living in zones where contraband is rife. Rather, as Titeca and Quitoriano underscore in their chapters in this volume, it can be an essential means of livelihood generation and coping in situations in which economic opportunities are sparse and state support limited or non-existent.

However, even while acknowledging the broad stabilizing effect smuggling and the contraband trade can have, it is clear that smuggling can, and in a growing number of instances, has transformed into something destabilizing and threatening to communities located on its periphery. Frequently, such a shift coincides with the emergence of structured organized crime groups seeking to dominate or monopolize an emergent trade in high-value contraband (Herbert, 2019).

The last 30 years have manifest a rising challenge by transnational organized crime, both globally and specifically along key smuggling and trafficking routes, posing a growing challenge to local communities, states, and regions (Walker, Kemp, Shaw, and Reitano, 2021). Institutions have become compromised, inequalities become more evident, and violence has risen, while at the same time becoming increasingly difficult to resolve.

Under these circumstances, the line between crime and the state has become blurred. In a rising number of instances, organized crime groups have functionally supplanted authorities, both in rural and borderland smuggling zones and urban areas where contraband markets are concentrated, establishing zones where criminal governance is a de facto reality for large swaths of population.

Though still an exception to the norm, situations in which smuggling, or areas astride contraband routes, come to be dominated by organized crime groups are important to focus upon for several reasons. First, they are substantially destructive to often vulnerable populations, menacing them with violence, coercion and exploitation, with risks especially concentrated upon women, girls and youth. (Gastelum Felix, 2017; Thomas and Pascoe, 2018; Burger, 2019). Communities face the preoccupation of lives consumed by violence, or fear that their youth will be recruited, voluntarily or not, by criminal actors (Burger, 2019). Further, efforts by organized crime groups to control smuggling routes can lead to the targeting, taxation or

DOI: 10.4324/9781003043645-31

exclusion of forms of smuggling which do support local livelihoods, further menacing the livelihoods of often vulnerable and marginalized populations.

Further, the emergence of organized crime in a contraband zone can be highly visible, sometimes by design, when covered by local and international media (Lantz, 2016). This visibility, and the political pressure it can induce, can in turn skew the policy responses of governments on public safety issues more broadly, impacting both organized criminal actors and smugglers more broadly, with the latter category often far less able to weather securitized government efforts than the former.

The challenge in countering transnational organized crime is often perceived to be a binary struggle between states and criminal organizations. Responses and lessons learned often emanate from this, heavily focused on what states should do or what aid can be extended to make state capacities more effective. These responses broadly fail to acknowledge that state actors can also play a significant role in criminal predation, or that with the communities most affected, longstanding failures in service delivery mean that state institutions have little legitimacy (Reitano and Hunter, 2016). Rarely are the local communities that face the challenge posed by organized crime analyzed and recognized as actors with agency, resources, and capacities, who often hold innovative and inspiring lessons on how to surmount criminal conflicts, promote better local governance and identify opportunities to shift beneficial forms of smuggling from criminalized to licit economic opportunities.

While often vulnerable, community members are neither static nor powerless actors. Their members can be criminal participants, victims, and advocates for accountability – sometimes all within the same family. In numerous cases, communities have sought to respond to the challenge posed to their families and societies by organized crime and alter the status quo, taking robust, yet non-violent approaches to build resilience within their communities (Olson, Shirk, and Wood, 2014).

Community resilience as a practice is not new. Rural and indigenous communities have long self-organized to protect their people and sustain their livelihoods against acute challenges, including environmental degradation, natural disasters and structural violence. Community resilience remains, however, imprecisely understood and ephemerous, to the detriment of at-risk communities and the international community seeking to help them through programmatic intervention. Community resilience against transnational organized crime as a concept is even more nascent, with limited attention given to the approach by governments and civil society actors. The intersections among insecurity, insufficient or threatened livelihoods, violence and the breakdown of the rule of law touch on all themes where civil society action has become more prominent and important.

This chapter focuses on building understanding of community resilience as a concept and in practice as a means of addressing the negative impacts on communities in contexts where smuggling economies have become penetrated or dominated by organised crime groups.[1] The chapter begins by offering a definition of community resilience, including the identification of the actors involved, and offers illustrative examples of resilience approaches. Next, it offers illustrative examples of resilience-building approaches. Third, the challenge posed to resilience efforts, by both criminal and government actions, is detailed. Fourth, it analyzes the counter-intuitive resilience offered by smuggling and illicit economies, and the risks posed to such stability by securitized approaches to organized crime. Finally, the chapter concludes with a brief set of reflections on resilience, and avenues forward for research and activism.

The analysis in this chapter is derived from the Global Initiative Against Transnational Organized Crime's work on the issue. Beginning in 2015, the organization began to document community responses to organized crime, largely as a means to present those voices into international development discussions. This chapter is based on that work, as well as further programmatic work done by the Global Initiative with resilience actors between 2017 and 2021.[2]

The concept of resilience to transnational organized crime

While the practices involved in resilience are ancient, the concept of resilience as a development tool is relatively new, emerging from the Disaster Risk Reduction field and coming into wider usage only since the 1990s (United Nations, 1994; Kimber, 2019). Over the last three decades, resilience has, however, been widely adopted in a variety of different fields, such as development, peacebuilding and counter-crime, and by different actors, including various United Nations agencies, donors (including the United States and the United Kingdom), and various international NGOs (Norris et al., 2008; Van Metre and Calder, 2016; Barbieri, Fessler, Hermes, and Lehne, 2019; DFID 2011; Seelke and Finklea, 2016).

The concept of resilience as applied to organized crime is newer, and in many ways still evolving. Conceptual work on the issue largely started to crystalize in the late 2000s and early 2010s (see, for example, Felbab-Brown, 2011; Davis, 2012), accompanying an increasing focus by international donors on efforts to support directly efforts to buttress communities against criminal violence and threats, including in the 2011 bilateral U.S.–Mexico "Beyond Merida" strategy, which encompassed an explicit focus on resilience (Seelke, 2021). Since that point, donor interest in the subject has grown, along with efforts to clarify and expand the field, including by authors such as Olson, Shirk and Wood, Carpenter and Cooper, Gastelum Felix, Thomas and Pascoe, Maringira and Gibson, Gutierrez, and Bird (Olson, Shirk and Wood, 2014; Carpenter and Cooper, 2015; Gastelum Felix, 2017; Thomas and Pascoe, 2018; Maringira and Gibson, 2019; Gutierrez, 2020; Bird, 2021).

Despite a rising interest in resilience by academics and practitioners focused on organized crime, the broader concept of resilience remains relatively elastic and loosely defined (Imperiale and Vanclay, 2020). Gastelum Felix has defined resilience as "the capacity of any system…to respond to and recover from shocks and stressors that threaten and/or disrupt its structure and functional capacities" (Gastelum Felix, 2017). Shocks are "sudden events that impact on the vulnerability of the system and its components," while stressors are "long-term trends that undermine the potential of a given system or process and increase the vulnerability of actors within it" (DFID, 2011).

Resilience capacity is inherently a multilevel concept, identifiable at the individual, familial, community, and national levels, with the capacity of each of those levels reenforcing – or weakening – that of the others (Barbieri, Fessler, Hermes, and Lehne, 2019). Crucially, each of the levels, and actors within each level, do not need to respond in the same way to shocks and stressors. Rather, the emergence of different responses – as long they are diffused and shared and not mutually incompatible – is broadly beneficial, increasing the chances that shocks and stressors will be surmounted or recovered from (Van Metre and Calder, 2016). Resilience capacity also necessarily operates along a dynamic continuum rather than being an end state: the same community can increase or decrease resilience capacity depending on the confluence of endogenous and exogenous factors, such as the shocks and stressors, the actors involved, and the broader political, social or security context.

It is important to note that a number of different actors, operating at different levels, can play a role within resilience building efforts and contribute to countering the negative impacts of transnational organized crime. This can include governments, especially those at the local level. However, situations in which the worst impacts of organized crime are manifest and where resilience needs are most acute exist due to failed institutional responses, often where the state is weak, complicit, or non-existent. For this reason, it is import to focus on resilience at the community level, undertaken through actors such as community members and other non-state actors, such as civil society organizations, religious forums, and local media organizations.

Gender is a key component of multi-actor analysis around resilience. In part, such a focus is essential as while both men and women are involved in organized crime, the vulnerability and impact of involvement can differ by sex, and forms of vulnerability within communities can be similarly stratified by gender (Shaw and Skywalker, 2017; Ghanem, 2020; Bird, 2021). Therefore, the design of approaches to resilience – especially those meant to engage directly with participants – necessarily need to be tailored with an eye towards gender dynamics in order to achieve success. In approaching resilience building, it is essential to recognize that women often play vitally important roles. They are able, for example, to leverage traditional gender roles to interrupt effectively cycles of violence via negotiation and the creation of safe space. However, they often have only limited representation in or access to the shaping of formal responses to organized crime (Bird, 2021). The inclusion of a gender lens is acutely important for programs and activities which seek to 'build back better,' in order to ensure that the programs and initiatives address, rather than entrench, gender based structural inequality and representation (Bird, 2021).

When applied to organized crime issues, the abstractions in the above definitions become clearer. Gastelum Felix and Tennant argue that "when applying resilience building to situations affected by organized crime, communities need to respond to not only long-standing negative situations (stressors such as embedded corruption, culture of extortion or protection etc.), but also immediate negative impacts (shocks such as an assassination or a sudden campaign of violence and/or intimidation)" (Gastelum Felix and Tennant, forthcoming). Further, as responses to the negative impacts of organized crime similarly are inherently multilevel, and multi-approach, actors within the same community, stratified by gender or social markers, for example, can adopt different approaches to transgressive violence or predation, even as national level authorities adapt tools at their disposal to do the same. Finally, on the issue of continuum, a community or family may hold well developed strategies for addressing impacts of stressors linked to some forms of the illicit economy, such as handling extortion or predation, but may be ill-prepared to respond if the context of the local illicit economy shifts, such as if a violent drug trafficking organization begins to operate in the area in which they live (Herbert, 2019).

It is important to distinguish the concept of resilience from that of resistance or contestation. In instances in which organized crime has emerged as a destabilizing threat, some communities have sought to counter it via the formation of community self-defence groups or militias (International Crisis Group, 2013; Lagrange and Vircoulon, 2021). This, however, differs substantially in aim and act from resilience, which according to Thomas and Pascoe, involves non-violent approaches to shocks and stressors (Thomas and Pascoe, 2018). Such a differentiation is key both in approach and impact, with numerous cases underscoring that the move towards the development of armed groups often can be a gateway to further shocks and criminality, with little positive impact on long term stressors (International Crisis Group, 2013).

Emanating from this, approaches to community resilience building to counter organized crime should be conceptualized as "a transformative process of strengthening the capacity of people and communities to effectively respond to and recover from the shocks and stressors of pervasive criminal governance" (Barbieri, Fessler, Hermes, and Lehne, 2019). In practice, resilience building aims to build structures to enable communities to weather adverse events or to recover to a status quo ex-ante after the emergence of an acute challenge. When possible, however, the aim is to fuse the two aspects, endeavor to assist communities in 'building back better' by identifying and supporting novel solutions and resilience activities to ensure that if similar challenges reoccur in the future, communities are better placed to lessen or dodge the damage (Gastelum Felix and Tennant, forthcoming).

Forms of resilience building

Forms of resilience, and the resulting nature of resilience-building activities, are situation specific. There is no 'one size fits all' approach. Rather, they differ based on a variety of factors, including the nature of the organized crime challenge, the interplay of stressors and shocks, a community's internal dynamics and existent coping strategies, the nature of broader engagement and capacity of the state, and the structure and nature of local illicit economies (Amerhauser and Kemp, 2021).

For this reason, resilience building is a bottom-up exercise, rooted in engaging with and supporting local actors, and often highly dependent on their social capital, the "links, shared values and understandings that enable individuals and groups to trust each other and work together" (Gastelum Felix, 2017). Such actors understand both the structure and impact (positive and negative) of local illicit economies and the formal and informal networks and social capital which exist within local communities (Gastelum Felix, 2017, Thomas and Pascoe, 2018).

As noted, the specific forms of resilience building are necessarily locally grounded. However, at a broad level, resilience activities can include activities designed to address directly issues of violence, improve community cohesion, offer individual or group support to victims or at-risk populations (including current or former criminal actors), buttress information sharing and awareness raising on resilience and crime issues, and strengthen connections and capacities within communities.

Below are some particularly important approaches which the authors have documented amongst organizations operating throughout the globe. The approaches are not exhaustive; rather, they are illustrative examples which underscore both the dynamism and the contextually tailored approaches undertaken by communities, civil society organizations and other non-state actors in confronting the challenges posed by organized crime.

The first, and most immediately important for communities menaced by organized crime related killings or disappearances, is violence interruption. Gang mediation by community members, aimed not at eliminating organized crime, but at addressing the acute negative impact it poses, has emerged in recent decades as a particularly important strategic approach (Sharkey, Torrats-Espinosa and Takyar, 2017). Outside of Cape Town, South Africa, the *Manenberg Safety Forum* has been deeply involved in such mediation. As Roegchanda Pascoe, chairperson of the Safety Forum, noted, "Whether we like it or not, we must live with them [gangs], so it is important for us to engage with them because we have to share the space with them. It was through this realization that our work in gang mediation started" (Thomas and Pascoe, 2018).

The second is the creation of 'safe spaces,' such as youth centres. Such safe spaces are not just meant to be physically safe from violence, but also to offer a space removed from criminal stresses and pressures, diverting those who might otherwise be targeted by organized crime actors. This can help to break the cycle of organized crime recruitment and offer pathways away from crime for those already enmeshed within illicit economies (Amerhauser and Kemp, 2021). In Cali, Colombia, the organization *Vicaria para la Reconciliación y La Paz* builds safe spaces for youth, especially those who previously were involved in gang activity. Yesid Perlaza, from the organization, noted the importance of providing an avenue of escape for such youth.

Youths see that someone has been able to escape from their condition of violence, of drug dependency, or the condition that allowed them to be out of legality. To become part of legality is important because it gives them hope. They have lost hope, they have lost faith, what we want is for them to recover hope and faith in institutionalism and to aspire to that offer which is limited but is always present. It's bringing institutions to the territories, taking away that space from criminal networks, and preventing them from having offers for their criminal activities.[3]

The work of *Vicaria para la Reconciliación y La Paz* took on added importance during the COVID-19 pandemic, when youth involved in the organization's programmes were mobilized to help the community, via the delivery of food and sanitary information. Such an activity was both an example of efforts by the community to stabilize itself in response to the immediate threat posed by the disease, and a manifestation of longer-term efforts to 'build back better', with the youth previously involved in organized crime, and stigmatized for it, using their involvement to change the way the community perceived of them.

Another example, in Tanzania, is the development of safe spaces for drug users. There the Salvage CSO provides support and shelter to drug users, focusing in particular on women. The aim is to offer opportunities for harm reduction, access to psycho-social services and a means of reintegrating drug users into the community.

Third is the provision of support to individuals at risk or impacted by organized crime. This does not only entail protective support, but also legal, financial, health and education assistance. Practically this can take the form of violence shelters, hotlines, and reintegration assistance for community members previously involved in illicit economies (Amerhauser and Kemp, 2021).

In Haiti, for example, the CSO *Rapha* has worked to address the issues of human trafficking and sexual exploitation. This is particularly important for the country, as, in recent years proliferating violence by criminal armed groups has triggered a crisis of forced internal displacement in a number of disadvantaged and marginalised communities. This displacement, exacerbated by continuing insecurity, has led to a situation of extreme social and economic vulnerability for those displaced, and exposed, many – particularly women and children – to an increased risk of sexual exploitation.

To address this, *Rapha* has sought to assist and aid victims directly, as well as build the resilience of high-risk communities and improve the capacity of state protection structures. In February 2020, *Rapha* launched a program to identify and help vulnerable people, via the provision of psychosocial and medical care to both victims of sexual exploitation and heads of household in vulnerable communities. Gerson Nozea, from *Rapha*, explains that "among the victims, families internally displaced due to organised crime now have access to safe housing, women heads of households have launched income-generating initiatives, and a network of cooperation and support has been created for women heads of small business enterprises."[4]

Fourth is information sharing and awareness. While local information on the manifestations of organized crime and criminal governance may exist, broader knowledge about organized crime, the nature of challenges in other locales or regions, and successful resilience efforts elsewhere is often limited or non-existent. This, in turn, effectively poses "a structural barrier to building resilience" (Gastelum Felix and Tennnant, forthcoming). Non-state organizations focused on research, journalism and education are keenly important in addressing these gaps, though often these same organizations need support and time to build the specific knowledge on organized crime issues (Amerhauser and Kemp, 2021).

Finally, resilience activities are – fundamentally – about community building. Ideally, resilience activities should be aimed both at retarding the key challenges communities face, and enhancing issues and ethical approaches communities hold dear (Amerhauser and Kemp, 2021). The latter, in particular, is keenly important within the 'build back better' approach to resilience.

Community building, however, does not simply entail the strengthening of bonds within geographically distinct communities, but also the building of a community of individuals and organizations working on resilience building issues. At a local level, such connectivity is particularly important to prevent large numbers of unconnected and uncoordinated actors and initiatives within a given community fragment rather than reinforce resilience building efforts (Davis, 2012).

There is, however, also a utility in strengthening global bonds amongst resilience actors. As will be detailed in greater depth in the following section, resilience building can be a dangerous activity, with efforts often surveilled by both governments and criminal organizations, and activists sometimes harassed, intimidated and attacked.

Challenges to resilience building

The narratives of building and rebuilding resilience are arguably powerful and positive, offering an avenue to marginalized communities and individuals to non-violently address challenges emanating from organized crime. However, they are not easy. The situations in which communities seek to enhance resilience are frequently unsafe, and rife with spoilers – including both criminals and states – whose interests run counter to or differ from those of communities. Simply, individuals, organizations and communities working on resilience often do so at great cost to themselves, while menaced by an ever-growing set of challenges.

The most dire challenge facing resilience proponents is physical violence and murder. Targeted killings – especially those of activists involved in countering environmental crime and journalists reporting on organized crime – have long been an issue, but it has become more acute over the last two decades as criminal groups have grown in global scope and power. In Mexico alone, 137 journalists were killed between 2000 and 2020 (Triana, 2021). Mexican journalist Javier Valdez, murdered on 17 May 2017, once explained the risks he faced, noting:

> In Culiacán (Mexico), living is dangerous, and working as a journalist means treading an invisible line drawn by the bad guys from both the drug cartels and the government – a sharp floor covered with explosives (The Global Initiative Against Transnational Organized Crime, 2020).

As intimated by Valdez, the risk comes not just from organized crime actors. Police and other security forces officials, acting either as hired assassins or due to complicity in criminal activity, have also been implicated in the killing of journalists and activists (The Global Initiative Against Transnational Organized Crime, 2020).

The goal of such killings if often two-fold. In part, the killings are aimed at silencing actors and halting initiatives which criminal actors perceive as threatening their business interests or a status quo advantageous to them. In some instances, such as with journalists, the goal can also be to prevent the dissemination of information highlighting links between criminals and state actors.

Targeted killings, however, are also intended to intimidate, implicitly threatening the broader social networks, community and society of those killed. Murder is not the only form of intimidation which resilience actors, and their communities, face. In a number of instances documented by the authors, criminal actors have resorted to cyber harassment or physical threats. In others, criminal actors have publicly sought out activists, overtly querying community members as to the activist's location and activities.[5] In some cases, state agents have been implicated in intimidation efforts, including targeting family members of murdered journalists (The Global Initiative Against Transnational Organized Crime, 2020; Amerhauser and Kemp, 2021; Triana, 2021).

Resilience activists have also been menaced by a rise in legal intimidation. Defamation suits, for example, have emerged as key approaches by actors seeking to target and deter individuals and activists working against organized crime. One activist who had been reporting on crime and corruption issues around the illicit mining industry, was sued for defamation by one of the alleged criminals involved. The suit led to the temporary seizure of the activist's organization, as well as other harassment of the organization's staff. Despite the ultimate dismissal of some lawsuits, the process can often be ruinously expensive for activists, forcing a halt to their activities and deterring others from becoming involved in resilience work.

Intimidation has always been a key tool of TOC activities, such as extortion and territorial control, due to the limited risk it involves for criminal actors, with police and security forces often less likely to investigate or prosecute it. Intimidation, however, can have a particularly acute chilling effect on efforts to buttress community resilience, impacting both the willingness of community members to discuss the challenges they face and efforts to address them (Connolly, 2019; Gastrow, 2021).

Apart from active threats from criminal actors meant to halt and deter resilience work, there are also inherent risks in the nature of some specific forms of resilience building. The most direct of these is gang mediation, where resilience actors are seeing to limit violence between antagonistic, often heavily armed groups of youth. One Liberian mediator explained that that "with gang violence, you have the physical situation where you can be physically attacked if people misunderstand your position while you're trying to facilitate."[6]

In addition to the challenges detailed above, resilience actors also face some very specific risks posed by states and state agents. While in an ideal situation, the latter actors should be proponents of resilience building, too often communities face predatory states that view resilience- building efforts with deep distrust. Amerhauser and Kemp, writing about resilience in the Western Balkans note that "In some cases, positions [between governments and CSOs] become entrenched to the point that one or both sides regard the other as 'the enemy,' which is unfortunate given that fighting organized crime should be a shared goal" (Amerhauser and Kemp, 2021).

Antipathy and mistrust of resilience actors by governments can sometimes lead to the intentional weaponization of state resources, to include physical assaults or murder by state agents, or intimidation via the legal system. However, more frequently, state efforts which curtail the activities of resilience actors occur via broader policy or legal initiatives.

Moves in recent years to expand defamation laws, especially to encompass speech on social media platforms, are one example of this, as detailed previously on legal intimidation (International Press Institute, 2020; Guterres, 2020). In some cases, such as in Mexico and Niger, government actors, or those linked to powerful officials, have been protagonists in such suits seeking to halt reporting on corruption or organized crime links (Edmonds-Poli, 2014; The Global Initiative Against Transnational Organized Crime, 2020).

Anti-Money Laundering and Terrorist Financing (AML/CTF) policies have also emerged as a problematic issue for resilience actors. In some instances, this is due to the instrumentalization of such policies by governments to harass and target resilience actors, such as in Serbia in July 2020, when the government issued a list of journalists and NGOs who bank accounts were to be reviewed for AML/CTF violations (Amerhauser and Kemp, 2021). Such instrumentalized approaches can be a particular issue in locales where criminals and state actors are closely interlinked (Knoote and Malmberg, 2021).

However, a more sustained challenge emanates from the underlying structure of AML/CTF legislation, including best practices promoted by international organizations. The Financial Action Task Force (FATF), a key AML/CTF standard setter, has recommended the regulation of the non-profit sector since the 1990s. This despite both FATF and other international actors, such as the World Bank and European Commission, acknowledging the limited risk NGOs pose for terrorist financing (Knoote and Malmberg, 2021).

FATF's promotion of non-profit regulation has furthered efforts by governments to control and target NGOs, all under the patina of an AML/CTF approach. This, in turn has led to operational, financial, and legal ramifications for such organizations. Already limited donor support for resilience activities against organized crime are further impeded by the difficulty recipient organizations have in navigating and adhering to strict AML/CTF requirements (Amerhauser and Kemp, 2021). Knoote and Malmberg, in reviewing the issue, note a "policy incoherence on the national and international arena: the very organizations whose mandate is to fight organized crime, corruption or terrorism, are being hampered in their valuable work by CFT/AML regulations" (Knoote and Malmberg, 2021).

Smuggling, stabilization and the risk of securitization

Securitized approaches to organized crime, smuggling and illicit markets are a final aspect of official policy which shape the activities and challenges of resilience actors. Much of this hinges on the counterintuitive stabilizing impact of some forms of smuggling and illicit markets. As a range of chapters in this volume have noted, in areas where economic opportunities are limited, smuggling and illicit markets are a key livelihood support strategy for local communities. This is especially the case for contraband activities in which barriers to entry are low and financial stakes widely distributed (Herbert, 2019).

Activities which contravene national laws do not necessarily contravene local social norms, nor are they considered taboo. Herbert and Gallien underscore, for example, that on the Tunisia-Algeria border, low level smugglers rarely perceive their activities to be deviant, even if they are criminal, with one Tunisian smuggler explaining "What we do is not really illegal trafficking" (Herbert and Gallien, 2020). This dynamic is not limited only to individuals directly involved in smuggling, but rather is reflected in the broader social context of many communities where smuggling or illicit trade is perceived as a livelihood necessity. Witbooi underscores this, noting that "research conducted on gangs elsewhere in Jamaica, particularly in Kingston, suggests a significant degree of tolerance, if not support, for the social benefits that these illicit activities bring vulnerable communities" (Witbooi, 2020).

Officials too can allow tacitly some forms of smuggling, turning a blind eye to cross-border commerce as long as specific norms and unofficial rules are adhered to by smugglers (Herbert, 2019; Gallien, 2019). This is often based upon the rationalization that the risks of destabilization and protests in the borderlands substantially exceed the dangers posed by low level smuggling (Hanlon and Herbert, 2015).

The advent of new security threats, including violent organized crime groups or terrorist networks perceived to be enabled by smuggling networks, can change this calculus, however. In such circumstances, states can seek to adopt blunt, security-focused strategies as a means of mitigating the risk.

However, government efforts to address nominally illegal activity and markets via securitized approaches that do not incorporate alternative development efforts acceptable to local communities risk primarily impacting small scale smugglers. Such actors have limited ability to surmount concerted government security or border closure campaigns, which, in turn can lead to destabilization of borderland communities.

In North Africa, for example, the governments of Tunisia, Algeria and Morocco substantially shifted their border security strategies between 2011 and 2020, moving from defacto tolerance of low-level smuggling to militarized approaches which sought to halt smuggling and other unauthorized cross-border movement. The net impact of this shift was to create a crisis in the region's borderlands, leading to an increase in social tension, irregular migration and involvement in more violent forms of criminality, such as drug trafficking (Herbert and Gallien, 2020). Similar unintended consequences can be seen with other securitized approaches, including that of early 'Mano Dura' policies in Central America's Northern Triangle or initiatives pursued in Afghanistan around narcotics cultivation (Jones, 2014; Goodhand, 2009; Gutierrez, 2020; Koehler, Rasool and Ibrahimkhel, 2021).

Thus, even in cases in which state intentions are nominally positive, poorly thought through policy approaches to informal and illicit economies, especially on what is meant to replace them, lead to a negative effect on community livelihoods and security. This, in turn, can increase the need for resilience actors, both to address the negative ramifications of state action and to address criminal entrepreneurs – such as drug traffickers in North Africa – who seek to profit from the upending of previously established markets and systems to increase their own power and influence.

Finally, securitized approaches also pose a risk to resilience actors, especially those perceived to oppose government approaches or maintain connections to criminals (such as resilience actors involved in gang mediation). In such instances, resilience actors can face investigation, harassment and physical violence by state agents not due to the initiatives they promote, but rather due to the broader social networks they and their communities exist within.

Conclusion

As the chapters in this book underscore, the negative impacts which manifest when smuggling economies have become penetrated or dominated by organised crime groups has emerged as a increasing global challenge. Much of the attention has focused on the macro-level impacts, such as state capture, rule of law erosion, and the functional ejection of state presence from areas dominated by organized crime actors. The micro-experience of organized crime has been more opaque, such as how communities deal with heightened insecurity and the rise of criminal governance. However, such a micro-focus is important, because it is out of these local contexts that some of the most active and successful efforts to deal with the impacts of organized crime are emerging.

In a vast range of countries and contexts globally, community activists, journalists and NGOs are working, often in circumstances of acute personal risk, to aid communities impacted by organized crime in addressing the damaging ramifications of the phenomenon. These resilience efforts are, in effect, efforts at stabilization from below, grounded in local context and responsive to local needs. Support of them should be key components of national and donor efforts to address organized crime.

National and international supporters, however, should not make the mistake of viewing community resilience as an end state in itself. Resilience is instead a multi-level continuum, with different levels – individual, family, community, national – deploying coping strategies to different effect at different times as organized crime risks and threats change (Davis, 2012). Because of this, support should be both durable and focused at connecting resilience actors with their peers, to ensure that good practices and approaches can be spread, innovated and employed.

Communities and crime wars

International actors – including both donors and the research community – should also remain attuned to the challenges faced by local individuals and organizations working on resilience. Those working on the ground are doing so against an ever-increasing set of challenges, and often at great personal risk.

Finally, while the focus of this chapter has largely been on how communities act to build resilience in the absence of the state, or its capture by criminal actors, promoters of resilience should not lose sight of the need to bring the state back into the conversation. Ultimately, if community efforts to counter organized crime are to be effective and durable, the state must play a role. The challenge then is to build trust and connections between state officials and community actors, and ensure that local knowledge and understanding fits both local administration and more national level responses to organized crime. This is particularly challenging, and yet highly salient, in communities where livelihoods are predicated upon smuggling and forms of petty contraband, and which the risk of destabilization is significant if state approaches to combat organized crime are bluntly applied.

The challenge posed by transnational organized crime is likely to continue to grow in the coming years and decades. This in turn, necessitates that those in the international community – such as governments, civil society, and academia – continue to work to support those resilience actors working on the ground and promulgate the novel solutions and approaches they come up with.

Notes

1   The authors would like to emphasize that while smuggling and organized crime are interrelated, they should not be construed as synonymous. Organized crime groups can emanate from smuggling networks, as the advent of high value goods leads to heightened barriers to entry, and a subsequent concentration of power and profit within specific groups and individuals. They can also become involved in taxing smugglers moving goods across a given territory, in some cases acting as gatekeepers on which individuals or groups can be active in smuggling activities. However, on a per person basis, members of organized crime groups are a distinct minority within the broader universe of smuggling.
2   Beginning in 2019, the Global Initiative Against Transnational Organized Crime launched the Resilience Fund to further support community and civil society responding to organized crime. The Resilience Fund not only provides financial support to its grantees but builds capacity of its beneficiaries by offering a learning curricula and networking opportunities, along with mentoring and other programmes to amplify the local impact of the projects and share lessons internationally, while building a global community of resilience actors.
3   Author Interview, Yesid Perlaza, remote, 2020.
4   Author interview, Gerson Nozea, remote 2020.
5   Author communication, activist, remote, April 2021.
6   Global Initiative interview, Yvette Chesson-Wureh, remote, September 2020.

References

Amerhauser, K., and Kemp, W. (2021). "Stronger together: Bolstering resilience among civil society in the Western Balkans." Policy Brief. The Global Initiative Against Transnational Organized Crime. https://globalinitiative.net/wp-content/uploads/2021/03/WBalkans-CSOs-web.pdf
Barbieri, A., Fessler, J.D., Hermes, M., and Lehne, K. (2019). "Synthesis report: Building community resilience: lessons learned for countering organized crime." Unpublished Thesis. Capstone Global Security Track Project of the Graduate Institute of Geneva.
Bird, L. (2021). "Mind the gap: The role of women in community resilience to organized crime." The Global Initiative Against Transnational Organized Crime.
Burger, V. (2019). "'If we speak up, we get shot down': Building resilience in Glebelands Hostel." The Global Initiative Against Transnational Organized Crime. https://globalinitiative.net/analysis/glebelands-hostel/

Carpenter, A. and Cooper, S. (2015). Transnational gangs and criminal networks: a contribution to community resilience a social network analysis of the San Diego/Tijuana Border Region. *Journal of Gang Research*, Vol. 22, No. 3, 1–24.

Connolly, J. (2019). "Building community resilience: responding to criminal and anti-social behaviour networks across Dublin South Central." Centre for Crime, Justice and Victim Studies, School of Law, University of Limerick. http://www.canaction.ie/wp-content/uploads/2019/12/Low-Res-Building-Community-Resilience-Report-FINAL.pdf

Davis, D. (2012). "Urban resilience in situations of chronic violence: Final report." MIT Center for International Studies and USAID.

DFID (2011). "Defining disaster resilience: A DFID approach paper." DFID. https://www.fsnnetwork.org/sites/default/files/dfid_defining_disaster_resilience.pdf

Edmonds-Poli, E. (2014). "The effects of drug-war related violence on Mexico's Press and democracy." In: Shirk, D., Wood, D., and Olson, E., eds. *Building Resilient Communities In Mexico: Civic Responses to Crime and Violence*. Washington, DC: Woodrow Wilson International Center for Scholars and Justice in Mexico Project.

Felbab-Brown, V. (2011). "Building resilience against organized crime." Brooking Institute: On the Record, posted 10 February 2011, retrieved 20 February 2021, available at: https://www.brookings.edu/on-the-record/building-resilience-against-organized-crime/

Felix, S.G. (2017). "Resilience in Sinaloa: Community Responses to Organized Crime." The Global Initiative Against Transnational Organized Crime. https://globalinitiative.net/wp-content/uploads/2017/08/Resilience-in-Sinaloa-community-responses-to-OC.pdf

Felix, S.G. and Tennant, I. (Forthcoming) "Understanding civil society efforts to build resilience to organized crime." In Allum, F. and Gilmour, S., eds. *The Routledge Handbook on Transnational Organized Crime*. London: Routledge.

Gallien, M. (2019). Informal institutions and the regulation of smuggling in North Africa. *Perspectives on Politics*, Vol. 18, No. 2, 79–106.

Gastrow, P. (2021). "Lifting the veil on extortion in Cape Town." The Global Initiative Against Transnational Organized Crime. https://globalinitiative.net/wp-content/uploads/2021/04/Lifting-the-veil-on-extortion-in-Cape-Town-GITOC.pdf

Ghanem, D. (2020). "The smuggler wore a veil: Women in Algeria's illicit border trade." Carnegie Endowment for International Peace.

Goodhand, J. (2009). "Bandits, borderlands and opium wars: Afghan state-building viewed from the margins." DIIS Working Paper 26, Danish Institute for International Studies.

Guterres, J. (2020). "Timor-Leste's draft defamation law will make it harder to curb corruption," The Diplomat, posted 10 August 2020, accessed 15 April 2021. Accessible at: https://thediplomat.com/2020/08/timor-lestes-draft-defamation-law-will-make-it-harder-to-curb-corruption/.

Gutierrez, E. (2020). "The paradox of illicit economies: Survival, resilience, and the limits of development and drug policy orthodoxy." *Globalizations*, Vol. 17, no. 6. doi: 10.1080/14747731.2020.1718825

Hanlon, Q. and Herbert, M. (2015). Border security challenges in the Grand Maghreb. US Institute of Peace, Peaceworks No. 109.

Herbert, M. (2019). "From contraband to conflict: Links between smuggling and violence in the borderlands of Meso-America and North Africa," PhD Dissertation, The Fletcher School of Law and Diplomacy, Tufts University.

Herbert, M. and Gallien, M. (2020). Divided they fall: Frontiers, borderlands and stability in North Africa. Institute for Security Studies, North Africa Report 6.

Imperiale, A.J. and Vanclay, F. (2020). "Top-down reconstruction and the failure to 'build back better' resilient communities after disaster: Lessons from the 2009 L'Aquila Italy earthquake." *Disaster Prevention and Management: An International Journal*, Vol. 29, No. 4, 541–555.

International Crisis Group. (2013). "Justice at the barrel of a gun: Vigilante militias in Mexico."Latin America Briefing no. 29. Brussels.

International Press Institute. (2020). "Concern as Albania looks to push ahead with controversial 'anti-defamation law." Posted 16 September 2020, accessed 14 April 2021. Accessible at: https://ipi.media/concern-as-albania-looks-to-push-ahead-with-controversial-anti-defamation-law/

Jones, N. (2014). "Understanding and addressing youth in "Gangs" in Mexico." In: Shirk, D., Wood, D., and Olson, E., eds. *Building Resilient Communities in Mexico: Civic Responses to Crime and Violence*. Woodrow Wilson International Center for Scholars and Justice in Mexico Project.

Kimber, L. (2019). "Resilience from the United Nations Standpoint: The Challenges of "Vagueness." In Wiig, S. & Fahlbruch, B., eds. *Exploring Resilience: A Scientific Journey from Practice to Theory*. Springer.

Knoote, F., and Malmberg, T. (2021). "Zero Risk Mentality: The damaging effect of AML/CFT measures for civil society." The Global Initiative Against Transnational Organized Crime. https://globalinitiative.net/analysis/financial-resilience/

Koehler, J., Rasool, G., and Ibrahimkhel, A. (2021). "Dynamic borderlands–The challenge of adapting to hardening borders in Nangarhar and Nimroz." *International Journal of Drug Policy*, Vol. 89. https://doi.org/10.1016/j.drugpo.2021.103117

Lagrange, M., and Vircoulon, T. (2021) "Criminals or vigilantes? The Kuluna gangs of the Democratic Republic of Congo." The Global Initiative Against Transnational Organized Crime. https://globalinitiative.net/wp-content/uploads/2021/06/Criminals-or-vigilantes-The-Kuluna-gangs-of-the-Democratic-Republic-of-Congo-GITOC.pdf

Lantz, A. (2016). The performativity of violence: abducting agency in Mexico's drug war. *Journal of Latin American Cultural Studies*, Vol. 25, No. 2. pp. 1–17.

Maringira, G. and Gibson, D. (Fall 2019). Maintaining order in townships: Gangsterism and community resilience in Post-Apartheid South Africa. *African Conflict and Peacebuilding Review*, Vol. 9, No. 2, pp. 55–74.

Norris, F., Stevens, S., Pfefferbaum, B., Wyche, K., and Pfefferbaum, R. (2008). Community Resilience as a Metaphor, Theory, Set of Capacities, and Strategy for Disaster Readiness. *American Journal of Community Psychology*, Vol. 41, 127–150.

Olson, E., Shirk, D., and Wood, D. (2014). "Building resilient communities in Mexico: Civic responses to crime and violence." In: Shirk, D., Wood, D., and Olson, E., eds. *Building Resilient Communities in Mexico: Civic Responses to Crime and Violence*. Woodrow Wilson International Center for Scholars and Justice in Mexico Project.

Reitano, T. and Hunter, M. (2016). "Protecting politics: Deterring the impact of organized crime on public service delivery." International IDEA, Stockholm.

Seelke, C.R., and Finklea, K. (2016). "U.S.–Mexican security cooperation: The Mérida initiative and beyond." Congressional Research Service. https://www.everycrsreport.com/files/20110815_R41349_fc727a70306d9822d728f2068377942ec03faca9.pdf

Seelke, C.R. (2021). "Mexico: Evolution of the Mérida Initiative, 2007-2021." Congressional Research Service. https://crsreports.congress.gov/product/pdf/IF/IF10578

Sharkey, P., Torrats-Espinosa, G., and Takyar, D. (2017). Community and the crime decline: The causal effect of local nonprofits on violent crime. *American Sociological Review*, Vol. 82, 1214–1240.

Shaw M., and Skywalker, L.L. (2017). "Gangs, violence and the role of women and girls: Cape Town." The Global Initiative Against Transnational Organized Crime.

The Global Initiative Against Transnational Organized Crime (2020). "Arrest of journalist Samira Sabou 'illegal' – RSF." Posted 18 June 2020, accessed 17 April 2021. Accessible at: https://globalinitiative.net/analysis/samira-sabou-arrest-niger/

The Global Initiative Against Transnational Organized Crime. (2020). "Faces of assassination: Bearing witness to the victims of organized crime." https://idpc.net/events/2020/06/faces-of-assassination-virtual-book-and-campaign-launch

Thomas, K., and Pascoe, R. (2018). "Being resilient - Learning from community responses to gangs in Cape Town: Reflections from a Manenberg Activist." The Global Initiative Against Transnational Organized Crime. https://globalinitiative.net/analysis/resilience_manenberg/

Triana, G. (2021). "The Forgotten Ones: Relatives of murdered and disappeared journalists in Mexico." The Global Initiative Against Transnational Organized Crime. https://globalinitiative.net/wp-content/uploads/2021/05/The-forgotten-ones-GITOC.pdfi

United Nations (1994). The Yokohama Strategy and Plan of Action for a Safer World: Guidelines for Natural Disaster Prevention, Preparedness and Mitigation. World Conference on Natural Disaster Reduction Yokohama, Japan, 23–27.

Van Metre, L., and Calder, J. (2016). "Peacebuilding and Resilience: How Society Responds to Violence." Peaceworks 121. United States Institute of Peace.

Walker, S., Kemp, W., Shaw, M., and Reitano, T. (March2021). The Global Illicit Economy: Trajectories of Organized Crime. The Global Initiative Against Transnational Organized Crime.

Witbooi, Emma. (2020). "Criminality and resilience: Rocky Point, Jamaica." The Global Initiative Against Transnational Organized Crime. https://globalinitiative.net/analysis/criminality-resilience-jamaica/

32

THE "WAR ON SMUGGLERS" AND THE EXPANSION OF THE BORDER APPARATUS

Lorena Gazzotti

Introduction

The website of the EU Directorate for Migration and Home Affairs includes a page dedicated to "migrant smuggling." It states that "migrant smuggling is a profitable business for criminal networks with estimated annual turnover reaching multiple billion Euros." It then goes on detailing that "Migrant smuggling is increasingly associated with serious human rights violations and deaths, in particular when it occurs by sea." The website continues by arguing that "The loss of migrants' lives at the hands of smugglers in the Mediterranean Sea is an acute reminder of the need to tackle migrant smuggling," an endeavor that justifies resorting to "all of the legal, operational, and administrative levers available" (European Commission, n.d.). Similar in both forms and content to speeches recited by both right-wing and left-wing European political leaders, this short extract exemplifies the role that the "smuggler" plays in current political discourses. Together with the archetypical figure of the "terrorist" (De Genova, 2010), the "homeless," or "the drug trafficker" (De Noronha, 2020), the "smuggler" quintessentially condenses the anxieties of late liberal societies: they are stigmatised as deviant because they do not conform to the established order, and they are therefore portrayed as a source of threat that conspires against the status quo.

Literature has now widely acknowledged that the public portrait of the smuggler as an inherently deviant, dangerous figure is deceiving. In this chapter, however, I will not focus on the mismatch between the realities and political fantasies about the "smuggler." Rather, this paper interrogates the "uses"[1] of smuggling. I ask: what political function does the figure of the "smuggler" fulfill in border control? I contend that the demonization of the smuggler enables the expansion of the border apparatus. Casting the "smuggler" as the main source of danger for people crossing the border irregularly (and for destination countries enacting restrictive migration policies) displaces attention away from the structural sources that create a demand for human smuggling in the first place. Individualizing and pathologizing the dangers connected to smuggling facilitate the deployment of further border control measures. Following Rob Nixon's concept of "slow violence" (Nixon, 2011), I argue that anti-smuggling activities can be categorized into *fast control instruments*, that deploy military-style interventions focusing on *destroying* the infrastructures that facilitate irregular border crossing; and *slow control methods*, that aim at *transforming* potential migrants and former smugglers into immigration-law-abiding

444

DOI: 10.4324/9781003043645-32

subjects through welfare-like initiatives. Although they might not appear to be successful in their intent to disrupt smuggling networks and economies, these projects *do* succeed in advancing the border project: they further precarise the life conditions of migrant people, and they reinforce the idea that migration is a "problem" that can be "solved" through ad-hoc, time-bounded, rapid interventions.

The rest of the chapter unfolds into four sections. The first section explores the existing academic literature on smuggling, providing a more nuanced and complex understanding of the facilitation of irregular migration. The following section provides a framework to conceptualise the expansion and diversification of the bordering apparatus. I then move on to discussing the difference between "fast" and "slow" anti-smuggling instruments of smuggling control, and how they contribute (explicitly and implicitly) to the expansion of the border apparatus.

"Dangerous smugglers" vs. "moral smugglers"?

In both policy literature and journalistic prose, people smugglers are generally described as "inherently hypersexual and violence-driven men from the global South, members of all-mighty, hierarchical, transnational criminal organisations, involved in markets ranging from weapons trafficking to terrorism and from drug trafficking to nuclear smuggling" (Sanchez, 2016, p. 390). In its 'Migrant Smuggling FAQs', for example, UNODC specifies that "Migrant smugglers are criminals and not humanitarians. They are motivated by financial or material gain" (UNODC, n.d.). The report continues by specifying that "migrant smugglers often conduct their activities with little or no regard for the lives of the people whose hardships have created a demand for smuggling services." The International Organization for Migration (IOM) shares such universal views about the indifference of smugglers to their clients: in its 'IOM's comprehensive approach to counter migrant smuggling' report, the organisation describes migrant smugglers are predatory figures, asserting, 'once paid, smugglers often have little or no regard for the well-being of migrants, who are particularly vulnerable to abuse and exploitation' (IOM, n.d.).

Academic research, however, has proven that reality is much more complex (Stock, 2019). First of all, the relations between smugglers and migrants can fall on a wide spectrum between mutual trust and overt violence. Trust and ethical commitment can be essential to the relation between smugglers and migrants, as the former can be seen as care providers who help the latter fleeing a situation of unease and danger when wealthy countries have closed most legal channels for escape (Achilli, 2018; Vogt, 2016). Second, smuggling is not necessarily a secret practice occurring away from the prying eyes of the public. Rather, it can be a mundane activity that is deeply embedded in the local political economy of border regions (Vives, 2017). The demand and supply for smuggling should be understood in the broader context of increasingly securitized borders that generate a source of precarious income for people available to facilitate the crossing of labourers across the border (Sanchez, 2016). Regions that have become central hubs of irregular border crossing have seen the emergence of a parallel service economy that caters to potential border crossers and smugglers, composed of activities as unnewsworthy as "shops, boutiques, restaurants, grocery stores, bus and taxi companies, nightclubs, and pubs" (Achilli, 2018). In this context, the smuggler can be a member of the same community that navigates a complex economic landscape by juggling multiple social positions (Magallanes-Gonzalez, 2020). Third, smuggling is not necessarily a male-dominated economic activity. Building on fieldwork at the US-Mexico border, Sanchez highlights that "smuggling" writ large is undertaken also by women, working either to arrange crossings or to provide a range of services (like maintaining accommodation for potential crossers) that are intimately linked to the facilitation of irregular migration (Sanchez, 2016). Fourth, smuggling does not systematically take place far away from the eyes of the authorities. The latter are, in a lot of cases, informed and essential to the everyday working of irregular crossing (Achilli, 2018; Stock, 2019).

The fact that smuggling should not be systematically represented as a hyper-violent activity does not mean that the facilitation of irregular border crossing never relies on threat. Scholars have widely documented that migrants can be victims of sexual violence (Tyszler, 2019), kidnapping (Slack, 2019) and robbery (Magallanes-Gonzalez, 2020) at the hand of smugglers. The level of violence that smuggling implies, however, is intimately linked to the expansion of border securitization policies. In her piece on irregular migration between Senegal and Spain, Luna Vives points out that before 2005, most smuggling was conducted occasionally by Senegalese fishermen, who had the skills to sail the Ocean, and who belonged to the same communities where their clients originated (and that could therefore more easily be held accountable for their wrongdoings). The criminalization of smuggling, however, discouraged this kind of occasional smuggler, paving the way for larger, foreign, criminal organisations to take their place in the facilitation of irregular migration. The change in actor determined an increase in vulnerabilities: migrants were deprived of the accountability systems that provided them with guarantees against deception and threat, and the business of smuggling became the monopoly of people with no experience in sailing in Senegalese waters (Vives, 2017).

"The dangerous smuggler" and the expansion of the border apparatus

The unwavering attention that political leaders cast on the figure of the "dangerous smuggler" is part of an established pattern of evidence-averse policy-making that characterizes the field of migration. The EU, in fact, tends to adopt policy responses to migration phenomena that are at odds with the existing evidence on the topic. Most important is the perseverance of European governments in adopting ever-more restrictive migration policies to curb immigration, even though scientific evidence exists that prove that tighter borders do not halt existing migration flows. Rather, they oblige migrant people to travel irregularly and to take more dangerous routes (Andersson, 2014). *Evidence-averse* policy-making happens despite the fact that national governments express a public commitment to *evidence-based* policy-making, implemented through the funding of research programmes (Baldwin-Edwards et al., 2019). The fact that migration policies are rooted in biased perceptions and racist stereotypes should not be understood as a question of "misinformed" public discourse or policy-making (see also Ferguson, 1994). Rather, it depends on the fact that policy-making is influenced by a number of competing factors, from the bureaucrat's background to the broader political context (Baldwin-Edwards et al., 2019). Building on his work on development programs in rural Africa, James Ferguson argued that seemingly 'apolitical' policy reports fulfil a precise political function. By providing a representation of social problems where "politics is conspicuous by its absence" (Ferguson, 1994: 66), these reports prepare the ground for technical intervention, that claim to solve complex social, political and economic issues through the deployment of "highly standardized operations" (Ferguson, 1994: 69).

Although Ferguson writes about a starkly different political field, his observations apply to the analysis of anti-smuggling policies. Casting attention on the figure of the "smuggler" obscures the political conditions that make the service of smugglers necessary in the first place, and that make border areas and migration routes more generally so dangerous for people racialized as "migrant others" (Gross-Wyrtzen, 2019). This enables a massive expansion of the border apparatus (Carling and Hernández-Carretero, 2011). In the past three decades, anti-smuggling activities have proliferated across the North and the South. European countries, the US and

The "war on smugglers"

Australia have adopted laws criminalizing irregular migration and its facilitation. Their partner countries in the Global South followed suit, juggling between externalization pressure and desire to strategize migration as a diplomatic tool (Ben Jémia, 2012; Khrouz, 2016). In aid-recipient countries qualified as countries of "transit" or of "origin," the implementation of anti-smuggling infrastructure was supported by donors as part of their border externalization efforts (Watkins, 2017). Anti-smuggling interventions can be divided broadly in two categories: military-style interventions implemented by traditional security actors (like the police and the army); and welfare-like interventions, implemented by non-traditional security actors like non-governmental organisations (NGOs) and international organisations (IOs).[2] In the aftermath of the 2015 migration "crisis," for example, the EU has funded a plethora of anti-smuggling and anti-trafficking activities through its EU Trust Fund for Africa, including a €42 million project on "Support to Integrated border and migration management" in Libya, a €44 million project on "Support to the integrated border and migration management" in Morocco, and a €8 million project supporting "Rapid Economic Impact Action Plan in Agadez" (PAIERA). The first two projects work according to a clear military approach, as they aim at expanding the capacity of the Moroccan and Libyan state apparatus to surveil their land and sea borders. As we will see later in this chapter, the PAIERA project, instead, was based on a softer approach, aiming at dismantling smuggling by providing alternative work opportunities to those facilitating irregular migration movements in Niger.

The proliferation of military/humanitarian responses to smuggling could be conceptualized in terms of a combination between "fast" and "slow" instruments of border control. In a seminal book, Rob Nixon draws a distinction between a form of direct violence that is "immediate in time, explosive and spectacular in space, and as erupting into instant sensational visibility" (Nixon, 2011, p. 2) and "slow violence," "a violence that occurs gradually and out of sight, a violence of delayed destruction that is dispersed across time and space, an attritional violence that is typically not viewed as violence at all" (Nixon, 2011, p. 2).[3]

Fast control

Fast violence instruments deployed to counter smuggling operate in a deductive fashion, through the *destruction* of the social and logistical infrastructures enabling smuggling. Scholars have pointed out that border policing focuses on three different types of smuggling infrastructures: infrastructures of waiting, through the destruction of makeshift camps (Tyszler, 2019) or the eviction of residents from temporary accommodation in areas hosting people waiting to cross (Bajalia, 2020); infrastructure of crossing, through the interception, seizing and destruction of vessels used by irregular migrants and their facilitators (Garelli & Tazzioli, 2018); and infrastructures of community, through the forcible dispersal and relocation of migrants away from the borders, either through arrest and forcible abandonment in areas far away from the border and from urban centres, or through relocation to other reception or detention centres (Gazzotti & Hagan, 2020; Tazzioli, 2019). Such techniques of destruction and dispersal have become commonplace at the French-UK border, especially in the Calais region (Hagan, 2020), at the French-Italian border, especially in Ventimiglia (OXFAM, 2018), and at the Spanish-Moroccan border, mostly in the Moroccan regions surrounding the Spanish enclaves of Ceuta and Melilla (Gazzotti & Hagan, 2020). In the latter case, police forces tend to attack migrant camps in the early morning, destroy migrant shelters and set the remainder on fire, then force migrant people on buses that forcefully lead them to areas in the Centre and South of Morocco, in areas far away from the border, and often far away from the main urban centres. Such destruction and dispersal campaigns have continued even after the outbreak of the

Lorena Gazzotti

COVID-19 pandemic, leaving migrant people particularly vulnerable to the risk of infection and of destitution (Gross-Wyrtzen, 2020).

Although these military-style initiatives operate through fast violence, political leaders often justify them as humanitarian in nature. In 2016, French president Hollande defined the dismantling of the migrant camp in Calais, which become famous as "The Jungle," as responding to a "humanitarian urgency" generated by migrants spreading false rumours and unduly attracting potential border crossers to the North of France:

> Everybody must understand that the Calais Jungle is an impasse for migrants. It is also, I know, an action field for smugglers that let [migrants] believe this illusion that it will be possible to cross the border.
>
> It is also necessary to inform those that think that a life here is possible and that at a certain point this will open. No, it will not open (Hollande, 2016, translation mine).

Similarly, Garelli and Tazzioli highlight that the anti-smuggling purpose of the EU's Operation Sophia was framed as humanitarian. It aims at protecting migrants by preventing them access to unsafe migration routes, and by decreasing the logistical capacity of smugglers to prey on migrants by charging them exorbitant prices for extremely risky journeys (Garelli & Tazzioli, 2018). In Morocco equally, the dismantling of migrant camps in the North was disguised in a humanitarian nature, and justified as both responding to fighting smuggling networks and of redirecting people to cities where integration might be easier (Benjelloun, 2017). These discourses depict destruction as a way to protect migrants from the risks of border crossing, and as such makes them more acceptable in the eyes of the public. This obviously obscures the fact that, beyond the violence to which migrants might be exposed during anti-smuggling operations, the latter potentially leave migrants without any form of shelter, without any alternative legal crossing pathway, and potentially stuck in countries like Libya.

Slow control

Compared to fast instruments of control, slow violence distinguishes itself by being less physical, less recognizable and, thus, less likely to meet resistance (Gazzotti, 2021). Slow methods of border control include protracted waiting to be regularized, granted asylum, or resettled, the exclusion from healthcare, education and work, and a structurally higher vulnerability to exploitation. These are forms of containment that are less legible, but no less assertive, than building fences (Gross-Wyrtzen, 2019) because they are based on a "discontinuous 'hold' over migrants' lives," made of some sites and moments in which migrants are highly controlled and others in which their movements are managed through (partial) non-governing, not-seeing and non-registration" (Aradau & Tazzioli, 2019, p. 201).

As I mentioned earlier, anti-smuggling activities too can rely on methods that are much more mundane than military-like interventions, and on actors that lie beyond the security apparatus of the state. NGOs and IOs, in particular, have been coopted in the implementation of anti-smuggling activities based on welfare-like methods. These include information campaigns (Oeppen, 2016; Pécoud, 2010; Williams, 2019), and the re-deployment of former smugglers or "would-be" migrants into alternative business opportunities (Gazzotti, 2018; Howden & Zandonini, 2018; Tazzioli, 2014). Information campaigns have become quite popular as an instrument deployed to curb people's willingness to rely on smugglers to cross the border irregularly. The campaigns thus try to dismantle "false myths" about smugglers; for example, they would spread false rumours about the journey conditions and the living opportunities in the destination countries to deceive "potential clients" into travelling (Oeppen, 2016). These campaigns are generally premised on the belief that, if given correct information about the "realities" of the journey, "would be migrants" would make better decisions about their potential journey. According to policy-makers, the "right" decision corresponds to refraining from migrating, or to migrating legally (even though legal migration avenues are only accessible for an extremely limited audience of people). Rather than disrupting smuggling through methods that destroy physical spaces, disperse communities, and physically constrain people, information campaigns operate in intimate, non-conventional security spaces. Information leaflets are attached to the walls of a community centre, or they are distributed at football matches (Andersson, 2014). In other cases, messages revealing "the real truths" about migration are included in speeches recited by religious leaders during services (Watkins, 2020), or screened before movies projected in open-air, donor-funded mobile cinemas (Heller, 2014). These information campaigns thus try to disrupt smuggling by leveraging on the feelings of fear, compassion and empathy that migrants might have (Williams, 2019). In other words, they hope to unmake smuggling by shaping the subjectivity of 'potential' migrants, by influencing their capacity of decision-making, by transforming them into actors that think and move according to the logics of the border.

The provision of vocational training and alternative business opportunities to both "potential migrants" and former smugglers is another form of slow policing that aspires to disrupt the facilitation of irregular migration not through destruction, but by fulfilling the needs and aspirations through other means. Labour has always played a central role in border control strategies, and on development-based security interventions more broadly (Gazzotti, 2018). Since the early 2000s, donors, NGOs and IOs have on many occasions resorted to labour integration programmes to immobilise different categories of migrants, or 'potential' migrants. All these programmes were based on the (simplistic) belief that employment, often in the form of precarious jobs, could alone constitute an alternative to emigration (Rodriguez, 2015). Such projects have been recently trialled in Niger, where the approval of the 2015 Law Against Illicit Smuggling of Migrants, which criminalized the facilitation of irregular migration, disrupted the human smuggling business, which was deeply embedded in the local political economy of Agadez and the surrounding region. The imposition of tighter border control norms by Nigerien authorities, under the pressure of the EU, thus considerably increased unemployment levels in an area already marked by very high poverty rates (Comolli, 2019). The EU thus decided to implement the Action Plan for Rapid Economic Impact in Agadez (PAIERA) programme. Funded through the EU Trust Fund for Africa, the €8-million programme aimed at reconverting the former smuggling economy writ large – not only the people arranging the crossing and driving people through the desert, but also those providing services (namely "owners of hostels or brothels [*maison close*] that accommodate migrants," "the prostitution sector that developed alongside migrant smuggling," and "the business owner of legal activities that developed alongside smuggling") (EU Commission, n.d.). According to an article published by Open Migration, around 6,000 former "migration players" in the Agadez region submitted applications for projects to be funded by the PAIERA programme, which granted up to 1500,000 CFA (around €2,300) to start new businesses (Zandonini, 2017). Like information campaigns, labour-based approaches to anti-smuggling also individualise the responsibility for disrupting irregular migration onto the single (former) smuggler, smuggler's client, or indirect beneficiary from the smuggling business. Building on a sedentary and colonial approach to human development and wellbeing (Bakewell, 2008; Landau, 2018), these projects thus try to shape the subjectivity of potential migrants, smugglers and their communities to produce law-abiding subjects who make a living through licit rather than illicit means (the latest including all migration or smuggling-related endeavours).

Lorena Gazzotti

On the "unintended effects" of the military/humanitarian war against smugglers

Whether anti-smuggling operations are actually effective in reducing smuggling is a source of debate. In Morocco, activists and journalists label destruction-and-dispersal policies as "nonsense." Migrants forcibly displaced to the Centre and South of the country, in fact, often go back to their places of residence within a few days (Gazzotti and Hagan, 2020). This specific anti-smuggling operation, therefore, does not seem "effective" because it does not achieve its stated intent – i.e., dismantling smuggling networks or keeping migrants away from the physical borders of the state. Similarly, both researchers and the International Organization for Migration (IOM) have raised doubts regarding the capacity of information campaigns to curb the propensity for irregular migration and the actual magnitude of existing migratory flows. Brachet found that information campaigns lacked cultural sensitivity, and paradoxically utilised symbols associated with health and prosperity, which induced more people to leave (Brachet, 2016). Hernandez-Carretero and Carling, instead, argue that information campaigns do not compound the fact that taking the risk to pursue dangerous border crossing activities might be considered socially acceptable in areas with high-emigration rates (Hernández-Carretero & Carling, 2012). IOM researchers, instead, found that rigorous evidence on efficiency was scarce, and that information campaigns, in other words, had become widespread as a border control tool in spite of any consideration about whether they actually worked or not (IOM GMDAC, 2018). Similar critiques exist for the PAIERA programme (Howden & Zandonini, 2018): local stakeholders claim that the economic packages provided by the programme are too meagre to facilitate the creation of alternative jobs for the over 5000 former smugglers living in the region. In the field of migration control, anti-smuggling policies are not the only ones to be implemented despite not being effective even on their own terms: Ruben Andersson brands the entire border economy as absurd, because it keeps on expanding and reproducing itself even though irregular migration continues unabated (Andersson, 2014).

Although anti-smuggling activities might not be effective in curbing smuggling and irregular migration tout-court, this does not mean that they do not do anything. Much to the contrary, these activities expand control over the mobility of people moving from marginalized communities in the South to the North in ways that are not captured in project factsheets or in journalistic prose. In Morocco, for example, dispersal policies aiming at dismantling smuggling networks activate multiple mechanisms of dispossession that keep migrants both far away from the border and at the margins of Moroccan society. Although many migrants manage to go back to their places of residence, many others remain stuck in the areas where they have been abandoned due to lack of funding to buy return tickets or to the refusal of public transport companies to carry people profiled as irregular migrants. The destruction of one's belongings and the forcible displacement to other areas, where employment opportunities are scarce or the working conditions are exploitative, prevent people from really settling and enjoying the economic and personal security needed to have a decent life. Many migrants get stuck in a state of hyper-mobility, in a cycle of mobility and forced displacement that leads them to wander from city to city, in an unbearable state of living (Gazzotti & Hagan, 2020).

Similarly, information campaigns or labour programmes aiming at converting the smuggling economy into a licit market might not reduce the structural causes creating the need for the facilitation of irregular border crossing in the first place. However, they do create the feeling that smuggling can be managed through a set of light-touch, technical instruments that do not put into question the status quo, including the existence of restrictive migration policies, the stark inequalities and economic precarity affecting border areas, and the existence of a tradition

The "war on smugglers"

of migration in areas of origin and transit. Although military and humanitarian responses to human smuggling might appear neatly distinct, they both consolidate restrictive migration policies: they displace attention away from the structural causes that produce irregular migration, smuggling, and border violence in the first place; they pathologise smuggling and irregular migration as 'deviances' that need to be prosecuted; and they legitimise security-based interventions aimed at containing people deemed dangerous to the security of countries in the Global North.

Conclusion

The ramping up of border surveillance policies around the world has transformed human smuggling into the target of both hard and soft security interventions. In this landscape, the figure of the "smugglers" has become demonized as a source of threat for both migrants (who are deceived into and abused during dangerous border crossings) and destination countries (whose borders and integrity are supposedly violated by irregular migrants and their facilitators). Academic literature has widely discarded the idea of "smugglers" as inherently dangerous and deviant figures. Scholars have highlighted that a more accurate understanding of "smuggling" should read this activity within the situated moral and political economy of borders. Depending on the context, the relationship between smugglers and their "clients" can thus lie on a variegated spectrum ranging from overt violence to trust and care. Furthermore, smuggling can be a mundane activity that is deeply embedded in the local economy of border regions. Nevertheless, this biased representation has remained commonplace in policy discourses, to the point of being upheld as a justification for militarized border interventions.

In this chapter, I have argued that casting attention on the "dangerous smuggler" as a societal enemy (which endangers both migrant people *and* the population in countries of destination) is strategical. By obscuring the complex, political causes of irregular border crossing, demonizing smugglers allows policy-makers to tighten the objective of border intervention to a series of time-bound, space-bound, manageable interventions. This process of strategy reduction and technicalisation thus facilitates the reproduction of the migration control apparatus, which expands into a number of heterogenous interventions aimed at disrupting the business model of smugglers. Building on the work of Rob Nixon, I argued that anti-smuggling operations could be divided into *fast* and *slow* policing instruments. Fast methods of smuggling policing rely on military-style interventions, implemented by actors close to the traditional circuits of state security. They aim at disrupting smuggling through destruction – of migrants' gatherings, of the spaces where migrants wait, of the infrastructures used to cross. The violence that characterize these interventions is deeply physical – it acts through the destruction and annihilation of things, spaces, and people themselves. Slow instruments of anti-smuggling rely on a radically different from of intervention, that takes the form of welfare-like initiatives promoted by actors that lie outside the traditional circuits of state security. Rather than focusing on the physical *destruction* of smuggling infrastructures, slow anti-smuggling interventions utilize a *productive* approach to border control, which is less physical in nature as it does not operate at the level of the body or of the physical space, but rather aims at shaping the subjectivities of both potential migrants, former smugglers, and the communities revolving around the smuggling business.

Notes

1   I paraphrase here the title of James Ferguson's piece on the "uses" of neoliberalism (Ferguson, 2010).
2   Whilst seemingly paradoxical, the combination of such different types of intervention has become

commonplace in contemporary conflicts. In a 2003 article, Michel Agier explained the symbiosis between humanitarian and militarized intervention as "the left and right hand of the empire." Building on Bourdieu, Agier argues that the humanitarian apparatus (the left hand) is left to mend the damages created by armed operations (the right hand) – in a sinister symbiosis where "one hand [...] strikes, the other one [...] heals" (Agier 2003: 67). However, conceptualizing the military-humanitarian security apparatus in terms of a left and right hand risks to understate the explicit (rather than collateral) control functions performed by "softer" interventions.

3   Other scholars have named this form of chronic dispossession as "abandonment," or a technique of governance premised on the "state's selective presence and absence in community members' lives" (Denyer Willis, 2018, p. 333), which operates through "exhaustion, destitution, continual surveillance, paternalist policies, and formal and informal incarceration" (Gross-Wyrtzen, 2020: 8).

References

Achilli, L. (2018). The "Good" Smuggler: The Ethics and Morals of Human Smuggling among Syrians. *The ANNALS of the American Academy of Political and Social Science*, 676(1), 77–96. https://doi.org/10.1177/0002716217746641

Andersson, R. (2014). *Illegality, Inc.: Clandestine Migration and the Business of Bordering Europe* (1st edition). University of California Press.

Aradau, C., & Tazzioli, M. (2019). Biopolitics Multiple: Migration, Extraction, Subtraction. *Millennium*, 48(2), 198–220. https://doi.org/10.1177/0305829819889139

Bajalia, A. G. (2020). Dima Africa, Daily Darija: Im/migrant Sociality, Settlement, and State Policy in Tangier, Morocco. *The Journal of North African Studies*, 1–20. https://doi.org/10.1080/13629387.2020.1800212.

Bakewell, O. (2008). 'Keeping Them in Their Place': The Ambivalent Relationship Between Development and Migration in Africa. *Third World Quarterly*, 29(7), 1341–1358.

Baldwin-Edwards, M., Blitz, B. K., & Crawley, H. (2019). The Politics of Evidence-based Policy in Europe's 'migration Crisis.' *Journal of Ethnic and Migration Studies*, 45(12), 2139–2155. https://doi.org/10.1080/1369183X.2018.1468307

Ben Jémia, M. (2012). La Tunisie, cerbère des frontières européennes. *Plein droit*, 73, 35–38.

Benjelloun, S. (2017). Nouvelle politique migratoire et opérations de régularisation. In M. Alioua & J.-N. Ferrié (Eds.), *La nouvelle politique migratoire marocaine* (pp. 35–76). Konrad Adenauer Stiftung.

Brachet, J. (2016). Policing the Desert: The IOM in Libya Beyond War and Peace. *Antipode*, 48(2), 272–292. https://doi.org/10.1111/anti.12176

Carling, J., & Hernández-Carretero, M. (2011). Protecting Europe and Protecting Migrants? Strategies for Managing Unauthorised Migration from Africa. *The British Journal of Politics and International Relations*, 13, 42–58. https://doi.org/10.1111/j.1467-856x.2010.00438.x

Comolli, V. (2019). Niger: Curtailing Migration has Unintended Consequences, International Institute for Strategic Studies. https://www.iiss.org/blogs/analysis/2019/11/csdp-curtailing-migration-niger

De Genova, N. (2010). Antiterrorism, Race, and the New Frontier: American Exceptionalism, Imperial Multiculturalism, and the Global Security State. *Identities*, 17(6), 613–640. https://doi.org/10.1080/1070289X.2010.533523

De Noronha, L. (2020). *Deporting black Britons: Portraits of deportation to Jamaica / Luke de Noronha*. Manchester University Press, 2020.

Denyer Willis, L. (2018). "It Smells Like a Thousand Angels Marching": The Salvific Sensorium in Rio de Janeiro's Western Subúrbios. *Cultural Anthropology*, 33(2), 324–348. https://doi.org/10.14506/ca33.2.10

European Commission. (n.d.). *Migrant Smuggling*. https://ec.europa.eu/home-affairs/what-we-do/policies/irregular-migration-return-policy/facilitation-irregular-migration_en

Ferguson, J. (1994). *The Anti-Politics Machine: Development, Depoliticization, and Bureaucratic Power in Lesotho* (New edition). University of Minnesota Press.

Ferguson, J. (2010). The Uses of Neoliberalism. *Antipode*, 41, 166–184. https://doi.org/10.1111/j.1467-8330.2009.00721.x

Garelli, G., & Tazzioli, M. (2018). The Humanitarian War Against Migrant Smugglers at Sea. *Antipode*, 50(3), 685–703. https://doi.org/10.1111/anti.12375

Gazzotti, L. (2021). *Immigration Nation. Aid, Slow Control, and Border Politics in Morocco*. Cambridge University Press.

Gazzotti, L. (2018). From Irregular Migration to Radicalisation? Fragile Borders, Securitised Development and the Government of Moroccan Youth. *Journal of Ethnic and Migration Studies*, 45(1), 1–22.

Gazzotti, L., & Hagan, M. (2020). Dispersal and Dispossession as Bordering: Exploring Governance Through Mobility in Post-2013 Morocco. *Journal of North African Studies*. https://doi.org/10.1080/13629387.2020.1800209.

Gross-Wyrtzen, L. (2019). *Bordering Blackness: The Production of Race in the Morocco-EU Immigration Regime*. PhD thesis, Clark University.

Gross-Wyrtzen, L. (2020). Policing the Virus: Race, Risk, and the Politics of Containment in Morocco and the United States." Roundtable on Borders and the State in Light of COVID-19. *Security in Context*. https://www.securityincontext.com/publications/borders-roundtable-policing-the-virus

Hagan, M. (2020). The Contingent Camp: Struggling for Shelter in Calais, France. In T. Scott-Smith & M. Breeze (Eds.), *Structures of Protection? Rethinking Refugee Shelter*. Berghahn Books.

Heller, C. (2014). Perception Management – Deterring Potential Migrants Through Information Campaigns. *Global Media and Communication*, 10(3), 303–318. https://doi.org/10.1177/1742766514552355

Hernández-Carretero, M., & Carling, J. (2012). Beyond "Kamikaze Migrants": Risk Taking in West African Boat Migration to Europe. *Human Organization*, 71(4), 407–416. https://doi.org/10.17730/humo.71.4.n52709742v2637t1

Hollande, F. (2016). *Déclaration de M. François Hollande, Président de la République, sur l'action des forces de sécurité et le démantèlement du campement de migrants, à Calais le 26 septembre 2016*. https://www.vie-publique.fr/discours/200512-declaration-de-m-francois-hollande-president-de-la-republique-sur-la

Howden, D., & Zandonini, G. (2018). Niger: Europe's Migration Laboratory. *Refugees Deeply*. https://www.newsdeeply.com/refugees/articles/2018/05/22/niger-europes-migration-laboratory

IOM. (n.d.). *IOM's comprehensive approach to counter migrant smuggling*. https://www.iom.int/sites/default/files/our_work/DMM/IBM/IOM-Approach-to-counter-migrant-smuggling-Brochure.pdf

IOM GMDAC. (2018). *Evaluating the impact of information campaigns in the field of migration: A systematic review of the evidence, and practical guidance*. https://gmdac.iom.int/sites/default/files/papers/evaluating_the_impact_of_information_campaigns_in_field_of_migration_iom_gmdac.pdf

Khrouz, N. (2016). *La pratique du droit des étrangers au Maroc. Essai de praxéologie juridique et politique*. PhD thesis, unpublished. Université Grenoble Alpes.

Landau, L. B. (2018). A Chronotope of Containment Development: Europe's Migrant Crisis and Africa's Reterritorialisation. *Antipode*, 15(7). https://doi.org/10.1111/anti.12420

Magallanes-Gonzalez, C. (2020). Sub-Saharan Leaders in Morocco's Migration Industry: Activism, Integration, and Smuggling. *Journal of North African Studies*. https://doi.org/10.1080/13629387.2020.1800213.

Nixon, R. (2011). *Slow Violence and the Environmentalism of the Poor*. Harvard University Press.

Oeppen, C. (2016). 'Leaving Afghanistan! Are you sure?' European efforts to deter potential migrants through information campaigns. *Human Geography*, 9(2), 57–68.

OXFAM. (2018). *Nulle part où aller. L'échec de la France et de l'Italie pour aider les réfugié-e-s et autres migrant-e-s échoué-e-s à la frontière vers Vintimille*.

Pécoud, A. (2010). Informing Migrants to Manage Migration? An Analysis of IOM's Information Campaigns. In *The Politics of International Migration Management* (pp. 184–201). Palgrave Macmillan.

Rodriguez, A.-L. (2015). Three Stories About Living Without Migration in Dakar: Coming to Terms With The Contradictions of the Moral Economy. *Africa*, 85(2), 333–355. https://doi.org/10.1017/S0001972015000042

Sanchez, G. (2016). Women's Participation in the Facilitation of Human Smuggling: The Case of the US Southwest. *Geopolitics*, 21(2), 387–406. https://doi.org/10.1080/14650045.2016.1140645

Slack, J. (2019). *Deported to Death: How Drug Violence Is Changing Migration on the US–Mexico Border/Jeremy Slack*. University of California Press.

Stock, I. (2019). *Time, Migration and Forced Immobility: Sub-Saharan African Migrants in Morocco/Inka Stock*. Bristol University Press.

Tazzioli, M. (2014). *Spaces of Governmentality: Autonomous Migration and the Arab Uprisings*. Rowman & Littlefield International.

Tazzioli, M. (2019). The Politics of Migrant Dispersal. Dividing and Policing Migrant Multiplicities. *Migration Studies*, mnz003. https://doi.org/10.1093/migration/mnz003.

Tyszler, E. (2019). *Derrière les barrières de Ceuta & Melilla. Rapports sociaux de sexe, de race et colonialité du contrôle migratoire à la frontière maroco-espagnole*. PhD thesis, Université Paris 8, unpublished.

UNODC. (n.d.). *Migrant Smuggling FAQs*. https://www.unodc.org/unodc/en/human-trafficking/migrant-smuggling/faqs.html#m6

Vives, L. (2017). The European Union–West African Sea Border: Anti-immigration Strategies and Territoriality. *European Urban and Regional Studies*, 24(2), 209–224. https://doi.org/10.1177/0969776416631790

Vogt, W. (2016). Stuck in the Middle With You: The Intimate Labours of Mobility and Smuggling along Mexico's Migrant Route. *Geopolitics*, 21(2), 366–386. https://doi.org/10.1080/14650045.2015.1104666

Watkins, J. (2017). Bordering Borderscapes: Australia's Use of Humanitarian Aid and Border Security Support to Immobilise Asylum Seekers. *Geopolitics*, 22(4), 958–983. https://doi.org/10.1080/14650045.2017.1312350

Watkins, J. (2020). Irregular Migration, Borders, and the Moral Geographies of Migration Management. *Environment and Planning C: Politics and Space*, 2399654420915607. https://doi.org/10.1177/2399654420915607.

Williams, J. (2019). Affecting Migration: Public Information Campaigns and the Intimate Spatialities of Border Enforcement. *Environment and Planning C: Politics and Space*, 2399654419833384. https://doi.org/10.1177/2399654419833384

Zandonini, G. (2017). "I'm Not a Criminal": The Story of a Former Passeur in Niger. *OpenMigration*. https://openmigration.org/en/analyses/im-not-a-criminal-the-story-of-a-former-passeur-in-niger/

INDEX

Note: *Italicized* page numbers refer to figures, **bold** page numbers refer to tables

AAA (American Anthropological Association) 79, 86
ABORNE (African Borderlands Research Network) 18, 26
ABP (Afghan Border Police) 202, 205
Abraham, I. 53, 144, 145, 385
Abrar, C. 335
Aceh, Indonesia 48
Ackello-Ogutu, C. 68
adulteration of petroleum products 262, 265; *see also* petroleum smuggling
Afghan Border Police (ABP) 202, 205
Afghan National Police (ANP) 202, 205
Afghanistan 5, 9, 86; armed conflicts and drug trade in 355; borderland brokers in 118–131; borders 124, 125, 200; civil war economy 370, 372–373; conflict zones 369; map of *125*; opium trade in 196–211; postcolonial trades 371; rebel revenues from smuggling in 398
Africa: food riots 273; migrant smuggling 316; smuggling at sea 413
African Borderlands Research Network (ABORNE) 18, 26
African clandestine economies 30–40; and model shopping 31–33; overview 30–31
African Great Lakes region: border economies 134–137; concentric circles 138–139; infrastructure for smuggling in 138–139; politics of scale in 139–140; transnational cross-border trade in 134–141
African Political Systems (Meyer Fortes and Evans-Pritchard) 81
African Rift Valley 136
Agnew, J. 109, 110, 114
Ahmad, A. 369–379
AK-47 rifles 50; *see also* arms trafficking
Al Shabaab 46–47
alcohol smuggling 102–103
Aldeen, S. 308

Alexander, M. 186
Algeria 374; border security 440; postcolonial trades 371
Ali, A. 96
alkalos (village chiefs) 100
Al-Qaeda 291
Al-Qaeda in the Islamic Maghreb (AQIM) 374, 376
Amerhauser, K. 438
American Anthropological Association (AAA) 79, 86
American Political Science Association (APSA) 79
AML/CTF (Anti-Money Laundering and Terrorist Financing) 438–439
amphetamines 388
Anaconda Plan 361
Andorra 253
Andreas, P. 52, 287, 389
Angola: cross-border smuggling in 20–21; diamond smuggling in 24, 400
ANP (Afghan National Police) 202, 205
Ansar al-Dine 291
ant contraband 173
Anti-Agricultural Smuggling Act of 2016 (Philippines) 275
Anti-Money Laundering and Terrorist Financing (AML/CTF) 438–439
anti-smuggling policies 319–320
apex brokers 121, 126–128; *see also* brokers
APSA (American Political Science Association) 79
ARC-GIS software 55
archipelagic waters 415
archival documents 52
Argentina 8, 171, 191; rice exports 274
armed conflicts 9–10
Armed Revolutionary Forces of Colombia (FARC) 188, 192
armed youth 33
Arms Trade Treaty (ATT) 214, 223

Index

arms trafficking: academic debates on 215–216; advantages of trafficked arms 217; authorized trade 216; categories 216; and collectors 217; comparison to other types of smuggling 223; countering 220–221; extent of 218–219; illicit prices 219; and instrumental need for arms 217; instrumentalist view on 215; international and regional agreements and regulations 222–223; international assistance in countering 221–222; localising perspectives on 23; main sources of arms 216–217; overview 4, 5, 213–214; in the Philippines 53; primary significance 213–214; and recirculation of illicit arms 219–220, *220*; semi-legal trade 216; state-sanctioned illicit trade 216; substantive view on 215; supply and demand of illicitly trafficked arms 216–217; and symbolic role for weapons 217; in West Africa 101–102; wholly illicit trade 216
Arrow Boys 160–165
Arua boys 148–149
ASA (Association of Social Anthropologists of the UK) 79
Asante 99
Association of Social Anthropologists of the UK (ASA) 79
Asycuda software 21
Australia: migrant smuggling in 319–320; rice exports 274
Austria 306; research ethics in 78
Avramopoulos, D. 303
Awumbila, M. 331
Ayalew, L. 63
azad visa system 335
Azande People 163
Aziz, H 128–129

Bach, D. 33
BaHema 136
BaNande 136
Bangladesh, human smuggling in 326, 327, 334–336
Bank of Uganda 67, 69
Barre, S. 373
barriers to entry 390–391
Barron, P. 53
Baud 110
Baud, M. 109, 110
Bayart, J.-F. 33
Bayat, A. 146
BaYira 136
Bazenuissa-Ganga, R. 33, 50
behaviors, quantifying 69–72
Belmokhtar, M. 247
Benford's law 66
Benin 34–35, *67*, 68, 69, 70, 101
Bensassi, S. 69, 70
Bermuda 362

berri kefach (door openers) 330
Bewley-Taylor, D.R 185
Beyond Meridca strategy 433
Bhagwati, J 72
Bhagwati, J. 62–63, 64, 66
Bhatia, J. 9, 118–131
Bierschenk, T. 31
bilateral trade 72
biopolitics 110
Bird Ruiz-Benitez de Lugo, L. 341–350
BIZNET 277
Blattman, C. 71
blind spots 120
blockade 361–365
blood cotton 361–365
blood diamonds 34, 355, 400
blue trade 25, 26, 252
Boko Haram 39, 46–47
Bolivia: coca growing in 188–189, 191; cocaine production 185, 190
bonded warehouses 20–21
border effects 119
border regimes, as interactive orders 119
border zone 108
bordering 109–112
borderities 110
borderland brokers 118–131; apex brokers 121, 126–128; definition of 120; effects of 121–122; as friction specialists 121; life histories of 124–129; in Nangarhar, Afghanistan 126–128; in Nimroz, Afghanistan 128–129; overview 118; political economy of 122–123; positionality of 121; tertiary brokers 121
borderlands 3, 6; definition of 108; economies 134–137; and frontiers 108–109; and localised smuggling 19–28; overview 107–108; as spaces of innovation and transformation 119; as trading spaces 119–120
border-making: and control of resources 97; defensive logic in 97; types of 157
borders 95–105; alcohol smuggling 102; and bordering practices 109–112; definition of 108; gun smuggling 101–102; irruption of 103–104; opium smuggling 102; overview 107–108; securitization of 113; territorialism perspective 110; vernacularization of 111
borderscapes 110
Botswana 69
Bourne, M. 213–214
Bout, V. 296
Brazil 8, 113, 171
Brazzaville 97
Brecht, B. 25
Brenner, D. 9–10, 397–406
Brenton, P. 70
bribery 48
British American Tobacco 253

Index

brokers 118–131; apex brokers 121, 126–128; definition of 120; effects of 121–122; as friction specialists 121; life histories of 124–129; in Nangarhar, Afghanistan 126–128; in Nimroz, Afghanistan 128–129; overview 118; political economy of 122–123; positionality of 121; tertiary brokers 121

Brown, J. 358

Bruwer, C. 411–428

Buen Guerdane, Tunisia 266

Bukavu/Cyangugu 98

bunkering of petroleum 262

Burke, W.J. 69

Burma; *see* Myanmar

Burundi 37, 67

Cambodia: rice exports 275; wildlife trafficking in 232

Cameroun 34

Canada: alcohol smuggling 102–103; border smuggling 113; wartime trading in 1812 359–361

cannabis 3, 5

capillary pattern 112

Carling, J. 450

Carpenter, A. 433

Carrera, S. 306–308

Carry (transport providers) 333–334; *see also* human smuggling/trafficking

Cartes, H. 173

Castells, M. 287

Catholics 103

CDC (Center for Disease Control) 346

Celestin, K. 70

Center for Disease Control (CDC) 346

Central African Republic (CAR) 156–165

Central Intelligence Agency (CIA) 399

Cerdanya 98, 101

Chad 34–35, 345

Chad Basin 34, 36, 39

Chalendard, C.R 65

Chalfin, B. 39

Chalmers, D. 165

Chambers, R. 82

Chand, S 233

Chiapas, Mexico 218

Chile 184–185, 191

China 28, 64; drug smuggling in 292; migrant smuggling from 314, 315; rice exports 274; rice smuggling in 276; smuggling at sea 51; smuggling in 28; tax avoidance 22; trade with Hong Kong 64; trading corridors **123**; wildlife trafficking in 230, 231, 232, 234

Chirundu (Zimbabwe) 24–25

Chouvy, P. 53

cigarette smuggling 5, 247–256; global illicit trade 248–249; licit goods 249–250; overview

247–248; tobacco industry involvement in 252–255

Ciudad del Este 8

Ciudad del Este, Paraguay 171–173

civil society 146

Civil War 361–365

civil war economies 369–379; Afghanistan 372–373; Algeria 374; laws in 375–377; Mali 374–375; and modern borders 370; old trade routes 370–372; overview 369–372; and postcolonialism 370–371; and rebel taxation 370; and smuggling 378–379; Somalia 373–374

Clandestine Crossings (Spener) 83

Clark, A 165

clearing agents 70

Clifford, J 81

Clunan, A.L. 288

coastal states: archipelagic waters 415; contiguous zone 415–416; and exclusive economic zone 416; internal waters 414–415; jurisdiction 413–414; territorial sea 415

coca chewing 185–186

cocaine 21; centers of production 189; colonial regulation 184; history 184; prices 187

cocaine smuggling 183–193; and armed conflicts 355; and gangs 188; geopolitics of 183–186, 190–192; history 184–185; input-output structure 289–291; prices 187; supply chains 187–188, 190–192; territoriality 291–293; and violence 188–189; war against cocaine 185–186

coffee smuggling 63

cold tapping 264

Cold War 287, 373

Colombia: armed conflicts and drug trade in 355; coca growing in 189, 191; cocaine production 185, 187–188, 189, 190; cocaine smuggling in 183, 293; safe spaces 435–436

colonial regimes 2, 97–98

comercio hormiga 173–174

Commission of Enquiry into the Coca Leaf 185

Commission of Narcotic Drugs (CND) 185

Communist Party of Burma 402

community based natural resource management (CBNRM) 236, 239–241

community resilience 431–441; actors in building 433–434; capacity 433; challenges to resilience building 437–439; and community building 436–437; concept of 431–433; definition of 433; forms of resilience building 435–437; and gender 434; information sharing and awareness 436; overview 431–433; and safe spaces 435–436; securitization risks 439–440; and smuggling activities 439–440; support to individuals affected by organized crime 436; and violence interruption 435

Confederates 361–365

conflict commodities 355

Index

conflict minerals 10, 37
conflicts 9–10
Congo 98, 134–141
Congo-Uganda border 7
connection men 321, 331–333; *see also* human smuggling/trafficking; migrant smuggling
contiguous zone 415–416
Continental Army 357
contraband 3
contrabando de hormigas 173–174
Convention Against Illicit Traffic in Narcotic Drugs (1988) 185
Convention on Psychotropic Substances (1971) 185
Cooper, A. 111
Cooper, S. 433
Coordination of Azawad Movements (CMA) 344
copper 26
copper cathodes 24–25
corruption, welfare effect of 63
Council of Europe Agreement 427n29
COVID-19 pandemic 228–229
COVID-19 pandemic and human smuggling 341–350; anti-migrant sentiments 346–347; changes to smuggling mechanics 345–346; demand for human smuggling services 344; and organised crime groups 347–348; overview 341–342; responses 347–348; and restrictions on cross-border movements 352–354; risks for migrants 345–346
Cox, R 139
coyotes 321; *see also* migrant smuggling
crime wars 431–441; and intimidation 437–438; overview 431–433; resilience to 431–433; securitization risks 439–440; and smuggling activities 439–440; targeted killings by 437–438
criminal iatrogenesis 319–320
criminalization of smuggling 33
Croke, K. 71
cross-border trades 278–280; in African Great Lakes region 137; cross-border traders 69–72; typology of 25; *see also* borderlands
Customs Preventive Service (Gold Coast) 100

Dahomean kingdom 96
dangerous smugglers: and expansion of border apparatus 446–447; versus moral smugglers 445–446
Darfur 83
Dark Net 288
Dark Web 288, 292
Dávalos, L.M. 189
De La Rosa, N.P.C. 45–58
De Vries, L. 156–165
Deardorff, A. 63
demarcations 161

Demir, O. 66, 316
Democratic Republic of Congo 10, 26, 32; border crossing points 69; colonial regime 36–37; economic pacification in 400–402; gold smuggling 400–401; mapping smuggling in 46; petroleum smuggling 144, 262; rebel revenues from smuggling in 398; and restriction of border trade 400–402
Derby. E.H. 358
Dercon, S. 63
Deshingkar, P. 326–337, 334
deterritorialization 111
DFG (German Research Association) 79, 80
diamond smuggling 21, 24, 34, 355, 400
differentiated products 65
digital ethnography 84
Dilger, Hansjörg 79
dirty entanglements 6
Djankov, S. 69
Djibouti 372
Dobler, G. 19–28, 251
Dodd-Frank Wall Street Reform and Consumer Protection Act 400–401, 404
domestic consumption 63
domestic provisioning 171–173
doorstepping 56, 59n12
double-funnel 112
downstream smuggling 264–265
drug smuggling 2, 4, 113; and narco-economy 175–176; and narco-geography 292; and narco-guerrillas 355; and narco-terrorists 355; by sea 412; West Africa 34; women in 175; *see also* cocaine smuggling; heroin smuggling; opium trade
Duffield, M. 33, 34
Durand Line 371
Durán-Martínez, A. 183–193
Dutt, P. 63

Eastern Africa: ideological rehabilitation of smuggling in 36–39; violent modes of accumulation in 37
Eastern Europe 65
Eberhard-Ruiz, A. 69
Ebola 228
Economic Community of West African States (ECOWAS) 250
economic pacification 397–406; in Democratic Republic of Congo 400–402; and liberalisation of border trade 402–404; in Myanmar 402–404; overview 397; pitfalls of 399; and rebel revenue from smuggling 398–399; and restriction of border trade 400–402
Economist Intelligence Unit (EUI) 251
Ecuador: cocaine smuggling in 191; gasoline-cocaine flows in 294

458

Index

Egypt 22, 273; borderlands 86; ethics review boards 80; food riots 273; fuel smuggling in 266, 267; rice exports 274
El Salvador 188
Ellis, S. 136
emancipation 168
embedded research 86
Enemy Trade Act of 1812 (United States) 359
Enough Project 400
entry tax 387
ephiderenes 388
Escobar, P. 188
ethics 80–82
ethics of reciprocity 82
ethics review boards 78–80
Ethiopia 63; human smuggling in 326, 328, 330; postcolonial borders 372; trade gap 65
EU Charter of the Fundamental Rights 307
EU Directorate for Migration and Home Affairs 444
EU Facilitation Directive 306–307
EU Trust Fund for Africa 447
EU-Libya Migration treaty 331
European Research Council (ERC) 79–80
Evans-Pritchard, E.E. 81
everyday diplomacy 86
exchange rates 63
exclusive economic zone (EEZ) 416
The Extinction Market (Felbab-Brown) 234, 238, 240
extortion 48

Famine Early Warning Systems Network (FEWS NET) 68
FARC-EP (Revolutionary Armed Forces of Colombia-People's Army) 188, 192, 291, 296
fast control instruments 444, 447–448
FATF (Financial Action Task Force) 439
Fearon, J.D. 370
Felbab-Brown, V. 228–240, 234, 238, 240
Felix, S.G. 433, 434
feminism 168
Ferguson, T.J. 32, 446
Fezzan, Libya 83, 84
field stories 158–160
fieldwork: ethics in 80–82; hidden practices 83–86; morality in 80–82; securitization of 83–86
Fieldwork under Fire (Nordstrom and Robben) 86
Filipino Muslim Traders Association 277
Financial Action Task Force (FATF) 439
Firearms Protocol (2001) 223
firearms smuggling; *see* arms trafficking
Fisk, R. 86
Fisman, R. 64, 66
fixer agencies 86
flag states 413–414

flags of convenience 419–420
food riots 274
Forstater, M. 66
Fortes, M. 81
forum shopping 32
Foucault, M. 110
France 447–448
Frank B. 401
Freedom House 347
Freeman, C. 174, 177
front men 35
frontier effects 119
frontier zone 108
frontiers 96; definition of 108–109; as spaces of innovation and transformation 119; *see also* borderlands
fuel smuggling: adulteration 265; anti-smuggling laws 269; combatting 267–269; complicity 269; and control of oil and gas infrastructure 263; downstream smuggling 264–265; gasoline smuggling 294; and global consumption 260; in Libya 265–267, 269; in Mexico 269; midstream and diversion of unrefined products 263–266; modalities of oil and fuel theft 262; reducing incentives for 267–268; and retailing 264; sale of unrefined products 263; second-order effects 269; and subsidies 267; tapping of unrefined products 263–264; and thef 260–269; and transparency of oil sector 268; in Uganda 144–153, 269; upstream governance of production 261–262

Gaddafi, M. 374
gala kata visas 335
Galemba, R.B 176
Gallien, M. 1–14, 53, 247–256, 251, 294, 439
Gambia 63, 100–101
Garelli, G. 449
gasoline smuggling 291, 293–294, 294; *see also* petroleum smuggling
GATIA (*Groupe autodéfense touareg Imghad et alliés*) 377
Gazzotti, L. 444–451
GDP (gross domestic product) 113
gems 53
gender and smuggling 168–177; domestic provisioning 171–173; drug trade 175; gendered labour 173–176; girl gangs 169–170; higglering 174; and narco-economy 175–176; overview 168; suitcase traders 174
geo-tagging techniques 51
German Anthropological Association 79
German Research Association (DFG) 79, 80
Germany 65; cocaine production 184; research ethics in 78
Ghana 97; human smuggling in 327, 331–333; petroleum smuggling in 263

459

Index

Ghor Ghori bazaar 128–129
girl gangs 169–170
global database 52–53
Global Fishing Watch 422–423
Global Shadows (Ferguson) 32
Global South 326
globalisation, dark side of 2
godown tax 387
Godson, R. 295
Gold Coast 99–100
gold smuggling 24, 37, 400–401
Golub, S. 63
Goma/Giseny 98, 120
Goodhand, J. 9, 118–131
Google Earth 55
Gootenberg, P. 184, 189
Grant, U.S. 362
Great Lakes Region 70
green trade 25, 252
grey trade 25, 26, 252
Grisaffi, T. 192
gross domestic product (GDP) 113
Groupe autodéfense touareg Imghad et alliés
   (GATIA) 377
GSPC (Salafist Group for Preaching and
   Combat) 374
Guadalupe Hidalgo treaty (1848) 363
Guardia di Finanza (Italy) 266
Guatemala 188
Guild, E. 306–308
Guinea Bissau 83, 102
gun smuggling: academic debates on 215–216;
   advantages of trafficked arms 217; authorized
   trade 216; categories 216; and collectors 217;
   comparison to other types of smuggling 223;
   countering 220–221; extent of 218–219; illicit
   prices 219; and instrumental need for arms 217;
   instrumentalist view on 215; international and
   regional agreements and regulations 222–223;
   international assistance in countering 221–222;
   overview 213–214; in the Philippines 53;
   Philippines 53; primary significance 213–214;
   and recirculation of illicit arms 219–220, *220*;
   semi-legal trade 216; state-sanctioned illicit trade
   216; substantive view on 215; supply and
   demand of illicitly trafficked arms 216–217; and
   symbolic role for weapons 217; in West Africa
   101–102; wholly illicit trade 216
gunpowder smuggling 357–358
Guzman, "El Chapo" 114

Haiti 287, 436
Hampton, W. 361
Hansen, B. 62–63, 64
Harmonized System code 64
Hausa traders 99

Hausa-Fulani commercial groups 36
Hawiye-Abgal clan 374
Hawiye-Habr-Gidr clan 374
Heersmink, R. 165
Henig, D. 86
Herbert, M. 431–441, 439
Herman, E. 305
Hernandez-Carretero, M. 450
heroin smuggling: heroin production 196;
   input-output structure 290; in Moreh 388;
   smuggling at sea 421
Heym, S. 87
Heyman, J. 112
hidden trade 61–73; and bilateral trade 72; versus
   missing trade *62*; overview 61–62;
   quantifying 66–69
higglering 174
high seas 416–417; *see also* smuggling at sea
high-stakes smuggling 24
HIV/AIDS 228
Hobsbawm, E. 145
Hollande, F. 448
Hong Kong 64
Horizon 2020 79
Hornbacher, A. 81
hot tapping 263
hotel journalism 86
Hübschle, A. 170
human rights, and smuggling at sea 422
human smuggling/trafficking 4, 113, 303–310,
   444; anti-migrant sentiments 346–347; and *azad*
   visa system 335; Bangladesh 334–336; brokers
   329–330; Carry (transport providers) 333–334;
   changes to smuggling mechanics 345–346;
   connection men 331–333; corridors of 326; and
   COVID-19 pandemic 341–350; demand for
   human smuggling services 344; facilitators of
   304–305; and gendered circuits of labour
   circulation 327–328; in Ghana 331–333; in the
   Global South 326–337; for humanitarian reasons
   306–309; and infrastructure of migration 328;
   and irregular immigration 303, 326; and *kafala*
   system 330, 334–336; in Mediterranean
   303–304; and migrant smuggling 313–321; in
   Myanmar 333–334; and organised crime groups
   347–348; overview 303–304; protection of
   migrants in 303–305; reasons for countering
   303–304; responses 347–348; and restrictions on
   cross-border movements 352–354; risks for
   migrants 345–346; by sea 412; smuggled
   migrants' perspectives 306; as a socially
   embedded process 330; South-South human
   smuggling 326; through social networks
   305–306; *see also* migrant smuggling
Human Terrain System (HTS) 86
Human Trafficking Act (Ghana) 331–332

Index

humanitarian clause 306–308
Hüsken, T. 21, 22, 77–88, 105
Hussein, S. 262

Ibañez-Tirado, D. 86
Idler, A. 286–296, 289
illegal logging 24
illegality 22
illicit smuggling 4; governance structure 295–296;
  input-output structure 289–291, 290;
  institutional context 293–294; and insurgents
  384–395; interconnectedness of flows 287–289;
  intersections of flows 286–296; supply chain
  networks 289–296; and survival smuggling 293;
  territoriality 291–293; underworld 292;
  upperworld 292
Illicit Trade Environment Index 251
illicitness 22
import tax evasion 66
incidental intelligence 52
India: borders 9, 125, 200; drug smuggling in 292,
  388; human smuggling in 326; Land Ports
  Authority 384; Moreh border crossing 386–387;
  opium trade in 196, 199; rice exports 274; rice
  smuggling in 276; trade gaps 65; wildlife
  trafficking in 230, 232, 234
India-Myanmar border 9
Indian Reserve Battalion (IRB) 386
Indonesia 63; food riots 274; mapping smuggling in
  47, 48; profits from illicit trades in 53; rice
  smuggling in 272, 276; wildlife trafficking in
  234, 240
informal cross-border trade (ICBT) 3, 386–389
informal taxes 387–388
informal trade 3
informal traders 69–72
insurgents 384–395; and barriers to entry 390–391;
  ceasefires 391–393; incentivising smuggling by
  389–390; informal regulation of smuggling
  390–391; smuggling as source of revenue for
  398–399; suspension of operations 391–393;
  territorial control 391–393
internal waters 414–415
International Organization for Migration
  (IOM) 450
International Ship and Port Facility Security (ISPS)
  Code 419
International Tax and Investment Center
  (ITIC) 254
International Tracing Instrument (ITI) 223
Iran: borders 124, 125, 200; opium consumption
  196; opium trade in 196; smuggling at sea
  412, 413
Iraq 86; civil war economy 370
Islamic Legion 374
Islamic State- Khorasan Province (ISKP) 204–205
Islamic State of Syria and al-Sham (ISIS) 263, 288

Italy, rice exports 274
ivory 230, 233
Izard, G. 369

Jackson, S. 38
Jalalabad, Afghanistan 124
Japan: coca production 184; wildlife trafficking
  in 234
Jarreau, J. 70
Javorcik, B. 65, 66
Jibao, S. 70
Jonathan, G. 261
Joossens, L. 55
Jordan 262
jump scaling 137, 139–140

kafala system 330, 334–336
Kahya, Y. 316
Kaizen, J. 316
Karandahan Association of Tawi-Tawi 277
Karen rebellion 403, 404
Karzai, A.W. 128
Karzai, H. 377
Keen, D. 34
Kelman, J. 294
Kemp,W 438
Kenya 36, 54, 67, 69, 136; hidden trade 67, 69;
  livestock marketing in 44; postcolonial borders
  372; trade gap 65; wildlife trafficking in 230,
  233, 235, 236
Kesselring, R. 24
Khan, H.M. 126–128
Khmer Rouge 400
Khyber Pass 124
The King David Report (Heym) 87
King, W. 360
Kleemans, E. 315
Klute, G. 83
Knoote, F. 439
Koehler, J. 9, 118–131
Kony, J. 160, 162
Kovats-Bernat, C. 84
Kuki National Army (KNA) 386–387, 388–389
Kwass, M. 52

laissez-faire 112
Laos: opium trade in 196; wildlife trafficking in 232
Lara, F.J., Jr. 45–58, 50
large-scale informal/illegal crossings **123**
Law Against Illicit Smuggling of Migrants 449
lawless zones 7
Leander, A. 39
Lebanon 287
legal trade in illegal goods 24
Leopoldville (Kinshasa) 97
Lewis, H.S. 81

461

Index

Liberia 35
Libya 22, 281, 447; borderland smuggling 80, 83, 86; EU–Libya Migration treaty 331; illicit trade routes in 291; migrant smuggling 316, 331–332; petroleum smuggling 262; petroleum smuggling in 265–267, 269
Libyan National Oil Corporation 265
licit smuggling 4, 5, **123**
Likert scales 55
Lindquist, J. 329
livelihood trade 3
livestock trade networks 79
livestock trucks 54
localising smuggling 5–6, 19–28; blind spots of 22, 23–25; and goods by-passing border situations by air, sea, or in pipelines 24; and high-stakes smuggling 24; and legal trade in illegal goods 24; overview 19–20; remaining localised without being restricted to local 25–28; use of bonded warehouses in 20–21
Lomé 99, 101
Lord's Resistance Army (LRA) 160
lorry riders 47–48
lower-middle class women 48; *see also* women in smuggling
low-income countries 6
Lujala, P. 370

Macdonough, T. 359
MacGaffey, J. 33, 50, 136
Madison, J. 359
mafia entities 33
Mahmoud, H.A. 55
Malawi 68, 345
Malaysia: human smuggling in 326; mapping smuggling in 47, 48; profits from illicit trades in 53; rice imports 275; rice smuggling in 272, 276, 277–280
Mali 83; civil war economy 370, 374–375; colonial regimes 100; conflict zones 369; human smuggling in 344; postcolonial trades 371
Malinowski, B. 81
Malmberg, T. 439
Malta 266–267
Mandrin, L. 247
Mansfield, D. 9, 196
mapping 45–58; analytical approaches 53–55; archival documents 52; in-depth interviews 49–50; family histories 50; geo-tagging techniques 51; global database 52–53; key informants 49–50; limitations in smuggling studies 55–57; and lorry riders 47–49; and maritime voyagers 47–49; mediated interviews 50–51
maquiladoras 177
Marchal, R. 34

Marcus, G. 81
Mare Nostrum Operation 308
marijuana 136
maritime voyagers 47–48
market intermediaries 174
Marsden, M. 86
Marsh, N. 213–224
Martinez, O.J 110
Marx, K. 110
Mathys, G. 98
Mauritius 65
Mayer, S. 58n1
Mbaye, A.A. 63
McAdams, D. 163
McGaffey, J. 145
McLean, K. 163
McPherson, J. 364
Meagher, K 30–40
Médecins Sans Frontiers (MSF) 308
Meehan, P. 121
Menkhaus, K. 40
mental landscape of border residents 159
Mercosur Southern Common Market 171
Messiant, C. 34
Mexico: border smuggling 113; cotton smuggling 363; migrant smuggling from 315; petroleum smuggling in 269; targeted killings in 437; women smugglers in 175
Meyer, S.R. 334
middle-income countries 6
Migrant Offshore Aid Station (MOAS) 308
migrant smuggling 313–321; anti-smuggling policies 319–320; from China to the US 315; and criminal iatrogenesis 319–320; crisis of 313; as an economic activity 314; evidences of 315–317; and network theory 317–319; war on 444; *see also* human smuggling/trafficking
militarized trading networks 36–38
military-commercial networks 36
militias 114
Mindanao 52
Minutemen 114
mirror statistics method 64–65
Mishra, P. 65
missing trade 61–73; and bilateral trade 72; versus hidden trade *62*; overview 61–62; quantifying 64–66
mobile borders 113
model shopping 31–33
modernism 110–111
Moore, J.W. 170
Moradi, A. 69
moral smugglers 445–446
Morales, E. 192
morality 80–82
More, I. 120

Index

Moreh border crossing 384; actors 386–387; drug trade in 388; incentivising smuggling in 389–390; informal cross-border trade in 386–389; informal taxes 387–388; Mayang traders in 386–387; non-state armed groups in 388–389; traders in 386–387; *see also* borderlands; cross-border trades

Moro insurgency 50

Morocco 5, 83, 273, 447, 450, 440

morphine 196

mother ships, in tapping of petroleum products 263

Moultrie, W. 356–357

Mouride trading networks 36, 39

Mozambique 65, 68, 273, 345

mujahideen 373

Myanmar 9; 'Burmese Way to Socialism' 402; borders 9; economic pacification in 402–404; gun smuggling in 53; human smuggling in 326, 327, 333–334; Karen rebellion 403, 404; and liberalisation of border trade 402–404; opium trade in 196; rebel revenues from smuggling in 398; rice exports 275; suspension of operations 391–393; wildlife trafficking in 232

Myers, R.J. 69

NAFTA (North American Free Trade Agreement) 177

Najibullah, M. 373

Namibia 68; tax avoidance in 22; wildlife trafficking in 230

Nangarhar, Afghanistan 124, 126–128, 198–199; map of 204; opium smuggling in 203–206; Shadal bazaar 205

Narciso, G. 65

narco-economy 175–176

narco-geography 292

narco-guerrillas 355

narco-terrorists 355

narratives 156–165; Arrow Boys 160–165; as contraband 165; demarcations 161; field stories 158–160; overview 156–158, 158–160

Nasr Brigade 266

Nassau 362–363

National Rifle Association 215

National Union for the Total Independence of Angola (UNITA) 400

Nationalist Socialist of Council of Nagalim-Isak Muivah (NSCN-IM) 386, 389, 392–393

NATO (North Atlantic Treaty Organisation) 375

Netherlands 184

network specialists 9

network theory 317–319

New Jim Crow 186

Newman, D. 108, 109

Niger 34, 70, 345, 449

Nigeria 34–35; colonial regimes 101; heroin smuggling in 287; hidden trade 67, 67, 70;

mapping smuggling in 46; migrant smuggling 316; petroleum smuggling in 261, 263; trade gap 65

Nimroz, Afghanistan 124, 128–129; cross-border opium smuggling in 199–203; Iranian border 200, 200; map of 199

Nixon, R. 444

nongovernmental organisations (NGOs) 447

Nonneman, W. 316

non-state armed groups 388–389; and barriers to entry 390–391; ceasefires 391–393; incentivising smuggling by 389–390; informal regulation of smuggling 390–391; territorial control 391–393

non-timber forest products (NTFPs) 232

Nordstrom, C. 86

North American Free Trade Agreement (NAFTA) 177

North Atlantic Treaty Organisation (NATO) 375

North Korea, smuggling at sea 412

Northern Alliance 127

Northern Ireland 103

Nozea, G. 436

NSCN-IM (Nationalist Socialist of Council of Nagalim-Isak Muivah) 386, 389, 392–393

Nugent, P. 21, 77, 95–105, 105

number 4 (drug) 388

Obama's law 400

Obasanjo, O. 261

Obrador, A.M.L. 269

OCCRP (Organised Crime and Corruption Reporting Project) 253, 254

Oil-for-Food programme 262

Olken, B. 53

Olson, E. 433

Olson, M. 32

OPEC boys 144–153, 262, 269; Arua boys as predecessors to 148–149; as social bandits 149–151; as uncivil society 151–152; *see also* petroleum smuggling

Open Migration 449

Operation Blast Furnace (1986) 192

Operation Dirty Oil 266–267

opium 2, 5, 102

opium trade: actors in 209, 209; in Afghanistan 196–211; and armed conflicts 355; bribes in 202, 209; costs of smuggling 198–206, 202, 206, 207–208; countries in 196; cross-border smuggling in Nimroz 199–203; global values of 197; impact of violence and conflict 203–206, 207; income from 202, 204, 207; overview 196–198; prices 202–203, 204–205, 206; risk management in 208; safe passage in 207

Organised Crime and Corruption Reporting Project (OCCRP) 253, 254

Index

organised crime groups 6, 347–348; intimidation by 438; overview 431–433, 431–441; resilience to 433–435; securitization risks 439–440; smuggling activities 439–440; targeted killings by 437–438
original sin 66
Orwell, G. 164
Oshikango (Namibia) 20–21
ÓTuathail, G. 111

Paasi, A. 109, 110
PAIERA (Rapid Economic Impact Action Plan in Agadez) 447, 449, 450
Pakistan: border conflicts with Afghanistan 373; borders 124; food riots 274; opium trade in 196; postcolonial trades 371; rice exports 274; smuggling at sea 413
paper blockade 362
Paraguay 8, 113, 171–173
Pascoe, R. 434, 435
Pashtuns 121
passeurs 321; *see also* migrant smuggling
Paul, K. 65
pax mafiosa 112
Paz Zamora, J. 192
Peña, S. 107–115
Perkins, C. 111
Perlaza, Y. 435
personal networks and human smuggling 305–306
Peru: coca growing in 189, 191; cocaine production 185, 190
Peter, M. 83, 84, 85, 87
Petróleos Mexicanos (PEMEX) 264
Petroleum Facilities Guard (Libya) 266
petroleum smuggling: adulteration 265; anti-smuggling laws 269; combatting 267–269; complicity 269; and control of oil and gas infrastructure 263; downstream smuggling 264–265; gasoline smuggling 294; and global consumption 260; in Libya 265–267, 269; in Mexico 269; midstream and diversion of unrefined products 263–266; modalities of oil and fuel theft 262; reducing incentives for 267–268; and retailing 264; sale of unrefined products 263; second-order effects 269; and subsidies 267; tapping of unrefined products 263–264; and thef 260–269; and transparency of oil sector 268; in Uganda 144–153, 269; upstream governance of production 261–262
Philippines 66; Anti-Agricultural Smuggling Act of 2016 275; gun smuggling 53; pre-colonial border trades in 52; rice as political issue in 274; rice imports 275; rice smuggling in 272, 275, 276, 277–280
Pike, Z.M. 359
pimpineros 293

Pinochet, A. 185
Pinson, L. 213–224
Pitt, M.M. 63
Plan Colombia 186
Plan Dignidad (1997) 192
plantation slavery 174
Plonski, S. 121
poaching: actors and stakeholders 232–233; alternative livelihoods 239–241; bans on 235–238; and community based natural resource management 236, 239–241; criminal and militant groups in 235; as a global crisis 230–231; hunters and middlemen 232–233; law enforcement 237–238; and legal trade 238–239; licensing 238–239; overview 228–229; policy debates on 234–237; statistics 230–231; structures and patterns 231–234; suppliers 232; zoos as cover for 234
pokol-pokol trucks 48
poor governance 2
Popular Liberation Army (EPL) 296
post-modernism 110–111
pre-shipment inspection of imports 65–66
pressure tapping 263
PRI (Revolutionary Institutional Party) 189
price filter method 65
Primitive Rebel (Hobsbwam) 145
Profauna 240
profitability 9
Protestants 103
Protocol against the Smuggling of Migrants by Land, Sea and Air 313, 327, 346, 420
Protocol to Prevent, Suppress and Punish Trafficking in Persons Especially Women and Children 327

Qatar: free visa system 335; migrant smuggling in 335
quasi-smuggling 64

Raeymaekers, T. 7, 37, 38, 134–141
Raineri, L 313
Rapha 436
Rapid Economic Impact Action Plan in Agadez (PAIERA) 447, 449, 450
Rastrojos 290
RATIN (Regional Agricultural Trade Intelligence Network) 68
Reagan, Ronald, administration of 186
rebels 33, 384–395; and barriers to entry 390–391; ceasefires 391–393; incentivising smuggling by 389–390; informal regulation of smuggling 390–391; smuggling as source of revenue for 398–399; suspension of operations 391–393; taxation 370; territorial control 391–393
re-bordering 113, 114

Index

reflection sheet 79
Regeni, G. 83
Regional Agricultural Trade Intelligence Network (RATIN) 68
regulations 7
regulatory authority 35–36
Reno, W. 32, 33, 34, 40
rent-seeking behavior 112
resilience building: actors 433–434; capacity 433; challenges 437–439; concept of 431–433; definition of 433; forms of 435–437; and gender 434; information sharing and awareness 436; overview 431–433; and safe spaces 435–436; securitization risks 439–440; and smuggling activities 439–440; support to individuals affected by organized crime 436; and violence interruption 435
retailing of petroleum 262, 264
Revolutionary Armed Forces of Colombia-People's Army (FARC-EP) 291, 296
rhinos and rhino horns 230; *see also* wildlife trafficking
Riau Islanders 58n1
rice smuggling 272–283; barter as concealment of 276–277; and cross-border trade in rice 278–280; and dynamics of rice supply 274; historical perspective 276–278; overview 272–273; regional perspective 276–278; and rice security 273–274
rice trade networks 79
risk analysis 79
road bonds 21
Robbens, A.C.G.M. 86
Robins, P. 291–292
Roitman, J. 33, 34
Ross, M. 370
rubber 63
Rumford, C. 111, 114
Rwanda 36–37, 399; borders 69, 98; conflict minerals 37; hidden trade 67

Sabah 277–280, 278–280
safe spaces 435–436
Safety of Life at Sea (SOLAS) Convention of 1974 419
Sahlins, P. 95, 98
Salafist Group for Preaching and Combat (GSPC) 374
Salim Ben Khalifa, F. 266
Salt, J. 305
Sanchez de Lozada. G. 192
Sanchez, G. 320, 445
Santos, J.M. 192
SARS 228
Saudi Arabia: financing for Timber Sycamore 218; human smuggling in 326, 328
Save the Children 308

scale jumping 113–114
Scheele, J. 105
Schendel, W.V. 53
Schomerus, M. 156–165
Schuster, C. 8, 168–177
Scott, J.C. 3, 135
Sebha, Libya 291
securitization of borders 113
security archipelago 86
Sendero Luminoso (Shining Path) 188
Senegal 35, 63, 100–101, 102
Senegambia 98–101
Sequeira, S. 69, 71
Seram, Indonesia 240
Sever, M. 316
Seychelles 421
Shadal bazaar 205
shadow economy 32
shadow state 32, 35
shadow trade 3
Shankland, D. 83
shark fins 233
shatter zones 135
Shirk, D. 433
shocks 433
Siberian tigers 231
Siegel, D. 168
Sierra Leone 30, 35, 68, 69, 399
Silk Road 288
Silk Route 119
Sinaloa Cartel 114
Single Convention on Narcotic Drugs (1961) 185
siphoning of petroleum 262; *see also* petroleum smuggling
Siu, J. 70, 71
slow control methods 444, 448–449
slow violence 444
small arms and light weapons (SALW) 46–47
small-scale informal crossings **123**
smugglers 8–9; dangerous 445–447; definition of 96; moral 445–446
Smugglers, Secessionists & Loyal Citizens on the Ghana–Togo Frontier (Nugent) 77
smuggling: barriers to entry 390–391; and conflicts 9–10; content of 4–5; definition of 2–4, 77; gender and 168–177; localising 5–6, 19–28; overview 1; regulating 6; as source of rebel revenue 398–399; terminology 3–4; war on smugglers 444–451
smuggling at sea 411–428; archipelagic waters 415; bilateral and multilateral treaties on 418–419; challenges in responding to 419–422; coastal state jurisdiction 413–414; commodities 411–412; contiguous zone 415–416; dangers of 412–413; exclusive economic zone 416; flag state jurisdiction 412–413; flags of convenience 419–420; high seas 416–417; human rights

Index

concerns 422; internal waters 414–415; International Ship and Port Facility Security (ISPS) Code 419; opportunities in responding to 422–423; overview 411; private industry responsibility for vessel actions and illicit cargo 421; territorial sea 415; transportation modes 411–412; and UNCLOS 412–417; United Nations Convention against Illicit Traffic in Narcotic Drugs and Psychotropic Substances (Vienna Convention) 417–418; United Nations Security Council resolutions 418; vessels without nationality 420–421; and Vienna Convention 417

Smuggling of Migrants Protocol 313, 327, 346

smuggling studies 1, 4–5, 77; disciplines 10–11; embedded research 86; ethics in 80–82; ethics review boards 78–80; hidden practices 83–86; methodologies 10–11; morality in 80–82; motivations 10–11; overview 77–78; remotely managed research 84; securitization of 83–86; zone of danger 83

snakeheads 321; see also migrant smuggling

social bandits 144–153

social imaginaries 145–146, 147–149

social networks and human smuggling 305–306

Sokoto Caliphate 98

Somalia 32; civil war economy 370, 373–374; colonial polities 372; conflict zones 369; mapping smuggling in 46; postcolonial borders 372; smuggling at sea 413

Soudjin, M. 315

South Africa 24, 69; cigarette smuggling in 249–250, 252, 254; clearing agents 69–70; copper smuggling in 24; human smuggling in 326, 330, 343; migrant smuggling 345; resilience building in 435; tobacco control policy 249–250; wildlife trafficking in 230, 233, 236

South African Revenue Services (SARS) 252

South Sudan 156–157, 160–163

Southeast Asia 47, 135

Southern Philippines 52

South-South human smuggling 326

Spain 254; rice exports 274

Spener, D. 83, 315

SPLM/A (Sudan Peoples' Liberation Movement/Army) 103

Sri Lanka, human smuggling in 328

St. Eustatius 362

Stein, J. 305

Stolper, W.E. 63

Straits of Melaka 101

Strazzari, F. 83, 85, 87

stressors 433

Stroessner, A. 171

Sudan 36, 148

Sudan Peoples' Liberation Movement/Army (SPLM/A) 103

sugar 63–64

suitcase traders 174

Sulu Zone 272

Sulu, Philippines 58n1; cross-border trade in 54

surveillance 84–85

survival smuggling 293; see also illicit smuggling

Sustainable Development Goals 223

Switzerland 28; research ethics in 78

Syria 218, 262, 287; oil smuggling in 294; rebel revenues from smuggling in 398

Tagliacozzo, E. 102–103

Taiwan 184

Taliban 126–128, 204–205; political economy of 122

Tanzania 36, 68; safe spaces in 436

tapping of petroleum 262, 263–264

targeted killing 437–438

tariff evasion 9, 63, 65, 71, 249

tariffs 3; and trade gap 64

tarsilas 52

Tawi-Tawi, Philippines 48, 278–280; cross-border trade in 54

taxes 3; avoidance 22; cigarette taxes 250; entry tax 387; evasion 63, 66; godown tax 387; import tax evasion 66; informal taxes 387–388; rebel taxation 370

Tazzioli, M. 449

TBA (Tri-Border Area) 8, 171–173

Team Humanity 308

Tennant, I. 434

territorial expansion of states 2

territorial sea 415

territorial trap 109

territorialism 110

territoriality 291–293

terrorist organisations 6

tertiary brokers 121

Thailand 231; human smuggling in 326, 333–334; opium trade in 196; rice exports 274, 275; rice smuggling in 276; wildlife trafficking in 234

Thakur 9

Thomas, K. 434

Threepenny Opera (Brecht) 25

tigers 230–231, 233; see also wildlife trafficking

Tilly, C. 32, 39, 287, 320

Timber Sycamore 218

timber trade 24

Titeca, K. 38, 70, 144–153

tobacco smuggling 247–256; global illicit trade 248–249; industry involvement in 252–255; licit goods 249–250; overview 247–248

Togo 34–35, 97, 99

TOR network 288, 292

Traca, D. 63

trade gap, and tariff rates 64, 65

traders 69–72

466

Index

trading corridors, typology of 122–124, **123**
tramadol 292
transnational corporations (TNCs) 113
transnational infrastructure corridors **123**
transnational organized crime 431–441;
intimidation by 438; overview 431–433;
resilience to 431–433; securitization risks
439–440; smuggling activities 439–440; targeted
killings by 437–438
Transparency International 251
Trans-Volta 98–101
Traoré, M. 374
trialogues 49–51
Tri-Border Area (TBA) 8, 171–173
Triennial Plan 192
Trinkunas, H.A. 288
trucking of petroleum 262
Trump, Donald, administration of 191
Tuaregs 374–375
Tunisia 83; border security 440; petroleum
smuggling in 266
Turkey 262, 287
Turner, F.J. 108–109
Tyson, J. 69

Uganda 32; colonial regime 36–37; hidden trade
67–68, 69; OPEC boys 144–153; petroleum
smuggling in 144–153, 269; transnational
cross-border trade in 134–141
Ugandan People's Defense Forces (UPDF) 160
ul-Haq, Z. 274
UN Convention against Transnational Organized
Crime (UNCTOC) 313–314, 327
UN Programme of Action to Prevent, Combat and
Eradicate the Illicit Trade in Small Arms and
Light Weapons in All Its Aspects 223
UN Protocol against the Smuggling of Migrants by
Land, Air and Sea 305
uncivil societies 145–146
UNCTAD 21
underdevelopment 2
underworld 292
UNITA (National Union for the Total
Independence of Angola) 400
United Kingdom 103; cigarette taxes 250;
petroleum smuggling 265
United Kuki Liberation Front (UKLF) 386
United National Convention on Organized Crime
(UNODC) 347–348
United Nations Commission on Trade (UN
Comtrade) 53
United Nations Convention against Illicit Traffic in
Narcotic Drugs and Psychotropic Substances
(Vienna Convention) 417, 417–418
United Nations Convention against Transnational
Organized Crime (UNTOC): Article 2(a)

426n21; Article 3(2) 426n22; Migrant
Smuggling Protocol Article 8 (2) 427n25;
Migrant Smuggling Protocol Article 8 (7)
427n26
United Nations Convention on the Law of the Sea
(UNCLOS) 412–417; archipelagic waters 415;
Article 2 424n3, 424n7; Article 8 424n5; Article
110 426n16; Article 114 425n13; Article 15(1)
426n24; Article 32 424n6; Article 33 424n9;
Article 46 424n8; Article 55 425n11; Article 56
425n12; Article 73 424n10; Article 86 425n14;
Article 92(2) 427n31; Article 94 424n4; Article
98 424n2; coastal state jurisdiction 413–414;
contiguous zone 415–416; exclusive economic
zone 416; flag state jurisdiction 412–413; high
seas 416–417; internal waters 414–415;
territorial sea 415
United Nations Interregional Crime and Justice
Research Institute (UNICRI) 186
United Nations Office of Drugs and Crime
(UNODC) 187, 189, 197, 209, 316
United Nations Security Council (UNSC) 400,
418; Resolution 2240 427n28
United States 102; blood cotton 361–365; border
smuggling 113; Civil War 361–365; illicit trade
and conflicts in 355–366; migrant smuggling
from 315; migrant smuggling from China and
Mexico 315; research ethics in 78;
Revolutionary War and smuggling 356–359;
war against cocaine 185–186, 192; War of 1812
359–361; war on drugs 319–320; wartime
smuggling 356–365
upperworld 292
Uruguay, rice exports 274

Valdez, J. 437
Valueworks 28
Van den Boogaard, V. 71
Van Houtum, H. 111
Van Liempt, Ilse 303–310
Van Naerssen, T. 111
Van Schendel, W. 109, 110, 112, 144, 145, 385
Venezuela 191; cocaine smuggling in 293;
gasoline-cocaine flows in 294
Venkatesh, S. 169
vernacularization of borders 111
vessels without nationality 420–421
Vicaria para la Reconciliación y La Paz 435–436
Vienna Convention 417; Article 17(3) 426n18;
Article 17(4) 426n19
Vietnam 231; opium trade in 196; rice exports 275
vigilantes 114
Villanueva, S. 58n1
violence, and cocaine smuggling 188–189
Vives, L. 446
Vlassenroot, K. 37

467

Index

von Benda-Beckman, K. 31

Walther, O.J. 70
war economies 33–35
War of 1812 359–361
war on drugs 319–320
war on smugglers 444–451; dangerous smugglers
445–447; evidence-averse policy-making 446;
evidence-based policy-making 446; fast control
instruments 447–448; moral smugglers 445–446;
slow control methods 448–449; unintended
effects of 450–451
warlords 33
Washington, G. 357–358
weak states 2, 135
Weber, M. 112
Weberian bureaucratic model 31–32
Wei, S.-J. 64, 66
Weigand, F. 1–14, 251, 294, 385
welfare 63
West Africa 31, 67, 70, 96; colonial revenue logics
in 98–101; criminalization of smuggling in 33;
GDP 35; regulatory authority 35–36; war
economies 33–35
West Nile region, smuggling in 147–149
Western Equatoria 162
Westphalian nation-state 111
WHO Framework Convention on Tobacco
Control (FCTC) adoption 250
wildlife trafficking 4, 5, 228–240; actors and
stakeholders 232–233; alternative livelihoods
239–241; bans on 235–238; and community
based natural resource management 236,
239–241; consumers 231–232; criminal and
militant groups in 235; as a global crisis
230–231; hunters and middlemen 232–233;
laundering within 234; law enforcement
237–238; and legal trade 238–239; licensing

238–239; overview 228–229; policy debates on
234–237; structures and patterns 231–234;
suppliers 232; zoos as cover for 234
Wilks, Ivor 99
Williams, P. 295
Wise, S. 362
Wiseman, E. 70
women in smuggling 168–177; domestic
provisioning 171–173; drug trade 175;
emancipation hypothesis 168–169; gendered
labour 173–176; girl gangs 169–170; higglering
174; and narco-economy 175–176; overview
168–169; suitcase traders 174
Wong, A. 233
Wood, D. 433
World Bank 48
World Health Organization (WHO) 250
World is Yours (WY) tablets 388
writing culture debate 81

Xiang, B. 329

Yang 66
Yar'Adua, U.M. 261
yellow fever 228
Yugoslavia 399

Zaire 148; mapping smuggling in 46
Zambia 24–25, 28; gold smuggling 24
Zambian Copperbelt 26
Zapatista uprising (1994) 218
Ziranj, Afghanistan 124–125
Zimbabwe 24–25, 343; wildlife trafficking in 230
zones of danger 83
zones of refuge 135
zoonotic diseases 228–229
zoos 234

Printed in the United States
by Baker & Taylor Publisher Services